2nd Edition

XML

Black Book

Natanya Pitts

President and CEO *Keith Weiskamp*	**XML Black Book 2nd Edition**

President and CEO
Keith Weiskamp

Publisher
Steve Sayre

Acquisitions Editor
Charlotte Carpentier

Marketing Specialist
Tracy Rooney

Project Editor
Dan Young

Technical Reviewer
Bill Schindler

Production Coordinator
Laura Wellander

Cover Designer
Jody Winkler

Layout Designer
April Nielsen

CD-ROM Developer
Chris Nusbaum

Limits of Liability and Disclaimer of Warranty

The author and publisher of this book have used their best efforts in preparing the book and the programs contained in it. These efforts include the development, research, and testing of the theories and programs to determine their effectiveness. The author and publisher make no warranty of any kind, expressed or implied, with regard to these programs or the documentation contained in this book.

The author and publisher shall not be liable in the event of incidental or consequential damages in connection with, or arising out of, the furnishing, performance, or use of the programs, associated instructions, and/or claims of productivity gains.

Trademarks

Trademarked names appear throughout this book. Rather than list the names and entities that own the trademarks or insert a trademark symbol with each mention of the trademarked name, the publisher states that it is using the names for editorial purposes only and to the benefit of the trademark owner, with no intention of infringing upon that trademark.

The Coriolis Group, LLC
14455 N. Hayden Road
Suite 220
Scottsdale, Arizona 85260

(480) 483-0192
FAX (480) 483-0193
www.coriolis.com

Library of Congress Cataloging-in-Publication Data
Pitts, Natanya.
    XML black book / Natanya Pitts.-- 2nd ed.
        p.   cm.
    Includes index.
    ISBN 1-57610-783-3
    1. XML (Document markup language)   I. Title.
QA76.76.H94 P4944   2000
005.7'2--dc21   00-064451
                                                                              CIP

Printed in the United States of America
10 9 8 7 6 5 4 3

The Coriolis Group, LLC • 14455 North Hayden Road, Suite 220 • Scottsdale, Arizona 85260

Dear Reader:

Coriolis Technology Press was founded to create a very elite group of books: the ones you keep closest to your machine. Sure, everyone would like to have the Library of Congress at arm's reach, but in the real world, you have to choose the books you rely on every day *very* carefully.

To win a place for our books on that coveted shelf beside your PC, we guarantee several important qualities in every book we publish. These qualities are:

- *Technical accuracy*—It's no good if it doesn't work. Every Coriolis Technology Press book is reviewed by technical experts in the topic field, and is sent through several editing and proofreading passes in order to create the piece of work you now hold in your hands.

- *Innovative editorial design*—We've put years of research and refinement into the ways we present information in our books. Our books' editorial approach is uniquely designed to reflect the way people learn new technologies and search for solutions to technology problems.

- *Practical focus*—We put only pertinent information into our books and avoid any fluff. Every fact included between these two covers must serve the mission of the book as a whole.

- *Accessibility*—The information in a book is worthless unless you can find it quickly when you need it. We put a lot of effort into our indexes, and heavily cross-reference our chapters, to make it easy for you to move right to the information you need.

Here at The Coriolis Group we have been publishing and packaging books, technical journals, and training materials since 1989. We're programmers and authors ourselves, and we take an ongoing active role in defining what we publish and how we publish it. We have put a lot of thought into our books; please write to us at **ctp@coriolis.com** and let us know what you think. We hope that you're happy with the book in your hands, and that in the future, when you reach for software development and networking information, you'll turn to one of our books first.

Keith Weiskamp
President and CEO

Jeff Duntemann
VP and Editorial Director

Look for these related books from The Coriolis Group:

Active Server Pages Solutions
by Al Williams, Kim Barber, and Paul Newkirk

Java Black Book
by Steven Holzner

XHTML Black Book
by Steven Holzner

Also recently published by Coriolis Technology Press:

Windows 2000 Active Directory Black Book
by Adam Wood

Windows 2000 System Administration Black Book
by Stu Sjourwerman, Barry Shilmover, and James Michael Stewart

Windows 2000 TCP/IP Black Book
by Ian McLean

About the Author

Natanya Pitts is an information analyst for Powered, a Web-based education organization, in Austin, Texas. Her primary activities are developing and maintaining the XML portion of a Web-based information delivery system. She also teaches Web related classes for several online universities.

Natanya has authored, co-authored, or contributed to more than a dozen Web and Internet related titles, including the first version of this book and XML In Record Time. Natanya has also taught classes on HTML, Dynamic HTML, and XML at several national conferences (including MacWorld, Networld + Interop, and HP World), as well as at the NASA Ames Research Center. Contact Natanya Pitts at **natanya@io.com**.

Acknowledgments

First and foremost I'd like to thank Ed Tittel for giving me the opportunity to work on this book. In addition, I'd like to thank Mary Burmeister for driving me crazy reminding me to turn in my chapters—I wouldn't want your job—and for being such a great editor and making me sound good. I'd also like to thank all the other authors who contributed to this book: Frank Boumphrey, Ted Wugofski, Verne Pence, Toivo Lainevool of **www.xmlpatterns.com**, Bill Brogden, Chris Bryant, and especially Chris and Margaret Minnick of Minnick Web Services— you all made this book possible. Chris and Margaret wrote chapters no one else wanted and helped tremendously with the author review process—thank you, thank you, thank you! Special thanks to my beloved husband, Robby, and to my lovely daughter, Alanna. All things are easier because you are a part of my life. Thanks to my parents, Charles and Swanya, for always believing in me and supporting me. And finally, thanks to my furry fuzzball, Gandalf, for keeping me company while I work.

Contents at a Glance

Table of Contents

Chapter 18
Building Web Pages with XHTML **493**

Chapter 19
Processing XML **519**

Introduction

Thanks for buying the *XML Black Book*. It covers the fascinating metalanguage known as the Extensible Markup Language, or XML. Webmasters, Web content developers, database experts, and all kinds of IT professionals are turning to XML to help them represent structured data in useful ways, especially when that data must be delivered to its consumers via the Web.

In fact, XML offers two profound reasons why it's worth investigating—and using—for all kinds of information management tasks, whether for delivering Web content or organizing other content and code:

- The *X* in XML stands for *extensible*. In plain English, this means XML allows you to develop any kind of markup you might need to capture, organize, and deliver data to users. In this book, you'll learn how to define and use your own custom or customized XML markup.

- More than 100 defined XML markup languages—known as XML *applications*—already exist. They are ready for you to use to capture everything from e-commerce transactions, to chemical or mathematical formulae, to genealogies, and much, much more. You can pick up many complete XML applications and use them immediately. In this book, you'll learn how to locate and use a number of interesting XML applications, as well as how to identify and analyze other XML applications to see if they apply to your data-handling needs.

In this book, you'll find some background information about XML's origins and history. However, the book is primarily focused on using XML to solve real-world information delivery problems, including general coverage of markup languages, a comparison of XML to HTML, and how to build, validate, and transform XML markup for everyday use. You'll also learn how to manage the presentation of XML documents using a variety of style sheets, how to manage linking and references, and about working with XML namespaces. The XML applications covered in this book include the Channel Definition Format (CDF), the Extensible Hypertext Markup Language (XHTML), the XML Path Language (XPath), the XML Pointer Language (XPointer), and the XML Linking Language (XLink). In addition, you'll find out how to work with databases, program with XML, and more.

Is This Book for You?

The *XML Black Book* was written with the intermediate or advanced user in mind. Among the topics covered, you'll find the following issues explored and explained from a theoretical perspective, and then illustrated with a plethora of real-world examples:

- The principles and practices involved in using markup languages such as XML, XHTML, and HTML, along with information about how to design custom XML markup for special data-handling and data presentation needs. In addition, you'll learn all the details on the pieces and parts that make XML markup work (element, attributes, entities, and more). We also explain how to use customized markup to create formal Document Type Definitions (DTDs) for mechanical validation and error checking.

- How XML documents are processed when accessed through the Web, including how they can be easily translated into plain-vanilla HTML for delivery to the broadest possible Web audience.

- How to manage the presentation of XML documents (or HTML translations of such documents) using the Cascading Style Sheet (CSS) language or working with the Extensible Stylesheet Language (XSL), plus how to create and extend hyperlinks in XML documents using XML applications for links, paths, and pointers (external document or resource references).

- How to work with a variety of existing XML applications, including CDF and XHTML. In addition, you'll learn how to build and process your own XML-based applications to make your structured data readily available for customers, users, and partners. Included is coverage of how to link XML applications and data stored in database management systems (DBMSs).

- A tour of a recommended collection of XML software tools, including various editors, XML-capable Web browsers, parsers, and processors, plus conversion tools, databases, content management and publishing systems, and useful XSL Transformations (XSLT) utilities that will allow you to translate XML markup to HTML for Web delivery.

All in all, you'll find the kind of coverage of XML concepts, tools, and technologies that you'll need to learn to make effective use of this powerful data-handling tool in your own IT infrastructure, especially when Web access to that information is required.

How to Use This Book

Although XML-savvy readers can pick and choose what they investigate in this book, I strongly recommend that those readers who are not already using and building XML in their IT environments tackle this topic by reading sections one through three of this book in sequence. Doing so will provide a good, general background on XML terms, topics, and tools so you can understand what XML is and how it can apply to your data-handling needs.

This book is divided into five sections, along with a set of appendices and other back matter:

- Section one introduces the basic concepts that describe XML, and the capabilities it can deliver. Chapter 1 covers markup languages in general, provides a rationale for XML, and covers its history, motivation, specifications, and typical uses. Chapter 2 explains the structure of an XML document and the kinds of functions it can perform. Chapter 3 compares XML to HTML and provides a set of guidelines to help you decide when to use either markup language, and for what purposes. Chapter 4 takes the topics covered in the first three chapters and explains how they apply to understanding and solving real-world problems, in the light of available alternatives.

- Section two covers the internals of XML, from the DTDs that describe XML markup in Chapter 5 to the various activities involved in defining and creating XML documents to capture specific content. Chapter 6 covers XML markup elements, which provide the building blocks and define the structure for XML documents. Chapter 7 explains how to create content using XML. Chapter 8 explains XML attributes and how they help condition and control XML document content. Chapter 9 covers XML entities, which define standard character sets and text and can also be used to capture and simplify common document elements and contents.

- Section three covers XML extensions, style sheets, and linking mechanisms that can be used to manage how XML documents appear when viewed, and how the documents interconnect with one another. Chapter 10 covers CSS, an external appearance management markup language that works with both HTML and XML. Chapter 11 covers XSL, an XML-specific style language, particularly how its transformation capabilities (XSLT) can be used to turn content represented using XML markup into HTML pages. Chapters 12 through 14 cover the various link-, path-, and pointer-handling applications for XML that support a vastly enriched and more powerful hyperlinking mechanism for XML documents. Finally, Chapter 15 introduces and explains XML namespaces, which make it possible to incorporate pre-defined standardized XML markup in documents without having to incorporate the DTDs that govern the documents.

- Section four covers two important XML applications that many sites will want to exploit. First, Chapter 16 explores the general mechanism of defining and using XML applications. Then, Chapter 17 covers the XML application CDF; CDF allows Web sites to deliver ongoing streams of news, documents, code, or other information to users who sign up for such delivery. Chapter 18 covers an

XML-based re-implementation of HTML called XHTML. The chapter explains why XHTML is better than HTML (simply put, because it follows the same rigid, formal rules that govern XML) and how to translate HTML into XHTML.

- Section five provides information intended to teach readers to understand how XML works and how best to use its capabilities. For those reasons, we call this part the "XML Users Guide." In Chapter 19, we explain how XML documents are parsed and processed when an XML-capable browser, editor, or parser reads the markup. In Chapter 20, we explain the components that make up a complete XML solution for data delivery—be it over the Web or through some other means. In Chapter 21, we describe how to interconnect XML with database management systems to allow XML documents to access or update a database's contents as part of its capabilities. Finally, in Chapter 23, we describe the contents of an ideal XML software toolbox, and cover the various kinds of editors, browsers, parsers, and other XML-savvy software tools that you'll want to think about adding to your toolbox—should you decide to do things the XML way.

- The back matter for this book includes two appendices, a glossary, and an index. Appendix A provides a detailed and useful compendium of XML resources on- and offline. Use this appendix to learn about the latest and greatest XML specifications and applications, and to ferret out the best XML-capable tools and technologies. Appendix B contains the XML specification; use it to understand the inner workings of XML in more detail. The glossary provides plain-language definitions for the many technical terms that are part and parcel of the XML world; use it to figure out what we're really trying to say. Finally, the index can provide a speedy and direct way to identify topics of interest when you want to use this book as a reference tool and get to those topics as quickly as possible.

After you've read the first three parts of this book (or if you already have the necessary background), you can pick and choose the topics in the sections that you find most appealing. Here again, these chapters build on one another, so those who are not terribly XML-savvy will also benefit from a sequential read-through of those chapters.

After you've read or skimmed the material in this book, it really comes into its own. This book is intended as a problem-solving tool to help you get the most out of your organization's data and documents. After you've learned the lay of the land, you can use this book to investigate specific topics, markup languages, or tools in a variety of ways. We recommend that you peruse the index to see if your specific areas of concern are addressed therein—in many cases, they will be, and you can flip right to the appropriate page. Otherwise, you will find the detailed table of contents quite useful—once you understand what its terms really mean—and can uncover the information resources you need through a process of stepwise refinement. Don't forget to check out the supplementary materials at the back of the book.

In general, I recommend that you use this book first and foremost to familiarize yourself with XML terms, concepts, markup, tools, and techniques. After that, you should use it to attack any problems or information delivery needs you discover that might be amenable to "the XML treatment."

The *Black Book* Philosophy

Written by experienced professionals, Coriolis *Black Books* provide immediate solutions to global programming and administrative challenges, helping you complete specific tasks, especially critical ones that are not well documented in other books. The *Black Book*'s unique two-part chapter format—thorough technical overviews followed by practical immediate solutions—is structured to help you use your knowledge, solve problems, and quickly master complex technical issues to become an expert. By breaking down complex topics into easily manageable components, our format helps you quickly find what you're looking for, with the diagrams and code you need to make it happen.

As you work your way through the contents of this book, please note that all of the numbered code samples are also available on the CD-ROM that accompanies this book. Should you decide to re-use any of our work, you won't have to worry about re-keying our code listings to get them up and running. You will also find that some of the tools discussed in Chapter 23 are included on the CD-ROM for your evaluation or use (depending on their owner's licensing terms) so that you can use them to investigate the information included in the book, and to create, debug, validate, test, and deploy your own XML markup as your needs may dictate.

Above all, take the time to explore and ponder what XML can do for you. If your experience is like mine (we use custom XML markup for our test and course engines for Web delivery; to capture information about our books, courses, and tools; and to transform XML markup into HTML for Web delivery on our own Web site), you'll find that the number of uses for XML depends more on the time and energy you can put into creating them than any inherent limitations in this flexible, powerful technology. Enjoy!

I welcome your feedback on this book; I'd like to hear whatever you may have to say about it—positive, negative, or otherwise. You can either email The Coriolis Group at **ctp@coriolis.com** or email me directly at **natanya@io.com** (Natanya Pitts). Errata, updates, and more are available at **www.lanw.com/books/errata**.

Chapter 1

Markup Languages

In Depth

Most likely, you've picked up this book to learn what the Extensible Markup Language (XML) is and how to implement it. You'll definitely learn all that and more; but before we jump into the subject at hand (later in this chapter and in subsequent chapters), you should know a little bit about the theory behind markup languages and the differences between XML, Standard Generalized Markup Language (SGML), and Hypertext Markup Language (HTML). A solid understanding of markup languages is a prerequisite of learning how to develop XML documents. Without such knowledge, you won't be able to apply the concepts and practices to your own document development.

In this chapter, we explain what a markup language is, the various components of markup languages you should familiarize yourself with, and what today's current markup languages offer. In addition, we give you a brief overview of XML's history and some insight into why a need exists for XML.

The Basis of Style and Markup

Take a good look at this book. Thumb through it, and you'll quickly notice consistency in its design and layout. Chapter titles and text are displayed in consistent fonts. In addition, section headings are a specific height, and sidebars and tips are easy to recognize. To get this consistent look and to speed up the publication process, specific styles—or *rules*—were created to accommodate the different types of information presented in the book. When the designers got together and created the styles, they outlined the styles and detailed their attributes, assigning names to particular kinds of text and formatting that could be easily identified.

For example, consider the style named Code (which you see applied to lines of code). The designers created this style to specify how text that is used to code XML documents should appear in this book. To separate code that you need to type from text that you should read, the designers made sure the code looks a certain way: They used a font similar to what you might see on a computer screen. But the designers didn't stop there. They went through the entire book and specified which text should appear in which fashion by defining the role each bit of text plays in the document (paragraph, heading, and so on). The final display of text is determined by the style sheet and depends entirely on the role the text plays in the document.

After the roles were defined and specifics for their attached styles were determined, electronic versions of the styles were created. For this particular book, the styles were created in Microsoft Word (an application commonly used in the book-publishing industry). Special binary instructions built into the word-processing program allow the editors to specify certain formatting instructions and then assign names to them. The collection of formatting rules, with specific user-defined names, is called a *style sheet*. When the authors need a specific style, it's selected from a list of styles and applied to the text. Regardless of who writes what, the look and feel of the book is consistent throughout. The styles are carried with the document, providing designers, editors, and authors with quick-and-easy access to a consistent format.

When chapters are exchanged electronically, Microsoft Word reads the list of styles and then displays the text in the format based on the style applied. The authors don't see any of the specialized instructions that turn the simple text into bold, 24-point, Times New Roman text, nor do they type any specialized commands to invoke a particular format. Instead, they simply indicate which text they want formatted a certain way by choosing a style from the style menu, and that text is displayed with the proper formatting both on the screen and on the printed page.

Programs such as PageMaker, QuarkXPress, FrameMaker, and even Microsoft Word display text and accompanying styles just as they appear when they're printed. Unlike word processors of old (in which the formatting commands consisted of a string of text before and after the information that required formatting), today's software programs store the formatting instructions in binary format. However, if you try to open a Microsoft Word file with an application that doesn't understand Word's formatting commands, you'll see mostly gibberish (the remains of the formatting commands) at the top of the file, and then maybe some of the actual text below all that gibberish.

Many software packages have built-in translators that read and convert files (and their associated styles), and those translators were built with other software packages. However, after a file is converted from one format (for example, Microsoft

Word) to another format (for example, WordPerfect), the file is inexorably changed. The format is converted from one file format to the other. The styles are different, so although the roles of the text in the document may be the same, they are described differently.

However, some standardized types of document formats, such as Rich Text Format (RTF), actually display the instructions used to control the style of the text—in much the same way you could see formatting information in older word processors. RTF uses a set of commands to format text, and if other programs understand and can interpret RTF files, those files can be shared between different word processors and even different applications. If you look at an RTF file, you can get a feel for how such formatting languages are interpreted, both on screen and by printers, and how the formatting languages are able to display text in a particular way. With RTF, collections of text, technically called *ASCII codes*, represent the formatting or markup of the text. Here's an example of how the RTF markup language formats a simple paragraph:

```
\keepn\par\sb240\b0
Now is the time for all good men to come to the aid of their country.
```

As you can see, each markup command starts with a backslash (\). In this particular formatting language, these commands can be entered on a single line and they tell either the display software or the printer how to format the paragraph that follows. Specifically, the commands perform the following functions:

- *\keepn*—Instructs the display software or the printer to keep this paragraph with the next paragraph.
- *\par*—Instructs the display software or the printer to start a new paragraph.
- *\sb240*—Places a 12-point space before the paragraph.
- *\b0*—Turns off bold formatting.

Because this paragraph is formatted using RTF, which follows a particular set of rules and contains a certain number of commands, any word processor or other application that has an RTF interpreter can view and properly display it. It wouldn't matter if this paragraph was created on a Macintosh, a mainframe, or a Windows PC. The file is saved as an ASCII file, so the paragraph will display as intended as long as the application used to view the file (be it a word processor, browser, or even spreadsheet) includes an RTF interpreter.

The Concept of Markup

RTF handles the on-screen and printed display of text. It does so with commands placed inside the actual file. To alter the appearance of the file, you must open the file and make changes. For example, you can't just apply a different set of rules to make all text bold, 24-point font without opening the file. You can't have different processors process the data found in the file in different fashions. And, although you can create various styles, those styles aren't tied to specific sections of the content. For example, you can change the style of all paragraphs that have the Code style applied to them, but all of those "coded" paragraphs may not appear the same. Why? Because some of those paragraphs may have additional formatting applied. For example, the author of the document may decide to add bold formatting to a style already defined with italics. RTF would allow that, because it does not require the text to adhere to strict style rules.

Therefore, although RTF serves to describe how text can be formatted, it doesn't work well with more complex formatting. It offers too many exceptions, and it fails to provide a true structure to define the entire document. RTF and other such formatting languages simply help present the information, rather than provide a more detailed structure for the document. In the previous code snippet, the only command that actually describes the structure of the document, and the role the text plays in it, is the **\par** (paragraph) command that serves to indicate that the following text is a unique paragraph.

Markup languages are much more structured than formatting languages such as RTF. Markup languages, such as the Standard Generalized Markup Language (SGML) and the Extensible Markup Language (XML), go beyond the simple formatting languages to create specific, detailed structures for documents. Unlike formatting languages, markup languages have the following characteristics:

- Markup languages describe the structure of the text within the document. Explicit rules determine where specific document structures begin and end. These explicit rules create a well-defined, almost tree- or outline-type structure from which the styles sheets work to display the information.

- Content is separate from formatting. Formatting is usually handled through the use of style sheets, which are separate instructions that describe how various sections of the document should be formatted. With style sheets, you can change formatting without changing content.

- After a specific element is tagged, formatting changes affect all occurrences of that element.

Like formatting languages, markup languages require applications that can read text described with codes—called *markup elements*—and then display or process the text accordingly.

When you describe a document's content with the same set of markup elements, the document can be processed by many different types of software, each of which can apply different processing instructions to the marked-up text. For example, a Web-based financial-analysis processor may pull out only the relevant numerical data from a reporting document and display that on the screen. A page-layout processor, however, might include all the header and footer information in addition to the text-formatting information, gather all the data for printing, and insert page numbers and footnote references in the appropriate places. With markup languages, such as SGML, different processing instructions can be associated with the same file.

Descriptive languages such as RTF concentrate on formatting and displaying the entire file. Markup languages, on the other hand, map the document structures, identifying (essentially mapping) each specific document structure by its function and leaving the formatting to separate style sheets on each device that will display the document.

With structured markup languages such as XML, you also have more searching flexibility. Not only can you search for any word as you can in a standard Web page, but you can also search within the various elements of a document. For example, you may want to search for just header information, or you may want to search in specific headings, such as the chapter headings in a book.

Generalized Markup Languages: HTML, SGML, and XML

We've been talking about markup languages, but let's get a bit more specific about the various generalized markup languages with which you may be familiar.

HTML: Its Place

We'll start by examining HTML. As you probably know, HTML is relatively simple to use and quick to implement; and although it's simplistic, it offers enough capabilities to deliver documents over the Internet in the form of Web pages or HTML-formatted email. It uses element tags to identify limited document structures, such as the head and body. And in the same document, HTML elements also define the way in which the document is viewed on a Web page. Although HTML is technically a markup language, in reality, it's used as a formatting language to guide the display of content in a Web browser.

Plug-ins provide HTML the only close approximation to the extensibility provided by XML. Plug-ins offer the ability to view different types of data within a Web page. They are external programs that are implemented in the HTML document by the inclusion of the HTML **object** element. The **object** element allows Web developers to embed non-HTML and non-text data, such as multimedia presentations and audio and video files, in a Web page. The **object** element's attributes identify the file type of the object (movie, Macromedia Flash presentation, and so on), and based on that type, the browser adds a specific plug-in to the Web browser's display that is capable of handling the file. If the user doesn't have the right kind of plug-in, the browser prompts the user to specify another application on his or her computer to read and display the file.

The problem with plug-ins is that they are developed with the sole intent of displaying proprietary data. This proprietary distinction means a plug-in that displays Adobe Acrobat documents most likely won't display Excel spreadsheet data. In addition, plug-ins also handle how the data is viewed rather than its structure; therefore, they may not be aware of certain structural elements. The plug-in technology is akin to creating and using proprietary browser elements. Both of these methods (plug-technology and using proprietary browser elements) mean that not every user will be able to take advantage of the data.

SGML: The Granddaddy of Them All

SGML is a markup language that is widely used in high-end information-publishing arenas. You'll find SGML used in technical writing, where the need to handle complex, large documents across platforms is common. SGML is also used in the automotive industry, the health-care field, many areas of the telecommunications industry, and just about any place where large volumes of text need to be structured in easily accessible formats.

SGML has been used extensively for many years, even before it became an International Organization for Standardization (ISO) standard in 1986. It has a broad range of support, because it has a tremendous number of features suited specifically for text-based applications. That's also the reason users avoid SGML: The language is very complex. Plowing through the more than 500 pages of specifications is a daunting task that many text-processing professionals simply don't have time for, especially when they want to convert their documents from paper to the Web. SGML's complexity also makes it difficult for software programmers to incorporate into desktop software applications. That fact is a factor in the small number of applications that implement SGML into their core subset of programming instructions. It also contributes to the high price tag on SGML-enabled applications, such as FrameMaker—although the user base exists, the cost for adding such features is expensive. Murray Maloney, coauthor of *SGML on the Web*, published by Prentice Hall, put it best, "HTML is the low-end Volkswagen of markup languages, and SGML is the high-end Rolls Royce."

XML: The Simpler Subset

When Web-site designers and developers started pushing the limits of HTML far beyond its capabilities, the need for a more extensive language became apparent. HTML provides only a limited set of elements for structuring a document, so using it is relatively easy. Sure, designers could try to use browser-specific elements that both Netscape and Microsoft offered, but doing so raised the possibility of shutting out users of other browsers. So, most designers realized that if they wanted to do anything advanced, they couldn't do it with HTML. They had to use a separate scripting language, such as JavaScript, or some Common Gateway Interface (CGI) scripting language, such as Perl.

But these options didn't give designers full control over the real structure of the document, let alone the structure of the data. To solve this dilemma, XML was created. XML is a subset of SGML, which means that XML offers many of the same complex features but, luckily, in a much more manageable fashion. The best part of XML is that it uses only the specific features of SGML that are needed to deliver information over the Internet or an intranet. Unlike SGML documents, XML documents are relatively easy to create and use on the Web, particularly now that both Netscape and Microsoft have added a great deal of support for XML in the latest versions of their browsers. (See Chapter 2 for more information on the support of XML in Internet Explorer and Netscape Navigator.)

XML provides a wide range of features that aren't found in HTML, including:

- The ability to define your own elements and attributes. These elements and their start and end tags along with their attributes help you to define the structural elements of the document, much like SGML's elements do.

- The ability to nest document structures within other document structures to create complex documents.

- The ability to check for valid document structures during processing.

The Differences between XML and SGML

You should be aware of the differences between XML and SGML, even if you've never developed a document in SGML. Although XML is derived from SGML, many differences exist between XML and SGML. The easiest way to explain these differences is to say that XML is a much smaller language. In other words, it's a subset of SGML. SGML's specification is more than 500 pages long, whereas XML's specification is a mere 50 pages. As a result, although XML can handle a wide range of documents, it's not intended to handle all the complex data SGML can handle. It's also easier to write a parser for XML than for SGML.

Another difference between SGML and XML is the need to validate documents. SGML documents must first be validated and used with a Document Type Definition (DTD). SGML documents must also use style sheets to display the information within the document. A DTD is not required with XML documents, and validation is not always needed (although XML documents must be well formed— see Chapters 3 and 5). Basically, all an XML document needs is a style sheet to be displayed within any type of textual formatting. If the XML document won't be displayed, it doesn't even need a style sheet. This major difference makes XML documents more portable and more accessible over the Web than SGML documents. With XML, less "baggage" is carried with the document, and that means reduced document storage needs. XML gives documents flexibility, which is definitely needed on the Web.

Specifically, XML is different from SGML in these ways:

- XML is simpler and created specifically for use over the Internet.
- XML documents take less time to create than SGML documents.
- It's much easier to write applications that interpret XML documents than it is to write applications that interpret SGML documents.

However, similarities do exist between the two languages. The similarities make it easy to convert XML documents to SGML, although converting SGML documents to XML documents can be a little more time consuming. Specifically, XML and SGML are alike in these ways:

- Both support a wide variety of applications.
- XML is fully compatible with SGML.
- Both use style sheets to format content.
- Both XML and SGML documents use concise structures.

The Differences Between XML and HTML

You're probably already familiar with HTML, so let's spend a few minutes examining the major differences between HTML and XML. You could say that XML is a more advanced markup language than HTML. If you were to take that simplistic statement one step further, you could say that HTML is used mainly for presentation of content and XML is used for structuring data. But there's more to it than that.

XML is in no way a replacement for HTML. And it isn't just HTML with extra elements thrown in, although the XML specification is much larger than the HTML specification. Remember that although HTML is an application of SGML, and XML is a subset of SGML, HTML and XML differ considerably. Specifically, XML allows you to define your own elements for particular purposes. Other than that, the differences are most notable in the problems XML serves to solve. You could say that XML is a fix to the particular problems that are encountered when using HTML. With XML, you have:

- Better control over layout via style sheets.
- The use of multiple types of hyperlinks.

- The ability to deliver any type of information over both the Internet and intranets.

- Fewer problems displaying long pages.

As you can tell, the differences between HTML and XML are more than just format versus content, although that is one major selling point for XML. Let's take a look at some of these particular HTML problems and how XML can solve them.

Better Control over Layout via Style Sheets

The current implementation of HTML contains a problem that designers have wrestled with since its inception: HTML includes formatting and content within the same document. This characteristic creates problems when a designer wants to change the overall look and feel of an entire site. To do that with HTML, a designer must manually change each page.

Cascading Style Sheets (CSS) were developed as a style-sheet mechanism for HTML to help Web designers overcome the issues associated with storing format and content information in the same document. However, poor browser support for CSS, combined with the lack of desire on the part of Web developers to depart from established coding practices, has made CSS unpopular and not widely implemented. Because CSS predates XML, and XML developers recognize it as an immediately available tool for styling their documents, CSS is more popular with XML developers and will be a viable style sheet solution for XML documents.

Although CSS is a great tool for driving the display of HTML and serves as a good starting point for styling XML, it isn't robust enough to meet all of XML's needs. The Extensible Stylesheet Language (XSL) is an XML-specific style sheet mechanism that is advanced enough to drive the display of even the most complex XML documents.

NOTE: *See Chapter 10 for more information on CSS and Chapter 11 for more information on XSL Transformations (XSLT)—one of the parts of XSL.*

With XML, the layout is separate from the content; therefore, when a designer wants to change the layout of a site, he or she simply changes the attached style sheet. The content stays intact. This method is a major change to the HTML concept and also provides a much more flexible format for delivering the same information through a variety of mechanisms. Style sheets can be used to format the same content for display across a variety of applications.

Even though the latest implementation of HTML (version 4.01) allows you to work closely with style sheets, the difference is that XML allows you to associate styles with structural elements. As a result, you can quickly format styles for particular structural elements, such as entities that declare images, specific paragraph formats, and even styles for different types of linking mechanisms.

NOTE: *HTML has been retooled as XHTML to fit under the XML umbrella as an XML vocabulary. XHTML represents the future of HTML and the general move of all content description to a paradigm in which content is separated from display. Chapter 18 discusses XHTML in more detail.*

The Use of Multiple Hyperlinks

Is your browser's Back button a little worn out? It's no wonder, because the current implementation of HTML only allows for single-direction linking (backward or forward)—and backward and forward are not the only directions many Web users want to go. No convention exists for multiple-linking formats that allow multidirectional linking based on the role the document plays. Where do current HTML sources take you? To other resources, whether they are Web pages, search engines, chat rooms, and so on.

So, what does XML offer in the way of linking that HTML leaves out? Specifically, XML provides a standard model for linking through its linking specification, XML Linking Language (XLink). With HTML, only character data types are used with a link location or Uniform Resource Locator (URL). Entities are not incorporated. URLs also don't include notations that segment different data types. You can link to a document or to a marked spot in a document, but you can't use the context of a document (elements, attributes, and so on) to link to a spot based on its surrounding text. This linking is relatively simplistic.

Linking in XML, however, is more complex. XML offers advanced linking through XLink by:

• Giving you control over the semantics of the link.

• Using extended links that involve more than two resources.

• Using pointers to external references through the use of extended pointers, or the XML Pointer Language (XPointer), to dig deep into a document using its content and link to a very specific spot.

We can easily explain all these different linking functions by examining the current linking method used in HTML. A simple link provides a way to identify a certain single source, whereas XLink allows you to express relationships between more than two resources. (Chapter 12 examines the various linking options available in XML.)

Briefly, advanced linking options provide XML documents with:

- Bidirectional links.

- Externally managed links (links that can be managed outside the document content itself).

- Links that provide access to a ring of sites or let the user open multiple windows.

- Links with multiple sources attached.

- Attributes associated with links.

Better Control of Long Documents

As you've probably noticed when you try to bring up a long Web page with today's browsers, HTML doesn't allow you to pick and choose which sections you want to view. The problem is that HTML does not allow for easy manipulation of and linking among multiple sections in a single document; it only allows the **head** or **body** sections. So, if you—the designer—want to create a single long document with links to its various sections, you need to either break the document into smaller Web pages with simple hyperlinks connecting them, or incorporate frames. But again, frames usually point to multiple documents, not to an entire document with separate sections.

To explain this problem with HTML in more detail, we'll use this book as an example. This chapter is more than 10 pages long and has many sections. If we were to place it on the Web, we would have to make it smaller so the reader wouldn't have to wait hours for the document to load. At the same time, we would need to provide the reader with the ability to jump back and forth between sections, either in a logical format or randomly. There's also the possibility of making a mistake and accidentally placing the wrong heading element at the wrong location, which would hinder the flow of the document.

If we tried using the **frameset** element to place the chapter into frames, we'd also run into problems with those readers who don't have frame-enabled browsers. And again, we could incorrectly identify a heading and ruin the flow of the text. Also, if we were to divvy up the chapter and place the parts into different pages, we would lose the ability to allow full-text searching.

TIP: XML promises to fix this particular problem simply because all XML documents are highly structured and well formed. XML won't let you cut as many corners as HTML does, and through the use of various section elements, XML gives you a way to break a single document into segments and then use a display tool that presents it as a single document with various levels. Such a presentation tool might display this multilevel structure in much the same way Windows Explorer presents folders and subfolders in a hierarchical fashion.

XML Should...

By now, you should understand the theory of markup languages, their features, and their applicable uses. Based on the basic theory of how markup languages work and the role that XML should play as a markup language for disseminating information over the Web and the Internet, the World Wide Web Consortium (W3C) has defined exactly what features XML should offer, as outlined in these guidelines:

- *XML shall be straightforwardly usable over the Internet.* XML should be simple enough for current Web designers to pick up and quickly put to use. It's designed to be used with proven Web features, such as linking, elements, and attributes. Making the move from HTML to XML may require the acquisition of new skills, but it shouldn't be a painful experience.

- *XML shall support a variety of applications.* XML should be useable in any kind of solution or application and not be restricted to a handful of applications. The types of applications should be varied, as well.

- *XML shall be compatible with SGML.* Any SGML processor should be able to interpret XML documents. This provides an extensible way to expand XML to more than just Web users. There should be no problem working with SGML or XML documents when you're using SGML-specific applications.

- *It shall be easy to write programs which process XML documents.* Developers won't or shouldn't shun XML because it's too difficult to write desktop or personal applications that process XML documents. The old theory, "If you build it, they will come," is supposed to apply to XML. The easier it is to develop XML applications, the more likely users and developers will embrace it.

- *The number of optional features in XML is to be kept to the absolute minimum, ideally zero.* The idea is to keep XML as simple and efficient as possible.

- *XML documents should be human-legible and reasonably clear.* XML documents should be interpretable not only by a parser or browser, but also by people. XML documents should be so readable that anyone can interpret the content and intent.

- *The XML design should be prepared quickly.* The actual design of XML has been on the fast track since its first proposal in 1996. Acceptance and implementation should happen at an even faster pace than was the case with HTML.

- *The design of XML should be formal and concise.* If the standard is well-established and detailed, there's less room for error by the user agents or authors.

- *Terseness in XML markup is of minimal importance.* The actual elements or markup should be self-explanatory. Instead of for example, the **p** element to specify a paragraph, the element would be named **paragraph**, because that name is complete and spelled out. Likewise, instead of **vlink**, the element would be named **visistedlink**. This makes XML documents easier for people to read and identify exactly what the elements are used for. Of course, because developers can write their own XML elements, there's no guarantee that they will develop element names that make sense to all people.

- *XML documents shall be easy to create.* For XML to catch on like HTML has, XML documents should be as easy to create. By incorporating structure, XML documents should also be easier to understand.

By now, you should have a firm grasp of what a markup language is and the differences between the various types of markup languages. Next, we'll provide you with a short history of XML and let you know why a need existed for it.

The Short History of XML

XML really began in the 1960s when IBM started working on the Generalized Markup Language (GML). The developers needed a way to easily describe and exchange documents with most of the formatting left in place. They decided a generalized markup language—something that could provide a universal set of instructions—would work best, so they embarked on the long and arduous task of creating something that was extensible enough to work across different platforms. However, the process of creating and implementing such a language and gaining widespread support for it wasn't easy.

Work on GML continued for many years, although acceptance was not quick or universal. Then, in 1986, ISO decided to adopt IBM's version of this generalized markup language, which was now known as SGML. Almost 20 years after the concept was established, SGML became the markup language for many sophisticated documentation systems. It provided a standard way to create, present, and exchange documents with other users regardless of the system or platform used. SGML also gave large organizations the flexibility to create their own document formats, offering a high level of sophistication not available previously. However, as we mentioned earlier, with this high level of sophistication came problems. Mainly, the language was *too* sophisticated and *too* complex for many users, particularly when it came to publishing smaller documents.

The Path to and Need for XML

When the Web came into worldwide focus in the early 1990s, SGML was tapped as the perfect language to use to develop a subset markup language that could, in turn, create Web pages. The features of SGML allowed a certain functionality that was perfectly suited for the delivery of documents across disparate systems. Tim Berners-Lee at the European Center for Particle Physics (CERN) developed HTML, which was a simplified SGML application. The maintenance and development of HTML was soon taken over by the W3C.

HTML caught on quickly because it lacks most of SGML's complexity but still provides a fair number of SGML features, within a relatively simple group of pre-defined elements. The document-sharing features of SGML and the limited number of elements made HTML and the Web enormously popular in a very short time. HTML initially provided the standard way by which Web pages could be easily created on one platform, placed on a server, and viewed on different platforms. HTML, the Graphics Interchange Format (GIF) image file format, and then the Joint Photographic Experts Group (JPEG) image file format allowed document and graphic interchange as well as interoperability between operating systems, browsers, and computers. As we've mentioned, HTML is relatively easy to use, and it's useful for the display of information.

Virtually anyone could easily develop a Web page using only a few elements. No specialized programming knowledge was required and no real structure needed to be followed. In some cases, you could even bend the rules a bit—leaving out a quotation mark here, a closing tag there—and the document would still display. HTML demanded little of its developers and, in return, provided a way for millions of people to make millions of Web pages.

In addition, HTML does not provide any standards beyond the visual representation portion of the Internet's communication layer. Suppose you want to search a site. Because no standards currently exist for intelligent searches, you're at the mercy of whatever technology the site developer employs; and in many cases, that may be none at all. In addition, HTML's element set is limited to describing a particular kind of information: data that is paragraph based and textual in nature. Although you can use HTML to describe catalog entries or financial data, you're really just envisioning how that information might look on a page—listed in a multi-column table, for example—and fitting your information into the elements that HTML has to offer. With HTML, you only have text embedded within markup elements, which drive the display in a tabular format on a computer screen. Therefore, you may have a problem if you want to use the data described with HTML for something other than display on a Web page. You can't easily derive anything about the data, such as its role or function in relation to other pieces of data, from this very simple markup.

HTML's simplicity quickly became its downfall. With its relatively easy text-oriented features and linking options, it worked well in the early days of Web development. But as prices for computers dropped in the mid-1990s and more systems were shipped with multimedia features, the strain on HTML began to show. Developers quickly demanded more out of HTML and out of Web browsers. They wanted to create, enhance, and tie in more and more sophisticated features and options to Web pages. They wanted to make the Web the portal into anything and everything, from databases to cameras, to videos, to radio stations. Seeing this need, many browser manufacturers quickly began creating their own customized element sets or features, such as plug-ins, that extended the capability of the browser.

Browser developers, such as Netscape and Microsoft, began adding their own elements into browsers. The result was a hodgepodge of Web features, many of which could be viewed on only one brand of browser. The rampant modification of the HTML standard put a strain on developers, who had to keep up with all these new enhancements and feature sets. It also proved difficult for users, who simply wanted to view information across global networks with whatever browser or computer they had. Many sites were no longer compatible with standard browsers; pages that didn't load correctly or crashed computers entirely befuddled users.

HTML also offers little capability for personalization. Hypertext Transfer Protocol (HTTP) cookies provide some level of personalization when a visitor browses a site, but this type of personalization is limited. Sites such as Microsoft's Investor or Expedia take Web-site personalization a step further by allowing data exchange between the user's personal computer and the site. For example, the Investor site exchanges data with the popular personal financial management program Quicken to record, track, and display portfolio information—but it doesn't accomplish this feat through standard methods. The browsing visitor must be using Internet Explorer on a Windows-based platform, which means that the protocols, programs, and scripting methods used are tied to a particular operating system and browser.

Although proprietary in nature, such systems do demonstrate the Internet's potential—specifically, the Web can offer tremendous personalization and interchange between local and remote systems. However, for these capabilities to be embraced throughout the Internet development community, we must move beyond the simple information-access and display standard HTML currently offers. Instead, there must be "an information understanding standard: a standard way of representing data so software can better search, move, display, and otherwise manipulate information currently hidden in contextual obscurity," according to Microsoft's Site Builders Network XML section.

If you've worked with HTML at all, you know that it cannot provide the kind of capabilities Microsoft describes. It would literally be impossible for HTML alone to provide standard ways for the following types of data interchange:

- Sharing subscriber data among insurance companies.

- Decoding and processing electronic payment information.

- Exchanging information about legal issues among lawyers, courts, judges, and litigants.

- Sharing patient prescription and drug interaction information among doctors and pharmacists.

- Creating company catalogs and sharing them with clients and salespeople, allowing both to place and to take orders, browse the catalog, and view order information.

If you've encountered these types of data exchange on the Web, you may be wondering what handles the data exchange, if HTML doesn't do it. HTML displays the results of searches or displays a form that will be sent to a remote CGI script or database. Some sites might use Active Server Pages (ASP) or another Web application server; others might use Perl to interface with structured query language (SQL) databases. The point is, there's no standardization, and HTML alone cannot accomplish any of these feats.

TIP: *Although HTML is limited, that doesn't mean it's broken or that people will stop using it. It's just that HTML wasn't designed to do all that the burgeoning Web world has demanded of it. HTML is still a useful tool for building Web pages, and it plays a different role than XML does in the dissemination of information. Many current XML solutions use a combination of XML and HTML to deliver information to users via Web browsers. For a more detailed discussion of the differences between HTML and XML and how to use both to meet your needs, read Chapter 3.*

Soon, the strain of all these incompatibilities and limitations all but sucked the life out of HTML. Why wasn't HTML, this subset of the hugely capable SGML, able to withstand the pressure? Basically, unlike SGML, HTML wasn't extensible. It had no room to grow, which, in the computer world, was a signal of certain and almost impending death. Sure, browser manufacturers such as Netscape and Microsoft could add their own elements. But you, as a developer, were stuck with several choices. You could:

- Use HTML.

- Use limited browser-specific elements.

- Create scripts that attached to outside resources.

- Forget the whole thing and give up.

The realistic solution was to come up with an extensible, expandable, flexible markup language that can use many of the best features of SGML while still utilizing all the great options HTML has to offer. The best of both worlds meant creating something in between SGML and HTML: XML is the best of both worlds.

XML is the Web's solution to a wide-scope markup language for exchanging data of all types. XML is a set of rules that you can use to build your own sets of markup elements that fit your data like a glove. In reality, XML is a meta-markup language, which is a markup language for defining markup languages. Organizations, individuals, and industries alike already use XML to build sets of markup that describe their information accurately so they can begin to leverage the infrastructure of the Web without forcing their data to fit into a single mold. XML 1.0 is the standard that guides the development of markup languages using XML.

The Beginning of XML

The evolution of XML started back in 1996. Publishing gurus and Web nerds got together and came up with an idea to create a subset of SGML. This subset would work specifically on the Web, be extensible (or expandable), and use all the advanced structural markup features without the complexity of SGML.

The first working draft of the XML specification was published in November 1996. Not too much later, in January 1997, the first XML parser appeared; and in March 1997, the first XML applications, such as Lark, became available. Then, in the fall of 1997, support for XML was implemented in Microsoft's Internet Explorer. Finally, in February 1998, the XML 1.0 recommendation was published, and support for this new Web-based development language grew.

What Is XML?

XML is designed to give developers the tools needed to produce new kinds of applications—advanced applications that span not only simple Web pages, but also databases, electronic commerce systems, and virtually any display system possible. XML can do this because, unlike HTML, XML describes data. XML concentrates on forming the data that will be presented and leaves the presentation to the device that displays it (with a little help from style sheets).

XML also brings great promise to intranets by giving developers the ability to link to databases regardless of the system used. More importantly, XML gives developers the ability to create customized data structures for particular industry-specific needs. These data structures and databases can be viewed with a variety of devices, without the need for custom-built interfaces to view the same data on each different display device. Eventually, no more warning signs will appear on sites saying "Best Viewed With Netscape" or "This Site Requires Internet Explorer." Instead, any XML-enabled browser will be able to interpret and display the data created with XML.

Chapter 2

The 10,000-Foot View of XML

In Depth

In this chapter, we provide you with your first XML example and identify the components of an XML document. We let you know which versions of the main browsers support XML and give you a little background on this support. Then, we examine the XML specification itself, as well as the process XML had to go through to make it past the World Wide Web Consortium (W3C), the governing body, if you will, for Web-based markup.

The XML specification changes and evolves yearly. It's important for you to understand how to read the specification and make sense of its changes, deletions, and additions. We'll also briefly cover the different subsets of XML, known as *XML vocabularies*, giving you a glimpse of what vocabularies are available now and how you can implement an XML vocabulary in your development process.

TIP: *See Chapter 20 for an in-depth look at the XML vocabularies.*

XML Example

The Extensible Markup Language (XML) has attracted tremendous interest and support since it was first formulated in 1996. It provides a standard way to describe content and, more specifically, it offers a means to create data structures in a flexible manner. XML uses the standard metaphor of element tags to mark up content based on a set of rules created by the document's developer. This set of rules is called the *Document Type Definition (DTD)*, and it allows developers to use XML markup to describe a variety of documents, such as:

• A standard document that can contain text and links to graphics and external resources.

• A more structured document or record, such as a Hypertext Markup Language (HTML) form with a true structure encoded within the document. This category could include a purchase order, a medical prescription, an address book, or other types of documents with specific fields.

• An object with data and methods, such as a Java bean or Component Object Model (COM) object.

• Database records that can be presented through a Web page, based on requests that browsing visitors submit to the database query engine.

- Meta-content, such as the content of an Internet Explorer channel.

- Anything else that provides data exchange between computers and people, or between computers and computers or other types of processing machines.

Although XML isn't a new technology, solid Web browser support for it is only beginning to emerge. To build solutions today that will work with a variety of Web browsers and make your data accessible to as many users as possible, you can create XML documents and use HTML (or XHTML) to present the content. XML also allows you to *repurpose*, or redefine and display, the content from a single source to a variety of different display mechanisms. For example, you could store data in a single database on a server, extract it into documents that incorporate XML markup elements to represent the data's structure, and then parse out the data to a number of different displays, including Web browsers, personal digital assistants (PDAs), and wireless phones. Each display mechanism uses a different set of rules to drive how information is presented. However, by not linking your information to any single display device, you can leverage it so it's viewable on all display devices.

Here's a real-world example of how you might use XML. Suppose you own a restaurant. You store your menu in a database and you have a variety of menu-display devices. Customers view the menu on a little palmtop computer that you distribute as they come in the door. The waitpersons use the same type of handheld devices to take orders. Orders are transmitted to the kitchen's receiving unit, which displays the order on a larger, touch-sensitive screen. Then, when the chef prepares the meal, he or she marks off the order with the stroke of a pen.

Your takeout and delivery customers get their information about the specials of the day and the rest of your menu via your Web site. Some of your customers like to subscribe to the Daily Specials channel you've set up using Internet Explorer's Channels feature, which means your menu database gets lots and lots of use. You use the same database to manage your stock quantities. When someone orders a meal and the chef marks the order as prepared and delivered, the stock levels in your food database are adjusted accordingly. Using additional Web automation tools, an order is automatically placed with your suppliers when quantities get low.

All the information in your database is used and reused in a variety of ways by your customers, your waitpersons, and your chefs. The relationships between the individual orders and the food database do not necessarily reside in the schema data described by either the database of orders or the database of food. Instead, they are extensions defined by the instance of an order. This kind of solution is possible using XML and a variety of XML-aware software tools.

TIP: *The current discussion of XML is theoretical and is intended to show what XML can do, rather than how it does it. Chapter 4 includes a more technical discussion of the different elements of three real-world XML solutions. The majority of other chapters in the book include more detailed discussions of different aspects of XML, as well as hands-on examples that you can use as you begin implementing your own XML solution.*

In the previous scenario, XML provides all the structural representations of the data. The following code helps explain this point further:

```
<meal><entree>Chicken Cordon Bleu</entree></meal>
```

In this example, we included the **entree** element not so much to separate the entree from the rest of the meal record, but rather to indicate that, in addition to being a part of the meal, it's the entree the customer ordered. If your manager wanted a report containing all of the meals ordered, he could generate it. Because some people may only order dessert for their meal, he could also pull up all the entrees instead of the meals. Customers could also conduct their own searches to find out, for example, how many people ordered the Cordon Bleu and, if they are provided, read comments about the meal.

This example may work for the food and beverage industry, but what if the user wants to use XML to define and keep track of medical data, such as prescriptions? Because XML allows you to develop elements to suit your own needs, you could define elements that represent various items, such as dosages, generic drug names, doctors' names, patients names, and so forth. XML allows you to develop documents that have terms and definitions specific to the needs of the user. The specifications you use to describe your documents are placed in a DTD that can potentially be used with many other documents. A DTD is a document that sets the structure for your XML data. You can reference the DTD as a separate document (external) or it can be placed within the XML document itself (internal).

NOTE: *You don't actually need to have a DTD to build an XML document, but we've found that DTDs help us build consistent and useful documents. Chapter 5 goes into the details of when you need a DTD and when you don't.*

Because the data is separate from the presentation, the same XML data (whether it's a menu or a prescription) could be presented in multiple ways on the user's desktop or laptop. It could even be presented on a hand-held device. An XML document, by itself, does not specify whether or how its information should be displayed—the XML document merely contains the data. With the help of style sheets, HTML is used to display the data in a Web page, or on a wireless phone, or via a PDA. Either the Web server serving up the document or the browser displaying the document handles the conversion from XML data to whatever presentation markup is needed to display the data on a particular device.

TIP: *XML doesn't work alone. The XML 1.0 specification only provides the rules for how to build markup languages to describe data. XML is supported by a wide range of other technologies (such as the style sheets mentioned earlier) that make display, linking, searching, and other data manipulations possible. Section three of the book is devoted to the discussion of XML's companions and the roles they play in a total XML solution.*

XML looks a lot like HTML, and it should, because both are derived from the same source: the Standard Generalized Markup Language (SGML). Like an HTML document, an XML source document is made up of elements, each of which has a start tag and an end tag (unless it's an empty element). The information between the tags, if there is any, is called the *content*. However, unlike HTML, XML allows for an unlimited set of elements that indicate what the data means, not how it should look. For example, this HTML element

```
<b>Cordon Bleu</b>
```

specifies that the name of the entree appears in bold-face text in the menu. However, this XML element

```
<entree>Cordon Bleu</entree>
```

defines the same information as an entree. The key difference between the two elements (**b** and **entree**) is that the HTML element specifies how the content should be displayed, and the XML element describes its function. It's entirely up to the developer of the XML document to determine which elements are used and what content is placed within those elements' tags. With HTML, the developer has to choose from a predetermined list of elements to display the data.

Whereas XML describes data, the rules for how to order and display the data are left up to the style sheet mechanism. This approach allows the same information to be displayed in a variety of formats based on which style sheet is specified for a particular display. Let's take a closer look at some of the components of XML, how they work, and why becoming familiar with them is so important.

TIP: *Chapter 1 includes a key discussion of the basic theory of markup and how it should be used to describe data rather than how data is displayed. If you're new to markup or have only used HTML to drive the display of a Web page, be sure to read the information on markup theory carefully. One of the keys to using XML successfully is understanding how to use markup correctly.*

XML Components

If you've worked with HTML, you're already familiar with XML's basic components. If you haven't worked with markup before, the components of markup are straightforward and easy to learn. The main XML components are:

- Elements

- Attributes

- Entities

- DTDs

The following sections describe these pieces of XML that you will use to construct your XML masterpiece.

WARNING! HTML gurus beware: You may have a hard time grasping some of the concepts of XML because HTML is a language that allows you to break all sorts of rules and requires little knowledge other than what a few elements do. With XML, on the other hand, you aren't just painting a picture on a page—you're constructing a document. Therefore, you need to follow many rules.

Elements

In XML, an *element* is something that describes a piece of data. An element is comprised of markup *tags* and the element's content. Most elements have both a start and an end tag (except empty elements). The paragraph element in HTML has both a start and an end tag, as shown in the following example:

```
<p>Now is the time for all good men
to come to the aid of their country.</p>
```

The paragraph element specifies to an XML processor what role the data contained within the start and end tags plays in a document. In XML, elements are really just storage containers for data. Every XML document has one main element that contains or holds all the data for the entire document. The following example will help you visualize exactly what we mean:

```
<book>
  <head>
    <title>XML Black Book</title>
    <toc>
      <item>Introduction</item>
      <item>Chapter</item>
      <item>Index</item>
    </toc>
  </head>

  <body>

    <introduction>
      Welcome to the XML Black Book
    </introduction>
```

```
    <chapter>
      <heading>Introduction</heading>
      <p>In this book, we hope to examine everything there is about XML...</p>
    </chapter>
  </body>
  <index>
      List of INDEX content
  </index>
</book>
```

The **book** element holds all the content of this document and is technically re-ferred to as the *document element*. All the other elements, such as the **index** element, are *subelements* nested below the **book** element. More specifically, the **book** element is the *parent*, and the rest of the elements are the *descendents*, or *children*. The **heading** element, then, is actually a child of the **chapter** element, which in turn is a child of the **body** element. All these elements create the struc-ture of the book; none of them creates the look and feel of the book when the document is displayed by a particular device.

Elements can contain a number of different types of content, including:

- Character data, such as text you would place in a document.

- Other elements, called *subelements* or children, as outlined in the preceding paragraph.

- **CDATA** sections, which are sections of the XML document that include literal data that the XML processor will ignore, such as scripting code that might be used to specify a JavaScript.

- Processing instructions

- Comments

- White space

- Entity references

You declare elements using a DTD either within the XML document or in a sepa-rate document by specifying the following information:

```
<!ELEMENT elementname content>
```

TIP: *For more information on elements, check out Chapter 6. Also, throughout this book, we represent "placeholder" names by putting them in italics.*

Attributes

Attributes are elements' best friends. They allow a single element to describe a general class of content, such as paragraphs or meals, and yet still provide specific information about the use of each element. Attributes are basically just sources of additional information about an element. Attributes are always explicitly assigned to elements and are designed to work with them.

Think back to the restaurant example and the **meal** element we specified. To know whether the meal was prepared, we could create an additional element and call it **prepared**. However, by creating this element, we're creating an additional element that describes the **meal** element. Instead, we can create an element attribute and specify the status of the meal within the element, as shown in the following example:

```
<meal prepared="no">Chicken Cordon Bleu</meal>
```

After the addition of this attribute, we can search the database of orders for all the meals that have not been prepared. Of course, as we did with the element, we declare our attribute within the DTD that governs the menu document. The basic syntax for defining attributes is:

```
<!ATTLIST ElementName
AttributeName Type Default
(AttributeName Type Default...)>
```

TIP: *For more information on attributes, how to create them, and how to use them in XML documents, check out Chapter 8.*

Entities

Entities are virtual storage units in an XML document. You can keep all kinds of information in an entity—from a graphics file to a snippet of frequently used text and XML markup. XML actually supports two different kinds of entities: *general* and *parameter*. Without getting into the major differences, an entity is simply any piece of data—whether text or binary data—that you want to reference in a document. Parsed entities, which are collections of text and markup, are processed by the XML processor as part of the document. Some examples of parsed entities are:

- A reserved character that XML uses as part of its syntax, such as the less-than (<) and greater-than (>) signs used to build markup tags.

- A collection of text and markup that you don't want to have to type repeatedly throughout the document, such as a copyright statement or standard footer.

For example, you need to specify a less-than sign and a greater-than sign in the content of an XML document. If you place the signs themselves (< and >), the XML processor assumes you're defining the start or end tag of an XML element. Therefore, the following sentence would return an error in an XML processor:

```
<sentence>In Math class, I never could grasp which symbol to use
to specify the greater-than sign, the < or the >.</sentence>
```

Instead, you need to use a general entity that is built into XML and used to specify such reserved characters. For the less-than sign, the entity is **<** and for the greater-than sign, it's **>**. After you replace the symbols with the appropriate entities, the code looks like this:

```
<sentence>In Math class, I never could grasp which symbol to use
to specify the greater-than sign, the &lt; or the &gt;.</sentence>
```

The display of the previous code would look something like this:

```
In Math class, I never could grasp which symbol to use
to specify the greater-than sign, the < or the >.
```

You can also use general entities to specify more mundane character data that you simply don't want to type again and again. For example, if you're tired of typing your address repeatedly on your Web pages, you could define an entity, such as **address**, that contains your address. Then, just as you specified a general entity to depict a reserved character (as shown in the previous example), you could specify the entity you created throughout your document using **&address;**. In this chapter's Immediate Solutions section, we show you how to do just that.

Entities that contain binary files, such as audio clips and graphics are officially called *unparsed entities* because the XML parser doesn't try to process them. These entities play by a slightly different set of rules than parsed entities do. XML also supports parameter entities for use in DTD building to help you create clean and easy-to-manage DTDs. In HTML, entities are only used to represent non-ASCII and reserved characters. In XML, however, entities are powerful tools that you'll use over and over to make both DTD and data management easier.

TIP: *Chapter 9 covers all the rules of building and using the different types of XML entities.*

Document Type Definitions

The DTD is an optional construct that provides all the markup tools used to create XML documents. In the most basic terms, a DTD is a separate unit from the main XML document that provides a set of rules for the XML document to which it's attached. A DTD sets the instructions for the structure of the XML document and defines which elements will be used in the document. In our previous restaurant example, the **entree** element would be declared in the restaurant's DTD along with all the other elements. Document entities are also declared in the DTD. Think of a DTD as a road map and rulebook for your XML document. The following features of an XML document are outlined within the DTD:

- The element types that will be allowed within the XML document

- The characteristics of each element type, including attributes and the type of content each element can have.

- Any notations that can be encountered within the document (see the section titled "Sections of the XML Specification" for more information on notations)

- The entities that can be used within the document.

It may sound like no rules govern XML, but that's not true. Sure, XML not only lets you develop your own elements and attributes, or specific rules, for those elements, but you can also create several different types of entities and then define how those XML constructs should work together. The rules of XML govern exactly how you build DTDs and then use the constructs you've defined in the DTDs to build XML documents.

XML's rules are outlined in a document called the XML *specification*. The specification outlines exactly how elements must be declared and how XML must be constructed in order for XML processors (which interpret XML code) to process the XML information properly and send it to the Web browser for display. Later in this chapter, you'll examine the XML specification and how to understand its rules.

Support for XML in Web Browsers

You're probably thinking, "Why would vendors support something like XML—a markup language that serves to take away their competitive advantage?" True, XML does level the playing field greatly; but the features vendors have already placed in their browsers will still be supported and developed. More importantly, however, instead of using their own specialized languages, the browser vendors can use XML to develop their own XML applications. Such XML applications have already been developed and are continuing to be developed and placed within the latest versions of browsers. Microsoft's Internet Explorer Channel Definition Format (CDF) is a prime example of how XML helps to augment a browser. Vendors will continue to create new XML applications and most likely will continue to add their own elements.

Currently, XML is supported in a variety of browsers, editors, parsers, and development products. Both Internet Explorer versions 4 and 5 offer XML support, although the support is somewhat limited in version 4. And, Netscape added XML support in Navigator version 4.6. Both companies implement XML in varying ways and to varying degrees. Let's take a look at how each company implements XML in its browsers.

Microsoft Internet Explorer

Microsoft is actually one of the first vendors to add XML support to its browser. Obviously, Microsoft saw how beneficial XML support could be for its product, and how, in conjunction with scripting languages, it extends the browser's functionality. XML support appeared first in Internet Explorer 4 and continues to extend to Internet Explorer 5. Let's look at the type of support each version of Internet Explorer offers.

TIP: *In this chapter, we simply want to give you an idea of what you can expect so you'll realize the wide range of support XML already has. If you need detailed information about XML support within browsers, visit the browser's Web site.*

Internet Explorer 4

Internet Explorer was the first browser to offer a relatively complete array of support for XML. The browser is bundled with a C++ parser, which is used to parse XML documents. The parser also supports the XML object model. The object model offers the developer the ability to interact with and manipulate individual XML elements as independent objects. With Internet Explorer, XML elements become objects, which in turn can be referred to and manipulated by programming and scripting languages to perform whatever function you want them to perform.

In terms of displaying XML, Microsoft provides the XML Data Source Object (XML DSO) feature. This feature, which uses the data-binding facility in Dynamic HTML, displays XML as HTML. However, XML support in Internet Explorer 4 doesn't stop there. Internet Explorer 4 also includes a technology preview release of the Microsoft Extensible Stylesheet Language (MSXSL) processor. This processor lets developers turn XML data into HTML using a style sheet to define the presentation rules for the XML data.

WARNING! MSXSL is different from the current W3C Extensible Stylesheet Language (XSL) specifications and working drafts. Any work you do with MSXSL won't be portable to any other system and doesn't include support for the latest XSL syntax and capabilities. Chapter 11 discusses XSL in more detail.

Internet Explorer 5

Never wanting to stay too far behind the curve, Microsoft once again upgraded its popular Internet Explorer browser and added quite a few new XML-related features. The folks at Redmond have extended XML support in this version considerably, and undoubtedly Microsoft will continue to include as much XML-specific code in subsequent versions.

First, Microsoft has shored up the inconsistencies and instabilities that are some-what apparent in Internet Explorer 4. This means that when you're viewing XML documents, your browser is less likely to crash. The code for Internet Explorer 5 matches the XML 1.0 specification, whereas version 4 had some incompatibilities. Also, version 5 works as an optional validating processor. A Java parser is also slated to become part of the browser.

Internet Explorer 5 now allows embedding of XML in HTML and includes a new XML-based feature called *scriptlets*. Scriptlets allow you store the JavaScript code outside of the page, which means you can more easily manage your scripts. Microsoft has also added behaviors to style sheets. You can use Cascading Style Sheets (CSS) rules to guide the display of XML elements.

TIP: *Microsoft's implementation of XML is actually quite good. In addition to basic support for XML, Microsoft has developed a variety of XML tools that are free and easy to use. You can read more about Internet Explorer 5's implementation of XML at **http://msdn.microsoft.com/xml/default.asp**.*

Netscape Navigator

Admittedly, Netscape has been much slower at jumping on the XML bandwagon. Microsoft included XML support in its browser in the fall of 1997, but it took Netscape much longer to display specific XML support in Navigator. It wasn't until spring 1998 that Netscape announced that a future component of Netscape Communicator would provide true XML support. However, after Netscape realized the need for XML implementation in its browser, the amount of support the company outlined far outpaced Microsoft's first XML offering.

Netscape originally showed off its support of XML at an XML developer's conference in early 1998. The company presented its new browser—now named Communicator 4.6—displaying XML documents. At the conference, Netscape vowed to fully support XML as a data and metadata syntax.

To support XML, Netscape placed an XML parser within the browser and added application support for the XML Linking Language (XLink) specification. Netscape 4.6 also includes support for XML namespaces. In an effort to display all this XML code, Netscape, like Microsoft, takes advantage of CSS, which formats the text encoded within the XML elements.

Netscape does all this through the emerging standard framework for metadata called the *Resource Description Framework (RDF)*. RDF is an XML vocabulary that provides a single mechanism for organizing, describing, and navigating information on Web sites. With RDF, a single interface—Communicator—manages and integrates information from Web sites, push channels, bookmarks, email, and legacy database systems. Undoubtedly, Netscape will add even more support in the future as its browser and server products continue to evolve.

TIP: *For more information on Netscape's XML implementation, see Netscape's Developer Network at **http:// developer.netscape.com**.*

The XML Specification

The World Wide Web Consortium (W3C) can best be described as the Web's governing body. This organization sets the standards for the languages used to deliver information to Web users. The W3C was responsible for formulating HTML and is doing the same with XML. Having a single governing body decide how the language should evolve creates a standard to which software developers can adhere.

Many companies and individuals have contributed to the creation of the XML specification. A short list of those individuals and companies includes Jon Bosak of Sun, Tim Bray of Textuality and Netscape, Jean Paoli of Microsoft, Dave Hollander of Hewlett-Packard, Eve Maler of ArborText, and Joel Nava of Adobe. All of the people and companies involved have offered or submitted ideas, information, and programming support to help write what is known as the XML 1.0 specification. This specification is a relatively small document (about 50 pages) that outlines the semantics of XML. The entire list of editors and contributors is listed at the end of the specification.

The XML specification is the most important document you need to study if you plan to learn XML inside and out. It's basically the official definition of how XML works and how you should use XML to design DTDs, elements, attributes, and entities. It's not the easiest thing to read and understand, however, which is why we include a section in this chapter about the specification and, more importantly, about how to decipher some of the rather cryptic information contained in it. If you plan to create your own DTDs, you need to learn exactly how to read the specification and put the information to good use, because the document defines what is and isn't legal for XML.

WARNING! The specification may have changed since this book was written. For the most up-to-date information on the specification, check out www.w3.org/XML.

At the time this book was written, the XML 1.0 specification was finalized and reviewed by the W3C members and endorsed by the W3C director as an official W3C recommendation. The XML Core Working Group is already hard at work updating the current XML specification. A variety of other working groups are turning out supporting technologies left and right to make XML a complete set of specifications.

How Specifications Are Created

When a markup language such as XML is created, it goes through a lengthy process. First, the need is realized, and the W3C forms a working group to address the issue and create a specification. Specifications must be formally approved by the W3C's membership, which is made up of many industry software and hardware leaders. A working draft is created, followed by a proposed recommendation, and then a final recommendation.

The working group submits a working draft to the W3C director as a proposed recommendation. After the director approves the document, it becomes the official proposed recommendation that is forwarded to the W3C membership. The membership votes on whether the recommendation should become an official W3C recommendation, which signals widespread support for the proposed topic. The W3C advisory committee votes yes, yes with comments, or no. If a no vote is cast, the committee thinks the entire recommendation should be abandoned. If a yes or a yes with comments vote is cast, the recommendation is adopted, press releases are sent out, and testimonials are gathered.

Overview of the XML Specification

The XML specification, like most others, is divided into a number of sections, each describing a certain part of the language. The specification itself is a simple document that can be read within your Web browser or viewed in a variety of other formats. Because we know the document can be quite daunting at first glance—and we wish someone had explained it to us the first time we read it— we'll outline exactly how to read it. The entire specification is included in Appendix A of this book; therefore, you might want to flip back and forth between this chapter and the specification as you learn how to interpret and understand the document. Each W3C specification, by the way, is written in almost the same format, so learning how to read the XML specification will help you understand other W3C recommendations.

At the top is the header section (see Figure 2.1). It includes the version number, the various formats in which you can view the specification, and the names and email addresses of the editors. This section also provides links to all versions of the specification. Make sure you look for the latest version; previous drafts of the document may not contain the most up-to-date information.

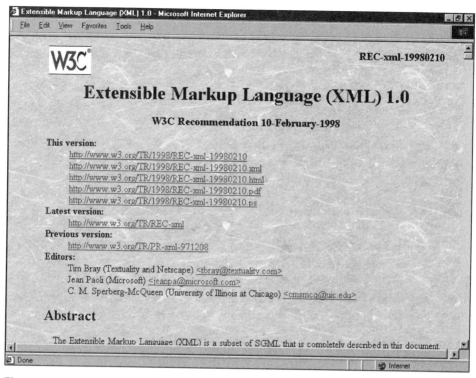

Figure 2.1   The XML specification header.

Following the header is a brief abstract that describes what the specification is and does. The abstract spells out exactly what XML is in a succinct fashion:

"The Extensible Markup Language (XML) is a subset of SGML that is completely described in this document. Its goal is to enable generic SGML to be served, received, and processed on the Web in the way that is now possible with HTML. XML has been designed for ease of implementation and for interoperability with both SGML and HTML."

The next section is called "Status of this Document." It describes the current status of both the specification and the recommendation process. This section also outlines exactly who is responsible for the document and where you can gather more information about XML. Finally, it includes information about the terminology that appears in the document and the standards used throughout. A hyperlinked table of contents and an introduction follow the status section.

After the introduction, which includes a statement of the goals of XML, appears a list of terms (with definitions) used throughout the specification. The next section provides the complete syntax for creating and using XML documents and includes examples and syntax definitions for each component of XML, such as elements, entities, CDATA sections, and so on.

The next section includes some additional appendices that list references and information about character classes, XML and SGML, and character encodings. The document ends with more links and information about the people responsible for developing the specification.

Sections of the XML Specification

Let's quickly examine each section of the specification, so you can find the information you need. The hypertext links that are highlighted throughout the specification will take you to explanations of the various terms and concepts and point you to additional information in other sites and other XML-related specifications.

Section 1: Introduction

The introduction gives you a brief overview of XML. Within a single paragraph, it introduces you to the basic concepts, such as entities, characters, character data, and markup. It also outlines the origins and goals of XML. You should read and understand the terminology in this section, because it will help you understand the rest of the specification.

Section 2: Documents

The "Documents" section describes what an XML document is and what makes a document well-formed and valid. It lists the elements used in a document and defines how documents should be expressed. This section also outlines the character data and markup syntax used in documents. It shows you how to include comments in an XML document, and what processing instructions look like and how they should be specified. It explains the DTD and its declaration, how to handle white space, and how to define different languages within the document.

Section 3: Logical Structures

The "Logical Structures" section explains which elements can appear in an XML document and how empty elements and end-tags are used. In this section of the specification, you learn how well-formed XML documents are created and what attribute values need to be declared. If you need to know how to specify an element, an attribute, or an empty element, this is the section you need to read. You'll also learn what content is valid element content and how to properly nest elements and work with mixed-content data. Finally, this section explains how to declare attribute lists.

Section 4: Physical Structures

The "Physical Structures" section describes everything you would ever want to know about entities. In technical terms, entities are storage units that can appear in XML documents. Both character and entity references are defined and explained, as are parsed entities. You'll learn how XML interprets character and entity references. Character encodings and how XML processors treat entities and references are discussed at some length. Predefined entities and notation declarations are also listed within this section.

Section 5: Conformance

The "Conformance" section explains how XML processors work. If you plan to develop XML processors, or if you simply want to know how processors deal with data (in other words, process it), you need to read this section. If you don't really care what goes on behind the scenes, you can skip this section. The section has plenty of links to information about XML processing.

Section 6: Notation

The "Notation" section is the actual formal grammar used in the XML specification. It's somewhat boring, but it helps explain the various notations used throughout the specification. We suggest that you read this section first so you can familiarize yourself with the notations.

Appendices

The "Appendices" section lists all the references that are used throughout the specification. This section will be useful if you need additional information or want to contact the people who actually helped write the specification.

How to Read and Understand the Specification

Knowing how to read the specification is paramount to really understanding how XML is structured. You need to understand six major sections; the first three are helpful for those who are simply building XML documents and not creating XML processors. You should pay close attention to the second section, "Documents," because it includes the definitions for such things as well-formed documents, elements, and other XML components. Although we cover most of what is included in the specification, we think you should read through the entire document at least twice. The first reading will give you an overview, whereas the second reading will allow the information to sink in.

TIP: *One of the best ways to read the XML specification is to use Tim Bray's Annotated XML Specification. This site is both frame- and Java-enabled. The important parts of the specification are annotated and explained in plain English (as opposed to the technical jargon the actual specification is written in). You'll find the Annotated XML Specification at* **www.xml.com/pub/axml/axmlintro.html**.

You should pay special attention to the boxes of text you'll see throughout the specification, along with the hypertext links. The boxed text defines the *production rules*, which are necessary for creating well-formed or valid XML code (see Figure 2.2).

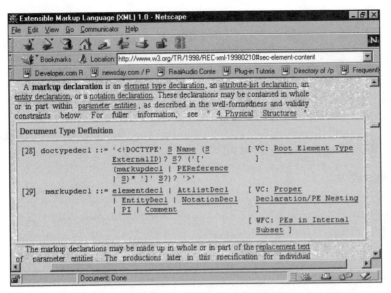

Figure 2.2   A sample production rule from the XML specification.

To understand the specification, you need to know how to read the production rules. The specification follows what is called the Extended Backus-Naur Form (EBNF) notation, which was developed by computer scientists in the 1960s as a way to standardize syntax rules for computer languages. It's basically a standard notation for stating the syntax of any formal computer language, and it can be a bit difficult to read.

Production Rules

Reading a production rule is much like reading a mathematical equation. Basically, the statement on the right side of the equal sign is equivalent to the statement on the left. Here's what a standard production rule looks like:

```
[1] symbol ::=expression
```

The number within the bracket is the number of the production rule. In the specification, production rules appear in boxes, as do the examples. The difference between a production rule and an example is that an example has no number. The word ***symbol*** refers to the rule's name. The **::=** symbol separates the symbol from the expression. The word ***expression*** refers to the definition of the *symbol* or what the symbol is supposed to do.

Before you can really understand them, you should know the rules for production rules. These rules are part of the EBNF syntax. First, let's take a look at the production rule for comments (remember that **[15]** specifies the production rule; the actual rule follows):

```
[15] Comment ::= '<!--' ((Char - '-') | ('-' (Char - '-')))*'- - >'
```

The rules for the production rules are as follows:

- The elements will appear within the production rule in the order in which they should appear in the XML document.

- A vertical slash or pipe character (I) between symbols—as shown between the first character and second character specification in the preceding code example—indicates that only one option can be chosen and included with the element.

- Any information that is placed within parentheses is called a unit. A *unit* is a pattern used to match a specific set of inputs.

- Comments within the production rule itself are specified by the */* text representation.

- An asterisk (*), when not used within comments, specifies that a symbol can appear zero or more times within the production rule.

- Characters or symbols that are enclosed in square brackets ([ ]) define a range of values or a list of values from which you can choose.

- If a left square bracket is followed by a caret symbol—for example, [^&]*, the characters or symbols that follow the [and ^ symbols must be excluded from the definition. Some exclusions are nested within already defined symbols, and some exclusions include an asterisk that isn't within comments. Remember that the asterisk tells you that certain characters are excluded.

- Any characters that are within single or double quotation marks are considered literals.

- A plus sign (+) means one or more symbols must occur.

- The **S** stands for white space within a literal character string.

- A rule followed by **[VC:...]** must apply if the resulting XML document is to be valid. **VC** stands for *validity constraint.*

- A rule that starts with **[WFC:...]** must apply if the XML document is to be well formed. Pay particular attention to these types of rules because you need to follow them to create a well-formed document. **WFC** stands for *well-formedness constraint.* See Chapters 3 and 5 for more information on well-formed XML documents.

An Overview of XML Applications

By now, you know that XML gives developers the ability to create their own sets of elements, their own attributes, and even their own entities. Because of this flexibility, all sorts of vocabularies (or sets of XML markup) can be created as standards for various industries or types of Web functions. An XML *vocabulary* is a set of markup for describing a particular structure and syntax to meet a particular need. For example, the Mathematical Markup Language (MathML) is an XML vocabulary that allows the XML developer to describe the different pieces and parts of mathematical equations. The specifics of MathML are defined in an XML DTD. Think of XML as the grammar, and the particular application—such as MathML—as the vocabulary.

Collections of different XML applications have already been created. These various XML applications fall into a variety of categories. Three of the more extensive categories are:

- *Horizontal-industry applications/vocabularies*—Push-based delivery, software distribution, searching/filtering, e-commerce, and so on.

- *Vertical-industry applications/vocabularies*—Pharmaceuticals, telecommunications, aerospace, and so on.

- *Internal applications/corporate vocabularies*—Internal data processes.

A handful of horizontal, vertical, and industry-specific internal XML applications either have already been developed or are being developed, with more on the way every day. Sometimes referred to as *frameworks*, some of the most popular applications include:

- *Channel Definition Format (CDF)*—Lets developers publish Web-based content automatically to subscribers through a variety of different methods, such as Web browsers, Active Desktop components, HTML-formatted email, and/or Web crawlers. A *channel* is a set of HTML-formatted documents that can be sent to a client in a group or individually. The channel is defined through XML, and information such as the sub-elements contained within the channel, the update schedule, and the delivery mechanism are part of the definition. This is an example of a horizontal vocabulary.

- *Chemical Markup Language (CML)*—Invented by British chemists for the purpose of exchanging descriptions of formulas, molecules, and other chemical specifications between people and computers. CML is used to accomplish such tasks as rendering 2D and 3D molecules. This is an example of a vertical vocabulary.

- *Mathematical Markup Language (MathML)*—Created primarily for supporting the need to display and exchange mathematical formulas and symbols. MathML is used in specialized applications to render mathematical content and notation over both the Internet and an intranet. This is an example of a vertical vocabulary.

- *Open Financial Exchange (OFX)*—Used by both Intuit's Quicken and Microsoft's Money. This vocabulary framework sets the standard for communication among financial software applications and financial institutions. This is an example of a vertical and internal vocabulary.

- *Open Software Description (OSD)*—Uses unique XML elements to describe the delivery of software applications over the Internet. Microsoft and Marimba understood there was a need to create a standard for distributing software over the Internet. Their OSD standard's elements describe such things as the version of the product, the platform on which the product should work, and the upgrade mechanism. Software packages can be delivered using CDF, which means software can now be updated with a push method on a specific schedule. This is an example of a horizontal vocabulary.

- *Resource Description Framework (RDF)*—Specifies general-purpose Web metadata, such as security information, content information, subject-heading information, copyright notices, and so on. RDF is a standard framework that can include many other vocabularies. This is an example of an internal vocabulary.

- *Synchronized Multimedia Integration Language (SMIL)*—Assists developers in integrating multimedia into their sites. SMIL provides a standardized way to describe multimedia and the various components needed to use, display, and manipulate multimedia on the Internet. This is an example of a vertical vocabulary.

- *Web Interface Definition Language (WIDL)*—An object-oriented XML application, best described as an automation tool used to enable automation of all interactions with HTML and XML documents. WIDL-defined services map existing Web content into program variables, making Web resources available, without modification, in formats suited for integration with diverse business systems. This is an example of a horizontal and internal vocabulary.

XML has come a long way in a short period of time. It has gathered a great deal of support from those in the Web-development community who want more than just a simple display markup language, such as HTML. The XML specification includes the new features XML offers and gives you a detailed outline of how XML is structured. By now, you should be familiar with the specification and know how to access it.

Immediate Solutions

Classifying an XML Document

Most XML documents are built according to a DTD, and should reference that DTD either in the beginning of the document, after the XML declaration (**<?xml version="1.0"?>**) and before the content of the document, or within the document type (DOCTYPE) declaration that specifies the DTD. For example, if you want to specify a DTD called memo.dtd, which was created for memo-type documents and stored on a remote server with the URL **http://www.site.com/dtd**, you would supply the following line of code after the XML declaration:

```
<!DOCTYPE memo SYSTEM "http://www.site.com/dtd/memo.dtd">
```

This DOCTYPE declaration points to the specific location of the DTD, and specifies that **memo** is the document element that holds all the text and markup in the document. **SYSTEM** specifies that the DTD can be found on the current computer system. Remember, DTDs are comprised of elements, attributes, and entities, so you can build your own DTDs and essentially create your own elements. In the following section, you get a quick peek at how to declare elements, specify their attributes, declare entities, and use character entities that are already part of the XML standard.

NOTE: *This is just a bit of XML to whet your whistle. Other chapters in the book, which are devoted to the different components of XML DTDs and documents, will give you a complete overview of each component and show you several immediate solutions for using each to meet a variety of needs.*

Defining an Element

To define an element, simply decide what name you want to use and what kind of information or markup it should hold. You use the name to build elements throughout the XML document with start and end tags. The element is composed of letters, digits, periods, dashes, underscores, or colons, and it must always be enclosed in angle brackets. The text **!ELEMENT** is used to define it as an element. An element can describe a variety of different kinds of content, including, but not limited to:

- *A mixed-content declaration*—Allows for both elements and character data
- *A list of elements*—Specifies a single- or multiple-element tag listed within the content section of the element declaration
- *The keyword EMPTY*—Specifies that the element contains no content
- *The keyword ANY*—Allows the element to contain any type of data or markup

To create an element named **paragraph** with the content type specified as **ANY**, insert the following code:

```
<!ELEMENT paragraph ANY>
```

Related solutions:	Found on page:
Using the **ANY** Keyword to Declare Elements	164
Using the **EMPTY** Keyword to Declare Elements	165

Using an Element to Tag Content

To tag content with the element you've just defined, place a start tag and an end tag around the content. Before you do, however, you must ensure that the element's content type matches the type of content in the document. If the element type is a list of other elements, only those elements specified in the definition of the element can be included within the start and end tags. To use the **paragraph** element you've just defined to mark up content, place the opening **paragraph** tag and the closing tag around the content you want to specify as a paragraph, as follows:

```
<paragraph>This is the paragraph element's content.</paragraph>
```

Defining an Attribute

When you define an attribute to further clarify the meaning of an element, you declare it like you declare an element. Attributes are tied to elements. Attribute specifications can appear only within start tags and empty element tags. The attribute declaration's first value is the name of the element to which it applies. You can include the element attribute directly after the element declaration in the

DTD or the document, although it's not required. After you've specified the name of the element the attribute is associated with, you specify the attribute definition list, which consists of the attribute name, the attribute type, and any predefined values you want to include. All attribute names must follow the same naming conventions as elements. To define an attribute for the **paragraph** element defined in the previous section, use the following code:

```
<!ATTLIST paragraph
          TYPE     CDATA     #IMPLIED>
```

Related solution:	Found on page:
Specifying String Attributes	194

Placing a Character Entity in a Document

To use special reserved characters within a document, you need to use a character entity that has already been defined within the XML standard. For example, if you want to use the ampersand sign (&) in the name of a company, you need to specify the XML character entity that represents the ampersand (**&**), because the ampersand is used to specify built-in character entities.

Entities that represent reserved characters always start with an ampersand, are followed by the entity name, and are closed by a semicolon at the end of the entity name. No additional white space is permitted inside the entity. To specify a built-in ampersand entity, place the following code within the content of your XML document:

```
&amp;
```

This code can be used anywhere within the content of an XML document; for example:

```
Welcome to the X,M &amp; L Consulting Firm!
```

The content, once processed, would display as follows:

```
Welcome to the X,M & L Consulting Firm!
```

Related solution:	Found on page:
Using Character Entities in XML Documents	227

Creating Your Own Entity

To create your own entities that hold bits of text and markup, you must first declare them in your DTD as you do elements and attributes. The name of the entity can be made up of letters, digits, periods, dashes, or underscores, and must begin with a letter or an underscore. The value of the entity, called the entity *definition*, must be enclosed in quotes and can contain any well-formed markup. The syntax of an entity declaration is the entity element, **!ENTITY**, followed by the name of the entity, and then the entity declaration. To define an entity specifying that the expansion of **xml** is **the Extensible Markup Language**, include the following code in your XML document's internal DTD:

```
<!ENTITY xml "the Extensible Markup Language">
```

Using the Entity You Have Declared

After you declare an entity, you can place it anywhere within the content of the XML document. The entity reference must start with an ampersand (**&**), include the entity name, and end with a semicolon (**;**). Case is important, so if, for example, you've defined an entity in all uppercase letters, you must also use uppercase letters when you place the entity notation in the document. To place the previously defined entity in your document, use the following code where you want the entity value to display within the content:

```
The future of the Web is closely tied to &xml;.
```

This would be processed through the XML processor and displayed within the XML application accordingly:

```
The future of the Web is closely tied to the Extensible Markup Language.
```

Reading the XML Specification

The XML specification is a difficult document to digest in a single pass. However, you must read the specification and familiarize yourself with it. Although it isn't a tutorial, the XML specification is the definitive guide to the XML syntax and to the rules for creating XML documents and XML options, such as entities, elements, and attributes. In this section, you'll learn how to locate the latest version of the specification and how to read and interpret it.

Locating the Latest Version of the XML Specification

The XML specification is located at the W3C's Web site (**www.w3.org/XML**). To locate the most up-to-date version of the specification, follow these steps:

1. Start your browser, and type "http://www.w3.org/XML" in the address field.

2. Click on the Events/Pubs link at the top of the page.

3. Locate and click on the Extensible Markup Language (XML) 1.0 link. All other links lead to either older versions or other XML-related specifications still in the works.

4. This link should take you to the most recent version of the specification. If it doesn't say Latest Version, scroll down until you see a Latest Version link, and click on it.

Understanding the XML Specification

This section is meant to give you some practice reading the XML specification. You learn how to navigate the specification and find the sections you need. Follow these steps:

1. Locate the latest version of the specification.

2. Scroll to the table of contents.

3. Locate Section 6 (Notation) in the table of contents, and click on the link to move to the Notation section of the document.

4. Read through the brief list of notations so you'll know when certain character strings specify various parameters in XML syntax. After you've familiarized yourself with the notations, scroll back to the table of contents at the top of the specification.

5. Click the link entitled 3.3 Attribute-List Declarations. This section includes information about defining attributes.

6. Read the first section about what an attribute is and what can be included in an attribute list. Take a look at the production rules [52] and [53]. Note what needs to be included within the attribute list definition in the production rule box.

7. Read through the rest of the attribute information until you get to the section Validity Constraint: Fixed Attribute Default. The blue box displays an example of how you can create an attribute list with a fixed value set as the default. This is a real-world example you can use or modify—it is not just the production rule syntax as is specified in most of the production rule boxes.

8. For a clearer understanding of the XML specification, make sure you also read through Tim Bray's Annotated XML Specification located at **www.xml.com/pub/axml/axmlintro.html**. You must be using a frame-enabled or Java-enabled browser to read the Annotated XML Specification.

Chapter 3

XML and HTML Compared

In Depth

Although the Web has a lot to offer, the past technologies used to develop Web pages are fairly out-of-date. For example, HTML's limitations are becoming more and more apparent and have all but stymied the creativity that visionary designers like yourself thrive on. Sure, tables let you do some nifty things, and you can do some tricks with dynamic HTML (DHTML). However, tables barely offer you the ability to handle the dynamic data you have tucked away in those company databases. Also, DHTML doesn't do much good if only half your visitors are able to take advantage of your site. XML, when it's combined with the Extensible Stylesheet Language (XSL), provides answers to all your nondynamic and dynamic dilemmas. It brings data to the Web—and at just the right time—in a much better way than HTML and in a more compatible fashion than browser-specific options.

In this chapter, you'll learn why HTML has reached its breaking point and what you can do about it. Specifically, you'll learn how you can use XML to move beyond the limitations of HTML. In addition, you'll learn how closely related the two markup languages really are. In fact, the next generation HTML, XHTML, has been designed using XML.

At this point, you should be ready to graduate from using the **blink** element, and you're probably chomping at the bit to test your XML wings. If so, read on and you'll learn the right habits for creating good XML. You'll learn where HTML has lost its momentum and, more importantly, some of the pitfalls you might run into when you're designing your first XML document. Finally, you'll learn what is involved in converting your existing HTML documents to XML.

From HTML to XML

Almost all documents on the Web are stored in HTML format or are transformed into HTML format by some form of server-side scripting. Because only a small set of HTML elements is defined, there's no need to transmit any additional language specifications or document definitions with an HTML document; therefore, documents can be transmitted quickly. In addition, you can build an HTML document quickly using any of the defined elements—the HTML specification dictates the rules, and you follow them. Sure, you can mix and match elements to create whatever effect you want, but just like thousands of other HTML developers, you're restricted to using the defined elements to describe and create your documents. Although it's easy to create documents this way, doing so severely limits your development capabilities. Specifically, HTML doesn't allow the developer to extend or structure the design of the document.

HTML's Lack of Extensibility

When you first learned about the various elements HTML offered, mastering them may have seemed like a daunting task. Not only did you have to memorize all those elements and what they did, but you also had to remember their attributes (the key features each element tag offered). But after a while, with only 40-odd major element tags to learn, using HTML tags probably became second nature. When you wanted something to appear bold within the browser, you used the **b** element. If you needed a different font size, you used the **font** element and specified the **size** attribute. And if you wanted to place a link to another document on the page, the anchor element (**a**) with a Uniform Resource Locator (URL) as the value of the **href** attribute worked just fine.

But what if you wanted to define a special element to specify that the text was actually a date? Or what if you wanted the ability to mark up your document and specify where certain types of data were located? You can mix and match HTML elements to get a variety of results on the screen, but you can't create your own element tags and give them specific attributes. In an HTML document, there's no way to describe the data you're presenting—and this lack of extensibility has brought HTML to the breaking point. HTML is great for displaying data, but it doesn't allow developers to extend beyond the limited parameters of the predefined elements. We'll examine this limitation in greater detail in the section "The Differences Between XML and HTML" later in this chapter and show you how limiting HTML can be when you consider the type of data you're presenting.

HTML's Lack of a Clearly Defined Structure

HTML fails to provide any clearly defined structure for documents. Outside of scripting, you cannot present a database full of data by using just HTML. HTML doesn't define a clear hierarchy to the data. Instead, every document created in HTML is flat.

The document has no *real* depth; however, links inside of and away from the document *imply* data hierarchy. This characteristic creates a problem for you when you're designing the data within a document and a problem for users when they're discovering the data.

From the design perspective, you must think ahead, break apart the data manually, and then create a visual representation of the data. Creating a static HTML representation of data is not only time consuming for you, the developer, but also for visitors to your site. It prevents visitors from really discovering the data you have to offer in their own unique ways. Visitors must take your word that the data is presented in the best way it can be. Just think how many times you've run across a site and thought, "I can't find a thing here." Chances are, you looked for another site where the presentation of information was logical and allowed you to easily find what you needed. With XML, you can create structures for data that are separate from how the data is formatted. This allows the actual presentation of the data to be much more flexible than is possible with HTML.

HTML's Lack of Structure Validation

HTML documents have very little structure, which makes it quite difficult for applications to check for structural validity. More importantly, HTML lacks support for any kind of language specification that applications use to check for valid document structure. The browser simply views the data and displays it. The developer of the HTML document may have left out the **head** element or accidentally placed the **body** element before the **head** element. In such a case, the browser may leave out some content because of the odd structure, causing problems for those who came to the site for information.

NOTE: *You can, however, check the validity of your HTML documents yourself. The W3C offers an online validator in which you just plug in your URI and it tells you whether your document is valid or not. Go to **http://validator.w3.org/** for details.*

The Differences between XML and HTML

XML is an excellent vehicle for manipulating structured data on the Web. Because of HTML's ability to present data, the two markup languages complement each other. When you stop considering the presentation of data and start concentrating on the structure of documents, you start to see XML's usefulness. Unlike HTML, XML is an excellent markup language for building complex Web applications. Don't worry—your knowledge of HTML will actually help you learn XML (however, note that XML is not HTML). The transition from HTML to XML will be quicker, and the concepts outlined in the XML specification will be easier to understand.

XML is an excellent language to use when you've outgrown the simple presentation options HTML has to offer. Microsoft Internet Explorer supports XML with the data-binding capability of DHTML and the Channel Definition Format (CDF), and Netscape Navigator offers similar support. Because both of today's popular browsers support the Document Object Model (DOM), the elements you're accustomed to using can now be defined in XML as objects. As a result, you can program them through scripting languages, giving them the ability to come alive and not just blink. This extensibility makes XML the ideal language to use when you need to display dynamic data on different platforms.

To you, the developer, all this means that you can now supply your site with a plethora of dynamic content, and you don't have to worry about any of HTML's limitations. XML not only lets you specify dynamically changing data in your documents, but it also allows you to create data sources that can be used for a variety of purposes, which in turn makes interoperability between applications on a server or client machine and your site a reality.

In more basic terms, XML and HTML differ in three major aspects:

• With XML, you can define your own set of elements and attribute names whenever you need to.

• With XML, document structures can be nested to any level of complexity, assuming they are following the XML rules of proper nesting.

• XML documents can contain an optional description of the document's grammar so other applications that need to perform validation on the document's structure can do so.

As you may have gathered by now, XML differs from older versions of HTML in some relatively fundamental ways. That doesn't mean learning XML requires you to tear down everything you've ever learned about using HTML. As a matter of fact, you'll soon see that XML and HTML look very similar and work in much the same way. Because both XML and HTML originate from Standard Generalized Markup Language (SGML), the granddaddy of markup languages, features such as syntax, elements, rules, and design principles are similar.

Comparing HTML Code to XML Code

Both XML and HTML use or are made up of elements. You may not be familiar with the term *elements*, but you've used elements again and again. Most likely, you're familiar with the term *tags* because in HTML, elements are most often called tags. Tags are actually just parts of elements. Specifically, tags either start or end elements. In technical terms, a tag is a singular entity that opens or closes an element. The **<cite>** tag—which in HTML marks up citation text—is an example of an opening tag (or start tag). The tag **</cite>** is used to close the citation element. Both the start and end tags and the content enclosed between them represent the entire element.

HTML and XML use elements to itemize text that should be marked up, which in turn is used to describe the content of a document. When you start examining XML more closely, you'll notice that there is one major difference between HTML and XML. Unlike HTML, XML's primary purpose is to describe the structure of data: HTML is geared more towards describing how the content should be displayed. Never in your wildest dreams have you used HTML to describe content. You've used it to display content, not structure it. With XML, the Web developer can mark up the contents of a document by describing it in terms of its relevance as data.

The easiest way to explain the difference is by looking at a relatively simple example, which we'll expand upon throughout this chapter. HTML code, such as the following, should be familiar and easy to read:

```
<p>Gone With the Wind</p>
```

It's obvious that this line of code simply describes the content of a paragraph. When the previous code is processed through an HTML browser, the text specified within the **p** element is displayed with whatever other content is included in the page. And that's the point. Specifically, HTML *displays* the content of this paragraph element.

This kind of markup language works fine if all you want to do is display the information with the paragraph element. But think about how you might want to use this content in the future. You might want to create a database of your favorite movies—a database that could easily be searched by anyone who visits your site. Instead of just *displaying* the content of the paragraph element, you may want to *access* it as data. In that case, you could do one of two things: You could use a scripting language that interfaces with a database, or you could use XML. How? First, you would specify which elements to use to mark up the titles of movies (in this case, *Gone With the Wind*). In XML, you can create an element to specify that the words in the title *mean* something (as shown in the following example) instead of creating an element that just displays text:

```
<film>Gone With the Wind</film>
```

You could use a style sheet to display the content of the **film** element (and the rest of the XML document) in any way you chose, and the **film** element would create a structure for your document; one that would follow a certain function and form. For example, you might set up one style sheet to display this film information on a Web browser, specifying that if the user had a Palm Pilot, a specific style sheet would be used to display the same information on a smaller screen. HTML is the display language and XML is the structure language.

How XML and HTML Fit into the Web

By now, you should have a relatively good concept of what XML offers and the limitations of HTML. You should also realize that it's time you start looking at your data as data and not just as text that needs to be displayed. XML will shine the most with data applications that can't be structured by simple HTML. Examples include the following:

- Applications that send the same data across the Web to users who have different display mechanisms

- Applications that require some sort of intelligent agent to customize and tailor the information discovery for individual user needs

- Applications that require perusal through or mediation between two or more similar databases

- Applications for which the processing is done on the client side rather than on the server side

There's no doubt you could meet all of these requirements by using the Common Gateway Interface (CGI), Java, or Visual Basic to create server- or client-side scripts or even by using browser plug-ins. But think about the constraints you impose on the user with these methods. For example, users must go through one extra step if they have to download a plug-in to see your data. They must also know *how* to download plug-ins, know if the plug-in is browser specific, and have a computer that is capable of running it. These requirements may severely limit the number of users who can view your data.

The philosophy of XML is that the data format used to deliver the information should not bind the user or even the developer to a particular delivery engine, set of content-creation tools, or even scripting language. XML is meant to offer a vendor-independent platform regardless of whether you're developing or displaying XML data.

HTML's Loss of Standardization

Because XML doesn't limit you to a certain set of elements like HTML does, you can create your own set of elements—a library, if you will—that constructs the foundation of a document. You can name these elements whatever you want or create whatever attributes you need to associate with certain elements. You can't do this with HTML, although as you've probably discovered, browser manufacturers have been creating elements that are specific to their own browsers. The problem is that the World Wide Web Consortium (W3C) has not standardized the browser-specific elements. If you want to use browser-specific elements, your visitors must be using that particular browser and, in most cases, a particular version of the browser.

Disparity in HTML Tools

We haven't examined HTML or XML editing tools yet, but we'll say a few words about how HTML tools are not always your best friends. Many tools perform code murder. Why is this? The problem is fourfold.

3. XML and HTML Compared

First, browsers are relatively forgiving of bad HTML code, because so much bad HTML was *grandfathered* into the Web.

Second, different HTML editors may supply browser-specific elements that work only on one type (or even one version) of a browser. If you're using this type of editor, you're not creating consistent HTML code that can be used across the board by virtually any user.

Third, HTML editors are not always consistent with the elements they place within the content of your document. For example, Claris Home Page places the proper start and end tags (**<p></p>**) for specifying a paragraph element in your document, but Netscape Composer doesn't. Instead, it simply places a single **<p>** tag in the document or, in some cases, replaces what you thought was a carriage return with what really is a line break specified by the **
** tag.

Let's create two versions of a simple Web page: one using Netscape Composer and another using Claris Home Page. The page simply says, "Now is the time for all good men to come to the aid of their country." We've broken it down to three lines by pressing the Enter key at the end of each line. We've also added a simple Graphics Interchange Format (GIF) image to the end of our sentence. Now, let's compare the code we get from each Web-composing application. Here is the code Netscape Composer generated:

```
<HTML>
<HEAD>
<META NAME="Author" CONTENT="C.Kirk">
<META NAME="GENERATOR" CONTENT="Mozilla/4.05">
</HEAD>
<BODY>
<P>Now is the time for all good men to come
<BR>to the aid of their
<BR>country. <IMG SRC="picture.gif" HEIGHT=240 WIDTH=10>
</BODY>
</HTML>
```

Now, let's take a look at the same page generated by Claris Home Page:

```
<HTML>
<!--This file create at 7/17/00 at 12:00 AM by Claris Home
Page version 3.0-->
<HEAD>
<META NAME="GENERATOR" CONTENT="Claris Home Page 3.0">
<X-CLARIS-WINDOW TOP=42 BOTTOM=469 LEFT=4 RIGHT=534>
<X-CLARIS-TAGVIEW MODE=minimal>
</HEAD>
```

```
<BODY BGCOLOR="FFFFFF">
<P>Now is the time for all good men to come</P>
<P>to the aid of their</P>
<P>country. <IMG SRC="picture.gif" HEIGHT=240 WIDTH=10
ALIGN=bottom></P>
</BODY>
</HTML>
```

Notice that even simple things, such as the paragraph element, are different. Claris Home Page used the **p** element between lines instead of the **br** element, even though we pressed the same key on the keyboard. Also, notice that Claris Home Page specified white as the page background color but Composer didn't, although we used it in both page-layout programs.

This code disparity even in simple documents is a big problem. Both pages display exactly the same way in both Netscape Navigator and Internet Explorer, but that's not to say that they would appear identically on other browsers. More importantly, the code is different, which means that converting documents from HTML to XML can be a chore—especially if you're using a variety of HTML tools (almost all of which add their own little nuisances and quirks). Because of this lack of standardization, it's hard to catalog, view, and print documents throughout the Web. A standardized approach may sound boring, but in the end, it's less time-consuming and allows the developer to spend more time developing the content instead of cleaning up sloppy or inconsistent code.

Finally, until recently, new elements were being introduced almost hourly when new versions of browsers and new HTML specifications hit the street. To keep up with these additions to HTML, Web page editors had to update their HTML page-creation tools frequently or hand-code the new HTML elements.

How can XML help? XML requires a document to be *well formed*. Each element must be a combination of start tag and end tag (unless it's an empty element), and elements must be nested properly. The XML specification is all about structure. The minute you declare a document to be an XML document, you must follow the rules of the specification, or the foundation of your structure will fall flat. XML editors can't be as loose with XML code as HTML editors are with HTML code—there are just too many rules to follow.

XML to the Rescue

XML gives you the flexibility that HTML doesn't. For example, if the **film** element (described earlier in the "Comparing HTML Code to XML Code" section) doesn't explain the film well enough and doesn't help differentiate between certain kinds of films, you can create an element that does. For example, let's say you wanted to differentiate between black-and-white and color films. You could create another element named **bw-film** and use it this way:

```
<bw-film>Bringing Up Baby</bw-film>
```

This element works great for this particular case. But if you wanted to offer the ability to access all films on your site regardless of whether they are color or black and white, and if you wanted to differentiate between such things as versions, dates, and so on, you could take your **film** element one step further. You could create attributes to describe more specific types of **film** element characteristics. HTML has a specific set of elements, and each element has a specific set of attributes that you can't add to or change; but with XML, you can create and change attributes for elements.

Not only can you create names for your elements, but you can also define names you want for element attributes. If you use attributes with your **film** element, you can easily describe any film you want. You can use a variety of attributes and allow all elements and their content to be viewed or searched. So in this case, it makes more sense to create an attribute instead of an element that describes the element as black-and-white or color. So, now you can specify whether a film is black-and-white, silent, or created in a particular year—all using attributes. In the following line of code, the **film** element specifies a black-and-white film:

```
<film color="no">Bringing Up Baby</film>
```

Let's take this example a bit further, so you can see how expansive XML is. Suppose more than one version of a movie exists, such as the thriller *Godzilla*. The preceding example has only one attribute to describe the **film** element. With XML, you can create multiple attributes to describe the elements more specifically. The following code shows another attribute that specifies the year the film was made:

```
<film color="yes" year="1998">Godzilla</film>
```

Sure, this process makes marking up a document a lot more work, and it's certainly more complex than just placing the paragraph element in front of the film title. However, when you get specific with your markup, you're able to distinguish between when the word *Godzilla* is referring to a film and when it's referring to your last blind date. It also helps you differentiate between one version of the movie *Godzilla* and another. By structuring the document and creating this kind of foundation, you make it much easier to catalog and find data in a document. It's not that XML works better than HTML in all circumstances—it just gives you more features and options than HTML for dealing with detailed data.

Why HTML Isn't the Ticket Anymore

Although the previous example probably gave you a glimpse into how XML provides better structure to documents, to understand why HTML simply won't do it for you anymore, you need to know what HTML does well and what it does poorly. Both XML and HTML are called *markup languages*, and for a time, you could convince most people that HTML *was* being used for markup. After its popularity grew, however, people began to stretch HTML to the max, and the limitations started to show. For example, because HTML doesn't specify structured data, on a site that lists films, their actors, and their directors, a user searching for a specific actor—for instance, "Robert Redford"—would get all the films Redford was in as well as all the films he directed.

As you already know, the problem with HTML really lies in the fact that HTML handles the display of data relatively well but has no clue about how to handle the structure of the data. When you start designing a Web site, you'll quickly realize that, although displaying data is what HTML does best, it can't handle displaying data on a variety of platforms. HTML will still be useful for designing Web sites or intranets, but developers now need to decide which projects will work best with HTML and which will more easily fit within XML.

Let's look at a simple example that will illustrate the differences between HTML and XML. Suppose you have a chunk of data (some corporate manuals and some brochures) that you need to display on a variety of platforms. You have on-the-road salespeople using hand-held Palm Pilot computers. You also have corporate businesspeople sitting at their desks using Netscape Navigator as their browser. In addition, your customers use a multitude of different computers—from Macs to Windows-based PCs. If you wanted to use HTML to deliver the data to everyone involved, you would most likely have to create separate pages of the same data for each type of user. For example, you would have to set up pages specifically for the Navigator users. Then, you would set up a site specifically for customers who could take advantage of the special features Internet Explorer offers. In addition, you would have to condense more pages into a document the hand-held computer users could view quickly. Then, when the data changed, you would have to plow through all the different types of pages and make the changes, which would be a laborious process with a high likelihood of error. Let's take a closer look at why HTML doesn't work for everything you will do on the Web or within an intranet.

Why HTML Doesn't Work for Handling Data

HTML was created to provide a quick and simple solution for displaying documents on a variety of platforms. Initially, the documents consisted mainly of text and included a few graphics and maybe a link or two that pointed to a single document or particular section of a document. Because of a variety of factors—including bandwidth constraints, incompatibility between file formats, and lack of multimedia PCs—the idea of offering video, sound, and access to databases wasn't even considered in the early days. HTML was really meant more for accessibility to relatively bland text-based documents than to a diverse selection of files, formats, and data. HTML can display text and simplistic formatting, but it can't do what page-description languages, such as PostScript, can do. In 1994, as the popularity of the Web increased, developers and designers quickly realized HTML's limitations. Specifically, they found that it couldn't or didn't offer the following features:

- The ability to publish one chunk of data in a variety of ways and to a variety of display devices

- Linking options that were more complex than simple one-way links

- Flexibility to structure and describe different types of data

- Control over how the data is displayed

The Differences between HTML and XML Syntax

Let's examine the differences and similarities between XML's and HTML's language syntax. Although differences exist, you'll probably be surprised to learn that the two languages have plenty of similarities—especially if you've followed the rules of creating good HTML markup. If you've practiced creating good HTML markup, it will be easier for you to convert existing HTML documents to XML. Let's start by examining what HTML lets you get away with; then we'll see what XML requires, and whether those requirements also exist in HTML.

TIP: *If you follow the suggestions in this section and format your XML code accordingly, your documents will be well formed.*

No More Sloppy Documents

With HTML, you can get away with creating sloppy documents. How many times have you viewed the source of an HTML document and found a dizzying array of mistakes, missing elements, and just downright sloppy code? Some of the problems are due to people not knowing proper HTML syntax, whereas others are due to HTML editors that simply haven't kept up with the changes in HTML. Because most of today's browsers are relatively forgiving, a lot of these *faux pas* are glossed over, and the data is displayed regardless. With HTML, you can be sloppy without great fear of retribution. For example, if you leave out the closing tag in the anchor element (**</a>**) when you specify a link to another document, the rest of the text from that point on turns into one big hypertext link—but the information still displays. It may not display the way you intended, but it displays nonetheless.

However, with XML, you can't be sloppy. As a matter of fact, the first objective for designing any XML document is that it be well formed. Tags must be nested properly and start tags must have end tags. If one end tag is missing, your XML processor will return an error—you can't slide by with sloppiness in XML the way you can in HTML. And this is a good thing. It means that the end user won't be left wondering if the document is displaying as it should. Not only is the data and information displayed properly, but the structure of the data is also clearly and accurately defined.

Declaring Your Markup Language

XML recommends that you tell the parser the document is an XML document. With HTML, you can get away with not declaring which markup language will be used. You could be using HTML 2 or HTML 4, and the browser usually figures out how to display the data. With XML, you should declare that your document is an XML document and what version of the XML specification you plan to use. (Note that currently XML 1.0 is the only version available.) You do so using the XML declaration, which is a small string of code that appears at the top of any XML document. This declaration shows the processor that this document is an XML document. The XML declaration looks like this:

```
<?xml version="1.0"?>
```

Starting and Ending with Tags

All XML elements have a start tag and an end tag. If you've created even a single Web page, you've used at least one element in your effort to create an HTML document. For example, you may have used the **title** element to specify the title of the Web page. To tell the browser where the title begins and ends in an XML document, you need to use a start tag and an end tag, as shown in this example:

```
<title>This is the title of my Web page.</title>
```

In the past, when you developed your HTML pages, you may have used the paragraph element's start tag (**<p>**) without its end tag (**</p>**). This is something many developers have chosen to do for one reason or another, such as to save typing time. With XML, however, every time you use a paragraph element with the start tag, specified as **<p>**, you must also use its accompanying end tag, **</p>**. You might be surprised (as we were with our code) to see how many start tags and how few end tags you've used throughout your HTML code. You'll need to make sure your HTML document has end tags before you can convert it to XML.

Watching out for Empty Elements

Empty elements need to be formatted correctly in XML documents. Lots of developers have created thousands of HTML pages and probably never knew there was such a thing as an empty element. But they are used frequently, not only in HTML but also in XML. For example, in HTML the image element is defined by the **<img>** tag. To specify a link to the file.gif image file in HTML, you would type the following code:

```
<img src="file.gif">
```

This is considered an empty element because no content is associated with it. Element content is the stuff found between the element's start tag and the element's end tag. The value "**file.gif**" is the **src**, or source-attribute value, and it's not considered content of the **img** element. However, **<img src="file.gif">** is still a tag (and an element). Because it has no content, you probably wouldn't think of adding an end tag to this element declaration. Remember, however, that in XML, every start tag must have an end tag. So, what do you do with elements that don't normally offer content but still require you to specify an end tag? You can do one of two things. You can specify the element as an empty element, sans content, by doing what comes naturally:

```
<img src="file.gif"></img>
```

Or you can do what comes naturally in XML—something you'll find you do a lot if you use CDF to develop channels. You can specify the empty element in this fashion (which is the preferred way to specify empty elements in XML documents):

```
<img src="file.gif"/>
```

Go through your HTML documents and you'll start to realize how many empty elements exist in your code. By doing so, you'll get an indication of how much work you have to do to convert HTML documents to XML documents.

Placing Quotes around Attribute Values

While we're on the subject of elements, and because we just looked at one empty element that included an attribute, let's talk about how XML requires quotes around attribute values. In some circumstances, HTML attributes can be written without quotes, even though it's recommended that you always use quotes around attribute values. Take, for example, the following line of code:

```
<q cite=www.mysite.com>XML is fun</q>
```

Notice that no quotes appear around the attribute value—HTML does not require you to place quotes around the **cite** attribute value. The **q** (quotation) element's **cite** attribute value of **www.mysite.com** will work fine in HTML. However, if this same line of code is placed in an XML document, the parser returns an error. With HTML, this code simply signals to the browser that the quote comes from **www.mysite.com**; the browser will interpret the value regardless of whether quotes appear. However, in XML documents, quotes are required. For our XML document to be well formed, the preceding code example would need to be changed to the following:

```
<q cite="www.mysite.com">XML is fun</q>
```

It doesn't matter whether you use single or double quotes as long as you're consistent. Also, in HTML, a standalone attribute is written as follows:

```
<hr noshade/>
```

However, in XML, every attribute must have both a name and a value. Therefore, the previous code is written as follows in XML:

```
<hr noshade="noshade"/>
```

Nesting Tags

Tags need to be nested correctly in XML documents. If you're a careful developer, you may already nest your tags correctly in your HTML documents. If so, when it comes to being a top-notch XML developer, you're halfway there. To nest tags properly, you close first what you opened last. For example, although this code listing would work just fine in HTML, it wouldn't work in XML:

```
<i><b>This text is bold and italicized.</i></b>
```

This code wouldn't work in XML because we didn't close the **b** element first as we should have; it was the last tag we opened. Nesting tags correctly is important in XML, because so much of the XML document depends on the parser knowing where things begin and end. The following line of code illustrates the proper way to nest bold and italic elements:

```
<i><b>This text is bold and italicized.</b></i>
```

Ignoring White Space

With HTML, white space is ignored. Go ahead. Press the spacebar a hundred times between text while you're writing your HTML code in your favorite text editor. What do you get? Most likely a sore thumb. Only a single space is recognized.

That's why developers were so happy when tables were invented—tables allowed more control over the placement of text or graphics.

With XML, however, the content of any element is treated as data, which means it's possible to indicate to an XML processor that certain whitespace is *significant* and should be preserved. For example, the following code

```
<film>Gone With the        Wind</film>
```

is not the same as

```
<film>Gone With the Wind</film>
```

When you create an XML document, you must pay attention to extra spaces in your element content. You must also clean up any sloppy HTML code you want to convert so the content is represented as you intended.

TIP: *To make sure that whitespace is preserved in an element, you can use the **xml:space** attribute in that element. However, you must remember to declare the **xml:space** attribute if you're going to use it. See Section 2.10 of the XML specification in Appendix A for more information.*

Specifying Character Data

In XML documents, unlike HTML, it's possible to indicate to the processor that certain data should not be checked for markup. This is done by creating a CDATA section. Data in which an XML processor will not look for the < or & symbols, which usually indicate the beginning of markup or entities, is called unparsed character data. One use for CDATA sections is to include the contents of a script within an XML data source. Because scripts may contain characters that otherwise might be interpreted as XML markup, it's often easier to tell the XML processor to simply ignore these characters than to use entity references (such as **<** and **&**) to hide these characters. The following code shows the syntax of a CDATA section:

```
<![CDATA[Information]]>
```

A CDATA section begins with **<![CDATA[** and ends with **]]>**. Inside of these combinations of characters, you can put anything except for **]]>**. The XML processor will ignore any markup inside of the **[Information]** section, but the information will still be part of the element. Another good example of a use for CDATA sections is for XML tutorials. For example, if the following element were written without a CDATA section, it would cause an error. Because of the CDATA section, this element can be parsed without a problem:

```
<example>
<![CDATA[ Certain characters, such as &, <, >, ", and ' need to be enclosed
in CDATA sections or escaped using entity references.]]>
</example>
```

Case Sensitivity

Unlike HTML, XML is case sensitive. You'll read it here, and you'll read it again and again, because it's such an important concept for developers: XML is case sensitive. Why is this so important to remember? Because in HTML, case is not important, and if you're like most HTML developers, you may not have typed your element names in lowercase. In fact, you may have used both uppercase and lowercase throughout your documents with no ill effects. However, when you specify elements and attributes in XML, you must use the same case. We suggest you use lowercase. This element markup

```
<director>Don Simpson</director>
```

is not the same as

```
<DIRECTOR>Don Simpson</DIRECTOR>
```

It wouldn't be interpreted the same through the XML processor, because the element name, **director**, is lowercase in one instance and uppercase in another. You should start looking through the code you plan to convert from HTML to XML to make sure you've been consistent.

Defining Entities

In XML, you can define entities. Have you ever found yourself endlessly typing the same character data again and again on your Web pages? Unlike HTML, XML allows you to create your own entities to specify certain characters or groups of characters you use repeatedly in documents. With HTML, character entities specify reserved characters, such as the open angle bracket (<); but no convention exists for creating your own entities to specify characters other than reserved characters. For more information about creating XML entities, check out Chapter 9.

Defining XML Applications

XML can define new applications. Imagine having not only the flexibility to define a document's structure, but also the ability to create your own Web-based applications in a single markup language. Unlike HTML, XML can be used to define new applications. CDF and the Resource Description Framework (RDF) are two prime examples of *XML applications*—applications that use XML to define their capabilities, elements, and syntax. With CDF, you can create customized delivery channels for a variety of display types, such as HTML-formatted email, Active Desktop items, and even Windows screen savers.

Because HTML doesn't allow you to define any of your own elements, you're stuck with elements that cannot be combined or changed in any way to create your own application. The closest you can come to such a thing in HTML is scripting, either with Java, JavaScript, CGI scripting on the server side, or VBScript. And even then, you have to learn an entirely different language and its syntax. With XML applications, you already know the rules. You have to learn the individual elements and their attributes, but you still follow the same structural concepts that XML requires.

Developing Your Own DTDs

HTML uses a universal DTD that defines the rules and syntax of all the elements you use This universal DTD limits your ability to extend your HMTL documents. The DTD specifies where you can use various elements in a document, in what order you can use them, and what attributes you can use. Because XML is primarily a system for defining your own language for your own Web documents, you develop your own set of rules for the elements you create—and hence, your own DTD, if you choose. You can also use a DTD already defined for your particular industry.

Related solution:	*Found on page:*
Creating and Specifying DTD	142

A Quick HTML-to-XML Conversion

Let's take a quick look at how a simple HTML document can be converted to XML. We'll build on the example used earlier in this chapter and convert an HTML movie-oriented page to an XML data document. This site describes the videotaped movies of someone we'll name Bobby Diggins. Here's the HTML code we'll start with:

```
<h1>Bobby Diggins' Video Library</h1>
<table>
  <tbody>
   <tr>
     <td>Shag</td>
     <td>Bringing Up Baby<td/>
     <td>As Good As It Gets</td>
     <td>The Graduate</td>
     <td>Godzilla</td>
     <td>Godzilla</td>
     <td>Psycho</td>
   </tr>
  </tbody>
</table>
```

Notice that we've used the **table** element to give the HTML document a kind of hierarchical look and feel, although the data has no true structure. We just placed the movie titles within the table as we saw fit. If someone wanted to search this document for a particular title, the search feature of the browser would simply move through the document, stopping at each occurrence of the word the visitor was looking for. If the visitor was looking for *Gone With the Wind* and Bobby included a reference to another movie with the word *wind* in its title, the search feature would stop on that movie, too.

TIP: *For an interesting glimpse at how a Web page can be made over, check out Microsoft's XML column, "Help, My Web Page Needs a Makeover," located at **http://msdn.microsoft.com/xml/articles/xml041398.asp**. It's an interesting step-by-step look at using a variety of scripting options to convert from HTML to XML.*

If we look more closely at the document, we really don't know what Bobby owns. Does he own two copies of *Godzilla*? Maybe. Perhaps he owns the original version. Then again, he could own the Japanese version, or maybe the 1998 version. To answer such questions, we need to convert this document to XML, so we can use XML's flexibility to create our own elements for our own purpose.

First, let's consider what elements we need. We need an element called **film** and maybe one called **colorfilm**. No wait, that won't do. What if we want to access all the black-and-white *and* color films? We couldn't do that if we separated the types of films into two different elements. Instead, we need to make sure we create the appropriate attributes to specify the types of films for which we might want to search. The attributes can specify whether the film is in color, what year the film came out, maybe whether it has sound, or possibly whether it's a foreign film. These attributes allow us to get specific with each film without putting the films into different predefined categories. Then, we can incorporate more complex searches and not leave out a single film.

TIP: *If you want more information on how to create elements, see Chapters 6 and 7. For more information on creating attributes, check out Chapter 8.*

Now, let's convert our HTML document into an XML document. The following code uses our **film** element along with several attributes we've declared:

```
<library>
  <owner>Bobby Diggins</owner>
  <films>
    <film color="yes" year="1984">Shag</film>
    <film color="no" year="1945">Bringing Up Baby</film>
    <film color="yes" year="1997">As Good As It Gets</film>
```

```
        <film color="yes" year="1969">The Graduate</film>
        <film color="no" year="1935">Godzilla</film>
        <film color="yes" year="1998">Godzilla</film>
        <film color="no" year="1954">Psycho</film>
    </films>
</library>
```

Looking at the XML code, you can now tell more about the films Bobby has in his video library. Specifically, you now know he has two different versions of the film *Godzilla*: the original and the 1998 remake. You also know that he has a collection of both black-and-white films and color films. But what else can we gather from this XML document? In the next section, you'll learn how XML creates a document tree structure that can be referenced in a variety of ways. Knowing about how XML structures data, compared to HTML, will help you in the conversion process.

The XML Document's Tree Structure

When you create a document in HTML or XML, you're creating a tree structure that represents the elements used in the document. The difference between HTML and XML is that the XML tree structure tends to place more meaning on the relationship of the elements.

The HTML tree structure adds very little meaning to the HTML document. Sure, there are the **head** and **body** elements, which signal to the HTML browser that it should place the title information or meta-tag information in the proper places. These elements also specify where the body content should begin and end. But after that, your document really has no structure, even if you use header elements—**h1**, **h2**, **h3**, and so on. Because of the unstructured method with which HTML works, you could easily place an **h2** element before an **h1** element, and the structure of the document wouldn't be affected. Because HTML just displays—and doesn't really interpret—the elements as structures, the content within these elements would still display, regardless of whether you use them in the proper place.

But XML is different. When you create an XML document, you're really defining a hierarchy and specifying elements, subelements, and so on. If we were to create a diagram of Bobby's video library document, it would look something like Figure 3.1.

TIP: *Microsoft's CDF is a prime example of how an XML application follows a structured format. Open a channel in Internet Explorer, and if the channel contains subelements and the subelements contain additional content or elements, you'll see a tree structure. For more information on CDF, read Chapter 17.*

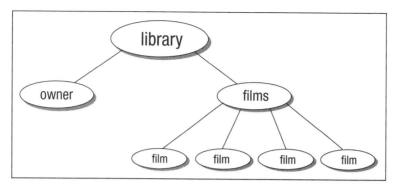

Figure 3.1   An example of how the video library is structured.

Every XML document has a single root element, and all the other elements branch off from this root element. This arrangement is different than HTML, in which a document has only two separate sections: the **head** section and the **body** section. To illustrate this point, Figure 3.2 shows the Windows 98 Explorer window displaying its directory structure. The root element is My Computer, and all the subelements are branches from the root.

In our previous XML document example with Bobby's video library, the **library** element is the root element. From this root element, all other elements—often referred to as *descendants*, or *children*—branch off. This is an important concept

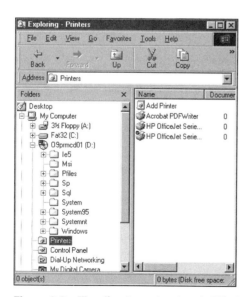

Figure 3.2   The directory structure in Windows 98 Explorer is much like an XML
            document's structure.

to grasp and one you probably didn't pay much attention to when you were creating HTML documents. In fact, you were probably more concerned about where the HTML elements appeared on the page than about which elements were descendants of other elements. To create effective XML documents, you should start thinking about the structure of the document and leave the look of the document to the style sheets. When you work with large documents or a lot of data, it's imperative that you pay attention to structure, so the data falls into the right places.

Taking Markup a Bit Further

In our video library example, we created a relatively structured data document. The elements we used helped create the structure and specify that certain data represents films. We can, however, take the markup a bit further and mark up specific text in the document. We can mark up the document much as we would with HTML—but instead of describing how the data should look, we're actually designating certain pieces of text as important pieces of data. For example, if we were to take the following sentence

```
In the Graduate, a movie produced in 1969,
Dustin Hoffman made his major film debut.
The critics all agreed that he was an emerging
talent who would soon make it big.
```

and use XML to mark it up in an effort to make the text more explicit, we would come up with code that looks like this:

```
<review subject-type="film">
In
<film color="yes" year="1969">The Graduate</film>,
A movie produced in
<year>1969</year>,
<actor>Dustin Hoffman</actor>
made his major film debut. The critics
all agreed that he was an emerging talent
who would soon make it big. </review>
```

If we mark up the text within the document as shown in the preceding code example, we make it possible for a program to search for films that feature Dustin Hoffman as an actor or films that were produced in 1969. It would be almost impossible to offer a search feature such as this if we used current HTML elements.

Good XML and HTML Design

Most of what you'll read about good HTML design focuses on using specific elements to achieve a certain effect in the *display* of data. But good design, regardless of whether you're using XML or HTML, depends on some basic rules for structuring the site and, more importantly, for planning for the site. It's important to remember the following guidelines:

- Specify a reason for your site.

- Define or know your intended audience.

- Know what hardware and software your users will need to view your site.

- Know your own limits and the limits of your site.

- Plan your site.

- Structure the flow of your site by creating a site map.

- Don't forget the importance of navigational controls.

- Test, test, test, and retest your site.

Notice that none of these design principles relates specifically to the capabilities of any language. Instead, they outline a larger concept of site design. Let's take a look at each of these principles in more detail.

TIP: *For more tips on site design, check out the article "Building a Better Interface" in the Web Graphics section of CINet Central's Site Builder site at **www.builder.com/Graphics/UserInterface**.*

Specify a Reason for Your Site

The first thing you need to do is specify a reason for your site. You don't have to declare it outright on the site itself, but as the developer, you need to know exactly why you're designing your site. Do you want to inform, promote, dazzle, or teach? (If you have a development team, make sure its members also know the purpose of the site.) If the purpose of your site is to share information about your favorite movies, for example, information about your dog would seem out of place to your visitors.

If the site is made up of simple, informative, short bits of information, is XML really necessary? HTML may be all you need for those nifty, eye-catching brochures. But do they really need to be XML documents, especially if they are more for show than for data? If, however, you need to keep data and add to it over time, XML may be the solution. Suppose you want to set up a list of available homes for sale in a given market. You want to allow visitors to pick and choose their potential homes based on the criteria they supply in a form instead of having to wade through link after link. In this case, you would need to seriously consider XML.

When you specify your site's purpose and keep it in clear focus, you'll begin realizing what elements you'll need, how the information should be structured, and—more importantly—which markup language you need to use.

Define Your Audience

The audience will dictate exactly how you structure your data. In some cases, the audience can dictate whether HTML will be better suited for your site than XML. Not everyone will be perfectly matched to your site. If you're creating a site that lists all the places you could travel to in Alaska, your audience will undoubtedly be vacationers; however, your audience could also include travel agents or tour guides. In addition, you may have different types of vacationers, such as hikers, adventure seekers, bed-and-breakfast guests, cruisers, and/or senior citizens. Make sure you cater to the largest segment of your intended audience. If only 10 percent are hikers, it would be counterproductive to fill the site with hiking information and lose the visitors who simply want a relaxing cruise.

Is your site the local alternative weekly newspaper with several years' worth of archived stories that you want to present to your visitors (both on the Web and in printer-friendly format)? If so, you may need to consider XML. However, if all the visitors want to do is read the latest quick clips of news bytes, HTML may be a better alternative.

Determine Your Visitors' Requirements

It's amazing how many sites are designed in-house with high-speed connections but are never viewed with what most of the site's audience will use—low-speed connections to the Internet. Determining user requirements is more important than designing around your own system's capabilities. Ask your potential users what types of connections they have, what software they use, and how they want to view and manipulate data on your site. This input will help dictate exactly what types of information you can offer and in what format. If your site is on an intranet, the design considerations are different than if you're designing for Internet users.

Find out what your audience will want to do once they make it to your site. It's useful to know what languages and browsers they will be using. If most of your visitors will be using only one type of browser and they speak English, you can use HTML to create your site. But if you want to accommodate a wider range of users, XML would probably work better, because you can create different displays of the same data. And if your audience wants to search your site quickly and easily, you should use XML. Knowing your audience and, more specifically, knowing what they expect from your site will help you determine which features you need to implement.

Know Your Limits

To implement XML, you need to know whether your server can handle the site and whether you can handle the demands the site will place on you and your coworkers. Microsoft's Internet Information Server (called Internet Information Services in Windows 2000), with its Active Server Pages, offers a great deal of flexibility, not only with HTML-only sites, but also with XML-enabled sites. If you plan to offer multimedia features, remember to consider the amount of bandwidth your site will need.

It's very important for you to know your server's capacity and what programs you can run on it. Consider what processing you can or should run on the server and what processing you can off-load to the client. And speaking of clients, make sure your system is capable of handling the maximum number of simultaneous requests you think it will get. Ensuring security features and knowing the security configuration is also an important component of planning correctly for your site.

Although it's not a technical consideration, it's important to understand what your own requirements are in terms of time, money, and stress. You need project-management capabilities as well as a good eye for graphic design. In addition, you'll need to know good grammar and have good editing skills if you plan to provide textual content. If a site requires a lot of updating and you work two full-time jobs, you may want to consider finding someone to help. Your role may best be played out as the builder of the site, leaving the Webmaster duties to another person.

The idea, of course, is that you keep the information dynamic. With HTML, you'll forever be adding new pages, changing old ones, keeping track of links, finding and deleting dead links, and updating graphics. With XML, creating dynamic sites is much easier.

Plan Your Site

This goes without saying, but you would be surprised how many people don't plan their sites properly. When you plan your site, you determine not only what its purpose will be and the tools you'll need, but also its structure. When you use XML, you need to spend more time planning the site's structure so you can determine what elements and attributes you'll need to create and what style sheets are needed for displaying the content. Also, proper planning gives you an opportunity to know exactly what links—and the kinds of links—are needed. This information will help you define what markup language you should use. If you simply need to link from one document to another, HTML may work for you. But if you need to create more complex structures, only XML will do.

Create a Site Map

After you determine your site's purpose, its capabilities, and the types of documents and links it will include, the next thing to do is put it down on paper. Create a road map of your site. Where will the links take the visitor? What pages are descendants of other pages? What internal and what external documents, scripts, and applications will be used, and how will they be invoked?

A visual road map will help you determine where things will go and will prevent your visitors from getting lost in "hyperspace." If you can't visualize the organizational structure of your site before you begin, you'll soon be lost in the numerous pages you've created.

Don't Forget Navigational Controls

Navigational controls are one of the most important design features used in creating a successful site. It doesn't matter whether your site is mainly HTML or XML—navigational controls are necessary. But without a good document structure or a clear road map, navigational controls can lead you to one dead end after another. You can use a template or index cards, or you can sketch your road map on a paper napkin. Remember to include navigational controls that will lead the visitor back to square one, or at least back to the preceding page. Although XML allows more complex linking structures, the principles of good navigation still apply. Navigational controls should be apparent to visitors so they can move freely within the site, and they should consistently take visitors where they ask to go.

TIP: For an excellent example of how to design Web sites, check out IBM's Web Design Guidelines at **www-3.ibm.com/ibm/easy/eou_ext.nsf/publish/572**.

Test the Site

Take the site for a spin, but make sure you bring along some friends to see how well it drives for them. Failure to test a site is a key design flaw of which many developers are guilty. The site may work great at ISDN speeds, but how does it work with a 56Kbps modem? Maybe it's a masterpiece on your 21-inch screen, but how well does it display on a lowly 13-inch screen? You may have been able to easily pluck and pull data out within your intranet, but will all that plucking and pulling work from miles away over the Internet?

It doesn't matter whether you're developing HTML or XML documents. What matters is that you test the site and that you test it on a variety of platforms, on a variety of machines, and in a variety of locations.

Immediate Solutions

Determining Whether to Use XML or HTML

Before you start converting all your HTML documents to XML, you should learn a few simple steps that will speed up the process. These steps reinforce what you just learned about the differences and similarities between HTML and XML. First, you should determine whether the document is better suited for HTML or XML. Use Table 3.1 as a quick reference guide to help you determine exactly which markup language to use.

Fixing HTML Problems

When you convert from HTML to XML, you should do some initial spot-checking of your HTML documents to see exactly where your problems may lie and what you need to do to fix them. You may need to use a text editor with find-and-replace capabilities to handle some of the more mundane changes, or you might want to write a script (depending on your development platform) to make some of the changes automatically, especially if your code inconsistencies are recurrent. Here are the issues you need to address when you convert a document from HTML to XML:

Table 3.1   Determining whether to use XML or HTML.

Problem	Solution
Does the data consist of a few simple pages and graphics, much like you would find in a brochure?	Use HTML
Does the data require advanced searching so users can get what they need out of the site?	Use XML
Will the data be viewed on a variety of different platforms or appliances?	Use XML
Does the content stay relatively static?	Use HTML
Do you need to interface the data between different machines or database engines?	Use XML
Are you having problems with your existing site in terms of users getting lost or not being able to find what they need?	Use XML
Will the site have primarily multimedia, such as sound clips or videos?	Use HTML, possibly with plug-ins

- Did the same developer or HTML editor prepare all the HTML code? If not, find out what pages were developed by which developer or editor and group them together. Doing so will help you spot patterns of inconsistency.

- Place the XML declaration at the top of all the documents you want to convert. If you leave the **html** element, browsers will still interpret the data within in the document as HTML. By placing the following code as the first line in your document, you'll prepare the document to be parsed as XML:

```
<?xml version="1.0"?>
```

- Convert all your elements and attributes to lowercase. (The next generation HTML, called XHTML, is case sensitive, and all elements and attributes are in lowercase.)

- Make sure all your elements have both a start tag and an end tag—even elements you're used to specifying with no end tag (which are called empty elements in XML), such as **br** or **hr**. In these cases, you can either use a closing tag such as **</br>** or close the tag within the element, by using **
. Make sure you convert the empty element **<img> to **<img/>**.

- Make sure all element attributes' values are quoted. For example, if you're specifying the height of a graphic, make sure you enclosed the size in quotes. For example:

```
<img src="file.gif" height="410" width="210"/>
```

- Make sure your HTML elements are nested correctly. Close first what you opened last.

- If you want to specify certain characters as data, make sure you use the CDATA section in the DTD or use the built-in XML entities.

Moving from HTML to XML

After you've decided which documents should be converted to XML and which should stay as HTML pages, and after you've cleaned up your HTML code and readied it for XML, the following checklist will help the transition go more smoothly:

- Define the structure of your document, specifying what the root and its various descendants will be.

- Identify the specific elements, attributes, and entities you will need.

- Create the XML DTD.

- Decide which style sheets will be required to display the data and the steps you need to take to create the style sheets.

- Set up a testing procedure that will help you identify early on what kinds of problems you will encounter in the conversion process. Take sample HTML pages from the various groups of HTML code you have collected, clean them up, and then convert the pages to XML documents. Run them through an XML processor to see how many errors you encounter. Then, identify the steps you need to take to fix the problems.

- Determine what server and additional programs and scripts you'll use to complement the data you'll be converting.

Designing Your Site

It doesn't matter whether you keep most of your HTML pages and add a few XML documents or whether you convert all your HTML pages to XML. Either way, you should design your site according to some specific design principles.

Planning Ahead

Planning ahead means understanding the direction you plan to go and who you will cater to once you get there. Poll your potential audience to find out the following information:

- What do they expect from your site?

- What specific data are they looking for and how do they want to access it— through a search engine or via simple links?

- What browsers and versions are they using?

- What appliances are they using to view your site? Are they using PCs, hand-held computers, or Web TVs?

- What demands will they put on your site?

Sketching Out the Site

When you sketch out the site, you need to create not only a road map, but also a navigational structure:

- Create an element hierarchy. Specify the element that will be your root element and what elements will branch off and be nested within other elements. Sketch out the hierarchy to show the relationships the elements will have with one another.

- Create a document or page hierarchy. Specify what pages will go where and what links will move the user in what direction. An easy way to do this is to use index cards or popular outlining programs. Determine where the user can or should go next and how the user gets back to where he or she wants to go within your site.

- Make sure you define the various sections of documents so you can refer to them in groups, either in your general document structure or within links. Consider building your site with depth, making the content on each page relatively short.

- When you sketch out your site, consider using identifiable elements to help users know where they are and where they can go next. Consider giving users the flexibility to jump to various sections in your site in a variety of ways, not just in a linear fashion.

- Make sure none of your documents are orphaned in any way. Always allow access to both the previous location and the home page or main menu.

- Make sure your site is organized in a way that your users, and not just you, will recognize. The structure you use internally may not make sense to anyone outside your organization. Take time to view other sites' organizational structure to get ideas on how to create an understandable navigational flow.

Tools for Integrating HTML and XML

You can use two types of tools to integrate HTML and XML. The first type of tool simply checks for well formedness, alerting you to problems with the document so you can correct them. Many XML editors have this tool built in. In addition, free tools to check XML syntax are available online. One such tool is Userland Software's XML Syntax Checker at **http://frontier.userland.com/stories/ storyReader$1092**.

The second type of tool fixes problems automatically. One of the more popular tools is HTML Tidy, which is available as freeware as a W3C Open Source project. The home page for HTML Tidy is **www.w3.org/People/Raggett/tidy**. From this home page, you can download versions of HTML Tidy that run on almost any platform.

HTML Tidy is a command-line program that you run from the Windows console. To run HTML Tidy, type the following into the Windows console:

```
tidy -asxml source.html >dest.html
```

This command line transforms the source.html file into the dest.html XML file. A variety of other command-line options are available, some of which we have listed in Table 3.2.

Table 3.2   Commonly used HTML Tidy command-line options.

Pattern	Definition
-wrap 72	Wrap text at column 72 (default is 68)
-upper or **-u**	Force tags to uppercase (default is lowercase)
-clean or **-c**	Replace **font**, **nobr**, and **center** tags with Cascading Style Sheets (CSS)
-numeric or **-n**	Output numeric rather than named entities
-errors or **-e**	Only show errors
-quiet or **-q**	Suppress nonessential output
-xml	Use this when input is well-formed XML
-asxml	Convert HTML to well-formed XML
-asxhtml	Convert HTML to XHTML
-raw	Leave characters greater than 128 unchanged upon output
-ascii	Use ASCII for output and Latin-1 for input
-latin1	Use Latin-1 for both input and output
-iso2022	Use ISO2022 for both input and output
-utf8	Use UTF-8 for both input and output
-mac	Use the Apple MacRoman character set
-config *<file>*	Set options from a configuration file named *<file>*
-f *<file>*	Write errors to the named *<file>*
-modify or **-m**	Modify original files
-version or **-v**	Show the version
-help or **-h**	List command-line options
-tidy-mark: no	If yes (the default), add a **meta** element indicating that the file has been "tidied"
-input-xml: yes	Use the XML parser rather than the error-correcting HTML parser
-output-xml: yes	Generate a pretty-printed well-formed XML file
-add-xml-pi: yes	Add an XML processing instruction
-add-xml-decl: yes	Add the XML declaration when outputting XML or XHTML
-output-xhtml: yes	Generate a pretty-printed XHTML file
-add-xml-space: yes	Add **xml:space="preserve"** to elements such as **pre**, **style**, and **script** when generating XML
-new-empty-tags: tag1, tag2	Declare new empty elements; required if the input includes previously unknown tags
-new-inline-tags: tag1, tag2	Declare new non-empty inline tags; required if the input includes previously unknown tags
-new-blocklevel-tags: tag1, tag2	Declare new non-empty block-level tags; required if the input includes previously unknown tags

You can also use TidyGUI, which is a GUI version of HTML Tidy written by André Blavier. TidyGUI is very easy to use, and it's free. You can download it from **http://perso.wanadoo.fr/ablavier/TidyGUI/**. It's so easy we don't go into much detail here. All you have to do is load the source file and click the Tidy button. Your results will look something like Figure 3.3.

An alternative to using the command-line HTML Tidy or TidyGUI is to use one of the HTML editors that has integrated HTML Tidy. For example, HTML-Kit is a nice freeware HTML editor that integrates HTML Tidy. You can find HTML-Kit at **www.chami.com/free/html-kit**.

Let's take a look at how you could use HTML-Kit. We'll start with an ugly (in other words, not well formed) HTML file shown in Listing 3.1:

Listing 3.1   An HTML file that's not well formed.

```
<HTML>
  <head>
  </head>
  <body>
    <h2>Moving From HTML To XML<h2>
    <p>After you've decided which documents should be converted and which
        should stay as HTML pages, and after you've cleaned up your HTML
        code and readied it for XML, the following checklist will help the
        transition go more smoothly:
    <ul>
      <LI>Define the structure of your document, specifying what the root
          and its various descendants will be.
```

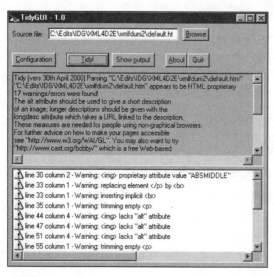

Figure 3.3   Example output from TidyGUI.

```
        <li>Identify the specific elements, attributes, and entities you will
             need.
        <LI>Create the XML DTD.
        <li>Decide which style sheets will be required to display the data
             and the steps you need to take to create the style sheets.
        <li>Set up a testing procedure that will help you identify early
             on what kinds of problems you will encounter in the conversion
             process. Take sample HTML pages from the various groups of HTML
             code you have collected, clean them up, and then convert the
             pages to XML documents. Run them through an XML processor to
             see how many errors you encounter. Then, identify the steps you
             need to take to fix the problems.
        <li>Determine what server and additional programs and scripts you'll
             use to complement the data you'll be converting.
     </ul>
</body>
</HTML>
```

Now, to convert this file into well-formed HTML, follow these steps:

1. Open HTML-Kit and select the option to open an existing file. We've named this file 0304.htm. You'll see something similar to Figure 3.4.

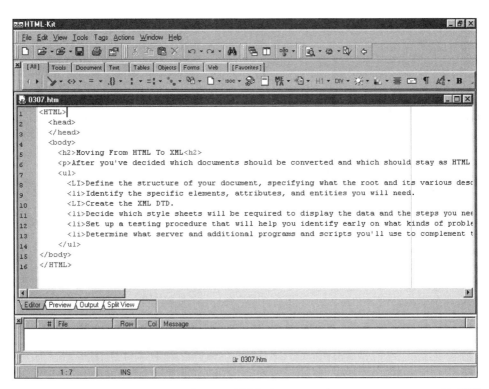

Figure 3.4   A very ugly (not well-formed) HTML document that we want to convert to XML.

2. Select Actions|Tools|HTML Tidy|Convert To XML from the menu. This function runs HTML Tidy and puts the transformed document into a new window, as seen in Figure 3.5.

The Messages window at the bottom of the screen will report any errors in the original document that were repaired. If you want to change some of the HTML Tidy preferences, select the Edit|Preferences and then select the TIDY tab shown in Figure 3.6.

The now conformed XML looks like Listing 3.2:

Listing 3.2   A valid XML document.

```
<?xml version="1.0"?>
<html>
<head>
<title></title>
</head>
<body>
<h2>Moving From HTML To XML</h2>
```

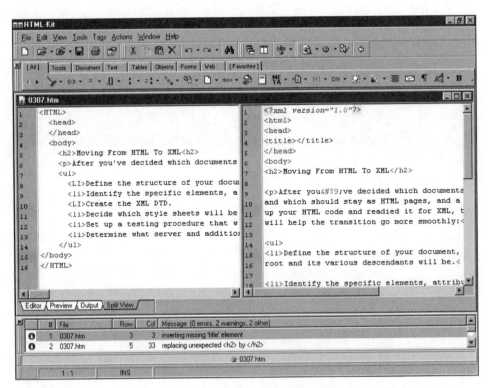

Figure 3.5   The result of running a document through HTML Tidy in HTML-Kit.

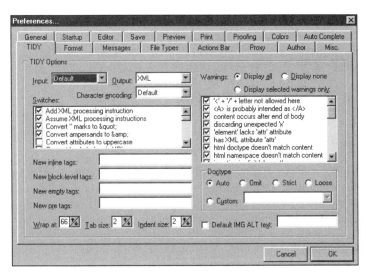

Figure 3.6   The HTML Tidy preferences in HTML-Kit.

```
<p>After you&#39;ve decided which documents should be converted
and which should stay as HTML pages, and after you have cleaned
up your HTML code and readied it for XML, the following checklist
will help the transition go more smoothly:</p>

<ul>
<li>Define the structure of your document, specifying what the
root and its various descendants will be.</li>

<li>Identify the specific elements, attributes, and entities you
will need.</li>

<li>Create the XML DTD.</li>

<li>Decide which style sheets will be required to display the
data and the steps you need to take to create the style
sheets.</li>

<li>Set up a testing procedure that will help you identify early
on what kinds of problems you will encounter in the conversion
process. Take sample HTML pages from the various groups of HTML
code you have collected, clean them up, and then convert the
pages to XML documents. Run them through an XML processor to see
how many errors you encounter. Then, identify the steps you need
to take to fix the problems.</li>
```

```
<li>Determine what server and additional programs and scripts
you&#39;ll use to complement the data you&#39;ll be
converting.</li>
</ul>
</body>
</html>
```

Chapter 4

Implementing XML in the Real World

In Depth

XML is becoming a key component in a variety of implementations across all fields and businesses. XML offers the extensibility that HTML doesn't have; and at the same time, XML offers the ability to interface with existing legacy systems. Many software vendors are incorporating XML features into their software. You'll find XML features in Web servers, XML editors, XML parsers, databases, and standard desktop document-creation and -management systems, such as those found in the latest version of Adobe FrameMaker. XML is perfect for any solution that requires the more structured capabilities of a markup language without the complexity of the Standard Generalized Markup Language (SGML). Data described with XML is easily shared and converted; thus XML breaks down the data barrier often caused by proprietary software.

In this chapter, we explore the benefits XML offers most solutions that depend on information and data. This discussion is aimed at helping you understand where XML fits into a total solution. (If you're a programmer trying to convince your boss that XML is the way to go, we suggest you pass this book to your boss and ask him or her to skim this chapter.) We examine the various reasons why XML fits so well in the data world and why the switch from HTML to XML is a natural progression.

Many Reasons for Implementing XML

In this chapter, you're introduced to solutions that utilize XML in one form or another. The Web sites and the companies discussed in this chapter used a variety of XML-enabled software programs, database engines, editors, browsers, parsers, and glued-together code to make the complete connection between different systems, XML, and the Web. In some cases, sites use only a comprehensive Document Type Definition (DTD) with some additional lines of code and a few scripts. Other sites use extensive Structured Query Language (SQL) databases, XML editors, DTDs, and Microsoft Internet Information Services (IIS) servers.

NOTE: IIS in Windows NT and earlier was called Internet Information Server. In Windows 2000, it's known as Internet Information Services.

We won't kid you; in most of these systems, it took more than just a few lines of code to create a cohesive system. But the XML that is used throughout makes data transfer from one system to the next possible. In each scenario, we introduce you to the problem, outline the solutions, and then review how XML and other products (such as Insight's Enigma, Chrystal's Astoria, and other XML-based software programs) help do the trick. As you read through each story, remember that without XML, these systems would continue to work in a proprietary fashion, offering little, if any, connectivity and compatibility between systems.

We'll start by examining how XML fits within the solution to help extend the data used in the solution. Then, we'll explain how various components of XML work well within the solutions and why other markup languages, such as HTML, leave the corporations looking for a better alternative. Finally, we'll recap with an overview of how several companies are using XML to handle their data needs. These companies cover a broad spectrum of businesses, all with varying data needs. Each business deals with data that needs to flow from one location or one user to the next. Each business has decided to standardize on intranet technology, which means that whatever method they choose must eventually interface to the browser's desktop. These companies and their problems are:

- *Siemens*—This company needed an integrated timecard system that would allow employees to track their time and attendance and relay this information to their managers.

- *RivCom*—This company needed to offer clients the ability to monitor job requirements and pass along those requirements to prospective employees and the human resources department.

- *DataChannel*—This company offers an "extended" channel application that helps many companies, including magazines, push information to users' and employees' desktops.

There's no doubt that XML is primed for the information world. Not only does it offer many of the features SGML offers, but it also provides them without the complexities of SGML. It also includes the extensibility HTML simply can't offer. Yet, its benefits go beyond extensibility and reduced complexity. With some experience and trial and error, XML DTDs and documents are easy to create—especially as more and better tools become available. In general, XML components make it easier to manage the various architectures of intranets and extranets. XML can revolutionize the corporation's document management, electronic data interchange, and information planning with relatively little investment and a small learning curve.

XML is very flexible. It can perform many of the tasks HTML and server-side scripts currently perform. It can also interface with existing legacy systems and databases, which means developers really don't have to choose between using disparate systems. XML can bring systems together and, in some cases, even replace them. Development staffs don't have to learn a wide array of programming languages, and they don't have to worry about developing intranet sites around a particular browser for which they must use specialized elements. Instead of spending so much time developing the look of a site, developers can spend time on the content and structure.

With XML, solutions aren't tied into specific vendors or languages or even operating systems. You can use the data in your XML solution on multiple operating systems, across platforms. In addition, if the developer (or you as the developer) decides to move from one browser to another, there's no need for recoding. (We discuss this topic in more detail in the "Why Cross-Platform Compatibility Is Important" section later in this chapter.) XML is one of the most flexible and versatile markup languages available because it allows you to create the elements you need to build the document structure you want.

Although flexibility is a key selling point for XML, there are numerous other reasons for replacing many HTML and script-oriented documents as well as other types of documents:

- XML offers cross-platform compatibility between systems, browsers, and external applications.

- Standardized DTDs can be used across the company or across industries; and in some cases, a DTD may already exist for the data type in your solution.

- XML documents can be used on more than just the Web and can be read within existing SGML environments.

- The same XML document can be repurposed, so it can be viewed on a variety of display devices without having to restructure the data. The Extensible Stylesheet Language (XSL) or style sheets allow for better control over presentation and provide the ability to keep the content and display together for better management.

- XML documents can off-load information to the client and reduce the load on servers.

- The creation of entities can reduce development time and allow for character and group standardization.

- Links can be used to create multiple actions in a simultaneous fashion, which allows you to link to multiple sources.

- XML is based on strict syntax rules, which forces documents to be more readable and to follow certain design standards. Just a few shortcuts can lead to out-of-sync data.

Before we examine some of the important features XML offers in more detail, let's discuss why the way XML handles documents is better than the way other popular document-management systems, such as Portable Document Format (PDF) and even HTML, handle them.

Comparing Basic Document Formats to XML

More and more companies are moving toward using intranets to help manage documents, document creation, and document distribution. Just think about how many documents you handle every day, including email messages, memos, and corporate manuals—you could work with hundreds of documents in a single day. XML lets you handle a wide variety of documents in a relatively simple, hierarchical fashion.

When you compare other document creation systems—such as HTML, Adobe's PDF file format, or even various word-processing systems, such as Microsoft Word—none of them offers the hierarchical option XML does. HTML, PDF, and Word all create documents, but they really have no document-management capabilities. Unless you create your own hierarchical structure, handling many Word documents is difficult at best. Finding information stored within these types of documents is even more frustrating. By using XML's hierarchical document-handling capabilities, users can pick and choose the exact data they want without having to plow through all the rest. Unlike HTML and other technologies, such as PDF, XML allows you to store documents in parts, not in a hodgepodge.

Because XML separates the content from the presentation, it's easier for search engines, scripting tools, and programming or scripting languages to work with the XML data. Presentation elements don't get in the way. Document structures can be matched within existing systems. Search queries can specify the exact level in the XML document where the user needs to search for information. And all the information can be parsed, processed, and then passed to a standard Web browser.

The Problems Associated with HTML

Even though XML has been around for a while, HTML is definitely still the standard for delivering information over the Internet or an intranet, partly because HTML is relatively easy to create, manipulate, and present. Yet, with this ease, comes many problems for corporations. First, information technology departments must decide on standards for such tasks as creating files, delivering information, and storing, converting, and searching for information on the company's servers. Although the official World Wide Web Consortium (W3C) standards govern HTML, those standards are not enforced by Web browsers or other HTML tools. In reality, HTML requires no conformity to any basic standard. HTML browsers are notoriously forgiving, which means document structures usually correspond to what the designer wants, not what the corporation needs. The standards that support XML require that documents be at the very least well formed, and at the most, valid. Vendors of XML tools have the XML standards to help guide the development of conforming and standard documents.

Spend a few minutes on your company's intranet or the Internet viewing various documents' HTML source code, and you'll see that different designers sometimes use different tags and features to accomplish the same thing. Structure? What structure? That's usually the question. The only structure HTML designers have to deal with is simple **head**, **frame**, or **body** sections. Everything else is left up to interpretation. There's little or no document validation. The terms *well formed* and *valid* have almost no meaning within the HTML world. Searching for documents across your network requires a lot more on the back end in terms of scripting and processing. And if a search facility isn't instituted, you must try to figure out the designer's plan on your own.

With HTML, you have to create chunks of data, parse them down into workable sizes, and then think ahead to create hyperlinks that will allow users to jump through the site to the information they need. XML, on the other hand, does all this automatically. Its tree structure, which is almost like a table of contents, not only makes it easier for humans to pick out the data they want, but it also makes it easier for computers to obtain the data components they need. These strict structural requirements make XML a much more sophisticated document-management system than HTML.

Because an XML document does not, by itself, specify whether or how its information should be displayed, it still needs to work with HTML. The XML data merely contains the facts of the document. HTML is great for presentation but not for searching or indexing vast amounts of data. No facilities exist within HTML to organize data, describe the content, or specify the various elements that could be searchable. HTML does, however, offer the ability to reference scripting languages, which makes it an ideal system to work with XML data files. XML can provide a means for embedding arbitrary data and annotations within HTML, which extends the possibilities for Web-based applications that use HTML and scripts.

For example, suppose you have an XML-based bookstore database. You want your employees to be able to search the online database and your customers to be able to place orders. Both employees and customers would use a standard Web browser to find the information they need. However, the HTML doesn't find the information for them—instead, the individual data records are expressed in XML on the back end, and the results are expressed to the users in HTML. To construct the results, the Web server or the Web browser needs to convert the XML data records into some form of HTML or use a Java applet or scripting language to fetch and display the data.

With XSL (the language used to create XML style sheets for display or transformation), you can create a collection of programming rules that define how to pull information out of an XML document and transform it into another format, such as HTML. Because XSL uses a declarative method to structure style sheets, people can grasp XSL concepts more quickly than if, for example, they were programming the display of the data in another language, such as C++.

Related solution:	*Found on page:*
Defining Basic XSLT Style Sheet Constructs	293

The Problems Associated with PDF

Because of the amount of textual information exchanged in the corporate environment, from policy and procedure manuals to stock reports, the concept behind Adobe's PDF seemed to make sense when it first hit the market several years ago. PDF provides a way to essentially print the contents of any type of document (whether it's a word processing document or a spreadsheet) to a file while still using the fonts inherent in the system that created the file. The electronic file, which is entirely platform independent, can then be passed from computer to computer. If users have the Acrobat Reader software or the Acrobat Reader plug-in is installed in their browsers, they can read, search, and print the file in the format in which the original designer created it.

PDF has gained a substantial amount of support, and many Web sites—particularly Web sites for software companies and corporate intranets—use this technology. But PDF has some document management problems. PDF is basically a display technology—it deals little with document format or structure. In essence, a PDF file is simply a snapshot of a file and has limited capabilities. Documents can be searched, but only within the individual document itself.

XML, on the other hand, is more capable of handling and managing documents, because it provides structured information that a wide variety of applications can understand. You have full control over which applications are deployed on your corporate network to view and manipulate XML documents. Better still, with such structured documents, you can provide a more effective way to search for information—users can base a search on a document's structure instead of just searching for words on a page. And, XML lets you specify how the document is presented, whereas the layout and format of PDF documents are hard-coded in the page.

NOTE: *In the past few months, many XML-based content management systems have begun to offer publishing of XML-based content to a variety of formats, including both HTML and PDF. Because some documents really should be disseminated as PDF files—especially highly formatted documents such as marketing materials and forms—the ability to save your information as XML and then publish it to the appropriate format is very attractive. Visit* ***www.xmlsoftware.com/dms/*** *to find out more about these types of content management systems.*

4. Implementing XML in the Real World

Standardization Is the Key

Although XML provides flexibility, you may find that one of the most significant benefits it offers information solutions is that XML documents are highly structured. The need for structure can mean using industry DTDs or simply creating a template for data input that everyone can use. Already, companies such as Chrysler and Ford have come up with a standard set of element tags for the automotive industry. And the Open Financial Exchange (OFX) format is an XML application created specifically for consumer financial transactions by Intuit, Checkfree, and Microsoft. It provides a standard mechanism for transferring financial data from the consumer to the merchant and then to the bank or bankcard company.

MasterCard International, along with AT&T, Hewlett-Packard, and Wells Fargo, is leading an initiative for an XML-based application for financial information interchange—the Open Trading Protocol (OTP). It will help financial companies transfer information about their clients through disparate financial systems without the need to replace their existing systems. XML could provide a conduit that passes information from one financial institution to the next.

All of these groups chose XML because of its ability to structure data and, at the same time, offer a tremendous amount of flexibility. Because XML is quickly becoming an industry standard, more industry-specific DTDs will be created. And XML is flexible enough that an entirely new programming language can be created for your particular industry. In addition, XML can be used in conjunction with binary systems or client-side scripting languages, such as JavaScript, to extend its functionality.

However, this doesn't mean that binary-based architectures should be tossed in favor of XML—they often work well together. In fact, many vendors that currently offer multi-tier applications that use binary messaging technologies are already looking to XML as a means of providing more efficient data exchange. Their goal is to eliminate data redundancy and foster data reuse. When you add XML to binary messaging transports, you can often leverage the strengths of each to create a more manageable distributed environment.

Standardizing a Simple Memo

Let's consider why standardization from the document-structure standpoint is important. Take a simple example, such as a consultative services proposal. In the worst-case scenario, although everyone may use the same word processor, employees could be creating their own templates for proposals, with various fonts and all sorts of sections, headers, and conventions. There is no standardization; employees may even refer to the company name in a variety of ways.

Even in the best-case scenario, in which everyone uses one memo template, various body text formats might be used. Some users may put everything in one paragraph, others may use spaces instead of tabs to line up information in columns, and still others may simply use the table option to create columns. Certain advanced users may use style sheets, and others may use only the most basic formatting rules.

You can use XML to define the entire structure of the memo, leaving the content up to the author and the formatting up to the style sheet. The user simply fills in the information, and the XML document, with its accompanying DTD and style sheet, does the rest. The structure of all proposals is the same—with optional elements included where necessary—so when employees need to search for a section outlining a particular scope of work, they simply search the **scope** element. Because there's a structure and a defined element for the scope of work section, users don't have to view each document to find the information they need. Each proposal that contains content for the **scope** element can be accessed quickly.

Entities can be created to further standardize the information included in a memo. For example, if the company name is XYZ Consulting Partners Limited, you can create an entity that everyone within the organization can use in his or her memos. Doing so will ensure that the use of the company name is consistent and correct. The following line of code is an example of an entity declaration in a company's memo DTD:

```
<!ENTITY coname "XYZ Consulting Partners Limited">
```

When employees need to reference the company name in their documents, they simply insert the entity reference and let the XML parser do the rest. The parser takes the information defined for the entity, locates instances where that entity is referenced in the XML document, and replaces it throughout the document. When it finds the entity reference, it expands the entity and replaces the reference with the information defined for the reference. The code to include the entity reference in memos would look like this:

```
Here at &coname; we pride ourselves on quality consultations.
```

After the code is parsed, the results would look like this:

```
Here at XYZ Consulting Partners Limited we pride ourselves on
quality consultations.
```

Entity references don't have to be simple, however. They can also contain entire sections of documents. For example, specialized clauses for the contracts department could easily be inserted by referencing the intended entity. Groups of Web-page links could be combined in a single entity and referenced on a single Web page. If a link changes, you simply change the link in the entity—you don't have to worry about changing it in your XML document or throughout a collection of XML documents.

XML Provides Development Standards

XML provides both XML document developers and XML document authors an easy-to-use, easy-to-learn set of rules. Because of the XML design principles and the ability to create XML documents in standard text format, XML documents and DTDs are usually readable by both humans and computers. Yet, documents built on a set of nested elements can grow complex as multiple layers of detail are added.

Although documents can be complex, XML can still easily interface with other systems. It supports a number of standards for character encoding, allowing it to be used by a variety of different computing languages, including Java and C++. When XML is combined with a standard application programming interface (API), programmers can build applications relatively easily. One such example is the Simple API for XML (SAX), a free cross-platform API. Parsers are also available in C++, C, JavaScript, Tcl, and Python, to name a few programming languages.

Standardization in Terms of Data and Display

With XML, you can use the style-sheet features for formatting and displaying XML content or you can create scripts that turn the XML data into HTML-formatted information. This ability allows developers and designers to create centralized document formats that can easily be revised without fear of disturbing the actual content or additional programming functionality. Style sheets can be shared by many XML documents. And a single XML data file can be displayed on a variety of systems, including Web-based and even portable phone systems.

The way in which the information is displayed depends on how the style sheet has been constructed. The XML data itself knows no boundaries, which means documents no longer have to be created for particular browsers. Companies aren't required to settle on one browser platform or another—with XML, the display is left up to standardized style-sheet mechanisms set forth in XML's XSL. Because all the information about style sheets can be stored in a centralized location and then passed to the browser for processing on the client end, most XML files require less bandwidth to display than their HTML cousins require.

Information and data can be processed at the user's end (if the user has an XML-compatible browser or viewing tool), so users can extract the XML data from documents and keep it in their own systems if the XML content has been cached there. Doing so would make it easy for users to manipulate and view the information. Price lists, catalog information, the latest news, and company bulletin board information could all be cached, with scheduled updates delivered as necessary. In addition, because the information is formatted in XML and stored locally, it could easily be searched and read offline, extending the capabilities of the content.

XML's modular document and design approach means that XML content editors can edit, programmers can program, and designers can get back to designing without having to worry about content. And because you can link XML files to various programming and scripting languages, many pages can be generated on the fly when a user makes a request for XML data.

All in all, XML requires a solution developer to think ahead about how to structure documents and how the delivery of content will take place. XML also forces groups within an organization to come together to create DTDs and standard elements, attributes, and entities. Even though XML as a data definition language is very structured and often carefully controls document development, the style sheet languages associated with XML are flexible enough for designers to create their own style sheets to format information as they see fit.

A prime example of this language's flexibility was demonstrated at the 1997 Seybold conference, when XML was just starting to catch on in the developer community. One conference presentation highlighted the flexibility of XML by creating a complete data set for the *Wall Street Journal* newspaper. This data set information was loaded, processed, and displayed in a variety of views, each accommodating a particular type of reader. One page was created for the desktop Web user, another for the hand-held computer user, and another for the actual print product. All information was culled from the same data source, but the display changed based upon the user's preference and the associated style sheet.

Why Cross-Platform Compatibility Is Important

XML files are actually just text files, so they're immediately compatible across platforms. They aren't written for a specific operating system, and they don't require anything more than a text editor and a sharp mind to create. Therefore, there's no need to scrap existing systems or buy new software or hardware just to implement XML. XML is a much easier language to implement than binary-based messaging technologies, such as those implemented on the CORBA or Distributed Component Object Model platform.

XML gives corporations flexibility to store data in a text format without the fear that it will become obsolete or incompatible with future systems. Because the element tags are not specific to a particular browser, corporations aren't limited to one browser or another. Documents can reside on different servers and can easily be moved from one system to another. The only thing you need to do when you move XML data between locations (from a Unix server to a Windows NT Server, for example) is double-check both relative and external references.

Namespaces in XML

You may wonder how a DTD can be used across networks and how conformity can be maintained when everything in XML is extensible. XML inherently provides a mechanism for developers to invent new element names and publish them so more than just the internal network can use them. This functionality is called *namespaces*.

Under the namespaces specification, every element name is subordinated to a Universal Resource Identifier (URI). The URI ensures that even if two developers choose the same name for a particular element, the element name remains unambiguous. The namespace facility lets developers define their own dictionary of elements and XML terms to be used not only on an internal network but also on a public network, such as the Internet. The easiest way to explain how it works is to show you some markup that contains namespaces, such as Listing 4.1.

Listing 4.1   Some markup that contains namespaces.

```
<?xml version="1.0"?>
<invoice>
    <order>
       New Macintosh iMac
    </order>
    <purchasedby>John B.</purchasedby>
    <siteb:digital-signature xmlns:siteb="http://www.siteb.com/siteb.dtd">
       6787409
    </siteb:digital-signature>

    <order>
       Pentium II Computer
    </order>
    <purchasedby>Harry Smith</purchasedby>
    <site:digital-signature xmlns:site="http://www.site.com/site.dtd">
       x8931kx
    </site:digital-signature>
</invoice>
```

What does this code mean? It means that you can use elements that reference other DTDs within your own markup, but without combining DTDs. In Listing 4.1, the digital signature elements refer to two separate DTDs:

```
<siteb:digital-signature xmlns:siteb="http://www.siteb.com/siteb.dtd">
```

```
<site:digital-signature xmlns:site="http://www.site.com/site.dtd">
```

The element **siteb:digital-signature** is really the **digital-signature** element defined by the **siteb** DTD that is housed at **http://www.siteb.com/siteb.dtd**. The colon between the namespace (**siteb**) and the element (**digital-signature**) lets the XML processor know that the element is based on a different DTD than the rest of the document.

Using this element-naming convention helps clearly define where the namespaces are located. However, namespaces do not specify processing instructions; they simply tell the person or machine viewing the document where the elements originated. Namespaces keep the element and attribute names straight, not only in your network but also across the Internet.

Related solution:	Found on page:
Using Elements from a Namespace in an XML Document	409

Standardized Character Set and Encoding

All information in XML uses standard character sets and encoding. In fact, all XML information, from the DTD to the actual content, uses Unicode text, which means the elements, attributes, notations, and entity declarations have a standard character set and method of encoding. XML supports the full representation of all international character sets, making it a truly universal markup language.

You can choose to use one of several encodings when you create your documents, including ISO-8859-1, ASCII, UTF-8, and UTF-16. The default is the UTF-8, or 8-bit encoding. You must use the same encoding throughout the entire document. Parsers, processors, browsers, servers, and other applications, such as Java, must also use Unicode; and, surprisingly, programming languages such as Java already do.

XML Integrates with Existing Systems

Because XML data is text only, the content can easily be integrated with existing systems. This can be done through tabular matching methods, using scripting languages, or by simply importing the data directly into the existing systems. XML has no proprietary control over the data, and whatever data is stored in the XML document can easily be extended. You can use XML to provide a link between disparate systems. It can interface with Web browsers, databases, editors, and other applications to exchange data.

You can send the client the data it needs, and the client can massage the data according to its specification. This means less server load and less bandwidth requirements because the server isn't being accessed for every piece of information. Also, because XML documents conform to structural standards to be well formed, there's no sloppy code. In addition, many standard relational database systems can be used as a means for deploying XML-based messaging systems. Because documents conform to structural standards, data in XML systems can easily be used not only as Web documents but also as other documents, such as email messages.

Related solution:	Found on page:
Knowing When to Use XML With a Database	581

How Organizations Are Using XML

XML already has a jump-start in the business world in many respects. SGML has been used for years in the U.S. Government Printing Office, IBM, the U.S. Department of Defense, and the Internal Revenue Service. With everything moving toward the Web, the IRS will most likely begin to store tax form information in an XML-enabled database that can then be used to dynamically generate Web pages. These Web pages could be tax forms or they could provide information about taxpayers and the amount of taxes they have already paid. Because the information would not be stored in PDF file format, the taxpayer would no longer need to download a separate application to view or print tax forms or taxpayer information.

Government agencies aren't the only entities using XML. Ericsson Incorporated, a division of the Swedish telecommunications equipment manufacturer, has licensed a software development product called the Web Automation Toolkit from a company called webMethods (find more about them at **www.webmethods.com**). Ericsson plans to use this XML-based tool to create a link between the Web and its wireless telephones. Because XML can use style sheets to display information in almost any format the developer chooses, people can use wireless phones to search directory databases stored on a Web server the same way they do on their computers at home.

A group of designers are using webMethod's Automation Toolkit to create a search mechanism to help reduce the time it takes to find and retrieve images off CD-ROMs. The images, which are used in both print and television advertising, are sold by various stock photography agencies. Finding the right image for the job used to mean searching Web sites, books, and CD-ROMs for the perfect piece. Using webMethod's Automation Toolkit, CD-ROM searches are cached and cataloged. Designers can use the search information again and again to quickly find the images they need without having to go back through each CD-ROM.

The healthcare industry is also jumping on the XML bandwagon in an effort to share patient data across various types of systems and networks. A group of healthcare-related vendors and service providers called the Health Level 7 (HL7) standards body (**www.hl7.org/**) has a standard called the Health Level Seven Standard that enables the exchange of medical information. This exchange does not occur because of a vendor-based standard software package, but with XML and some SGML. The idea is to structure the patient data in such a way that the information can quickly move from one system to the next instead of tying it to a single vendor solution. This system allows patients to take their medical records with them and be assured that the same information will be valid at whatever healthcare facility they choose.

If a hospital needs to consult with the patient's insurance company, the hospital could theoretically use a standard Web browser to connect to the insurance company's system and then pull up the medical information and records it needs for the patient's care. XML allows an open platform for this data. This is just one of many industry-specific proposals being introduced to the W3C; expect many more in the future.

A good example of an XML application that has made its home in corporate America to facilitate communications and a distributed, but effective, work environment is Channel Definition Format (CDF). Although this application was originally intended to let Web developers push Web site content to users, its uses have been expanded to keep employees up-to-date and to provide them with access to the information they need to do their jobs. Many companies are using CDF to deliver company-wide information at times when network usage is at a minimum.

DataChannel has implemented CDF in its ChannelServer software. You can think of ChannelServer as a kind of extended version of Microsoft's CDF, because it takes the idea of push technology and maximizes the features to deliver documents to the user's desktop in one complete, easy-to-program package. ChannelServer consists of three major components:

- A Web server to transmit the content of the channels and to process user logins.

- A database that contains the channel content, presentation information, and a list of users and groups who can access the information.

- A dynamically generated Java applet, which is downloaded to users each time they log in to the Web server.

4. Implementing XML in the Real World

Here is how ChannelServer works. First, you create users and groups who are authorized to access certain content stored in the database. Any authorized user can create a new channel and publish information to the rest of the organization with a few clicks of the mouse button. Unlike Microsoft's CDF, users don't have to know anything about HTML or XML—they simply need to know what content they want to send and the list of users who should receive the information.

Because the information is transmitted through a Web server, it's viewable through any standard Web browser, regardless of the computer the intended recipient uses. Mac, Windows, and even Unix users can easily view the channel information. There's no need for specialized browser software or specialized programming. Netscape Navigator 3 and higher or Microsoft Internet Explorer 4 and higher can be used. ChannelServer is not browser specific like Microsoft's CDF or Netscape's Netcaster XML-based push technology.

When new information becomes available or updates to existing information are required, ChannelServer uses scripting to locate the list of subscribed users, pushes (automatically sends) the information to the user, and dynamically generates a new Web page or pages on the user's desktop. The user doesn't have to go to a particular server or Web site or even login to email to get the new information. No additional software or downloads are required.

Each ChannelServer database and server can be set up so only certain people within the organization have permission to send or receive information. Five levels of permissions are available, and those who publish the content can specify who can and cannot see the information. For example, if the human resources department has recently completed the results of an employee benefit survey, it can share the information electronically with the managers of the company but keep all other employees from seeing confidential data. Groups of users can be defined, and those groups can have certain restrictions placed on them for subscribing, viewing, and publishing content.

Best of all, this type of XML-based application requires no knowledge of HTML. Multiple data types can be used for the content, including Word, PowerPoint, or even Excel documents. All these documents are considered part of the **ITEM** element within the ChannelServer software, which then extracts the metadata from the document specified as content and dynamically creates an XML file that can be processed over the network.

Currently, several large organizations are using ChannelServer. One such company, an investment firm, uses it to send exchange investment information and commodity trading tips to its thousands of traders in 380 offices worldwide. Another organization, a large employment firm, uses it to send human resources information to its employees. The company also uses ChannelServer to send resumes of potential clients to its employees instead of clogging the email server with large files saved in Word document format.

XML at Work: The Siemens TimeCard System

With more than 7,000 employees to keep track of, Siemens needed to find a better way to manage employee time and save money simultaneously. They needed a way to track, transfer, and analyze information about employee time cards and records. The Siemens TimeCard System, also called the Time and Attendance System, is entirely Web based. A Microsoft IIS server handles the flow of data, distributing it to the various resources—employees, managers, and the accounting system. The system was developed by Open Minded Solutions, a company that creates specialized human resource applications that can be deployed over intranets. Open Minded Solutions first creates the data structure in XML and then provides a link to the data so employees can use the Internet Explorer browser to view it. The Siemens system easily integrates with Microsoft Office 2000, providing ways to view, exchange, and read XML data that is stored on the existing IIS server.

4. Implementing XML in the Real World

NOTE: *The information in this section was derived from the Siemens Web site. For more information on the Siemens system, visit* **http://mothra.odi.com/content/XML/Siemens/siemens.htm**.

A great deal of planning went into setting this system up. Various pieces of data were reused throughout the employee Time and Attendance System. An employee can log in to the time-card system, and his or her time card data—including a work history, such as where the employee logged in and logged out—can be shared among supervisors, human resources, and accounting. Here's how the system works:

- The employee submits time cards electronically through a Web page form. The information about the employee—for example name, type of employee, shift, and employee identification number—is placed at the top of the time-card form after the employee logs in. This employee information is stored in the Siemens Directory Database, and the application uses the employee's Windows login to automatically identify the user. All of this is done on the fly and the page is dynamically generated. If the employee has a set schedule, the schedule is generated based on the current date and the employee's work schedule. Before the user can enter the hours worked, the application checks for system availability, authenticates the user, and checks for data incompatibility.

- This information is saved to the server, which stores it in the correct location and, if necessary, forwards it to the appropriate manager.

- The manager approves the time card. The information stored within the electronic time card is tied to the company's HR records, so standard reusable information, such as name, social security number, and department, can be quickly displayed when the manager pulls up the employee time-card record.

- The time card is validated against payroll records based on a pay code specified in the employee record. Pay codes specify certain rules and pay-rate tables that provide information such as hourly rate, frequency of pay, and so forth.

- If a manager will not be available during the time-card processing period, he or she can temporarily delegate the approval authority to a subordinate because the managerial information, such as approval routing, is tied to the HR and organizational system.

- If the manager doesn't know the phone number of the person to which he or she wants to delegate authority, he or she can look it up in the corporation-wide directory database, which is also tied into HR and payroll records.

- The employees use only the information they need to access the various documents. Most of the data is processed locally on the client machine, thereby reducing the load on the server.

Constructing the System

XML provided Siemens with a way to develop such an elaborate system by simplifying the development process. Regardless of what the data is or how it's accessed—whether it's an employee punching in electronically through a Web-based form or a manager viewing the results of a payroll through an email message—XML provides a standardized data structure. The Document Object Model (DOM) was used to write additional data-intensive applets for the client.

First, the design team considered what information needed to be seen by both employees and managers. They created the data model by considering how a simple time card worked and what fields it contained. The time card became the structural model for their timecard DTD, which is shown in Listing 4.2.

Listing 4.2   The Siemens employee timecard DTD.

```
<!-- Siemens Employee Timecard>
<!ELEMENT timecard(paycodes?,submitted?,approved?)-->
<!ATTLIST timecard
period CDATA #IMPLIED
serial CDATA #IMPLIED
fullname CDATA #IMPLIED
email CDATA #IMPLIED
manager CDATA #IMPLIED
department CDATA #IMPLIED
exempt CDATA #IMPLIED
status CDATA #IMPLIED
type CDATA #IMPLIED
shift CDATA #IMPLIED
```

```
days CDATA #IMPLIED
hours CDATA #IMPLIED
effective CDATA #IMPLIED
>
<!ELEMENT paycodes(paycode*)>
<!ELEMENT paycodeEMPTY>
<!ATTLIST paycode
batch CDATA #REQUIRED
period CDATA #IMPLIED
code CDATA #REQUIRED
mon CDATA #REQUIRED
tue CDATA #REQUIRED
wed CDATA #REQUIRED
thu CDATA #REQUIRED
fri CDATA #REQUIRED
sat CDATA #REQUIRED
sun CDATA #REQUIRED
total CDATA #REQUIRED
submitted CDATA #IMPLIED
submitter CDATA #IMPLIED
approved CDATA #IMPLIED
approver CDATA #IMPLIED >

<!ELEMENT submitted (PCDATA)>
<!ATTLIST submitted
date CDATA #IMPLIED
serial CDATA #IMPLIED
fullname CDATA #IMPLIED>

<!ELEMENT approved (PCDATA)>
<!ATTLIST approved
date CDATA #IMPLIED
serial CDATA #IMPLIED
fullname CDATA #IMPLIED>
```

Next, the design team created a DTD that models the existing Directory Database, which contains all the information about the employee—from name to serial number to pay rate. Then, they used XML's search ability to match the fields in the two DTDs in an effort to populate the initial timecard Web-page entry form. Now, when the employee logs on, information about the employee is generated on the fly to the Web page and displayed.

From that point, it was a matter of managing all the data that flowed in and out of the Web pages, IIS server, and various databases. The design team used a product called ObjectStore to manage the data. ObjectStore is an object database management system that provides native storage for structured data such as XML,

C++ objects, or Java objects. The Open Minded Solutions developers realized that using such an object-oriented database meant they did not have to write or maintain any mapping code to match the structure of the XML document with other data systems.

One important element that had to be managed and that worked well in XML was the pay period. The DTD to define the pay periods is shown in Listing 4.3.

Listing 4.3   The Siemens DTD to define pay periods.

```
<!-- PayPeriods-->
<!ENTITY #default system>
<!ELEMENT payperiods - o (payperiod*)>
<!ATTLIST payperiods
future CDATA #REQUIRED
history CDATA #REQUIRED
schema CDATA #REQUIRED
period CDATA #IMPLIED
>
<!ELEMENT payperiod EMPTY>
<!ATTLIST payperiod
week CDATA #REQUIRED WEEK_DATE
cycle CDATA #REQUIRED PAY_PERIOD
holiday CDATA #REQUIRED HOL_WEEK
batch CDATA #REQUIRED LAST_BATCH_NUM
current CDATA #REQUIRED CURR_PROCESS
calculate CDATA #REQUIRED CALC_DATE
>
```

If, for some reason, you need to adjust the pay period (such as for holidays), the XML developer simply adds a holiday attribute to the payperiods DTD. Because the software stores all the information in an object database, when a new branch from the overall element tree is added, the ObjectStore software simply adds a pointer to the new element attribute object.

After all the information is entered, the manager (who has his or her own DTD) processes the time card. Email messages are sent to employees, notifying them that their time cards have been accepted. All the data is reused once again in the email message by simply picking it out of the XML DOM. The manager DTD, shown in the following code, creates the data structure for the managerial information needed to process the time card:

```
<!-- Siemens Manager-->
<!ELEMENT manager(departments,delegations,others)>
<!ATTLIST manager
```

```
serial CDATA #REQUIRED SERIAL
fullname CDATA #REQUIRED FULLNAME
>
<!ELEMENT departments(department*)>
<!ELEMENT delegations(department*)>
<!ELEMENT others(department*)>
<!ELEMENT department EMPTY>
<!ATTLIST department
depart CDATA #REQUIRED DEPART
>
```

The ObjectStore software supports cross-references between the DTDs because it stores the relationships between the objects in the XML DTDs in its database. After that information is used, pointers are stored in memory so the information can again be easily accessed.

Continuing, if the manager is to approve the time cards, the Time and Attendance System needs to surmise the department for which the manager has approval authority. Because managers may delegate that authority, the system has to be able to check not only the current manager's authority, but also any temporarily designated manager's authority. That means a separate DTD is needed to cross-reference any delegated managers and their authority:

```
<!-- Siemens Employee Timecards-->
<!ENTITY % timecard.dtd system "timecard.dtd">
<!ELEMENT department(payee*)>
<!ATTLIST department
depart CDATA #IMPLIED DEPART
period CDATA #IMPLIED WEEKEND_DATE
>
<!ELEMENT payee(timecard*)>
<!ATTLIST payee
serial CDATA #REQUIRED SERIAL
fullname CDATA #REQUIRED FULLNAME
manager CDATA #IMPLIED MANAGER
department CDATA #IMPLIED DEPT
email CDATA #IMPLIED MAIL_STOP
>
%timecard.dtd;
```

After this information has traversed through the ObjectStore database and the signing authority has been verified, it can be passed to the final payroll and accounting systems. ObjectStore can retain and forward the information on to the various systems as required, and the final paycheck can then be processed.

Using XML as a Conduit between Systems

By using XML and combining it with an object-oriented database that understands XML, the developers reduced the overall amount of code that needed to be written for all this information to be processed. This is a prime example of how XML can act as a conduit between systems, carrying information back and forth from time card to Web page form to company directory database and finally on to the payroll system. Siemens anticipates saving $500,000 a year by reducing duplication, data entry errors, and redundancy.

Examining RivCom's Competence Gap Analysis Tool

RivCom, a consulting firm in England (**www.rivcom.com**), used XML to create a rather elaborate system for Shell Services International. The Competence Gap Analysis Tool helps Shell employees in all divisions determine the exact skills sets required for jobs within the organization and rank each skill in the skill set by level of importance to the job. The tool can also be used to analyze individual employee skill sets and drive staff development as well as hiring. The database behind this system is complex and extensive, and it includes detailed information on all jobs and job requirements at Shell as well as employees and their skills.

XML is the perfect data format for this system because Shell is a worldwide organization and its employees use a variety of different hardware and software platforms. The system data needs to be accessible across all platforms and XML meets that requirement. XML is also flexible enough to allow a processing system (the Competency Gap Analysis Tool, in this case) to provide multiple views of the same information without reformatting that information.

The RivCom solution to Shell's needs was dubbed the RivComet. RivComet stores data in XML and uses style sheets to drive the display of the data. Client software can access and manipulate the data without taxing servers, and the costs of development and maintenance are low compared to those associated with a proprietary file format. Most display changes simply require changes to style sheets, and updating the DTD and the backend database can easily expand the data store.

Because browser support for style sheets is still immature, RivCom uses an ActiveX control embedded in Internet Explorer to parse and process the style sheets that drive the display of the XML data. The XML markup that describes the data in the system breaks down each information component so select bits of information can be removed, modified, or added as necessary. Listing 4.4 is an example of a portion of the XML file used to accomplish this task.

NOTE: *This example is taken from the RivCom overview of the RivComent solution at* **http://www.rivcom.com/ rivcomet/linked/cgat/overv.htm**.

Listing 4.4 A portion of the XML file that shows job requirements.

```
<comp ID="cpcf1" required="0" indiv="0">
<title>Delegation</title>
<desc>
Creates appropriate scope of work, authority,
and schedules for staff and is able to delegate work
in the confidence that at least the desired output
will be achieved.
</desc>
</comp>


<comp ID="cpcf2" required="0" indiv="0">
<title>Respect</title>
<desc>
Demonstrates a fundamental respect for,
and a genuine interest in, people at work,
understands individuals and provides caring support for
them at times of need.
</desc>
</comp>
```

In this example, the attributes of the **comp** element are **required** and **indiv**. Both are set to zero (**0**), which indicates that no competency levels for this particular job have been set yet. When competency levels have been set, the style sheets determine how the information will be displayed.

RivCom decided not to use HTML to create the resulting files. Instead, all of the information displayed in the Web page is actually generated on the fly by the RivComet ActiveX control. The RivComet ActiveX control was also developed as a Netscape plug-in for those users who prefer Navigator over Internet Explorer.

The RivComet Active X control (or Netscape plug-in) builds a display of XML information in a Web browser by using JavaScript to get the name of the XML file to be displayed, calling a Windows API to retrieve the actual XML, and applying a style sheet to the retrieved data. The ActiveX control combines the retrieved data and the style sheet to generate a final display for the user in HTML.

NOTE: *As Web browser support for XSLT becomes more mature, the ActiveX control will be obsolete in this solution. Another option might be to convert the XML data to HTML on the server side instead of in the ActiveX control in the browser. However, this would place a heavier burden on the servers. This solution is a good example of an implementation that will change over time as vendor support for XML improves.*

Immediate Solutions

Comparing HTML to XML

In this section, we'll examine how HTML and XML compare for creating and delivering some standard data. The following information needs to be delivered over the Web with a standard Web browser. The company in this example is a bookstore with an online catalog that needs to be accessed by customers and other vendors. The following elements need to be created, so that individuals can interact with the online bookstore:

- *ISBN*—The publishing industry's identifying number for each book
- *Title*—The title of the book
- *Author*—The author of the book
- *Publisher*—The publisher's name
- *Price*—The retail price of the book
- *Book club price*—Special discount price for book club members

Before XML, you might have considered creating a Web page for each book you have in inventory or stock on a regular basis. You might even place your list of books in your own database and add reviews and publicity information from a variety of sources to the final Web page for each book.

After you've switched to XML, created a bookstore DTD, and created style sheets to present the information in a variety of ways, you can do away with the Web pages. You can also do a lot more with a lot less, especially in terms of processing the information:

- *Automate*—Automate the process of ordering. If a publisher comes out with a new book and uses the same DTD you use to describe the book, you immediately have that book in your catalog. If a publisher uses a different DTD, you can use XSL Transformations (XSLT) to convert information described by the publisher's XML to your XML. You can also automate the order process by providing key information for each order. It doesn't matter what system you use, because you can easily pull the data out of your database, construct it in XML, and pass it to the book reseller's systems.

- *Provide better searching*—Not only will you be able to provide better searching for your employees, but you can also provide better searching for those using your online system. All books are now cataloged by the same elements and can easily be searched across these elements.

- *Exchange data with publishers and other suppliers*—Because the data is structured in a standard format, you can exchange information with suppliers and publishers. Information may contain comments and reviews about the books, pricing information, sales history, and so on. This information can easily be sent to their systems to help track marketing and sales promotions.

- *No worry about the browser*—You no longer have to worry about whether your online customers have the latest software. The store employees no longer have to answer calls about browsers or where to locate the right browser to view your site. If you want to create a page that uses specific features of a new browser, you can simply adjust the formatting of the style sheets, leaving all the data intact. Also, you can easily create a style sheet for Palm Pilot or mobile phone users without worrying about structuring or re-purposing content just for those devices.

Analyzing an XML Implementation

As XML becomes a more popular technology and is part of more information solutions, you'll have more implementations to use as examples as you plan your own solutions. Before you choose to use an XML implementation as an example, it's a good idea to look at exactly how the implementation works and what role XML plays in it. In general you want to come away from your analysis of the XML implementation with a good understanding of the following:

- What is the goal of the implementation?

- What kind of information does the implementation revolve around?

- Is the implementation built from scratch to meet a particular need or is it an update to an existing system?

- What other systems does the implementation interact with?

- What platform or platforms does the implementation run on?

- Is the implementation home-grown or does it use canned XML systems? Is it a combination of both?

Before you can decide if an implementation is a good example, you need to be sure that it matches some of your basic design and deployment requirements.

Chapter 5

DTDs in XML

In Depth

A Document Type Definition (DTD) is the foundation from which XML documents are created. You can create your own DTDs or use predefined DTDs from a wide variety of industries, such as investing, software development, and scientific research. Whether you create your own DTD or use a predefined DTD, you need to know what a DTD is, how it's constructed, how it works, and how it drives the development of XML documents.

NOTE: *DTDs are not required. You can build XML documents that don't have DTDs and still use them in many XML documents. We recommend that you build DTDs for most documents. If the XML processor uses a validating parser you need to supply a DTD for your document.*

Creating a DTD is one of the first steps in structuring your XML documents properly. DTDs provide the XML parsers with information, and they provide you with a guide to building standardized XML documents. In this chapter, we show you how to read, understand, and create DTDs. We also give you criteria to determine when an external DTD is needed and when to use an internal DTD. In addition, we explore why you might want to use previously defined DTDs and let you know when you should consider building your own DTD.

NOTE: *The W3C is working on replacing DTDs with XML Schema. See the W3C site at **www.w3.org/XML/Schema.html** for more information.*

What Is a DTD?

A DTD defines what markup components you can use to describe the different parts of a document. It includes a set of element and attribute declarations and the entities, notations, and comments you want to use to describe your data. In addition, the DTD outlines how you can and cannot use these components, what kind of content they can contain, and whether they are required or optional pieces of the document. Basically, a DTD is a set of rules that you use to guide your production of XML documents. Usually, a DTD has been well thought out and tested to be sure it can be used to accurately describe a particular kind of content, such as a stock ticker entry or a mathematical equation.

The easiest way to explain what a full DTD looks like and how it works is to quickly examine one. The following is an example of an internal DTD for a relatively simple document and is meant to demonstrate how a DTD looks and operates:

```
<!DOCTYPE doc [
<!ELEMENT doc (subject, date, address, memo)>
<!ELEMENT subject (#PCDATA)>
<!ELEMENT date (#PCDATA)>
<!ELEMENT address (#PCDATA)>
<!ELEMENT memo (#PCDATA)>
<!ENTITY publisher "The Coriolis Group">
]>
```

The DTD is contained within the **<!DOCTYPE doc [ ]>** marker, which specifies that the **doc** element is the *document element*. A document element is simply the XML element that contains all the other elements and content in a document. Inside the DTD are five element declarations, contained within **<!ELEMENT>** marker, and one entity declaration, contained within an **<!ENTITY>** marker. All of these declarations and markers are described in detail later in the chapter. Before we delve into the different components of the DTD, let's look at Listing 5.1 to see how the DTD is actually used to drive the structure of information in a document.

Listing 5.1   Using a DTD to drive the structure of information in a document.

```
<?xml version="1.0" encoding="UTF-8" standalone="no"?>
<!DOCTYPE doc [
<!ELEMENT doc (subject, date, address, memo)>
<!ELEMENT subject (#PCDATA)>
<!ELEMENT date (#PCDATA)>
<!ELEMENT address (#PCDATA)>
<!ELEMENT memo (#PCDATA)>
<!ENTITY publisher "The Coriolis Group">
]>
<doc>
<subject>XML Black Book Memo</subject>
<date>July 5, 2000</date>
<address>
    14455 N. Hayden Road, Suite 220, Scottsdale, AZ 85260
</address>
<memo>
    This memo is to alert you that the new version
    of the XML Black Book has now been printed. Published
    by &publisher;, this book outlines everything you
    need to know about XML.
</memo>
</doc>
```

The constructs in the DTD are reflected in the document itself. Of course, knowing what information you should include in each construct (such as including a valid date in the **date** element) requires some knowledge of the purpose and design goals of the DTD. Understanding how to use a DTD to guide document development and using the DTD correctly are two different things. Currently, we're only concerned with how to interpret a DTD and use it to describe data.

Let's take a closer look at our example DTD to get a feeling for what each line of code does in terms of defining the document. Here's a quick rundown of the most important components of this document:

- **<?xml version="1.0" encoding="UTF-8" standalone="no"?>**—The XML declaration specifies that the document is an XML document. It's the first line of instructions that is sent to the parser. For more specific information about the XML declaration, see "The XML Declaration" section later in this chapter.

- **<!DOCTYPE doc [**—The DOCTYPE declaration indicates that the DTD components are about to be defined. The components can then be defined within the declaration, called an *internal DTD*, as in our example DTD. Or, the declaration can point to a set of components contained in an external file, called an *external DTD*. In some cases, a DOCTYPE declaration may include both internal and external DTD components. Later sections in the chapter include more information on internal and external DTDs. The declaration also specifies the **doc** element as the document element.

- **<!ELEMENT doc (subject, date, address, memo)>**—Defines the list of elements for the root **doc** element. This element declaration tells the parser that the root element **doc** must contain the child elements **subject**, **date**, **address**, and **memo** and that they must appear in this order within the document. If they don't, any tool that attempts to process the document and validate it against the DTD will return an error.

- **<!ELEMENT subject (#PCDATA)>**—Defines the element **subject** and specifies that the element will contain parsed character data, or data that a processor will try to process and treat as XML information. Chapter 6 discusses the kind of content an element can contain in more detail.

- **<!ELEMENT date (#PCDATA)>**—Defines the element **date** and specifies that the element will contain parsed character data.

- **<!ELEMENT address (#PCDATA)>**—Defines the element **address** and specifies that the element will contain parsed character data.

- **<!ELEMENT memo (#PCDATA)>**—Defines the element **memo** and specifies that the element will contain parsed character data.

- **<!ENTITY publisher "The Coriolis Group">**—Defines the parsed entity, **publisher**, and specifies that the value for this entity is **The Coriolis Group**.

When a processor encounters the entity reference in a document, it replaces the entity name (**&publisher;**) with the entity value, **The Coriolis Group**.

- **]>**—Indicates the end of the DTD.

- **<doc>...</doc>**—Contains the XML document that is driven by the DTD. See Table 5.1 for a rundown of how the document content reflects the DTD components.

A DTD drives the way you build XML documents. It's as simple as that. The actual components of a DTD may exist directly inside a document or may be included in a reference file linked to the document. Regardless of the physical location of the DTD components, a DTD is considered part of an XML document. The DTD defines the parameters of the document, and the document holds data in a way that conforms to those parameters. To work with DTDs, you need to be familiar with their terminology and constructs. The next several sections of the chapter review the terminology and concepts associated with DTDs, and include cross-references to those chapters that cover the full functionality of these components in all realms of XML.

Table 5.1 How DTD components are reflected in a document.

DTD Component	Document Component	Description
<!ELEMENT doc (subject, date, address, memo)>	**<doc>...</doc>**	Element named **doc** that must contain one instance each of the **subject**, **date**, **address**, and **memo** elements
<!ELEMENT subject (#PCDATA)>	**<subject>Today's Memo</subject>**	**subject** element that contains text
<!ELEMENT date (#PCDATA)>	**<date>July 5, 2000 </date>**	**date** element that contains text
<!ELEMENT address (#PCDATA)>	**<address> 14455 N. Hayden Road, Suite 220, Scottsdale, AZ 85260 </address>**	**address** element that contains text
<!ELEMENT memo (#PCDATA)>	**<memo>...</memo>**	**memo** element that contains text
<!ENTITY publisher "The Coriolis Group">	**&publisher;**	Parsed entity that equates the code **&publisher;** in a document with the phrase **The Coriolis Group**

Declarations

A *declaration* defines the specifics about the elements, attributes, entities, and notations you want to use to describe content in your document, as well as any special instructions you might want to pass to the XML processor. A DTD is comprised entirely of declarations. When you learn to build and read DTDs, you're really learning to build and read declarations.

The first two lines of most XML documents contain two declarations: the XML declaration and the document type declaration (DOCTYPE declaration). Unlike other declarations (element, attribute, entity, and notation), the XML declaration and the DOCTYPE declaration don't construct the document. They don't explain the structural role of any particular element or attribute. Instead, they tell a processor what standards to use, what type of document is being processed, and where the DTD that actually drives the document is stored. Looking once again at the two lines of code in the sample document from the previous section, you see the XML declaration and the DOCTYPE declaration:

```
<?xml version="1.0" encoding="UTF-8" standalone="no"?>
<!DOCTYPE doc [
```

> **NOTE:** There's a difference between the terms DTD (Document Type Definition) and DOCTYPE declaration (document type declaration). The DTD holds all the declarations that guide a document's development. The DOCTYPE declaration holds the DTD itself, or points to the DTD's location in an external file. The DOCTYPE declaration points the processor to the DTD—it connects the DTD to the document. Think of it as the glue that binds the document to the definition that explains the document. Therefore, within the DOCTYPE declaration, you find the components of or links to the DTD.

The XML Declaration

The first line in the example document (Listing 5.1) is called the XML declaration, and it tells the processor to use version 1.0 of the XML specification to process the document as an XML document. Currently, version 1.0 is the only version of the specification; but as new versions become available, you can indicate which processor applications can and cannot process the document based on the version of XML the processor recognizes. The second part of the XML declaration specifies what kind of character encoding will be used for the document. In this example, we use the 8-bit Unicode character-encoding scheme, which is XML's default character-encoding scheme, but we could also specify 16- or 32-bit or, depending on the parser, a variety of other character encoding schemes. The "Parts of a DTD" section later in this chapter provides further insight into the issues of character encoding, and Chapter 9 discusses the topic in even more detail.

Related solutions:	Found on page:
Declaring a Text-Encoding Scheme for Entities	226

The final piece of information that we include in our XML declaration is called the *standalone document attribute*. It specifies whether an XML document stands alone or whether it relies on an external declaration. For example, if the value is set to **"yes"**, the document is self-sufficient and doesn't use an external DTD. In other words, a standalone XML document contains all the pertinent information within itself.

A value of **"yes"** also tells an XML processor to ignore any declarations that point to external references (such as DTD information included in an external file). A value of **"no"** or omitting the **standalone** attribute tells the processor that it should process external declarations. When you set the standalone attribute to **"no"**, you're simply telling the XML processor that the document can reference any external declarations. However, doing so doesn't mean that you must include external references—only that the processor should accept and process any if they're noted in the document.

When do you set the standalone declaration to **"no"** and when do you set it to **"yes"**? As we've mentioned, if your document relies on an external DTD, you need to set the value to **"no"**. You can set the value to **"yes"** if you aren't using external references at all and if you're only using the general entities that are specified as part of the XML language, such as ampersands, greater-than or less-than symbols, apostrophes, or quotation marks.

The DOCTYPE Declaration

The second line of code is called the DOCTYPE declaration, and it's used to associate the XML document with its corresponding DTD. Following **<!DOCTYPE** is the name of the document element. In the case of an internal DTD, the list of declarations that make up the DTD follows the document element in the declaration and is contained within brackets (**[ ]**). If you're referencing an external DTD, you simply identify the location of the DTD in the declaration immediately following the document element. If you're combining internal and external DTDs, you first point to the external DTD and then use brackets to include internal DTD elements. The next section, "Storing DTDs" discusses the ins and outs of DTD location and references in detail.

NOTE: *If you're going to include a DTD in your document, include the DOCTYPE declaration after the XML declaration but before the first element (the document element). If you try to place the DTD any place else in the document, an XML processor will spit out the document along with an error message telling you to rearrange your document. For more information on DTD-less documents, see the section "To DTD or Not to DTD" later in the chapter.*

5. DTDs in XML

Storing DTDs

As we mentioned earlier in the chapter, the declarations that make up a DTD can be stored within the document (internally) or in a separate file (externally). Internal DTDs combine all the declarations that comprise a document's DTD. Internal DTDs are specified with the following code within the DOCTYPE declaration:

```
<!DOCTYPE document_element [ DTD goes here]>
```

In the example we've worked with so far in the chapter, the DTD is stored internally:

```
<?xml version="1.0" encoding="UTF-8" standalone="no" ?>
<!DOCTYPE doc [
<!ELEMENT doc (subject, date, address, memo)>
<!ELEMENT subject (#PCDATA)>
<!ELEMENT date (#PCDATA)>
<!ELEMENT address (#PCDATA)>
<!ELEMENT memo (#PCDATA)>
<!ENTITY publisher "The Coriolis Group">
]>
```

External DTDs are also referenced within the DOCTYPE declaration, but the actual declarations that make up the DTD are stored in an external file. The name of the external DTD doesn't have to correspond in any way to the XML document, but it must have the three-letter extension .dtd. For example, if your XML document is named bizmemo.xml, you might want to name the DTD memo.dtd, instead of something like xyz.dtd.

Storing your DTDs externally is beneficial because a single DTD can be used and reused with literally thousands of documents. This is one of XML's most powerful features. Having the ability to create a single DTD to encompass a variety of documents that are based on a common structure makes it possible for you to create standardized ways to store and describe information for presentation across a variety of devices.

Public and System DTDs

Within a DOCTYPE declaration, you can identify an external DTD reference as a *public DTD* or a *system DTD*. You can use publicly available DTDs that have already been defined for a particular need, or you can use your own locally developed DTD. When you use a publicly available DTD, you need to use the keyword **PUBLIC** within the DOCTYPE declaration when you specify the DTD. When you use your own DTD, you need to use the keyword **SYSTEM**. Here's an example of a DOCTYPE declaration that references the public XHTML DTD (XHTML is a reformulation of HTML under the umbrella of XML; Chapter 18 is devoted to the subject):

```
<!DOCTYPE html PUBLIC "-//W3C//DTD XHTML 1.0 Strict//EN"
"DTD/http://www.w3.org/DTD/xhtml1-strict.dtd">
```

The public identifier structure used by XML for publicly available DTDs is the same structure used for Standard Generalized Markup Language (SGML) public identifiers. If the specified entity or DTD is an International Organization for Standardization (ISO) standard, you must start the DTD with **ISO**. If it's not an ISO standard, but the standard is officially approved by a standards body, start the declaration with a plus sign (**+**); if it's not officially approved by a standards body, start the declaration with a minus sign (**-**). Following the identifier are two forward slashes (//) and then the owner of the DTD. If we dissect the DOCTYPE declaration in the preceding example, we find that the DTD specified is not standard and that the W3C owns this DTD. We also find that the name of the DTD is **DTD XHTML 1.0 Strict** and it's located at **http://www.w3.org/** in the **DTD** directory.

Now, let's see an example of what a DOCTYPE declaration looks like when you specify a DTD stored on a local system:

```
<!DOCTYPE book SYSTEM "http://www.site.com/dtds/book.dtd">
```

This declaration includes just the keyword **SYSTEM** followed by the location and file name of the DTD. The **SYSTEM** keyword allows you to specify the location of any DTD (not just DTDs that are recognized standards) using a URI.

Combining Internal and External, Public and System DTDs

The actual DTD that guides your document may be a combination of an internal DTD and an external DTD, as well as a system-specific DTD and a publicly available DTD. As long as the DTDs are syntactically correct and are written according to the XML specification, you can mix and match DTDs all you like. If a publicly available DTD meets most, but not all, of your needs, you can reference it as an external DTD in your DOCTYPE declaration and then add your own declarations in an internal DTD to augment the public DTD. This example combines the external XHTML DTD with the sample memo DTD from earlier in the chapter:

```
<?xml version="1.0" encoding="UTF-8" standalone="no"?>
<!DOCTYPE html PUBLIC "-//W3C//DTD XHTML 1.0 Strict//EN"
"DTD/xhtml1-strict.dtd"
[
<!ELEMENT doc (subject, date, address, memo)>
<!ELEMENT subject (#PCDATA)>
<!ELEMENT date (#PCDATA)>
<!ELEMENT address (#PCDATA)>
<!ELEMENT memo (#PCDATA)>
<!ENTITY publisher "The Coriolis Group">
]>
```

The document element is **html,** and the complete DTD for this document combines all the declarations in the XHTML DTD with the declarations listed in the internal memo DTD. The most common use of this feature is not to mix and match the elements and attributes from multiple DTDs into a single DTD, but is instead to define entities that are specific to the document within the internal DTD. Chapter 9 discusses the ins and outs of entity placement in more detail.

WARNING! Although you can use the DOCTYPE declaration to combine declarations from several DTD sources into a single DTD, you may want to think twice before you do so. A DTD developer usually builds all the components in the DTD to work well together. If you introduce new elements from another DTD into the fray, you may find that the combined collection of components doesn't work well together. If a DTD isn't meeting your needs, consider reengineering it instead of simply adding to it to ensure that all the components are compatible.

To DTD or Not to DTD

XML documents don't necessarily require a DTD to work well, unlike SGML documents, which always require a DTD. Because XML was fashioned to work within the constraints of the Web, sometimes a DTD simply doesn't work because of bandwidth limitations. Often, developers will work with a sample set of data and build elements and attributes around that data to get a good idea of what constructs will be needed to describe similar kinds of data. They then work backward from the DTD-less markup they've created to build a functional DTD.

So, how do you know when you need a DTD and when you don't? And how do you know when you should make it internal and when you should make it external? Several mitigating factors will help you decide:

• *Structurally complex documents more often have external DTDs.* With an external DTD, you can create a certain amount of standardization. Doing so makes the document more coherent, because DTD users will have to follow certain rules.

- *The more people and data involved, the more useful a DTD is.* Remember that the whole point of a DTD is to help predefine data structures so you can achieve consistency across documents that contain that data. The more data you have and the more people there are who need to share the documents you have to deal with, the harder it is to maintain that consistency. If everyone has a standard to work from, your consistency problems will be effectively solved (barring human error, of course—but that's what validating parsers are for).

- *Small documents don't require external DTDs.* Unless you want to standardize every single bit of data in your company, you should consider not creating a DTD for simple correspondence (for example, one-page memos or faxes).

- *Some Internet-oriented documents don't require DTDs.* If you have bandwidth constraints, an external DTD may cause more bandwidth overhead.

- *Non-validating XML processors don't require a DTD.* When you use a non-validating XML processor that only checks for well-formedness, you don't need an external DTD.

Although we've given you guidelines to help you determine when you should include a DTD and when doing so isn't required, you really should consider creating an external DTD for complex documents and documents with data that will be shared among many users. By creating and keeping DTDs in a separate file, they're not only reusable, but also easier to manage, update, and change. You can also prevent people from changing the DTDs.

External vs. Internal DTDs

After you've decided to create a DTD, you need to determine if it should be stored internally or externally. The size of the document is only one consideration. Other factors to take into consideration are reusability of the DTD and portability of the document.

Internal DTDs

When you create a document, the first thing you should ask yourself is whether the document needs to be self-contained. A self-contained document can be moved from system to system without losing components. You can use the document on your local system without being connected to the Internet. You can also place a self-contained document on a disk or cartridge drive and carry it with you. And any XML processor can process it without having to look for an accompanying DTD.

Another reason for placing the DTD information within a single file is to cut down on the amount of processing time and the amount of bandwidth required to load, parse, and display the file. Sometimes, it's more efficient to place the DTD within the document so the XML processor only has to read one file—not two, three, or more—to display the information. Finally, when you use an internal DTD, you create a self-contained file that is both valid and complete. Any XML processor can process it without having to look for an external DTD.

External DTDs

Although they add a certain amount of overhead, processing time, and bandwidth requirements, it's usually better to use external DTDs. External DTDs offer many benefits, especially in the areas of managing, updating, and editing documents. Here are just a few reasons you would want to use an external DTD:

- *If you use an external DTD, you can use public DTDs.* A public DTD may have all the capabilities you need. Instead of reinventing the wheel, you can use a DTD that someone else has already built, which means your document structure will be standard. Updates to a public DTD are automatically incorporated within your documents.

- *With small documents, you can focus on content.* Instead of worrying about the structure of a small document, you can focus on creating the content. You can use an externally stored DTD so you don't have to worry about putting all the information about the document structure within a small document. For quick documents that need to match a particular structure, an external DTD is preferable.

- *External DTDs provide for better document management.* With external DTDs, you can easily create a set of documents that define rules for specific needs. Then, you can edit and update the DTD as required without having to open the XML content document, much as you would when reformatting a style sheet. Also, instead of entering the same information again and again, you enter the information once. You don't have to worry about whether you've entered the same element name in a variety of documents.

Parts of a DTD

As with any great masterpiece, you need to use certain building blocks to construct your DTD. Everything about the document—from the entities to the elements that help construct the document—is defined in the DTD. A DTD contains no content, only definitions.

TIP: *You must use the correct XML syntax when you create your DTDs. Otherwise, your document won't parse, and you'll have nothing but errors. Learn the syntax for declaring elements, attributes, and entities. If you need more information on how to read the XML specification, review Chapter 2. Information on elements, attributes, and entities is described in detail in Chapters 6, 7, 8, and 9.*

When you think about it, the entire document rests on the shoulders of the DTD. It not only defines the elements, attributes, and entities of the document, but it also describes everything that can be contained within the document. The DTD actually accomplishes many things, including:

- Defines and provides the names of all the elements used in the document.

- Defines how elements may (and in some cases must) be used together to describe information.

- Defines and provides the names of all the attributes used in a document.

- Defines all attributes (and their default values) for each element.

- Defines and provides the names and the content of all the entities used in the document.

- Specifies the order in which elements and attributes must appear in the document.

- Outlines any comments that may help clarify the structural context of the document.

The DTD makes it possible for the document content to be marked up and then displayed properly when it's parsed. To construct a well-defined DTD, you must first know exactly what individual parts are included. DTDs include the following:

- Character data, including normal character and special character data

- White space characters

- Entities

- Elements, including their start and end tags (unless they're empty elements)

- Attributes

- Comments

- Processing instructions

Each part is used to create DTDs that make up both well-formed and valid XML documents. Let's examine each part briefly.

TIP: *We discuss both well-formed and valid documents later in this chapter.*

Character Data

The smallest piece of a DTD is a single character. So, how does a single character help form a well-designed DTD? It's simple: Characters make up the content of the document and also the content of entities, elements, attributes, and even comments. Character data specifies a certain process, marks up data, or represents some type of information.

Character data can be a mixture of text and markup information. When that happens, you have *mixed content*. Here's an example of what mixed content looks like:

```
<subject>Creating DTDs</subject>
<information>This section will help you understand
how to create well-designed DTDs.</information>
```

All characters used in the DTD and the document itself within XML are based on the ISO 10646 character-encoding scheme, commonly referred to as Unicode. You can use Unicode to represent the same characters across different platforms. It supports encoding schemes for 8-bit, 16-bit, and 32-bit character sets.

Some special characters, however, are reserved and are used within XML to signify certain functionality. For example the left angle bracket (<) is used to indicate element and attribute declarations, as well as to identify the beginning of a tag for an element used in an XML document. With the help of Unicode, you can use these special, reserved characters within the content of a document without worrying that the processor will indicate an error in processing. Unicode helps create *internal entities*, which are reserved entities that specify various reserved characters. Table 5.2 lists several reserved characters and their Unicode hexadecimal assignments along with the escape character strings used to denote them in an XML document.

TIP: *For more information about Unicode, check out the official Web site at* **www.unicode.org**. *Chapter 9 includes an in-depth discussion of how to represent non-ASCII characters in your XML documents.*

White Space Characters

White space is simply empty space between characters. However, white space can be more than just space. It can also be one of the following characters:

Table 5.2   Reserved characters in XML.

Character	Unicode Assignment	Escape Character String
<	<	<
>	>	>
&	&	&

- The space character (Unicode character **#x20**)

- The line feed (Unicode character **#xD**)

- The tab character (Unicode character **#xA**)

- The carriage return (Unicode character **#x9**)

You can combine any of these characters in a string of character data. XML processes white space by using *white space handling*. XML processors read all white space along with all other characters in a document. However, you need to describe to the XML processor when white space is significant by using the **xml:space** attribute within the attribute list. For example, if you want to signify that white space is important and needs to display in the document itself, you would define the following within the attribute list:

```
<!ATTLIST listing xml:space
      (default | preserve) "preserve">
```

Entities

While we're on the subject of characters, we might as well discuss entities. XML provides a mechanism that makes it easy to create information that will be placed in the document repeatedly and will help you maintain the document over time. This mechanism is called an *entity* and unlike HTML, with XML, you get to create your own entities. An entity is a component, be it text or other data, that can be substituted into a document based on a declaration. The component can be a text string or any type of file; that's right, entities can also reference entire files. That means an entity could reference a masthead, a chapter in a book, or anything to which a reference can point. Because entities allow text and files to be substituted into a document, they can be used to replace values when a document is parsed and displayed.

TIP: *Chapters 1 and 2 discuss the roles entities play in markup in general and XML in specific. Chapter 9 is entirely devoted to the ins and outs of entities.*

It's our opinion that entities are by far the easiest portion of the DTD to create, because in their most basic form, entities provide a mechanism to specify content without much effort. Entities are also the most complex, because you can do so much with them. There are two types of entities: parsed entities and unparsed entities. The following example focuses on parsed entities that associate an entity name or keyword with a text string or file, as well as on unparsed entities, which associate an entity name or keyword with content that may be non-textual (such as a graphic). All other kinds of entities are discussed in Chapter 9.

For example, if you use copyright information again and again in a document, you could create an entity with the following code:

```
<!ENTITY copyright "Copyright 2000">
```

Then, you would specify the entity within the document by using the entity reference, as follows:

```
All this information is &copyright;.
```

The previous code would display as follows when the document is parsed:

```
All this information is Copyright 2000.
```

You can also create entities that reference entire files to be inserted into the document. You use the **SYSTEM** keyword to identify the URL of the file. **SYSTEM** is a reserved keyword that tells the XML processor the referenced external entity is in a file. The following code inserts a file into an XML document (note that the URL used is just an example):

```
<!ENTITY adddata SYSTEM "http://www.adn.com/docs/document.xml">
```

When the XML processor encounters the **adddata** entity, it processes the file and then replaces the entity with the processed contents of the file.

You can also use this type of code to include other types of files—for example, the image file for a logo. Entities that reference non-text files are called *unparsed entities*; they are not parsed by the XML parser, but are instead handled by an application you specify in the DTD. You specify an application or processor to handle the file using the keyword **NDATA**. **NDATA** is used as a pointer to a previously declared notation to specify which application will process the entity reference. The following code allows you to insert a graphic into an XML document and have it processed as a GIF file, and not as any other type of file:

```
<!ENTITY adnlogo SYSTEM
"http://www.adn.com/images/logo.gif" NDATA gif >
```

WARNING! You can reference parsed entities anywhere in a document, but you can only reference an unparsed entity in the value of an element's attribute.

Therefore, when you use the **adnlogo** entity in a document, the processor uses the GIF notation to determine how to handle the entity.

TIP: *You can use the **NOTATION** declaration to declare the GIF notation. When you create a notation, identify the URL of the helper application using the **SYSTEM** keyword and the following code (note that **iviewer.exe** is the application that can display the GIF file):*

```
<!NOTATION gif SYSTEM "http://site.com
```

Elements

Because elements are fully explained in Chapter 6, we only discuss them briefly here. Elements construct the parts of a document. You have full control over what elements you create and use in your XML documents. You usually create elements and their content right after you specify the XML processing instruction and DOCTYPE declaration at the top of a DTD with external DTDs, or at the top of an XML document when creating internal DTDs. An element declaration looks like this:

```
<!ELEMENT name content>
```

For example, if you were creating an online parts ordering system, you could declare the part number element named **partno** and specify that this content can be parsed character data. To do so, you would include the following code in your DTD:

```
<!ELEMENT partno (#PCDATA)>
```

You can declare as many elements as you need in the DTD. Yet, depending upon how you structure the elements in the DTD, you may or may not need to use all those elements in your XML document. Or, depending upon how you specify the elements' content, you may need to use one element before you use another. You determine such element preferences in the DTD. For example, to specify that the element **name** must contain two other elements, **first** and **last**, and that **first** has to appear before **last**, you declare the elements in your DTD in this order:

```
<!ELEMENT first (#PCDATA)>
<!ELEMENT last (#PCDATA)>
<!ELEMENT name (first, last)>
```

Attributes

Attributes help describe exactly what elements are, the kind of information that must be placed in them, and the order in which the information should be placed. Attributes can be placed directly after an element has been declared, or you can place them in groups (*attribute lists*) after all elements have been declared within the DTD. It's best to declare the element and then declare its attribute list because doing so makes it easier to read the DTD. You'll know exactly what element has been declared and what attributes are specified if you follow the element with its attribute list.

A list of attributes is defined for an element using the **ATTLIST** assignment to specify exactly what can and cannot be placed in an element and what information is required. Because a document's elements are completely configurable, you're free to create attributes as necessary.

This is where the tough part begins. Although attributes help clarify what content the elements can contain, they require more information than elements because they further clarify what an element does. Therefore, their construction is a bit more complex; you really have to think about your elements and how to describe them not only to humans, but also to parsers. The parser that reads the XML DTD document uses the attributes to set certain flags, such as whether an order has been processed. The application in turn uses this flag to determine if data can be edited.

The basic format of an attribute is specified through the use of the **ATTLIST** assignment, as shown in the following code:

```
<!ATTLIST elementname attributename type default_usage>
```

If we break down this string of code from left to right, this is what we have:

- **!ATTLIST**—Begins the attribute-list declaration.

- *elementname*—Names the element to which the attribute is associated. Attributes can appear directly after elements or anywhere within the DTD. You need to include this information because, in many cases, the attribute doesn't follow the actual element it describes.

- *attributename*—Specifies the name given to the attribute. You can give your attribute just about any name you want (within the limitations specified by the XML 1.0 and XML Namespaces recommendations). The attribute name is significant when you need to reference it while using an application and when someone's reading your document and trying to make sense of it.

- *type*—Specifies whether the attribute will be a string type, tokenized type, or enumerated type.

- *default_usage*—Specifies the default values that can be used with attributes. Some of the default values used are:

  - **#IMPLIED**—A value is optional for this attribute. The processor should notify the system when no value is set, but the document can still be considered valid.

- **#FIXED**—The value is fixed and cannot be changed. The document is not valid if the attribute is used with a value different from the default.

- **#REQUIRED**—A value is mandatory for this attribute. If no value is set, the document is not valid.

For example, suppose you want to declare an element called **last** and you want to create an attribute named **format** for it. You want to specify that this attribute must contain character data (**CDATA**) and not markup data. In addition, you want the content of the element to be required; this tells the processor to return an error if no content is specified for this element's attribute. The code would look like this:

```
<!ELEMENT last (#PCDATA)>
<!ATTLIST last
          format    CDATA    #REQUIRED>
```

TIP: *You can do many things with attributes and use them to closely control what information is contained in a document and what form that information should take. To learn more about the various attribute options you can declare in your DTD, see Chapter 8.*

Comments

Comments are important in any DTD. They not only help you remember what you placed in the DTD, but they also help others know the purpose for certain elements or attributes you create. Remember, one of the XML design principles is that XML data be humanly legible and easily understood. With a few well-placed comments, you can ensure that this design principle is followed. Here is the syntax for a comment:

```
<!-- comment -->
```

The first part, **<!--**, signifies the start of the comment, and **-->** signifies the end. If you've worked with HTML, this comment format probably looks very familiar to you. With the exception of two hyphens (--), anything can be placed within the comment itself. No part of the comment is displayed or processed by the parser. Comments can be on a single line or broken up and placed on multiple lines. For example:

```
<!-- The information
specified in this document
outlines the document structure. -->
```

You should use a lot of comments when you first start creating XML documents. Consider the DTD shown in Listing 5.2, which was created by David Megginson. He has fully commented the entire DTD. He has indicated each element's purpose and specified where the entities start. When you read Listing 5.2, you'll understand what the author's intentions were when he created each element, attribute, and notation, because he identified each with a comment. Each section that describes a particular set of DTD components is commented. As you can see, it doesn't matter where you place the comments. Placing them frequently throughout the DTD makes it easier to read and understand. Even the end of the DTD is described in detail.

Listing 5.2   A novel DTD.

```
<?xml encoding="UTF-8"?>
<!--
******************************************************
novel.dtd: A simple XML DTD for marking-up novels.
Copyright (c) 1997 by David Megginson.
******************************************************
-->
<!-- Content model for phrasal content -->
<!ENTITY % phrasal "#PCDATA|emphasis">
<!-- ******** -->
<!-- Elements -->
<!-- ******** -->

<!-- The top-level novel -->
<!ELEMENT novel (front, body)>

<!-- The frontmatter for the novel -->
<!ELEMENT front (title, author, revision-list)>

<!-- The list of revisions to this text -->
<!ELEMENT revision-list (item+)>

<!-- An item in the list of revisions -->
<!ELEMENT item (%phrasal;)*>
<!-- The main body of a novel -->
<!ELEMENT body (chapter+)>
<!-- A chapter of a novel -->
<!ELEMENT chapter (title, paragraph+)>
<!ATTLIST chapter
   id ID #REQUIRED>

<!-- The title of a novel or chapter -->
<!ELEMENT title (%phrasal;)*>
```

```
<!-- The author(s) of a novel -->
<!ELEMENT author (%phrasal;)*>

<!-- A paragraph in a chapter -->
<!ELEMENT paragraph (%phrasal;)*>

<!-- An emphasized phrase -->
<!ELEMENT emphasis (%phrasal;)*>

<!-- **************** -->
<!-- General Entities -->
<!-- **************** -->

<!--
  These really should have their Unicode equivalents.
-->

<!-- em-dash -->
<!ENTITY mdash "--">

<!-- left double quotation mark -->
<!ENTITY ldquo "``">

<!-- right double quotation mark -->
<!ENTITY rdquo "''">

<!-- left single quotation mark -->
<!ENTITY lsquo "`">

<!-- right single quotation mark -->
<!ENTITY rsquo "'">

<!-- horizontal ellipse -->
<!ENTITY hellip "...">

<!-- end of DTD -->
```

Processing Instructions

Processing instructions are information for applications and are passed through to the application by the XML processor. For example, the following processing instruction could be used in an XML document to indicate to an application that uses the data, for example, a Web browser, that it should apply the style sheet that is indicated to the contents of the document in which this instruction appears:

```
<?xml-stylesheet href="MyStyle.xsl" type="text/xsl"?>
```

Every processing instruction must start with **<?** and end with **?>**. The contents of a processing instruction begin with a target name. The target name is generally used to indicate the application (for example, an XSL processor) that will use the data contained in the processing instruction. The target name may not be the letters "xml" in any combination of upper and lowercase. These names (xml, Xml, xMl, xmL, and so on) are reserved for use by the XML declaration.

Valid and Well-Formed Documents

In addition to the parts that make up a DTD, you need to know the difference between valid and well-formed documents: Valid XML documents require a DTD, and well-formed documents don't. Knowing which components you need to include if you want to create valid or well-formed XML documents is important when creating an XML document that will parse correctly and not return errors.

Well-Formed XML Documents

If you want an XML processor to process a document correctly, the document must be *well formed*, which means that the document and the code markup conform to the rules of XML syntax. Well-formed XML documents don't require a DTD to be valid XML files. However, there's a little bit more to it—certain rules determine whether a document is well formed:

- The document must be surrounded by a single outermost root element, or document element.
- No attribute can appear more than once in the same start tag.
- Elements must be nested properly and must have matching open and close tags (unless the element is an empty element).
- Parameter entities must be declared before they can be used, and all entities except XML predefined entities must be declared.
- You can use unparsed entities only if you have declared them as **ENTITY** or **ENTITIES**. They cannot be referenced in the content.
- All entities, elements, and attributes are case sensitive and therefore, must be referenced correctly.
- String attribute values cannot contain references to external resources.
- Always use **<** to represent the literal character **<**, use **&** to represent the literal character **&**, use **"** to represent a literal quotation mark inside of an attribute's value and **'** to represent a literal apostrophe inside of an attribute's value. See Chapter 9 for more information on entities.

If your document doesn't follow these conventions, it's not well formed and therefore it's not considered an XML document. You should check the XML specification for more information about well-formed XML documents. If you violate any of the specification's rules, your parser will give you a fatal error. The XML parser will report the error to the XML application and may not continue to process the document.

Here's an example of a very simple, well-formed document:

```
<?xml version="1.0"?>
<body>
This is the body of a well-formed document.
</body>
```

Valid XML Documents

A valid XML document is a well-formed document that also adheres to the specifications of a DTD. To break it down, a valid document has all of these characteristics:

- Valid documents follow the XML specification rules (well-formedness rules).

- The document has a corresponding DTD, either internally, externally, or both.

- The document complies with the rules of the associated DTD.

Well-formed documents obey the XML specification rules, whereas valid XML documents require conformation to both the XML specification and the DTD that accompanies the document. All valid XML documents are well-formed, but not all well-formed documents are valid. For instance, a well-formed document that doesn't use a DTD is not valid, but it is also not invalid. Because it has no associated DTD, it has no validity characteristics.

Here's an example of a valid document:

```
<?xml version="1.0"?>
<!DOCTYPE body
[
<!ELEMENT body (#PCDATA)>
]>
<body>This is a well-formed and valid document.</body>
```

You need to know what makes documents valid and well-formed so you'll know why your processor is returning errors. The best thing to do is read through the XML specification, which is included in Appendix B of this book and is available online at **www.w3.org/XML/**.

The Road to Good DTD Design

To create a well-designed DTD, you must know how the parts of your document work together. Because XML is all about structure, you must plan ahead before you start developing the DTD; therefore, you know exactly which building blocks you need to structure your documents. It's kind of like building a house. If you were going to build a stucco house, you wouldn't go to the hardware store and buy truckloads of siding; instead, you would buy stucco material. Building a DTD is somewhat the same. You need the right building materials before you can start the job, and that means you need to determine what kinds of documents you're going to create. For example, you could create technical manuals, an online book, or an automated office system with structured elements for faxes, memos, and reports. You can create a plethora of different types of documents.

After you determine what kind of document you're going to create, you need to sketch out on paper exactly which elements, attributes, entities, and notations you need in order to construct the perfect DTD for the job. You should also consider whether other people will be involved in the project. You may not know all the necessary elements because someone else may be doing the actual content creation. During the planning stage, it's imperative that you include everyone who will be involved in the project.

You should examine the document flow as well as the document content. How you structure your DTD may very well be determined by what external organizations will use the information and what requirements they may have. It's important that you know how documents will relate to one another and what constraints outside forces may place on your documents. It doesn't really matter if the DTD you're building is for a small company or a major publishing house. The steps in document analysis and creation are all the same:

1. Define the environment in which existing documents work.
2. Define the external requirements for your internal documents.
3. Define and outline the elements needed for both internal and external use.
4. Define how the elements will relate to one another and to outside elements.
5. Define the flow of information from one document to the next.
6. Determine what other systems will utilize the data.
7. Document how the flow of information works, along with the elements, attributes, entities, and notations defined in the DTD.
8. Create the DTD model.
9. Parse the DTD to check for errors.

10. Test the DTD with trial content.

11. Resolve any outstanding issues.

12. Supply the DTD to everyone involved in the project.

These steps work toward a logical progression, from analyzing the problem the DTD will solve, to parsing the DTD, to checking for errors. Without proper planning, your DTD may not accommodate the markup that is necessary for the people involved.

If you break down an XML document, you find two types of information: the content and the markup. The content determines what the markup will be. Before you create the DTD, you should examine existing content that will be used or incorporated into your XML document. In addition, make sure you evaluate any restrictions or policies that may be associated with these documents. The attributes you develop for the elements you create may depend on existing restrictions. For example, a document may require part numbers with orders; therefore, you could create an element that requires a part number with all orders.

After you know what documents you already have and the restrictions they impose, the next step is to ask yourself what purpose your DTDs will serve for both the documents you have and those you'll create. If you're creating a site to take online orders, you need to structure your documents with the correct elements and attributes listed in proper order in the DTD. You might also consider creating another set of documents to handle purchase orders, and those documents might use the same DTD. For example, if you're working with a government agency, what are their requirements for invoicing? In other words, what types of information need to be maintained? Asking yourself these questions will help you determine which elements are required and which attributes will help further define them. To visualize exactly how all the elements will work together, create a project map that outlines all the information and the information flow.

5. DTDs in XML

Immediate Solutions

Defining the Elements

Before you can create your DTD, you need to know not only how to define the elements, but also how to choose which elements to define. For an example, let's take a quick look at something almost everyone is familiar with: a newspaper. If you were creating an online newspaper, you would need to consider that the information may eventually be made available via an online search archive. You might also want to send the newspaper to subscribers and to other news agencies via email. In addition, companies may want to buy the photos or graphics.

In a section of a newspaper, you could have multiple instances of any or all of the following: page numbers, articles, bylines, pictures of editors, editor email addresses, callouts, headlines, and/or quotes. You need to create elements that will work with the printed version, the Web-site version, as well as the email version. The elements should also be interfaced with a database system that will allow both reporters and readers to search for particular articles based on keywords. So, knowing all this, you could define the following elements for this particular newspaper:

- **newspaper**—The root element. Although our example considers only a single section of the newspaper, you should remember that the section is just a part of a larger entity.

- **section**—The secondary element. Each newspaper will have at least one section, and each section will have multiple parts, such as articles and graphics. The **section** element may have such attributes as the section name, section location, section page numbering scheme, and more.

- **headline**—Usually a single sentence that defines the content of the article that follows. The **headline** element should always appear before the **story** element and may include other elements, such as the **subhead** element.

- **subhead**—An optional secondary headline that further defines the article that follows. This element is not required, but it should always follow the **headline** element and be placed before the **story** element.

- **byline**—The name of the article's author. It always appears before the **story** element but after the **headline** or **subhead** element.

- **lede**—A separate element that basically consists of the first paragraph of the **story** element. The lead is the teaser that brings the reader into the story. The **lede** element follows the **byline** element but appears before the **story** element.

- **story**—The content. The **story** element contains several attributes that further explain the story. Those attributes may be the names of all the authors and editors of the story along with date and the edition in which the story appears.

- **pullquotes**—Quotes from stories that may be displayed beside the articles.

We won't discuss *all* the elements a newspaper would require, but these will give you an idea of some of the more important elements. Now that you have an idea of some of the elements you need to turn this newspaper section into an XML document, we're ready to sketch the element relationships and hierarchies.

Understanding Element Relationships and Hierarchy

Sketching the element relationships and hierarchy will help you define not only the elements, but also the attributes each element needs. Here's what you need to define for each element:

- Sequence

- Relationship to other elements

- Hierarchy

- Occurrence

Before we move too far ahead, let's take a look at the novel DTD we showed you in Listing 5.2 to see how sequence, hierarchy, occurrence, and relationships to other elements evolve within a DTD.

In Listing 5.3, we've stripped out the comments so you can see only the elements, attributes, and entities to get an idea of how the DTD was created and how you can create your newspaper DTD. We recommend that you expose yourself to as many DTDs as you can; therefore, you get an idea of how to write them and how others create them. We've also removed the general entities, so you can concentrate on the elements and attributes. You'll see one parameter entity in Listing 5.3 because it's referenced in some of the elements—we cover entities later in the "Defining the Entities" section.

Listing 5.3   A novel DTD without the comments and general entities.

```
<?xml encoding="UTF-8"?>
<!ENTITY % phrasal "#PCDATA|emphasis">
<!ELEMENT novel (front, body)>
<!ELEMENT front (title, author, revision-list)>
<!ELEMENT revision-list (item+)>
<!ELEMENT item (%phrasal;)*>
<!ELEMENT body (chapter+)>
<!ELEMENT chapter (title, paragraph+)>
<!ATTLIST chapter
  id ID #REQUIRED>

<!ELEMENT title (%phrasal;)*>
<!ELEMENT author (%phrasal;)*>

<!ELEMENT paragraph (%phrasal;)*>
<!ELEMENT emphasis (%phrasal;)*>
```

Now, let's examine the structure. The main element is called **novel**. It contains two other elements, **front** and **body**. The **novel** element is considered the root element and everything branches from it. The next big branches, so to speak, are **front** and **body**, and from those, smaller branches sprout. The **front** element must appear before the **body** element. We know this because the **front** element, along with the **body** element, is listed in the content of the **novel** element.

As we move through the code, we see that the **front** element contains **title**, **author**, and **revision-list** elements. The **title** element is simple; its content is specified in the entity outlined at the very beginning of the code. It is the same with the **author**, **paragraph**, and **emphasis** elements. The **front** element requires that the **title**, **author**, and **revision-list** be listed in that order.

The **chapter** element contains the **title** and **paragraph** elements. The **title** element must appear first, and at least one **paragraph** element must exist within the **chapter** element. We know this because of the plus sign after the **paragraph** element name.

So, here's the kind of structure this document offers:

```
novel
  front
    title
      author
        revision-list
          item
```

```
body
   chapter
      title
       paragraph
```

By evaluating other DTDs, you can quickly get an idea of how your DTDs might also be structured. The easiest way to get a handle on your element relationships is to look at how others handle theirs. Once you do, you're ready to create your own relationships.

Organizing the Elements

Let's go back to creating a newspaper DTD. First, you should sketch how the sequence and hierarchies of the elements will work. We'll start with the overall concept of the newspaper and drill down to more specific pieces. Because you already know what major elements you'll use, you need to start with the main root element—the **newspaper** element—and determine what other elements will branch off this root. The best way to determine the other elements is to start small and work your way up. As described earlier, every newspaper has sections; so this simple code structure makes sense:

```
<newspaper>
   <section>
   </section>
</newspaper>
```

Now, if you break down the **section** element a bit more and define the next level, each section will have articles, which means the following code is valid:

```
<newspaper>
    <section>
      <article>
      </article>
    </section>
</newspaper>
```

Considering that newspapers have multiple sections and each section can have multiple articles, you should structure your elements so they can be repeated throughout the newspaper. When you do that, each section is on the same level as any other section, and all the subelements, such as the **article** element, are nested within the **section** element. Therefore, this code is also valid:

```
<newspaper>
    <section>
       <article>
       </article>
```

```
        <article>
        </article>
    </section>

    <section>
        <article>
        </article>

        <article>
        </article>

        <article>
        </article>
    </section>

</newspaper>
```

TIP: *As you build your document structure, you may notice that you need an attribute for the* **section** *element: a* **title** *attribute. This is just one attribute example. You will need other attributes for other elements. When you lay out the structure in this manner, you can start to visualize all the components you'll need.*

Now that the major elements are in place, you can concentrate on refining the individual elements that will make up the rest of the structure. Let's further define the **article** element. Each **article** element will contain a **headline** element. The **headline** element contains one subelement (or minor element), which is called **subhead**. The **subhead** element will be the secondary headline, so to speak. It's not a child of the **article** element, because although it's part of the **article** element, it actually relates directly to the **headline** element and not the **article** element. The code looks like this:

```
<article>
    <headline>
        <subhead>
        </subhead>
    </headline>
<article>
```

Next, the **article** element would contain the **byline**, **lede**, and **story** elements. You'll start by specifying the **byline** element and then moving on to the rest:

```
<article>
    <headline>
    </headline>
    <byline>
    </byline>
```

```
    <lede>
    </lede>
    <story>
        <pullquotes>
        </pullquotes>
    </story>
<article>
```

WARNING! We're simply outlining our structure in this section. Although we're indicating our structure using standard start and end tag notations, we're not really creating the DTD or the XML document yet. Instead, we're outlining exactly how the elements will stack up in the DTD. The actual code we use to declare these elements and their relationships is much different.

Now, let's put it all together. Here's the code for the *structure* of our DTD:

```
<newspaper>
<section>
    <article>
        <headline>
            <subhead>
            </subhead>
        </headline>
        <byline>
        </byline>
        <lede>
        </lede>
        <story>
            <pullquotes>
            </pullquotes>
        </story>
    <article>
<section>
<newspaper>
```

Take away all the minor elements and the actual structure follows. You'll use this structure when you're creating the actual element declarations in your DTD:

```
<newspaper>
<section>
    <article>
        <headline>
        <byline>
        <lede>
        <story>
```

This simple sketch gives you a lot of information about the elements you're structuring:

- The **newspaper** element is the document element. From it, all other elements are created.
- Each **newspaper** must have at least one **section**.
- Each **section** must have at least one **article**.
- Numerous **section** elements can appear in the **newspaper** element, but only one **byline** element can appear within each **article** element.
- Only one **headline** element can appear within a single **article** element.
- Each article has only one **lede** element.
- There can be multiple **pullquotes** elements.

Declaring the Elements

Now that you know which elements to use, it's time to create the element declarations to include in the DTD. This section simply covers element declarations. The DTD won't be complete after this step, because you haven't determined or even specified which attributes need to be created. Although it may sound like we're jumping the gun, you need to define the elements and their structures before you define attributes or entities.

You declare elements by specifying the following information:

```
<!ELEMENT name content>
```

Because you know which elements contain other elements, you start with the first root element, **newspaper**. It contains one element, **section**. But remember, you can have multiple sections, so the following code defines your **newspaper** element:

```
<!ELEMENT newspaper (section+)>
```

This line of code defines an element named **newspaper**, which can contain an element named **section**. You add the plus sign after the **section** name to signify to the XML processor that valid XML documents can contain more than one **section**.

Using what you know about declaring elements, continue creating the element list. Remember the structure we created previously:

```
<newspaper>
<section>
  <article>
    <headline>
```

```
<byline>
<lede>
<story>
```

Using this structure, you come up with a list of elements that looks like this:

```
<!ELEMENT newspaper (section+)>
<!ELEMENT section (article+)>

<!ELEMENT article (headline, byline, lede, story)>
<!ELEMENT headline (content, subhead?)>
<!ELEMENT story (storycontent, pullquotes+)>

<!ELEMENT byline (#PCDATA)>
<!ELEMENT lede (#PCDATA)>
<!ELEMENT content (#PCDATA)>
<!ELEMENT subhead (#PCDATA)>
<!ELEMENT storycontent (#PCDATA)>
<!ELEMENT pullquotes (#PCDATA)>
```

Let's examine what some of this code means before you create the attributes that further explain these elements. First, you already know that the **newspaper** element contains the **section** element and that there can be more than one **section**. Second, the **section** element contains the **article** element, and it can contain more than one **article**.

Next, the **article** element must contain **headline** first, followed by **byline**, **lede**, and finally, **story**. The **headline** element can contain parsable character data (**#PCDATA**), as is defined in the **content** element. And it can contain a **subhead** element, which also contains parsable character data. However, the **subhead** element can be optional, as specified by the inclusion of the question mark (**?**).

TIP: *If you need more information about how to declare the content for elements or what various element notations mean, see Chapter 7. It outlines all the special notations used to define certain structural elemental context.*

Defining the Attributes

Now that you have an idea of what elements you need, the number of times they can occur, and their relationship to other elements, the next step is to define which attributes are required by those elements. After you define the elements for the document, you provide additional information about those elements to the XML processor in the form of attributes.

Here's an example of an attribute for the **article** element that helps further define exactly what the **article** element can contain:

```
<!ELEMENT article (headline, byline, lede, story)>
<!ATTLIST article
          authors    CDATA    #REQUIRED
          editors    CDATA    #IMPLIED
          date       CDATA    #IMPLIED
          edition    CDATA    #IMPLIED>
```

The first line of the preceding code declares the element. The second line declares the attribute list and identifies the element that it goes with. The following four lines define four attributes for the **article** element, which are:

- **authors**—Several authors might contribute to the story. Although the reader may not care who the multiple authors are, the newspaper editor may, especially when handing out Pulitzer prizes.

- **editors**—By including this piece of information as an attribute, you link the story to the actual editor or editors who helped make this particular masterpiece readable.

- **date**—This attribute helps further define the article and date-stamps it. You could create an element that defines the date of the newspaper. However, in this particular instance, a **date** attribute for the **article** element allows you to more easily search on the date for a particular article.

- **edition**—This could be the attribute for either the **newspaper** or **article** element, but in this example, you create it as an attribute for the **article** element.

Notice in the previous code that the only data required is the name of the authors. Everything else is implied (with the **#IMPLIED** attribute). All information is contained in character data.

When to Use Attributes and When to Use Elements

Sometimes, it's hard to know when to use attributes and when to use elements. Although, in our opinion, elements are used to define the structure of an object and attributes are used to define the aspect of that object, you could easily create an attribute when it should be an element and vice versa. The easiest way to determine whether you should use an attribute or an element is to follow these guidelines for attribute usage:

- Attributes define a particular aspect about an element, such as size, height, weight, or color.

- Attributes define formatting information. Such attributes further define the appearance of an element.

- Attributes locate an object in the document—for example, a footnote, a graphics file, or a cross-reference.
- Attributes locate external objects, such as links.

Note that these guidelines are not set in stone. You may have other factors influencing your decision, such as corporate guidelines, personal style, or the design requirements of the application.

To determine whether an item should be an element or an attribute, think about whether the object needs further explanation or whether the item in question actually defines a new object. If it relates to another element you have defined, it's probably an attribute. If it's similar but actually describes an entirely new object, it's probably an element. Determining which to declare can sometimes be tough, but if you sketch out your structure first and then determine the relationships, you'll quickly see when to create elements and when to create attributes.

Defining the Entities

5. DTDs in XML

So far, you've defined the necessary elements as well as their attributes for your newspaper DTD. With the exception of some additional data, such as the name of the newspaper and possibly the copyright information, you're almost finished defining the parts of the DTD. The name of the newspaper and the copyright information need to be included on almost every page of the paper, but you don't want to type them again and again. XML provides a mechanism that makes it easy to create information that will be placed in the document repeatedly and will help you maintain the document over time. This mechanism is called an *entity*.

In our example, you can define an entity for your newspaper's name along with some basic copyright information. Then, you add this information to the DTD in the form of entities. The code for such information looks like this:

```
<!ENTITY newspaper "Hometown Post">
<!ENTITY copyright "Copyright 2000">
<!ENTITY publisher "James Wright">
```

After you define these entities in your DTD, you can reference them in your XML document, like this:

```
All contents are &copyright; by the
&newspaper;, &publisher;, publisher.
```

When the XML processor encounters the **&copyright;** entity, it replaces the entity with its value, **Copyright 2000**. The previous line of code would look like this when it's parsed and displayed:

```
All contents are Copyright 2000 by the
Hometown Post, James Wright, publisher.
```

One reason to use entities is that they make documents easier to maintain. For example, if the publisher decides to move up the corporate ladder and is replaced, you can simply replace the value of the entity reference instead of having to replace the publisher's name throughout the entire document.

Entities can also be used to insert symbols into a document. For example, you can use an entity to insert the Pulitzer prize icon in the newspaper's editorial page, or new column bugs can be easily replaced when columnists have their pictures retaken.

Creating and Specifying the DTD

By now, you have almost all the components you need to create the DTD. You know about the structure of the document. You also know which elements you'll use, and you have a grasp on which attributes will be used to further explain those elements. You also know which entities will be included in the DTD. All that's left is for you to put all this information together along with some well-placed comments, and you'll have a valid DTD.

Let's go through the entire process from start to finish. You start by creating the elements and the attributes for each element. You should use as many comments as you can to make the DTD as humanly readable as possible. Because a newspaper DTD could actually encompass many, many elements, we can't show you how to create the entire DTD here; but we can show you enough to get an idea of how a DTD is created.

After you decide which elements to use, you need to formally declare these components in the DTD. The DTD, as you'll recall, can be either **PUBLIC** or **SYSTEM**, and can be stored either locally or remotely. An external DTD is generally stored in a text file with the extension .dtd. The structure of the DTD has five separate parts:

- Document types
- Elements
- Attributes
- Entities
- Comments

TIP: *You can start creating a DTD by building all the elements, but doing so may be counterproductive. It's best to start with a few elements and attributes, parse them, and build up from there. It may be more difficult to troubleshoot your DTD with thousands of lines of code to pore through.*

When you create a DTD, you should save all DTDs, XML data, and display information in standard, text-only format. You can use the standard Windows Notepad application to create the file, or you could use a variety of different products, including XML Pro by Vervet Logic software (**www.vervet.com**). Regardless of the editing software tool you use, it is recommended that you specify what type of encoding the document uses by including a text declaration at the top of the document. A text declaration resembles an XML declaration, except that the **version** attribute is optional, and it's used in external parsed entities (such as an external DTD), for example:

```
<?xml encoding="UTF-8"?>
```

Next, it's a good idea to add a comment that will identify the DTD and its purpose, as well as author information and a copyright notice:

```
<!--
***************************************************
newspaper.dtd: This is a sample DTD for marking up
newspapers. Copyright The Coriolis Group, 2000.
***************************************************
-->
```

Now, you need to indicate which entities you plan to use. Actually, entities can be placed anywhere in the DTD, but because they can also be used within various elements, it's a good idea to define them at the beginning of the DTD. Here's the code used in the DTD to specify entities (note that we're adding on to the existing portions of the DTD so you can see it as it's built):

```
<?xml encoding="UTF-8"?>
<!--
***************************************************
newspaper.dtd: This is a sample DTD for marking up
newspapers. Copyright 2000, James Wright.
***************************************************
-->
<!-- Entities -->
<!ENTITY newspaper "Hometown Post">
<!ENTITY copyright "Copyright 2000">
<!ENTITY publisher "James Wright">
```

Next, you declare the elements that are necessary to construct the document. Creating the elements in order helps you further concentrate on the structure and hierarchy. Because any newspaper starts with the **newspaper** element as the root, you need to define it first. Then, you'll create the rest of the elements that branch off the main root element: **section**, **article**, **headline**, **byline**, **lede**, and **story**, in that order. Here's a small sample of how your DTD would look as you progress through the list of elements:

```
<?xml encoding="UTF-8"?>
<!--
****************************************************
newspaper.dtd: This is a sample DTD for marking up
newspapers. Copyright 2000, James Wright
****************************************************
-->
<!-- Entities -->
<!ENTITY newspaper "Hometown Post">
<!ENTITY copyright "Copyright 2000">
<!ENTITY publisher "James Wright">
<!-- Elements -->
<!ELEMENT newspaper (section+)>
<!ELEMENT section (article+)>

<!ELEMENT article (headline, byline, lede, story)>
<!ELEMENT headline (content, subhead?)>
<!ELEMENT story (storycontent, pullquotes+)>

<!ELEMENT byline (#PCDATA)>
<!ELEMENT lede (#PCDATA)>
<!ELEMENT content (#PCDATA)>
<!ELEMENT subhead (#PCDATA)>
<!ELEMENT storycontent (#PCDATA)>
<!ELEMENT pullquotes (#PCDATA)>
```

At this point, you need to include the attributes for the elements you've built. Place those attributes directly following the element declarations they describe. Your DTD now looks like this:

```
<?xml encoding="UTF-8"?>
<!--
****************************************************
newspaper.dtd: This is a sample DTD for marking up
newspapers. Copyright 2000, James Wright
****************************************************
-->
```

```
<!-- Entities -->
<!ENTITY newspaper "Hometown Post">
<!ENTITY copyright "Copyright 2000">
<!ENTITY publisher "James Wright">

<!-- Elements -->
<!ELEMENT newspaper (section+)>
<!ELEMENT section (article+)>

<!ELEMENT article (headline, byline, lede, story)>
<!ATTLIST article
        author  CDATA #REQUIRED
        editor  CDATA #IMPLIED
        date    CDATA #IMPLIED
        edition CDATA #IMPLIED >

<!ELEMENT headline (content, subhead?)>
<!ELEMENT story (storycontent, pullquotes+)>

<!ELEMENT byline (#PCDATA)>
<!ELEMENT lede (#PCDATA)>
<!ELEMENT content (#PCDATA)>
<!ELEMENT subhead (#PCDATA)>
<!ELEMENT storycontent (#PCDATA)>
<!ELEMENT pullquotes (#PCDATA)>

<!-- end of the DTD -->
```

You should end your DTD by adding a comment to specify to humans, not XML parsers, where the DTD ends. No conventions exist for signaling the end of the DTD to the XML processor. You might want it to parse this working DTD with a variety of different XML parsers. In Chapter 23, you'll find a discussion of some parsers that will help determine whether there are any problems with your DTD.

Using the DTD

Now that you have a working DTD, you need to specify it within your document. Because this DTD is externally stored, you need to include the following line of code in the actual content document:

```
<?xml version="1.0" encoding="UTF-8" standalone="no"?>
<!DOCTYPE newspaper SYSTEM "newspaper.dtd">
```

However, you need to know how to include other types of DTDs in your documents, as well.

Specifying an External DTD

To specify a DTD that is stored within a network (or on a local hard drive), include the keyword **SYSTEM** and the location of the DTD in your DOCTYPE declaration, as shown in the following code:

```
<!DOCTYPE book SYSTEM "http://www.mysite.com/dtds/name.dtd">
```

Specifying a Public DTD

To specify a public DTD that is stored in another location, include the keyword **PUBLIC** when you're describing the DTD. If the DTD is not an ISO standard, include a dash (-) before the notation that specifies the DTD, as shown in the following DOCTYPE declaration:

```
<!DOCTYPE book PUBLIC "-//CompanyXYZ//DTD book//EN"
 "http://www.mysite.com/dtds/book.dtd">
```

Specifying an Internal DTD

To specify an internal DTD (one that will be included within the XML document), include the entire DTD within the DOCTYPE declaration. Add the document element name and enclose the DTD within square brackets, as shown in the following DOCTYPE declaration:

```
<?xml version="1.0?>
<!DOCTYPE purchases
[
<!ELEMENT main (purchase)*>
<!ELEMENT purchase (date, account?, item+)>
<!ELEMENT date (#PCDATA)>
<!ELEMENT account (#PCDATA)>
<!ELEMENT item ((itemnumber, itemdescription, quantity)|#PCDATA)*>
<!ELEMENT itemnumber (#PCDATA)>
<!ELEMENT itemdescription (#PCDATA)>
<!ELEMENT quantity (#PCDATA)>
]>
```

Creating an Internal DTD

To create an internal DTD, you must specify all the elements and attributes within the XML document itself. The DTD components must be declared before the markup tags are used within the document. To create an internal DTD, follow these steps:

1. Specify that this is an XML document by including the XML declaration:

```
<?xml version="1.0" encoding="UTF-8"?>
```

2. Add the DOCTYPE declaration by adding the following code, which specifies the name of the DTD along with all the components that make the DTD:

```
<!DOCTYPE purchases [
<!ELEMENT main (purchase)*>
<!ELEMENT purchase (date, account?, item+)>
<!ELEMENT date (#PCDATA)>
<!ELEMENT account (#PCDATA)>
<!ELEMENT item ((itemnumber, itemdescription, quantity)|#PCDATA)*>
<!ELEMENT itemnumber (#PCDATA)>
<!ELEMENT itemdescription (#PCDATA)>
<!ELEMENT quantity (#PCDATA)>
]>
```

3. Use these elements within the document itself. You do this by marking up
   the document as you would any XML document, making sure you follow
   the rules specified in the internal DTD:

```
<item>
<itemnumber>3200
</itemnumber>
<itemdescription>External Outer Locking Value
</itemdescription>
<quantity>40
</quantity>
</item>
```

Creating an External DTD

For an external DTD, you must declare all the elements, attributes, and entities in
a separate file. You should use comments to indicate each group of components
you specify. In this example, you'll create a purchase order DTD with various
elements and attributes. To create an external DTD, follow these steps:

1. Specify the encoding that the DTD uses by including the following code:

```
<?xml encoding="UTF-8"?>
```

2. Document the file by adding comments to clearly describe what the DTD is and what elements will be declared next:

```
<!--
****************************************************
purchaseorder.dtd: This is a DTD for creating
a purchase order system.
****************************************************
-->
<!-- Entities -->
```

3. Declare the entities for the document so they can then be referenced within the element or attribute declarations if necessary. Define entity references by specifying the entity declaration followed by the entity name and the content of the entity. For example, the following code defines three different entities:

```
<!ENTITY Company "Purchase Orders R Us">
<!ENTITY Address "1111 West 34rd Street, Anytown, TX 11111 USA">
<!ENTITY Email "po@purchaseorders.com">
```

4. Declare the various elements you'll use within the document. Specify the element declaration, the name of the element, and then the content of the element. The content can be data, other elements, or even entities. The following code declares several different elements for the purchase order system:

```
<!ELEMENT main (purchase)*>
<!ELEMENT purchase (date, account?, item+)>
<!ELEMENT date (#PCDATA)>
<!ELEMENT account (#PCDATA)>
<!ELEMENT item ((itemnumber, itemdescription, quantity)|#PCDATA)*>
<!ELEMENT itemnumber (#PCDATA)>
<!ELEMENT itemdescription (#PCDATA)>
<!ELEMENT quantity (#PCDATA)>
```

TIP: The asterisk (*) after an element indicates that the elements between the parentheses are optional and repeatable. The plus sign (+) indicates that at least one of the subelements must appear within the main element, and the subelements can also be repeated. The comma (,) indicates that the items must appear sequentially, meaning the **itemnumber** element must precede the **itemdescription** element.

5. Create and include the attributes for each element that requires an attribute. To create an attribute, use the **<!ATTLIST** declaration followed by the name of the element the attribute is describing, the content of the attribute, and any default value. The attribute is usually placed after the element declaration. The following code is an example of an attribute declaration:

```
<!ELEMENT account (#PCDATA)>
<!ATTLIST account
        accountno CDATA #REQUIRED
        accountaddress CDATA #IMPLIED
        accounttype CDATA #IMPLIED>
```

6. After you add all the elements, attributes, and entities, indicate the end of the DTD to humans by including a comment line, such as the following:

```
<!-- end of the DTD -->
```

7. Save the file with the file extension .dtd. You can choose any name you like. Remember, however, that, like XML, many file systems are case sensitive—if you use uppercase in the file name, you also need to use uppercase when you declare the DTD in your DOCTYPE declaration. For example, if you saved a DTD with the file name purchase.dtd, this code in the XML document might result in the XML processor not being able to locate the DTD:

```
<!DOCTYPE purchase PUBLIC "-//CompanyXYZ//DTD purchase//EN"
"http://www.site.com/dtds/Purchase.dtd">
```

From the DOCTYPE declaration, you can then create the rest of the document and include the rest of the data. Now all you have to do is create the content. See Chapter 7 for more information on creating content in an XML document.

Chapter 6

Working with XML Elements

In Depth

Elements and attributes are the building blocks of XML. Element declarations within a Document Type Definition (DTD) specify the structure of the XML document and give you a set of guidelines to use as you build your document. Although XML elements may look the same and, in many ways, act the same as Hypertext Markup Language (HTML) elements, they are far more robust and powerful than HTML elements. XML elements give you the flexibility of designing your own document structure. In HTML, all of the elements are predefined for you. In XML, you can create your own set of elements that fit your content like a glove.

TIP: *Even if you're using someone else's DTD and aren't creating your own elements, it's still important for you to understand the structure of the data. Therefore, you should still read this chapter.*

In XML, elements are more than just tags used to mark up text for formatting in a document. Instead, elements construct and hold together the document, providing markup to tell the document and the processor what you want the document to do. Every XML document forms a treelike structure, with each element creating a branch of the tree. Elements can be nested, and all elements defined are nested below the *root*, or main, element of the XML document, which is usually referred to as a *document element*.

Developing and deploying XML elements involves two steps. The first is declaring the elements in a DTD and using them to describe data. The second is specifying how all the elements in a DTD should work together. Believe it or not, an element can contain several different kinds of content: other elements, text, or some combination of elements and text, to name just three. The way you define the kind of content each individual element can hold plays a large role in the way your documents are formed. In this chapter, we focus on the first step: the syntax you use to declare elements in your DTDs, and how to use those elements to create well-formed XML documents.

NOTE: *Although this chapter discusses the concept of element content on a very high level, Chapter 7 covers the details of defining element content. Because it's difficult to discuss elements without discussing attributes, this chapter will also skim the surface of how elements interact with attributes. Chapter 8 includes a full discussion of the many types of attributes you can use with elements and the syntax you use to both declare and use those attributes.*

Elements Revisited

If you've been diligently reading each chapter and following along with the Immediate Solutions examples, you should now know that elements are used to describe content in XML documents. You should also know that XML elements look like and work in much the same way as HTML elements. In XML, you can create your own elements and specify the element names to describe a particular section in a document, a piece of text, or special processing instruction. Element names can be anything you want them to be as long as you conform to the XML standards (discussed later in this section) and use descriptive element names. For example, **paragraph** is a more descriptive element name, for defining where the XML processor should start a new paragraph than just **p**.

NOTE: *The words* element *and* tag *are used interchangeably in most discussions of markup. In all our discussions, we use the word* element *to describe the set of tags that you use to describe content in an XML document. We also use the word* element *to describe those tags with attributes and content included in them. We only use the word* tag *if we're referring to the specific tags (opening and closing) that make up an element.*

Like elements in HTML, most XML elements are made up of two tags, and the tags are distinguished from the text used in the document by angle brackets (**<** and **>**). Both a start and end tag define or make up the element—for example **<example_tag>** (start tag) and **</example_tag>** (end tag). There is also an empty element, which contains only a single tag—for example **<empty_tag/>**. In general, a standard XML element contains information between the start and end tags; it can also contain attribute values, like this:

```
<paragraph type="general">This is a paragraph.</paragraph>
```

An empty element doesn't have any content. Only attributes and attribute values are allowed as data in an empty element, like this:

```
<picture src="my_picture.gif" />
```

The choice to use standard elements or empty elements depends entirely upon the content you want to describe. It makes sense to enclose entire paragraphs within the start and end tags of an element, but it doesn't really make sense to try to include those paragraphs in the element as attribute values, like this:

```
<paragraph text="This is a paragraph" />
```

In the previous markup, there's no way to apply other elements (such as emphasis indicators) to the paragraph text. In addition, your paragraph content won't be displayed. When you put content between the start and end tags of an element, you have an opportunity to use other elements with that text.

6. Working with XML Elements

Conversely, sometimes it makes more sense to use an empty element to embed information, such as a picture or other resource, in a document. A good rule to follow when building your elements is if the element needs to describe something, such as text, it should be a standard element. If it needs to embed something, such as a graphic or a piece of information, in the document, it should be an empty element. In the end, only experience and a good feel for your information will make the choice between the two easy.

All elements follow certain rules. Element names can consist only of letters, digits, periods, dashes, underscores, and colons. No spaces are allowed, and no reserved characters, such as the angle bracket, can be used in an element name. However, you can use other special characters to separate the type of content you want the element to display. For example, you can use the pipe character (|) to separate nested content and attributes. For more information about element content specification delimiters, see this chapter's "Specifying the Content of an Element" section.

As seen in the previous example, for every start tag used to specify an element, there must be an end tag, unless the element is empty. Empty elements use a slash (/) before the closing greater-than sign to indicate that they are empty. All elements must be properly nested, and all tag names must match for a document to be considered well formed. If you turned this book into an XML document, you would have **section**, **chapter**, **heading**, and **paragraph** elements (just to name a few). The following code is a brief example of how these elements and more might work and how certain elements could be nested within other elements:

```
<?xml version="1.0"?>
<book>
  <chapter>
    <chapter_title>Elements in XML</chapter_title>
      <section>Elements explained
        <paragraph>
          Elements are the building blocks of XML.
        </paragraph>
      </section>
  </chapter>
</book>
```

Notice how the **book** element defines the overall concept and context of the XML document, and how certain elements such as **paragraph** and **section** can easily be nested within **chapter** elements, which, in turn, are nested in the **book** element. Notice that each element starts and ends—although not all on the same line, or possibly even on the same page—with start and end tags. The nesting of elements is an important concept, because you define not only the structure of the document, but also the rules for where the various elements can be placed. You would not, of course, place a **paragraph** element before the **chapter_title** element. And with the nesting features of XML elements, you can specify these rules.

Nesting Elements

As you can see, elements not only help define the start of paragraphs within a document, but they also define where an XML document begins and ends. In actuality, as you saw in our book example in the previous section, the entire XML document is grouped within a single element, which is called the *document element* (which is the **book** element in our example). For a document to be well formed, there must be a single element that constructs the document and in which all other elements are nested: the document element.

The easiest way to understand the nesting concept is by conceptualizing a simple XML document in the form of one big box. Open that big box, and inside is a smaller box. Open that smaller box and you'll see an even smaller one. Open that box and another smaller box is inside. This concept of elements nested inside other elements that are nested inside other elements is technically referred to as *parent/child nesting*. The **book** element is the parent and the **chapter** element is the parent's child. However, the **chapter** element has its own child relationship in the form of the **section** element, which in turn is a parent to the **paragraph** element. Incestuous isn't it?

TIP: *In some XML documentation, you may see all parent/child-nested elements commonly referred to as* sub-elements. *You may also find all children of a single element, such as* **paragraph** *elements within a* **section** *element, referred to as* siblings.

Regardless of what you call them, this concept of nesting and parent/child elements is important for you to understand so you learn how to properly structure your document and where you should and can place various elements. After you understand the relationships of all your elements in the context of the entire document, you can structure your document accordingly.

Based on this parent/child nesting relationship, the document provides a root from which the markup tree structures grow and evolve. If you've experimented with any of the XML Java browsers, such as Jumbo, or even tried your hand at Channels (an XML-based application), you've probably experienced this parent/child/tree structure without even knowing it. If you click on a channel in Internet Explorer, the channel expands to show you all its children. Those children can have their own children, and so on. This structure is created through the use of elements.

From this tree structure, the outline of the document is created. The tree structure is also where various style sheets can be used on the elements within the document to format the text. Because of the tree structure, it's much easier to search XML documents than it is to search even a simple HTML document. In an XML document, you can look for and find a specific element based on it context or the other elements around it. As you'll learn in Chapters 13 and 14, the ability to point to an element based on its location in the document tree is crucial to many of the technologies that support XML.

Document Elements

As we've mentioned, the main element of any XML document—the element that is figuratively the big box in which all other boxes are placed—is called the document element. The document element often defines the concept of the document. For example, if you were defining an XML document as a memo, then after the XML declaration and the DTD, you would specify the document element as **memo**, as shown in the following code:

```
<?xml version="1.0"?>
  <memo>
  <to>John Smith</to>
  <from>Betty Lou</from>
  <subject>This memo</subject>
  <content>
  <alert>Please read carefully.</alert>
  <paragraph>Please make sure you read this memo.</paragraph>
  <closing>Thank you very much.</closing>
  </content>
</memo>
```

Notice that the **memo** element sets the structure of the file and makes this a well-formed XML document. Within the **memo** element are its children elements: **to**, **from**, and **subject**. However, **content**, although it's a child of **memo**, has children of its own. If you're a genealogy buff, you'll understand the concept of parents, children, and descendants. If we had placed the closing **content** tag before the closing **alert** tag, the document would not be considered well formed.

Now, take a look at the following code, and try to figure out why it *isn't* a well-formed XML document:

```
<?xml version="1.0"?>
<to>John Smith</to>
<from>Betty Lou</from>
<subject>This memo</subject>
<paragraph>Please make sure you read this memo,
<to>John Smith</to>.</paragraph>
<closing>Thank you very much</closing>
</memo>
```

Did you spot the problem? Notice that there are plenty of elements, but no document element is defined at the beginning. Nothing tells the processor (or you, the reader of this XML file) exactly what type of document this is going to be. Instead, this document jumps right into the thick of things with the **to** element, never once stopping to tell you what the XML document actually is or contains. The XML processor would assume **to** is the document element. However, the processor would quickly generate an error because only one document element is allowed and the **to** element shows up in two different places in this document. Also, because document elements cannot be nested, the **to** element would cause this document to error when processed.

To sum up, any XML document must have one—and only one—document element defined. If a DTD exists for the document element, it specifies what the document element must be. The document element can't be part of another element, and it can't be nested within other elements.

A Closer Look at Elements

By now, you know what an element looks like; but we've been somewhat carefree in our examples of elements, using only the most simplistic examples. We kept it simple because we wanted to first introduce you to the concept of elements, how they control the document structure, and how nesting elements creates the overall structure in XML documents. Now, it's time to get down to the nitty-gritty and look closely at elements and how they are declared.

When you declare an element in a DTD, whether it's an internal or external DTD, you start by following the proper syntax for declaring elements. The following line of code shows the proper syntax for the element declaration:

```
<!ELEMENT name content>
```

When you declare an element, you specify the name of the element so it can be referenced throughout the document. You also declare the type of content that can be used, such as character data, other elements, or nothing at all. The following example creates a **memo** element that can contain any kind of content

```
<!ELEMENT memo ANY>
```

NOTE: *See our warning about using **ANY** content in the "**ANY** Content" section later in this chapter.*

When you want to use this element within the XML document, you do so just as you would an HTML element: by specifying the element name and surrounding it with angle brackets. For example, after you declare the **memo** element in the

DTD, as shown in the previous example, you can put it to use in your document by doing this:

```
<memo>This is the text of the memo.</memo>
```

Notice that, as with HTML, you add the start tag and the end tag. Because you declared that this element can have any type of content, you can include text, other elements, or a combination of both. Notice also that you use **memo**, not **MEMO**, for the element name—the element name is case sensitive, just like almost everything else in XML. Therefore, the declaration

```
<!ELEMENT book ANY>
```

is not the same as

```
<!ELEMENT BOOK ANY>
```

As mentioned previously, the name you use for an element must be something that is descriptive and must not contain spaces or special reserved characters. Element names can only contain letters, digits, periods, dashes, underscores, and colons. You can use underscores or dashes when you want to create an element name that normally would have spaces between the words. For example, instead of **first name**, you can follow proper syntax and name your element either **first_name** or **first-name**.

Element names also should not imply any particular formatting. Instead, they should imply structure or content. It's not a good idea to declare an element with the name **24-point**, especially if what you really want to do is declare a **heading** element. The name **heading** is always preferred when you're specifying content that should be marked up as a heading. You may not always be able to keep your element names specific to their intended process, but whatever you do, remember to leave the formatting to the style sheets.

Specifying the Content of an Element

In addition to declaring the name of an element, you need to define the content of the element. That content may be characters, lists of elements, or specific keywords that signal to the processor certain information about the element. You can use four main types of element content:

- Element content
- Mixed content
- **ANY** content
- No content (empty content)

The following sections describe each kind of content briefly. Chapter 7 describes them in detail.

Element Content

Sometimes, you may want to include other elements instead of content in the content model specification. If an element's content model specifies that it can only contain other elements and no text, it's said to have *element content*. The benefit of allowing only other elements to be nested within an element is that you can specify which elements the parent element can contain, as well as how many instances of each element the parent element can contain, and even in which order child elements must appear. XML uses a specific set of notations to carefully define the kind of child elements a parent element can contain, as well as the rules of order and number that guide those elements. Chapter 7 covers these rules in detail.

Mixed Content

If an element contains anything other than elements (in other words, character data) or a combination of character data and child elements, then it's said to contain *mixed data*. When you declare mixed data for an element that contains both character data and child elements, you can't exert as much control over the order and number of the child elements, as you can with pure element content. However, mixed content is more flexible than element content. See Chapter 7 for more information on mixed content.

ANY Content

The **ANY** declaration does what it says—it allows any type of content (data) or element markup information. The element's content can use text, any another elements, or a mixture of both. If you want an element to accept any content indiscriminately, you specify **ANY** as its content. If you want to control what child elements an element can contain, even if the element can also contain parsed character data or character data, you need to use mixed content and specify those child elements individually.

WARNING! *The ANY declaration is usually only used during the development and testing phases of a DTD. It's very rarely used in a production DTD.*

As you can see, the **ANY** content declaration gives you tremendous flexibility. However, remember that you should be specific about the rules of content. You can use **ANY** whenever you want to, with whatever element you want to declare; but if you use it all the time, you're not following the proper XML document-development conventions. Those conventions strongly suggest that you declare elements that are as descriptive as possible to provide for a tight document that defines exactly where and which elements can be used in the various locations.

6. Working with XML Elements

Empty Elements

Many of your elements will have content, but sometimes you may want an element to have no content whatsoever. In that case, you declare empty element content by using the content keyword **EMPTY** in the element content specification. (Note that the word **EMPTY** is written in all caps because it's a reserved keyword.) The following is an example of the code you would use to do just that:

```
<!ELEMENT loginfo EMPTY>
```

In this example, we define an element called **loginfo** in preparation for a channel we're setting up with Microsoft's Channel Definition Format (CDF). We don't want to record any **loginfo** at this point, although we may change our minds later. In terms of content, we want to specify that this element records or contains no data, so we use the keyword **EMPTY** to turn off any content collection.

An empty element is one that has no textual context. Although empty elements can be used for just about anything, they are generally used as markers where something should occur. If we look at HTML, the **hr** element is an excellent example of an empty element and how the **EMPTY** content declaration works. The **hr** element inserts a horizontal rule or line across a Web page. As with any empty element, attributes are associated with the **hr** element. With its **size** attribute, you can specify the width or length of the horizontal rule. For example, the following code

```
<hr size="4" />
```

specifies a horizontal rule that is four pixels high. The **hr** element declaration looks something like this:

```
<!ELEMENT hr EMPTY>
```

TIP: *Remember that with XML, you must first declare the element name and then the content specification mode. Attributes are specified later, after the element and its content model have been declared. We cover attributes a little later in this chapter (see "Element Attributes") and discuss them in detail in Chapter 8.*

As you can see, when you declare an element's content model **EMPTY**, you do so by using the following syntax:

```
<!ELEMENT elementname EMPTY>
```

When you want to use these elements with the XML document, you can still use start and end tags. However, because they have no contextual information to envelop, empty elements can use a special format that standard elements don't allow. Although you *can* use start and end tags for the empty element within your document, you don't need to use them because there's nothing within the element to work with. Instead, when you use an empty element in your document, it's much easier to use a single tag—the element name—and a single slash to indicate that the element is an empty tag. The following is an example of an empty tag used in an XML document:

```
<logfile/>
```

Element Attributes

Attributes provide extra information about an XML element and its content. If an element is empty, attributes are generally used to provide additional content; but if the element has content, the attributes usually provide more information about the content. Either way, the attribute further defines the element in some fashion.

HTML offers some 70 elements and some 50 different attributes. In HTML, attributes extend the power of elements by specifying how the element can be formatted. Attributes further define how an element is to be used and what kind of content and information can be included within the element. For example, if you declare a **phone_number** element, the **location** attribute can be added to it to further clarify which location (home, office, cell, and so on) the phone number represents.

Even though declaring attributes is separate from declaring elements, the two work together to describe your content. Often, a child element that was created to define some content for another element could be more effective if it were an attribute. Sticking with the phone example from the previous paragraph, look at the following two approaches:

```
<phone_number>
    <location>Home</location>
    <number>555.555.1111</number>
</phone_number>
```

and

```
<phone_number location="home">555.555.1111</phone_number>
```

Which approach to further refining a phone number seems better? By making **location** an attribute instead of a child element, the markup to describe a phone number is less verbose and easier to use. Because you can also control the value of some attributes with predefined attribute lists, you can better control the information users include in their documents. However, before you build your elements and define the content that they can contain, you should carefully consider which attributes will go with those element's application as an additional consideration. You should also evaluate your element groups to be sure that an attribute isn't the better approach to providing additional information about a particular chunk of text. Note that Chapter 8 covers attributes in depth.

For the SGML-Savvy: A Word about Exceptions and Exclusions

Full Standard Generalized Markup Language (SGML) element content models allow for what are called *exceptions* and *exclusions*, which do just what their names imply—explicitly forbid or allow instances of certain element types in the element or within the element's children. However, XML does not give its elements such functionality. Instead, all element content models must be complete and explicit to prevent ambiguity.

Unfortunately, this means that it can be difficult to convert SGML and HTML DTDs to XML, because inclusions and exclusions are at a high level in the document structure. If you're converting SGML and HTML DTDs, you need to consider this point: If an SGML DTD includes exclusions or exceptions, you'll need to reproduce the DTD with exactly the same properties, but without the exceptions or exclusions. To do so, you have to make your newly converted XML DTD more or less restrictive.

Immediate Solutions

Declaring and Specifying a Single Element with Parsed Character Data

To declare a single element in the XML DTD, start with the element declaration **<!ELEMENT**, followed by the name of the element and the type of content it can contain. The following code declares the **paragraph** element as parsed character data:

```
<!ELEMENT paragraph (#PCDATA)>
```

Here's an example of how to use this element in the document (note that this is only a portion of an XML document):

```
<paragraph>
This is a paragraph.
</paragraph>
```

TIP: In this section, we give you a glimpse at how content models for elements work. Don't forget to refer to Chapter 7 for a complete review of all content model rules and synta

Declaring and Specifying a Single Element with Element Content

To declare a single element in the XML DTD with element content as the content model specification, use code like the following:

```
<!ELEMENT paragraph (#PCDATA)>
<!ELEMENT section (paragraph)>
```

The element used in the content model specification must be defined first, in order for the element content to be valid and, in turn, for the parser to not return errors. To use the element in the document, you include the following code:

```
<section>
<paragraph>
This is a paragraph.
</paragraph>
</section>
```

Declaring a Content Model with Both Character Data and Child Elements

When you want to include both content and elements, first specify the element and then list the character data and elements with vertical bars separating them. An asterisk (*) indicates that all the content—text and elements alike—can be used as many or as few times as necessary:

```
<!ELEMENT paragraph (#PCDATA | link | emphasis)*>
```

Declaring Element Types with the Same Content Specification

If you want to declare more than one element type with the same content specification and you're specifying element content, you must use a separate declaration for each type:

```
<!ELEMENT paragraph (#PCDATA)>
<!ELEMENT note (paragraph)>
<!ELEMENT section (paragraph)>
<!ELEMENT chapter (paragraph)>
```

Using the **ANY** Keyword to Declare Elements

Instead of specifying a content model specification, the content specification can include the keyword **ANY**. The **ANY** keyword allows for any character data or declared elements to be valid within the element content. You should use the **ANY** keyword sparingly, because you can end up with a document that is missing the rules and specifications that would make it tightly formed. To declare an element using the **ANY** keyword, use code similar to the following:

```
<!ELEMENT paragraph ANY>
```

You could then use this element any way you want—for example, to nest other elements within this element. The following code would be considered valid because the **paragraph** element has been defined to contain any data:

```
<paragraph>
<emphasis>
This paragraph uses both parsed character data and another
element labeled emphasis, which is an element that was
defined previously.
</emphasis>
</paragraph>
```

Using the **EMPTY** Keyword to Declare Elements

When you want to specify that an element may never contain any content, use the keyword **EMPTY** in the content model. The following code shows exactly how you can create an empty element content model specification:

```
<!ELEMENT rule EMPTY>
```

In this example, the **rule** element may never contain character data or any other element data, although the element can be nested with other elements in other element content model rules. In your XML document, you can use one of two forms to specify an empty element. The first code example supplies a single empty element tag:

```
<rule/>
```

The second form is the same model you would use with any other element. It includes both a start tag and an end tag. The code in the XML document would look like this:

```
<rule></rule>
```

Remember, if you use the second form, you cannot place anything between the two tags; if you do, the document will be invalid and the parser will return an error.

Chapter 7

Creating Content in XML

In Depth

Experienced Webmasters and Web site developers are fond of the phrase, "Content is king," with good reason. Internet and Web technologies were created with the express goal of storing and sharing information with as many people as possible who are working in a wide variety of computing and networking environments. Extensible Markup Language (XML) is no different. Markup describes a document's content; consequently, markup is content driven. Although XML is robust and extensible enough to allow developers to create their own Document Type Definitions (DTDs) and processors, it has very strict rules about how content should be defined in DTDs and included in XML documents. Both DTD and document developers must follow these rules to create well-formed and valid documents.

Content and markup work hand in hand in an XML document to create a well-structured and useful information-dissemination tool. Content in XML documents isn't limited to ASCII text and special character entities; it can also include other markup or no data at all. DTD developers must define what content each element in a DTD can contain; so, ultimately, DTDs define a strict set of content rules developers must adhere to when creating valid and well-formed documents. This chapter describes the three types of content used in XML, discusses how to evaluate a DTD and understand the content models of each individual element, and provides instructions for declaring content rules for elements during DTD creation. This chapter also includes a section on how to use parameter entities as shortcuts to quick and easy content declaration.

Important Content-Related Terms

Before we jump into our discussion of XML content, you must be familiar with a few words and phrases. The definitions go a long way toward explaining how the rules of content are used in XML DTD and document development. The following list includes the terms or phrases as we use them throughout the chapter—and, indeed, as they're used in the XML world—followed by their definitions:

- *Content*—Anything found between the start and end tags of an element. Content can include element content, character data, or mixed content.

- *Element content*—Other elements (tag pairs) that can be included within an element. The elements that can be nested within a tag (and the order in which they must appear) are defined for each element within the DTD.

- *Character data*—The text (other than markup) included within document elements. Not all elements must necessarily allow character data as content; some can have only element content. As with element content, character data content must be defined by the DTD as part of an element's content.

- *Mixed content*—A combination of element and character data that can be included as content for any given element.

- *Content model*—The definition in a DTD of what content is allowed for any given element.

- *Parent element*—An element that has one or more elements as content. A parent element of a child element or elements may also be the child of another, higher-level element.

- *Child element*—An element that is contained (nested) within another element. A child element may also be the parent of other, lower-level elements.

- *Nesting*—A description of how elements are contained within one another.

- *Empty element*—An element that has no content of any kind.

The projects in this chapter's Immediate Solutions section focus on common tasks such as evaluating the content of an element in a DTD, defining different types of content for elements while building a DTD, using parameter entities in a content model, and creating the content model for elements in a DTD. If you're familiar with XML content, these definitions should serve as a quick reminder of the components of XML content; you can move on to the projects in the Immediate Solutions section for step-by-step instructions on creating content models in DTDs and content in XML documents. For those of you who aren't as familiar with the topic of XML content, the remainder of the introductory section will prepare you to use the projects in the Immediate Solutions section by taking a closer look at the concepts and components defined in the previous definition list.

Different Types of Content

As the definitions in the previous section indicate, any given XML element can take more than one kind of content. However, for an element to take any kind of content at all, the content and specific information about its order and requirement status must be included as part of the element's definition in the DTD. For a refresher on elements in general, refer to Chapter 6.

What Exactly Is Content, Anyway?

Content is anything found between the start and end tags of an XML element. That's a pretty generic and almost vague statement, but it's entirely accurate. Developers tend to think of content as the text that shows up on the screen or the text that an application or user interacts with, but that's only the beginning of the important role content can play in an XML document. In addition to the text between start and end tags, other child elements can be included to provide additional information about the content of both the child and the parent elements. For example, let's examine these two lines from an XML document:

```
<title>The XML Black Book, 2nd Edition</title>
<title>Creating Content in XML</title>
```

Although you can tell that the text between each pair of start and end **title** tags is probably the title of something, you don't really know what. It could be a book title, a chapter title, an article title, or even a presentation title. However, when the **title** tags become child elements of two new sets of parent elements, you learn quite a bit more about these two unspecified titles:

```
<novel>
    <front>
        <title>The XML Black Book, 2nd Edition</title>
    </front>
    <body>
        <chapter>
            <title>Creating Content in XML</title>
        </chapter>
    </body>
</novel>
```

A glance at the markup—based on David Megginson's novel DTD, first introduced in Chapter 5—reveals that "The XML Black Book, 2nd Edition" is the title of a book (this one) and "Creating Content in XML" is the name of a chapter found in this book (this chapter). The inclusion of both text and element content within the **front** and **chapter** elements demonstrates how one element (**title**) can be used in more than one place in the document (which would be an example of an efficient DTD) but describe a different kind of text in each place.

XML content is much more than just the text that the user or application sees. Instead, it's a combination of text and other elements that not only includes text for users and applications to interact with, but also provides a mechanism for describing the role of the text within the document in detail.

An element's content model describes what kind of content can legally be included within its start and end tags. XML differentiates among four different kinds of content:

- Element content
- Mixed content
- **ANY** content
- Empty content

Element Content

If an element's content model specifies that it can contain only other elements and no text, it's said to have *element content*. For example, this element content model, taken from the Open Software Description (OSD) DTD, indicates that the **DEPENDENCY** element can include either the **CODEBASE** or **SOFTPKG** element in its content, but it cannot contain other elements or text:

```
<!ELEMENT DEPENDENCY (CODEBASE|SOFTPKG)>
```

If you use this content model, the following XML markup is valid:

```
<DEPENDENCY>
    <CODEBASE />
    <SOFTPKG>...</SOFTPKG>
</DEPENDENCY>
```

CODEBASE is an empty element, so it doesn't have an end tag or content. **SOFTPKG** has its own content model that defines which elements and/or character data may be included within it. Based on the same content model, the following code is not valid:

```
<DEPENDENCY>
    <CODEBASE />
    This is some text describing the dependency.
    <SOFTPKG>...</SOFTPKG>
</DEPENDENCY>
```

The content model for the **DEPENDENCY** element does not include character data as part of the element's allowed content therefore the line of text is not legal and the code snippet is invalid.

Another example, taken from the Web Interface Definition Language (WIDL) specification (yet another proposed XML application), includes the following content model for the **BINDING** element:

```
<!ELEMENT BINDING ( VARIABLE | CONDITION | REGION )* >
```

The parentheses and asterisk (*) indicate that the **BINDING** element can contain zero or more instances of the **VARIABLE**, **CONDITION**, and **REGION** elements. For a full explanation of the notation used in content models, refer to the "Defining Element Content" section in this chapter's Immediate Solutions section.

Based on the content model for the **BINDING** element, this code is valid:

```
<BINDING>
    <VARIABLE />
    <CONDITION />
    <CONDITION />
    <CONDITION />
</BINDING>
```

The code includes one **VARIABLE** element, three **CONDITION** elements, and no **REGION** elements. All three elements that may be included within the **BINDING** element are empty tags, so they don't have content models; instead, they have extensive attribute lists that provide information for the software package that is processing the WIDL document.

Nesting Elements Correctly

When you nest one element inside another, always remember to close first what you opened last. All child elements must be closed before a parent element is closed, and the end tags of child elements may not be switched. For example, the following code is invalid:

```
<DEPENDENCY>
    <CODEBASE />
    <SOFTPKG>...</DEPENDENCY>
</SOFTPKG>
```

The parent element, **DEPENDENCY**, is closed before the child, **SOFTPKG**. To correct this problem, the two closing tags must be reversed, as follows:

```
<DEPENDENCY>
    <CODEBASE />
    <SOFTPKG>...</SOFTPKG>
</DEPENDENCY>
```

Because many DTDs, such as OSD, rely heavily on element content, it's important to be careful when nesting child elements within one another. Any number of XML and Standard Generalized Markup Language (SGML) editors, such as those described in Chapter 23, can help you avoid this nesting problem or catch it in document validation. However, it's always best to be aware of the open first, close last rule.

Mixed Content

As its name implies, mixed content is a combination of element content and character data. Character data is data that can contain only text and no other elements. In actuality, this is the simplest content model an element can contain. There's no need to worry about nesting elements correctly or which elements can be nested—the only content you can include between the start and end tags is plain old text. Among existing XML applications, it's surprisingly difficult to find examples of content models that call for only character data. Neither the WIDL nor the novel DTDs have any such elements. (The novel DTD uses a parameter entity—which is described in the "Including Parameter Entities in Content Models" section in the Immediate Solutions section—as part of the content model instead of a simple character data listing.) The OSD DTD has this element that uses character data:

```
<!ELEMENT title (#PCDATA) >
```

The **title** element can contain only text, as indicated by the **(#PCDATA)** notation in the element's content listing. Including any other elements within the **title** element will render an OSD document invalid; however, there's no limit to how much text can be included. The term **PCDATA** refers to *parsed character data*, which means that the XML parser will try to process the content, including entities.

CDATA Sections

Sometimes when an XML element is used in an XML document you see the following delimiter around PCDATA:

```
<![CDATA["
...some text and possibly markup here...
"]]>
```

This is a CDATA section. The term CDATA, which stands for *character data*, refers to content that you don't want your XML parser to process. If the CDATA section includes tags or other XML-like content, it won't be parsed. The most common use of CDATA is to include information in an XML file that you don't want the parser to try to read—for example, a client-side script written in JavaScript or VBScript. The parser passes content labeled as CDATA directly to a processor so it can handle the content.

To make things even more complex, character data content can also be called mixed content. Why? The important distinction is between element content (content that doesn't include any character data) and mixed content (content that does include character data). If an element can contain any character data at all, it's considered to have a mixed content model, even if the content model includes only character data.

Imagine a calendar DTD created to facilitate the organization of staff member time. An entry could include information about people, places, times, project references, and more. And because there's no way to categorize everything included in a calendar entry, it's useful to be able to enter undefined text. The following code defines the content model for the **entry** element:

```
<!ELEMENT entry (#PCDATA | date | place | time | person | project | phone)*>
```

The **entry** element can contain character data in addition to the **date**, **place**, **time**, **person**, **project**, and **phone** entities. The asterisk indicates that each entity can occur zero or more times in the contents of the **entry** element. Using this content model, you can create the following XML code:

```
<entry>
<date>August 1, 2000</date>
<place>Louis 106</place>
<time pm="pm">1:00PM</time>
<person>Mr. Cooper
    <organization>Computers Inc.</organization>
</person>
<project id="14568" />
<phone>555-5555</phone>
Don't forget to take a revised training manual and
marketing materials.
</entry>
```

This particular code snippet takes advantage of every available child element the **entry** element can contain. You also discover that the **time** element takes **pm** as an attribute, the **person** element is parent to the **organization** element, and the **project** element is an empty element that uses the **id** attribute to identify a project by number, possibly based on a company-wide billing and project-tracking solution. The following code is also based on the same content model:

```
<entry>
<date>November 3, 2000</date>
My birthday! Take myself to lunch.
</entry>
```

In addition to the character data, the **date** element is the only child element you use from the content model list. Even so, it's still valid code, because the content model does not say that all the listed elements must be included—only that they *can* be included.

If a parameter entity is used as part of a content model, it's considered mixed content instead of element content. For more on the role parameter entities play in content models, see "Including Parameter Entities in Content Models" in the Immediate Solutions section later in this chapter.

One of the most important differences between element content and mixed content is that content models that contain only element content can specify which child elements must be in the content of the parent element (which are optional) and in what order. When you use mixed content, everything is optional and no order can be imposed. These two different approaches to defining content can greatly affect DTD design. For more on this topic, see "Planning Content Models for a DTD" in this chapter's Immediate Solutions section.

ANY Content

Instead of carefully specifying what content any given element can take, developers can declare the content of the element as **ANY**. The syntax for this content model is:

```
<!ELEMENT name ANY>
```

where **name** is the element's name. Although this approach may seem like the easy way out, remember that parent and child elements can provide useful information about each other; and sometimes, you won't want one element to be included within another. For example, it would make no sense in the novel DTD to nest the **body** element within the **chapter** element or the **chapter** element within the **title** element. The whole purpose behind XML is to provide structural information about data, and the ability to nest elements within elements at will defeats this purpose. Instead, carefully structured content models provide well-structured documents. In our search of existing XML DTDs, we couldn't find a single instance of **ANY** content being defined in an element's content model.

EMPTY Elements

In some instances, an element is empty—that is, it can't contain any content at all—and it's listed as a singleton tag in an XML document. Examples from a familiar source, the Hypertext Markup Language (HTML), are the **img** (image) and **br** (line break) elements. Logically, there's no reason why either element should have content, because each element exists to insert something into a document, rather than to provide information about text or other elements. In XML, an **EMPTY** element is defined in the DTD using this notation:

```
<!ELEMENT name EMPTY>
```

Although the concept of an empty tag isn't new, the single tag used to include an empty element in a document is a bit different from your standard start tag. An empty element tag looks like this:

```
<element />
```

All empty tags must end with a slash just before the greater-than sign, or the document is invalid.

Looking through the various XML DTDs already being developed, we found several instances in which empty elements were used within regular elements to provide information in a structured way. Take this example from the OSD specification, as posted on the World Wide Web Consortium's (W3C) Web site at **www.w3.org/TR/NOTE-OSD**:

```
<IMPLEMENTATION>
    <OS VALUE="WinNT">
        <OSVERSION VALUE="4,0,0,0"/>
    </OS>
    <OS VALUE="Win95"/>
    <PROCESSOR VALUE="x86" />
    <LANGUAGE VALUE="en" />
    <CODEBASE HREF="http://www.foobar.org/solitaire.cab" />
</IMPLEMENTATION>
```

The operating system (**OS**), **PROCESSOR**, **LANGUAGE**, and **CODEBASE** elements all provide important information about the specific implementation of the software package being described. Except for the first instance of the **OS** element, all the other elements are empty, but they are hardly devoid of information. "Planning Content Models for a DTD" (in this chapter's Immediate Solutions section) discusses why using empty entities with predefined attributes and values is often better than allowing the document developer to provide structure information in regular character data.

Content-Based Markup vs. Presentation-Based Markup

Because HTML provided many of us with our first introduction to markup languages, we tend to view markup with the idea that it always describes content that will be presented or displayed in some way. Presentation-based markup describes data created with the idea that it will be visually presented—for example, on a computer screen, overhead, or printed page. Presentation-based markup, such as HTML, often focuses on the final look and feel of information, which leads to complex workarounds (such as using tables to control pages) and creating new methods for describing presentation-like style sheets.

However, XML was not created to describe only content that might be presented. Instead, XML is robust enough to describe information so it can be processed by one or more applications or delivered in ways other than traditional visual presentation (such as aurally or in Braille). Markup that describes content that isn't intended for display but that is instead intended to drive the functionality of an application or tool is known as *content-based markup*.

The novel and OSD DTDs, respectively, are perfect examples of presentation-based and content-based paradigms. The whole point behind the description of a novel's content is so that people can read the novel on screen or in print. The DTD is compact and concerns itself mostly with describing author, title, and paragraph information. This approach lends itself quite easily to one of several possible visual presentations.

The OSD DTD, on the other hand, is designed to provide information (the OS and processor requirements, as well as version and location information) about software packages. The goal of OSD is to facilitate the quick and easy download and update of software across a network without requiring the presence of a person at the computer while the installation or upgrade is being performed. The content OSD describes is not presentation-oriented information. Instead, the DTD concerns itself with describing the particulars of the software so the client computer can compare its parameters and installed software to determine if the package can be installed and, if so, which portions of the package it should download and from where.

The novel DTD leaves quite a bit of room for character data, and the OSD specification uses many empty elements with attributes that take one of several specified values. The novel DTD revolves around text, and the OSD DTD concerns itself with computer and software package information. The purpose that drives a DTD, whether it's based on content or presentation, greatly affects how content models are defined for each element in the DTD.

No rule says an XML application can't be both content and presentation-based; but as the DTD develops, certain portions will be reserved for information that will be presented, and others for information that will be processed or analyzed. In general, presentation-based markup allows developers more room for including their own freeform character data, and there will be more of it. Content-based markup will more closely control the amount of character data allowed and may opt to use attributes and values instead of developer-supplied information.

7. Creating Content in XML

The need for a markup language that supports both content- and presentation-based markup was one of the main motivations for the creation of XML. Although SGML is very good at creating both kinds of markup, its learning curve and implementation costs can be steep. Instead, XML provides the extensibility developers require to create DTDs to meet their needs (whether they are based on content, presentation, or both) without some of the complexities of SGML.

Immediate Solutions

Defining Parsed Character Data Content

If an element can only contain parsed character data content, its element description in the DTD takes this format:

```
<!ELEMENT name (#PCDATA)>
```

This content indicates that the element cannot contain any other child elements. The following code shows how the **note** element with a character-data-only content model would be described in the DTD:

```
<!ELEMENT note (#PCDATA)>
```

This markup is valid for the **note** element based on the element description:

```
<note>
This is some note text. This note can contain as much
text as necessary. However, it cannot contain any other markup.
</note>
```

However, this markup is not valid based on the content model for the **note** element:

```
<note>
This is some note text. <b>This markup is no longer valid</b>
because it contains additional elements nested inside of the
note element. The note element content model does not allow this.
</note>
```

Because elements that can contain only character data cannot take advantage of the strengths offered by the ability to contain other elements or by recursion (the ability to nest elements within themselves), character data is very rarely the only content an element can contain. Instead, character data is often combined with element content in a mixed content model.

Defining Element Content

You can create element models that allow only other elements to be nested within the described element. Character data, parsed or otherwise, is not allowed in the contents of the element. Elements contained within the described element are called child elements, and these child elements have their own content models, which may include other elements, character data, or both. As a result, the content model applies only to the first nesting level within an element.

Element content can specify which elements can be included as content, as well as the order in which they must appear, which are required, and which are optional. To specify this information, the content model uses a special set of notations, as outlined in Table 7.1.

The notations within the element content notation system can be combined to create complex descriptions of the elements that are allowed as child elements within a parent element. For example, this content model

```
<!ELEMENT entry ( date, place?, time, person+, project+, phone?)>
```

indicates that the **entry** element must contain one instance of the **date** element—and it must be first—followed by zero or one optional **place** element, a mandatory **time** element, one or more **person** elements, one or more **project** elements,

Table 7.1 The element content notation system.

Notation	Name	Description	Example
( )	Parentheses	Indicates a set of alternatives or a sequence of elements.	**<!ELEMENT caption (align I size)>**
I	Vertical bar	Separates elements in a set of alternatives.	**<!ELEMENT person (organization I client I partner I staff)>**
,	Comma	Separates elements in a sequence; elements must occur in the order listed.	**<!ELEMENT novel (front, body)>**
?	Question mark	Indicates that an element or set may occur zero or one time.	**<!ELEMENT caption (align, size?)>**
•	Asterisk	Indicates that an element or set may occur zero or more times.	**<!ELEMENT person (organization I client I partner I staff)*>**
+	Plus	Indicates that an element must occur one or more times.	**<!ELEMENT entry (date, place, time, person, project, phone)+>**

and an optional **phone** element. This carefully constructed content model ensures that important information such as the date, time, person, and related project information is included, but it provides flexibility for the **place** and **phone** elements because they might not be as necessary as the other information. Because the elements are separated by commas, they must occur in the order specified in the content model.

The Channel Definition Format (CDF) specification found on the W3C's Web site at **www.w3.org/TR/NOTE-CDFsubmit.html** includes the **Item** and **Schedule** elements, whose content models include only element content and use the following element content notation:

```
<!ELEMENT Item ( LastMod, Title, Abstract, Author, Publisher,
    Copyright, PublicationDate, Keywords, Category, Rating,
    Schedule, Usage )* >
<!ELEMENT Schedule ( StartDate?, EndDate?, IntervalTime?,
    EarliestTime?, LatestTime? ) >
```

The **Item** element can contain zero or more instances of several elements, and when it does, they must be included in the order listed in the content model. The **Schedule** element can take one of five optional elements, but if the elements are included, they can be included only once and must be in the order listed.

NOTE: *The CDF specification at the W3C doesn't reflect some of the real-world uses of CDF. However, the DTD at the W3C is a good example of a well-written DTD and is a valuable learning tool.*

Defining Mixed Content

Mixed content includes a combination of character data and element content. Unlike content models that include only element content, those that take mixed content cannot specify order or required values for the nested elements and data. Instead, a mixed data content model takes this format:

```
<!ELEMENT name (#PCDATA element | element | element |...)*>
```

The content list must be enclosed within parentheses, begin with the **#PCDATA** declaration, and be followed by an asterisk. Instead of using long lines of mixed content declarations, many DTDs include parameter entities in their mixed content. The next section "Including Parameter Entities in Content Models" addresses this technique.

Including Parameter Entities in Content Models

Parameter entities—entities that work only in the DTD to provide a shorthand notation for frequently used element groups—can be included in content models to make them more manageable and less cumbersome. For a detailed explanation of creating parameter entities, refer to Chapter 9. Parameter entities are included in an element's content model; they are prefaced by the percent sign (%) and followed by a semicolon (;), as shown in this syntax example:

```
<!ELEMENT name %entity;>
```

This sample code from the novel DTD provides an example of a parameter entity included in a content model:

```
<!ELEMENT item (%phrasal;)*>
```

This code indicates that the **item** element can include any content as defined by the **phrasal** parameter entity. The **phrasal** parameter entity is defined as:

```
<!ENTITY % phrasal "#PCDATA|emphasis">
```

Therefore, the **item** element can contain either character data or the **emphasis** element. This example does not lend much weight to the argument for creating parameter entities instead of just listing content within a regular content model. However, this example from the Technical Markup Language (TecML), found at **http://pcic.chem.pku.edu.cn/comp/cml/doc/dtd/htmldoc/tecml.html**, does. The content model for the **relation** element looks like this:

```
<!ELEMENT relation ((array | xvar), (array | xvar), %x.content;)>
```

This content model indicates that the **relation** element can nest either the **array** or **xvar** element twice in any order, as well as any other elements included in the **x.content** entity. The **x.content** entity, shown in the following code, also references the **x.descrip** entity:

```
<!ENTITY % x.content '(%x.descrip;, (array | xlist| xvar)*)'>
<!ENTITY % x.descrip '(xhtml?)'>
```

These two entities add zero or more **array**, **xlist**, and **xvar** elements into the fray, as well as an optional **xhtml** element. If we put this all together, the content model for the relation **element** would look something like this:

```
<!ELEMENT relation ((array | xvar), (array | Xvar), (xhtml?),
    (array | xlist| xvar|)*)
```

Although this description isn't too long, keep in mind that you can use the **x.content** entity in the content model descriptions of as many other elements in the DTD as necessary. It's much easier to type "%x.content;" than its equivalent over and over again. Additionally, the TecML specification is included as an entity in the Chemical Markup Language (CML) and Molecular (MOL) DTDs, so you can use the **x.content** entity in the content models of all the elements in those two DTDs, as well.

Entities are powerful tools, as Chapter 9 discusses in detail. When combined with content models, entities help DTD and document developers create well-structured and easy-to-read DTDs and documents.

Planning Content Models for a DTD

In many ways, content models can make or break an XML DTD. If the models contradict one another or do not work well together, the result could be invalid or unusable documents. Although it's the document developer's responsibility to follow the rules set forth in the element content models, it's up to the DTD developer to create a solid set of rules. Follow these steps to ensure your DTD's content models are viable:

1. Determine the goals and objectives of your DTD. This initial step helps you decide which elements you need in your DTD and which elements you don't need.

2. Make a list of all the elements you plan to include in the DTD and their descriptions. This process identifies the role each element will play in documents created for the DTD. For more information on elements, refer to Chapter 6.

3. Create a hierarchy showing how all the elements relate to one another. Make notes about initial ideas of what kind of content the elements might contain, but don't get too attached to your notes. In this phase, the roles and relationships among the elements will begin to become clearer than they were in Step 2.

4. Review your hierarchy and notes, paying close attention to those elements that will have child elements. Ask yourself:

   • In what order (if any) do the child elements need to appear?

   • Which child elements are required and which are optional?

   • How many times should you allow child elements to be included in content (only once or many times)?

- Will the child elements have children of their own?
- How will the children of child elements affect the parent element?
- Can the element contain instances of itself as child elements (recurs)?

These questions will no doubt lead to other, project-specific questions. The goal here is to keep examining your elements until you can see all the possible relations between them.

5. Create initial content models for each element and then take a break from your DTD development. After you've become intimately involved with a project, it becomes difficult to see your own mistakes. When you return to the project, you'll have a keener eye.

6. Develop a document for your DTD, focusing on using all the elements and their potential child elements. Document development helps flush out minor problems you couldn't see when you developed your content models. Make adjustments to your content models as necessary and keep working on your document until you have viable and solid content models.

7. Ask friends or colleagues to look over your content models and create documents for them. Be prepared to take criticism and remember that you asked for their help. Others will be able to find mistakes you might have missed or suggest a solution to a difficult problem. Even though your DTD isn't finished yet, errors at this stage in the game can be more difficult to fix later.

When you've developed your content models for an XML DTD account, you'll find that a large portion of your work is done. You'll still need to work on element attributes and entities, but the framework for your DTD will be firmly in place.

Chapter 8

Working with XML Attributes

In Depth

This chapter takes a careful look at the role attributes play in a Document Type Definition (DTD) and in document development, the types of attributes DTD designers can include in their XML applications, and the ways attributes can be used to describe information.

Attributes provide information about elements in much the same way that adjectives modify nouns. Attributes allow DTD designers to provide developers with a wide range of information description choices. Document developers can even add their own attributes to the internal subset of a DTD to meet individual document needs. Attributes provide a mechanism for extending or fine-tuning the meaning of XML elements and their content.

The ability to define your own elements and use the markup generated from the elements with an XML processor to create a customized solution for a specific need is the very essence of the power XML affords developers. There are no limits to the number and type of elements you can create. In addition, elements can be nested within each other level after level (as the content model allows) to describe complex relationships between information. Still, the element mechanism alone isn't always enough; it must be extended to provide more information about the element or its content. Attributes are the extension. This introductory section examines the role attributes play and describes the components that make up the attributes used in XML DTDs and documents in detail. If you're well versed in the roles and uses of attributes, you may turn directly to the Immediate Solutions for instructions on creating and referencing attributes.

The Role of Attributes in XML

In a nutshell, attributes provide extra information about an XML element and its content. If the element is empty, attributes are useful for tailoring the meaning of the element. If the element has content, attributes usually provide more information on how the content should be processed. Applications that incorporate empty elements—such as the Open Software Description (OSD) and the Channel Definition Format (CDF)—use a variety of attributes to allow developers to provide information to the processor in controlled and standardized ways, as this snippet of example code from the CDF specification shows:

```
<SCHEDULE STARTDATE="1997-03-24">
    <INTERVALTIME HOUR="6" />
    <LATESTTIME HOUR="3" />
    <EARLIESTTIME HOUR="1" />
</SCHEDULE>
```

The **INTERVALTIME**, **LATESTTIME**, and **EARLIESTTIME** elements all use the **HOUR** attribute to provide scheduling information for a channel.

Other DTDs use attributes to help document developers provide more detail about how the information described by the markup language should be presented. For example, the **mtable** element of the Mathematical Markup Language (MathML) can take up to 14 different attributes, all of which describe how the table should look when presented, including row and column alignment and spacing, as well as border information. By mixing and matching the attributes and their values, developers of MathML documents can create literally thousands of different table presentations. By itself, the **mtable** element only indicates that the information it contains is a table; but when the attributes are added, they bring the table to life.

Attribute Terminology

It's important to understand the meaning and specific uses of the following key attribute terms:

- *Attribute list declaration*—A listing in the DTD of all the attributes that can be used with a given element. This listing includes the attributes, their values and default value (if the values are fixed), and whether the attribute is required or optional.

- *Attribute specification*—An individual listing for a single attribute within the attribute list declaration.

- *Attribute name*—The name used to identify the attribute in the DTD and reference it in a document. Attribute names must always consist of a letter, underscore, or colon, followed by zero or more characters.

- *Attribute type*—The value that identifies the attribute as a string, tokenized, or enumerated attribute.

- *Attribute value*—A list in the specification of all the possible values an attribute can take; in a document, this is the specific value assigned to the attribute by the document developer.

In a DTD, the combination of a name, type, and value makes up a single attribute specification, and a group of attribute specifications makes up an attribute list declaration for an element. In a document, attributes and their values are part of a single instance of an element. Attributes apply only to that single instance of the element and must be referenced in every instance of a starting tag where they should be applied.

WARNING! Attribute values in both DTDs and documents must be enclosed in quotation marks. Both HTML and Standard Generalized Markup Language (SGML) are a bit more forgiving about the presence of quotation marks than XML is. In XML (and XHTML), if the quotation marks are missing in either the DTD or the document body, the document will be invalid and not well formed. XML editors that are being developed should support the automatic insertion of quotation marks around values in both DTDs and documents. If you need to use quotation marks as part of an attribute's value, they must be escaped using the " entity. You may also use the entities ' and & as part of an attribute's value to indicate single quotation marks and ampersands (&).

Types of Attributes

XML provides for three different attribute types:

- String attributes
- Tokenized attributes
- Enumerated attributes

Each attribute type can only take specific kinds of values, and for a document to be valid, the value provided in the attribute specification must match the declared type. The following sections describe each of the three attribute types. For specific instructions on creating attributes of each type, turn to this chapter's Immediate Solutions section.

String Attributes

String attributes take string data and are used to create attributes that allow the user to define any value they would like for the attribute. The **HOUR** attribute for the **INTERVALTIME**, **LATESTTIME**, and **EARLIESTTIME** elements of the CDF application (these elements were discussed earlier in this chapter) is an example of a string attribute. Another example is the **HREF** attribute for the **ITEM** element from the same specification, shown in this example code taken from the specification:

```
<ITEM HREF="http://www.foosports.com/intro.htm">...</ITEM>
```

NOTE: Throughout this chapter, you will see attributes and element names both uppercased and lowercased. We recommend lowercasing your element and attribute names in most instances. However, some of the DTDs we use as examples declare their elements and attributes in uppercase; therefore, we keep the markup as they intended.

Tokenized Attributes

Tokenized attributes refer to seven different types of predefined attributes that play a specific role in XML documents and that must have a particular kind of value. These seven attributes can't be used for anything other than their express purposes in an XML document or the document will be invalid. The tokenized attributes are as follows:

- **ID**—Provides a unique identifier for the element within the document. The value for an **ID** must always consist of a *name*—a letter, underscore, or colon followed by zero or more name characters (letters, digits, periods, dashes, underscores, colons, and a few others). If two or more elements have the same **ID**, the document is invalid.

- **IDREF**—Points to an element with the specified **ID** value. If an element identified by the **ID** is not included somewhere in the document and an **IDREF** attribute attempts to point to it anyway, the document is invalid.

- **IDREFS**—Points to two or more elements within the documents by using multiple **ID** listings separated by spaces.

- **ENTITY**—Points to an external entity. The value must consist of a name and must match both the name and case constructs of the external entity to which it points.

- **ENTITIES**—Points to two or more external entities by using multiple names separated by spaces.

- **NMTOKEN**—Takes a value that is an **NMTOKEN**—any mixture of name characters.

- **NMTOKENS**—Takes a value of two or more **NMTOKENS** separated by spaces.

Generally, the values of all tokenized attributes are character strings. Unlike string attributes, however, the strings used as values for tokenized attributes must conform to the rules of their specific tokenized types.

Enumerated Attributes

When an attribute includes a predefined list of options as its value, it's said to be *enumerated*. Enumerated attributes include a subset of attribute types that includes the notation type attribute and the general enumeration. A notation type attribute lists one of several notation types—defined elsewhere in the DTD—as a value. A general enumeration takes a series of **NMTOKENS** as values. The value for any enumerated attribute in an XML document must match one of the values listed in the attribute specification.

TIP: *When you work with values of mixed case, the following rules apply: All **ID**, **IDREF**, **IDREFS**, **NMTOKEN**, and **NMTOKENS** values are automatically converted to uppercase by XML, so these values are not case sensitive. However, XML does not convert **string**, **ENTITY**, or **ENTITIES** values to uppercase, so these values are case sensitive. We recommend using lowercase for all values and file names wherever possible to avoid any accidental case incompatibilities.*

Additional Attribute Specifics

In addition to providing name, type, and value information in any given attribute specification, you can also provide answers to three important questions about any attribute:

- Is its value fixed?
- What is its default value?
- Is the attribute required or optional?

Attributes can have a fixed value assigned to them that the document developer cannot change. In addition, a default value can be declared for any attribute—especially commonly used attributes—so the document developer doesn't have to enter the attribute to reference it. Finally, an attribute can be defined as required and must be included each time its element is used in markup; if the attribute is missing or its value is incorrect, the entire document is invalid. "Adding Attribute Specifics to an Attribute Specification" in this chapter's Immediate Solutions section, gives you more information on how to provide default values for an attribute, as well as how to designate the attribute as fixed or required.

Uses of Attributes

When designing your DTD, attributes should only be used when you want to associate a name-value pair with an element. If you want to associate more complex data, consider creating a new child element.

As already indicated, attributes provide an additional source of content and supply information about how an element's contents should be presented. Attributes are used in very different ways, depending on whether the markup is presentation or content based. Presentation-based markup concerns itself with how the document's content is displayed, whereas content-based markup focuses on providing well-formatted and standardized content for an XML processor to read and manipulate.

Attributes are used quite differently in these two types of markup. In presentation-based markup, attributes provide document developers with a mechanism that allows them to customize the document's final display and appearance. In contrast, the attributes in content-based markup focus more on providing document developers with a list of possible standard values and less on describing content within elements. No rule says a DTD has to lend itself to either presentation-based markup or content-based markup. Instead, a DTD can lend itself to both by including elements that are geared for both presentation and processing. MathML is a perfect example of a DTD that contains both presentation- and content-based elements, and it shows how their associated attributes play different roles depending on the role of each element.

TIP: *The examples in this section are taken from the MathML specification, located at **www.w3.org/TR/PR-math**, and are written by the authors listed at the top of the specification. The copyright on all information contained within the specification is retained by the World Wide Web Consortium (W3C).*

Of the presentation elements included in the MathML specification, its creators have this to say: "Presentation elements correspond to the 'constructors' of traditional math notation—that is, to the basic kinds of symbols and expression-building structures out of which any particular piece of traditional math notation is built."

Notation is a physical representation of a mathematical function, so it makes sense that the elements that focus on notation should be presentation oriented. Among the list of presentation elements included in the MathML application are those that describe how elements should be grouped horizontally; how spaces, subscript, and superscript should be addressed; and how square roots and fractions should be formed. These elements also use attributes to allow the document developer to provide his or her own specifics about these notations. For example, the **mtable** element (mentioned in the opening paragraphs of the chapter) takes the 14 presentation-related attribute-value sets shown in Table 8.1.

Although none of these attributes contributes significantly to the way a MathML processor crunches numbers, they do have quite a bit to do with the way the results of the number crunching are displayed. Although processing numbers is very important, the presentation of the results has a great deal to do with their value to the end user. For the curious, the attribute list declaration for the **mtable** element looks like this:

```
<!ATTLIST mtable    %att-tableinfo;
                    %att-globalatts;>
```

This attribute list declaration uses parameter entities to assign the attributes within the **att-tableinfo** and **att-globalatts** attribute lists to the **mtable** element. The **att-tableinfo** parameter entity defines the 14 presentation-related attributes, and the **att-globalatts** parameter entity defines 4 other attributes (**class**, **style**, **id**, and **other**). For more information on the creation of parameter entities, see Chapter 9.

Table 8.1   The mtable element's presentation-related attributes and values.

Attribute	Values	Default Value
align	top, bottom, center, baseline, axis, or *row number*	axis
rowalign	top, bottom, center, baseline, or axis	baseline
columnalign	left, center, or right	center
groupalign	*group alignment list*	left
alignmentscope	true or false	true
rowspacing	*number*	1.0ex
columnspacing	*number*	.8em
rowlines	none, solid, or dashed	none
columnlines	none, solid, or dashed	none
frame	none, solid, or dashed	none
framespacing	*horizontal numeric value* and *vertical numeric value*	0.4em 0.5ex
equalrows	true or false	true
equalcolumns	true or false	true
displaystyle	true or false	false

Related solution:	Found on page:
Creating Parameter Entities	221

On the content side of the fence, the **declare** element—clearly labeled as a content element—is used to set or change the default value of a mathematical object or to associate a name with an object. Its five attributes exist for the express purpose of assisting the element in its role; the element does so by allowing the document developer to use a strict set of predetermined values, a number, or a URL to provide information about the mathematical object. The attributes and their values are shown in Table 8.2.

Table 8.2   The declare element's content-related attributes and values.

Attribute	Values	Default Value
type	integer, rational, real, float, complex, complex-polar, complex-cartesian, or constant	real
scope	local or global	local
nargs	*number*	1
occurrence	prefix, infix, or function-model	function-model
definitionURL	*URL*	none

The **type**, **scope**, and **occurrence** attributes force users to choose from a list of values that provide detailed information about the object's mathematical type, in what scope it can be applied, and the occurrence of any operator declarations. The **nargs** attribute specifies how many arguments exist for function declarations, whereas the **definitionURL** attribute links to an external definition of the element's syntax.

Even if you're not math-savvy, it's easy to see that these attributes provide information about the element that the processor will use in its calculations, but that probably won't have much affect on the final presentation of the MathML document. The attribute list declaration for the **declare** element is as follows:

```
<!ATTLIST declare        %att-type;
                         %att-scope;
                         %att-nargs;
                         %att-occurrence;
                         %att-definition;
                         %att-globalatts;>
```

This attribute declaration is made up of more of those pesky parameter entities. For more information on parameter entities see Chapter 9.

Because the MathML DTD expressly defines content and presentation markup in separate categories, it's easy to see how the elements and their attributes act as functions of either content or presentation. It's likely that many of your DTDs will have both content- and presentation-oriented elements. Although you may not need to differentiate between them in the DTD in the same way the MathML DTD does, it's important to keep them separate in your own mind. As you begin to develop your elements, you'll notice that their role as either content or presentation markup will play a large part in which attributes you specify for the elements and how you define those attributes' values.

8. Working with
XML Attributes

Immediate Solutions

Specifying String Attributes

Use the following syntax to create string attribute specifications:

```
<!ATTLIST element
    attributename CDATA #IMPLIED|#REQUIRED|#FIXED>
```

The **element** is the name of the element to which the attribute applies, and **attributename** is the name you give the attribute and by which it will be referenced in the body of an XML document. The **CDATA** label defines the attribute's type (character data); it's required for every string attribute and indicates that the attribute's value will be text and numbers. You use one of the values of **#IMPLIED**, **#REQUIRED**, or **#FIXED** to indicate to the XML processor that the attribute is either implied, required, or fixed, respectively. Each attribute specification is discussed in "Adding Attribute Specifics to an Attribute Specification" later in this section.

Here's an example from the Open Software Description (OSD) DTD of a string attribute:

```
<!ATTLIST SOFTPKG
    VERSION CDATA #IMPLIED>
```

The **SOFTPKG** element takes the **VERSION** attribute, whose value is string data. This particular attribute is used to provide version information for the software package that is described using OSD markup. The attribute takes a string value because it would have been impractical for the developers of OSD to try to provide a list of all the possible version values software developers might use. Instead, this information can be entered "freestyle" by the developer of the document as dictated by the software package version.

Specifying Tokenized Attributes

Tokenized attributes take string values closely controlled by type. Use the following syntax to create tokenized attribute specifications:

```
<!ATTLIST element
    attributename TOKENTYPE #IMPLIED|#REQUIRED|#FIXED>
```

The ***element*** is the name of the element the attribute applies to, and ***attributename*** is the name you give the attribute and by which it will be referenced in the body of an XML document. The ***TOKENTYPE*** can be one of the following seven types (as described in the introductory sections of the chapter):

- **ID**
- **IDREF**
- **IDREFS**
- **ENTITY**
- **ENTITIES**
- **NMTOKEN**
- **NMTOKENS**

Your choice of one of the **#IMPLIED**, **#REQUIRED**, or **#FIXED** values indicates to the XML processor that the attribute is implied, required, or fixed, respectively. Here's an example from David Megginson's novel DTD of a tokenized attribute specification:

```
<!ATTLIST chapter
  id ID #REQUIRED>
```

This attribute is used to assign a unique ID number to each chapter in a document and is a required part of any **chapter** element. If a **chapter** element doesn't have an **id**, the document is invalid. Although the creator of the DTD could have made this a string value attribute instead of a tokenized attribute, a string attribute doesn't guarantee that its value must be unique. To make sure that each chapter has its own unique identifier, the DTD designer instead took advantage of the uniqueness requirement of the **ID** token and constructed a tokenized attribute instead of a string attribute.

Specifying Enumerated Attributes

Enumerated attributes include a set of possible values—each conforming to the **NMTOKEN** format—which the attribute can take, rather than a string value. Use the following syntax to create an enumerated attribute specification:

```
<!ATTLIST element
    attributename (A | B | C | ...) "DEFAULT"  #REQUIRED|#FIXED >
```

The *element* is the name of the element the attribute applies to, and *attributename* is the name you give the attribute and by which it will be referenced in the body of an XML document. The list of possible values is enclosed within parentheses and separated by vertical lines. It's generally best not to list a value more than once within any given value list, because doing so is redundant and incompatible with SGML standards. *DEFAULT* indicates which value should be the default if the user doesn't specify a value, and the **#REQUIRED** or **#FIXED** values indicate to the XML processor that the attribute is either required or fixed, respectively. Here's an example from the OSD DTD of an enumerated attribute specification:

```
<!ATTLIST DEPENDENCY
    ACTION (Assert|Install) "Assert">
```

This attribute assigns a value of either **Assert** or **Install** to the **DEPENDENCY** element, with **Assert** as the default. This attribute is not required, nor does it have a fixed value. Based on the presence of other application components, this attribute helps a client computer determine whether it should install the software package described by the OSD document. If **Assert** is the chosen value, the software package is installed only if other required components are already installed on the client computer. If these components are not installed on the client computer, the software package installation is skipped entirely. However, if the value of **ACTION** is **Install**, any missing required components are installed on the client machine, and then the described software package is installed. Because these two values provide the client machine with important information that can lead to the successful installation or intentional noninstallation of software, a consistent means of identifying the action had to be integrated into the DTD. By providing document developers with keywords to trigger different actions, the DTD designers guarantee that processing instructions will be transferred to the XML processor in a consistent and understandable manner. Neither a string nor a tokenized attribute could accomplish this.

A list of notations may also be used as values for an enumerated attribute, but each listed notation must be declared in the document's DTD using the following syntax:

```
<!NOTATION NAME PUBLIC/SYTEM "location">
```

For more on notations, review Chapter 5. The following is an example of an enumerated attribute that takes a list of notations as possible values:

```
<!ATTLIST DOCUMENT
    TYPE NOTATION (DOC | TXT | RTF | WPF) "DOC">
```

This attribute defines the file type for the **DOCUMENT** element (the default value is **DOC**). The options in the value list are described by the following notation statements in the DTD:

```
<!NOTATION DOC SYSTEM "/apps/docs/msword.exe">
<!NOTATION TXT SYSTEM "/apps/docs/pfe32.exe">
<!NOTATION RTF SYSTEM "/apps/docs/msword.exe">
<!NOTATION WPF SYSTEM "/apps/docs/wordperfect.exe">
```

If just one of the options listed in the value list isn't declared by a notation statement in the DTD, the entire document is invalid.

Adding Attribute Specifics to an Attribute Specification

In addition to providing name, type, and value information for an attribute, the attribute specification can include information that answers these three questions (as posed in the introductory portion of this chapter) about any given attribute:

- Is its value fixed?
- What is its default value?
- Is the attribute required or optional?

To answer these questions, attribute specifications use the following three mechanisms:

- **#IMPLIED|"*DEFAULT*"**
- **#FIXED**
- **#REQUIRED**

Any attribute of any type can have a default value set for it by including that default value in quotation marks just prior to the end of the attribute specification. If the attribute doesn't have a default value, the label **#IMPLIED** is used instead to indicate to the XML processor that a default value wasn't assigned and the processor should ignore the attribute altogether. The document type attribute specification used in the previous section also provides an example of a default value being assigned to an attribute:

```
<!ATTLIST DOCUMENT
    TYPE NOTATION (DOC | TXT | RTF | WPF) "DOC">
```

8. Working with
XML Attributes

The **DOC** inside the quotation marks at the end of the specification indicates to both the document developer and the XML processor that the **DOC** notation is the default value for the attribute if the developer doesn't supply one.

If the label **#FIXED** precedes its default value, the default value of the attribute is considered fixed and must be referenced in the document body exactly as it is listed in the attribute specification. The **#FIXED** label is usually associated with string or tokenized attribute types and not enumerated types (what's the point of having choices if the choice is made for you?) and is always used in conjunction with a default value. Fixed attributes are created by DTD designers to ensure that vital information is passed to the XML processor even if the document developer forgets to include it. An example of a fixed attribute follows:

```
<!ATTLIST MSWDOC
     TYPE NOTATION CDATA #FIXED "DOC">
```

This example combines a notation with a string attribute and a fixed label to ensure that any document described by the **MSWDOC** element is labeled as a Microsoft Word document, as declared in the **DOC** notation that would be declared in the DTD. The document developer cannot change the value of the **TYPE** attribute without invalidating the document.

Finally, the **#REQUIRED** label can be used to indicate that the attribute must be included with each instance of its element. The example of a tokenized attribute declaration from an earlier section also serves as an example of a required attribute:

```
<!ATTLIST chapter
  id ID #REQUIRED>
```

Each time the **chapter** element is used in the document body, it must include the **id** attribute. Because the **id** attribute is tokenized, the attribute's value must meet the specifications set up for the **ID** token. The result is an attribute specification that requires each instance of the **chapter** element to have a unique identifier. This is a good example of how specific types of attributes and the additional specification labels can be combined to ensure that the document developer provides a required set of information to the XML processor.

Combining Attribute Specifications to Form an Attribute List Declaration

An attribute list declaration is simply a group of attribute specifications given for a single element. The list declaration may include as many or as few attribute specifications as necessary and can contain any combination of string, tokenized, and enumerated specifications. The syntax for forming an attribute list declaration is:

```
<!ATTLIST ELEMENT
attribute specification
attribute specification
attribute specification
...>
```

Here is an example from the OSD specification of an attribute list declaration for the **CODEBASE** element:

```
<!ATTLIST CODEBASE FILENAME CDATA #IMPLIED>
<!ATTLIST CODEBASE HREF CDATA #REQUIRED>
<!ATTLIST CODEBASE SIZE CDATA #IMPLIED>
```

Notice that the attribute list declarations contain one attribute per listing. These three attribute list declarations could be legally combined into one list declaration, like this:

```
<! ATTLIST CODEBASE
    FILENAME CDATA #IMPLIED
    HREF CDATA #REQUIRED
    SIZE CDATA #IMPLIED>
```

Referencing Attributes in Markup

XML attributes are referenced in markup in the same way HTML attributes are referenced. The syntax is:

```
<element attribute="value">
```

The following rules apply to attributes referenced in markup:

- Attributes are listed after the element they modify and are separated from the element by a space.

- No spaces appear on either side of the equal sign in an attribute-value pair, and all attribute values in XML must be enclosed in quotation marks. If they are not, the document is invalid.

- Additional attributes may be assigned to an element (providing its attribute list declaration includes them) by listing them one after the other in attribute-value pairs separated by spaces.

- An attribute and its value can appear only once in any given instance of an XML markup element.

- An attribute-value pair applies only to the single instance of the XML markup element with which it is listed.

- Only those attributes and values assigned in an element's attribute list declaration can modify an element. Mixing and matching attributes is not allowed.

- One attribute can modify more than one element as long as it has been declared in an attribute list declaration for each element it modifies.

- Required attributes must be listed with each instance of their associated element. If they are not, the document is invalid.

- Fixed attribute values must be included exactly as specified by the attribute list declaration. If they are changed in any way or omitted, the document is invalid.

Planning for Element Attributes

The following steps outline a good way to go about planning the attributes for a DTD. You can use index cards to help you plan the attributes for your DTD. Use one index card for each element so you can group and regroup elements by function. To plan the attributes for a DTD, follow these steps:

1. Define the role and purpose of each element in as much detail as possible, one element to a card. This definition will be your first clue to what kind of attributes you'll need to assign to each individual element.

2. Compare all the element definitions and group similar elements.

3. Determine which, if any, attributes the elements will have in common and create lists of attributes that are common to several elements.

4. Use the lists of common attributes to create parameter entities to better organize your DTD.

5. Record the appropriate parameter entity or entities on the index cards of those elements that take attributes that are included in parameter entities.

6. Finalize the attribute lists for each element on the index cards.

7. Transfer the information from the index cards to attribute list definition statements and parameter entity declarations in your DTD.

Although the idea of using index cards may seem outdated, it will help you better define attributes for individual elements, as well as show the relationship between elements that have common attributes. The attributes for even the simplest DTD can be created from this process of definition and organization. The process also makes the creation and organization of complex DTDs easier.

Working with Attributes in XML Tools

Although a variety of XML development tools can be used to manipulate XML attributes, we only take a brief look at how to use two tools: XML Spy (**http://new.xmlspy.com/**) and Near & Far Designer (**www.opentext.com/ near_and_far**). XML Spy and Near & Far Designer both provide an integrated environment for developing XML DTDs.

With XML Spy, you create attributes just like you create elements—you make sure your cursor has selected an element in the main window and then you select an Insert Attribute menu item. Filling in the attribute data is much like filling in element data—you fill in fields and choose enumerated types from a window on the screen.

With Near & Far Designer, attributes are treated as properties of the elements. To create or manage an attribute, you select the attribute's element and then select the Edit|Attribute List menu item. Doing so displays a dialog box for managing your attributes.

If your DTD tends to be attribute rich, the XML Spy user interface may be more useful because it generally shows you what you're trying to manage. If your DTD tends to be more element oriented, the Near & Far Designer user interface may help hide information that is not immediately relevant.

To work with attributes in XML Spy, follow these steps:

1. Load your DTD into XML Spy.

2. Select an element and then select the XML|Insert|Attribute menu item. If you were to load the newspaper.dtd used in Chapter 5, you would see something like the screen shown in Figure 8.1.

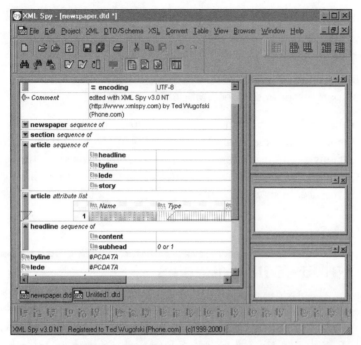

Figure 8.1   XML Spy displays an attribute list in the same window as the elements, very much like the DTD.

3. Click in an attribute's Name field and type the name of the attribute.

4. Click the Type field and select the attribute type from the list. In Figure 8.2, the attribute types are shown in a window near the right side of the screen. The attribute type can be a string attribute (**CDATA**), one of the seven token types (**ID**, **IDREF**, **IDREFS**, **ENTITY**, **ENTITIES**, **NMTOKEN**, or **NMTOKENS**), a **NOTATION** (which is covered in Chapter 9), or an enumerated type. (Note that when you select a field that permits only enumerated values, these values appear in a window to the right.) Double-clicking on the attribute type enters that value into the Type field.

Related solution:	*Found on page:*
Declaring Notations	225

5. Click the Presence field and select from the list of attribute value requirements: **#REQUIRED**, **#IMPLIED**, or **#FIXED**.

6. You may need to enter values for the Values and Default fields, depending on the attribute type.

7. While still selecting an attribute, select the XML|Insert|Attribute menu item to insert more menu items. After you type all your attributes, you will see something like the screen in Figure 8.3.

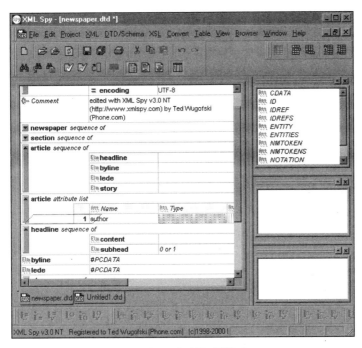

Figure 8.2   Selecting the Type field in XML Spy.

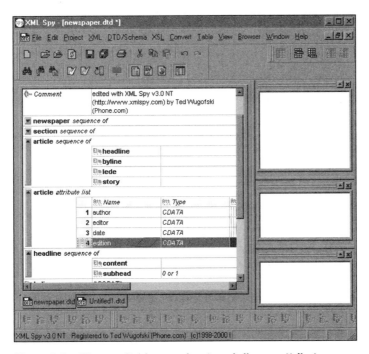

Figure 8.3   The result when you've *typed* all your attributes.

8. To modify an attribute in XML Spy, select the attribute in the main window and then click on the field that you want to change.

9. You can move attributes by clicking on the number of the attribute and then dragging the attribute to the proper location.

10. If you want to remove an attribute, select the number of the attribute and then select the Edit|Delete menu item.

To work with attributes in Near & Far Designer, follow these steps:

1. Load your DTD into Near & Far Designer.

2. Select the root node and then select the View|Expand All menu item. Doing so displays the entire document tree.

3. Select the element for which you want to create an attribute list.

4. Select the Edit|Attribute List menu item. If you loaded the newspaper.dtd used in Chapter 5, you would see something like the screen shown in Figure 8.4.

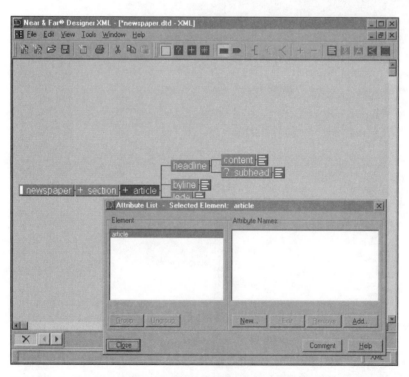

Figure 8.4   The Near & Far Designer user interface shows DTD elements in a graphical layout. Attributes, on the other hand, are displayed in a list box.

5. Click the New button to create a new attribute. Doing so displays another dialog box in which you fill in the attribute data. See Figure 8.5 for how this might look for the **author** attribute in our newspaper DTD.

6. After you fill in the appropriate information for an attribute, click OK to return to the previous dialog box.

7. In the Attribute List dialog box, click New to create any additional attributes.

8. To modify an attribute, select the element in the main window and then select the Edit|Attribute List menu item. Select the desired attribute from the list of attribute names and then click the Edit or Remove button.

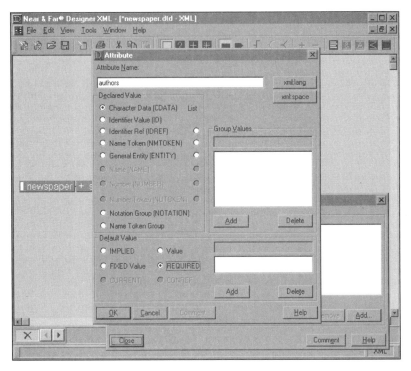

Figure 8.5   In Near & Far Designer, modifying attributes is performed through a straightforward dialog box.

Chapter 9

Creating and Including XML Entities

In Depth

An *entity* is a powerful Extensible Markup Language (XML) tool that allows Document Type Definition (DTD) and document developers to associate a text-based alias with non-ASCII text or unparsed resources and large or frequently used blocks of text and markup. DTDs that take advantage of the entities are well organized, easier to read and work with, and able to support thousands of nonstandard characters. Without entities, unparsed resources—such as image and audio files—cannot be included in XML documents.

In this chapter, we examine the different kinds of entities that XML supports and the crucial role each type of entity plays in DTD development. The Immediate Solutions section of this chapter provides instructions for constructing each kind of entity, as well as a complete listing of the entities that are used in XML documents to include the most common special characters defined in the ISO-Latin-1 character set.

What Is an Entity?

An entity is essentially a unit of storage. In the XML world, almost anything can be stored in a entity, including:

- Unparsed resources
- Blocks of text or markup
- Other XML documents
- Lists of attributes
- Content models
- Characters that are not part of the ASCII character set

In the Hypertext Markup Language (HTML), entities play a minor role in document development. Entities define non-ASCII characters using an ampersand (**&**), a text string, and a semicolon (**;**), as follows:

```
&textstring;
```

For example, this entity represents a less-than sign (**<**):

```
&lt;
```

Although entities play this role in XML as well, they can be used in a variety of other ways to simplify DTD organization and document construction. XML's sophisticated use of entities contributes in many ways to the language's extensibility and robustness, which are lacking in HTML. In fact, one of the more significant differences between modularized XHTML and traditional HTML is XHTML's use of entities.

Recalling that an entity is essentially a storage unit, the basic premise behind an entity is that the contents of the storage unit are associated with a name. Whenever the entity's name is invoked in an XML document, the entity's contents are inserted in place of the name, just as a less-than sign is displayed in place of the entity **<**.

The contents of an entity can be contained inside the entity's declaration or outside the entity's declaration. Not surprisingly, these are called internal entities and external entities, respectively.

The remainder of this introductory section discusses internal and external entities and provides a detailed description of each of the three types of entities: parsed, unparsed, and parameter entities. This chapter's Immediate Solutions section is devoted to instructions for referencing and creating entities and includes a listing of entities in common character sets.

Types of Entities

As mentioned previously, there are three types of entities; each of these three types can be declared as either internal entities or external entities. Regardless of the type of entity, all entities are declared in the same way in the DTD:

```
<!ENTITY name "content">
```

External and parameter entities throw in a few extra bits of information for good measure, but they still include the basic entity name and content information.

If the entity is declared inside the DTD, it's called an internal entity. If the entity is declared outside the DTD and is only referenced by the DTD, it's called an external entity.

Internal Entities

Internal entities are self-contained and do not reference any content outside of the DTD. The following code is an example of a group of internal entities taken from David Megginson's Novel DTD (**www.megginson.com/texts/darkness**):

```
<!-- em-dash -->
<!ENTITY mdash "--">

<!-- left double quotation mark -->
<!ENTITY ldquo "``">

<!-- right double quotation mark -->
<!ENTITY rdquo "´´">

<!-- left single quotation mark -->
<!ENTITY lsquo "`">

<!-- right single quotation mark -->
<!ENTITY rsquo "´">

<!-- horizontal ellipse -->
<!ENTITY hellip "...">
```

All of an entity's pieces—its name and complete content—are included within the declaration. Note that the content must be enclosed in quotation marks and each entity must have a name that is unique to both the internal and external subsets. If a name is used twice, the one listed last has precedence over the one listed first.

External Entities

In an external entity, the content portion refers to another storage unit using either a system or public identifier. Therefore, the declaration's content is really just the name of a file or other resource. The following example references the DocBook DTD.

```
<!ENTITY % DocBookDTD PUBLIC "-//OASIS//DTD DocBook XML V4.1.2//EN"
         "http://www.oasis-open.org/docbook/xml/4.0/docbookx.dtd">
```

This example references a file called **mypict.gif** stored on a local system:

```
<!ENTITY mypict SYSTEM "graphics/mypict.gif" NDATA gif>
```

Notice that both of the previous entity declarations include a specific file name or location. In the case of the second entity (with the **SYSTEM** identifier), this location will be used to locate the specified file on the system. In the case of the first entity (with the **PUBLIC** identifier), the path provided will be used if the XML processor is unable to locate the file using the formal public identifier (**-//OASIS//DTD DocBook XML V4.1.2//EN**). The idea behind this identification system is that files labeled as public can be retrieved from one of many places because they are widely available. Therefore, the XML processor can figure out the best place from which to get the file. System entities are usually specific to the document or set of documents, so there's no reason why they would be available any place other than on the local system. By differentiating between **PUBLIC** and **SYSTEM** when describing the entity, the DTD developer helps the XML processor know where to look for an entity.

Parsed Entities

A *parsed entity* is character data assigned as content to an entity name. When created for use in the content of a document, a parsed entity is called a *general entity*. When a parsed entity is referenced, the content of the entity is inserted in the document in place of the entity reference. The examples of internal entities from David Megginson's Novel DTD are also examples of parsed entities. These particular entities use names such as **ldquo** and **hellip** as aliases for punctuation marks such as the left double quote (") and ellipsis (...).

Parsed entities are especially useful for creating aliases to frequently used phrases and blocks of text or markup, as well as for inserting special characters. Please see "Common Entity Uses" later in this chapter for more examples of using parsed entities in XML documents.

Unparsed Entities

Anything that's not an XML-encoded resource, such as an audio or video file, is considered to be an *unparsed entity*. Not all unparsed entities are multimedia files; they can also include text or binary files that are not supposed to be processed as XML-encoded files. In contrast to parsed entities, the storage contents referenced by an unparsed entity are not automatically treated as XML markup and text. For any external unparsed resource to be referenced in an XML file, it must first be declared as an entity. Unparsed entities may only be used in attribute values.

In addition to the name and content portions, each unparsed entity declaration must have a notation. The unparsed entity's notation identifies the content's type. The only way to tell an unparsed entity from a parsed entity is by the notation. If you forget the notation, the XML processor will try to treat the entity as an XML-encoded resource, leading to invalid and virtually unusable files.

Our earlier example of an external system entity is also an example of an unparsed entity:

```
<!ENTITY mypict SYSTEM "graphics/mypict.gif" NDATA gif>
```

The **NDATA** portion of the declaration indicates that notation information follows and labels the entity as unparsed. In this example, the **gif** notation is assigned to the entity, so the XML processor will recognize the entity as a Graphics Interchange Format (GIF) file and not XML-encoded data. If we change the example to

```
<!ENTITY mypict SYSTEM "graphics/mypict.gif" NDATA tiff>
```

the processor will treat the file as a Tagged Image File Format (TIFF) file, even though its extension says "gif." Although it's important to remember to include the notation information for an unparsed entity, it's just as important to include the *correct* notation information. For the declaration to be valid, the notation name must also be declared in the DTD. For more on this subject, see "Declaring Unparsed Entities" in this chapter's Immediate Solutions section.

How unparsed entities are handled or displayed is ultimately up to the application that uses the XML data. In general, the application should know what to do with an unparsed entity based on its notation. The application may have built-in mechanisms to handle the unparsed entity, just as Web browsers can display GIF and Joint Photographic Experts Group (JPEG) files in addition to other types of multimedia resources. If the application can't support the entity type, it may automatically launch an external helper application to deal with the entity.

The types of unparsed entities you include in documents written for one DTD or another are driven by the purpose and functionality of the DTD itself. The Open Software Description (OSD) DTD is used strictly for describing software packages, so the chance that you'll want to embed an audio file in an OSD document is pretty slim. Knowing this, processors designed to work specifically with OSD probably won't know what to do with an audio file. When you include unparsed entities in your XML documents, always keep in mind the purpose and limitations of the DTD, as well as those of the associated XML processor.

Parameter Entities

A *parameter entity* is created as an alias for a group of elements—usually attributes or element content—that are used frequently within the DTD. Parameter entities are only allowed inside of the DTD subset and are reserved for use within the DTD to enhance organization and efficiency. Parameter entities differ from parsed entities and unparsed entities in that they are used only by the DTD—document authors never need to reference a parameter entity.

Parameter entities take a slightly different format than the entities we've seen so far. In addition to the name and content portions of the declaration, a percent sign (%) is also included before the entity name. An example of a parameter entity from the Novel DTD is:

```
<!ENTITY % phrasal "#PCDATA|emphasis">
```

The entity is invoked using the percent sign (instead of an ampersand) and its name is followed by a semicolon. Because parameter entities are reserved for use in the DTD, you will only see them included in other portions of the DTD. In the previous example, the parameter entity created an alias for a content model. Each time **%phrasal;** is included elsewhere in the DTD, it is an alias for the content model **#PCDATA|emphasis**, as shown in this element definition from the same DTD:

```
<!ELEMENT title (%phrasal;)*>
```

This element definition is the equivalent of:

```
<!ELEMENT title (#PCDATA|emphasis)*>
```

Because the phrasal content model is used repeatedly throughout the Novel DTD, it was more efficient to assign it to a parameter entity than to specify it multiple times.

Parameter entities can also be used to group frequently used attributes, as shown in this rather complex example from the TecML DTD. These entity declarations assign attributes to each entity name:

```
<!ENTITY % dictname '
        convention  CDATA      #IMPLIED
        dictname    CDATA      #IMPLIED
        '>

<!ENTITY % type '
        type        (%x.type;) #IMPLIED
        '>

<!ENTITY % fuzzy '
        fuzzy       (%x.fuzzy;) #IMPLIED
        '>

<!ENTITY % mime '
        mime        CDATA      #IMPLIED
        '>
```

```
<!ENTITY % targettype '
        targettype   CDATA        #IMPLIED
        '>


<!ENTITY % lang '
        lang         CDATA        #IMPLIED
        '>


<!ENTITY % units '
        units        CDATA        #IMPLIED
        '>
```

Parameter entities can also be included as content for other parameter entities, as the following example shows:

```
<!ENTITY % vararr '
        %dictname;
        %type;
        %fuzzy;
        %mime;
        %lang;
        %units;
        %targettype;
        '>
```

The parameter entity **vararr** includes the attributes for the seven previously defined parameter entities in one parameter entity. For an exercise in unpacking parameter entities nested within parameter entities, visit the XHTML 1.0 specification at **www.w3.org/TR/xhtml1/** at your leisure. This specification demonstrates masterful use of parameter entities in DTD organization.

Predefined Entities in XML

XML has five predefined entities that are native to its specification. These predefined entities are available to you when you're writing your XML-based DTD. You don't have to define these entities in your external or internal DTD subsets to use them. These entities are shown in Table 9.1.

Future XML editors should include support for predefined entities as well as extensive support for parsed, unparsed, and parameter entities. In a perfect world, the XML editors will be able to read a DTD and provide a pull-down list of entities, automatically replace text with predefined entities, and show warning messages when an entity referenced in a document isn't defined by the internal or external subsets of the DTD. In the Immediate Solutions section, we describe how two different XML editors handle entities.

Table 9.1   XML's predefined entities.

Character	Entity	Description
>	&gt;	Greater-than sign
<	&lt;	Less-than sign
&	&amp;	Ampersand
'	&apos;	Apostrophe
"	&quot;	Quotation mark

Common Entity Uses

As our descriptions of entities show, entities lend themselves to a variety of uses. We'll discuss some of the more practical uses in this section.

Aliasing Frequently Used Text and Markup

Frequently used text can include:

• Company and division names

• Document header and footer information

• Authorship attributions

• Other strings or blocks of text used more than once or twice in a document or set of documents

Frequently used markup (entities that include both text and markup) can include:

• Copyright information

• Document templates

• Press releases

• Product information

The benefits of using general entities in XML documents to represent frequently used bits of text and markup include:

• *Consistency*—Because it's declared as an entity, the text that replaces the entity name will be the same every time. Much human error is avoided using this method.

• *Changeability*—If a block of text or markup needs to be altered universally among a group of documents, it's much easier to change the content of an entity once and have the text automatically updated in every place the entity is referenced. If the text isn't referenced by an entity, each instance must be altered individually, which opens the door to missed and incorrectly changed text.

- *Efficiency*—It's much easier to type a short entity name than large amounts of text and markup. Using entities is also faster than cutting and pasting, and the text is altered more easily, as indicated in the preceding bullet point.

Any text or markup can be used as the content of a general entity. These entities can be stored internally for short snippets and externally for longer chunks of text and markup. As with any portion of an XML DTD or document, plan your general entities carefully to make sure your entities nest properly and don't violate the content models established in the DTD.

Including XML Documents within XML Documents

Lengthy documents are often easier to work with when they are split into a collection of smaller documents. By declaring the smaller documents as general entities in the larger, final document, each one is imported into the main document in place of its entity reference. A document created for the Novel DTD, darkness.xml, uses this approach to create one large document by embedding four smaller documents within it. The entities are defined like this:

```
<!ENTITY chapter.01
     PUBLIC "-//Megginson//TEXT Heart of Darkness, Chapter 1//EN"
     "chap01.xml">
<!ENTITY chapter.02
     PUBLIC "-//Megginson//TEXT Heart of Darkness, Chapter 2//EN"
     "chap02.xml">
<!ENTITY chapter.03
     PUBLIC "-//Megginson//TEXT Heart of Darkness, Chapter 3//EN"
     "chap03.xml">
<!ENTITY chapter.04
     PUBLIC "-//Megginson//TEXT Heart of Darkness, Chapter 4//EN"
     "chap04.xml">
```

The entities are then referenced in the body of the document using regular entity references, as follows:

```
<body>
&chapter.01;
&chapter.02;
&chapter.03;
&chapter.04;
</body>
```

When you use this method of document inclusion, remember that only the referring document can have a document type (DOCTYPE) declaration. The included files can only contain text and XML markup, or you'll have dueling internal DTD subsets to contend with, which will result in invalid files.

Organizing the DTD

As our example from the TecML DTD showed, entities—parameter entities specifically—can be used to help better organize a DTD and make it easier for humans to read. In addition, using parameter entities in a DTD has the same advantages as using parsed entities to represent text and markup in a document. Large content models and blocks of attributes that are frequently used in the DTD can be referenced quickly and can be altered and extended just as quickly.

Including Non-XML Resources

Because the world of information is not limited to text and markup, we need a way to include non-XML resources in XML documents. Unparsed entities provide this mechanism. Actually, they extend XML's support of resources to every possible file type. Although XML allows you to define any unparsed entity in the internal or external DTD subset, always remember that the XML processor must know what to do with the entity or its inclusion is useless. DTDs and applications should be clear about what type of entities they require and support, and document developers should keep the purpose and goals of the DTD and application firmly in mind when defining and referencing unparsed entities.

Although XML has changed the way developers look at markup, it hasn't changed bandwidth issues. Large files still take a long time to download over a network, regardless of which markup language you're using. Because XML supports file types, the temptation to embed unparsed entity after unparsed entity may be great. Always keep download time firmly in mind when you reference external entity files. The extensibility and functionality of XML will be irrelevant if users have to wait three hours to download all the files they need in a document set.

Representing Non-ASCII Characters

Although the use of the ASCII character set in markup ensures that XML documents will be portable from one computer to another—because ASCII is the universal language of computers—it somewhat limits the characters developers can use in their document creation. Although all the computers in the world speak ASCII, it's not sufficient to describe every resource in the world. To extend the character set available to XML documents, entities are used as aliases for special characters.

XML supports the ISO 10646 (Unicode) character-encoding scheme, which in turn supports a wide variety of character-encoding schemes. You can use a character's Unicode number or hexadecimal code to reference it, but we prefer to use standard character entity sets defined in the DTD instead. The Immediate Solutions sections on declaring text-encoding schemes and using character entities provide detailed information on extending your DTD and document character sets to support a wider variety of characters.

Immediate Solutions

Referencing Entities

Use this syntax to reference text and unparsed entities in an XML document:

```
&name;
```

For example, this entity

```
<!ENTITY mypict SYSTEM "graphics/mypict.gif" NDATA gif>
```

is referenced by:

```
&mypict;
```

Use this syntax to reference parameter entities in an XML DTD:

```
%name;
```

For example, this entity

```
<!ENTITY % DocBookDTD PUBLIC "-//OASIS//DTD DocBook XML V4.1.2//EN"
          "http://www.oasis-open.org/docbook/xml/4.0/docbookx.dtd">
```

is referenced by:

```
%DocBookDTD;
```

Declaring Internal Entities

An internal entity stores all information about an entity inside the entity's declaration statement. Internal entities can be declared in either the external or internal DTD subsets of a document and are used most often to define short parsed entities. Use the following syntax to declare internal entities:

```
<!ENTITY name "content">
```

As mentioned previously, the content must be enclosed within quotation marks, and each entity must have a name that is unique to both the internal and external subsets. If a name is used twice, the one listed last will have precedence over the one listed first. Examples of internal entities are as follows:

```
<!ENTITY html "Hypertext Markup Language (HTML)">
<!ENTITY xml "Extensible Markup Language (XML)">
<!ENTITY sgml "Standard Generalized Markup Language (SGML)">
```

This XML markup

```
The &html; was the first markup language to be implemented
by the masses. The &xml; bridges the gap between HTML and
the more complex &sgml;.
```

is the equivalent of:

```
The Hypertext Markup Language (HTML) was the first markup
language to be implemented by the masses. The Extensible
Markup Language (XML) bridges the gap between HTML and the more
complex Standard Generalized Markup Language (SGML).
```

Declaring External Entities

An external entity stores its name and a reference to another container—usually a file—that holds its contents. Use the following syntax to declare external entities:

```
<!ENTITY name (SYSTEM SystemId)|(PUBLIC PublicId SystemId)>
```

The inclusion of the **PUBLIC** or **SYSTEM** identifier differentiates an external entity from an internal one, and the content points to a file stored either on a local system or a well-archived public file, such as a public DTD.

For example, the following entity references the public version of the DocBook DTD:

```
<!ENTITY % DocBookDTD PUBLIC "-//OASIS//DTD DocBook XML V4.1.2//EN"
          "http://www.oasis-open.org/docbook/xml/4.0/docbookx.dtd">
```

This entity references a system version of the same file:

```
<!ENTITY % DocBookDTD SYSTEM "CML/docbookx.dtd">
```

9. Creating and
Including XML Entities

External entities with public identifiers don't usually provide exact file locations but do allow the processor to use the most easily accessible copy. By contrast, external entities with system identifiers must provide location-specific file names so the processor can locate the file.

Declaring Parsed Entities

Parsed entities can be defined as either internal or external entities. Any content referenced by a parsed entity is treated by the XML processor as XML content. To declare parsed entities, use either the internal or external declaration syntax:

```
<!ENTITY name "content">
<!ENTITY name (SYSTEM SystemId)|(PUBLIC PublicId SystemId)>
```

Parsed entities are the simplest form of XML entities and are used to reference non-ASCII characters, text strings, blocks of text, and marked-up text. An XML processor views the contents of a text declaration entity as a replacement for the entity references in the document.

Declaring Unparsed Entities

Unparsed entities are always defined as external entities, because their contents are always stored in external files and treated as non-XML content. Unparsed entity declarations must include a notation expression that describes what kind of resource the entity is referring to. Notations must also be declared elsewhere in the DTD in order for unparsed entities to be valid. The syntax for an unparsed entity is:

```
<!ENTITY name (SYSTEM SystemId)|(PUBLIC PublicId SystemId) NDATA datatype>
```

Without the **NDATA** identifier and a data type that matches a declared notation, the entity will be treated as a parsed entity. An example of an unparsed entity is:

```
<!ENTITY bp SYSTEM "docs/book-proposed.doc" NDATA DOC>
```

When you're working with unparsed entities, and entities in general, it's always important to remember that, for any entity to be referenced within an XML document, it must first be declared by an entity declaration. However, after an entity has been declared, it can be referenced as many times as needed. An entity that is declared in the external subset of a DTD can be referenced by all documents that reference the DTD, but an entity that is declared in the internal subset of a DTD can only be referenced by the document.

Creating Parameter Entities

Parameter entities are reserved for use within the DTD itself and are not used in documents created for any XML DTD or application. Parameter entities provide a simple alias for groups of frequently used content models or attribute groups. To include a parameter entity in a DTD, use the following syntax:

```
<!ENTITY % nnn "content model or attribute list">
```

A sample parameter entity from the TecML DTD is:

```
<!ENTITY % x.content  '(%x.descrip;, (array | xlist| xvar)*)' >
```

As this example shows, parameter entities can include other parameter entities in their content to create a nested effect that lends itself to clean and efficient DTD design. In a parameter entity, the single space to either side of the percent sign (%) is crucial. The spaces separate the sign from the entity declaration and the entity's name. If either space is missing, the entity will be invalid. To invoke a parameter entity within a DTD, simply use a percent sign (%) immediately followed by the entity's name and a semicolon (;), as shown here:

```
%x.content;
```

Including Parameter Entities in Content Models

Using parameter entities in the content models of an element can help make the element more manageable and less cumbersome. When parameter entities are included in an element's content model, they are prefaced by the percent sign (%) and followed by a semicolon (;), as shown in this syntax example:

```
<!ELEMENT NNN %entity-name;>
```

This sample code from the Novel DTD provides an example of a parameter entity included in a content model:

```
<!ELEMENT item (%phrasal;)*>
```

9. Creating and Including XML Entities

The previous code indicates that the **item** element can include any content defined by the **phrasal** parameter entity. If the **phrasal** parameter entity is defined as:

```
<ENTITY % phrasal "#PCDATA|emphasis">
```

the **item** element's content model can contain either character data or the **emphasis** element. In other words, the **item** element's content model is the same as if its declaration was:

```
<!ELEMENT item (#PCDATA|emphasis)*>
```

This may not seem very compelling, but let's look at a more complicated example— the Technical Markup Language (TecML). In this markup language, the content model for the **relation** element looks like this:

```
<!ELEMENT relation ((array | xvar), (array | xvar), %x.content;)>
```

The **relation** element's content model indicates that it may contain either an **array** or **xvar** element, twice in any order, followed by any other elements defined by the **x.content** parameter entity. The **x.content** parameter entity is defined as:

```
<!ENTITY % x.content '(%x.descrip;, (array | xlist | xvar )*)'>
```

As you can see, the **x.content** parameter entity contains an **x.descrip** parameter entity, which is defined as:

```
<!ENTITY % x.descrip '(xhtml?)'>
```

Therefore, the **x.content** parameter entity adds zero or more **array**, **xlist**, and **xvar** elements to the **relation** element's content model, as well as an optional **xhtml** element. If we put all of these together, the **relation** element's content model is written as:

```
<!ELEMENT relation ((array | xvar), (array | xvar), (xhtml?),
                    (array | xlist | xvar )*)>
```

Although this definition is not too long, other elements in the DTD may share many of the same parts of this content model. By using parameter entities to define commonly used parts of content models, you can reuse them across the DTD. In fact, as new DTDs are built upon an existing DTD, the new DTDs can reuse these parameter entities.

For example, the Chemical Markup Language (CML) and the Molecular Markup Language (MML) DTDs are based on the TecML specification. As a result, CML and MOL can use the **x.content** parameter entity in their content models.

Using Parameter Entities in Attribute List Declarations

In addition to their use in content models, parameter entities can be used in attribute list declarations to represent lists of frequently used attributes. To use a parameter entity in an attribute list declaration, you must first construct the parameter entity using this syntax:

```
<!ENTITY % entity-name 'attribute-specification
                        attribute-specification'>
```

The parameter entity can contain as many attribute specifications as desired; however, the entire group of attribute specifications must be enclosed by a pair of single quotation marks.

Each parameter entity may contain an attribute specification of any type or any combination of attribute specifications. Each attribute specification must adhere to the rules established for each different type of attribute. Parameter entities can also include other parameter entities.

After you define a parameter entity, you create an attribute list declaration using this syntax:

```
<!ATTLIST name %entity-name;>
```

More than one parameter entity can be used in an attribute list declaration, and parameter entities may be mixed with standard attribute specifications. For example, you can write:

```
<!ATTLIST name %entity-name;
               attribute-specification
               attribute-specification>
```

Parameter entities are useful for managing extensive and frequently used sets of attributes. In the MathML DTD, the **mtable** element provides a good example of how parameter entities may be used for attribute list declarations:

```
<!ATTLIST mtable %att-tableinfo;
                 %att-globalatts;>
```

If you look at the **att-globalatts** parameter entity, you find:

```
<!ENTITY % att-globalatts 'class CDATA #IMPLIED
                           style CDATA #IMPLIED
                           id    ID    #IMPLIED
                           other CDATA #IMPLIED'>
```

The **att-globalatts** parameter entity includes the **class**, **style**, **id**, and **other** attributes. These attributes are used frequently throughout the MathML DTD, so it's convenient to assign them to a parameter entity rather than list them for each of the many elements to which they're assigned.

If you look at the **att-tableinfo** parameter entity, you find:

```
<!ENTITY % att-tableinfo '%att-align;
                          %att-rowalign;
                          %att-columnalign;
                          %att-groupalign;
                          %att-alignmentscope;
                          %att-rowspacing;
                          %att-columnspacing;
                          %att-rowlines;
                          %att-columnlines;
                          %att-frame;
                          %att-framespacing;
                          %att-equalrows;
                          %att-equalcolumns;
                          %att-displaystyle;
                          '>
```

The **att-tableinfo** parameter actually consists of even more parameter entities. These parameter entities are declared using the following entity declarations:

```
<!ENTITY % att-align          'align CDATA #IMPLIED'>
<!ENTITY % att-rowalign       'rowalign CDATA #IMPLIED'>
<!ENTITY % att-columnalign    'columnalign CDATA #IMPLIED'>
<!ENTITY % att-groupalign     'groupalign CDATA #IMPLIED'>
<!ENTITY % att-alignmentscope 'alignmentscope CDATA #IMPLIED'>
<!ENTITY % att-rowspacing     'rowspacing CDATA #IMPLIED'>
<!ENTITY % att-columnspacing  'columnspacing CDATA #IMPLIED'>
<!ENTITY % att-rowlines       'rowlines CDATA #IMPLIED'>
<!ENTITY % att-columnlines    'columnlines CDATA #IMPLIED'>
<!ENTITY % att-frame          'frames (none | solid | dashed) #IMPLIED'>
<!ENTITY % att-framespacing   'framespacing CDATA #IMPLIED'>
<!ENTITY % att-equalrows      'equalrows CDATA #IMPLIED'>
<!ENTITY % att-equalcolumns   'equalcolumns CDATA #IMPLIED'>
<!ENTITY % att-displaystyle   'displaystyle (true | false) #IMPLIED'>
```

Although these single-line entities could have been declared as attribute specifications for the **att-tableinfo** parameter entity, they would have had to be declared again for any other element that used them. Instead, the use of the parameter entity means that these attributes can be used by any number of elements by simply including the name of the parameter entity. Doing so tends to make the DTD less error prone and more legible.

If you remove all the attribute specifications from the **att-tableinfo** and **att-globalinfo** parameter entity declarations and, instead, create a single attribute list declaration for the **mtable** element, it looks like this:

```
<!ATTLIST mtable
        class CDATA #IMPLIED
        style CDATA #IMPLIED
        id    ID    #IMPLIED
        other CDATA #IMPLIED
        align          CDATA #IMPLIED
        rowalign       CDATA #IMPLIED
        columnalign    CDATA #IMPLIED
        groupalign     CDATA #IMPLIED
        alignmentscope CDATA #IMPLIED
        rowspacing     CDATA #IMPLIED
        columnlines    CDATA #IMPLIED
        frame (none | solid | dashed) #IMPLIED
        framespacing   CDATA #IMPLIED
        equalrows      CDATA #IMPLIED
        equalcolumns   CDATA #IMPLIED
        displaystyle   CDATA #IMPLIED >
```

Declaring Notations

Notation declarations take a form similar to that of an external entity. The purpose of a notation is to help the XML processor deal with non-XML entities such as multimedia files and word-processing documents. Notations can be declared in either the internal or external subset of the document's DTD. Use this syntax to declare notations:

```
<!NOTATION name (PUBLIC|SYSTEM) "location">
```

A notation that links Microsoft Word to the **doc** data type might look like this:

```
<!NOTATION doc SYSTEM
"program_files/microsoft_office/office/winword.exe">
```

The notation declaration is the only place in XML where you're allowed to use a public identifier without providing a URI as well. For example,

```
<!NOTATION gif PUBLIC "-//CompuServe//NOTATION Graphics Interchange
                        Format 89a//EN">
```

The XML specification is flexible enough to allow XML processors to treat unparsed entities in any way necessary, which means that the processor doesn't necessarily have to view the entity in the application referenced by the notation. The processor might just use the referenced application to provide a general idea of how the resource should be treated if it has its own built-in mechanism for handling the file. Alternately, users might be able to specify how certain entities are processed and thus override the notation references entirely.

Declaring a Text-Encoding Scheme for Entities

Because XML supports Unicode, a variety of encoding schemes are available to DTD and document developers alike—including 8-bit, 16-bit, and 32-bit character encoding. The encoding scheme used in a particular document or DTD affects how non-ASCII characters are referenced using their Unicode decimal or hexadecimal code. If 8-bit encoding is specified and an entity declaration uses 16-bit encoding in its content, the XML processor might not be able to implement the entity when it's referenced.

A parsed entity must declare and adhere to a single encoding scheme, but that doesn't mean several external parsed entities, each with its own encoding scheme, can't be referenced by a single XML document. Using entities to represent large chunks of text or markup can be beneficial in this situation. Blocks of text that need more advanced encoding systems, such as 16- or 32-bit, can utilize entities; but those that only require 8-bit encoding do not have to. This arrangement makes for the most efficient use of character encoding. The more bits the encoding system includes, the more characters can be generated. However, the larger encoding systems also create large files that take more time to download.

In addition, if you need only a few of the 16- or 32-bit characters, you can reference them in individual character references and use the smaller 8-bit encoding system for the entire document. For example, if you need to use the Cyrillic letter "palochak" in your document—but no other Cyrillic letters—it's easiest and most efficient to create a character entity reference that includes the letter's Unicode hexadecimal number (**04C0**) preceded by **&#x** and followed by a semicolon, as shown here:

```
&#x04C0;
```

The default encoding scheme assumed by XML processors is ISO 10646 UTF-8, which is 8-bit character encoding. To declare otherwise, you need to use a *text declaration* that defines the character-encoding scheme your document uses. Its syntax is:

```
<?xml encoding="scheme name" ?>
```

A few examples of character-encoding scheme names include:

- UTF-8
- UTF-16
- ISO-10646-UCS-2
- ISO-10646-UCS-4
- ISO-8859-1 to -9
- ISO-2022-JP
- Shift_JIS
- EUC-JP

The Novel DTD includes this XML declaration:

```
<?xml version="1.0" encoding="UTF-8" standalone="no"?>
```

This example combines version and standalone information with encoding information, which is an effective and efficient way to provide three important pieces of information about the document to the XML processor at once.

The world of Unicode is so complex that it's not supported by HTML yet, but it may possibly be in the future. Unicode covers a wide variety of languages (human and scientific alike)—including Cyrillic, Greek, Thai, and Box Drawing—and a two-volume book has been written about it. For more information on Unicode, including charts and glyphs of characters and their hexadecimal codes, visit the Unicode site at **www.unicode.org**.

Using Character Entities in XML Documents

Character entity sets are large groups of general entities created to display non-standard characters in markup languages. Anyone familiar with HTML has used a character entity from one of these sets at least once in their coding career. Because Unicode is so complex and many developers would like to keep their documents within the 8-bit encoding system (and to help XML degrade gracefully to HTML), it's often useful to use the established ISO-Latin-1 character encoding sets—as well as a few others that are standard in HTML 4—with XML DTDs and documents. XML does not include native support for these specific entities. If you want to take advantage of a character set's entities, you must use a regular parsed entity declaration to reference them in the DTD. You don't have to include all the entities; just the ones you think you'll need. You can also store them all in easily accessible external files and make a habit of referencing them in your DTDs; therefore, you'll have a familiar and easy way to include nonstandard characters in your documents.

The remainder of projects in this section are devoted to listings of five useful character sets, including:

- The ISO-Latin-1 character set
- A mathematical character set
- The Greek letter character set
- The miscellaneous technical character set
- The miscellaneous symbol character set

These five character sets are part of HTML 4, but they certainly aren't the only entity sets you can include in your documents. They include some of the most commonly used non-ASCII characters, as well as some useful math symbols and Greek letters. For each set, we've included the complete Unicode entity declaration list followed by a table that shows each character, the numeric and/or character entity you can use to embed the character in a document, and a description of the character. (Listing 9.1 includes the ISO-Latin-1 character entity set, and Table 9.2 lists the ISO-Latin-1 character set. Listing 9.2 includes the mathematical, Greek, and miscellaneous character entity sets. Table 9.3 lists the mathematical character set, Table 9.4 lists the Greek character set, Table 9.5 lists the miscellaneous technical character set, and Table 9.6 lists the miscellaneous symbols character set.) Each entity declaration set includes a section on how to use an external entity declaration with a public identifier to reference the entity set, as seen in this example:

```
<!ENTITY % HTMLlat1 PUBLIC "ISO 8879-1986//ENTITIES Added
    Latin 1//EN//XML" "ents/iso-lat1.ent">
```

If you don't want to use a public identifier to reference an entire set of entity declarations, you can choose only those that you need, save them as internal entities or in a separate file, and reference them as an external parsed entity with a system identifier.

Using the ISO-Latin-1 Character Entity Set

The most common special characters are defined in the ISO-Latin-1 character set, shown in Listing 9.1. This character set includes common punctuation marks and frequently used symbols, such as the copyright and trademark indicators. The character set also contains entities for referencing accented characters in both lowercase and uppercase, as well as ligatures important to languages such as Spanish and German that use the Latin character set. The characters are shown in Table 9.2.

Listing 9.1   The ISO-Latin-1 character entity set.

```
<!-- Portions (C) International Organization for Standardization 1986
     Permission to copy in any form is granted for use with
     conforming SGML systems and applications as defined in
     ISO 8879, provided this notice is included in all copies.
-->
<!-- Character entity set. Typical invocation:
    <!ENTITY % HTMLlat1 PUBLIC
       "-//W3C//ENTITIES Latin 1 for XHTML//EN"
       "http://www.w3.org/TR/xhtml1/DTD/xhtml-lat1.ent">
    %HTMLlat1;-->

<!ENTITY nbsp    " "> <!-- no-break space = non-breaking space,
                                U+00A0 ISOnum -->
<!ENTITY iexcl   "&#161;"> <!-- inverted exclamation mark, U+00A1 ISOnum -->
<!ENTITY cent    "&#162;"> <!-- cent sign, U+00A2 ISOnum -->
<!ENTITY pound   "&#163;"> <!-- pound sign, U+00A3 ISOnum -->
<!ENTITY curren  "&#164;"> <!-- currency sign, U+00A4 ISOnum -->
<!ENTITY yen     "&#165;"> <!-- yen sign = yuan sign, U+00A5 ISOnum -->
<!ENTITY brvbar  "&#166;"> <!-- broken bar = broken vertical bar,
                                U+00A6 ISOnum -->
<!ENTITY sect    "&#167;"> <!-- section sign, U+00A7 ISOnum -->
<!ENTITY uml     "&#168;"> <!-- diaeresis = spacing diaeresis,
                                U+00A8 ISOdia -->
<!ENTITY copy    "&#169;"> <!-- copyright sign, U+00A9 ISOnum -->
<!ENTITY ordf    "&#170;"> <!-- feminine ordinal indicator,
                                U+00AA ISOnum -->
<!ENTITY laquo   "&#171;"> <!-- left-pointing double angle quotation mark
                                = left pointing guillemet,
                                U+00AB ISOnum -->
```

```
<!ENTITY not      "&#172;"> <!-- not sign = discretionary hyphen,
                                    U+00AC ISOnum -->
<!ENTITY shy      "&#173;"> <!-- soft hyphen = discretionary hyphen,
                                    U+00AD ISOnum -->
<!ENTITY reg      "&#174;"> <!-- registered sign = registered
                                 trade mark sign, U+00AE ISOnum -->
<!ENTITY macr     "&#175;"> <!-- macron = spacing macron = overline
                                    = APL overbar, U+00AF ISOdia -->
<!ENTITY deg      "&#176;"> <!-- degree sign, U+00B0 ISOnum -->
<!ENTITY plusmn   "&#177;"> <!-- plus-minus sign = plus-or-minus sign,
                                    U+00B1 ISOnum -->
<!ENTITY sup2     "&#178;"> <!-- superscript two = superscript digit two
                                    = squared, U+00B2 ISOnum -->
<!ENTITY sup3     "&#179;"> <!-- superscript three = superscript digit three
                                    = cubed, U+00B3 ISOnum -->
<!ENTITY acute    "&#180;"> <!-- acute accent = spacing acute,
                                    U+00B4 ISOdia -->
<!ENTITY micro    "&#181;"> <!-- micro sign, U+00B5 ISOnum -->
<!ENTITY para     "&#182;"> <!-- pilcrow sign = paragraph sign,
                                    U+00B6 ISOnum -->
<!ENTITY middot   "&#183;"> <!-- middle dot = Georgian comma
                                    = Greek middle dot, U+00B7 ISOnum -->
<!ENTITY cedil    "&#184;"> <!-- cedilla = spacing cedilla, U+00B8 ISOdia -->
<!ENTITY sup1     "&#185;"> <!-- superscript one = superscript digit one,
                                    U+00B9 ISOnum -->
<!ENTITY ordm     "&#186;"> <!-- masculine ordinal indicator,
                                    U+00BA ISOnum -->
<!ENTITY raquo    "&#187;"> <!-- right-pointing double angle quotation mark
                                    = right pointing guillemet,
                                      U+00BB ISOnum -->
<!ENTITY frac14   "&#188;"> <!-- vulgar fraction one quarter
                                    = fraction one quarter, U+00BC ISOnum -->
<!ENTITY frac12   "&#189;"> <!-- vulgar fraction one half
                                    = fraction one half, U+00BD ISOnum -->
<!ENTITY frac34   "&#190;"> <!-- vulgar fraction three quarters
                                    = fraction three quarters,
                                      U+00BE ISOnum -->
<!ENTITY iquest   "&#191;"> <!-- inverted question mark
                                    = turned question mark, U+00BF ISOnum -->
<!ENTITY Agrave   "&#192;"> <!-- latin capital letter A with grave
                                    = latin capital letter A grave,
                                      U+00C0 ISOlat1 -->
<!ENTITY Aacute   "&#193;"> <!-- latin capital letter A with acute,
                                    U+00C1 ISOlat1 -->
<!ENTITY Acirc    "&#194;"> <!-- latin capital letter A with circumflex,
                                    U+00C2 ISOlat1 -->
```

```
<!ENTITY Atilde "&#195;"> <!-- latin capital letter A with tilde,
                                  U+00C3 ISOlat1 -->
<!ENTITY Auml   "&#196;"> <!-- latin capital letter A with diaeresis,
                                  U+00C4 ISOlat1 -->
<!ENTITY Aring  "&#197;"> <!-- latin capital letter A with ring above
                                = latin capital letter A ring,
                                  U+00C5 ISOlat1 -->
<!ENTITY AElig  "&#198;"> <!-- latin capital letter AE
                                = latin capital ligature AE,
                                  U+00C6 ISOlat1 -->
<!ENTITY Ccedil "&#199;"> <!-- latin capital letter C with cedilla,
                                  U+00C7 ISOlat1 -->
<!ENTITY Egrave "&#200;"> <!-- latin capital letter E with grave,
                                  U+00C8 ISOlat1 -->
<!ENTITY Eacute "&#201;"> <!-- latin capital letter E with acute,
                                  U+00C9 ISOlat1 -->
<!ENTITY Ecirc  "&#202;"> <!-- latin capital letter E with circumflex,
                                  U+00CA ISOlat1 -->
<!ENTITY Euml   "&#203;"> <!-- latin capital letter E with diaeresis,
                                  U+00CB ISOlat1 -->
<!ENTITY Igrave "&#204;"> <!-- latin capital letter I with grave,
                                  U+00CC ISOlat1 -->
<!ENTITY Iacute "&#205;"> <!-- latin capital letter I with acute,
                                  U+00CD ISOlat1 -->
<!ENTITY Icirc  "&#206;"> <!-- latin capital letter I with circumflex,
                                  U+00CE ISOlat1 -->
<!ENTITY Iuml   "&#207;"> <!-- latin capital letter I with diaeresis,
                                  U+00CF ISOlat1 -->
<!ENTITY ETH    "&#208;"> <!-- latin capital letter ETH, U+00D0 ISOlat1 -->
<!ENTITY Ntilde "&#209;"> <!-- latin capital letter N with tilde,
                                  U+00D1 ISOlat1 -->
<!ENTITY Ograve "&#210;"> <!-- latin capital letter O with grave,
                                  U+00D2 ISOlat1 -->
<!ENTITY Oacute "&#211;"> <!-- latin capital letter O with acute,
                                  U+00D3 ISOlat1 -->
<!ENTITY Ocirc  "&#212;"> <!-- latin capital letter O with circumflex,
                                  U+00D4 ISOlat1 -->
<!ENTITY Otilde "&#213;"> <!-- latin capital letter O with tilde,
                                  U+00D5 ISOlat1 -->
<!ENTITY Ouml   "&#214;"> <!-- latin capital letter O with diaeresis,
                                  U+00D6 ISOlat1 -->
<!ENTITY times  "&#215;"> <!-- multiplication sign, U+00D7 ISOnum -->
<!ENTITY Oslash "&#216;"> <!-- latin capital letter O with stroke
                                = latin capital letter O slash,
                                  U+00D8 ISOlat1 -->
<!ENTITY Ugrave "&#217;"> <!-- latin capital letter U with grave,
                                  U+00D9 ISOlat1 -->
```

```
<!ENTITY Uacute "&#218;"> <!-- latin capital letter U with acute,
                                U+00DA ISOlat1 -->
<!ENTITY Ucirc  "&#219;"> <!-- latin capital letter U with circumflex,
                                U+00DB ISOlat1 -->
<!ENTITY Uuml   "&#220;"> <!-- latin capital letter U with diaeresis,
                                U+00DC ISOlat1 -->
<!ENTITY Yacute "&#221;"> <!-- latin capital letter Y with acute,
                                U+00DD ISOlat1 -->
<!ENTITY THORN  "&#222;"> <!-- latin capital letter THORN,
                                U+00DE ISOlat1 -->
<!ENTITY szlig  "&#223;"> <!-- latin small letter sharp s = ess-zed,
                                U+00DF ISOlat1 -->
<!ENTITY agrave "&#224;"> <!-- latin small letter a with grave
                              = latin small letter a grave,
                                U+00E0 ISOlat1 -->
<!ENTITY aacute "&#225;"> <!-- latin small letter a with acute,
                                U+00E1 ISOlat1 -->
<!ENTITY acirc  "&#226;"> <!-- latin small letter a with circumflex,
                                U+00E2 ISOlat1 -->
<!ENTITY atilde "&#227;"> <!-- latin small letter a with tilde,
                                U+00E3 ISOlat1 -->
<!ENTITY auml   "&#228;"> <!-- latin small letter a with diaeresis,
                                U+00E4 ISOlat1 -->
<!ENTITY aring  "&#229;"> <!-- latin small letter a with ring above
                              = latin small letter a ring,
                                U+00E5 ISOlat1 -->
<!ENTITY aelig  "&#230;"> <!-- latin small letter ae
                              = latin small ligature ae,
                                U+00E6 ISOlat1 -->
<!ENTITY ccedil "&#231;"> <!-- latin small letter c with cedilla,
                                U+00E7 ISOlat1 -->
<!ENTITY egrave "&#232;"> <!-- latin small letter e with grave,
                                U+00E8 ISOlat1 -->
<!ENTITY eacute "&#233;"> <!-- latin small letter e with acute,
                                U+00E9 ISOlat1 -->
<!ENTITY ecirc  "&#234;"> <!-- latin small letter e with circumflex,
                                U+00EA ISOlat1 -->
<!ENTITY euml   "&#235;"> <!-- latin small letter e with diaeresis,
                                U+00EB ISOlat1 -->
<!ENTITY igrave "&#236;"> <!-- latin small letter i with grave,
                                U+00EC ISOlat1 -->
<!ENTITY iacute "&#237;"> <!-- latin small letter i with acute,
                                U+00ED ISOlat1 -->
<!ENTITY icirc  "&#238;"> <!-- latin small letter i with circumflex,
                                U+00EE ISOlat1 -->
```

```
<!ENTITY iuml    "&#239;"> <!-- latin small letter i with diaeresis,
                                U+00EF ISOlat1 -->
<!ENTITY eth     "&#240;"> <!-- latin small letter eth, U+00F0 ISOlat1 -->
<!ENTITY ntilde "&#241;"> <!-- latin small letter n with tilde,
                                U+00F1 ISOlat1 -->
<!ENTITY ograve "&#242;"> <!-- latin small letter o with grave,
                                U+00F2 ISOlat1 -->
<!ENTITY oacute "&#243;"> <!-- latin small letter o with acute,
                                U+00F3 ISOlat1 -->
<!ENTITY ocirc   "&#244;"> <!-- latin small letter o with circumflex,
                                U+00F4 ISOlat1 -->
<!ENTITY otilde "&#245;"> <!-- latin small letter o with tilde,
                                U+00F5 ISOlat1 -->
<!ENTITY ouml    "&#246;"> <!-- latin small letter o with diaeresis,
                                U+00F6 ISOlat1 -->
<!ENTITY divide "&#247;"> <!-- division sign, U+00F7 ISOnum -->
<!ENTITY oslash "&#248;"> <!-- latin small letter o with stroke,
                                = latin small letter o slash,
                                U+00F8 ISOlat1 -->
<!ENTITY ugrave "&#249;"> <!-- latin small letter u with grave,
                                U+00F9 ISOlat1 -->
<!ENTITY uacute "&#250;"> <!-- latin small letter u with acute,
                                U+00FA ISOlat1 -->
<!ENTITY ucirc   "&#251;"> <!-- latin small letter u with circumflex,
                                U+00FB ISOlat1 -->
<!ENTITY uuml    "&#252;"> <!-- latin small letter u with diaeresis,
                                U+00FC ISOlat1 -->
<!ENTITY yacute "&#253;"> <!-- latin small letter y with acute,
                                U+00FD ISOlat1 -->
<!ENTITY thorn   "&#254;"> <!-- latin small letter thorn with,
                                U+00FE ISOlat1 -->
<!ENTITY yuml    "&#255;"> <!-- latin small letter y with diaeresis,
                                U+00FF ISOlat1 -->
```

Table 9.2   The ISO-Latin-1 character set.

Character	Character Entity	Numeric Entity	Description
		&#00; through &#08;	Unused
		&#09;	Horizontal tab
		&#10;	Line feed
		&#11; through &#31;	Unused
	&space;	&#32;	Space
!	&exclam;	&#33;	Exclamation mark

(continued)

9. Creating and Including XML Entities

233

Table 9.2   The ISO-Latin-1 character set *(continued).*

Character	Character Entity	Numeric Entity	Description
"	&quot;	&#34;	Quotation mark
#	&hash;	&#35;	Number
$	&dlr;	&#36;	Dollar
%	&pct;	&#37;	Percent
&	&amp;	&#38;	Ampersand
'	&apos;	&#39;	Apostrophe
(	&lparen;	&#40;	Left parenthesis
)	&rparen;	&#41;	Right parenthesis
*	&ast;	&#42;	Asterisk
+	&plus;	&#43;	Plus
,	&comma;	&#44;	Comma
-	&hyph;	&#45;	Hyphen
.	&per;	&#46;	Period (full stop)
/	&fwsl;	&#47;	Slash
0 through 9	&d0; through &d9;	0 through 9	Digits 0 through 9
:	&colon;	&#58;	Colon
;	&semi;	&#59;	Semicolon
<	&lt;	&#60;	Less than
=	&eq;	&#61;	Equals
>	&gt;	&#62;	Greater than
?	&ques;	&#63;	Question mark
@	&at;	&#64;	Commercial at
A through Z		A through Z	Letters A through Z (capitals)
[	&lsq;	&#91;	Left square bracket
\	&bksl;	&#92;	Reverse solidus (backslash)
]	&rsq;	&#93;	Right square bracket
^	&crt;	&#94;	Caret
_	&hbar;	&#95;	Horizontal bar
`	&grav;	&#96;	Grave accent
a through z		a through z	Letters a through z (lowercase)
{	&lcb;	&#123;	Left curly brace
|	&vbar;	&#124;	Vertical bar
}	&rcb;	&#125;	Right curly brace

(continued)

Table 9.2   The ISO-Latin-1 character set *(continued)*.

Character	Character Entity	Numeric Entity	Description
~	&til;	~	Tilde
		&#127; through	Unused
¡	&ixl;	¡	Inverted exclamation mark
¢	&cnt;	¢	Cent
£	&lbs;	£	Pound sterling
¤	&cur;	¤	General currency
¥	¥	¥	Yen
¦	&bvb;	¦	Broken vertical bar
§	&sec;	§	Section
¨	¨	¨	Umlaut (dieresis)
©	&cpy;	©	Copyright
ª	&for;	ª	Feminine ordinal
«	&glf;	«	Left angle quote, guillemet, left
¬	¬	¬	Not
	­	­	Soft hyphen
®	&trd;	®	Registered trademark
¯	&mac;	¯	Macron accent
°	°	°	Degree
±	&plm;	±	Plus or minus
²	&s2;	²	Superscript two
³	&s3;	³	Superscript three
´	&acc;	´	Acute accent
µ	&mic;	µ	Micro
¶	∥	¶	Paragraph
·	&mdt;	·	Middle dot
¸	&ced;	¸	Cedilla
¹	&s1;	¹	Superscript one
º	&mor;	º	Masculine ordinal
»	&glr;	»	Right angle quote, guillemet, right
¼	&f4;	¼	Fraction one-fourth
½	&f2;	½	Fraction one-half
¾	&f34;	¾	Fraction three-fourths
¿	&iqm;	¿	Inverted question mark

(continued)

Table 9.2   The ISO-Latin-1 character set *(continued)*.

Character	Character Entity	Numeric Entity	Description
À	&Agrave;	&#192;	Capital A, grave accent
Á	&Aacute;	&#193;	Capital A, acute accent
Â	&Acirc;	&#194;	Capital A, circumflex accent
Ã	&Atilde;	&#195;	Capital A, tilde
Ä	&Auml;	&#196;	Capital A, dieresis or umlaut
Å	&Aring;	&#197;	Capital A, ring
Æ	&AElig;	&#198;	Capital AE, diphthong (ligature)
Ç	&Ccedil;	&#199;	Capital C, cedilla
È	&Egrave;	&#200;	Capital E, grave accent
É	&Eacute;	&#201;	Capital E, acute accent
Ê	&Ecirc;	&#202;	Capital E, circumflex accent
Ë	&Euml;	&#203;	Capital E, dieresis or umlaut
Ì	&Igrave;	&#204;	Capital I, grave accent
Í	&Iacute;	&#205;	Capital I, acute accent
Î	&Icirc;	&#206;	Capital I, circumflex accent
Ï	&Iuml;	&#207;	Capital I, dieresis or umlaut
Ð	&ETH;	&#208;	Capital ETH, Icelandic
Ñ	&Ntilde;	&#209;	Capital N, tilde
Ò	&Ograve;	&#210;	Capital O, grave accent
Ó	&Oacute;	&#211;	Capital O, acute accent
Ô	&Ocirc;	&#212;	Capital O, circumflex accent
Õ	&Otilde;	&#213;	Capital O, tilde
Ö	&Ouml;	&#214;	Capital O, dieresis or umlaut
×	&times;	&#215;	Multiply
Ø	&Oslash;	&#216;	Capital O, slash
Ù	&Ugrave;	&#217;	Capital U, grave accent
Ú	&Uacute;	&#218;	Capital U, acute accent
Û	&Ucirc;	&#219;	Capital U, circumflex accent
Ü	&Uuml;	&#220;	Capital U, dieresis or umlaut
Ý	&Yacute;	&#221;	Capital Y, acute accent
ß	&szlig;	&#223;	Small sharp s, German (sz ligature)
à	&agrave;	&#224;	Small a, grave accent
á	&aacute;	&#225;	Small a, acute accent

(continued)

Table 9.2   The ISO-Latin-1 character set *(continued)*.

Character	Character Entity	Numeric Entity	Description
â	&acirc;	&#226;	Small a, circumflex accent
ã	&atilde;	&#227;	Small a, tilde
ä	&auml;	&#228;	Small a, dieresis or umlaut
å	&aring;	&#229;	Small a, ring
æ	&aelig;	&#230;	Small ae, diphthong (ligature)
ç	&ccedil;	&#231;	Small c, cedilla
è	&egrave;	&#232;	Small e, grave accent
é	&eacute;	&#233;	Small e, acute accent
ê	&ecirc;	&#234;	Small e, circumflex accent
ë	&euml;	&#235;	Small e, dieresis or umlaut
ì	&igrave;	&#236;	Small i, grave accent
í	&iacute;	&#237;	Small i, acute accent
î	&icirc;	&#238;	Small i, circumflex accent
ï	&iuml;	&#239;	Small i, dieresis or umlaut
_	&eth;	&#240;	Small eth, Icelandic
ñ	&ntilde;	&#241;	Small n, tilde
ò	&ograve;	&#242;	Small o, grave accent
ó	&oacute;	&#243;	Small o, acute accent
ô	&ocirc;	&#244;	Small o, circumflex accent
õ	&otilde;	&#245;	Small o, tilde
ö	&ouml;	&#246;	Small o, dieresis or umlaut
÷	&divide;	&#247;	Division
ø	&oslash;	&#248;	Small o, slash
ù	&ugrave;	&#249;	Small u, grave accent
ú	&uacute;	&#250;	Small u, acute accent
û	&ucirc;	&#251;	Small u, circumflex accent
ü	&uuml;	&#252;	Small u, dieresis or umlaut
ý	&yacute;	&#253;	Small y, acute accent
þ	&thorn;	&#254;	Small thorn, Icelandic
ÿ	&yuml;	&#255;	Small y, dieresis or umlaut

Using Math, Greek, and Miscellaneous Character Entity Sets

The math, Greek, and miscellaneous character sets allow authors to include mathematical and scientific notation in their documents without having to resort to the overkill of the MathML or CML vocabularies. Although you can use these entities to toss assorted mathematical operators and Greek letters into the fray, they don't provide a way to describe mathematical or scientific notation. If you need advanced notation capabilities, consider using a graphic of the notation or working with one of the newly developed vocabularies that specialize in advanced notation. Listing 9.2 shows the mathematical, Greek, and miscellaneous character entity sets. Table 9.3 lists the mathematical character set, Table 9.4 lists the Greek character set, and Tables 9.5 and 9.6 lists the miscellaneous character sets.

Listing 9.2   The mathematical, Greek, and miscellaneous character entity sets.

```
<!-- Mathematical, Greek and Symbolic characters for HTML -->
<!-- Character entity set. Typical invocation:
<!ENTITY % HTMLsymbol PUBLIC
"-//W3C//ENTITIES Symbolic//EN//HTML">
%HTMLsymbol; -->


<!-- Portions © International Organization for Standardization 1986:
Permission to copy in any form is granted for use with
conforming SGML systems and applications as defined in
ISO 8879, provided this notice is included in all copies.-->


<!-- Relevant ISO entity set is given unless names are newly introduced.
New names (i.e., not in ISO 8879 list) do not clash with any
existing ISO 8879 entity names. ISO 10646 character numbers
are given for each character, in hex. CDATA values are decimal
conversions of the ISO 10646 values and refer to the document
character set. Names are Unicode 2.0 names. -->


<!-- Latin Extended-B -->
<!ENTITY fnof      CDATA "&#402;" -- latin small f with hook =
     function= florin-->


<!-- Greek -->
<!ENTITY Alpha     CDATA "&#913;" -- greek capital letter alpha-->
<!ENTITY Beta      CDATA "&#914;" -- greek capital letter beta-->
<!ENTITY Gamma     CDATA "&#915;" -- greek capital letter gamma-->
<!ENTITY Delta     CDATA "&#916;" -- greek capital letter delta-->
<!ENTITY Epsilon   CDATA "&#917;" -- greek capital letter epsilon-->
<!ENTITY Zeta      CDATA "&#918;" -- greek capital letter zeta-->
<!ENTITY Eta       CDATA "&#919;" -- greek capital letter eta-->
<!ENTITY Theta     CDATA "&#920;" -- greek capital letter theta-->
```

```
<!ENTITY Iota     CDATA "&#921;" -- greek capital letter iota-->
<!ENTITY Kappa    CDATA "&#922;" -- greek capital letter kappa-->
<!ENTITY Lambda   CDATA "&#923;" -- greek capital letter lambda-->
<!ENTITY Mu       CDATA "&#924;" -- greek capital letter mu -->
<!ENTITY Nu       CDATA "&#925;" -- greek capital letter nu -->
<!ENTITY Xi       CDATA "&#926;" -- greek capital letter xi-->
<!ENTITY Omicron  CDATA "&#927;" -- greek capital letter omicron-->
<!ENTITY Pi       CDATA "&#928;" -- greek capital letter pi-->
<!ENTITY Rho      CDATA "&#929;" -- greek capital letter rho-->
<!-- there is no Sigmaf, and no U+03A2 character either -->
<!ENTITY Sigma    CDATA "&#931;" -- greek capital letter sigma-->
<!ENTITY Tau      CDATA "&#932;" -- greek capital letter tau-->
<!ENTITY Upsilon  CDATA "&#933;" -- greek capital letter upsilon-->
<!ENTITY Phi      CDATA "&#934;" -- greek capital letter phi-->
<!ENTITY Chi      CDATA "&#935;" -- greek capital letter chi-->
<!ENTITY Psi      CDATA "&#936;" -- greek capital letter psi-->
<!ENTITY Omega    CDATA "&#937;" -- greek capital letter omega-->
<!ENTITY alpha    CDATA "&#945;" -- greek small letter alpha-->
<!ENTITY beta     CDATA "&#946;" -- greek small letter beta-->
<!ENTITY gamma    CDATA "&#947;" -- greek small letter gamma-->
<!ENTITY delta    CDATA "&#948;" -- greek small letter delta-->
<!ENTITY epsilon  CDATA "&#949;" -- greek small letter epsilon -->
<!ENTITY zeta     CDATA "&#950;" -- greek small letter zeta-->
<!ENTITY eta      CDATA "&#951;" -- greek small letter eta-->
<!ENTITY theta    CDATA "&#952;" -- greek small letter theta-->
<!ENTITY iota     CDATA "&#953;" -- greek small letter iota-->
<!ENTITY kappa    CDATA "&#954;" -- greek small letter kappa-->
<!ENTITY lambda   CDATA "&#955;" -- greek small letter lambda-->
<!ENTITY mu       CDATA "&#956;" -- greek small letter mu-->
<!ENTITY nu       CDATA "&#957;" -- greek small letter nu-->
<!ENTITY xi       CDATA "&#958;" -- greek small letter xi-->
<!ENTITY omicron  CDATA "&#959;" -- greek small letter omicron-->
<!ENTITY pi       CDATA "&#960;" -- greek small letter pi-->
<!ENTITY rho      CDATA "&#961;" -- greek small letter rho -->
<!ENTITY sigmaf   CDATA "&#962;" -- greek small letter final sigma-->
<!ENTITY sigma    CDATA "&#963;" -- greek small letter sigma-->
<!ENTITY tau      CDATA "&#964;" -- greek small letter tau-->
<!ENTITY upsilon  CDATA "&#965;" -- greek small letter upsilon-->
<!ENTITY phi      CDATA "&#966;" -- greek small letter phi-->
<!ENTITY chi      CDATA "&#967;" -- greek small letter chi-->
<!ENTITY psi      CDATA "&#968;" -- greek small letter psi-->
<!ENTITY omega    CDATA "&#969;" -- greek small letter omega-->
<!ENTITY thetasym CDATA "&#977;" -- greek small letter theta symbol-->
<!ENTITY upsih    CDATA "&#978;" -- greek upsilon with hook symbol-->
<!ENTITY piv      CDATA "&#982;" -- greek pi symbol -->
```

```
<!-- Mathematical Operators -->
<!ENTITY forall   CDATA "&#8704;" -- for all -->
<!ENTITY part     CDATA "&#8706;" -- partial differential-->
<!ENTITY exist    CDATA "&#8707;" -- there exists, U+2203 ISOtech -->
<!ENTITY empty    CDATA "&#8709;" -- empty set = null set = diameter-->
<!ENTITY nabla    CDATA "&#8711;" -- nabla = backward difference-->
<!ENTITY isin     CDATA "&#8712;" -- element of -->
<!ENTITY notin    CDATA "&#8713;" -- not an element of-->
<!ENTITY ni       CDATA "&#8715;" -- contains as member-->
<!ENTITY prod     CDATA "&#8719;" -- n-ary product = product sign-->
<!-- prod is NOT the same character as U+03A0 'greek capital letter pi'
 though the same glyph might be used for both -->
<!ENTITY sum      CDATA "&#8721;" -- n-ary sumation -->
<!-- sum is NOT the same character as U+03A3 'greek capital letter sigma'
though the same glyph might be used for both -->
<!ENTITY minus    CDATA "&#8722;" -- minus sign -->
<!ENTITY lowast   CDATA "&#8727;" -- asterisk operator-->
<!ENTITY radic    CDATA "&#8730;" -- square root = radical sign -->
<!ENTITY prop     CDATA "&#8733;" -- proportional to -->
<!ENTITY infin    CDATA "&#8734;" -- infinity-->
<!ENTITY ang      CDATA "&#8736;" -- angle-->
<!ENTITY and      CDATA "&#8743;" -- logical and = wedge-->
<!ENTITY or       CDATA "&#8744;" -- logical or = vee-->
<!ENTITY cap      CDATA "&#8745;" -- intersection = cap-->
<!ENTITY cup      CDATA "&#8746;" -- union = cup-->
<!ENTITY int      CDATA "&#8747;" -- integral-->
<!ENTITY there4   CDATA "&#8756;" -- therefore-->
<!ENTITY sim      CDATA "&#8764;" -- tilde operator
                   = varies with = similar to-->
<!-- tilde operator is NOT the same character as the tilde -->
<!ENTITY cong     CDATA "&#8773;" -- approximately equal to-->
<!ENTITY asymp    CDATA "&#8776;" -- almost equal to = asymptotic to-->
<!ENTITY ne       CDATA "&#8800;" -- not equal to-->
<!ENTITY equiv    CDATA "&#8801;" -- identical to-->
<!ENTITY le       CDATA "&#8804;" -- less-than or equal to-->
<!ENTITY ge       CDATA "&#8805;" -- greater-than or equal to-->
<!ENTITY sub      CDATA "&#8834;" -- subset of-->
<!ENTITY sup      CDATA "&#8835;" -- superset of-->
<!ENTITY nsub     CDATA "&#8836;" -- not a subset of-->
<!ENTITY sube     CDATA "&#8838;" -- subset of or equal to-->
<!ENTITY supe     CDATA "&#8839;" -- superset of or equal to-->
<!ENTITY oplus    CDATA "&#8853;" -- circled plus = direct sum-->
<!ENTITY otimes   CDATA "&#8855;" -- circled times = vector product-->
<!ENTITY perp     CDATA "&#8869;" -- up tack = orthogonal to =
     perpendicular-->
```

```
<!ENTITY sdot    CDATA "&#8901;" -- dot operator-->
<!-- dot operator is NOT the same character as U+00B7 middle dot -->
    <!-- Miscellaneous Technical -->
<!ENTITY lceil   CDATA "&#8968;" -- left ceiling = apl upstile-->
<!ENTITY rceil   CDATA "&#8969;" -- right ceiling-->
    <!ENTITY lfloor  CDATA "&#8970;" -- left floor = apl downstile -->
<!ENTITY rfloor  CDATA "&#8971;" -- right floor-->
<!ENTITY lang    CDATA "&#9001;" -- left-pointing angle bracket = bra-->
<!-- lang is NOT the same character as U+003C 'less than'
or U+2039 'single left-pointing angle quotation mark' -->
<!ENTITY rang    CDATA "&#9002;" -- right-pointing angle bracket = ket-->
<!-- rang is NOT the same character as U+003E 'greater than'
or U+203A 'single right-pointing angle quotation mark' -->

<!-- Miscellaneous Symbols -->
<!ENTITY spades  CDATA "&#9824;" -- black spade suit-->
<!-- black here seems to mean filled as opposed to hollow -->
<!ENTITY clubs   CDATA "&#9827;" -- black club suit = shamrock-->
<!ENTITY hearts  CDATA "&#9829;" -- black heart suit = valentine-->
<!ENTITY diams   CDATA "&#9830;" -- black diamond suit-->
```

Table 9.3   The mathematical character set.

Character	Character Entity	Numeric Entity	Description
∀	&forall;	&#8704;	For all
∂	&part;	&#8706;	Partial differential
∃	&exist;	&#8707;	There exists
∅	&empty;	&#8709;	Empty set
∇	&nabla;	&#8711;	Nabla
∈	&isin;	&#8712;	Element of
∉	&notin;	&#8713;	Not an element of
∏	&prod;	&#8719;	n-ary product
ℜ	&sum;	&#8721;	n-ary summation
Σ	&minus;	&#8722;	Minus
∗	&lowast;	&#8727;	Asterisk operator
√	&radic;	&#8730;	Square root
∝	&prop;	&#8733;	Proportional to
∞	&infin;	&#8734;	Infinity
∠	&ang;	&#8736;	Angle
∧	&and;	&#8743;	Logical and

(continued)

Table 9.3   The mathematical character set *(continued).*

Character	Character Entity	Numeric Entity	Description
∨	&or;	&#8744;	Logical or
↔	&cap;	&#8745;	Intersection
≈	&cup;	&#8746;	Union
∨	&int;	&#8747;	Integral
∴	&there4;	&#8756;	Therefore
~	&sim;	&#8764;	Tilde operator
≅	&cong;	&#8773;	Approximately equal to
≈	&asymp;	&#8776;	Almost equal to
≠	&ne;	&#8800;	Not equal to
≡	&equiv;	&#8801;	Identical to =
≤	&le;	&#8804;	Less-than or equal to
≥	&ge;	&#8805;	Greater-than or equal to
⊂	&sub;	&#8834;	Subset of
⊃	&sup;	&#8835;	Superset of
⊄	&nsub;	&#8836;	Not a subset of
⊆	&sube;	&#8838;	Subset of or equal to
⊇	&supe;	&#8839;	Superset of or equal to
⊕	&oplus;	&#8853;	Circled plus
⊗	&otimes;	&#8855;	Circled times
⊥	&perp;	&#8869;	Up tack
•	&sdot;	&#8901;	Dot operator

Table 9.4   The Greek character set.

Character	Character Entity	Numeric Entity	Description
A	&Alpha;	&#913;	Capital letter alpha
B	&Beta;	&#914;	Capital letter beta
Γ	&Gamma;	&#915;	Capital letter gamma
Δ	&Delta;	&#916;	Capital letter delta
E	&Epsilon;	&#917;	Capital letter epsilon
Z	&Zeta;	&#918;	Capital letter zeta
H	&Eta;	&#919;	Capital letter eta
Θ	&Theta;	&#920;	Capital letter theta

(continued)

Table 9.4   The Greek character set *(continued)*.

Character	Character Entity	Numeric Entity	Description
Ι	Ι	Ι	Capital letter iota
Κ	Κ	Κ	Capital letter kappa
Λ	Λ	Λ	Capital letter lambda
Μ	Μ	Μ	Capital letter mu
Ν	Ν	Ν	Capital letter nu
Ξ	Ξ	Ξ	Capital letter xi
Ο	Ο	Ο	Capital letter omicron
Π	Π	Π	Capital letter pi
Ρ	Ρ	Ρ	Capital letter rho
Σ	Σ	Σ	Capital letter sigma
Τ	Τ	Τ	Capital letter tau
Υ	Υ	Υ	Capital letter upsilon
Φ	Φ	Φ	Capital letter phi
Χ	Χ	Χ	Capital letter chi
Ψ	Ψ	Ψ	Capital letter psi
Ω	Ω	Ω	Capital letter omega
α	α	α	Small letter alpha
β	β	β	Small letter beta
γ	γ	γ	Small letter gamma
δ	δ	δ	Small letter delta
ε	ε	ε	Small letter epsilon
ζ	ζ	ζ	Small letter zeta
η	η	η	Small letter eta
θ	θ	θ	Small letter theta
ι	ι	ι	Small letter iota
κ	κ	κ	Small letter kappa
λ	λ	λ	Small letter lambda
μ	μ	μ	Small letter mu
ν	ν	ν	Small letter nu
ξ	ξ	ξ	Small letter xi
ο	ο	ο	Small letter omicron
π	π	π	Small letter pi

(continued)

9. Creating and Including XML Entities

Table 9.4   The Greek character set *(continued)*.

Character	Character Entity	Numeric Entity	Description
ρ	&rho;	&#961;	Small letter rho
_	&sigmaf;	&#962;	Small letter final sigma
σ	&sigma;	&#963;	Small letter sigma
τ	&tau;	&#964;	Small letter tau
υ	&upsilon;	&#965;	Small letter upsilon
φ	&phi;	&#966;	Small letter phi
χ	&chi;	&#967;	Small letter chi
ψ	&psi;	&#968;	Small letter psi
ω	&omega;	&#969;	Small letter omega
υ	&thetasym;	&#977;	Small letter theta
ϒ	&upsih;	&#978;	Upsilon with hook
Π	&piv;	&#982;	Pi

Table 9.5   The miscellaneous technical character set.

Character	Character Entity	Numeric Entity	Description
⌈	&lceil;	&#8968;	Left ceiling
⌉	&rceil;	&#8969;	Right ceiling
⌊	&lfloor;	&#8970;	Left floor
⌋	&rfloor;	&#8971;	Right floor
〈	&lang;	&#9001;	Left-pointing angle bracket
〉	&rang;	&#9002;	Right-pointing angle bracket

Table 9.6   The miscellaneous symbols character set.

Character	Character Entity	Numeric Entity	Description
♠	&spades;	&#9824;	Black spade suit
♣	&clubs;	&#9827;	Black club suit
♥	&hearts;	&#9829;	Black heart suit
♦	&diams;	&#9830;	Black diamond suit

Using XML Tools to Create and Manage Entities

In this section, we take a brief look at how XML Spy (**http://new.xmlspy.com/**) and Near & Far Designer (**www.opentext.com/near_and_far/**) can be used to manage entities.

With XML Spy, you type entities almost the same way as you would in a text editor. The biggest advantage is that the XML Spy understands entities, so after you define an entity, it appears in a window for easy selection and insertion into other DTD elements and attributes.

Near & Far Designer hides the syntax by displaying well-labeled dialog boxes. However, Near & Far Designer does not fully understand entities and quickly converts them into the basic form.

To work with parameter entities using XML Spy, follow these steps:

1. Load your DTD into XML Spy.

2. Select an element and then select XML|Insert|Entity from the menu bar. If you load the "newspaper.dtd" used in Chapter 5, you would see something similar to Figure 9.1.

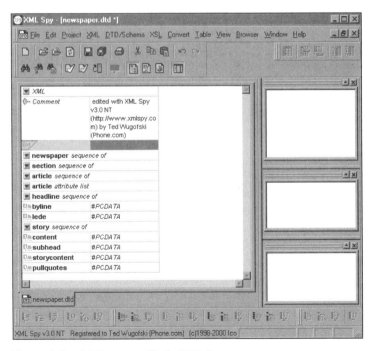

Figure 9.1   Adding an entity in XML Spy.

3. Select the field labeled Ent and type the name for the entity. For example, let's create an entity named **attr-id**.

4. Select the adjacent field and type the entity declaration. In this case, enter the string (quotes included) **"id ID #IMPLIED"**.

5. You can repeat the same procedure for the remaining parameter entities. In Figure 9.2, we've created two additional "simple" parameter entities: **att-class** and **att-style**, and then a more complex parameter entity, **common**, which includes references to the three other parameter entities.

6. After you define your entities, you can begin making references to them throughout your DTD. In this example, you'll use parameter entities to construct an attribute list. Create an attribute list for the **newspaper** element (we covered how to do this in Chapter 8). You should see something similar to Figure 9.3.

7. After naming the attribute list (in this example, name it **newspaper**), select the first Name field. Notice that the bottom-right pane contains a list of all available parameter entities.

8. Double-click on the desired parameter entity, and it will be assigned to the currently selected attribute declaration. After selecting the **%common;** parameter entity, the screen should look something like Figure 9.4.

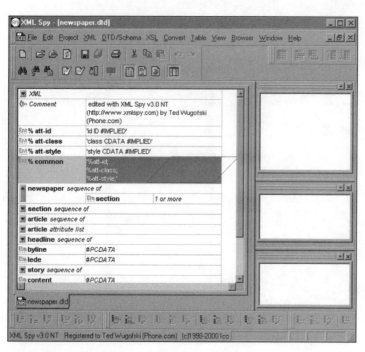

Figure 9.2   Adding more entities in XML Spy.

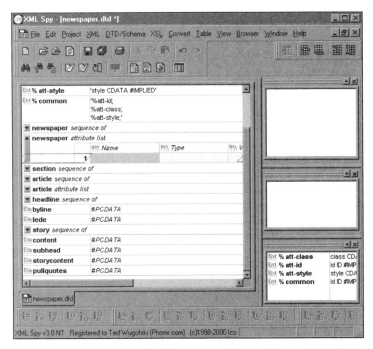

Figure 9.3   An attribute list for the **newspaper** element in XML Spy.

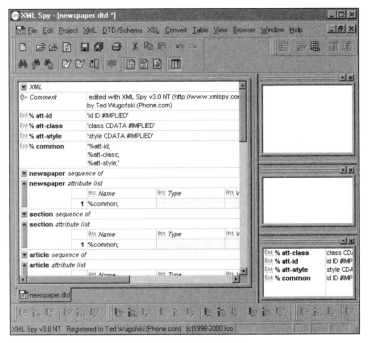

Figure 9.4   Assigning a parameter entity to an attribute declaration in XML Spy.

9. At this point, you may wish to repeat this procedure for the remaining elements in the DTD. Many markup-related DTDs will assign **id** and **class** attributes to elements so that authors can readily apply Cascading Style Sheets (CSS).

To work with entities using Near & Far Designer, follow these steps:

1. Load your DTD into Near & Far Designer.

2. To create an external parameter entity, select the Edit|External Parameter Entities menu item. Doing so displays the Edit External Parameter Entities dialog box shown in Figure 9.5.

3. Click the New button to display the External Parameter Entity dialog box (shown in Figure 9.6). This dialog box provides a simple form for entering the entity's name and identifier.

4. You're not going to define an external parameter entity right now, so click on the Cancel button and then the Close button to return to the main window.

5. To create an internal parameter entity, select the Edit|General And Other Entities menu item. Doing so displays the Edit General And Other Entities dialog box.

6. Click New to display the General And Other Entity dialog box shown in Figure 9.7. This dialog box provides several fields and radio buttons for creating the different types of entities we have described in this chapter.

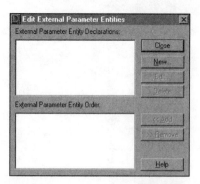

Figure 9.5 The Near & Far Designer Edit External Parameter Entities dialog box.

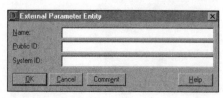

Figure 9.6 The Near & Far Designer External Parameter Entity dialog box.

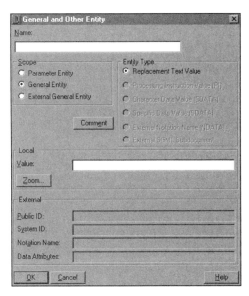

Figure 9.7   The Near & Far Designer General and Other Entity dialog box.

7. To create a parameter entity called **att-class**, type the string **att-class** in the Name field. Click the Parameter Entity radio button (located in the group of buttons labeled Scope). Type the entity declaration (**class CDATA #IMPLIED**) into the Value field.

8. Click OK to save the **att-class** entity. You may repeat this same procedure to create **att-id** and **att-style** parameter entities.

9. To create a more complex parameter entity, go to the Edit General And Other Entities dialog box and click New.

10. Type the string **common** in the Name field. Click the Parameter Entity radio button. Click the Zoom button, located near the Value field, to display the Entity Value dialog box shown in Figure 9.8. Type the appropriate values and click OK when you're finished.

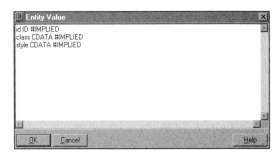

Figure 9.8   The Near & Far Designer Entity Value dialog box.

Chapter 10

Formatting XML Documents with Style Sheets

In Depth

Like any good markup language, XML exists to provide information about the structure and content of a document or set of documents. However, XML leaves issues of document style and presentation to the software package used to parse and process it. To help these applications, the creators of XML have considered some of the hard lessons learned during the development of HTML and implemented style sheet support as part of the overall XML strategy from the beginning. The markup governs content and structure, whereas associated style sheets govern how that content and structure is presented to the user.

The concept of style is not a new one. Nevertheless, the introduction of style sheets into the HTML world has been difficult at best. As with HTML, the various browsers handle the Cascading Style Sheets (CSS) that drive the display of XML documents differently. To get a glimpse of the different implementations of style sheets among the various Web browsers, visit the Web site at **http:// webreview.com/wr/pub/guides/style/mastergrid.html**.

Just as HTML developers are constantly frustrated and stumped by the differences in HTML rendering by various and sundry Web browsers, XML developers have run into compatibility problems with style sheets in different applications.

The situation is improving, however. As users continue to demand it, Web browser manufacturers are becoming increasingly compliant with style sheet standards. More importantly, because XML documents do not contain any formatting information or browser-specific elements, they're not limited to being displayed in Web browsers. XML data is currently being used and displayed by such diverse types of applications as hand-held computers, word processors, operating systems, and much more. With style sheets, developers can use the same XML document anywhere and be sure that it will be presented correctly by simply creating a custom style sheet for each different target application.

This chapter focuses on the role style sheets play in the presentation of XML documents and provides in-depth coverage of CSS—one of two style sheet languages that can be used to drive the display of XML documents. It also contains a discussion of the pros and cons of using CSS with XML, a full reference for creating CSS, and a complete rundown of all the CSS properties and values available to developers with the release of the most widely implemented version of CSS—CSS2.

The Case for Style Sheets

Because we've worked with Web documents both before and after style sheets were available, it seems obvious to us why anyone working with a markup language would want to use style sheets. However, we realize that not everyone worked with Web documents back in the early days, and perhaps the use of style sheets isn't as much of a no-brainer as we think it is. So, why should you use style sheets with XML? We have a three-part answer to that question:

- A single style sheet can drive the display of an unlimited number of documents.

- When markup is separated from style presentation, display rules are more efficiently created, more consistent, and easier to update, change, and manage.

- Multiple style sheets can easily be applied to the same document or set of documents as dissemination needs demand.

In following sections, we expand on each of these arguments so we can move on to the business of creating CSS.

One Style Sheet, Unlimited Documents

The style rules that drive the display of a Web page can be stored either within a document (internally) or in a separate file (externally). *Internal style rules*—those listed only in the document to which they pertain—are limited in application to the document in which they reside. However, *external style rules*—those that reside in a style-only document that is external to any other XML documents—apply to every document to which their document is linked. Therefore, in theory, a single external style sheet could be linked to, and define the style for, thousands of documents in a collection. Because an entire document collection relies on a single style sheet, you can change the style of the entire document collection simply by changing a single style sheet. After the change is made to the style sheet, the style rules of the documents linked to it will change by extension.

Separate Style from Markup for Improved Efficiency, Consistency, and Maintenance

Imagine that you've written a DTD that provides eight different presentation-related attributes for each paragraph of your document and five for each heading. Although this DTD obviously takes advantage of the extensibility of XML, you'll have to set all the attributes for every paragraph and heading every time they appear in your document or document collection. However, your paragraphs and headings probably fall into a variety of groups, or classes, because of their similar attribute settings. By adding a style sheet that defines the attribute settings for each class of paragraph or heading, you won't need to set them individually. Instead, you only need to classify the paragraphs and headings and let the style sheet do the rest.

The ability to link multiple documents to a single style sheet provides a mechanism for ensuring consistency of style and presentation across an entire document collection. As the Internet and intranets become the primary media for the dissemination of documents, consistency of style and presentation is essential. Document designers can use styles to provide readers with visual clues that help them familiarize themselves with the creators of the information they are browsing. For example, companies that have spent years creating a corporate image via logos and slogans can use those same elements to create familiarity with their Web content. Styles can also be used to provide both nontextual content and emphasis to textual content, thus making the overall interaction with the information more enriching and interesting for the user. Without a simple, standard mechanism for ensuring the consistency of these visual and nontextual clues, document designers would not be able to easily implement advanced styles and presentation layouts. Style sheets allow developers to set up styles once and apply them to a large number of documents quickly and easily.

The development of XML documents is only the beginning of a long commitment to the upkeep and maintenance of a document collection. New information is generated constantly, and with solid XML DTDs and accompanying style sheets in place, adding the information to the collection is simple.

One Document, Many Styles

Rarely is information created that won't be leveraged in some way and need to be presented in an entirely new light. Documents become bullet points. Bullet points become presentations. Presentations become outlines. Outlines become new documents. In addition, a single document may need to be presented across various media, such as Web pages, printed pages, wireless devices, and text read by a computer for the visually impaired. Public and private versions of documents are also common, just as it's common for portions of documents to be available only to those with the necessary access credentials.

Although it's possible to create a new iteration of a document to meet each display need, doing so isn't an efficient or resource-effective method for disseminating information for a single document, much less a collection of thousands of documents. Instead, several different style sheets can be written for a document or collection of documents and be applied to the content as dissemination needs require. Once again, efficiency and consistency are achieved, and a single iteration of a document can be manipulated to meet a wide variety of presentation and dissemination needs.

TIP: *We could go on and on about why style sheets are useful. We could even write an entire book about them—and we actually did: the* HTML Style Sheets Design Guide *from The Coriolis Group.*

If you've spent any time developing content for dissemination, you'll see almost immediately why style sheets are necessary and valuable tools. In the following section, we look briefly at the style alternatives available to XML developers and then move on to the Immediate Solutions section of this chapter, which shows you everything you need to know to create CSS style rules and style sheets and link them to existing documents.

XML Style Options

Currently, two style sheet options are available to XML developers:

- Cascading Style Sheets levels 1, 2, and 3 (CSS1, CSS2, and CSS3)
- Extensible Stylesheet Language (XSL)

CSS1 and CSS2 are existing standards, whereas CSS3 and XSL are under development by the World Wide Web Consortium (W3C) and related groups. XSL is divided into two separate specifications:

- *Extensible Stylesheet Language (XSL)*—A syntax for driving the display of XML documents
- *XSL Transformations (XSLT)*—A syntax for converting a document from one XML DTD to another

XSL, the formatting mechanism built specifically for XML, is still under development and isn't well supported among browsers or other tools, which means it's currently not a useful tool for driving the display of XML documents. Therefore, the two most practical uses of style sheets with XML are:

- Using CSS to drive the display of XML documents in browsers that support XML
- Using XSLT to convert documents from any flavor of XML to HTML and then using traditional display mechanisms to publish the HTML for all Web browsers

Given that these are the two practical approaches to styling XML documents, the remainder of this chapter focuses on using CSS with XML, and Chapter 11 covers using XSLT to convert XML documents from one DTD to another.

Related solution:	*Found on page:*
Defining Basic XSLT Style Sheet Constructs	293

The Pros and Cons of Using CSS with XML

There are several reasons you would want to use CSS with XML, but there are also reasons you would not. As you work more with XML and related style sheet languages, you'll find that each has its appropriate uses, as do the various XML vocabularies. Luckily, you won't be obligated to try to force CSS or XSL to do what you want them to because each provides a solution for very different needs. The following list includes some of the advantages of using CSS:

- CSS is easy to learn and implement. Because CSS was originally designed for HTML, it was created to be a simple yet elegant solution to the issues of style on the Web.

- CSS is already utilized in the Web community. As the implementation of CSS improves among Web-related vendors, it will naturally be used as an XML style solution as well as an HTML style solution.

- CSS works with HTML. While we wait for the integration of XML into the Web world, many XML documents will be translated into HTML for mass-market dissemination. Because CSS already works with HTML, it will be relatively simple to create style sheets for HTML documents that are produced from XML documents.

However, CSS does have a downside when it's implemented with XML (as described by Jon Bosak in his WWW6 STEP/XML Presentation—you can download it from **http://lists.w3.org/Archives/Public/w3c-sgml-wg/msg04740.html**):

- CSS cannot generate text.

- CSS cannot grab an item from one place and use it again in another place.

- CSS is not a programming language; it does not support decision structures, and it cannot be extended by the style sheet designer.

- CSS is oriented toward Western languages and assumes a horizontal writing direction.

- CSS uses a simple box-oriented formatting model that works for current Web browsers but will not extend to more advanced applications of the markup, such as multiple column sets.

- CSS has no concept of sibling relationships.

XSL makes up in many ways for what CSS lacks. Even though CSS isn't the perfect tool for styling XML, it does provide an easy-to-implement immediate solution for driving the display of style sheets. If you're new to the world of style sheets, CSS also provides a gentle introduction to how style sheets work and why they're such useful tools.

Immediate Solutions

Working with a Living Example

If you've ever used CSS with HTML, you'll take to using CSS with XML like a duck to water. All the mechanisms are the same, selectors and property definitions take the same format, and the property/value combinations from which you have to choose are identical. If you treat HTML as an XML vocabulary, then you've used CSS with XML. The only difference in using CSS with other XML vocabularies is that the elements to which you apply style rules are different for each vocabulary.

NOTE: *In this section, we work with CSS2, the most current version of CSS. CSS3 is in development, but it's not stable nor is it implemented by any major display tools. After you get the hang of CSS, upgrading to a new version is simply a matter of learning what new style tools you have at your disposal.*

Throughout this Immediate Solutions section, we use David Megginson's novel DTD (previously dissected and discussed in Chapter 5) for our examples. Listing 10.1 contains the full version of the DTD.

Listing 10.1   The novel DTD.

```
<?xml encoding="UTF-8"?>


<!--
**************************************************************************
novel.dtd: A simple XML DTD for marking-up novels.
Copyright (c) 1997 by David Megginson.
**************************************************************************
-->

<!-- Content model for phrasal content -->

<!ENTITY % phrasal "#PCDATA|emphasis">

<!-- ******** -->
<!-- Elements -->
<!-- ******** -->
```

```
<!-- The top-level novel -->

<!ELEMENT novel (front, body)>

<!-- The frontmatter for the novel -->

<!ELEMENT front (title, author, revision-list)>

<!-- The list of revisions to this text -->

<!ELEMENT revision-list (item+)>

<!-- An item in the list of revisions -->

<!ELEMENT item (%phrasal;)*>

<!-- The main body of a novel -->

<!ELEMENT body (chapter+)>

<!-- A chapter of a novel -->

<!ELEMENT chapter (title, paragraph+)>
<!ATTLIST chapter
  id ID #REQUIRED>

<!-- The title of a novel or chapter -->
<!ELEMENT title (%phrasal;)*>

<!-- The author(s) of a novel -->
<!ELEMENT author (%phrasal;)*>

<!-- A paragraph in a chapter -->
<!ELEMENT paragraph (%phrasal;)*>

<!-- An emphasized phrase -->
<!ELEMENT emphasis (%phrasal;)*>

<!-- **************** -->
<!-- General Entities -->
<!-- **************** -->
<!--
   These really should have their Unicode equivalents.
  -->
<!-- em-dash -->
<!ENTITY mdash "--">
```

```
<!-- left double quotation mark -->
<!ENTITY ldquo "´´">

<!-- right double quotation mark -->
<!ENTITY rdquo "``">

<!-- left single quotation mark -->
<!ENTITY lsquo "´">

<!-- right single quotation mark -->
<!ENTITY rsquo "`">

<!-- horizontal ellipse -->
<!ENTITY hellip "...">

<!-- end of DTD -->
```

The Simple Style Formula: Selector+ Declaration=Style Rule

Every style rule has two parts:

- *The selector*—The markup element to which the style rule is applied
- *The declaration*—Specific information about how the element should be presented

Declarations are made up of property and value combinations that define what aspect of the element's display is affected and how it's affected. The declaration **margin-left: .5in** indicates that the left margin of the element to which the declaration applies should be half an inch. Declarations are enclosed in curly braces— { and }. The property to be affected is listed first and is followed by a colon and the value the property should take.

All style rules use this syntax:

```
selector {property: value}
```

Therefore, a sample style rule that assigns a left margin of half an inch to the **author** element would be:

```
author {margin-left: .5in}
```

Case Doesn't Count, but Punctuation Does

CSS rules require a very specific syntax in which case is irrelevant but punctuation makes all the difference. Braces, colons, semicolons, periods, and commas all have defined roles in CSS rule notation. If you use a comma instead of a period, or a colon instead of a semicolon, your style sheets will break. When you debug CSS style sheets, always check the accuracy of your punctuation. The section "Exploring the Role of Punctuation in CSS" (later in this chapter) includes a table that details the meaning of each punctuation mark as it applies to CSS. Note that only the case is irrelevant in the CSS syntax. When you reference an XML element in CSS, the case of the element must match the case declared in the XML DTD.

Grouping Selectors in Style Rules

Occasions will arise when you'll want to apply the same declaration (or set of declarations) to more than one selector. You could—with the help of cut and paste—generate a long series of style rules with different selectors but the same declarations, as shown in this code snippet:

```
author {margin-left: .5in}
title {margin-left: .5in}
revision-list {margin-left: .5in}
```

But thanks to the grouping mechanisms built into CSS, that's not necessary. You can include all three selectors in one style rule. Simply separate the selectors with commas and follow the entire group with the common declaration (or declarations, as discussed in the following project):

```
author, title, revision-list {margin-left: .5in}
```

Grouping Declarations in Style Rules

Just as it's convenient to group selectors in style rules to apply one declaration to many selectors, it's useful to be able to apply several different declarations to one selector, or to a group of selectors. More often than not, you'll want to affect multiple aspects of an element's presentation. You could—once again, with the help of cut and paste—generate a long series of style rules with the same selector but different declarations, as follows:

```
author, title, revision-list {margin-left: .5in}
author, title, revision-list {color: navy}
author, title, revision-list {font-family: Arial}
author, title, revision-list {font-style: oblique}
```

This method quickly becomes cumbersome and lengthy. With CSS, you can group declarations. Simply separate multiple declarations within the curly braces of a single selector with semicolons, as shown here:

```
author, title, revision-list {margin-left: .5in;
                              color: navy;
                              font-family: Arial;
                              font-style: oblique;
                              }
```

The style rule takes on a slightly different format when it includes several declarations. (Note that this formatting isn't required by CSS.) Each declaration is moved to its own line, all are indented so they line up underneath the beginning of the first declaration, and the final curly brace resides on its own line. We could have listed the entire rule on one line. However, listing each rule on its own line, putting the final curly brace on the last line by itself, and adding white space makes it easier for the developer to read and modify the rule.

Including Special Declaration Groupings for Individual Properties

Some properties have their own special rules for grouping declarations. This creates a type of CSS shorthand that allows you to create style rules quickly and easily. For example, box properties, such as margins, use the {1, 4} notation to indicate the values that should be assigned to each of the four sides of an element box. The syntax looks like this:

```
selector {margin: 1 2 3 4}
```

You can include up to four values after the colon in the declaration, but each number you add changes the way the values are applied to the element's box. The numbers are interpreted in this manner:

- *One number*—The value is applied to all four sides of the element's box.
- *Two numbers*—The first value is applied to the top and bottom of the element's box, and the second to the left and right sides.

- *Three numbers*—The first value is applied to the top, the second to the bottom, and the third to the right and left sides of the element's box.
- *Four numbers*—Each number is applied to a different side of the element's box in the order of top, bottom, left, and right.

The following style rules provide an example of this notation at work. In this style rule **title** elements will have a margin of 10 percent on all four sides:

```
title {margin: 10%}
```

In this style rule, **title** elements will have a margin of 10 percent on the top and bottom and a margin of 20 percent on the left and right:

```
title {margin: 10% 20%}
```

In this style rule, **title** elements will have a margin of 10 percent on the top, 20 percent on the bottom, and 15 percent on the left and right:

```
title {margin: 10% 20% 15%}
```

In this style, rule, **title** elements will have a margin of 10 percent on the top, 20 percent on the bottom, 15 percent on the left, and 5 percent on the right:

```
title {margin: 10% 20% 15% 5%}
```

Other property families also have their own built-in shorthand notation. For example, the **background** property combines the values of six other background properties—**background-color**, **background-image**, **background-repeat**, **background-attachment**, and **background-position**—into one declaration. This long style rule

```
author {background-color: white;
        background-image: url(myback.gif);
        background-repeat: repeat-x;
        background-attachment: fixed;
        background-position: 50%;
        }
```

can be reduced to this shorter rule and still retain the same meaning:

```
author {background: white url(myback.gif) repeat-x fixed 50%}
```

The projects found later in the section provide details of all the properties and values, as well as the details of the property families that support special declaration groupings. All of them will take one of the two shorthand formats discussed in this project.

Using Class as a Selector

Often, you want to use the same element to describe similar content but you want to apply different style rules to different instances of the element based on the kind of content the element describes. For example, in addition to standard paragraphs, you might have two classes of **paragraph** elements: **summary** and **abstract**. You not only want to class both kinds of content as paragraphs, but you also want to find a way to build slightly different formatting rules for each one.

To create multiple instances of the same element, each with its own style rule, CSS allows you to use the **class**-attribute to provide additional information in an element that you can use in a selector. In a selector, follow the element name with a period and the class name. To link the rule to a specific instance of the element, use **class="*string*"**, where "*string*" is the same as the class name given after the element name in the style rule. The syntax for both the style rule and its invocation are:

```
selector.class {property: value}

<element class="string">...</element>
```

Using our previous example of **summary** and **abstract** classes of paragraphs, the following two style rules apply to two different classes of a paragraph:

```
paragraph.summary {font-size: 90%;
                   font-color: navy;
                   border: 3pt;
                   }

paragraph.abstract {font-size: 85%;
                    font-color: black;
                    font-weight: bold;
                    }

<paragraph class="summary">This is a summary paragraph.</paragraph>

<paragraph class="abstract">This is an abstract paragraph.</paragraph>
```

263

10. Formatting
XML Documents with
Style Sheets

If a selector includes class information and an element is used without including the appropriate **class-** attribute, the style rule will not be invoked for that instance of the element. This fact allows you to build a generic style for most instances of an element and then build specialty styles for different classes of the element.

Megginson's novel DTD includes a **title** element that can be used to include either a title for the entire book or a title for a chapter. What if you want to create a separate style for each of the two titles based on the type of title (book or chapter)? Creating two separate style rules that are both linked to **title**, as follows, wouldn't work:

```
title {color: navy;
       font: 36pt Arial;
       background-color: teal;
       border-style: double;
       margin-top: 5%;
       margin-left: 10%;
       margin-right: 10%;
       }
```

```
title {color: teal;
       font: 18pt Arial;
       background-color: navy;
       border-style: groove;
       margin-left: 15%;
       margin-right: 15%;
       }
```

The second style rule would simply override the first, and the second rule would be used to present all instances of the **title** element. You probably don't want to rewrite that DTD to have two separate types of titles. Instead, to create two separate style rules for two different instances of the same element, you can differentiate them by class. The new style rules would look like this:

```
title.book {color: navy;
       font: 36pt Arial;
       background-color: teal;
       border-style: double;
       margin-top: 5%;
       margin-left: 10%;
       margin-right: 10%;
       }
```

```
title.chapter {color: teal;
     font: 18pt Arial;
     background-color: navy;
     border-style: groove;
     margin-left: 15%;
     margin-right: 15%;
     }
```

This markup invokes the book and chapter style rules, respectively:

```
<title class="book">This is the book's title.</title>
<title class="chapter">This is a chapter title.</title>
```

If you use the **title** element without specifying a class, neither style rule is invoked.

Using Context as a Selector

Creating a **class** attribute for every element in a DTD is not the only way to create style rules that apply only to certain instances of an element. Instead, an element's context can be used as a selector. To specify the context rules an element must meet before it can be considered a candidate for a style rule, simply list the elements included in the context in the order that they will appear. For example, this style rule

```
front title  {color: navy;
     font: 36pt Arial;
     background-color: teal;
     border-style: double;
     margin-top: 5%;
     margin-left: 10%;
     margin-right: 10%;
     }
```

specifies that only **title** elements nested within **front** elements should have this style rule applied to them. To invoke this style rule, the markup needs to take this format:

```
<front><title>The book's title goes here.</title></front>
```

In the same way, this style rule indicates that it should be applied only to **title** elements nested within **chapter** elements:

```
chapter title {color: teal;
     font: 18pt Arial;
     background-color: navy;
     border-style: groove;
     margin-left: 15%;
     margin-right: 15%;
     }
```

The following markup is required to invoke this style rule:

```
<chapter><title>The chapter's title goes here.</title></front>
```

These two style rules work well with the novel DTD because both the **front** and **chapter** elements require **title** elements, and a **title** element cannot stand alone outside of the front matter or chapter; therefore, you've covered all the title bases. You don't have to create a third title style without context information because you know a valid document won't include a **title** element that doesn't fit one of your two predefined context models.

When you use context as a selector, the element names that make up the selector portion of the style rule are separated by spaces only, not by commas. If you include commas, you'll create a group of selectors instead of a single, context-based selector. Elements linked to the style rules must be nested in the order defined by the style rule. Because DTDs must provide specific information about what content, in what order, is required or optional for all elements, you should study the DTD closely when you create rules that use context as a selector. Chapter 7 discusses element content in detail.

NOTE: *The different versions of the "big two" browsers have varying support for the selector feature; therefore, you should experiment to determine which approach works best for the target browser(s).*

Exploring the Role of Punctuation in CSS

The previous discussions of the syntax of style rules (including the different grouping and selector methods) show that CSS relies heavily on a variety of punctuation marks for the creation and interpretation of style rules. Table 10.1 recaps the role that each punctuation mark plays in creating style rules.

TIP: *For additional help in debugging your style sheets—especially to catch punctuation mistakes—run your Cascading Style Sheets through the Web Design Group's CSS validator, CSS Check, found at **www.htmlhelp.com/tools/csscheck**.*

Table 10.1   Punctuation rules in CSS.

Character	Name	Role
{	Left curly brace	Begins a declaration
}	Right curly brace	Ends a declaration
:	Colon	Separates the property and its value in a declaration
,	Comma	Separates multiple selectors in a selector grouping
;	Semicolon	Separates multiple declarations in a declaration grouping
.	Period	Separates the element and the class name in a selector when class is used as a selector
	Space	Separates elements in the selector when context is used as a selector, or separates values in a declaration when certain property family shorthand notations are used

Using Measurement Units in CSS

CSS supports a wide variety of units, including standard measurements, percentages, and specific URL and color notation systems. This flexibility allows developers to assign the appropriate units, as dictated by the presentation aspect being defined, without having to perform laborious measurement conversions. In general, measurements in CSS are either absolute or relative. An example of an absolute measurement is **1in**, whereas **75%** is a relative measurement. One inch is one inch, no matter how you look at it, but a percentage changes as its whole changes; for example, 75 percent of 1 inch is .75 inches, but 75 percent of 2 inches is 1.5 inches. Table 10.2 lists each measurement mechanism available in CSS with its abbreviation and its type (absolute or relative).

Table 10.2   Units of measure in CSS.

Name	Abbreviation	Type	Notes
Centimeter	**cm**	Absolute	
Em	**em**	Relative	Equal to the width of the display font's letter *m*.
Ex	**ex**	Relative	Equal to the height of the display font's letter *x*.
Inch	**in**	Absolute	
Millimeter	**mm**	Absolute	
Percentage	**%**	Relative	
Pica	**pc**	Absolute	
Pixel	**px**	Absolute	Pixels are different from device to device. A pixel on a screen that has a display resolution of 1024x768 is smaller than one with a screen resolution of 640x480.

Using URLs in CSS

URLs are defined in CSS using this syntax:

```
url(resource address)
```

The URL listed inside the parentheses can be a local URL, whose location is relative to the file to which the style sheet is attached, or a fully qualified URL. Here's an example of a URL as a value for a CSS property:

```
title {background-image: url(background.gif)}
```

Remember, for an image to be included as part of an XML document, it must be defined in the document's DTD as an unparsed entity. In this case, however, the image is not part of the XML document; it's part of a style sheet. Therefore, it doesn't need to be defined in the DTD.

TIP: CSS supports the hexadecimal color notation system used with HTML documents.

Reading Property Definitions

The next several projects provide a detailed discussion of the properties that are available for creating CSS style rules. For each property, we'll include the following:

- *Property name*—The property's name exactly as it should appear in the style rule
- *Description*—A brief description of which aspect of an element the property affects
- *Syntax*—The exact code used to call the property and the values it takes
- *Values*—Lists of all the values that are valid for the property (Table 10.3 provides descriptions of value notations)

Although CSS2 is a full specification, it's still not supported completely in a variety of display tools. The following projects focus on those properties that are part of CSS1 and work well across multiple display tools. For a full view of the CSS2 recommendation, and to keep up with the development of CSS3, visit the W3C's CSS site at **www.w3.org/Style/CSS**.

Table 10.3   Descriptions of value notations for property values.

Value	Description	Example
<value>	A specific type of value	*<percentage>; <length>*
Value*	A value that is repeated zero or more times	*[[<family-name>l<generic-family>],]**
Value?	A value that is optional	*[/<line-height>]?*
Value{X,Y}	A value that must occur at least *X* times and at most *Y* times	*[<length>l<percentage>lauto]{1,4}*
Keyword	A keyword that must appear exactly as listed	**thin**
XlY	A list of possible values; only one may be used	**thin l medium l thick**
XllY	A list of possible values; one or more may be used	*<font-style>* ll *<font-variant>* ll *<font-weight>*
[items]	A group of items	**[thin l medium l thick l** *<length>* **] {1,4}**

Using the Box Property Family

The box properties govern the margins, padding, height, width, and border aspects of any element. Table 10.4 lists each property and its description, syntax, and values.

Utilizing the Classification Property Family

The classification properties govern the way white space and lists are displayed. Table 10.5 lists each property and its description, syntax, and values.

Table 10.4   Box properties.

Property	Description	Syntax	Values
margin-top	Sets the size of an element's top margin	**margin-top:** *<value>*	*<length>* l *<percentage>* l auto
margin-right	Sets the size of an element's right margin	**margin-right:** *<value>*	*<length>* l *<percentage>* l auto
margin-bottom	Sets the size of an element's bottom margin	**margin-bottom:** *<value>*	*<length>* l *<percentage>* l auto

(continued)

Table 10.4   Box properties *(continued)*.

Property	Description	Syntax	Values
margin-left	Sets the size of an element's left margin	**margin-left:** *<value>*	*<length>* I *<percentage>* I auto
margin	Sets the size of all four element margins at one time	**margin:** *<value>*	[*<length>* I *<percentage>* I auto]{1,4}
padding-top	Sets the amount of space between an element's content	**padding-top:** *<value>*	*<length>* I *<percentage>*
padding-right	Sets the amount of space between an element's content and its right border	**padding-right:** *<value>*	*<length>* I *<percentage>*
padding-bottom	Sets the amount of space between an element's content and its bottom border	**padding-bottom:** *<value>*	*<length>* I *<percentage>*
padding-left	Sets the amount of space between an element's content and its left border	**padding-left:** *<value>*	*<length>* I *<percentage>*
padding	Sets the padding size for all sides of an element at one time	**padding:** *<value>*	[*<length>* I *<percentage>*]{1,4}
border-top-width	Sets the width of an element's top border	**border-top-width:** *<value>*	thin I medium I thick I *<length>*
border-right-width	Sets the width of an element's right border	**border-right-width:***<value>*	thin I medium I thick I *<length>*
border-bottom-width	Sets the width of an element's bottom border	**border-bottom-width:** *<value>*	thin I medium I thick I *<length>*
border-left-width	Sets the width of an element's left border	**border-left-width:** *<value>*	thin I medium I thick I *<length>*
border-width	Sets the width of all four element borders at one time	**border-width:** *<value>*	[thin I medium I thick I *<length>*]{1,4}
border-color	Sets the color for all four sides of an element's border	**border-color:** *<value>*	*<color>*{1,4}

(continued)

Table 10.4   Box properties *(continued)*.

Property	Description	Syntax	Values
border-style	Sets the style for all four sides of an element's border	**border-style:** *<value>*	**[none I dotted I dashed I solid I double I groove I ridge I inset I outset]{1,4}**
border-top	Sets the width, color, and style of an element's top border	**border-top:** *<value>*	**<border-top-width> I <border-style> I <color>**
border-right	Sets the width, color, and style of an element's right border	**border-right:** *<value>*	**<border-right-width> I <border-style> I <color>**
border-bottom	Sets the width, color, and style of an element's bottom border	**border-bottom:** *<value>*	**<border-bottom-width> I <border-style> I <color>**
border-left	Sets the width, color, and style of an element's left border	**border-left:** *<value>*	**<border-left-width> I <border-style> I <color>**
border	Sets the width, color, and style for all of an element's borders	**border:** *<value>*	**<border-width> I <border-style> I <color>**
width	Defines an element's width	**width:** *<value>*	*<length>* I *<percentage>* I **auto**
height	Defines an element's height	**height:** *<value>*	*<length>* I **auto**
float	Shifts a floating box to the left or to the right, determining how other content should flow around the box	**float:** *<value>*	**left I right I none**
clear	Identifies which sides of an element's box may not be adjacent to an earlier floating box	**clear:** *<value>*	**none I left I right I both**

Table 10.5   Classification properties.

Property	Description	Syntax	Values
display	Defines how an element should be displayed	display: *\<value\>*	block I inline I list-item I none
white space	Defines how white space within an element should be rendered	white-space: *\<value\>*	normal I pre I nowrap
list-style-type	Specifies the type of marker to be used within a list	list-style-type: *\<value\>*	disc I circle I square I decimal I lower-roman I upper-roman I lower-alpha I upper-alpha I none
list-style-image	Identifies an image to be used as a list-item marker	list-style-image: *\<value\>*	*\<url\>* I none
list-style-position	Defines whether text in a list should be displayed inside or outside the list-item marker	list-style-position: *\<value\>*	inside I outside
list-style	Defines the list-style type, position, and marker image URL	list-style: *\<value\>*	*\<list-style-type\>* II *\<list-style-position\>* II *\<url\>*

Using the Color and Background Property Family

The color and background properties govern the way color and background images are linked to elements, as well as the positioning and scrolling status of images. Table 10.6 lists each property and its description, syntax, and values.

Table 10.6   Color and background properties.

Property	Description	Syntax	Values
color	Specifies an element's color	color: *\<color\>*	*\<color\>* I inherit
background-color	Specifies an element's background color	background-color: *\<value\>*	*\<color\>* I transparent
background-image	Specifies an image to be attached as the background for an element	background-image: *\<value\>*	*\<url\>* I none
background-repeat	Defines how an element's background image should be repeated	background-repeat: *\<value\>*	repeat I repeat-x I repeat-y I no-repeat

(continued)

Table 10.6   Color and background properties *(continued)*.

Property	Description	Syntax	Values
background-attachment	Defines whether an element's background image is fixed in the browser window or scrolls with the element	background-attachment: *<value>*	**scroll I fixed**
background-position	Sets the position of an element's background image in relation to the element	background-position: *<value>*	**[*<percentage>* I *<length>*]{1,2} I [top I center I bottom] II [left I center I right]**
background	Defines an element's background color and image, as well as how the image repeats its attachment, and its position	background: *<value>*	*<background-color>* I *<background-image>* I *<background-repeat>* I *<background-attachment>* I *<background-position>*

Exploring the Font Property Family

The font properties provide font specifics for document elements. Table 10.7 lists each property and its description, syntax, and values.

Investigating the Text Property Family

The text properties provide text specifics for document elements. Table 10.8 lists each property and its description, syntax, and values.

Table 10.7   Font properties.

Property	Description	Syntax	Values
font-family	Specifies the font in which to display the element's text	font-family: [[*<family-name>* I *<generic-family>*],]* [*<family-name>* I *<generic-family>*]	*<family-name>* *<generic-family>* **serif** (ex: "Century Schoolbook") **sans-serif** (ex: Helvetica) **monospace** (ex: Courier) **cursive** (ex: Zapf-Chancery) **fantasy** (ex: Western)

(continued)

Table 10.7   Font properties *(continued)*.

Property	Description	Syntax	Values
font-size	Sets the size of text	**font-size:** *<absolute-size>* | *<relative-size>*	*<absolute-size>* **xx-small | x-small | small | medium | large | x-large | xx-large** *<relative-size>* **larger | smaller** *<length>* *<percentage>*
font-style	Defines the element's font style	**font-style:** *<value>*	**normal | italic | oblique**
font-variant	Specifies whether the text should be rendered as normal or small caps	**font-variant:** *<value>*	**normal | small-caps**
font-weight	Defines how dark or light text should be	**font-weight:** *<value>*	**normal | bold | bolder | lighter | 100 | 200 | 300 | 400 | 500 | 600 | 700 | 800 | 900**
font	Defines all the font properties in one property/value set	**font:** *<value>*	**[** *<font-style>* | *<font-variant>* | *<font-weight>* **]?** *<font-size>* **[/** *<line-height>* **]?** *<font-family>*

Table 10.8   Text properties.

Property	Description	Syntax	Values
word-spacing	Defines the amount of space between the words in an element	**word-spacing:** *<value>*	**normal |** *<length>*
letter-spacing	Defines the amount of space between the letters in an element	**letter-spacing:** *<value>*	**normal |** *<length>*
text-decoration	Defines how the text in an element should be decorated	**text-decoration:** *<value>*	**none | [underline | overline | line-through | blink]**

(continued)

Table 10.8   Text properties *(continued)*.

Property	Description	Syntax	Values
vertical-align	Defines how an inline element should be positioned relative to its parent	*element* vertical-align: *<value>*	baseline I sub I super I top I text-top I middle I bottom I text-bottom I *<percentage>*
text-transform	Defines the case in which the text in an element should be rendered (regardless of the case it is typed in)	text-transform: *<value>*	none I capitalize I uppercase I lowercase
text-align	Defines how text in an element should be aligned relative to its parent element and the page	text-align: *<value>*	left I right I center I justify
text-indent	Defines how much the first line of a block-level element should be indented	text-indent: *<value>*	*<length>* I *<percentage>*
line-height	Sets the amount of space between lines in an element	line-height: *<value>*	normal I *<number>* I *<length>* I *<percentage>*

Linking Style Sheets to XML Documents

In June of 1999, the W3C published a recommendation that defines how you should link style sheets to XML documents. The basic syntax for linking a style sheet to an XML document is to use an **xml-stylesheet** processing instruction, which looks like this:

```
<?xml-stylesheet href="style_file.css" type="text/css"?>
```

You can read the complete, yet compact, recommendation at **www.w3.org/TR/xml-stylesheet/**.

NOTE: *Many great resources are available on the Web for building CSS and using them with your XML documents. Search your favorite Web browser using the keywords Cascading Style Sheets.*

Chapter 11

Translating XML Documents with XSL Transformations

In Depth

The Extensible Stylesheet Language (XSL) is a style sheet mechanism that is customized for XML. XSL has two parts: a vocabulary for formatting documents and XSL Transformations (XSLT), which is a language for transforming one XML document into another XML document.

With XSLT, you can convert an XML document to HTML or other XML vocabularies. With XSL, you can tell an XML processor or browser exactly how you want your XML documents displayed. XSL is the ultimate formatting language for XML, and it's easy to learn and implement.

Chapter 10 examines Cascading Style Sheets (CSS) as an option for creating style sheets for XML documents. Although this style mechanism has solid strengths and qualities that make it suitable for working with XML, the bottom line is that CSS was created to work with HTML. On the other hand, XSL is designed to work specifically with XML and the vocabularies created with it.

Related solution:	Found on page:
The Simple Style Formula: Selector+Declaration=Style Rule	259

Although the World Wide Web Consortium (W3C) has not finished defining the XSL formatting vocabulary, the W3C has finalized its recommendation for XSLT. This chapter describes how you can use XSLT to transform an XML document into another XML document or into an HTML document. This chapter's Immediate Solutions section focuses on how to create the various constructs found in an XSLT style sheet, combine them to form a cohesive style sheet, and integrate the style sheet with one or more XML documents. In addition, it discusses some of the tools that are available for working with XSLT.

Presently, the most practical use of XSLT is converting XML documents to HTML (and XHTML) documents for Web-publishing purposes. Therefore, the Immediate Solutions section focuses on this use of XSLT in the majority of its examples. We're not suggesting that XSLT isn't good for anything other than XML-to-HTML conversions; we chose this approach because it's a useful way to create examples with a point of reference everyone can understand and a means to show the immediate uses of XSLT.

What Are XSL and XSLT?

As discussed in previous style chapters, XML should be used strictly to provide information about the structure of a document. XSL is a language used to express style sheets in XML. As mentioned in the previous section, XSL consists of two parts: XSLT and a formatting vocabulary.

Although XSLT was originally invented to solve the problem of transforming an XML document into a document using the XSL formatting vocabulary, it can be used independently of XSL to transform between any two XML documents.

An XSLT document describes the rules for transforming a source document's tree structure into a *result tree*. These rules take the form of a collection of patterns and templates. The patterns in the XSLT document are matched against the source document. When a pattern is matched, the content of the matching elements is used to fill in the XSLT template, which then becomes part of the result tree.

This process means that the result tree is completely separate from the source tree. In fact, the structure of the resulting document can be different than the source document—elements can be reordered, reorganized, or removed altogether.

The Status of XSL and XSLT

XSLT became a W3C recommendation in November 1999. At the time this book was written, XSL was still in the working draft stage.

What does this mean to the XML developer? The best advice is that you can feel pretty comfortable if you're using XSLT to transform a document from one XML language to another (as long as you are using a tool that is compliant with the XSLT recommendation).

You should be cautious, however, if you're using the formatting aspects of XSL (which are still in a working draft stage). Don't get so attached to a style sheet that you aren't willing to modify it as XSL evolves.

If you're desperate for a solid style sheet mechanism that won't change every few months, you might consider using the tried-and-true CSS technologies discussed in the previous chapter. CSS is particularly useful if you use XSLT to transform your XML document into XHTML and then apply the style sheet.

Practical Uses for XSLT

As we mentioned in the previous section, XSLT was originally invented to transform XML documents into documents using the XSL formatting vocabulary. It was quickly discovered that XSLT had far greater use outside of XSL, and it therefore became its own recommendation.

The ability of XSLT to move data from one XML language to another is quite useful when you're interfacing between two distinct data networks, as with electronic data interchange (EDI) and electronic commerce. XSLT is also commonly used to transform XML documents into XHTML documents. This transformation is particularly useful given the availability of HTML browsers and CSS processors. See the Immediate Solutions section of this chapter for more on how to implement XSLT in real-world situations.

Important XSLT Terms

Any XSLT discussion includes the repeated use of several key terms. Therefore, you need to be familiar with the following terms:

- *Source tree*—The tree of elements and element content in the original document.

- *Result tree*—The tree of elements and element content in the document after transformation.

- *Template rule*—The cornerstone of an XSLT style sheet. Template rules consist of two parts: a pattern and a template.

- *Pattern*—The portion of a template rule that specifies the set of conditions in which an element in the source tree matches the template rule.

- *Template*—The portion of a template rule that specifies what is instantiated in the result tree when the template rule is applied (i.e., when the template rule's pattern matches an element in the source tree).

The Immediate Solutions section of this chapter discusses the creation of each of these XSL components and describes the roles they play in an XSLT style sheet.

The xsl:stylesheet Element

The root element of an XSLT style sheet is the **xsl:stylesheet** element. A minimal XSLT document looks like this:

```
<xsl:stylesheet version="1.0"
xmlns:xsl="http://www.w3.org/1999/XSL/Transform">
... template rules ...
</xsl:stylesheet>
```

NOTE: *If you want to, you can use the **xsl:transform** element instead of the **xsl:stylesheet** element. These two elements are considered synonymous.*

The **xsl:stylesheet** element's **version** attribute is required. Currently, the only available value is 1.0. Check **www.w3.org/Style/XSL/** for the latest updates on the available versions.

The **xsl:stylesheet** element may contain a variety of top-level elements. Some of the more useful include:

- **xsl:import**
- **xsl:include**
- **xsl:strip-space**
- **xsl:preserve-space**
- **xsl:attribute-set**
- **xsl:variable**
- **xsl:param**
- **xsl:template**

In general, these elements can occur in any order within the **xml:stylesheet** element; the exception to this rule is the **xsl:import** element, for which the order is relevant.

xsl:import

The **xsl:import** element is used to import another XSLT style sheet. For example:

```
<xsl:import href="uri-reference" />
```

The **xsl:import** element's **href** attribute value is a Universal Resource Identifier (URI) that references the style sheet to be imported. The order in which style sheets are imported determines the precedence of one template rule over another. In general, the last style sheet imported has a higher precedence than a previously imported style sheet (with the importing style sheet having the highest precedence).

xsl:include

The **xsl:include** element is used by an XSLT style sheet to include another XSLT style sheet. For example:

```
<xsl:include href="uri-reference" />
```

The **xsl:include** element's **href** attribute value is a URI that references the style sheet to be included. The included style sheet brings along its template rules and definitions as if they had been copied into the style sheet at the location of the **xsl:include** element.

Unlike the **xsl:import** element, the template rules included by the **xsl:include** element have the same precedence in the importing style sheet as any other template rule in the style sheet.

xsl:strip-space

The **xsl:strip-space** element specifies which elements in the source document should be removed from the document tree if they contain only white-space characters (and they don't have an ancestor that preserves white space):

```
<xsl:strip-space elements="tokens" />
```

The value of the **xsl:strip-space** element's **elements** attribute is a set of white-space-separated element names.

xsl:preserve-space

The **xsl:preserve-space** element specifies which elements in the source document should not be removed from the document tree even if they contain only white-space characters:

```
<xsl:preserve-space elements="tokens" />
```

The value of the **xsl:preserve** element's **elements** attribute is a set of white-space-separated element names.

xsl:attribute-set

The **xsl:attribute-set** element defines a named set of attributes:

```
<xsl:attribute-set name="qname">
... attributes ...
</xsl:attribute-set>
```

The **xsl:attribute-set** element provides a means for you to apply the same set of attributes to many different elements. The **xsl:attribute-set** element can contain one or more **xsl:attribute** elements:

```
<xsl:attribute name="qname">
... value ...
</xsl:attribute>
```

Therefore, if you want to define an attribute set for styling a section header, you might write:

```
<xsl:attribute-set name="section-header">
   <xsl:attribute name="font-family">Baskerville</xsl:attribute>
   <xsl:attribute name="font-size">18pt</xsl:attribute>
   <xsl:attribute name="font-weight">bold</xsl:attribute>
</xsl:attribute-set>
```

xsl:variable

The **xsl:variable** element binds a name to a value:

```
<xsl:variable name="qname">
... value ...
</xsl:variable>
```

The **xsl:variable** element's **name** attribute value is a string that can be used else-where in the style sheet. The substituted value can be as simple as a string that is commonly used throughout the style sheet or as complicated as additional XSLT markup.

xsl:param

The **xsl:param** element also binds a name to a value:

```
<xsl:param name="qname">
... value ...
</xsl:param>
```

The difference between the **xsl:param** and **xsl:variable** elements is that the **xsl:param** element is used to pass a value to a named template (as well as a style sheet), much like a parameter is passed to a function. You'll learn about named templates later in this chapter.

xsl:template

The **xsl:template** element defines a template rule:

```
<xsl:template match="pattern" name="qname" priority="value">
... template ...
</xsl:template>
```

The **xsl:template** element's **match** attribute specifies the pattern that is com-pared with the elements in the source tree. The **name** attribute is used to create a named template. The **priority** attribute is used when more than one template rule matches a node in the source tree. We'll talk about conflict resolution later in this chapter. The contents of the **xsl:template** element define how the matching element and its element content are transformed.

First, we'll explain how to use basic templates; then we'll explain how to use named templates.

Template Rules

The **xsl:template** element has two basic parts: the pattern of the rule and the output template. The **xsl:template** element's **match** attribute specifies the pattern, and the element content specifies the template.

The first template in your style sheet is usually used to create the root element in the result tree. For example, if you want your result tree to be an XHTML document, you write:

```
<?xml version="1.0"?>
<xsl:stylesheet version="1.0"
xmlns:xsl="http://www.w3.org/XSL/Transform/1.0"
xmlns="http://www.w3.org/1999/xhtml">

    <xsl:template match="/">
        <html>
            <xsl:apply-templates />
        </html>
    </xsl:template>

    ... remaining templates ...
</xsl:stylesheet>
```

When the pattern is matched (as specified by the value of the **match** attribute), the **html** element is added to the result tree. The "/" pattern is used to match the root node of the source tree. For other elements in the document, you simply set the value of the **match** attribute to the element's name.

The **xsl:apply-templates** element tells the XSLT processor to process the content of the root element. This recursion allows you to traverse through the rest of the source tree.

It will help to have a concrete example that demonstrates how these rules apply. Consider the XML document in Listing 11.1 that contains employee information.

Listing 11.1   An XML document that contains employee information.

```
<?xml version="1.0"?>
<?xml-stylesheet
    type="text/xsl" href="C:\WINNT\PROFILES\twugofsk\Desktop\XSLT\test.xsl"?>
<employees>
  <person status="part-time">
    <name><firstname>Jane</firstname> <lastname>Doe</lastname></name>
```

```
        <department>Human Resources</department>
        <phone>555-2300</phone>
        <mobile>555-5423</mobile>
    </person>
    <person status="part-time">
        <name><firstname>Harry</firstname><lastname>Smith</lastname></name>
        <department>Accounting</department>
        <phone>555-2301</phone>
    </person>
    <person status="full-time">
        <name><firstname>Jeff</firstname><lastname>North</lastname></name>
        <department>Accounting</department>
        <phone>555-2310</phone>
        <mobile>555-1029</mobile>
    </person>
    <person status="full-time">
        <name><firstname>Bobby</firstname><lastname>Diggins</lastname></name>
        <department>Information Systems</department>
        <phone>555-4458</phone>
    </person>
</employees>
```

The XSLT style sheet shown in Listing 11. 2 could be used to transform Listing 11.1 to XHTML.

Listing 11.2   An XSLT style sheet used to transform Listing 11.1 to XHTML.

```
<?xml version="1.0"?>
<xsl:stylesheet version="1.0"
xmlns:xsl="http://www.w3.org/1999/XSL/Transform"
xmlns="http://www.w3.org/1999/xhtml">

    <xsl:template match="employees">
        <html>
            <body>
                <xsl:apply-templates />
            </body>
        </html>
    </xsl:template>

    <xsl:template match="person">
        <p>
            <xsl:value-of select="name/lastname" />
        </p>
    </xsl:template>

</xsl:stylesheet>
```

The **xsl:value-of** element computes text by extracting text from the source tree:

```
<xsl:value-of select="string-expression"/>
```

The **xsl:value-of** element's **select** attribute is an expression that is converted into a string and stored as a text node in the result tree. In our example, this would result in generating the following document:

```
<html>
<body>
<p>Doe</p>
<p>Smith</p>
<p>North</p>
<p>Diggins</p>
</body>
</html>
```

The **xsl:template** element's **match** attribute can have a variety of patterns. Use Table 11.1 as a quick reference guide to various patterns for matching templates. These are just samples of the various ways in which you can match nodes in the source tree.

After you have matched nodes in the source tree, you will generally iterate over the matched nodes and either match additional nodes or select parts of the document tree relative to the current node. XSLT uses a new W3C recommendation

Table 11.1   Common patterns for matching templates.

Pattern	Definition
match="E"	Matches any element **E**.
match="*"	Matches any element.
match="E|F"	Matches any element **E** and any element **F**.
match="E/F"	Matches any element **F** with element **E** as its parent.
match="E//F"	Matches any element **F** with element **E** as an ancestor.
match="/"	Matches the root node.
match="text()"	Matches any text node.
match="processing-instruction()"	Matches any processing instruction.
match="node()"	Matches any node other than an attribute node and the root node.
match="id('W11')"	Matches the element with the unique ID W11.
match="E[@class="foo"]	Matches any element **E** whose class attribute is **"foo"**.
match="E[F]"	Matches any element **E** that contains an element **F**.

called the XML Path Language (XPath) for identifying parts of the document tree. In addition to the previous examples, XPath provides mechanisms for selecting nodes. Two of the more useful mechanisms are selecting by an axis and selecting using a predicate.

The *axis* specifies the tree relationship between the current node and the desired node. It allows you to locate children, descendents, and ancestor nodes. Table 11.2 summarizes the various expressions for specifying axes.

XPath introduces *predicates* for selecting nodes relative to the current node. These predicates may be used for the value of the **xsl:apply-templates** element's **select** attribute or the **xsl:value-of** element's **select** attribute. Table 11.3 lists some common predicates and their meaning.

Table 11.2 XPath axis expressions.

Axis	Definition
child	Contains the children of the current node.
descendent	Contains the descendents of the current node. A descendent is a child, or a child of a child, and so on. The descendents never include attribute or namespace nodes.
parent	Contains the parent of the current node.
ancestor	Contains the ancestors of the current node. An ancestor is a parent, or a parent of the parent, and so on. Unless the current node is the root node, the ancestor will always include the root node.
following-sibling	Contains all the siblings that follow the current node. The **following-sibling** axis never includes **attribute** or **namespace** nodes.
preceding-sibling	Contains all the siblings that preceded the current node. The **preceding-sibling** axis never includes **attribute** or **namespace** nodes.
following	Contains all the nodes that follow the current node. The **following** axis excludes descendents of the current node as well as **attribute** and **namespace** nodes.
preceding	Contains all the nodes that preceded the current node. The **preceding** axis excludes ancestors of the current node as well as **attribute** and **namespace** nodes.
attribute	Contains all the attributes of the current node.
namespace	Contains all the **namespace** nodes of the current node.
self	Simply contains the current node.
descendent-or-self	Contains the current node and the descendents of the current node.
ancestor-or-self	Contains the current node and the ancestors of the current node.

Table 11.3   Common predicates for selecting nodes.

Predicate	Meaning
select="E"	Selects the **E** elements that are children of the current node.
select="*"	Selects all elements that are children of the current node.
select="text()"	Selects the text node children of the current node.
select="@name"	Selects the **'name'** attribute of the current node.
select="@*"	Selects all attributes of the current node.
select="E[1]"	Selects the first **E** element that is a child of the current node.
select="E[last()]"	Selects the last **E** element that is a child of the current node.
select="*/E"	Selects all **E** elements that are grandchildren of the current node.
select="E//F"	Selects the **F** elements that are descended from the **E** elements that are children of the current node.
select="//"	Selects the root node.
select="//E"	Selects all **E** elements descended from the root node.
select="//E/F"	Selects all **F** elements that are children of all **E** elements descended from the root node.
select="."	Selects the current node.
select=".//E"	Selects all **E** elements descended from the current node.
select=".."	Selects the parent of the current node.
select="../@name"	Selects the **'name'** attribute of the parent of the current node.
select="E[@name='foo']"	Selects all **E** elements that are children of the current node and whose **'name'** attribute has the value **'foo'**.
select="E[@foo and @bar]"	Selects all **E** elements that have both a **'foo'** attribute and a **'bar'** attribute.

For example, you could create an XSLT style sheet that displays only those employees who have mobile phone numbers by writing the markup in Listing 11.3.

Listing 11.3   The markup used to create an XSLT style sheet that displays only those employees who have mobile phone numbers.

```
<?xml version="1.0"?>
<xsl:stylesheet version="1.0"
xmlns:xsl="http://www.w3.org/1999/XSL/Transform"
xmlns="http://www.w3.org/1999/xhtml">

<xsl:template match="employees">
    <html>
        <body>
            <xsl:apply-templates />
```

```
        </body>
    </html>
</xsl:template>

<xsl:template match="person">
        <xsl:apply-templates select="mobile" />
</xsl:template>

<xsl:template match="name">
    <xsl:value-of select="lastname"/>
</xsl:template>

<xsl:template match="mobile">
    <xsl:apply-templates select="parent::node()/name" />:
    <xsl:value-of select="text()" />
    <br/>
</xsl:template>

</xsl:stylesheet>
```

This style sheet generates the following document:

```
<html xmlns="http://www.w3.org/1999/xhtml">
<body>Doe: 555-5423<br/>North: 555-1029<br/>
</body>
</html>
```

The **xsl:value-of** element is only one way of creating nodes in the result tree. XSLT provides mechanisms for creating text, elements, attributes, processing instructions, comments, and numbering. See the Immediate Solutions section to find out how these elements are used.

The **xsl:element** element is used to create an element with a computed name:

```
<xsl:element name="qname" >
    ... template ...
</xsl:element>
```

The **xsl:element** element is useful if the node in the source tree has an attribute value or some other feature that determines which element you want to create in the result tree. For example, if you want to create a node based on the value of an element's class, you might write:

```
<xsl:element name="{@class}">
    ... template ...
</xsl:element>
```

The **xsl:attribute** element is used to create an attribute with a computed name:

```
<xsl:attribute name="qname">
   ... template ...
</xsl:attribute>
```

The **xsl:attribute** element is useful if the node in the source tree has a value that affects an attribute in the corresponding node in the result tree. For example, if you want to create a hyperlink, you might write:

```
<xsl:template match="pattern">
   <a>... template ...
   <xsl:attribute name="href">
      <xsl:value-of select="string-expression">.htm
   </xsl:attribute>
   </a>
</xsl:template>
```

Named Templates

In the previous section, you saw how you can use patterns to match template rules to nodes in the source tree. XSLT also provides a mechanism for directly invoking a template by its name. Doing so is very useful if you want to reuse a template throughout a complex style sheet.

To name a template, you set the **xsl:template** element's **name** attribute to the name of the template, as follows:

```
<xsl:template name="qname">
   ... template ...
</xsl:template>
```

To use the named template, you use the **xsl:call-template** element from within another template:

```
<xsl:template match="pattern">
   ... start of template ...
   <xsl:call-template name="qname"/>
   ... rest of template ...
</xsl:template>
```

Consider the previous XML document of employee information. If you want a style sheet that displays information in a table, you might write the markup in Listing 11.4.

Listing 11.4   The markup for a style sheet that displays information in a table.

```
<?xml version="1.0"?>
<xsl:stylesheet version="1.0"
xmlns:xsl="http://www.w3.org/1999/XSL/Transform"
xmlns="http://www.w3.org/1999/xhtml">

<xsl:template match="employees">
   <html>
      <body>
         <table>
            <tr><th>Last</th><th>First</th><th>Dept</th><th>Tel</th></tr>
            <xsl:apply-templates/>
         </table>
      </body>
   </html>
</xsl:template>

<xsl:template match="person">
   <xsl:call-template name="contact"/>
</xsl:template>

<xsl:template name="contact">
   <tr>
   <td><xsl:value-of select="name/lastname"/></td>
   <td><xsl:value-of select="name/firstname"/></td>
   <td><xsl:value-of select="department"/></td>
   <td><xsl:value-of select="phone"/></td>
   </tr>
</xsl:template>

</xsl:stylesheet>
```

This XSLT style sheet would generate the document in Listing 11.5.

Listing 11.5   The document generated by the markup in Listing 11.4.

```
<html xmlns="http://www.w3.org/1999/xhtml">
<body>
<table>
<tr><th>Last</th><th>First</th><th>Dept</th><th>Tel</th></tr>
<tr>
<td>Doe</td>
<td>Jane</td>
<td>Human Resources</td>
<td>555-2300</td>
</tr>
```

```
<tr>
<td>Smith</td>
<td>Harry</td>
<td>Accounting</td>
<td>555-2301</td>
</tr>
<tr>
<td>North</td>
<td>Jeff</td>
<td>Accounting</td>
<td>555-2310</td>
</tr>
<tr>
<td>Diggins</td>
<td>Bobby</td>
<td>Information Systems</td>
<td>555-4458</td>
</tr>
</table>
</body>
</html>
```

Resolving Conflicts: Rule Arbitration

As in CSS, with XSLT, it's possible for more than one template rule to match a node in the source tree. XSLT has several rules for resolving these conflicts.

First, when a node in the XML document matches more than one template rule, all template rules that have a lower import precedence are removed from consideration. As you may recall, the last rules imported through the **xsl:import** element have precedence; only rules in the importing style sheet have a higher precedence.

Second, all remaining rules are prioritized based on the value of the **xsl:template** element's **priority** attribute. If you do not specify the value for the **priority** attribute, it's computed based on the specificity of the rule.

The template rule with the highest priority is processed. If more than one template rule still matches the source node, the XSLT processor may signal an error or it must choose the matching template rule that occurs last in the style sheet.

Immediate Solutions

Defining Basic XSLT Style Sheet Constructs

TIP: *Every XSLT document is an XML document; therefore, it must adhere to all of XML's syntactical rules that govern well-formed and valid documents.*

The root element for an XSLT style sheet is the **xsl:stylesheet** element. Every XSLT style sheet should begin and end with opening and closing **xsl:stylesheet** tags.

Use this code to begin an XSLT style sheet:

```
<?xml version="1.0"?>
<xsl:stylesheet version="1.0"
    xmlns:xsl="http://www.w3.org/1999/XSL/Transform">
    ...rest of stylesheet ...
</xsl:stylesheet>
```

The **xsl:stylesheet** element declares that the document is an XSLT document and sets up the remainder of the document to describe style rules for elements in the document to which the style sheet is linked.

Some XSLT processors (such as the one that is included with Microsoft Internet Explorer) require you to refer to this style sheet in the XML document that serves as the source tree. Use the **xml-stylesheet** processing instruction (PI) to reference an XSL style sheet in an XML document:

```
<?xml-stylesheet href="/styles/main-style.xsl" type="text/xsl" ?>
```

Creating Template Rules

Template rules associate nodes in a source tree with a template that creates nodes in a result tree. The nodes in the source tree correspond to all of the elements, attributes, content, and namespaces used in the source document. The nodes in the result tree correspond to the elements, attributes, content, and namespaces in the generated document.

Use this syntax to create a basic template rule:

```
<xsl:template match="pattern">
... template ...
</xsl:template>
```

Patterns and templates are created using their own syntactical constructs. Consider the newspaper DTD we used in Chapters 5 and 8. The following template rule matches the **newspaper** element to **html** and **body** elements in an HTML document:

```
<?xml version="1.0"?>
<xsl:stylesheet version="1.0"
xmlns:xsl="http://www.w3.org/1999/XSL/Transform"
xmlns="http://www.w3.org/1999/xhtml">
  <xsl:template match="newspaper">
    <html>
      <body>
        <xsl:apply-templates/>
      </body>
    </html>
  </xsl:template>
</xsl:stylesheet>
```

The **xsl:template** element's **match** attribute specifies a pattern that matches the first (and only) child of the root node of the source document. When this rule matches the **newspaper** node in the source document, the template creates an **html** element node and a **body** element node.

The **xsl:apply-templates** element tells the XSLT processor to continue processing the children of the source document's root node (in other words, the rest of the document).

Declaring a Pattern

Patterns describe a source tree's nodes to which the template portion of a template rule is applied. Create a basic pattern using this syntax:

```
<xsl:template match="pattern">
... template ...
</xsl:template>
```

The **xsl:template** element's **match** attribute specifies which nodes in the source tree should be affected by the rule.

The newspaper template rule from the previous section is an example of the simplest form a pattern can have:

```
<xsl:template match="newspaper">
  <html>
    <body>
      <xsl:apply-templates/>
    </body>
  </html>
</xsl:template>
```

This template rule will match any element whose name matches the value of the **match** attribute. You could extend this rule to include several other elements in our newspaper DTD:

```
<?xml version="1.0" encoding="UTF-8"?>
<xsl:stylesheet version="1.0"
xmlns:xsl="http://www.w3.org/1999/XSL/Transform"
xmlns="http://www.w3.org/1999/xhtml">

<xsl:template match="newspaper">
  <html>
    <body>
      <xsl:apply-templates/>
    </body>
  </html>
</xsl:template>

<xsl:template match="section">
  <xsl:apply-templates/>
</xsl:template>

<xsl:template match="article">
  <div class="article">
    <xsl:apply-templates/>
  </div>
</xsl:template>

</xsl:stylesheet>
```

In this example, we iterate through the **section** elements and the **article** elements. Each **article** element is placed inside of a **div** element.

There are a variety of other ways in which you can match template rules to nodes in the source document. Refer back to Table 11.1 for a list of the more commonly used matching patterns.

Matching Children and Descendents

In addition to matching by element name, you can match an element's children by using the **/** symbol to separate the name of the parent element and the name of the child element. For example:

```
<xsl:template match="parent-pattern/child-name">
    ... template ...
</xsl:template>
```

Returning to our newspaper DTD, you could write two simple template rules that format the **headline** element's content child element and subhead child element:

```
<xsl:template match="headline/content">
  <h2><xsl:value-of select="text()"/></h2>
</xsl:template>

<xsl:template match="headline/subhead">
  <b><xsl:value-of select="text()"/></b><br/>
</xsl:template>
```

The first template rule matches any **content** element that is a child of a **headline** element. The second template rule matches any **subhead** element that is a child of a **headline** element. Each of these rules takes the text contained by the element and places it inside an HTML element (the **h2** and **b** elements, to be specific).

You're not limited to matching the child of an element; you can also match an element's descendents using the **//** symbol. Doing so might be useful if the DTD has a deep hierarchy and you want to select all the elements regardless of whether they're children, grandchildren, or farther down in the hierarchy. For example, if you want to select all the articles in the newspaper, regardless of which section they were in, you would write:

```
<xsl:template match="newspaper//article"/>
   ... rest of template ...
</xsl:template>
```

Matching Attributes in a Pattern

Attributes are used to better define elements within an XML document. With XSLT, you can also match a pattern against an element's attribute values.

To specify this type of template rule, you write:

```
<xsl:template match="E[@foo='bar']">
... template ...
</xsl:template>
```

This rule selects all **E** elements that are children of the current node and that have a **foo** attribute with value **bar**.

Matching Multiple Patterns

Template rules can apply to multiple patterns by using a vertical bar (|) symbol. If the pattern matches any of the patterns separated by the | symbol, the template is applied. For example, if you want to apply the same template to the **subhead** element and the **byline** element, you write:

```
<xsl:template match="headline/subhead | byline">
  <b><xsl:value-of select="text()"/></b><br/>
</xsl:template>
```

Although this example shows two patterns, you can add additional patterns if you see fit.

Selecting the Value of a Child Element

The first part of a template rule is the pattern used to match the rule with nodes in the source tree. The second part of a template rule is the template used to transform the source tree into the result tree.

The most common way to copy the value of a child element into the result tree is to use the **xsl:value-of** element. For example, if you want to copy the **story** element's **storycontent** child element into the result tree, you would write:

```
<xsl:template match="story">
  <p><xsl:value-of select="storycontent"/></p>
</xsl:template>
```

The **xsl:value-of** element's **select** attribute value is set to the name of the child element that you wish to copy.

Selecting the Value of a Text Element

You can select the text children of the current node by using the **xsl:value-of** element and setting the **select** attribute to "**text( )**". We used this selector previously, when we created the template rule for matching the **headline** element's content child element:

```
<xsl:template match="headline/content">
  <h2><xsl:value-of select="text()"/></h2>
</xsl:template>
```

Applying Templates to Specific Elements

Previously, we described how you use the **xsl:apply-templates** element to apply template rules to all the children of an element. Sometimes, you'll want to be more selective about which children to process. You can accomplish this by setting the **xsl:apply-templates** element's **select** attribute to specify which children should be processed.

Returning to our venerable newspaper DTD, let's create a template that applies only to the **pullquotes** elements. Because you want this template to generate content near the top of the result tree, you specify the rule in which you match the **section** element:

```
<xsl:template match="section">
  <ul><xsl:apply-templates select=".//pullquotes"/></ul>
  <xsl:apply-templates/>
</xsl:template>
```

This template rule creates a **ul** element that contains the results of applying the templates against all **pullquotes** elements that are descendents of the current **section** element. The . symbol indicates the current node (the **section** element) and the **//** symbol indicates descendents.

Let's also create a template rule that matches the **pullquotes** element:

```
<xsl:template match="pullquotes">
  <li><xsl:value-of select="text()"/> (See
    <xsl:value-of select="../../headline/content" />)
  </li>
</xsl:template>
```

This template rule creates an **li** element that has two **xsl:value-of** elements. The first **xsl:value-of** element inserts the text of the **pullquotes** element into the list item (**li**). The second **xsl:value-of** element inserts the text of the **pullquotes** element's grandfather's **headline** element's **content** element.

Generating Numbers

In addition to generating text from the element and attribute content, you can create numbers using the **xsl:number** element. For example, if you want to create a numbered header for each section in your newspaper, you can rewrite the template rule that applies to the **section** element:

```
<xsl:template match="section">
  <h1>Section <xsl:number value="position()" format="1" /></h1>
  <ul><xsl:apply-templates select=".//pullquotes"/></ul>
  <xsl:apply-templates/>
</xsl:template>
```

This template inserts an **h1** element into the result tree. This **h1** element contains the text *"Section"* followed by white space and then the value of a counter indicating the position of this **section** element in the source document.

Setting Attribute Values

Most of the time, you'll probably set attribute values directly in the style sheet. We did this when we created the template for the **article** element:

```
<xsl:template match="article">
  <div class="article">
    <xsl:apply-templates/>
  </div>
</xsl:template>
```

In this template, we set the **div** element's **class** attribute to the value **"article"**. This approach may work most of the time, but sometimes you'll want to set an attribute value based on a dynamic value.

The **xsl:attribute** value provides a mechanism for dynamically setting an attribute value. For example, you might use the **xsl:attribute** element to create an anchor at the beginning of each article:

```
<xsl:template match="article">
  <a>
    <xsl:attribute name="name">
      <xsl:value-of select="headline/content" />
    </xsl:attribute>
  </a>
  <div class="article">
    <xsl:apply-templates/>
  </div>
</xsl:template>
```

The **xsl:attribute** element always appears as the first child of the element it's modifying. The **xsl:attribute** element's **name** attribute is set to the name of the attribute you want to modify, and the **xsl:attribute** element's content is the value assigned to that attribute. In this example, the value of the **a** element's **name** attribute is set to the name of the article.

Likewise, you can create a link to this anchor by adding an **a** element to the **pullquote** element's matching template rule:

```
<xsl:template match="pullquotes">
  <li>
    <xsl:value-of select="text()"/> (See <a>
      <xsl:attribute name="href">
        #<xsl:value-of select="../../headline/content"/>
      </xsl:attribute>
    <xsl:value-of select="../../headline/content" /></a>)
  </li>
</xsl:template>
```

In this template, we added an **a** element and set the **href** attribute to the text **#** followed by the name of the article. The **#** is necessary because we're referring to a fragment anchor located within the current document.

Putting It All Together

The XSLT style sheet that results from our previous examples looks something like Listing 11.6.

Listing 11.6   XSLT style sheet that results from our previous examples.

```
<?xml version="1.0" encoding="UTF-8"?>
<xsl:stylesheet version="1.0"
xmlns:xsl="http://www.w3.org/1999/XSL/Transform"
xmlns="http://www.w3.org/1999/xhtml">

<xsl:template match="newspaper">
  <html>
    <body>
      <xsl:apply-templates select="section"/>
    </body>
  </html>
</xsl:template>

<xsl:template match="section">
  <h1>Section <xsl:number value="position()" format="1" /></h1>
  <ul><xsl:apply-templates select=".//pullquotes"/></ul>
  <xsl:apply-templates/>
</xsl:template>

<xsl:template match="article">
  <a>
    <xsl:attribute name="name">
```

```
      <xsl:value-of select="headline/content" /></xsl:attribute>
  </a>
  <div class="article">
    <xsl:apply-templates/>
  </div>
</xsl:template>

<xsl:template match="headline/content">
  <h2><xsl:value-of select="text()"/></h2>
</xsl:template>

<xsl:template match="headline/subhead|byline">
  <b><xsl:value-of select="text()"/></b><br/>
</xsl:template>

<xsl:template match="lede">
  <p><b><xsl:value-of select="text()"/></b></p>
</xsl:template>

<xsl:template match="story">
  <p><xsl:value-of select="storycontent"/></p>
</xsl:template>

<xsl:template match="pullquotes">
  <li><xsl:value-of select="text()"/> (See <a>
    <xsl:attribute name="href">
     #<xsl:value-of select="../../headline/content" /></xsl:attribute>
    <xsl:value-of select="../../headline/content" /></a>)
  </li>
</xsl:template>

</xsl:stylesheet>
```

Now, let's apply this style sheet (Listing 11.6) against the following XML document in Listing 11.7.

Listing 11.7 The XML document to which we're going to apply the style template in Listing 11.6.

```
<?xml version="1.0" encoding="UTF-8"?>
<!DOCTYPE newspaper SYSTEM
  "D:\LANWrights\XML Black Book\Ch11\newspaper.dtd">
<?xml-stylesheet type="text/xsl"
  href="D:\LANWrights\XML Black Book\Ch11\newspaper.xsl"?>
<newspaper>
  <section>
    <article>
```

```
    <headline>
        <content>First Article</content>
    </headline>
        <byline>By Yogi Bear</byline>
        <lede/>
        <story>
           <storycontent>
             This is the beginning of the first article.
           </storycontent>
           <pullquotes>A pullquote from the first article.</pullquotes>
        </story>
    </article>
    <article>
      <headline>
        <content>Second Article</content>
        <subhead>The subheading</subhead>
      </headline>
        <byline>By Betty Boop</byline>
        <lede/>
        <story>
           <storycontent>
             This is the beginning of the second article.
           </storycontent>
           <pullquotes>A pullquote from the second article.</pullquotes>
        </story>
    </article>
  </section>
  <section>
    <article>
      <headline>
        <content>Third Article</content>
      </headline>
        <byline>By Krazy Kat</byline>
        <lede/>
        <story>
           <storycontent>
             This is the beginning of the third article.
           </storycontent>
           <pullquotes>A pullquote from the third article.</pullquotes>
        </story>
    </article>
  </section>
</newspaper>
```

The generated document would look something like Listing 11.8.

Listing 11.8   The result of combining Listings 11.6 and 11.7.

```html
<html>
<body>
<h1>Section 1</h1>
  <ul>
    <li>A pullquote from the first article.
       (See <a href="#First Article">First Article</a>)
    </li>
    <li>A pullquote from the second article.
       (See <a href="#Second Article">Second Article</a>)
    </li>
  </ul>
<a name="First Article"></a>
<div class="article">
<h2>First Article</h2>
<b>By Yogi Bear</b><br>
<p><b></b></p>
   <p>This is the beginning of the first article.</p>
</div>
<a name="Second Article"></a>
<div class="article">
<h2>Second Article</h2>
<b>The subheading</b><br><b>By Betty Boop</b><br>
<p><b></b></p>
   <p>This is the beginning of the second article.</p>
</div>
<h1>Section 2</h1>
  <ul>
    <li>A pullquote from the third article.
       (See <a href="#Third Article">Third Article</a>)
    </li>
  </ul>
<a name="Third Article"></a>
<div class="article">
<h2>Third Article</h2>
<b>By Krazy Kat</b><br>
<p><b></b></p>
  <p>This is the beginning of the third article.</p>
</div>
</body>
</html>
```

Your generated document is likely to be different depending on the white space you added in your XSLT style sheet. HTML is insensitive to white space, and your document may look different because we added white space for readability.

11. Translating XML Documents with XSL Transformations

Using Tools to Build XSLT Style Sheets

The XSLT and XPath recommendations are still rather new; however, there are a few robust XSL tools already available, such as the following:

- *Xalan*—**http://xml.apache.org**
- *XT*—**www.jclark.com/xml/xt.html**
- *Saxon*—**http://users.iclway.co.uk/mhkay/saxon/index.html**
- *LotusXSL*—**www.alphaworks.ibm.com/tech/LotusXSL**

For XSLT editors, try the following:

- *Stylus*—**www.exceloncorp.com/products/excelon_stylus.html**
- *XML Style Wizard*—**www.infoteria.com/en/contents/download/**
- *IBM's XSL Editor*—**www.alphaworks.ibm.com/tech/xsleditor**

Microsoft Internet Explorer (IE, beginning with version 5.5 beta) has a fairly good XML parser that handles both XSLT and XPath. Another good tool is XML Spy (**www.xmlspy.com/**), which also requires the Microsoft IE 5.5 beta (presumably, later versions of IE will work as well).

If you only have IE 5.5 beta, you can simply use any text editor (such as Notepad) to create your XML DTDs, XML documents, and XSLT style sheets. Make sure that your XML document refers to your XSLT style sheet using the following processing instruction:

```
<?xml-stylesheet href="/styles/main-style.xsl" type="text/xsl" ?>
```

Also, make sure that your XSLT style sheet refers to the correct XSLT namespace:

```
<?xml version="1.0"?>
<xsl:stylesheet version="1.0"
   xmlns:xsl="http://www.w3.org/1999/XSL/Transform">
   ...rest of stylesheet ...
</xsl:stylesheet>
```

XML Spy, on the other hand, provides a nice GUI for managing your DTDs, XML documents, and XSLT style sheets. To create a new XML document in XML Spy, follow these steps:

1. Start with the newspaper DTD, and load it into XML Spy using the File|Open menu item. You'll see a window similar to Figure 11.1.

2. After you load the DTD into XML Spy, you can create an XML document by selecting File|New. This menu item displays the Create New Document dialog box, shown in Figure 11.2, which allows you to choose the type of file you want to create.

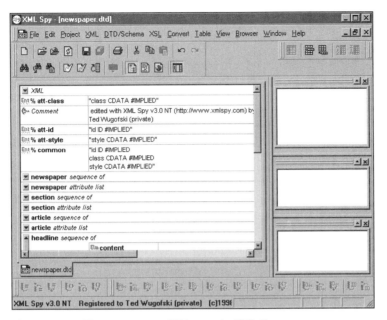

Figure 11.1   The newspaper DTD open in XML Spy.

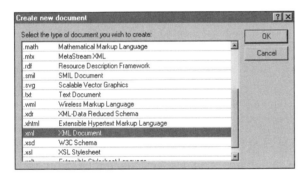

Figure 11.2   The XML Spy Create New Document dialog box.

3. Select the .xml XML Document type and click OK.

4. You're asked if you want to associate the new document with an existing schema or DTD. Select the DTD radio button and click OK to display a dialog box that allows you to browse to a DTD.

5. Click the Window button and select the newspaper DTD that is currently loaded into XML Spy. Click OK to return to the development environment. The window displays the newly created XML document, as shown in Figure 11.3.

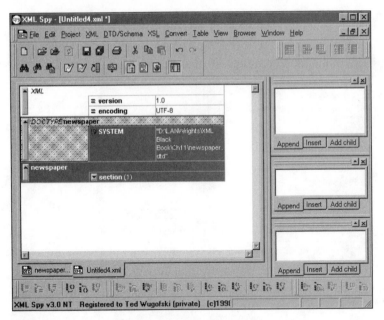

Figure 11.3   The newly created XML document.

In the development environment, you can populate the XML document as you see fit.

To create the XSLT style sheet, follow these steps:

1. Select File|New and then select the .xslt Extensible Stylesheet Language menu item. Doing so displays a blank XSLT style sheet, as shown in Figure 11.4.

2. Put your cursor after the **xsl:stylesheet** start tag and begin typing your template rules. When you're done, you should see something similar to Figure 11.5.

3. Make sure you save everything, of course. When you're done with your XSLT style sheet, select the XML document, and select XSL|Assign XSL. This menu item displays a dialog box for selecting the associated XSLT style sheet. Make sure you select the style sheet currently in the window.

4. After you've assigned the style sheet, select XSL|XSL Transformation. This menu item will run the XSLT processor and generate an output window, as shown in Figure 11.6.

TIP: *The View/Text View menu item also lets you look at the generated markup. This feature is particularly useful when debugging your XSLT style sheets.*

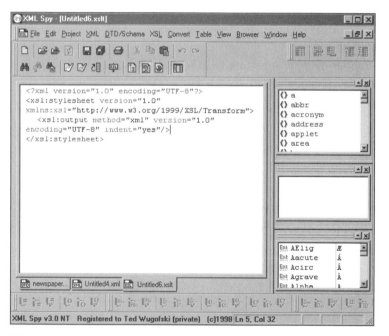

Figure 11.4   A blank style sheet in XML Spy.

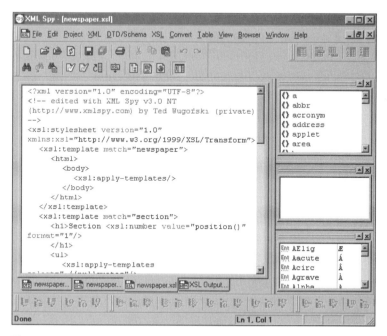

Figure 11.5   A sample style sheet in XML Spy.

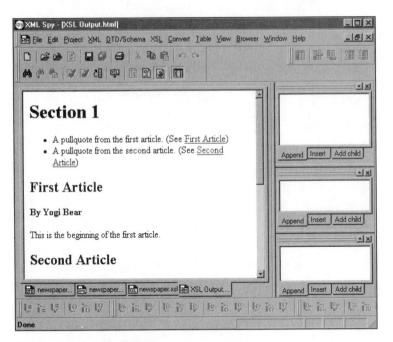

Figure 11.6   An XML Spy output window.

Chapter 12
Linking in XML: XLink

In Depth

A large part of the Web's success is a result of its hyperlinking capabilities. Users are always just a click away from any resource on the Internet. Hyperlinking provides ways of finding, organizing, and relating resources that provide Web users with the power to access massive amounts of information. When XML was first introduced, it lacked the type of standardized linking features that Web users were accustomed to with the Hypertext Markup Language (HTML). XML documents needed a standardized way of linking to other resources so that XML could also take part in the vast supply of information available over the Internet.

The XML Linking Language (XLink) is the World Wide Web Consortium's (W3C's) attempt to standardize this important feature of the Web. XLink brings the robust, easy-to-use features of the Web's current linking system to the world of XML, and extends it to provide even more powerful ways to link the Internet's resources. The combination of XML's flexibility and the power of linking will make the future of the Web even more exciting than it is today. This chapter explores XLink and shows the new capabilities this linking language will bring to XML documents.

TIP: *The XLink specification is currently in the candidate recommendation stage. Some of the information in this chapter may be subject to change. Check* **www.w3.org/XML/Linking** *for the most up-to-date information.*

An Overview of Linking in XML

Before we go into the details of XLink, we'll first examine simple hypertext links and how they work in HTML. This information provides a backdrop based on familiar concepts from which we'll expand to explore the capabilities of XLink.

In the world of hypertext, a *link* is a connection to another resource. A *resource* can be anything that's accessible over a network. If you've developed any HTML Web pages, you're probably already familiar with links and the element used to specify them. In HTML, links to other resources are created using the anchor (**a**) element with an **href** attribute, which specifies the location of the resource. The following example shows a typical linking element in HTML:

```
<a href="http://www.site.com/index.html">The Index of My Site</a>
```

A Web browser such as Netscape Navigator or Microsoft's Internet Explorer will display this fragment of HTML as underlined text: for example, <u>The Index of My Site</u>. When a user clicks on the underlined text, the Web page at **http://www.site.com/index.html** will be displayed in the browser.

An HTML link consists of a *starting resource*, which is the area that the user clicks on, and an *ending resource*, which is the Web page that the user sees after the area is clicked. The starting resource is the content that appears between the opening and closing **a** tags—in this case, the text **The Index of My Site**. Because this resource is part of the linking element itself, it's known as a *local resource*. The ending resource is indicated by the **href** attribute—in this case, the Web page referred to by **http://www.site.com/index.html**. Because this resource is located elsewhere, it's known as a *remote resource.*

The behavior of the link is predefined by the HTML specification. It states that when a link is selected, the ending resource will be retrieved and displayed in the browser. Using a link is also known as *traversing* a link. This traversal has a direction associated with it, which is also specified by the HTML specification. The direction is from the local resource (the content between the opening and closing **a** tags) to the remote resource (**http://www.site.com/index.html**).

The remote resource specified can be any Web resource, such as another Web page, a file stored on a file transfer server, a script that allows you to query a remote database, or even a connection to a remote video camera. You can also specify other types of documents, fragments of documents, and even links to multimedia resources, such as video or audio files. The **href** attribute specifies the remote resource using the Universal Resource Identifier (URI) format. The following are examples of the types of URIs that can be used in an **href** attribute to connect to a variety of resources:

- **ftp://ftp.is.co.za/rfc/rfc1808.txt**—To connect to an FTP server.

- **mailto:mduerst@ifi.unizh.ch**—To connect to an email address.

- **test/text.html**—To connect to a Web page that is relative to the current base URL.

- **http://www.mycompany.com/one.html#anchor-one**—To connect to a specific location in the given Web page.

NOTE: *Even though XLink specifies that you use a URI format, the **href** is commonly a Universal Resource Locator (URL), which is a specific type of URI. In this chapter, we use the term URL, even though URI is more technically correct, because URL is more familiar; and, in practice, it's the type of URI used most often. To learn more about the differences between URIs and URLs, see the W3C's document on the subject at **www.w3.org/Addressing**.*

When the developers of XML's linking mechanism set out to create XLink, they knew they needed a language that was capable of representing the same types of links that are used in HTML documents. Therefore, links in XLink had to have the following characteristics:

- The link can be traversed from a local resource to a remote resource.
- The link goes to a single destination.
- The link's effect on the graphical user interface (GUI) is determined by the GUI itself and not the link.
- The link is activated by the user.
- Remote resources are specified with a URL.

However, simple HTML links are limited, and the language had to be powerful enough to support more advanced linking concepts. Therefore, XLink needed additional functionality to include the following capabilities:

- Because XML allows developers to define their own links, they must be able to attach the linking markup to any element.
- Links need to have both human- and machine-understandable labels.
- Developers must be able to provide the XLink application with specific information about how links must be processed.
- Link transversal can be activated in ways other than by the user.
- Links don't have to be one-way links.
- Links can be described from outside of the resources they connect.
- Links can contain more than two resources.
- Each starting and ending pair of resources in a link can have different traversal behaviors.

In XLink, the type of link that is equivalent to an HTML link is referred to as a *simple link*. Simple links connect one piece of an XML document to another Internet resource; it can be another XML document or any other resource accessible over the Internet. A simple link can include the following information:

- The element used to specify the link. In HTML, this is the **a** element; however, in XLink, it could be any element.

NOTE: The **img** element also provides links to graphics files.

- The starting resource that indicates to the user that this is a link. The starting resource is always the contents of the element used to specify the link.

- Any instructions that specify to the browser or the software what the link should do, such as display the other document in a new window or replace the contents of the current window with the new document.

- Whether a link has to be clicked on or whether the link is activated when the document is loaded.

- Whether the link will reference an entire document or a specific part of an XML resource. Note that this capability is provided by the XPointer language. (See Chapter 14 for more information on XPointers.)

Related solution:	Found on page:
Adding a Simple XPointer to an XML Link	383

The following is a simple XML link similar to the HTML link we examined earlier in the chapter:

```
<go xlink:type="simple" xlink:href="http://www.site.com/index.html">
The Index of My Site</go>
```

As you can see, this link is very similar to the HTML anchor (**a**) element, with a few additions. First, the element name used for a link is not fixed. Unlike HTML, where the **a** element specifies that the element will be a link, no one XLink element specifies a link. Instead, you use the XLink attribute **xlink:type**. The **xlink** part of this attribute name is called a *namespace prefix*. Any valid linking element must have an attribute named **type** that belongs to the XLink namespace. The value of this attribute, **simple**, indicates that this is a simple link. Another difference from HTML is the namespace prefix attached to the **href** attribute. Again, attributes recognized by an XLink application must be in the XLink namespace.

TIP: *To learn more about namespaces, see Chapter 15.*

XLink offers much more than simple inline links. In fact, XLink offers a variety of link types, link actions, and link capabilities, which can be defined using the XLink language. In this way, you actually construct your own links and linking action.

The entire linking mechanism in XML is defined in three subcomponents or parts: XLink, XPointer, and XML Base:

- *XLink*—Specifies how links are inserted into XML documents and where the links can point. XLink specifies how the links in a document are recognized as links and not just as content or element or attribute information. It gives you the ability to link objects and/or other resources, internally or externally.

It's a language that allows you to create your own link elements and create a kind of link database.

- *XPointer*—Allows you to specify precise subparts of an XML document instead of just pointing to the entire document. HTML limits pointing to parts of a document that have an ID or are named using the **a** element. XPointers are used with URLs and help define a particular fragment of a document. Basically, XPointers govern the fragment identifier that goes into a URL when you link to a resource in an XML document.

- *XML Base*—Allows you to specify the base URL for the purpose of resolving relative URLs in links. A single, new attribute called **xml:base** can be included in any element to set a base URL other than that of the base URL of the document itself.

TIP: *If you're interested in reading more about the three linking-related specifications, check out* **www.w3.org/XML/ Linking**. *For a detailed discussion of XPointers, see Chapter 14.*

Why are there three separate specifications just for linking? Why didn't the W3C include the linking portion of XML in the actual XML specification? The answer to both these questions is a basic design principle: modularity. A super-specification that contains information from all the specifications would be large and difficult to understand. In addition, software based on such a specification would take a long time to develop. Then, every time a part of the specification changed, all the software that relies on the specification would need to change. It's easier to understand and implement the specifications for the various XML-related concepts if they're separate.

XML Linking Terms

Before we go any further, we should clearly define some of the terminology and components of XLink. You need to know and understand them to work with the Immediate Solutions section of this chapter and to understand the XLink specification itself. The following terms are used in the XLink specifications:

- *Link*—A relationship between resources or parts of resources.

- *Linking element*—An element that specifies the existence of a link. This linking element contains attributes and other linking elements that describe the link's characteristics. The anchor (**a**) element in HTML is a linking element. Any element in an XML document is a potential linking element.

- *Resource*—A service or piece of information that can be addressed. A resource can be a file, an image, a document, a document fragment, a program, database query results, or a sound file. More specifically, a resource can be anything that can be referenced by a URL.

- *Inline link*—A link that serves as one of its own resources. More specifically, an inline link is one where the content of the linking element acts as a resource. An example of such a link is the HTML **a** element.

- *Locator*—A piece of data (provided as part of a link) that identifies the resource and can be used to locate the resource. A locator is a resource's address specified by a URL.

- *Participating resource*—A resource that is part of a link. Any resource is a potential link and becomes a participating link when it's identified by a locator as part of the link.

- *Local resource*—The content of an inline linking element. If the document that contains the link is one of the link's resources, the document is a local resource.

- *Remote resource*—A participating resource that is pointed to by a locator. It can be a resource accessed across a network, or a different part of the document where the link appears.

- *Traversal*—The action of using a link to access a resource. Traversals are often initiated by a user action. Think of a traversal as the activation of a link in order to access its ending resource.

- *Multidirectional link*—A link that can be traversed from either resource. It's more than just a link that provides a mechanism to go back to a previously visited resource or link; the traversal can start from either end.

- *Arc*—Specifies how to traverse a link. It can include information about the direction of the traversal, and what behavior is expected when the link is activated.

- *XLink application*—Any software that processes an XML document according to the XLink specification.

All these link components are put together to form different types of links, which are covered in "The Details of XLink" section later in this chapter. For now, you should be familiar with the following linking terms:

- *Simple link*—An XLink link that uses the **href** attribute to point to only one remote resource. Simple links can take on several different attributes, including **role** and **show**, and are always inline links that connect the local resource to one remote resource.

- *Extended link*—An XML link that can include several resources and doesn't have to be an inline link. Each combination of starting and ending resources can have different arcs associated with it, giving different behaviors for each traversal.

The Origins of XLink

Now that you're familiar with some basic XLink terminology, you need to know where XLink came from and what previous linking technologies helped form the XLink specification. The XLink specification was first called the Extensible Linking Language (XLL), and then it was XML-Link. Finally, the W3C decided on its final name, XLink. XLink provides the mechanism to link resources to each other using XML syntax. The ideas used in XLink came from a variety of other linking specifications. The three standards that have been most influential in XLink's development are HTML, HyTyme, and the Text Encoding Initiative Guidelines (TEIP3). If you have previous experience with any of these standards, it should be relatively easy for you to understand what XLink offers. If you're not familiar with these linking technologies, here's a quick overview:

- *Hypertext Markup Language (HTML)*—HTML helped define several Standard Generalized Markup Language (SGML) element types that represent single directional links to resources regardless of the type of protocol—Hypertext Transfer Protocol (HTTP), File Transfer Protocol (FTP), Gopher, Telnet, and so on—used to connect to those resources. HTML **a**, **img**, and **form** elements are all examples of linking elements.

- *HyTime*—HyTime, which is used within the SGML specification, defines the inline and out-of-line link structures and some semantic features, including traversal control and presentation of objects.

- *Text Encoding Initiative Guidelines (TEIP3)*—The TEIP3 guidelines provide structures for creating links, aggregate objects, and link collections.

Numerous other linking systems have also contributed to the creation of the XLink specification, including Dexter, FRESS (which stands for the File Retrieval and Editing System), MicroCosm, and InterMedia. More specifically, however, XML's linking specification builds upon HTML and actually works toward preserving the HTML linking structure. One of the original design goals of XLink was for it to be backward compatible with HTML. However, because XLink's global attributes are required to be in the XLink namespace, this compatibility is not possible. The structure of XLink simple links is as close to HTML syntax as possible to allow easy translation between the two formats.

TIP: *XLink is a candidate recommendation as of July 3, 2000. Check it out at the W3C's site, **www.w3.org/TR/xlink**. This specification is considered stable, and it should be very close to the current version when it does become a recommendation.*

XLink Design Principles

When the group that put together the XLink syntax gathered, it had specific goals in mind in terms of how XLink should operate and function, not only on the Internet, but also within XML documents. In this section, you'll find out how links are designed in XLink. Knowing these design principles will help you implement links in your documents. The following is a summary of the design principles governing XLink as defined by the W3C:

- *XLink shall be straightforwardly usable over the Internet.* This principle simply means that, because you have no control over resources outside your own network, and because you cannot control the result each link provides, the linking feature should not be unusable in circumstances dictated by the Internet. Because sites move, pages are deleted, and information changes, XLink must accommodate broken links, resources that cannot be located, and links that take the user in the wrong direction. XLink must also support multidirectional links in software applications. Interoperability and internationalization is also important.

- *XLink shall be usable by a wide variety of link usage domains and of classes of linking application software.* When you use XLink, there should be no favoritism of one domain over another. Regardless of where the link points are or what type of document the link is stored in—for example, a cross-reference in a technical publication or a link to a Web page—there should be no preference. In addition, there should be no preference for browsers, application software, or editing systems that are used to create, display, or process the links. Browsers are not the only software used on the Internet, and links should be equally useful for all types of applications.

- *The XLink expression language shall be XML.* The premise here is that any link structure must follow the XML element and attribute syntax. Because you can design your own link elements, you need to supply the characteristics of the link in the same way you do when you create and specify any element.

- *The XLink design shall be prepared quickly.* XLink is a critical piece for the next generation Web infrastructure, and a specification must be available to ensure interoperability among applications. If the specification takes too long to prepare, each application will invent its own linking mechanism, and there will be no compatibility between them.

- *The XLink design shall be formal and concise.* The linking language should be explained in such a way that it does not confuse readers. The idea is that the specification doesn't confuse how the links relate to each other and the XML syntax used to define the links.

- *XLink shall be human-readable.* Don't you wish everything in the computer world followed this rule? Actually, it means more than just making sure links are readable. The link structures may be in compressed, encrypted, or binary form when transmitted or internally processed, but they must be in text form within the XML document to be considered XLink links.

- *XLink links may reside outside the documents in which the participating resources reside.* To offer scalability and relief from HTML linking limitations, XLink must support sophisticated out-of-line linking. This principle allows for situations in which links are defined in one document, but the resources specified by the links exist in other documents.

- *XLink shall represent the abstract structure and significance of links.* There should be some small indication about basic link behavior. The designers of the XLink specification didn't want to encourage procedural markup; they wanted to indicate what basic link behavior is acceptable.

- *XLink must be feasible to implement.* Although some of the features of linking may be difficult to implement because of their complexity, linking should be possible to implement. It is not a requirement of the specification to make the implementation easy.

Knowing these design principles before you start creating links will help you design your links appropriately. If you want to read more about the XLink design guidelines, see the specification at **www.w3.org/TR/NOTE-xlink-principles**. Next, we review the actual link process.

An Overview of XLink

XLink extends HTML's concept of linking in several ways. A link defined with XLink is an explicit relationship between two or more data units or portions of data units. XLink provides not just one, but two types of link elements: the standard inline link that provides unidirectional connections to resources, and extended links that can be either inline or out-of-line connections to resources, and can be multidirectional. Behavioral and semantic information can also be added to links. Thus, XML linking goes far beyond the basic hyperlinking mechanism HTML offers. XLink offers the ability to have sophisticated links that can be processed in a standard way.

One of XLink's features lets you create multidirectional links. *Multidirectional links* are more than just links that take the visitor forward to a particular location, as is the case with HTML. Multidirectional links mean that you can start the link traversal on either end of the link.

When a developer creates a link with XLink, metadata can be added to the link. This metadata specifies the behavior of the link—that is, how and when link traversal should occur. The roles of links, resources, and arcs can also be specified, including human- and machine-understandable data.

XLink also allows you to define links that are in a different location than the resources to which they refer. The idea behind this ability is that the links and cross-references to other sources can be scalable and maintainable. By allowing links to be separated from source documents, you can maintain links by modifying a single document. In the following section, we examine the components of XLink and the details of creating links in an XML document.

The Details of XLink

As mentioned earlier, one of XML's features lets you define your own linking elements. Unlike HTML, XLink allows you to define any element type to be used as a link. XLink does not define any elements; it only defines the attributes you use to specify linking characteristics. You use these attributes to indicate which elements are XLink elements. You must define these attributes in the XLink namespace, which is:

```
http://www.w3.org/1999/xlink
```

The attributes from this namespace can be inserted into a document like this:

```
<myElement
  xmlns:xlink="http://www.w3.org/1999/xlink"
  xlink:type="simple"
  xlink:href="/foo.html">
    This is my link
</myElement>
```

The previous XML fragment defines an element that has two attributes from XLink's namespace: **type** and **href**. In the examples used in this section of the chapter, the namespace declaration (**xmlns:xlink="http://www.w3.org/1999/xlink"**) is left out and the prefix **xlink** is always used for XLink attributes. In your code, you need to use the namespace declaration, and the examples in the Immediate Solutions section of this chapter will include it. XLink defines 10 attributes, all of which are covered throughout this chapter.

Defining a Simple Inline Link

As mentioned earlier, a simple inline link connects to a single, remote resource. This resource is really anything that can be reached by using a locator and can include graphics, documents, database queries, or streamed movies. You define the locator the same way **href** attributes are defined in HTML.

When defining unidirectional external links in XLink, you use the simple link type that includes a URL. Because of the XLink design, simple links in XLink are similar to HTML anchor (**a**) links. They have only one locator, which (like the **href** attribute in the HTML **a** element) specifies the URL. The following code shows valid, simple XLinks:

```
<a xlink:type="simple" xlink:href="http://www.site.com/default.html"/>
<a xlink:type="simple" xlink:href="/default.xml"/>
<a xlink:type="simple"
xlink:href="http://www.site.com/default.xml#sectiona/">
```

In XML, a simple link carries all the linking information in the linking element itself. Although it sounds straightforward, creating a simple link in XML is a bit more time-consuming than creating one in HTML. It takes a little more than just the **a** element and the **href** attribute to specify a link.

Specifying Link Elements

Of course, when you specify a link, you must first specify the element that signifies the link. To do so, you create an **xlink:type** attribute for the element in the Document Type Definition (DTD). Then, you use that element and its attributes as you would any element within an XML document. For example, we'll define an element called **link** and specify the attributes of the element using the following code:

```
<!ELEMENT link (#PCDATA)>
<!ATTLIST link
     xlink:type   CDATA     #FIXED    "simple"
     xlink:href   CDATA     #REQUIRED >
```

Now, let's explain what this code does. First, we create an element called **link** that can use any parsed character data (**PCDATA**—see Chapters 6 and 7 for more information on **PCDATA**). Next, we define the attribute list for the element. The first attribute is **xlink:type**. This attribute specifies that the element is a link. Any element that contains this attribute clarifies that this element acts as a link. The link is also a simple link because we declare the value as **simple**. Possible values for the **xlink:type** attribute are **simple** and **extended**, which identify linking elements, and **locator**, **arc**, **resource**, and **title**, which identify other related types of elements and are discussed in the "Extended Links and Linking Groups" section later in this chapter. Simple links in XML are links that point forward to another single locator or URL. With a simple link, there are no restrictions on the contents of the element.

The **xlink:type** attribute declaration signals to the XLink application that this attribute is a link. Any element declared in a DTD that you plan to use as a link must include this attribute. If you specify the attribute in the DTD as a fixed value, as we did in the previous code, you don't have to specify it in every instance of the element. This allows you to use the element in a document like this:

```
<link xlink:href="/test.html">click here!</link>
```

An XML parser automatically assigns the **xlink:type** attribute with a value of **simple** for this element; therefore, you don't need to include the attribute in this instance of this document.

Next, we declare the **href** attribute. The locator attribute, **href**, works almost the same as the HTML **href** attribute works for the **a** tag, but it's been extended, as you'll see later. You can specify more about a simple link than the type and the locator (**xlink:type** and **xlink:href**, respectively). You can also define link behavior and semantics. We cover these in the following sections.

NOTE: *Other information about links, such as formatting the appearance of links, is outside the scope of the XLink language. The processing software that recognizes links is responsible for defining this information in an application-specific way.*

12. Linking in XML: XLink

Defining Link Behavior

After you define the locator of a simple link, you probably want to specify what behavior is initiated when the link is traversed. The link's behavior is specified with two attributes: **show** and **actuate**. These attributes specify just the link's behavior, not the mechanism used to create that behavior. According to the XLink specification, link-processing software companies are free to devise their own processing mechanisms. This division of labor allows the software to be suited to a particular user environment and processing mode. What makes sense for a traditional browser might not make sense for voice-based browsing or a Web-crawling robot.

The **show** and **actuate** attributes are optional, which means that they don't need to be included in order for XLink processing software to be able to use the link. However when defining your own document types, there's no reason for the attributes to be optional. Depending on the types of documents being created, it might make sense for each link to define which behaviors should occur when traversing the link.

Using the show Attribute

The **show** attribute defines what happens after the link is traversed (clicked). You can assign five different values to the **show** attribute:

- **embed**—Signifies that the resource should be inserted in the body of the resource at the exact location where the traversal started. In other words, after the link is chosen, the remote resource of the link is embedded at the location in which the link was specified. You achieve the same result in HTML using the following markup: **<img src="*file*.gif" >**.

- **replace**—Specifies that after the link is traversed, the specified resource should be loaded into the same presentation context. If the link is displayed in a window, the same window should be used to display the new resource. You achieve this same result in HTML using the following markup: **<a href="*file*.html" target="_self" >...</a>**.

- **new**—Indicates that upon traversal of the link, the designated resource should be displayed or processed in a new context, and it should not affect the context of the resource where the traversal started. In other words, the window where the link was located is not replaced, and a new window is displayed. You achieve the same result in HTML using the following markup: **<a href="*file*.html" target="_blank">...</a>**.

- **other**—Indicates that the behavior of the link traversal is unconstrained by XLink, but some additional markup indicates the behavior. The processing software should look for some other attributes or elements to determine the appropriate behavior, which allows the processing software to define new behaviors for itself.

- **none**—Indicates that the behavior of the link traversal is unconstrained by XLink, and that no other markup is available to help determine the behavior. The processing software is free to do whatever it sees as appropriate.

Using the actuate Attribute

The **actuate** attribute is used to specify when a link should be activated. It has four possible values:

- **onLoad**—Specifies that the remote resource should be retrieved as soon as the link is encountered. No additional action, such as a user click, has to take place for the remote resource to be displayed. You achieve the same result in HTML using the following markup: **<img src="file.gif" >**.

- **onRequest**—Specifies that the resource given in the **href** attribute should not display until some action occurs to request it. This action could be a user click, or a timer expiring in software. This behavior occurs in HTML when the **a** element is used, and the user needs to click the displayed text to request the new resource.

- **other**—Specifies that the timing of the link traversal is unconstrained by XLink, and some additional markup indicates the behavior. The processing software should look for some other attribute or element to determine the appropriate behavior, which allows for processing software to define new timing behaviors for itself.

- **none**—Specifies that the timing of the link traversal is unconstrained by XLink, and that no other markup is available to determine the behavior. The processing software is free to do whatever it sees as appropriate.

Here's a DTD fragment that extends our first simple link example using the behavior attributes:

```
<!ELEMENT link (#PCDATA)>
<!ATTLIST link
    xlink:type      CDATA      #FIXED     "simple"
    xlink:href      CDATA      #REQUIRED
    xlink:show      (new
                    |replace
                    |embed
                    |other
                    |none)                #IMPLIED
    xlink:actuate   (onLoad
                    |onRequest
                    |other
                    |none)                #IMPLIED>
```

TIP: *If you need help understanding some of the terms (such as **#FIXED** or **CDATA**), review Chapter 8, which defines the attribute terminology.*

The previous markup allows the document instance to use the behavioral attributes if it desires, for example:

```
<link xlink:href="/test.html" xlink:show="replace"
xlink:actuate="onRequest">
```

would create a link similar to a standard HTML anchor (**a**) element.

Defining Link Semantics

XLink also provides attributes that allow document creators to describe the meaning of simple links. There are three such attributes: **title**, **role**, and **arcrole**.

The title Attribute

The **title** attribute allows the document creator to add a human-readable description to the link. This attribute should contain text that adds information that helps the reader of a document know what is at the remote end of the link. For example, a browser might display pop-up text when the user moves his or her mouse pointer over the link. The exact use of this attribute is highly dependent on the specific application that uses the information. The **title** attribute is optional on a simple link.

The role Attribute

The **role** attribute is used to describe the meaning of the remote resource identified by the **href** attribute. This attribute is not meant for presentation to the user of a document, but instead, for the software that processes the link. The **role** attribute is a URL that uniquely identifies the role of the remote resource. This attribute allows software to identify the type of resource that is being pointed to by the locator. The Web was originally meant to be human-consumable. As it becomes increasingly machine-consumable, this type of machine-understandable information becomes increasingly important.

The details of the resource identified by the **role** attribute URL are not specified by XLink. As a result, the application that processes the link decides what to do with the information. For example, if you create a document that represents an employee, and the employee information is stored in a separate XML document, a fragment of the document might look like this:

```
The employee of the month is
<employee_link xlink:type="simple"
               xlink:href="/bob_smith.xml"
               xlink:role="/roles/person">
Bob Smith
</employee_link>
```

Because the link points to an XML document that represents a person, the **role** is a URL that contains information about what the person's role is.

When you create document types, you need to establish unique URLs that represent roles. Soon, standards may be set for these role URLs. Industry groups are getting together to define schemas for different purposes. These efforts are easily extended to define the role URLs need to link these documents.

The arcrole Attribute

The **arcrole** attribute is similar to the **role** attribute, but instead of specifying the role of the remote resource, the **arcrole** attribute specifies the role of the relationship that the ending resource has with the starting resource. This relationship can be read as "*start* HAS *arcrole end.*" Like the **role** attribute, the value of the **arcrole** attribute is a URL that identifies the role. Here's an example of how you would use the **arcrole** attribute:

```
<person xlink:type="simple"
        xlink:href="/betty_smith.xml"
        xlink:role="http://www.example.com/roles/person"
        xlink:arcrole="http://www.example.com/relationships/mother"
        xlink:title="Click here to see information about Bob's mother">
Bob Smith
</person>
```

In the previous markup, the **arcrole** attribute specifies the relationship between two people. It adds meaning to the connection between the local resource, **Bob Smith**, and the remote resource specified by the **href** attribute (**/betty_smith.xml**). It can be read as "Bob Smith HAS mother Betty Smith".

Extended Links and Linking Groups

In this section, we'll show you how extended links work in XLink. Extended links offer you a standardized, nonproprietary way to create relationships among different resources. Extended links add several new element types that add data to the link. Here's an example of an extended link:

```
<moviereview xlink:type="extended">
    <locator xlink:type="locator"
             xlink:href="/PulpFiction.html"
             xlink:role="http://www.example.com/roles/Movie"/>
    <locator xlink:type="locator"
             xlink:href="/Siskel/review6253.html"
             xlink:role="http://www.example.com/roles/Review"/>
    <locator xlink:type="locator"
             xlink:href="/Ebert/review87354.html"
             xlink:role="http://www.example.com/roles/Rebuttal"/>
</moviereview>
```

The **moviereview** element is a linking element that contains three **locator** child elements, each of which adds a resource to the link. As you can see, an extended link can connect to any number of resources, not just one resource like simple links. All three of the resources in the previous example are linked. Traversals can exist for each resource to the other two resources in the link. Let's look at what's available with extended links, and how to implement these details.

Creating Extended Links

Extended links are created in much the same way as standard, simple links. However, instead of specifying **simple** in the **xlink:type** attribute value, you specify **extended**. Four other element types are also available: **resource**, **locator**, **arc**, and **title**. You can use these new element types to expand the capabilities of an extended link. Each of them allows you to add data about the resources and relationships involved in extended links. Here's an example of the code you would place in the DTD to create an extended link:

```
<!ELEMENT elink (locator*, resource*, arc*, title?)>
<!ATTLIST elink
  xlink:type     CDATA #FIXED "extended"
  xlink:role     CDATA #IMPLIED
  xlink:title    CDATA #IMPLIED>
```

Notice that this extended link markup's attribute declarations are similar to the simple link's, but there are two major differences. First, for the extended link, we specify the **xlink:type** attribute as **extended**. We also leave out the **href, show, actuate**, and **arcrole** attributes. If we don't specify these attributes, how do we specify this information for extended links? We do so by creating other elements that the **extended** element relies on to create the additional information. We declare the content of the **elink** element to allow several child elements, each of which has special meaning to XLink applications. Each of these new element types is examined in detail in the following sections.

The **role** and **title** attributes in extended links play slightly different roles than they did in simple links. In simple links, these attributes refer to the ending resource; in extended links, these attributes apply to the link as a whole. The **role** attribute specifies a machine-understandable role for the entire link, and the **title** attribute specifies a human-understandable meaning for the entire link.

Creating locator Elements

Here's an example of a DTD definition for a **locator** element:

```
<!ELEMENT locator (title?)>
<!ATTLIST locator
          xlink:type     CDATA   #FIXED "locator"
          xlink:href     CDATA   #REQUIRED
          xlink:role     CDATA   #IMPLIED
          xlink:title    CDATA   #IMPLIED
          xlink:label    NMTOKEN #IMPLIED>
```

The **locator** element carries the information we need for remote references that belong to the extended link. This element can appear as a direct child element of an extended link. The **href** attribute has the same role in an **extended** link as it does in a **simple** link; its value is a URL that identifies a remote resource. The **role** and **title** attributes are also similar to the same attributes in the **simple** link; they define semantic information about the remote resource. The **label** attribute is an identifier for the **locator** (we'll examine identifiers in more detail when we look at **arc** elements).

Next, we use the **elink** and **locator** elements within an XML document. To include an extended link, we specify the first element we created, **elink**, and then use the **locator** element within the **elink**'s content. Here's an example:

```
<elink xlink:title="Popular Nevada ToURLst Destinations"
       xlink:role="http://www.toURLst.com/destinations">
  <locator xlink:title="Las Vegas"
           xlink:href="http://www.lasvegas.com/ "
           xlink:role="http://www.example.com/roles/city"/>
  <locator xlink:title="Hoover Dam"
           xlink:href="http://www.hooverdam.com/ "
           xlink:role="http://www.example.com/roles/dam"/>
  <locator xlink:title="Groom Lake"
           xlink:href="http://www.groomlake.com/ "
           xlink:role="http://www.example.com/roles/militarybase"/>
  <locator xlink:title="Reno"
           xlink:href="http://www.reno.com/"
           xlink:role="http://www.example.com/roles/city"/>
</elink>
```

12. Linking in XML: XLink

If an XLink application processes this document, it could do several things with the information found in the document. If the application presents travel information to a user, it could display the choices in a pop-up menu or in a table. The user could select any of the choices, and possibly move progressively from one resource to the next. Because these locators also have the semantic **role** attribute, the processing software could display more sophisticated behavior. If the user had previously indicated an interest in cities, the software might display only the resources it found with the **role** of **http://www.example.com/roles/city**, and display navigation options only for Las Vegas and Reno.

This link, however, is also multidirectional, which allows processing software to present links from one of the remote resources listed here to the others. For example, if a user were browsing the document about Las Vegas, **http://www.lasvegas.com**, the browser could display options to navigate to any of the other resources here. The browser could perhaps display a menu entitled Other Popular Nevada Tourist Destinations that had menu options for the Reno, Hoover Dam, and Groom Lake sites.

Creating resource Elements

The next type of sub-element within extended links we'll look at is the **resource** type element. Here's a DTD definition for a **resource** type element:

```
<!ELEMENT resource ANY>
<!ATTLIST resource
  xlink:type   CDATA    #FIXED "resource"
  xlink:role   CDATA    #IMPLIED
  xlink:title  CDATA    #IMPLIED
  xlink:label  NMTOKEN #IMPLIED>
```

The **resource** element adds a participating local resource to an extended link. The **resource** element, along with its content, makes up the local resource. Because this is a local resource, there's no **href** attribute as in a **locator** element. The **role**, **title**, and **label** attributes have the same function they do for **locator** elements. Here's an example of a document that uses the previous definition along with the **elink** and **locator** elements:

```
<elink>
  <resource xlink:role="http://www.movies.com/movie">
    <title>Matrix, The</title>
    <date>1999</date>
  </resource>
  <locator xlink:role="http://www.movies.com/person"
           xlink:title="Keanu Reeves"
           xlink:href="http://www.movies.com/people/KeanuReeves.xml"/>
  <locator xlink:role="http://www.movies.com/person"
           xlink:title="Laurence Fishburne"
           xlink:href="http://www.movies.com/people/LaurenceFishburne.xml"/>
</elink>
```

The previous example shows a link that brings together three resources: one local and two remote. The local resource contains information about a movie, and the two remote resources point to information about two actors in the movie. The local resource is specified using the **resource** element, and the contents of it are data about the title and the date. The local resource also has a **role** attribute, which indicates to applications that the resource is a movie.

Creating arc Elements

The next element type we'll look at is the **arc** element. Here is a DTD definition for the **arc** element:

```
<!ELEMENT arc (title?)>
<!ATTLIST arc
          xlink:type    CDATA    #FIXED    "arc"
          xlink:title   CDATA    #IMPLIED
          xlink:arcrole CDATA    #IMPLIED
```

```
xlink:show    (new
              |replace
              |embed
              |other
              |none)      #IMPLIED
xlink:actuate (onLoad
              |onRequest
              |other
              |none)      #IMPLIED
xlist:from    NMTOKEN     #IMPLIED
xlist:to      NMTOKEN     #IMPLIED>
```

The **arc** element is used to specify traversal information among participating resources of an extended link. The **arc** element identifies which traversals are being described using the **from** and **to** attributes. Each of these attributes must match a **label** attribute on the **locator** or **resource** element. Here's an example of a document:

```
<elink>
  <locator xlink:label="A" xlink:href="http://www.foo.com/x1.xml"/>
  <locator xlink:label="B" xlink:href="http://www.foo.com/x2.xml"/>
  <locator xlink:label="C" xlink:href="http://www.foo.com/x3.xml"/>
  <arc xlink:from="A" xlink:to="B" xlink:title="link from x1 to x2"/>
  <arc xlink:from="C" xlink:to="A" xlink:title="link from x3 to x1"/>
</elink>
```

The previous document has six possible traversals:

- x1 to x2

- x1 to x3

- x2 to x1

- x2 to x3

- x3 to x1

- x3 to x2

There are two **arc** elements in the link, each of which adds a title for one of the traversals. The first **arc** adds a title for the traversal from x1 to x2, and the second arc adds a title for the traversal from x3 to x1. The other four traversals that are involved in the link have no extra information added to them, and XLink processing software is free to use the traversals in any way.

It's possible to group two or more resources by giving them the same name. This grouping allows **arc** elements to describe more than one traversal at a time. Here's an example of how it's done:

```
<elink>
  <locator xlink:label="A" xlink:href="http://www.foo.com/x1.xml"/>
  <locator xlink:label="A" xlink:href="http://www.foo.com/x2.xml"/>
  <locator xlink:label="B" xlink:href="http://www.foo.com/x3.xml"/>
  <arc xlink:from="A" xlink:to="B" xlink:actuate="onRequest"/>
  <arc xlink:from="B" xlink:to="A" xlink:actuate="onRequest"/>
</elink>
```

In this example, **actuate** behaviors are specified for four of the possible six traversals. Because the label **A** is applied to the first two resource elements, the first **arc** element specifies the **actuate** behavior for two traversals: x1 to x2 and x1 to x3. The second **arc** element adds behavior for two more traversals: x3 to x1 and x3 to x2. The two remaining traversals, x1 to x2 and x2 to x1, have no **actuate** behavior specified, and again, the software processing this link is free to do whatever it sees fit.

There's one more way for you to use the **arc** element to specify information for multiple traversals. If the **to** or **from** attribute is missing from the **arc** element, the element applies to all appropriate traversals. For example, if an **arc** element is **<arc xlink:from="A" xlink:title="A title">**, the title is used for every traversal from each resource labeled **A** to every other resource in the link.

The **arc** element also allows for three additional attributes: **arcrole**, **show**, and **actuate**. These attributes have the same meaning they do in a simple link. The **show** and **actuate** attributes specify the behavior of the traversal, and the **arcrole** attribute specifies the relationship the ending resource has with the starting resource.

Creating title Elements

The last type of element is a relatively simple one: the **title** element. Here's a DTD definition for a **title** element:

```
<!ELEMENT title ANY>
<!ATTLIST xlink:type    CDATA #FIXED      "title">
```

Having a **title** element instead of using just a **title** attribute provides you with more flexibility. For example, the **title** element content can contain extra markup, or allow different titles for different languages. The following demonstrates both of these situations:

```
<elink>
  <title xml:lang="en">A <b>large</b> book!</title>
  <title xml:lang="fr">Une <b>grande</b> livre!</title>
  ...
</elink>
```

An application processing this link could display either of the titles, depending on the user's language preferences. The titles also contain additional markup (the **b** element).

The **title** element can appear as a direct child of many element types. You can use it within the **extended**, **arc**, and **locator** elements. As shown in the previous XML fragment, multiple **title** elements can appear as direct children of these other elements. How these multiple titles are used is up to the processing software.

Linkbases

As you've seen in some of the examples in this chapter, it's possible to define links where no local resources are involved. These are called *third-party links*. It's also possible to create an inbound link that involves a traversal from a remote resource to a local resource. XML documents created to contain a collection of third-party and inbound links are called *linkbases*. XLink gives linkbase documents some special treatment.

There are several reasons for creating linkbases. A creator of a series of documents may want to collect all the links needed for the documents in one place for easier maintainability. If all the links must be changed, it's easier to edit just one document instead of finding links in many documents. The creator of the links also might use linkbases if he or she does not have the ability to edit the document that contains a starting resource. Links can still be created in a separate document, and then an XLink application can read the original documents and add the linking information before it's displayed to the user.

For example, the following XML document contains information about a person called **person123.xml**:

```
<person>
  <name>Fred Smith</name>
  <address>12 Main St.</address>
</person>
```

There's also a picture of the person in the **pic11.jpg** file. If we want to create a link between the person's name in the previous XML document and the picture file contained in a linkbase, the linkbase document might look like this:

```
<linkbase>
  <link>
    <locator
       xlink:label="name"
       xlink:href="person123.xml#xpointer(/person/name)"/>
```

```
    <locator
        xlink:label="picture"
        xlink:href="pic11.jpg"/>
    <arc actuate="onRequest"/>
  </link>
</linkbase>
```

This document uses a URL in the form of an XPointer that points at the **name** element in the **person 123.xml** document.

TIP: *For a detailed discussion of XPointers, see Chapter 14.*

The problem is, how does the application know about the linkbase document when it loads the **person123.xml** document? How will it know that when the user selects the **name** element, a picture should be displayed? The XLink language specifies a special link type for this situation, as shown here:

```
<elink>
  <locator xlink:label="person" xlink:locator="/person123.xml"/>
  <locator xlink:label="linkbase" xlink:locator="/linkbase.xml"/>
  <arc
      xlink:from="person"
      xlink:to="picture"
      xlink:actuate="onLoad"
      xlink:arcrole=" http://www.w3.org/1999/xlink/properties/linkbase"/>
</elink>
```

When an application encounters this link with an **arc** element that has the **arcrole** value **http://www.w3.org/1999/xlink/properties/linkbase**, it knows that this is a specialized link that provides the location of a linkbase. In this case, because the starting point of the **arc** is the person document, and the **actuate** attribute is **onLoad**, the linkbase is loaded whenever the person document is loaded. These links differ from other links in that they are not meant to be used immediately; they should be stored and used when they're needed.

This special value of the **arcrole** attribute is not the only way an application can find linkbases. Each application is free to find linkbases in any suitable way—for example, through configuration files, asking for user output, or crawling the Web with a robot. Linkbases can also be chained together; that is, one linkbase can contain a reference to another linkbase. An application can follow these chains for as long as it desires.

Immediate Solutions

Creating a Simple Link

A simple XLink link with minimal attributes takes the following syntax:

```
<element xlink:type="simple" xlink:href="URL">...</element>
```

Here, the ***element*** can be any element that is allowed in the document, ***xlink*** is a namespace prefix that refers to the XLink namespace, and ***URL*** is a locator for the resource being linked to. In a valid XML document, these attributes must be declared in the DTD, just as any other attribute is. This means that when you create a new document type, you must decide which elements are used as linking elements and declare them appropriately in the element declaration.

TIP: *XLink links rely heavily on the syntax for creating elements and attributes. To review these subjects, revisit Chapters 6 and 8.*

To create a simple link, create an element as you normally would, but specify the **xlink:type** attribute as **simple**. For example, to create a **simple** link, this DTD can be used:

```
<!ELEMENT simple ANY>
<!ATTLIST simple
    xmlns:xlink    CDATA  #FIXED      "http://www.w3.org/1999/xlink"
    xlink:type     CDATA  #FIXED      "simple"
    xlink:href     CDATA  #REQUIRED>
```

This DTD starts by declaring the element you want to use as the link in your DTD—in this case, **simple**. Next, the XLink namespace prefix is specified as **xlink**. Then, the **xlink:type** attribute is added with a fixed value of **simple**. Finally, the **xlink:href** attribute is specified as a required attribute.

NOTE: *If other attributes are needed for this element, they can be included without interfering with the linking attributes.*

Using a Simple Link in the Document

To use the **simple** link in an XML document, simply use it as you would any other XML element. The only thing that makes it special is that an XLink application knows how to process the link's attributes. Here's an example of how you would use the **simple** link you created in the previous section:

```
<?xml version="1.0"?>
<simple
  xmlns:xlink="http://www.w3.org/1999/xlink"
  xlink:type="simple"
  xlink:href="http://www.site.com/info.xml">
    This is my link to XML.
</simple>
```

Using the DTD from the previous section as its document type, a **simple** link could be written as follows:

```
<?xml version="1.0"?>
<!DOCTYPE simple  SYSTEM "simple.dtd">
<simple xlink:href="http://www.site.com/info.xml">
  This is my link to XML.
</simple>
```

The namespace declaration and **xlink:type** attribute are not needed because they were declared as fixed for the **simple** element. You can include any content and attributes you want in the element, but the **href** attribute must appear because it's a required attribute.

Specifying a Link's Semantics

A simple link's semantics, or meaning, are defined by three different attributes: **title**, **role**, and **arcrole**. As mentioned earlier, the **title** attribute gives a human-readable description to the remote resource specified by the link, and the **role** and **arcrole** attributes supply additional information to software processing the links. They both take URLs as values. Using unique URLs for **role** and **arcrole** attributes allows for a more intelligent Web. Search engines that are aware of **role** attributes can scan the Web and organize links much more intelligently than they do now. Current search engines must guess at the meaning of links and Web pages by parsing content meant for humans and trying to make sense of it. By tagging information with these new types of machine-understandable properties, a much more organized Web can exist. The W3C calls this new vision *The Semantic Web*.

The **role** attribute in a simple link specifies the role of the remote resource in the link. The **arcrole** attribute specifies the role of the relationship between the local and remote resources. For example, here's a document that links a baseball manager, Yogi Berra, to his baseball team, the New York Yankees:

```
<?xml version="1.0"?>
<manager xmlns:xlink="http://www.w3.org/1999/xlink"
        xlink:type="simple"
        xlink:href="http://www.baseball.com/teams/NYYankees.xml"
        xlink:role="http://www.baseball.com/properties/team"
        xlink:arcrole="http://www.baseball.com/properties/managed"
        xlink:title="Click here to see the Yankees Team">
Yogi Berra
</manager>
```

You can see that the **role** attribute specifies that the remote resource is a baseball team, and the **arcrole** specifies that the local resource Yogi Berra is a manager of the remote resource. This link also supplies a user-readable **title** attribute.

Controlling Link Behavior

Link behavior describes how and when a link is traversed and works with simple links as well as extended links. HTML **a** elements typically have user-invoked and replacing behavior. These HTML links cannot be activated without a click from the user, and unless they are specified by the **target** element, the contents of the linked resource generally replace the contents of the page where the link was initiated. XML provides a bit more flexibility with the **actuate** and **show** attributes. Remember, the values of the **actuate** attribute are **onLoad**, **onRequest**, **none**, and **other**.

Here's an example of a simple link that needs to be activated by a user:

```
<?xml version="1.0"?>
<website xmlns:xlink="http://www.w3.org/1999/xlink"
        xlink:type="simple"
        xlink:href="http://www.w3.org"
        xlink:actuate="onRequest">
W3C
</website>
```

If, however, the link should be traversed as soon as the application comes across it, the markup would be as follows:

```
<?xml version="1.0"?>
<website xmlns:xlink="http://www.w3.org/1999/xlink"
        xlink:type="simple"
        xlink:href="http://www.w3.org"
        xlink:actuate="onLoad">
W3C
</website>
```

The **show** attribute controls how linked resources are processed and displayed. Remember, its values are **embed**, **new**, **replace**, **none**, and **other**.

By combining the **actuate="onRequest"** and **show="new"** attributes and values in the following code, the link is set to open the W3C's home page in a new window at the user's request:

```
<?xml version="1.0"?>
<website xmlns:xlink="http://www.w3.org/1999/xlink"
        xlink:type="simple"
        xlink:href="http://www.w3.org"
        xlink:actuate="onRequest"
        xlink:show="new">
W3C
</website>
```

If, however, you change the attributes to **actuate="auto"** and **show="embed"**, the contents of the W3C's Web site will be directly embedded into the document where the link traversal began. Fragments of different XML documents can be combined into a single XML document automatically by using this attribute combination. It's also useful for automatically embedding header and footer information into documents.

Predefining Link Attributes in the DTD

As discussed in the In Depth section of this chapter, you need to indicate which of your elements will be linking elements when you create a DTD. To allow the creation of links in an XML document, you can include any or all of the linking attributes in an element's attribute list declaration. When you include the linking attributes, you can specify how these attributes will be used to control the links specified when using the element. For example, you can use the **xlink:type** attribute in an element's attribute declaration list and include with it a fixed value of **simple**, using this syntax:

```
<!ATTLIST element xlink:type CDATA #FIXED "simple">
```

This attribute declaration indicates that the *element* can take the **xlink:type** attribute of type **simple** whose content is **CDATA** (character data). Because the type is fixed, simple links made from this element must always be simple, and the element in the document does not need to specify it. If the element is used as a linking element in an extended resource, the document will be invalid. In the **website** element example from the previous section, the **link** attribute can be affixed to the element by using this code:

```
<!ELEMENT website ANY>
<!ATTLIST website
    xmlns:xlink  CDATA    #FIXED "http://www.w3.org/1999/xlink"
    xlink:type   CDATA    #FIXED "simple"
    xlink:href   CDATA    #IMPLIED>
```

A link is now made with the **website** element as the linking element in this way:

```
<?xml version="1.0"?>
<!DOCTYPE website SYSTEM "website.dtd">
<website xlink:href="http://www.w3.org">W3C</website>
```

The only difference in the XML markup now is that the **xmlns:xlink="..."** and **xlink:type="simple"** attribute-value pairs are missing. Still, if you're planning on creating lots of links, the less typing you have to do, the better. If you use this convention, simple XML links begin to look much like HTML links—except, of course, the linking elements are different and the **href** attribute has a namespace prefix.

Other attributes can also be declared to ensure that a locator is named and default values for the **show** and **actuate** attributes are set. The following code specifies that, in addition to a fixed simple link status, the **website** element has a required **href** attribute, a required **role** attribute, and the default values **embed** and **onLoad** are specified for the **show** and **actuate** attributes, respectively:

```
<!ELEMENT website ANY>
<!ATTLIST website
    xlink:type    CDATA   #FIXED "simple"
    xlink:href    CDATA   #REQUIRED
    xlink:role    CDATA   #REQUIRED
    xlink:show    (embed
                  |replace
                  |new
                  |none
                  |other)       "embed"
```

```
xlink:actuate (onLoad
               |onRequest
               |none
               |other)        "onLoad">
```

Notice that the **title** and **arcrole** attributes are not included in this attribute dec-laration. Also, if you don't want the document author to be able to use the **other** and **none** values of the **show** and **actuate** attributes, you can leave them off.

Creating an Extended Link

Sometimes simple links are not adequate to represent complex linking situations, including:

- Supplying any number of local and remote resources
- Specifying a traversal from its remote resource to its local resource
- Attaching a **title** to the single hardwired **arc**
- Attaching a **role** or **title** to the local resource
- Attaching a **role** or **title** to the link as a whole

Unlike simple links, extended links involve more than just a single element. An **extended** element type can contain **locator**, **resource**, **arc**, and **title** elements as children. The DTD definition for an extended link for use with families could look like Listing 12.1.

Listing 12.1   The DTD definition for an extended link for use with families.

```
<!ELEMENT family (family-name?, family-member*, relations*)>
<!ATTLIST family
    xmlns:xlink   CDATA     #FIXED "http://www.w3.org/1999/xlink"
    xlink:type    CDATA     #FIXED "extended"
    xlink:role    CDATA     #FIXED "http://www.family.com/properties/name"
    xlink:title   CDATA     #IMPLIED>

<!ELEMENT family-name (#PCDATA)>
<!ATTLIST family-name
    xlink:type    CDATA     #FIXED "resource"
    xlink:role    CDATA     #FIXED
"http://www.family.com/properties/familyname">

<!ELEMENT family-member (name?)>
<!ATTLIST family-member
    xlink:type    CDATA     #FIXED "locator"
```

```
    xlink:role     CDATA     #FIXED "http://www.family.com/properties/person"
    xlink:href     CDATA     #REQUIRED
    xlink:label    NMTOKEN   #IMPLIED>

<!ELEMENT name (#PCDATA)>
<!ATTLIST name
    xlink:type     CDATA     #FIXED "title">

<!ELEMENT relation EMPTY>
<!ATTLIST relation
    xlink:type     CDATA     #FIXED "arc"
    xlink:to       NMTOKEN   #REQUIRED
    xlink:from     NMTOKEN   #REQUIRED
    xlink:arcrole  CDATA     #REQUIRED>
```

Listing 12.1 shows several of the possibilities that are allowed in extended links that are not allowed in simple links. We'll look at a document based on this DTD:

```
<?xml version="1.0"?>
<!DOCTYPE family SYSTEM "">
<family>
  <family-member xlink:href="/person1.html"/>
  <family-member xlink:href="/person2.html"/>
  <family-member xlink:href="/person3.html"/>
</family>
```

If you look at the DTD declaration for the first element declared, **family**, you see that it has three fixed attributes: **xmlns:xlink**, **xlink:type**, and **xlink:role**. Here's what these fixed attributes do:

- **xmlns:xlink**—Declares a namespace prefix **xlink**, which is used to identify the namespace for all the XLink-specific attributes.

- **xlink:type**—Signals that this element is an XLink extended link element type.

- **xlink:role**—Declares the purpose of this link, which is to link various members of one family.

When you create the **family** element in the document, you do not need any attributes for it because the three fixed attributes are added by any standard XML parser.

The **family** element has three children elements, which are all **family-member** elements. Again, these elements have fixed attributes, so they're automatically identified as **locator** elements, with the role of **http://www.family.com/properties/person**. The required **xlink:href** attribute is provided for each of these elements to identify three different people who belong to this family.

Because you haven't specified anything else about this link, the software processing it is free to do whatever it wants with the link. A GUI application displaying this document could display the remote resources to the user as clickable options, or it might automatically retrieve the remote resources and display the contents of them as a single document. It could also display just one of the documents and then present options to the user to navigate to the other two people.

You can add data about the traversals involved in this link. To do so, add **label** attributes to the **family-member** elements and then add **relation** elements to include the traversal data. Here's an example:

```
<?xml version="1.0"?>
<!DOCTYPE family SYSTEM "family.dtd">
<family>
   <family-member xlink:label="bob"    xlink:href="/person1.html"/>
   <family-member xlink:label="sally"  xlink:href="/person2.html"/>
   <family-member xlink:label="junior" xlink:href="/person3.html"/>
   <relation
       xlink:start="bob"          xlink:end="sally"
       xlink:actuate="onRequest"  xlink:show="new"
       xlink:arcrole="http://www.family.com/properties/wife"/>
</family>
```

The **relation** element includes traversal data, because the **xlink:type** attribute has a fixed value **arc** on the **relation** element. This **relation** element adds data about the traversal from **"bob"** to **"sally"**. It specifies behavior with the **actuate** and **show** attributes. The **onRequest** value of the **actuate** attribute means that the XLink application will wait for some action, such as user input, before the link is traversed. Specifying **new** for the **show** attribute means the document will be displayed in a new window or frame. Finally, the **arcrole** attribute specifies the relationship that the ending resource has to the starting resource. In this case, the relationship is read as "Bob has wife Sally". This example shows just one **arc**-type element, but you can add as many of these elements as are needed.

Next, let's add a local resource to this document. In the DTD, the **family-name** element is a local resource element:

```
<?xml version="1.0"?>
<!DOCTYPE family SYSTEM "family.dtd">
<family>
   <family-name>Smith</family-name>
   <family-member xlink:href="/person1.html"/>
   <family-member xlink:href="/person2.html"/>
   <family-member xlink:href="/person3.html"/>
</family>
```

This example adds the family's name, Smith, as a local resource. It's very similar to the remote resources, but the information is contained in this document itself, instead of being referenced by a URL.

As a final example, here's how **title** elements can be added:

```
<?xml version="1.0"?>
<!DOCTYPE family SYSTEM "family.dtd">
<family>
  <family-member xlink:href="/person1.html">
    <name>Bob Smith</name>
  </family-member>
  <family-member xlink:href="/person2.html">
    <name>Sally Smith</name>
  </family-member>
  <family-member xlink:href="/person3.html">
    <name>Junior Smith</name>
  </family-member>
</family>
```

In this case, each family member gets a **name** element. The **name** element has a fixed **xlink:type** value of **title** so that XLink applications can identify it as a title, which gives a human-readable name to each of the remote resources, thereby allowing an application to show some reasonable text when displaying navigation options to the user.

Creating Linkbases

Linkbases are XML documents that contain a collection of links. Here's an example of a DTD that defines a linkbase element:

```
<!ELEMENT linkbaseloader ((startresource+, linkbase+, loader)*)>
<!ATTLIST linkbaseloader
    xmlns:xlink   CDATA     #FIXED "http://www.w3.org/1999/xlink"
    xlink:type    CDATA     #FIXED "extended">

<!ELEMENT startresource EMPTY>
<!ATTLIST startresource
    xlink:type    CDATA     #FIXED   "locator"
    xlink:label   CDATA     #FIXED   "start"
    xlink:href    CDATA     #REQUIRED>
```

```
<!ELEMENT linkbase EMPTY>
<!ATTLIST linkbase
    xlink:type    CDATA    #FIXED  "locator"
    xlink:label   CDATA    #FIXED  "linkbase"
    xlink:href    CDATA    #REQUIRED>

<!ELEMENT loader EMPTY>
<!ATTLIST loader
    xlink:type    CDATA    #FIXED  "arc"
    xlink:role    CDATA    #FIXED
    "http://www.w3.org/1999/xlink/properties/linkbase"
    xlink:from    CDATA    #FIXED  "start"
    xlink:to      CDATA    #FIXED  "linkbase"
    xlink:actuate (onLoad
                  |onRequest) #IMPLIED>
```

This document shows an example of how to use the linkbase:

```
<?xml version="1.0"?>
<!DOCTYPE linkbaseloader SYSTEM "linkbaseloader.dtd">
<linkbaseloader>
   <startresource xlink:href="http://www.w3.org/TR/REC-xml"/>
   <linkbase xlink:href="http://www.examples.com/annotations/xmlspec.xml"/>
   <loader xlink:actuate="onLoad"/>
</linkbaseloader>
```

This link specifies that whenever the XML specification is loaded from **http://www.w3.org/TR/REC-xml**, the linkbase document should be loaded from **http://www.examples.com/annotations/xmlspec.xml**. The application should then render the XML specification to show any links it found in the annotation document. In this way, the author of the linkbase is able to add annotations to the specification without modifying the original document.

Linking in XML Documents Using Tools

Unfortunately, there's currently very little tool support for XLink. This is the case mainly because XLink has not yet reached the W3C's recommendation status. Because the language is not yet in its final form, any tools written would need to be updated whenever the specification is updated. Very few tool vendors can afford the time and effort it takes to keep pace with the specification and go through many sets of changes to keep current. We hope that after the specification is a recommendation, vendors will create many tools that support XLink. In this section, we review one product—X2X from empolis—that has stayed fairly current with the XLink specification, and we also look at using XSL Transformations (XSLT) to transform XLink links into HTML.

TIP: *As always, keep an eye on **www.xmlsoftware.com** for the latest software.*

Using X2X by empolis

X2X is a commercial product by empolis. They have an evaluation version available for download from their Web site (**www.empolis.co.uk**). X2X allows you to create and maintain a collection of third-party links, and provides ways to merge documents with the links. At the time of this writing, X2X uses a slightly out-of-date version of the XLink specification, but the company intends to update its product to track the latest changes.

X2X consists of three major parts: the X2X Server, the LinkBase Explorer, and the X2X Proxy Server. The X2X Server interacts with a database to store and maintain links. It can also merge third-party links with the original documents that the links refer to, or compose documents from different sources based on templates. The X2X Server has both a Java Application Programming Interface (API) and a socket-based interface for non-Java applications. The LinkBase Explorer provides a graphical interface you use to add, maintain, and query links that have been stored in a database by the server. Linkbases can be imported into the server from XML documents and exported back out from the server.

Here's an example of the link insertion that X2X will do. First, create a sample XML document that contains the name and city of a person. Save this file as **data\fred.xml**:

```
<?xml version="1.0"?>
<test>
<person ID="fred">
  <lastname>Flintstone</lastname>
  <firstname>Fred</firstname>
  <city ID="bedrock">Bedrock</city>
</person>
</test>
```

Next, you create a linkbase document with two resources. One resource is the city element from the previous document; its URL is **data\fred.xml#ID(bedrock)**. The second resource in the linkbase identifies a document with additional information about the city:

```
<linkbase xmlns:xlink="http://www.w3.org/1999/xlink">
<link xlink:type="extended"
      xlink:title="city-links">
  <locator xlink:type="locator"
           xlink:href="data\fred.xml#ID(bedrock)"
           xlink:title="Freds City Name"
           xlink:role="\properties\cityname"/>
  <locator xlink:type="locator"
           xlink:href="data\bedrock.xml#ID(bedrock)"
           xlink:title="Bedrock"
           xlink:role="\properties\city"/>
</link>
</linkbase>
```

Using the LinkBase Explorer's **import** option, you load this linkbase into the server database. Then, when you select the fred.xml document and choose the Resolve option of the Explorer, a merged document is saved. The resulting document is shown here:

```
<?xml version="1.0" ?>
<test>
<person ID="fred">
  <lastname>Flintstone</lastname>
  <firstname>Fred</firstname>
  <city ID="bedrock">
    <xlink:link xmlns:xlink="http://www.w3.org/1999/xlink/namespace/"
                ID="ID(bedrock)"
                xlink:title="city-links">
      <xlink:locator title="Bedrock"
                     role="\properties\city"
                     href="data\bedrock.xml#ID(bedrock)"/>
    </xlink:link>
  Bedrock
  </city>
</person>
</test>
```

TIP: *This document does not quite meet the requirements of the latest XLink specification: The namespace is incorrect, no* **xlink** *prefix appears on some of the attributes, and elements are declared in the* **xlink** *namespace. empolis will be upgrading X2X to implement the latest version of the specification. Check the empolis Web site for updates to the product.*

The interesting thing to see here is that a new XML document has been produced that has the elements of the original fred.xml document with an XLink link inserted within the **city** element. The original document has not been changed during this process.

The X2X product also contains a Proxy Server to make using the tool easier in a Web environment. The Proxy Server allows documents to be retrieved from the Web with links inserted into them based on linkbases in the X2X Server.

Using XSLT

You can use XLink markup before it's widely supported in other tools by using Extensible Stylesheet Language Transformations (XSLT) to convert XLink links into HTML links. XSLT is a transformation language for XML (see Chapter 11 for more details). The transformation is relatively straightforward when you're dealing with simple links. For example, suppose you have the following document, which contains two simple links:

```
<test xmlns:xlink="http://www.w3.org/1999/xlink">
  <link xlink:type="simple" xlink:href="http:\\www.w3.org\XML">XML</link>
  <link xlink:type="simple"
        xlink:href="http:\\www.w3.org\XML\linking.html" xlink:show="new">
    XML Linking</link>
</test>
```

You can use the following XSLT style sheet to convert this document into an HTML page:

```
<?xml version="1.0"?>
<xsl:stylesheet version="1.0"
                xmlns:xsl="http://www.w3.org/1999/XSL/Transform"
                xmlns:xlink="http://www.w3.org/1999/xlink"
                exclude-result-prefixes="xlink">
<xsl:output method="html"/>

<xsl:template match="/">
  <html><body>
    <xsl:apply-templates/>
  </body></html>
</xsl:template>

<xsl:template match="*[@xlink:type='simple']">
  <p><a>
    <xsl:attribute name="href">
      <xsl:value-of select="@xlink:href"/>
```

```
      </xsl:attribute>
      <xsl:if test="@xlink:show='new'">
        <xsl:attribute name="target">_blank</xsl:attribute>
      </xsl:if>
      <xsl:apply-templates/>
    </a></p>
  </xsl:template>

</xsl:stylesheet>
```

This is a relatively simple example. The first template rule matches the root element and creates an HTML page. The second template rule matches any element with an **xlink:type** attribute that has the value **simple**. For each **xlink:type** attribute with a value of **simple**, an HTML **a** element is created. In addition, if an **xlink:show** attribute with the value **new** is found, the **target** attribute of the **a** element is set to **_new**, which causes the browser to display the remote resource in a new browser window. Here's the result of processing these documents using an XSLT engine:

```
<html>
<body>
  <p>
   <a href="http:\\www.w3.org\XML">XML</a>
  </p>
  <p>
   <a href="http:\\www.w3.org\XML\linking.html"
      target="_blank">XML Linking</a>
  </p>
</body>
</html>
```

If you also needed extended links, you would have to create more sophisticated pages, perhaps using JavaScript or Dynamic HTML. Creating HTML pages from XML using XSLT is already a popular way to use XML, and creating extended links is just a natural extension of that use.

TIP: *Look for more complete sets of style sheets for converting XLink elements to HTML on the Web. One is available at* **http://www.thefaactory.com/xlink2html**.

Chapter 13

Building Paths in XML with XPath

In Depth

When the separate World Wide Web Consortium (W3C) working groups were developing the Extensible Stylesheet Language (XSL) and the XML Linking Language (XLink), it became apparent that both of these languages shared a common need to locate parts of documents. In the interest of simplicity and to spare XML developers from having to learn two separate languages for the same task, XML Path Language (XPath) was developed to fulfill the needs of both languages. XPath 1.0 became a W3C recommendation on November 16, 1999.

As you saw in Chapter 11, XSL Transformations (XSLT), the transformation part of XSL, uses XPath to locate nodes in the source tree that are to be transformed. In Chapter 12, you saw how XLink uses XML Pointer Language (XPointer) to identify document fragments for use in links. XPointer, in turn, uses XPath to address parts of XML documents.

What Is XPath?

XPath is a language used by both XSL and XLink to address parts of XML documents. Like XSLT, XPath represents an XML document as a tree of nodes. Elements, text, attributes, and so forth are represented in XPath as nodes. Because of the hierarchical structure of XML, the result of representing a document as nodes resembles a tree. We explore the concept of node trees in detail in the "Document Trees and Nodes Explained" section later in this chapter. For now, imagine that an XML document resembles a family tree. The top of the tree is a single node (the *root node*), and every other node in the tree is related in some way to the root node. These relationships create the branches of the tree.

XPath gets its name from its use of Uniform Resource Locator (URL)-like paths for navigating the hierarchical (tree) structure of XML documents. For example, to locate **name** elements that are children of **person** elements that are children of the root element, you use the following XPath expression:

```
/child::person/child::name
```

This example uses the full XPath syntax, which is fairly easy to read and to learn. When you identify a very specific part of a large document, the syntax can be fairly wordy. For example, the following expression selects the third **para** element child of the fourth **chapter** element child of the **book** element:

```
/child::book/child::chapter[position()=4]/child::para[position()=3]
```

Fortunately, you can abbreviate XPath expressions in various ways. Most people who write XPath expressions use the abbreviated syntax. Using abbreviations when possible, the previous example could be written as follows:

```
/book/chapter[4]/para[3]
```

XPointer, which is an extension of XPath, can in turn use the previous expression as follows:

```
xpointer(/book/chapter[4]/para[3])
```

This XPointer expression can then be used as a fragment identifier for an XLink:

```
<myElement
  xmlns:xlink="http://www.w3.org/1999/xlink"
  xlink:type="simple"
  xlink:href="/foo.html#xpointer(/book/chapter[4]/para[3])">
    This is my link
</myElement>
```

As you saw in Chapter 11, XSLT uses XPath expressions inside of the **select** attribute of various elements and inside certain other attributes (those that are specified as attribute value templates). For example, the following XSLT element uses an XPath expression to output the value of the **name** attribute of the context node:

```
<xsl:value-of select = "@name"/>
```

XPath is a flexible and powerful language. Besides simply finding specific locations in XML documents, XPath can also be used to compute values, perform pattern matching, and more, as you'll see in the following section.

The XPath Syntax

The most basic structure in XPath is the *expression*. The result of evaluating an expression is called an *object*. For example, when an XPath processor evaluates the following example, the result is the string (or text) object that contains the text **"Hello"**:

```
string("Hello")
```

XPath objects are always one of the following four types:

- *Node-set*—An unordered list of nodes without duplicates
- *Boolean*—A value of true or false
- *Number*—A floating-point number (a positive or negative integer or a number containing a decimal)
- *String*—Character data

The environment in which an XPath expression is evaluated is called its *context*. Any application that runs XPath expressions (for example, an XSLT or XPointer processor) must make certain information available to the XPath expression. This information includes:

- The current node that the application using the expression is evaluating. This node is called the *context node*.
- The *context size* and the *context position*. These values indicate the size of the context (for example, the number of nodes in a document) and the position of the context node, respectively.
- Variable bindings, which map variable names to their values.
- The XPath function library.
- The set of namespace declarations that apply to the expression.

Although both XPointer and XSLT are required to supply context information to the XPath processor, they differ in how they determine the context information.

There are several types of XPath expressions. The most commonly used of these is the *location path*.

Location Paths

Location path expressions find node-sets in an XML tree by specifying their position in relation to the *context node*, or in relation to the document root. Just as URLs or XLinks can be either relative or absolute, a location path that starts at the current node is called a *relative location path*, and a location path that starts at the document root is called an *absolute location path*. For example, the following example shows a relative location path that finds all the **para** nodes that are descendants (children, grandchildren, and so on) of the current node:

```
descendant::para
```

If this XPath expression were applied inside a **para** element in an XML document, it wouldn't find any matching nodes. You can make a relative location path into an absolute path the same way in XPath as in Unix operating systems and URLs—simply add a forward slash to the beginning of the path. The following location path selects all the **para** elements in the document:

```
/descendant::para
```

Before we get too deep into the syntax of location paths, let's look at some more examples. Table 13.1 shows some of the various ways that location paths can be used to find content in XML documents.

TIP: *When used in a location path, the asterisk (*) functions in much the same way as it does in many operating systems—as a wildcard character. It says, "Select everything that meets the criteria specified."*

Now that you've seen a variety of examples of location paths, let's look at each part of the location path more closely.

Location Path Steps

All location paths are made up of one or more *steps*. Each step represents a level of depth in the XML hierarchy. Like URL paths, steps in XPaths are divided by a forward slash (/). Let's take a look at an example of a path with multiple steps:

```
/descendant::Chapter/descendant-or-self::text()
```

The first step in the example is **descendant::Chapter**, and the second step is **descendant-or-self::text( )**. The function of the second step is dependent upon

Table 13.1 **Examples of location paths.**

Location Path	Description
child::node()	Selects all the children of the current node. If this expression were used in an HTML document and the context node was the **html** element, the **head** and **body** elements would be selected.
attribute::color	Selects the **color** attribute of the context node.
/descendant::para[position()=3]	Selects the third **para** element in the document.
child::table[child::row]	Selects the **table** children of the context node that have at least one **row** child.
preceding-sibling::chapter	Selects the previous **chapter** siblings of the context node.
ancestor::*	Selects all ancestor elements (parents, grandparents, and so on) of the context node.
/descendant::text()	Selects all the text nodes in the document.
/descendant::price/preceding-sibling::*	Selects all preceding siblings of each **price** element in the document.
/descendant::chapter/descendant-or-self::text()	Selects all text nodes that are in the **chapter** element and its descendants.

the function of the first step. That is, the first step selects all **Chapter** elements of the document. The second step then selects all **text** nodes that are descendants of the **Chapter** element.

Location Path Axes

The first section of each location path step is called the *axis*. This is the word that appears to the left of the double colon (::). The axis specifies the relationship between the context node and the nodes that are selected by the step. XPath defines 13 axes; we'll review them one by one and explain their functions:

- **child**—Selects children of the context node. *Children* are nodes that are on the next level down in the tree hierarchy.

- **descendant**—Selects descendants of the context node. *Descendants* include the nodes on the next level down in the hierarchy, and also the nodes on every level below that—that is, the children, grandchildren, great-grandchildren, and so on.

- **parent**—Selects the node of which the context node is the child, as long as the context node is not the root node.

- **ancestor**—Selects ancestor nodes of the context node—that is, the parents, grandparents, and so on.

- **following**—Selects nodes that follow the context node in the document, except descendants of the context node, attribute nodes, and namespace nodes. When used with the following markup, the location path **/descendant::personalinfo/ following::*** selects only the **jobinfo**, **position**, **startdate**, and **manager** nodes:

```
<employee>
    <personalinfo>
        <name>Joe Jones</name>
        <birthdate>05/22/65</birthdate>
    </personalinfo>
    <jobinfo>
        <position>Web Developer</position>
        <startdate>08/04/1998</startdate>
        <manager>no</manager>
    </jobinfo>
</employee>
```

- **preceding**—Selects nodes that precede the context node in the document, except ancestors of the context node, attribute nodes, and namespace nodes. The location path **/descendant::startdate/preceding::*** selects the **position**, **personalinfo**, **name**, and **birthdate** nodes in the previous markup, but nothing else.

- **following-sibling**—Selects nodes on the same level as the context node that comes after the context node. For example, the location path **/descendant:: quantity/following-sibling::*** , when used with the XML structure in the following markup, selects the **address**, **city**, and **state** nodes, but not the **item** node:

```
<order>
    <item>Tennis Ball</item>
    <quantity>6</quantity>
    <address>1805 Main St.</address>
    <city>Smithton</city>
    <state>ME</state>
</order>
```

- **preceding-sibling**—Selects nodes on the same level as the context node that comes before the context node in the document. For example, you can use the location path **/descendant::quantity/preceding-sibling::*** to select the **item** node in the previous markup, but not the **address**, **city**, or **state** node.

- **attribute**—Selects attributes of the context node.

- **namespace**—Selects the namespace of the context node.

- **self**—Selects just the context node itself.

- **descendant-or-self**—Selects the context node and its descendants. For instance, if you use the location path **/descendant::personalinfo/ descendant-or-self::*** with the markup in the previous employee example, you select the nodes **personalinfo**, **name**, and **birthdate**.

- **ancestor-or-self**—Selects the context node and its ancestors (parents, grandparents, and so on).

Location Path Node Tests

The second part of the location path step is called the *node test*; it's separated from the axis by a double colon (::). You've already seen node names used as node tests in the previous examples. You can use several other node tests, namely:

- *The asterisk (*)*—Selects all nodes of the type specified by the axis. That is, the location step **child::*** selects all child elements of the context node.

- **text( )**, **comment( )**, *and* **processing-instruction( )**—Select nodes of the type specified. For example, **/descendant::text( )** selects any text nodes in the document. Likewise, **child::comment( )** selects any comment nodes within the context node.

- **node( )**—Selects all node types. For example, **/descendant::node( )** selects every node in the document.

Location Path Predicates

Predicates are used in a location path step to filter the resulting node-set into a new node-set. That is, they further refine the set of nodes selected by the location path. Predicates are enclosed in square brackets to the right of the node test. For example, the following code selects the fifth **para** child of the context node:

```
child::para[position()=5]
```

The node-set produced by **child::para** would contain *all* **para** child elements of the context node. The new location path step, with the predicate **[position()=5]** added, selects only the fifth **para** child element.

The XPath specification defines axes as either forward or reverse axes. A *forward axis* selects the context node or nodes that come after the context node in the document. A *reverse axis* selects the context node or nodes that come before the context node. See Table 13.2 for a list of which axes fall into which categories.

The previous example demonstrates the use of the **position** function as a predicate with a forward axis, **child**. The **position** function also works with reverse axes, but in the reverse of the document order. For example, the location path

```
/descendant::name[position()=2]/ancestor::*[position()=3]
```

selects the **classics** node from the markup in Listing 13.1.

Listing 13.1   The **classics** node is selected from this markup.

```
<bookinventory>
<classics>
<book>
    <title>Great Expectations</title>
    <author>
        <name>Charles Dickens</name>
        <born>1812</born>
        <died>1870</died>
        <nationality>English</nationality>
    </author>
    <protagonist>Pip</protagonist>
</book>
<book>
    <title>Oh, Pioneers!</title>
    <author>
        <name>Willa Cather</name>
        <born>1873</born>
        <died>1947</died>
        <nationality>American</nationality>
```

13. Building Paths in XML with XPath

```
      </author>
      <protagonist>Alexandra</protagonist>
   </book>
   </classics>
   </bookinventory>
```

In this case, the first location step, **/descendant::name[position()=2]**, selects the second **name** node in the document (**Willa Cather**). The second step, **ancestor::*[position()=3]**, selects the ancestor node three positions up the hierarchy from the context node (**Willa Cather**), which is **classics**.

Predicates can also contain location paths. Using this functionality, XPath can define the nodes to be included in the resultant node-set even further. For example, the code

```
child::table[child::row]
```

selects the **table** children of the context node that contain at least one **row** child.

Any XPath expression can be used as a predicate. You'll find a detailed examination of XPath expressions in the following section. But let's take a look at some example predicates that use a variety of expressions and how they function in Table 13.3.

Table 13.2   Categorization of axes.

Category	Axes
Forward axes	**child, descendant, following, following-sibling, descendant-or-self**
Reverse axes	**parent, ancestor, preceding, preceding-sibling, ancestors-or-self**
Neither	**self, attribute, namespace**

Table 13.3   Example predicates used in location paths.

Location Path	Function
/descendant::employee[last()]	Selects the last **employee** node in the document.
ancestor::*[count()]	Returns the number of ancestor nodes of the context node.
child::employee[attribute::secretary and attribute::assistant]	Selects all **employee** child nodes of the context node that have both the **secretary** and **assistant** attributes.
/descendant::price[number()>"4.95"]	Selects all **price** nodes in the document that contain a text node whose value, when converted to a number, is greater than 4.95.
/descendant::description[contains(text(),"deluxe")]	Selects all **description** nodes in the document that contain a text node with the word "**deluxe**" in it.

Abbreviated Syntax

As you can probably imagine from the examples you've seen so far, complex expressions in XPath can become quite lengthy. Fortunately, abbreviated XPath syntax has been developed to alleviate this problem. The abbreviated syntax is fairly straightforward and arguably more intuitive than standard XPath syntax.

The most commonly used abbreviation is the omission of the **child** axis altogether. Essentially, the **child** axis is the default axis of any location step. For example, **/child::book/child::title** can be abbreviated as **/book/title**.

The following list outlines additional common abbreviations:

- **attribute::** can be substituted with **@**
- **/descendant-or-self::node( )/** can be substituted with **//**
- **self::node( )** can be replaced by **.**
- **parent::node** can be replaced by **..**
- **[position( )=3]** can be replaced by **[3]**

With these abbreviations at our disposal, many of the previous examples can be shortened quite a bit. See Table 13.4 for a list of translated example paths.

XPath Functions

All XPath processors are required to support a set of standard functions, called the *core function library*. These functions fall into four categories:

- *Node-set functions*—Used to return node-sets
- *Boolean functions*—Used to test whether a condition is true or false
- *Number functions*—Used to facilitate the use of numbers in an expression
- *String functions*—Used to select and manipulate string values

Let's take a look at the functions included in each category.

Table 13.4   Abbreviated syntax examples.

Original Path	Abbreviated Syntax
/child::person/child::name	/person/name
/descendant::name[position()=2]/ancestor::* [position()=3]	/descendant::name[2]/ancestor::*[3]
child::employee[attribute::secretary and attribute:: assistant]	employee[@secretary and @assistant]
/descendant-or-self::node()/child::para	//para
/descendant::personalinfo/descendant-or-self::*	/descendant::personalinfo//*
self::node()/descendant-or-self::node()/child::para	.//para
child::table[child::row]	table[row]

Node-set Functions

Node-set functions are used in location path predicates to further refine the members of a node-set. Table 13.5 lists each node-set function and its purpose. The word in parentheses (when present) indicates the type of value (also known as an *argument*) that the function acts upon, if any. A question mark after the type of argument indicates that there may be more than one argument.

Boolean Functions

Boolean functions select nodes that are either equal to a condition or not. Table 13.6 lists the boolean functions and their purposes.

Number Functions

Number functions are used to incorporate mathematical functions into XPath expressions. The number functions are shown in Table 13.7. For example, the **sum** function can be used to total prices or quantities in an XML document.

Table 13.5   Node-set functions.

Function	Description
id(*object*)	Selects elements by their unique **id** attribute.
last()	Selects the last node that meets the criteria specified in the location step.
position()	Selects the node that is in the specified position in the node-set.
count(*node-set*)	Counts the number of nodes in the node-set.
local-name(*node-set?*)	Returns the local part of the expanded name of the first node in the node set that is passed to it as an argument. For example, if the expanded name (the element, preceded by its namespace) of an element is **http://www.w3.org/1999/xhtml:body**, the local-name function returns just **body**.
namespace-uri(*node-set?*)	Returns the namespace URI of the expanded name of the first node in the argument node-set. So, if the expanded name of the first node in the argument node-set is **http://www.w3.org/1999/xhtml:body**, the **namespace-uri()** function returns **http://www.w3.org/1999/xhtml**.
name(*node-set?*)	Returns a qualified name (QName) that represents the expanded name of the first node in the argument node-set. Note that a QName is an element name that contains the prefix that represents the namespace URI. For example, the QName **xhtml:body** might represent the expanded name **http://www.w3.org/1999/xhtml:body**.

Table 13.6   Boolean functions.

Function	Description
not(*boolean*)	Selects all nodes that do not meet the condition of an additional boolean function placed between the **not** function's parentheses.
true()	Selects all nodes that meet a condition.
false()	Selects all nodes that do not meet a condition.
lang(*string*)	Selects all nodes that are in a particular language. If a node contains the attribute **xml:lang** and its value is equal to the string in the **lang** function, the node is selected.
boolean(*object*)	Converts an object to a boolean. Can be used to test whether an object is empty.

Table 13.7   Number functions.

Function	Description
sum(*node-set*)	Returns the sum of all numerical string nodes in the node-set.
floor(*number*)	Returns the largest number that is not greater than the argument and is an integer.
ceiling(*number*)	Returns the smallest number that is not less than the argument and is an integer.
round(*number*)	Returns the number that is closest to the argument and is an integer. In other words, it rounds a number to the nearest integer.
number(*object?*)	Converts an object to a number. Can be used to convert a boolean value to 1 or 0 (from true or false) for use in an expression. A numerical string value is converted to the nearest IEEE 754 number, and a non-numerical string is converted to NaN, which indicates that it is not a number.

String Functions

String functions are used to select and manipulate string values; they are shown in Table 13.8. These functions can be useful in location paths for selecting nodes that start with or contain certain words, for example.

Document Trees and Nodes Explained

As mentioned at the beginning of this chapter, XPath models XML documents as trees of nodes. In other words, XPath does not actually work with the XML document that is input to it. Instead, an XPath processor creates a representation of the document in its memory. This representation of an XML document is called a *data model*.

Understanding the reasons for creating an abstraction of an XML document requires that we take a step back and look at the big picture. Listing 13.2 shows a well-formed XML document:

Table 13.8   String functions.

Function	Description
concat(*string, string, string**)	Concatenates the argument strings.
starts-with(*string, string*)	If the first argument string starts with the second argument string, the function returns true. It can be used to select nodes that start with a certain word.
contains(*string, string*)	If the first argument string contains the second argument string, the function returns true. Similar to the **starts-with** function, it can be used to select nodes that contain a certain word.
substring-before(*string, string*)	Returns the substring of the first argument string that precedes the first occurrence of the second argument string in the first argument string, or the empty string if the first argument string does not contain the second argument string. For example, **substring-before("2000/11/25","/")** returns **2000**.
substring-after(*string, string*)	Similar to the **substring-before** function. For example, **substring-after("2000/11/25","/")** returns **11/25**, and **substring-after("2000/11/25","20")** returns **00/11/25**.
substring(*string, number, number*?)	Returns the part of the string argument that starts at the position specified by the first number, with the substring length specified by the second number. If the third argument is missing, the function returns the part of the string starting at the position specified, and continues to the end of the string argument.
string(*object*?)	Converts an object to a string.

Listing 13.2   A well-formed XML document.

```
<?xml version="1.0"?>
<?start music intro.mp3?>
<sitcom>
  <opening_credits>
    <title>Funny People with Nice Clothes</title>
    <star>Bobby McBobby</star>
    <star>Jean Jeanny</star>
  </opening_credits>
<laughter/>
  <scene location="apartment">
  </scene>
</sitcom>
```

This document contains various types of XML structures, including elements, a processing instruction, attributes, and text. A data model provides a standard way to describe these parts. Without a data model, a programmer who wants to access a part of this document needs to have an intimate knowledge of XML syntax. For example, each program that uses XML data would have to say something like "A tag is marked by angle brackets. XML elements have an opening tag and a closing tag. The text in the opening tag is the name of the element."

Because the syntax of an element and the other parts of XML documents are the same for all well-formed XML documents, it's possible for programmers to not have to worry about these details. With a data model, a programmer, or an XPath expression, can simply say, "Show me the third element named **scene**."

When you work with an abstraction (or model) of the document, it's much easier to work with the data. Each node in the document tree model represents a part of your XML document. Figure 13.1 shows how XPath represents Listing 13.2.

When XPath creates a node tree of a document, it records the order of the nodes. A node's position in the order is based on the order in which the first character of the XML representation of each node occurs in the XML representation of the document. For example, in the previous example, the **opening_credits** element comes before the **scene** element. This order is preserved in the XPath tree and is called the *document order*. In perhaps the most unnecessary definition in the entire XPath specification, *reverse document order* is defined as the reverse of document order. In other words, the last node in reverse document order is the first node in document order.

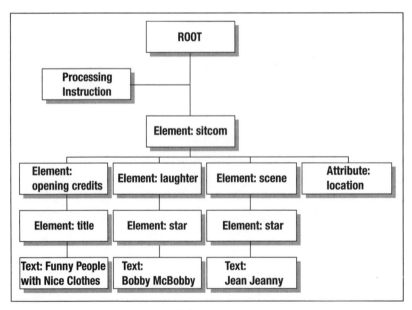

Figure 13.1   How XPath represents Listing 13.2.

A few common-sense rules govern node trees:

- Just as an XML document can have only one root element, a node tree may have only one root node.
- The root node is always the first node in document order.
- Nodes cannot share children.
- Each node in a tree, except for the root node, has only one parent node.
- The descendants of a node are the children of the node and the descendants of the children of the node. This statement, of course, says that all the children, grandchildren, great-grandchildren, great-great-grandchildren, and so forth are descendants of a node.

XPath's model of an XML document is created using the seven different types of nodes, which we discuss in detail in the following sections:

- Root nodes
- Element nodes
- Text nodes
- Attribute nodes
- Namespace nodes
- Processing instruction nodes
- Comment nodes

Root Node

The root node is the root of the tree. All the nodes in a tree are the descendants of the root node. Processing instruction and comment nodes that occur outside the document element are the children of the root node. For example, in the following document, the comment that is outside the document element (in this case, **employees**) is considered a child of the root node, and the comment that is inside of the **employees** element is a child of the **employees** element:

```
<?xml version="1.0"?>
<!--This is the beginning of the employee list.-->
<employees>
<!--Here's the first employee.-->
<employee number="1">
  <name>
    <first>Albert</first>
    <last>Jones</last>
  </name>
</employee>
</employees>
```

Element Nodes

The tree contains an element node for every element in the XML document. The element node's name is made up of the element in the document's name. The children of an element node are the element nodes, processing instruction nodes, comment nodes, and text nodes in the element's content.

An element node may have a unique identifier. In documents that use Document Type Definitions (DTDs), attributes of the type ID can be defined for elements. If an element has an **id** attribute, it can be used to select nodes in XPath.

Text Nodes

Character data in XML documents is represented in XPath as text nodes. Character data includes **CDATA** sections as well as the text contents of elements. Attribute values and text in comments and processing instructions are not turned into text nodes.

Text nodes always have at least one character, and they will contain as much content as is necessary for there never to be a text node immediately preceding or following a text node in document order. For example, no matter how long the text contents of the **monologue** element are in the following example, only one text node is created.

```
<?xml version="1.0"?>
<script>
  <monologue>
    To be, or not to be, that is the question:
Whether 'tis nobler in the mind to suffer
The slings and arrows of outrageous fortune;
Or to take arms against a sea of troubles,
And by opposing, end them: to die, to sleep
No more; and by a sleep, to say we end
The heart-ache, and the thousand natural shocks
That flesh is heir to; 'Tis a consummation
Devoutly to be wish'd. To die, to sleep,
To sleep, perchance to dream; Ay, there's the rub,
For in that sleep of death, what dreams may come,
When we have shuffled off this mortal coil,
Must give us pause.
  </monologue>
</script>
```

Attribute Nodes

An element's attributes produce attribute nodes in the node tree. The element is the parent of its attribute nodes. The attribute node, however, is not the child of the element. At first glance, this would seem to be a contradictory relationship. Upon further examination, however, it actually does make sense.

Because an attribute is a component of the element node itself, when you use the XPath expression **/child::employee/attribute::id**, you select the **id** attribute of the **employee** element, not the **id** attribute of any child elements of **employee**.

Namespace Nodes

Each element has a namespace node for every namespace that is in scope for that element. The relationship between a namespace node and an element node is similar to the relationship between attribute nodes and element nodes. The element node is the parent of the namespace node, but the namespace node is not the child of the element node. In a graphical representation of a tree containing namespace nodes, the namespace and attributes are usually shown at the same level as the element.

An element will have one namespace node:

- for every attribute of the element whose name starts with **xmlns:**

- for every attribute of an ancestor element whose name starts **xmlns:**—unless the element itself or a nearer ancestor redeclares the prefix

- for an **xmlns** attribute, if the element or some ancestor has an **xmlns** attribute

Related solution:	*Found on page:*
Using Elements from a Namespace in an XML Document	409

Processing Instruction Nodes

A tree contains a processing instruction node for every processing instruction in the document, excluding any processing instructions that occur in the DTD. This means that if you declare a DTD inside an XML document, any processing instructions in the definition itself do not result in nodes in the tree created by XPath.

TIP: For more information on declaring DTDs, both as external documents and inside XML documents, please see Chapter 5.

Comment Nodes

A comment node is created in the node tree for every comment in the document, excluding any comments in the DTD.

Throughout this chapter, you've seen that XPath is a complex and powerful tool for selecting locations and node-sets in XML documents. When used with XSLT and XPointer, the possible applications for XPath are many and varied.

Immediate Solutions

Building an XPath with the Full XPath Syntax

In this section, you learn how to create XPaths using the full XPath syntax to select the different parts of an XML document. The document from which you'll select nodes is shown in Listing 13.3.

Listing 13.3   The XML document from which you'll select nodes.

```
<?xml version="1.0"?>
<cats_at_the_pound>
 <cat id="ca001">
    <name>Moby</name>
    <age_in_months>3</age_in_months>
    <weight_in_pounds>3</weight_in_pounds>
    <breed>Domestic Short Hair</breed>
 </cat>
 <cat id="ca002">
    <name>Stinky</name>
    <age_in_months>5</age_in_months>
    <weight_in_pounds>5</weight_in_pounds>
    <breed>Domestic Long Hair</breed>
 </cat>
 <cat id="ca003">
    <name>Buster</name>
    <age_in_months>36</age_in_months>
    <weight_in_pounds>12</weight_in_pounds>
    <breed>Domestic Short Hair</breed>
 </cat>
 <cat id="ca004">
    <name>Hep</name>
    <age_in_months>9</age_in_months>
    <weight_in_pounds>9</weight_in_pounds>
    <breed>Abyssinian</breed>
 </cat>
</cats_at_the_pound>
```

Using XPath, you can select various combinations of nodes from this document. Our first XPath expression simply selects all the names of the cats. To create this location path, follow these steps:

1. Decide whether you need to use a relative or absolute location path. For this example, use an absolute location path. Absolute location paths start with a slash (/).

2. Decide how the location path should navigate the XML tree to get to the **name** element inside each **cat** element. For example, should the XPath expression navigate the tree in document order (from the top down) or in reverse document order? Sometimes you might want to navigate a document in reverse order, but this probably isn't one of them. For this example, this step is pretty clear: navigate in document order.

3. Choose an axis for the first location step. The axis is the first part of a location step. The axis can be one of the following:

   - **child**
   - **descendant**
   - **parent**
   - **ancestor**
   - **following-sibling**
   - **preceding-sibling**
   - **following**
   - **preceding**
   - **attribute**
   - **namespace**
   - **self**
   - **descendant-or-self**
   - **ancestor-or-self**

   It's possible for you to select the **name** element using any one of several of these axes. For example, you could simply write the following XPath expression:

   ```
   /descendant::name
   ```

   This expression would select every name in the document. This expression could lead to a problem, however. If this document contained another section with **dog** elements, the previous XPath expression would also select the names of the dogs.

   Perhaps the best way to start this expression, then, is to use the **child** axis to specify that you only want the names of the cats. You could write the first location step in this path as follows:

   ```
   /child::cats_in_pound
   ```

4. Select the **name** nodes that are descendants of the **cats_in_pound** node. By choosing to use the **descendant** axis, you're able to skip a level in the XML document hierarchy. For example,

```
child::cat/child::name
```

describes the same node-set as

```
descendant::name
```

but the latter is a more efficient way of coding this location step.

5. Your final XPath to select the names of all the cats in the document is:

```
/child::cats_in_pound/descendant::name
```

Now, suppose you want to do something a bit more complicated. Imagine that the pound wanted to put an advertisement in the local newspaper featuring the adult cats that are available for adoption. You would need to select all the names of the cats that are over 12 months old. To do this, follow these steps:

1. Because the node-set you want to create (names of cats in the pound that are over 12 months old) is a subset of the node-set you just created in the previous example (names of cats in pound), you can use the XPath from the previous example as the starting point for your new XPath:

```
/child::cats_in_pound/descendant::name
```

2. To modify this XPath so it only returns the **name** nodes of cats older than 12 months, you need to add a predicate refining the resultant node-set:

```
[child::age_in_months[number()>12]]
```

Note that this predicate has another predicate nested inside it. The first predicate, **[child::age_in_months]**, refines the current node-set to those nodes with a child node called **age_in_months**. The nested node, **[number()>12]**, further refines the node-set to only those nodes that have child nodes called **age_in_months** with values greater than 12.

3. Your final XPath that selects the names of all cats with an age greater than 12 months is:

```
/child::cats_in_pound/
descendant::name[child::age_in_months[number()>12]]
```

Building an XPath with the Abbreviated XPath Syntax

As you've seen in the previous examples, XPath syntax gets very wordy very fast. Almost any useful XPath is rather lengthy. Fortunately, you can use abbreviated syntax to help you keep the length of your XPath syntax to a minimum. In this section, you convert the final XPath from the previous section into abbreviated syntax, and also create a new XPath in abbreviated syntax.

Converting an XPath to Abbreviated Syntax

In this example, you convert the final XPath from the previous section to abbreviated XPath syntax. Follow these steps:

1. Start with the following XPath in full syntax:

```
/child::cats_in_pound/
descendant::name[child::age_in_months[number()>12]]
```

2. Eliminate all **child** axes from the XPath, because **child** is the default axis, and as such does not need to be stated:

```
/cats_in_pound/descendant::name[age_in_months[number()>12]]
```

This is actually all that can be done to abbreviate this expression. None of the other axes or predicates can be abbreviated.

Creating a New XPath with Abbreviated Syntax

Very complex XPaths can be shortened significantly when using abbreviated XPath syntax. Let's look at an example of how to build an XPath using abbreviated syntax.

In this section, you'll build an XPath to extract nodes from an XML document with the structure shown in Listing 13.4.

Listing 13.4   An XML document that you'll extract nodes from using an XPath.

```
<?xml version="1.0"?>
<clothes>
    <item id="w00230" ordered="yes" name="checkered_blouse">
        <order id="00678">
            <quantity>1</quantity>
            <size>10</size>
            <name>Mary Duncan</name>
            .
            .
            .
```

```
      </order>
      <order id="00892">
         <quantity>1</quantity>
         <size>14</size>
         <name>SueAnn Lawson</name>

            .

            .

            .

      </order>
      <order id="01288">
         <quantity>1</quantity>
         <size>7</size>
         <name>Frances Gilman</name>

            .

            .

            .

      </order>
   </item>
   <item id="w00550" ordered="yes" name="striped_blouse >

         .

         .

         .

   </item>
      .

      .

      .
</clothes>
```

Suppose that you want to select the third order for each blouse you have for sale. Here are the steps required to construct an abbreviated location path to select this node-set:

1. Select all **item** nodes in the document that are children of the **clothes** node (the document may include other top-level nodes that aren't shown in the code snippet). Using the abbreviated syntax, this code is as follows:

   ```
   /clothes/item
   ```

2. Refine this node-set to include only the **item** nodes whose **ordered** attribute is equal to **yes** and whose **name** attribute contains the word **blouse**. The following code accomplishes this, using predicates and functions:

   ```
   /clothes/item[@ordered[text()="yes"] and
   @name[contains(text(), "blouse")]]
   ```

   Remember, the **@** symbol is short for the **attribute** axis.

3. Select the third **order** of each **item** from this node-set. You accomplish this by adding a new step that selects the **order** children of the current node-set members that are in the third position, as follows:

```
order[3]
```

4. Your final XPath is:

```
/clothes/item[@ordered[text()="yes"] and
@name[contains(text(),"blouse")]]/order[3]
```

If you'd written this XPath in full syntax, it would read as follows:

```
/child::clothes/child::item[attribute::ordered[text()="yes"] and
attribute::name[contains(text(), "blouse")]]/order[position()=3]
```

Obtaining Tools to Build XPaths

A variety of tools are available for working with XPath expressions. Because XPath is used with XML applications such as XSLT and XPointer, many of the tools available for these languages also include XPath capabilities.

However, you can use several standalone XPath tools to experiment with and learn to use XPath:

- *XPath 1.0 Interactive Expression Builder*—XPath 1.0 Interactive Expression Builder is a Web-based tool written by Aaron Skonnard for building XPath location paths. It can be found at **http://staff.develop.com/aarons/bits/ xpath-builder/** and is shown in Figure 13.2. The Interactive Expression Builder allows you to load an XML document into your Web browser (Internet Explorer 5 and MSXML 3.0 are required). You can then type an XPath expression into a form field, and the nodes that are selected by that expression are highlighted in the XML document.

- *XPath 1.0 Compressor*—XPath 1.0 Compressor is another Web-based tool written by Aaron Skonnard. It can be found at **http://staff.develop.com/ aarons/bits/xpath-compress/**. As shown in Figure 13.3, XPath 1.0 Compressor allows you to input an XPath expression that uses the full XPath syntax; it displays the abbreviated version of the expression.

- *XML Style Wizard*—Infoteria's XML Style Wizard allows you to specify an XML file; it then generates an XSL file to transform the XML document into a simple HTML document. XML Style Wizard creates XSLT markup based on your answers to a few questions and the nodes that you select in the input document. You can view the resulting XSL document to see how XPath expressions are used in XSLT.

- *XML Spy*—XML Spy (**www.xmlspy.com/**) is an Integrated Development Environment (IDE) for XML. Among its many capabilities is a function called Copy XPath. Copy XPath creates an XPath expression that points to the currently selected element or attribute in an XML document. This XPath expression can then be pasted into an application that uses XPath, such as XSLT or XPointer expressions.

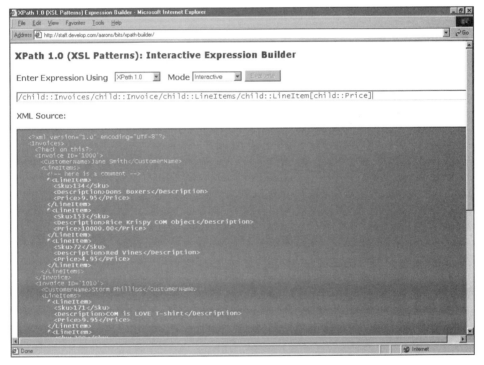

Figure 13.2   Interactive Expression Builder displaying an example document.

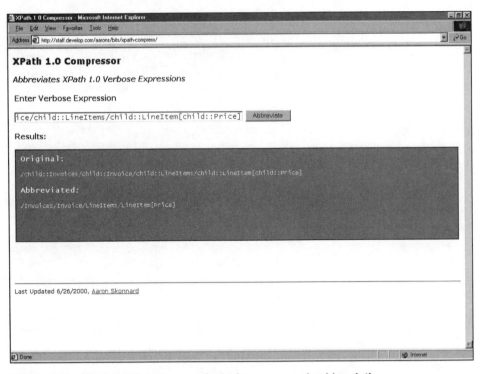

Figure 13.3   XPath 1.0 Compressor displaying an example abbreviation.

Chapter 14

References within Links: XPointer

In Depth

The flow of information across the Internet becomes increasingly complex every day. What once consisted of just words and pictures now contains structured information about every subject imaginable. It's now possible to get up-to-date weather reports, stock quotes, sports scores, and much, much more on the Internet. Although the Hypertext Markup Language (HTML) displays this information well, it doesn't work very well with the structure of the data. This is where XML takes over: It organizes documents into logical sections quite efficiently.

Even though XML documents are structured, you still must be able to navigate through the structure in an effective manner. The World Wide Web Consortium (W3C) addresses this issue with the XML Path Language (XPath), XML Linking Language (XLink), and XML Pointer Language (XPointer) specifications. This chapter describes XPointer and how it relates to structured and non-structured documents. In addition, you find out what you can do with XPointer.

The Purpose of XPointer

In HTML, you use HTML hyperlinks (the anchor element) to link standard documents. You can even use the **#name** reference in the anchor (**a**) element to jump to specific locations within those documents. So what does XPointer provide beyond what is currently available with HTML? XPointer gives you the ability to create links to any part of any document, without having to place anchor (**a**) elements in that document. As a result, XPointer allows you to link to specific parts of not only documents on your own site, but also on sites that you don't own.

TIP: XPointers haven't been around long. This technology is currently a candidate recommendation that closed on September 7, 2000. Sections of this chapter are based on this specification. You can go to **www.w3.org/TR/xptr** to find out more.

XPointer is an extension of the XPath expression language (which was covered in Chapter 13). Like XPath, XPointer is used to identify parts, or fragments, of XML documents. When used as part of an XLink, an XPointer expression is therefore called a *fragment identifier*.

Related solutions:	Found on page:
Building an XPath with the Full XPath Syntax	365
Building an XPath with the Abbreviated XPath Syntax	368

Listing 14.1 shows a segment of an XML document that we'll be using as an example throughout this chapter.

Listing 14.1   An XML document segment.

```
<artists>
  <artist>
   <name>Beethoven</name>
   <genre>Classical</genre>
   <songs>
      <song>Moonlight Sonata</song>
      <song>Silence Concerto</song>
   </songs>
  </artist>
  <artist>
   <name>Elvis</name>
   <genre>Rock</genre>
   <songs>
      <song>Hound Dog</song>
      <song>Blue Suede Shoes</song>
      <song>Heartbreak Hotel</song>
   </songs>
  </artist>
</artists>
```

14. References within
Links: XPointer

This segment describes musical artists, the type of music they play, and some of the music they've performed. XML makes this document very structured; therefore, it's fairly easy to see that three of Elvis's songs are listed in this document (**Hound Dog**, **Blue Suede Shoes**, and **Heartbreak Hotel**) and that his musical genre is **Rock**. As you saw in Chapter 13, it's useful for you to think of the document in Listing 14.1 in terms of a tree structure, as shown in Figure 14.1.

Imagine that you wanted to link directly to the portion of this document that contains information about Elvis. If this were an HTML document, you would need to add an **a** element to the document with a **name** attribute. You could then link to the named section of the document by adding an HTML fragment identifier to the URL of the document in your link, for example:

```
<a href="artists.html#Elvis">Here is the information about Elvis</a>
```

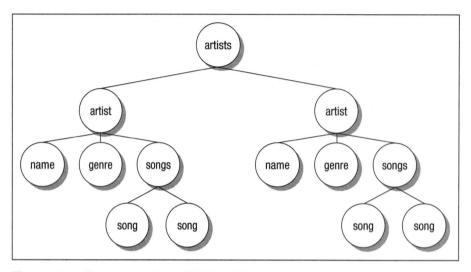

Figure 14.1   The tree structure of Listing 14.1.

XLink, as mentioned previously in this chapter and in Chapter 12, allows you to link to part of documents without having to attach names to the target. The following sample XLink shows how you can link to the portion of the document that contains information about Elvis using XLink and XPointer:

```
<myElement
   xmlns:xlink="http://www.w3.org/1999/xlink"
   xlink:type="simple"
   xlink:href="/artists.xml#xpointer(/artists/artist[name/text()='Elvis'])">
      Elvis info
</myElement>
```

This link will point to **artist** nodes in the document that have a **name** child with a value of **Elvis**. As you can imagine, this way of identifying fragments is much more flexible than adding anchors to the target document. Using XPointer, the target document can be changed a great deal and this link will still function.

Using XPointer with XLink, it's possible to link to any part of any document, as well as to multiple parts of a document. For example, you could create an extended link that links to all of the works by Beethoven, or you may want to find all the artists who belong to a specific genre, such as **Rock**. Taking it even further, you may want to know the last song a particular artist wrote. Finally, it's even possible to link to a substring of characters within an element, such as a word within the title of a song.

An endless number of applications could benefit from XPointer. Here are some examples:

- An online shopping catalog.

- An employee manual in which you need to reference information about a specific topic.

- A database of animals that is organized so you can locate information about a specific group of animals.

- A cookbook that can instantly list all the recipes that use a specific ingredient.

The possibilities are endless.

Linking Within a Document

When the W3C developed the XPointer specification, its goal was to create a means to address or create links to the internal structure of a document. The link could be to a specific point, element, attribute, character string, or relative position within the document. The specification does not discuss what should happen when a link is actually followed: This action is usually decided by the browser or other application software that is traversing the link. One browser may jump to the link in the document and highlight the resulting information; another may show a graphical representation between the two pieces of information. Search engines or data storage systems may use the links in entirely different ways. The XPointer specification is written in a way that makes it very flexible. XPointer also has a very simple syntax, which makes it easy to read and develop links in.

Linking to Other Resources

As the Web evolves, the number of links in existence will grow exponentially—and not just between text-based documents. There will be (and already are) links to many different types of media, ranging from images, to sound clips, to movie clips, and more. Before you can connect to a resource, it must be capable of having you link to it. This link is called a Uniform Resource Identifier (URI). URIs encompass the familiar Uniform Resource Locators (URLs), which are the common locators used to navigate to specific pages on the Web, as well as Universal Resource Names (URNs), which are universal names that are mapped to the required resource, whatever it may be.

TIP: *XPointer and XLink are based on two well-defined standards that have been in place for some time: the Text Encoding Initiative (TEI) and Hypermedia/Time-based Structuring Language (HyTime). These standards originated in the publishing world. If you would like to read more about the TEI guidelines, go to* ***www.uic.edu/orgs/tei/p3/***. *For information on HyTime, go to* ***www.hytime.org***.

How XPointers Work

In the previous sections, we discussed what an XPointer is capable of linking to, at a theoretical level, and you saw an example of an XPointer expression being used as a fragment identifier. In this section, we'll look more closely at the syntax and inner workings of XPointer.

Let's look at an example of linking in its simplest form. You're at one location and want to move to another location or piece of related information. You should be able to follow a link to the desired resource. This ability is what makes the Web so powerful. With HTML, you create links using the **a** element; for example, you could link from text or an image to another page or possibly somewhere else within that page by using the **#*name*** fragment identifier. Although this system has served the Web quite well, wouldn't it be nice if you could go to the exact spot you're looking for in a 1,000-page document without having to download the entire document? HTML-style fragment identifiers help a bit, but they only point to some sort of flag in the document—not to the important data located in the page.

Moving to an exact location within a resource should be a natural extension to moving to the resource in the first place. When you're using XPointer, it's that easy!

First, let's examine how you would get to the XPointer part of the W3C site using a standard browser:

1. Type "http://www.w3.org" in the browser's address bar.
2. Press the Enter key, and the default page is loaded.
3. To get to the specific page dealing with XPointer, which happens to be in a subdirectory under the previous site, you add the appropriate path to the end of the current location, for example, **http://www.w3.org/TR/xptr**.
4. To jump to a specific point within that document (such as the definition for XPath), you add that part to the end of the current HTTP path, for example, **http://www.w3.org/TR/xptr#XPath**.

XPointer works in much the same way because its goal is also to navigate to specific fragments of a document. After you've reached the page you want, it's possible to add an XPointer expression to the end of your URI that takes you directly to the desired resource buried deep within a document without loading the entire document.

It's important to mention again why XML has so much more to offer than HTML. XML has structure, and every location in the target document becomes a resource to which you can link. It's also easier to create links to ranges by using two tags as starting and ending points in the document; doing so would be impossible using HTML.

For example, let's refer back to Listing 14.1, which describes the musicians. In the first XPointer example in the chapter, we used XPointer to find the **artist** element that contains information about Elvis. We did this by creating an expression that looked for **artist** children of the **artists** element that have **name** node with a **text** child with value of **Elvis**. This is just one way you can access the same information in this document.

You could also locate the same information using its position in the document. In our example, **Elvis** is the second artist in the document. To create a path to this part of the document, you need to get to the page initially using a link that contains the following URL:

```
http://www.musicians.com/artists.xml
```

Now, to get to the specific location in the document, you add a pound sign (**#**) followed by an XPointer expression that would guide you to **Elvis**:

```
#xpointer(/child:artists/child:artist[position()=2])
```

The final URL is as follows:

```
http://www.musicians.com/artists.xml#xpointer
(/child:artists/child:artist[position()=2])
```

From left to right, this code provides the following instructions: Go to the Web site called **www.musicians.com** where you'll find an XML document called **artists.xml**. When you reach that page, find a child node of the document node called **artists**. Select the second child node of that node called **artist**.

XPointer Syntax

We've reached the stage at which everything has been tied together as a working unit. We've gone through what an XPointer is, what it's capable of, and how it compares to regular links between documents using HTML. We also worked through an example in which we linked to a specific fragment of a document. The next step is to explain the XPointer language fully by discussing the syntax required to link to various sub-resources in a document.

TIP: *The information from this section has been taken from a candidate recommendation of the XPointer language. Because XPointer is not yet an official recommendation, this material should be considered work in progress that may change at a later date. The complete specification can be found at **www.w3.org/TR/xptr**.*

At the heart of the XPointer language is something called a *location*. A location is any point in an XML document that can be located using XPointer expressions. Locations are the XPointer equivalent to XPath nodes. A location set is the XPointer equivalent of an XPath node-set.

XPointer expressions use location steps separated by slashes to specify a specific resource in a document. Other important XPointer definitions include:

- *sub-resource*—Part of an XML document that is identified by an XPointer

- *point*—A position in XML data

- *range*—An identification of a selection of XML data using a starting point and ending point

- *singleton*—A location that consists of a single, contiguous portion of a document

The XPointer specification defines three types of XPointer expressions: full XPointers, bare names, and child sequences.

Full XPointers

Full XPointer expressions use the same syntax (plus a few additions) as XPath expressions (either abbreviated or unabbreviated). XPointer expressions start with a *scheme*. The scheme indicates the language of the XPointer. Currently, the only value that is allowed as the scheme is **xpointer**. In the future, the scheme will be used to indicate the version of XPointer that is being used, or a different language that is being used to locate document fragments.

Here are some examples of full XPointer expressions and what they do:

- **xpointer(child:html/child:body/child:h1)**—Points to all of the **h1** elements in an HTML document.

- **xpointer(/html/body/h1)**—Same as the previous example; points to all of the **h1** elements in an HTML document.

- **xpointer(paragraph[3])**—Points to the third **paragraph** child of the current location.

- **xpointer(id('Elvis'))**—Points to the element with an **ID** attribute with the value **'Elvis'**.

Full XPointers are the most flexible way to locate specific parts of documents. Much of the complexity of XPath and the verbosity of XPointer can be avoided in many circumstances by using the two shorthand types of XPointer expressions. The first of these, Bare Names, is similar to HTML fragment identifiers.

Bare Names

Bare names are useful when you simply want to create an HTML-style fragment identifier. As you saw in the previous section, if you want to point to an element with an **id** attribute using the full XPointer syntax, you can use the following syntax:

```
xpointer(id('value'))
```

The bare-names shorthand method allows you to omit all of the fat and simply use the value of an attribute of the **ID** type as the fragment identifier. For example, to point to an element with an **id** attribute with the value of **Elvis**, you could use the following URL:

```
http://www.example.com/artists.xml#Elvis
```

Child Sequences

Child sequence addressing iterates through a series of values separated by slashes to find a location. For example, if you want to link to the third child of the second child of the root node, you could use the following child sequence as an XPointer expression:

```
/1/2/3
```

14. References within Links: XPointer

TIP: *The first part of a child sequence must either be the document node, which is represented by /1, or a bare name that corresponds to the id attribute of an element.*

XPointer Extensions to XPath

As mentioned earlier in this chapter, XPointer is an extension of XPath. Although it's possible to use XPointer quite successfully just by knowing XPath, there are several important concepts and functions that XPointer contains that are not in the XPath specification.

Ranges

An XPointer range location represents all of the XML structure between a start point and an end point. A range is not the same as a list of nodes or locations, because a range may contain only a part of a node.

XPointer has several functions that make it possible to work with ranges. Table 14.1 shows the functions, their syntax, and descriptions.

Table 14.1   XPointer functions, their syntax, and descriptions.

Function	Syntax	Description
range-to()	*location-set* range-to(*expression*)	The **range-to** function returns a range for each location in the context. For example, the following XPointer locates a range from the element with ID **Elvis** to the element with ID **Beethoven**: **xpointer(id('Elvis')/range-to(id('Beethoven')))**
string-range()	*location*-set string-range (*location-set*, *string, number?, number?*)	Returns a set of string ranges, or substrings in a string. For example, the following expression returns the fourth occurrence of the string **XPointers are fun** that occurs in a paragraph element: **string-range(//paragraph,"XPointers are fun")[4]**.
range()	*location-set* range(*location-set*)	Returns a range that contains the locations in the argument *location-set*. The argument *location-set* is the one in parentheses.
range-inside()	*location-set* range-inside (*location-set*)	Returns a range that contains the contents of the locations in the argument location-set.
start-point()	*point* start-point(*point*)	Returns a location-set that contains a point for the first point in every location in the input location-set.
end-point()	*point* end-point(*point*)	Returns a location-set that contains a point for the last point in every location in the input location-set.

Immediate Solutions

Adding a Simple XPointer to an XML Link

To build onto an existing URI, you know to follow the URI with a pound sign (#) and the XPointer terminology required to specify the desired document fragment.

WARNING! XPointers rely on links to function. Remember that they really are just an extension of a standard link that allows you to reference fragments of documents rather than entire documents. Make sure you're comfortable with XLink before moving on to XPointers. XLinks are covered in detail in Chapter 12.

The pound sign separates the document fragment from the rest of the identifier. Actually, the URI is optional. If it's given, the XPointer will link to that resource; then it will search for the desired document fragment. If the URI is not specified, the XPointer assumes that the document to link to must be the current document that contained the XPointer in the first place, and it searches there.

In our first example, you link to the W3C's Web site. After you reach that resource, you will navigate to the logo, which is situated somewhere on the page. The logo happens to have an ID of **logo**. Here's an XML document that uses a link to point to the logo:

```
<myLink
    xmlns:xlink="http://www.w3.org/2000/xlink"
    xlink:type="simple"
    xlink:href="http://www.w3.org#logo"
    xlink:title="Jump to the W3C logo!!"/>
```

This code takes you to **www.w3.org** and searches for a tag with an ID of **logo**. Try going there yourself. View the source, search for logo, and you should be able to find the same tag.

The following example is similar to the first, but the required document page is deeper in the site. In this example, you want to reach a resource location with an ID of **diet** located somewhere on a page called **whales.htm** on the Web site **www.animals.com**. Here's the appropriate code:

```
href="http://www.animals.com/mammals/whales.htm#diet"
```

Once again, think back to the idea behind linking to a subresource. In our example, you automatically assume you're going to be taken to some text that discusses the diet of a whale. In reality, however, almost anything could happen. You could see a film of whales eating, hear a sound clip, or see an image. This link could be combined with others to create a virtual document listing the diets of a variety of different types of animals. It all depends on what the client application plans to do with the subresource it's given.

TIP: *It's amazing to think that we can build virtual documents by pulling information from a variety of locations. There have been discussions on the ability to create link databases, which are entire Web sites that contain no information whatsoever, but instead draw the requested information from the appropriate sites and display a virtual document to the client consisting of many types of media.*

Creating XPointers with the Full XPointer Syntax

As discussed earlier, you may need to specify an exact location within an XML document, and sometimes a simple HTML-style fragment identifier can't give you what you require. Consider Listing 14.2, which we'll use to show you some examples of when you should use full XPointer syntax:

Listing 14.2   Example for using full XPointer syntax.

```
<customers>
  <customer id="1000">
    <name>Smith</name>
    <orders>
      <ordernum>111</ordernum>
      <ordernum>222</ordernum>
    </orders>
  </customer>
  <customer id="2000">
    <name>Taylor</name>
    <orders>
      <ordernum>333</ordernum>
      <ordernum>444</ordernum>
    </orders>
  </customer>
</customers>
```

Let's say you want to reference parts of the document using XPointer expressions. Before you get to that point, you have to decide on the starting point for your expression. The starting point is also known as the context node, or the context location. To start at the root of the document, you can begin your expression with a slash (/), just as in XPath.

However, let's assume you've already done some previous processing. You're at an order for a specific customer and you want to get back to the **customer** element from which you started to find the corresponding customer name. The XPointer function called **origin( )** will return you to where the traversal began.

Next, you want to jump to customer **2000** to review the associated information. The **id( )** tag allows you to specify an element with a unique **ID** attribute that matches the specific value you're looking for. Therefore, for our example, you use **id('2000')**, which takes you to the second customer.

After you establish a context location (either the root or the context node) within a document, you can start to navigate through the document to other meaningful locations. This is where thinking of an XML document as a tree-like structure full of nodes comes in very handy. The nodes are related to each other like a family, with children, parents, brothers, sisters, and so on. Your location source is just one relative in the tree that you use as a starting point to reach the rest of the family.

Creating XPointers with Ranges

Ranges require two arguments to fully identify the link being pointed to. Both arguments are relative to a location source and not to each other. We use Listing 14.3 to work through some examples of ranges.

Listing 14.3 Example for using ranges.

```
<groceries>
  <meats necessity="yes">
      <item>Steak</item>
      <item>Ribs</item>
      <item>Sausage</item>
      <item>Hamburger</item>
  </meats>
    <vegetables necessity="yes">
      <item>Corn</item>
    </vegetables>
    <dairy necessity="yes">
      <item>Milk</item>
    </dairy>
```

```
    <breads necessity="yes">
       <item>Bagels</item>
       <item>Cereal</item>
    </breads>
    <other>
       <item>Candy</item>
    </other>
</groceries>
```

Listing 14.3 is an example of a grocery list broken down into food groups. Let's say you want to select the second through fourth items in the **meats** category. You need to indicate a starting location and an ending location, as follows:

```
xpointer(/groceries/meats/item[2])/range-to(/groceries/meats/item[4])
```

The first part of this XPointer expression is a location path that specifies the starting point as the second **item** child of the **meats** child of the **groceries** child of the root. The location-set after **range-to** specifies the ending point. The range pointed to by this expression contains **Ribs**, **Sausage**, and **Hamburger**.

Creating XPointers with String Ranges

String ranges differ from the other types of ranges in that they select strings or positions between strings. Most of the other locators deal with nodes. The following XML document is used with the string range examples:

```
<poem>
    <title>How Much Wood</title>
        <line id="first">How much wood could a woodchuck chuck</line>
        <line id="second">if a woodchuck could chuck wood?</line>
        <line id="third">He would chuck as much as he could</line>
        <line id="fourth">if a woodchuck could chuck wood.</line>
</poem>
```

You use a string range to link to specific sections of text. A simple example is to link to all of the occurrences of **wood** in the second line of the poem, as follows:

```
xpointer(string-range(/poem/line[id('second')],"wood"))
```

You start with an absolute locator to find the location source of the second line. After you have this base, you can search the element for the first match of the desired string and place the location pointer at the first character in the word.

Now, let's make things a little harder. This time you want to link to just the first occurrence of the word **wood** in the second line:

```
xpointer(string-range(/poem/line[id('second')],"wood")[position()=1])
```

This was fairly easy to accomplish: You just add a predicate to the **string-range** function to tell it to get only the first result. The next example links to every instance of the characters **wood** that appears in the entire poem:

```
xpointer(string-range(/,"wood"))
```

For this example, XPointer uses the root as a starting point to link to the entire poem (you can use **descendant** here, as well). After you have the children, you can link to the first position of all occurrences of the string **wood**.

Remember that you can also move to the last occurrence of a string with markup similar to the following:

```
xpointer(string-range(/,"wood")[last()])
```

The previous line links you to the first character of the word **woodchuck** in the fourth line of the poem.

You may need to locate a specific substring in a document. A good example is when you want to link to a phone number and skip the first three digits that indicate the area code. Using the example document in this section, you can jump to the fourth character in the second line by not specifying a string to match, as follows:

```
xpointer(string-range(id('second'),"",4))
```

This line selects the letter **a** because it's located on the second line and is the fourth character in. If you think about what you've done so far, you should also be able to select characters starting from the end of the string instead of the beginning. To select the **?** at the end of the second line, you need to get to the end and then back up one character, as follows:

```
xpointer(string-range(id('second'),"",1)[last()-1])
```

We need to make one more point regarding the string ranges. In all the previous examples, after a match is made, the link exists at a point on or before a single character. You can add a fourth argument to the **string** keyword that will allow you to select a range of characters. In the previous document, the word **could** appears four times. This example creates links to all four of these occurrences and selects the entire word:

```
xpointer(string-range(/,"could",1,5))
```

This line states that the document should be traversed to locate every occurrence of the word **could**. When a match is found, the XPointer should start selecting text from the first character and select exactly five characters.

> **WARNING!** It's important to note that when performing string matching, the element text refers to all the character data in the element or elements selected, as well as any descendant elements. Any markup characters located in the text are ignored, and the pattern matching is exact. No normalization for uppercase or lowercase, spaces, or combining of characters is performed. For example, two words separated solely by a carriage return are not the same as two words separated by a space.

Bringing It All Together

Here's a final example that ties together the previous sections. In this example, you use XPointer expressions, ranges, and string ranges together to select a section of your poem. The goal is to select the text starting with the first occurrence of the string **wood** down to and including the last occurrence of the word **wood**. Here's the XPointer that will accomplish this task, followed by an explanation of each piece:

```
xpointer(string-range(/,"wood",1,4)[position()=1])/range-to(string-range(/
,"wood",1,4)[last()])
```

This XPointer first points to the first occurrence of the word **wood** and selects it. The second step in this XPointer is the **range-to()** function, which makes the string selected by the first expression into the starting point of a range. The second **string-range** function then selects the last occurrence of **wood** and makes it the end point of the range.

This final example is definitely more complex. Generally speaking, it's fairly straightforward to link to a wide variety of subsections within a resource. Although all the examples focus on XML documents as the target for an XPointer, remember that links can be made to many different types of resources if they support this technology. The future will see technologies such as XLink and XPointer being pushed further than ever in order to maintain more accurate storage and retrieval of information.

Finding XPointer Tools

This final section deals with some of the software that is available to start creating links using XPointer. Because of the nature of this technology, no software is specifically required to set up the links. In fact, a simple text editor will do just fine for most linking requirements and may be a good place to start. Specific tools can be used to make the linking easier and more efficient after the basic concepts have been mastered, such as the following:

TIP: *Additional descriptions and links to the actual sites for some of the tools outlined in this section can be found at* **www.xmlsoftware.com/xlink**. *Most of the tools and source code are either shareware or have some type of trial period associated with them.*

- *PSGML-XPointer.el*—**www.megginson.com/Software/psgml-xpointer.el**. This site provides source code for a PSGML add-on that will generate XPointers for any location in an XML or Standard Generalized Markup Language (SGML) document.

- *XPFilter*—**www.bitoek.uni-bayreuth.de/xml**. This Perl script can be used to filter and/or mark XML elements in an XML document through the use of XPointer location terms. You can download the source code and an example XPFilter module.

- *PyPointers*—**www.stud.ifi.uio.no/~lmariusg/download/python/xml/ xptr.html**. This product uses the XPointer location language to locate specific fragments in XML and HTML documents. It's a general parser combined with a portion that locates Document Object Model (DOM) nodes.

- *Link Manager*—**www.doczilla.com/product/index.html**. Link Manager uses HyTime, XLink, and XPointer to provide extended hyperlinking. It has the ability to look up XPointer locations in a DOM document and generate XPointers for DOM nodes.

Chapter 15

Namespaces in XML

If you need an immediate solution to:	See page:

In Depth

Namespaces have been around longer than XML. Traditionally, a *namespace* is simply unique names that belong to a collection. The words of a language belong to a namespace. For example, all the words of the English language belong to the English language namespace, and all the words of the Italian language belong to the Italian language namespace.

Moving closer to the computer world, all the names of tables in a relational database, for example, could belong to the *table-name* namespace of that database; and for each individual table, the names of the fields could belong to a *tables* namespace.

Namespaces have three important characteristics:

• A namespace is simply a collection of names.

• The names in the namespace are unique.

• The names usually have some good reason for being together.

Traditional namespaces are useful for identifying names. For example, the word *sex* in the Italian namespace translates to the number six. However, in the English namespace, it has a very different meaning. Note, however, that a namespace simply gives you a way to assign a name to a certain collection—it says nothing about the meaning or semantics of a name.

An XML namespace is a simple collection of names, such as the names of the elements and attributes pertaining to a certain XML document type.

Let's look at two simple documents:

```
<book>
  <title>English Regional Dialects</title>
</book>
```

and

```
<name>
  <title>Professor</title>
  <first>Henry</first>
  <last>Higgins</last>
</name>
```

The first document is simply a namespace with two names (**book** and **title**) belonging to the **book** document type. The second is a namespace with four names (**name**, **title**, **first**, and **last**) belonging to the **name** document type.

Let's see what happens if we combine the two documents, as in the following:

```
<name>
  <title>Professor</title>
  <first> Henry</first>
  <last>Higgins</last>
</name> wrote the book
<book>
  <title>English Regional Dialects</title>
</book>
```

It's obvious to us (as humans) that the first instance of the **title** element is from the namespace of the **name** document type, and the second instance is from the namespace of the **book** document type. However, a typical software application has no way to make this insight, and can't distinguish one use of the name **title** from the other. To distinguish the name **title** as belonging to either one namespace or the other, some identifying mechanism must be devised. This mechanism (XML namespaces) is the topic of this chapter. You can find out more about XML namespaces on the World Wide Web Consortium (W3C) Web site in the "Namespaces in XML" recommendation at **www.w3.org/TR/REC-xml-names/**.

Right away, however, notice that we have a problem. A traditional namespace is a collection of unique names. However, XML (and the Standard Generalized Markup Language, or SGML) allow us to use the same name for an element and an attribute. Therefore, the following is a perfectly legal XML document:

```
<cars type="German"><type>Porsche</type></cars>
```

When presented with the name **type**, however, how do you decide whether it's an element or an attribute? The answer is that in an XML document, elements and attributes must be distinguished one from another—and this makes an XML namespace different from a traditional namespace.

Furthermore, each element can (and does) use the same attribute name with different semantic meaning. For example:

```
<!ATTLIST  book
    title     CDATA     #IMPLIED
>
```

15. Namespaces in XML

```
<!ATTLIST  name
    title      (Dr.|Prof|Lord|Mr.|Mrs.|Ms.|Miss)      #IMPLIED
>
```

It's quite feasible that the previous attributes both appear in the same Document Type Definition (DTD). If you keep in mind that duplicate names can occur in an XML document, some of what may appear to be rather peculiar quirks of the XML namespace recommendation will become clearer. As you'll see, much of the confusion surrounding XML namespaces revolves around which attributes are in a given namespace, and which are not.

Combining Elements from Multiple Sources in a Single Document

Namespaces as they're used in XML are in fact very simple. They're simply a means of distinguishing elements from several document types that are combined in a single document. Before we go into details of the specification, let's consider what namespaces are and are not. When it comes to using the document types, the problem is a little more complex. Therefore, in the first part of this section, we'll just look at how to combine elements from multiple sources in a single document.

An XML namespace is (as already stated) simply a collection of element types and attribute names. This namespace is identified by a Uniform Resource Identifier (URI), which allows any element type or attribute name in an XML namespace to be uniquely identified by a two-part name: the URI of its XML namespace, and its local name.

It's important to realize that this two-part naming system is the only function of XML namespaces. Even though a URI is used as the name of the namespace, nothing has to exist at this URI. It's simply a way to define a unique name for our namespace. Specifically:

- This URI is not a pointer to a schema, DTD, or any information about the XML document. It's simply an identifier.

- XML namespaces are not a technology for merging different documents that use different schemas, although they could be used in such a technology.

Declaring XML Namespaces

Now, let's look at how to combine elements from multiple sources in a single document. Essentially, there are two ways to declare a namespace in an XML document:

- Use a default namespace declaration.
- Use a prefixed namespace declaration.

Default Namespace Declaration

A default declaration takes this general form:

```
xmlns="URI"
```

The declaration is placed on an element (it looks like an attribute but it's not; see "Declaring a Default Namespace" in the Immediate Solutions section). When the declaration occurs, it declares to any namespace-aware application that the element it's declared on is in the namespace belonging to that *URI*. The namespace also applies to any descendant element in the document tree, unless otherwise exempted or declared.

Prefixed Namespace Declaration

A prefixed namespace declaration takes this general form:

```
xmlns:alias="URI"
```

The declaration can be placed on any element, but it must be declared before it's used. This declaration informs namespace-aware processing software that any element that is prefixed by the *alias* name followed by the colon is in the namespace of the *URI* (see "Declaring a Prefixed Namespace" in the Immediate Solutions section). However, these prefixed elements must be in the scope of the namespace. In other words, they must either be on the same element on which the namespace is declared or they must be in a descendant element.

Qualified Names

When the name of an element type is preceded by a prefix followed by a colon, it's a *qualified element name*. An attribute that is so prefixed is also called a qualified name.

Namespace Scoping

The namespace declaration is considered to apply to the element on which it's declared as well as all elements within the content of that element. Here's an example of an XHTML document taken from the XHTML 1.0 recommendation:

```
<html xmlns="http://www.w3.org/1999/xhtml" xml:lang="en" lang="en">
  <head>
    <title>Virtual Library</title>
  </head>
```

```
<body>
  <p>Moved to <a href="http://vlib.org/">vlib.org</a>.</p>
</body>
</html>
```

In this example, all the elements are in the **http://www.w3.org/1999/xhtml** namespace because the namespace declaration occurs on the opening **html** element tag. All the other elements are descendants of the **html** element, and are thus said to be within the scope of the default element.

However, consider the following two XML documents:

```
<xdoc>
  <a xmlns:foo="http://myurl/mynamespace">
   <foo:b>In scope for namespace</foo:b>
    <c>some text</c>
  </a>
    <foo:b>Out of scope for namespace</foo:b>
</xdoc>
```

Only the descendant elements of the **a** element type are in scope for the **http://myurl/mynamespace** namespace; therefore, the first **foo:b** element belongs to the namespace, but the second does not. In fact, because the colon is a reserved character, the document, although well formed, could be considered illegal. Furthermore, the second **foo:b** element does not belong to any namespace. Also note that the **c** element, although it's in scope for the namespace, does not in fact belong to the **http://myurl/mynamespace** namespace.

The following, which uses a default method of declaration for the namespace, is really a different document:

```
<xdoc>
  <a xmlns="http://myurl/mynamespace">
   <b>In scope for namespace</b>
    <c>some text</c>
  </a>
    <b>Out of scope for namespace</b>
</xdoc>
```

Here, we use a default type of declaration; therefore, all the descendant elements of the **a** element default to the **http://myurl/mynamespace** namespace. Note that the second **b** element is not in any namespace.

Namespace Defaulting

Note that the default namespace is considered to apply to the element where it's declared (provided that that element does not have a namespace prefix of its own assigning it to another namespace), and to all elements with no prefix that are within the content of that element. Consider the following example:

```
<xdoc>
 <a xmlns="http://myurl/mynamespace">
    <b>In http://myurl/mynamespace namespace</b>
    <c>In http://myurl/mynamespace namespace</c>
 </a>

<l>
    <m>In no namespace</m>
    <n>In no namespace</n>
 </l>

<x xmlns="http://myurl/mynamesecondspace">
    <y>In "http://myurl/mynamesecondspace" namespace</y>
    <z>In "http://myurl/mynamesecondspace" namespace</z>
 </x>
</xdoc>
```

In this example, two namespaces are declared: one on the **a** element, and one on the **x** element. All the child elements are in their respective namespaces, and the **l**, **m**, and **n** elements (as well as the **xdoc** element) are not in any namespace. What happens, however, if a namespace is declared on the **xdoc** element?

```
<xdoc xmlns="http://myurl/rootnamespace">
 <a xmlns="http://myurl/mynamespace">
    <b>In http://myurl/mynamespace namespace</b>
    <c>In http://myurl/mynamespace namespace</c>
 </a>

<l>
    <m>In  no namespace</m>
    <n>In  no namespace</n>
</l>

<x xmlns="http://myurl/mynamesecondspace">
    <y>In "http://myurl/mynamesecondspace" namespace</y>
    <z>In "http://myurl/mynamesecondspace" namespace</z>
 </x>
</xdoc>
```

Now the entire document is in the scope of the **http://myurl/rootnamespace** namespace, and the **l**, **m**, and **n** elements all belong to this namespace. The other elements, of course, belong to their own namespaces. However, if for any reason the **l**, **m**, and **n** elements were not in the **http://myurl/rootnamespace** namespace, and were not in any namespace, they could be exempted from the default scope by giving them an empty namespace. A default namespace is undeclared by simply assigning an empty ("") value to the namespace declaration, for example:

```
<xdoc xmlns="http://myurl/rootnamespace">
 <a xmlns="http://myurl/mynamespace">
    <b>In http://myurl/mynamespace namespace</b>
    <c>In http://myurl/mynamespace namespace</c>
 </a>

<l xmlns="">
    <m>In no namespace</m>
    <n>In no namespace</n>
</l>

<x xmlns="http://myurl/mynamesecondspace">
    <y>In "http://myurl/mynamesecondspace" namespace</y>
    <z>In "http://myurl/mynamesecondspace" namespace</z>
</x>
</xdoc>
```

Now, the **l**, **m**, and **n** elements are not in any namespace.

In this final example, we show how default namespaces can be nested:

```
<xdoc xmlns="http://rootnamespace">
    <xtag>This is in the http://rootnamespace namespace</xtag>
    <a xmlns="http://anamespace">
        <b>This is in the http://anamespace namespace</b>

        <l xmlns="http://lnamespace">
            <m>This is in the http://lnamespace namespace</m>
              <x xmlns="http://xnamespace">
                    <y>This is in the http://xnamespace namespace</y>
              </x>
            <m>This is in the http://lnamespace namespace</m>
        </l>
      <b>This is in the http://anamespace namespace</b>
    </a>

    <xtag>This is in the http://rootnamespace namespace</xtag>
</xdoc>
```

Changing a Namespace

After a namespace has been put in scope, it remains in scope. In fact, it's impossible to unscope a namespace. The namespace can be changed, but it cannot be unscoped.

In the following example, both **foo** and **bar** are entered as namespaces on the root element, and are therefore in scope throughout the entire document. The namespaces recommendation specifically forbids the unscoping of a namespace that has been declared using a prefix:

```
<xdoc
xmlns:foo="http://foourl/"
  xmlns:bar="http://barurl/"
>
  <a>Not in a namespace</a>
  <foo:a>In the foo namespace</foo:a>
  <bar:a>In the bar namespace</bar:a>
  <foo:a  xmlns:foo="">In the foo namespace</foo:a>
  <!--The above is illegal-->
</xdoc>
```

Unlike the situation with a default namespace, **foo** cannot be changed to an empty string.

Changing a Namespace Prefix

A namespace prefix can be changed by the simple expedient of re-declaring it, as follows:

```
<xdoc
xmlns:foo="http://foourl/"
>
  <foo:a>In the http://foourl/ namespace</foo:a>
  <foo:a xmlns:foo="http://newfoourl/">
In the http://newfoourl/ namespace</bar:a>
</xdoc>
```

The previous constructs tend to be very confusing, and would probably never occur in a freshly authored document. These constructs are only likely to occur in machine-compiled documents from several sources. Freshly authored documents should follow a few simple rules.

Best Practice Rules

The best practice rules for XML document namespaces can be best summed up as follows:

- Use the default namespace on the root element.

- Use one default namespace, at most.

- Declare the prefixed namespaces as soon as possible, preferably on the root element.

- Do not use the same prefix for different namespaces.

- Use one prefix per XML namespace.

The following example shows a good use of namespaces.

```
<html
    xmlns="http://www.w3.org/1999/xhtml"
    xmlns:cat="http://libcat.org"
    xml:lang="en" lang="en">
  <head>
    <title>Virtual Library</title>
    <cat:number>12345</cat:number>
    <cat:type>Virtual Book</cat:type>
  </head>
  <body>
    <p>Moved to <a href="http://vlib.org/">vlib.org</a>.</p>
  </body>
</html>
```

These best practice rules guarantee that namespaces in your document are unique and easily understandable.

Combining Attributes from Multiple Sources in a Single Document

The entire previous section applied to elements. Applying namespaces to attributes is a little more complicated. Consider this simple XHTML document:

```
<html xmlns="http://www.w3.org/1999/xhtml" xml:lang="en" lang="en">
  <head>
    <title>Virtual Library</title>
  </head>
  <body>
    <p>Moved to <a href="http://vlib.org/">vlib.org</a>.</p>
  </body>
</html>
```

The **href** attribute belongs to the **http://www.w3.org/1999/xhtml** namespace, doesn't it? If you answered yes, you're wrong. The **href** attribute belongs to no namespace. The namespaces recommendation specifically states that a default namespace does not apply to attributes.

The reason is that in XML, unlike its predecessor SGML, you cannot declare global attributes. In fact, the same attribute can be used on several different elements, and can have quite different declarations and/or semantic meanings.

In Extensible Hypertext Markup Language (XHTML), for example, the **href** attribute is used on the **base**, **link**, **a**, and **map** elements, and the **src** attribute is used on the **script**, **img**, **iframe**, and **input** elements.

XML Namespace Partitions

The namespaces recommendation introduces the concept of *namespace partitions*, which allow namespace-aware software to assign attributes to a namespace. There are three partitions:

- *The all-element-types partition*—All elements in an XML document belong to this partition, and this is the partition that we've been talking about in most of the chapter so far.

- *The global attribute partition*—This partition contains all the global attributes in an XML document. Even though an attribute cannot be defined as global in an XML document, those that are in fact global, belong in this namespace.

- *The per-element-type partition*—All element types have an associated namespace in which the names of all unqualified (unprefixed) attributes of that element appear. Because the rules of XML do not allow duplicate attribute names, this is a traditional namespace. Thus, every unprefixed attribute is considered to belong to an element's private namespace.

Here's an example from the namespaces specification (found at **www.w3.org/ TR/1999/REC-xml-names-19990114/#ns-expnames**):

```
<section xmlns="urn:com:books-r-us">
<title>Book Signing event</title>
  <signing>
    <author title="Mr" name="Vikram Seth" />
    <book title="A Suitable Boy" price= "$22.95"
  </signing>
</section>
```

In this example, all the elements belong to the element-types partition of the namespace (**urn:com:books-r-us**), and all the attributes belong to the per-element-type partition of the namespace. In other words, they belong to the traditional namespace of the element, and it's the element, not the attribute, that belongs

15. Namespaces in XML

to the **urn:com:books-r-us** namespace. In other words, the attributes can be considered offspring of the element.

Here's a second example, also taken from the namespaces recommendation:

```
<RESERVATION xmlns:HTML="http://w3.org/TR/REC-html-4.01">
<NAME HTML:CLASS="largesansserif">Layman, A </NAME>
<SEAT CLASS="Y" HTML:CLASS="largeMonotype"> 33B</SEAT>
<HTML:A HREF="/cgi/bin/ResStatus">Check Status</HTML:A>
<DEPARTURE>1997-05-24t07:55:00 +1</DEPARTURE>
```

In this example, all the unqualified elements do not belong to any namespace.

The attribute **HTML:CLASS** belongs to the **http://w3.org/TR/REC-html-4.01** namespace. The element **HTML:A** also belongs to the **http://w3.org/TR/REC-html-4.01** namespace; however, the attribute of this element, **HREF**, belongs to the traditional namespace of that element and *not* to the **http://w3.org/TR/REC-html-4.01** namespace! If the example had shown **HTML:HREF**, it would have been an error because the **HREF** element is not a unique element in the **HTML** DTD—although any namespace-aware software that reads the document would not know that unless it had access to the DTD.

Linking Elements to a URL

A Uniform Resource Locator (URL) is a type of URI. A URL is typically used only as the URI because it's a unique name that also happens to be under the control of the person writing the document. In fact, any unique name, or URI, would do, and the specification only mentions in passing that it should be a URL reference. A URN could be used instead, as was the case in the first example in the last section. Although there's loose talk about "linking elements to a URL," as is the case in this section's heading, in fact no linkage to a URL occurs. It cannot be expressed strongly enough that there is no expectation that anything will be found at the URL. In fact, it's highly recommended that there be nothing at the URL—otherwise, some misguided software could initiate an unintentional denial of service attack!

The element is linked to the namespace name, and it just so happens that in most cases the namespace name is an URI.

The Namespaces Specification

The namespaces specification can be found at **www.w3.org/TR/REC-xml-names**. At first, this recommendation appears to be fairly simple; but it's probably accurate for us to say that very few recommendations have caused more argument and confusion than this one. It's a matter of public record that the recommendation delayed the publishing of the XHTML recommendation by about six months, and has also had an effect on other recommendations.

The problem is that the recommendation was rushed out because it was needed for the Resource Description Framework (RDF) recommendation, and the loose bits were never tied up. If ever there was an object lesson in the importance of recommendations being concise, this is it! Even the three authors of the recommendation have argued publicly about the meaning of some parts of the recommendation. Many of the arguments take on the air of medieval divines arguing about how many angels can dance on the head of a pin, but the real problem is that many implementations of applications that use the namespaces specification are not compatible with each other.

The main problems center around the partitions of the namespace, and whether attributes are indeed in the namespace.

The recommendation is divided into two parts:

• The normative main section

• The non-normative appendices

Unfortunately, for a full interpretation of the namespaces recommendation (especially as far as attributes are concerned), you should read the non-normative part. Indeed, the normative part does not make sense in places without the non-normative part.

The sections of the recommendation are as follows:

• *Motivation and Summary*—This section is quite straightforward and merely sets out the reasons why namespaces are needed.

• *Declaring Namespaces*—This section lays out the formal way to declare a namespace. (This process was covered earlier in the "Combining Elements from Multiple Sources in a Single Document" section.) It also defines what names may be used as prefix names. A prefix name must begin with a letter or an underscore, and then can contain all the characters allowed in an XML name *except* a colon (:). Note also the usual constraint that prefixes can't begin with *xml* in any case combination. This section also states that when a prefixed namespace declaration is used, the value of the namespace cannot be empty—although it can be if a default declaration is used.

• *Qualified Names*—This section gives the formal definition of a qualified name. In other words, a qualified name consists of a prefix, followed by a colon, followed by an attribute or element name.

• *Using Qualified Names*—This section formally describes how to use qualified names in elements. It also points out difficulties that can occur when a

15. Namespaces in XML

namespace declaration is declared in an external entity. Basically, although such a declaration is theoretically possible, it should never be done and therefore is not an issue.

- *Applying Namespaces to Elements and Attributes*—This section describes how to default a namespace. The last sentence of section 5.2 is a throwaway sentence that is responsible for much of the difficulty with this specification (remember that this sentence is normative): "Note that default namespaces do not apply directly to attributes." Section 5.3 contains the nonsensical second example that has also caused so much confusion when it comes to attributes.

- *Conformance of Documents*—This section lays out the basis for conformance of XML documents with the namespace specification. Essentially, this means that all element and attribute types, qualified or not, cannot contain more than one colon.

Appendix A of the namespaces recommendation is non-normative, which means that you don't *have* to read it. However, unless you read it, you cannot really understand how to treat attributes. The most common interpretation of how attributes are treated in the XML community was given in the previous major section; but, unfortunately, software exists that treat attributes in different ways. Because this section is non-normative, software developers are essentially entitled to treat an unprefixed attribute as either belonging in the same namespace as the element to which it's attached or belonging to no namespace at all.

Frequently Used Namespaces

Not unsurprisingly, most of the namespaces commonly used at the present time are under the control of the W3C. However, numerous organizations are using namespaced documents for their own internal uses and writing software to handle these namespaces.

Here's a list of some of the more commonly used namespaces:

- *Extensible Hypertext Markup Language (XHTML: **http://www.w3.org/ 1999/xhtml/**)*—Both Netscape and Internet Explorer (IE) 5 support this namespace in their latest browsers. Unfortunately, the latest release of IE 5.5 makes this the default namespace for the **style** and **class** attributes in its browser, whether they are declared or not. This does make it easy to style XML documents, and as the namespaces recommendation is written, it's probably legal; but it's probably not the behavior most people would expect. Note that IE 5 and Netscape browsers currently only recognize the **html** prefix, and not the actual name of the namespace. This behavior is likely to change in future issues of the browsers.

- *Extensible Stylesheet Language Transformations (XSLT: **http://www.w3.org/1999/XSL/Transform**)*—This namespace is recognized by all XSLT-compliant applications including IE 5+ browsers.

- *Mathematical Markup Language (MathML: **http://www.w3.org/Math/MathML**)*—This namespace is used in documents that use MathML.

- *Cascading Style Sheets (CSS: **http://www.w3.org/TR/css3-namespace/**)*—Note that this namespace still has the designation TR because CSS3 is not yet a recommendation. When it becomes a recommendation, the TR will be changed to the year it becomes a recommendation; for example, **http://www.w3.org/2000/css3-namespace/**.

- *RDF and dc*—The RDF and dc namespaces are usually used together in XHTML documents. Here's an example of their usage.

```
<xhtml xmlns="http://www.w3.org/1999/xhtml"
       xmlns:rdf="http://www.w3.org/1999/o2/22-rdf-syntax-ns#"
       xmlns:dc="http://purl.org/dc/elements/1.0/">


<head>
<title>Basic XMTML document with namespace declaration</title>
    <rdf:RDF>
       <rdf:description
          rdf:about="http://someurl.com"
          dc:creator="John Doe"
          dc:title="John's Web Page"
          dc:description="Home page for John Doe"
          dc:date"1999-01-01"
        />
    </rdf:RDF>
</head>
<body>
  <p>All the unprefixed elements are in the XHTML namespace.
   All the qualified elements and attributes are in the namespaces
   declared on the root element.</p>
</body>
</html>
```

- *Extensible Linking Language (XLink: **http://www.w3.org/2000/xlink**)*—The XLink document is just about to become a recommendation. Look shortly for XML browsers that will recognize the XLink namespace and link according to the specification's semantics. In the meantime, most people will use the **a** element from the XHTML namespace. Note that the semantics of this element are executed in both the latest IE 5 and Netscape browsers.

- *Scalable Vector Graphics (SVG:* ***http://www.w3.org/2000/svg-20000303-stylable***)—Currently, no browser company has incorporated SVG into its browsers, although Opera is promising to do so in its next release.

Remember that a namespace is just a namespace. To make an element or an attribute from the namespace do anything, you must write software that recognizes the namespace and then executes the appropriate semantics.

Immediate Solutions

Declaring a Default Namespace

In the following example, the **xdoc** and **greeting** element types are in the **http://www.hypermedic.com/mynamespace** namespace:

```
<xdoc xmlns="http://www.hypermedic.com/mynamespace">
  <greeting>Hello Namespaces</greeting>
</xdoc>
```

Here you have what appears to be an attribute named **xmlns** with a value that looks like an URI. In fact, it's not an attribute; it's a *namespace declaration*. This has important implications for XML application writers, because **xmlns** should not appear as an attribute information item but rather as a namespace declaration.

This declaration says that the **xdoc** element and all its descendant elements are in the **http://www.hypermedic.com/mynamespace** namespace, unless they're overridden.

Declaring a Prefixed Namespace

In the following example, just the **greeting** element type is in the **http://www.hypermedic.com/mynamespace** namespace:

```
<xdoc xmlns:foo="http://www.hypermedic.com/mynamespace">
  <foo:greeting>Hello Namespaces</foo:greeting>
</xdoc>
```

Here, you have a namespace declaration that is associated with the prefix **foo**. The declaration says that any tag prefixed by **foo:** that is also a descendant of the element on which it's declared is in the **http://www.hypermedic.com/mynamespace** namespace. Because the **xdoc** element is not prefixed with **foo**, it's not in this namespace. Note that the declaration must take place before the first use of the prefix.

In the following example, the **xdoc** element is prefixed with **foo:**. Therefore, the **xdoc** element (as well as the **greeting** element) is in the **http://www. hypermedic.com/mynamespace** namespace:

```
<foo:xdoc xmlns:foo="http://www.hypermedic.com/mynamespace">
  <foo:greeting>Hello Namespaces</foo:greeting>
</foo:xdoc>
```

To use namespaces at the present time, you must write custom code and use a namespace-aware parser. MSXMLII (the parser that comes with IE 5.5) is such a parser. The following simple example shows how a script can be used to identify a namespace in a document. After the namespace is identified, of course, the necessary behavior and semantics can be added by code.

Note that for the sake of simplicity, this example uses the proprietary Microsoft XML data island to import the simple XML file:

```
<html>
<title>Namespace Demo</title>
<xml id="simplexdoc">
 <xdoc>
   <a
     xmlns:dc="dublincore.org"
     xmlns:html= >
   <b>Books</b>
   <dc:title>Book Title</dc:title>
   </a>
 </xdoc>
</xml>
<script>
 var mydoc=simplexdoc
 if(mydoc.parseError!=0)
  {document.write(mydoc.parseError.reason)}
 else
  var xlist=mydoc.getElementsByTagName("dc:title")
  document.write(xlist.item(0).firstChild.data)
</script>
</html>
```

This simple example uses the syntax of the Document Object Model (DOM) to make a node list of all the qualified elements (**dc:title**) and prints the data content.

Using Elements from a Namespace in an XML Document

Here's an example that uses the **XHTML** and **Dublin** core namespace in an XML document. Note that this document will run in any XML parser; but when it's run in IE 5+ or the latest Mozilla browser, the semantics of the HTML namespace will be interpreted. Note that a style-sheet processing instruction is necessary if the document will be run in IE 5; otherwise, IE 5 will just give its default tree view.

The other important point to notice is that most applications will look to the prefix to identify the namespace rather than to the namespace itself. Although this is an incorrect interpretation of the namespaces recommendation, a few software writers are creating applications that behave this way.

Here's the example:

```
<?xml-stylesheet type="text/css" href=""?>

<xdoc xmlns:html="http://www.w3.org/1999/xhtml"
      xmlns:dc="dublincore.org"
 >

   <a> Is this a link?
   <html:style type="text/css">
    .redcolor{color:red;display:block;}
   </html:style>
   <html:h2 class="redcolor">Books</html:h2>
   <dc:title style="color:blue">Book Title</dc:title>
   <dc:author class="redcolor">John Doe</dc:author>
   <html:h2 html:style="color:green">A Failing Grace</html:h2>
   </a>
 </xdoc>
```

The following section describes how IE 5 interprets this document. A processing instruction is necessary in IE 5; otherwise, the browser will just give a default tree view:

```
<?xml-stylesheet type="text/css" href=""?>
```

The namespaces are declared:

```
<xdoc xmlns:html="http://www.w3.org/1999/xhtml"
      xmlns:dc="dublincore.org"
 >
```

IE5 does not treat the following as a link (it shouldn't, but see the **style** and **class** attributes that follow):

```
<a href=""> Is this a link?
```

IE 5 reads this style sheet:

```
<html:style type="text/css">
 .redcolor{color:red;display:block;}
</html:style>
```

The following markup appears with **h2** semantics, and the **class** attribute is interpreted:

```
<html:h2 class="redcolor">Books</html:h2>
```

Both the **style** and the **class** attributes are interpreted in the following lines. Because the namespaces recommendation is so poorly written with respect to attributes, it's difficult to decide whether this behavior falls within the meaning of the recommendation:

```
<dc:title style="color:blue">Book Title</dc:title>
<dc:author class="redcolor">John Doe</dc:author>
```

Here the **h2** semantics are interpreted (as they should be), but the **style** attribute is not interpreted:

```
<html:h2 html:style="color:green">A Failing Grace</html:h2>
```

Of course, applications do not have to interpret namespaced elements, but we strongly suspect that they are not interpreted because IE 5 does not recognize them as belonging to the XHTML namespace—and of course, it should.

This code closes the document:

```
 </a>
</xdoc>
```

The Future of Namespaces

Over the next two or three years, we can expect to see more and more applications becoming namespace aware. We can also expect to see specialized applications that will apply semantics to certain namespaces. It would be very nice if a second version of the namespaces recommendation was written that ties up all the loose ends and uncertainties created by the first recommendation.

Chapter 16

XML Applications

In Depth

XML offers the flexibility to create new vocabularies, which are actually applications that use XML. This flexibility allows organizations and industries to create their own elements, attributes, and entities that fully explain the structure of the specific types of data they use. Already, a handful of applications have been created for either industry-specific or subject-specific document types. For example, OpenMLS (a real estate listing management system) has created Document Type Definitions (DTDs) for real estate agents that specify the structure of data documents that hold information about properties for sale.

In this chapter, we'll explore the various available special-purpose applications and describe how they work. This chapter is not, however, meant to be a complete reference for each XML application we discuss. Each application is meant to solve a particular problem, and we'll show you how you can use these applications to your advantage. If you were going to create your own application, you may find that you can use one of the applications described in this chapter instead.

What Is an XML Application?

By now, you know that XML enables you to create your own set of elements, your own attributes, and even your own entities. XML defines how a vocabulary can be structured. *Vocabularies* are sets of XML components that can be used to define specific document structures. For example, in one of the earliest, widely used vocabularies, Channel Definition Format (CDF), XML provided the structure to define *channels* and their accompanying channel elements, called *items*. In other words, you can use XML to create your own language of sorts, and you can use this language to perform a variety of tasks, from displaying mathematical equations to remotely updating software on a networked computer.

With XML, you can construct your own set of components that define the structure of a document. As you've seen in previous chapters, you define this structure in the DTD, which lists all the elements, attributes, entities, and notation declarations. The DTD can be stored in a file outside of the XML document (external DTD) or it can be included in the content at the top of an XML document (internal DTD). You determine where the DTD is placed. When you really think about it, XML allows you to construct entirely new applications, not through conventional programming methods, but rather by defining the contextual structure of the document.

Many XML applications have emerged in the years since XML's introduction. Quite a few widely used XML applications already exist that you can use for a variety of functions, and dozens more are under development or up for consideration with the World Wide Web Consortium (W3C). In this chapter, we'll highlight the most popular applications, and also point you to those that are more industry specific.

Types of XML Applications

XML applications follow the XML syntax, so all you have to do to learn how to use them is familiarize yourself with the specific elements and their attributes. Most of the XML applications available today use fewer than 20 different elements, and many of these elements have only 1 or 2 attributes. As a result, the learning curve is relatively small.

As mentioned in Chapter 2, XML applications fall within one of three types:

- *Horizontal-industry applications/vocabularies*—Push-based delivery, software distribution, searching/filtering, electronic commerce, and so on

- *Vertical-industry applications/vocabularies*—Pharmaceuticals, telecommunications, aerospace, and so on

- *Internal applications/corporate vocabularies*—Internal data processes

The three different types of XML applications can be placed in one of these seven categories:

- Web and Internet applications
- Metadata and archival applications
- Multimedia, including graphics and speech applications
- Finance/commerce and business-oriented applications
- Scientific applications
- Education-oriented applications
- Language-oriented applications

Web and Internet Applications

As their name implies, Web and Internet XML applications work over the Internet or over the Web to either deliver content and programming information or enhance communication between computers over the Internet. The following are considered Web-oriented XML applications:

- *Channel Definition Format (CDF)*—Developed by Microsoft, CDF is an XML-based application that lets a developer use a variety of delivery mechanisms to publish collections of information, called *channels*, from any Web server to any Internet-compatible appliance. More information about this application can be found in the official specification at **http:// msdn.microsoft.com/workshop/delivery/cdf/reference/CDF.asp**.

- *Open Software Description (OSD)*—Also developed by Microsoft, OSD is used to describe software components, software versions, and the underlying structure of software packages and their components for delivery over a network. OSD can work in conjunction with CDF to update software over the Internet or over an intranet. More information about this application can be found on Microsoft's Web site at **http://msdn.microsoft.com/workshop/ delivery/osd/overview/osd_overview.asp** or on the W3C site at **www.w3.org/TR/NOTE-OSD.html**.

- *Distributed Authoring and Versioning on the World Wide Web (WebDAV)*— WebDAV is an Internet Engineering Task Force (IETF) proposed standard. It's an application specification that is intended to define Hypertext Transfer Protocol (HTTP) methods and semantics for creating, removing, querying, and editing Web pages remotely. WebDAV offers overwrite protection of files, structured views of sites, and the ability for more than one author to collaborate on a single site. More information can be found on the working group's Web site, **www.ics.uci.edu/~ejw/authoring**, and at **www.webdav.org**.

- *Wireless Application Protocol (WAP)*—This protocol offers standards for wireless network transmissions and for scaling across various transport options and device types. It was created by some of the leaders in the wireless communication industry, including Ericsson, Motorola, and Nokia. Information about this application can be found on the WAP organizing committee's Web site at **www.wapforum.org**.

- *UML eXchange Format (UXF)*—The UXF application was created for software developers as a mechanism for transferring Unified Modeling Language (UML) models. The application format is powerful enough to allow developers to express, publish, and exchange UML models universally. DTDs have already been created for this particular application and are available on the UML eXchange's Web site at **www.yy.cs.keio.ac.jp/~suzuki/project/uxf**.

- *Extensible Hypertext Markup Language (XHTML)*—XHTML is essentially HTML written in XML—that is, HTML 4 as an XML 1.0 application. XHTML 1.0 became a W3C recommendation in January 2000, and is slowly replacing HTML 4 as the core language of the Web. Because it's an XML application, XHTML 1.0 is stricter than HTML 4. All tags must be written in lowercase letters and be properly nested. In addition, all non-empty tags must have end tags, attribute values must be in quotes, and empty elements must be terminated with a closing slash. You can learn about the differences between XHTML and HTML at the official W3C XHTML site at **www.w3.org/TR/xhtml1/**. Chapter 18 of this book is dedicated to XHTML.

Metadata and Archival Applications

Metadata and archival applications handle certain kinds of data sets (those that may be specific to a particular industry, such as library sciences), multiple sets of data information, and data interchange between systems. The following XML applications are available, although they are in various stages of development:

- *Resource Description Framework (RDF)*—RDF is a framework specification that supports metadata and Web-based activities such as site maps, content ratings, search engine data collections, and distributed authoring. You can read the official RDF specification on the W3C's site at **www.w3.org/RDF**.

- *IMS Metadata Specification*—This specification uses XML to offer delivery of training materials over the Internet. It also supports the management of materials and types of data relating to Web sites. Essentially, this specification is meant to track students online, create reports of students' progress, exchange student records over the Internet, and work with various administrative learning systems. You can read more about this specification on the IMS Web site at **www.imsproject.org/metadata/index.html**.

- *Encoded Archival Description (EAD)*—This application, a full DTD, is used to develop a nonproprietary encoding standard for library documents, including indexes, archives, and any other type of holdings that may be found in libraries and museums. You can learn more about the EAD DTD at the Library of Congress Web site at **www.loc.gov/ead**.

- *Genealogical Data in XML (GedML)*—The GedML DTD was created to provide a standard method for presenting, exchanging, and manipulating genealogical data across a network and with other users. The intent is to make genealogical data exchange and searching easier. You can find out more information about GedML at **http://users.iclway.co.uk/mhkay/gedml/**.

Multimedia Applications

Multimedia XML-based applications use XML and its syntax to create standardized ways to present information over the Web—particularly graphics, video, and digitized speech. Applications such as the Synchronized Multimedia Integration Language (SMIL) and Scalable Vector Graphics (SVG) give developers the ability to work from a common development platform to use the interactive features of the Web to deliver feature-rich video and audio. These XML-based applications

16. XML Applications

are in various stages of specification completion. Check the W3C Web site (**www.w3.org**) regularly to track their status. The following XML-based applications fall into this category:

- *Synchronized Multimedia Integration Language (SMIL)*—The SMIL specification was approved as a W3C recommendation in 1998 and helps deliver multimedia content to the Web. SMIL allows developers to create and deliver television-like content with low bandwidth requirements. It also adds hyperlinking capabilities to the multimedia content, which make it possible for users to quickly move to other Web-based content. In addition, the hyperlinking capabilities give developers the ability to synchronize presentations. You can read more about SMIL at **www.w3.org/TR/REC-smil/**.

- *Scalable Vector Graphics (SVG)*—SVG is a language used to describe two-dimensional graphics in XML. The entire image is described by text, which can either be included in the XML document or exist as a separate file. SVG can be used to create three types of graphic objects: vector graphic shapes (paths consisting of straight lines and curves), images, and text. Images can be dynamic and interactive, allowing users to zoom in and out on the image from within the Web browser. Event handlers such as **onmouseover** and **onclick** can be assigned to any SVG graphical object. As of this writing (August 2000), SVG is a W3C candidate recommendation. Learn more about SVG at the W3C's SVG site at **www.w3.org/Graphics/SVG/**.

- *Java Speech Markup Language (JSML)*—The JSML specification, submitted to the W3C by Sun Microsystems, is intended to let developers create applications that annotate text for playback through speech synthesizers via the Java Speech Application Programming Interface (API). This data format provides detailed information about how the text should be spoken through the synthesizer. It describes the structure of the document, the pronunciations of words, and the phrasing and punctuation in the text. It also indicates how pitch, speaking rate, and other spoken characteristics should be noted. JSML uses the Unicode character set and follows XML standards for marking up text, so most languages can be processed to the API and then to the speech synthesizer. JSML specifications are currently being worked on by the W3C Voice Browser Working Group. See **www.w3.org/Voice** for more information.

Finance/Commerce and Business-Oriented Applications

Finance and commerce XML-based applications open a whole new world for consumers, financial institutions, and businesses. They allow consumers and businesses to use a standardized language to communicate. Consumers can transfer funds, check on accounts, and use their financial applications to track their investments regardless of the financial institution they're using. Without standardized XML applications, consumers and financial institutions would be forced to work with proprietary information and applications. The following XML-based applications are currently available or are in the process of being finalized:

- *Open Financial Exchange (OFX)*—OFX is a data format used to represent how financial information can be exchanged between an online financial service's server and client software, such as a browser. This format makes it possible for Microsoft's Money or Intuit's Quicken to connect to financial servers and exchange information about transactions and financial data stored on a user's computer. It allows banks, credit card companies, brokerage firms, and mutual fund markets to transmit and receive data over the Internet in a standardized way. It allows customers to pay bills, transfer funds, keep track of investments online, and buy mutual funds, stocks, and bonds regardless of the financial application they use. For more information about this financial exchange standard, check out the official OFX Web site at **www.ofx.net**.

- *XML/Electronic Data Interchange (XML/EDI)*—XML/EDI offers vendors a standard framework and format for describing different types of data used in processing invoices, payments, and project information. For example, a vendor could use the XML/EDI format to transmit an invoice to a customer electronically. The information in the invoice could then be searched, decoded, encoded, or manipulated so it could be displayed or printed. Using EDI dictionaries and XML ensures that information is displayed consistently and correctly regardless of the vendor or the customer. For more information on XML/EDI, check out the official home page at **www.xmledi.com**.

- *Internet Open Trading Protocol (IOTP)*—This IETF protocol provides a standard for exchanging data in Internet commerce. It will eventually be able to support a variety of payment systems and handle cases in which merchant functions (such as shopping, payment handling, delivery, and customer support) are performed on different sites. You can find more information on IOTP at the working group's homepage at **www.ietf.org/html.charters/ trade-charter.html**.

- *Information & Content Exchange (ICE)*—This proposed protocol is based on the XML standard and is intended to provide automatic, controlled exchange and management of online assets between business partners. ICE gives businesses a standard way to set up online relationships with other business and to transfer and share information. With ICE, businesses can easily partner with any number of affiliates to create online destinations such as syndicated publishing networks, Web superstores, and online reseller channels. You can find out more about ICE from its official Web site at **www.icestandard.org**.

Scientific Applications

Scientific XML-based applications allow scientists and mathematicians to exchange data in a standardized way. The applications set the language and syntax that can be used to specify such things as the constructs of an atom or how to properly display mathematical equations. The following scientific XML-based applications are some of the most widely used tools in this category:

- *Mathematical Markup Language (MathML)*—MathML is a W3C recommendation that provides a standard way to describe mathematical symbols and equations and how mathematical expressions should be displayed in Web pages. It also facilitates the use and reuse of mathematical and scientific content on the Web and in other applications, such as print typesetters and voice synthesizers. MathML can be used to encode both mathematical notation (for high-quality visual display) and mathematical content. You can find out more about MathML at **www.w3.org/Math**.

- *Chemical Markup Language (CML)*—CML was created to provide a way to describe molecular information and manage a wide range of chemical equation problems within a single language. It was also created to help chemists manipulate atoms and molecules as elements. CML offers standard document elements, such as footnotes, citations, and glossary terms, for inclusion in scholarly papers. CML provides the data format needed to represent chemical equations, molecules, formulas, and scientific data in a single standardized way, regardless of the application used. You can find out more about CML from its Web site at **www.xml-cml.org**.

- *Bioinformatic Sequence Markup Language (BSML)*—BSML is still in the comment phase, but it's intended to provide a standard method for encoding and displaying DNA, RNA, and protein sequence information between programs and data over the Internet. Although many proprietary software packages can display such information, no publicly available standard currently exists for graphic displays of sequences such as chromosomes and genetic material as well as physical maps of a variety of sequences. You can find out more about BSML and comment on the application by visiting the BSML Web site at **www.labbook.com**.

- *Telecommunications Interchange Markup (TIM)*—The TIM language is used to provide a standard mechanism for offering industry standards associated with the provision, procurement, and use of telecommunications equipment, products, and services. The group that is working on TIM, the Telecommunications Industry Forum (TCIF), was founded in June 1986 in an effort to promote understanding and implementation of global standards, guidelines, and emerging technologies involving electronic data interchange, electronic commerce, and bar coding. You can find out more about TIM from the TCIF Web page at **www.atis.org/atis/tcif/index.htm**.

Education-Oriented Applications

Actually, some of the XML applications listed previously could fall within this category, but the only educational application we discuss in this section is the Tutorial Markup Language (TML). As instruction, test-taking and -tracking, and educational development move toward the Web, you'll find more and more XML-based educational applications springing up.

TML was originally a Standard Generalized Markup Language (SGML) application, but it's been converted to XML to provide flexibility over the Internet. TML is an interchange format designed to separate the semantic content of a question from its screen layout or formatting. This format allows questions and answers to be searched, cataloged, and calculated easily. TML allows questionnaire developers to specify such items as how many attempts a test-taker has to answer a question, what the questions are, what choices you want to include for the answers, what the correct answers are, and what, if any, hints are available for the question. For more information about TML, check out the official TML Web site, which offers the full language set and examples, at **www.ilrt.bris.ac.uk/netquest/about/lang**.

Language-Oriented Applications

Language-oriented XML-based applications are not for spoken languages, but rather for computer languages and interchange between computer systems. By far, most XML-based applications currently fall into this category, because these applications help machines make decisions about the data stored in Web pages and in databases. If you're looking to develop true machine-based intelligent systems, you'll want to delve deeper into some of the following XML applications:

- *Translation Memory eXchange (TMX)*—TMX allows easier exchange of translation memory data between tools and/or translation vendors with little or no loss of critical data during the process. You can find out more about TMX through its official Web site at **www.lisa.org/tmx**.

- *Ontology Markup Language (OML)*—OML allows Web-page authors to annotate their Web pages so they can be read by machines and processed with intelligent agent software. You can read more about OML and the elements and attributes used with it at **www.ontologos.org/OML/OML%200.3.htm**.

- *Conceptual Knowledge Markup Language (CKML)*—CKML follows the philosophy of Conceptual Knowledge Processing (CKP). This processing language is used to represent knowledge and data analysis, which serves to create models for rational thinking, judgment, and decision making. It's an extension of the OML application.

- *OpenTag*—The OpenTag format helps create a standardized way to code diverse file types through the use of a common markup method. For example, suppose you have two files: one saved in RTF format and another saved in Hypertext Markup Language (HTML) format. Both files contain the same text and are formatted in the same fashion. Although the information and layout are the same, the encoding methods used to save the files are different. With OpenTag, you can use identical tags to output the files and display the data, but the formatting codes that were used to save the files originally are saved and later used to encode the files in their native formats. You can find out more about OpenTag from the official Web site at **www.opentag.com**.

XML Applications in Detail

Now, let's take a closer look at some of the more popular XML applications. This section is not meant as a full tutorial for each application. Instead, it will introduce you to the application, what it offers, and some of the elements used most often within the application. We recommend that you visit the official Web site for applications you're interested in for more information and examples.

We'll concentrate on the applications that have already been standardized and have a range of practical uses, such as exchanging financial data, software, mathematical information, or multimedia files. You will undoubtedly see some of these applications incorporated into many new browsers and servers. We'll examine the following five XML applications here and in this chapter's Immediate Solutions section:

- Channel Definition Format (CDF)
- Chemical Markup Language (CML)
- Mathematical Markup Language (MathML)
- Open Software Description (OSD)
- Synchronized Multimedia Integration Language (SMIL)

NOTE: *CDF is only covered briefly here and is not covered in the Immediate Solutions section, because it's a widely used XML-based application and Chapter 17 presents a complete discussion of CDF.*

Channel Definition Format (CDF)

CDF provides developers with a way to automatically publish Web-based content to subscribers through a variety of methods, such as a Web browser, an Active Desktop component, HTML-formatted email, or Web crawlers. A *channel* is a set of HTML-formatted documents that can be sent to individual clients or groups of clients. XML is used to define the channel. Information including the subelements contained within the channel, the update schedule, and the delivery mechanism are part of the definition.

Related solution:	Found on page:
Creating a Channel	473

Chemical Markup Language (CML)

CML was invented by British chemists specifically for exchanging descriptions of formulas, molecules, and other chemical specifications between people and computers within intranets or on the Internet. You can use CML for accomplishing such tasks as rendering 2D and 3D molecules or creating and publishing scientific papers.

CML lets you specify and represent very specific types of data (molecules) within a structured format. Although CML is an XML application, you need a specialized viewer to see the results of the data CML represents.

Why would you want to use CML? Because it's based on XML, a platform-independent markup language, it doesn't matter whether you develop the data on a Mac, PC, or Unix system. The information will still display, as long as you're using a browser that supports XML.

Just as with all other XML applications, the best way to understand CML (aside from getting a degree in chemistry) is to understand the CML DTD and the CML elements and their attributes. But first, let's take a quick look at molecular technology and some of the terminology you might need know to understand this application.

With CML, you can represent the following molecular information:

- Molecular structure
- Molecular sequence
- Quantum chemistry
- Inorganic crystallography
- Organic molecules
- Spectra

You create CML files as you do any other XML-based files. One way is to use a text processor, such as Notepad or Emacs. After you create your CML file and save it, you must parse the data file and view the results with a specialized CML viewer, such as JUMBO. JUMBO is written in Java and can be used with Java-enabled browsers or as a standalone application. As with any XML application, you must first declare the document to be a CML document in the DOCTYPE declaration at the beginning of the CML file. Then, every element you place must have a start tag and end tag, and all attribute values must be in quotes. In this chapter's Immediate Solutions section, you'll write a small CML data file that includes a few formulas. When you write your CML document, you can include any of the nine main CML DTD elements, which are explained in the following sections.

The array Element

The **array** element specifies an array of variables. You can use the **array** element to specify both one- and two-dimensional arrays. As is the case with every XML element, the **array** element must have a matching ending **</array>** tag. The following is an example of how the **array** element is used to declare a simple one-dimensional array:

```
<array>
1 3 5 7 9 10 11
</array>
```

The atoms Element

The **atoms** element is used to represent an atom or a list of atoms contained within a molecule. The element has over 20 attributes, including:

- **atomno**—Specifies the atom's serial number
- **atid**—Specifies the atom's unique identifier
- **attyp**—Specifies the atom type
- **elsym**—Specifies the atom's elemental symbol
- **isotope**—Specifies the atom's isotope
- **elno**—Specifies the element's atomic number

The bonds Element

The **bonds** element represents the chemical bond or connection between two atoms. You can specify an arbitrary number of arrays for carrying the bond information. The **bonds** element uses the following attributes:

- **atid1**—Specifies the atom identifier of the first atom within the bond
- **atid2**—Specifies the atom identifier of the second atom stored within the bond
- **bondid**—Represents the unique identifier for the bond
- **cylic**—Represents the bond's cyclicity
- **order**—Specifies the bond's order
- **parity**—Represents the parity of the bond
- **parids**—ATOMIDs used to reference the parity

The cml Element

You use the **cml** element to represent to the parser or browser that the document is a CML document, as shown in the following code:

```
<!DOCTYPE cml PUBLIC "-//CML//DTD CML//EN"
"http://www.ch.ic.ac.uk/chimeral/cml_10.dtd">
<cml title="This is a CML Document">
</cml>
```

Notice that the element requires a closing tag. You can place additional elements between the CML **title** declaration and the closing **cml** tag. Every CML document must include the DOCTYPE declaration, which specifies that the document is a CML document. The preceding example specifies a CML document with no content.

The formula Element

The **formula** element is used to describe the contents of the molecule—in other words, it defines what the molecule is. The following attributes are used to further represent the formula:

- **molwt**—Represents the element's molecular weight

- **stoichiom**—Represents the element's chemical composition, or stoichiometry

Here's an example of how the formula for water, H_2O, might be written:

```
<formula>
<xvar builtin="stoichiom">
H H O
</xvar>
</formula>
```

The mol Element

The **mol** element is the top-level container for molecular information. It represents the molecule, including the atoms, the bonds between the atoms if there are any, and the molecule's formula. The **atoms** and **bonds** elements can be used as subelements, or children, within the **mol** element.

The xaddr Element

The **xaddr** element is the easiest element of the bunch. It specifies the address of the person or organization that created the document. You can use the **xvar** element to separate the various elements of the address if you need to.

The xlist Element

You can use the **xlist** element as a generic container of information. It can include arrays, **xvariables**, or even other **xlists** to specify items such as chemical elements and compounds, lists of dates, lists of values, or anything else that needs to be specified in a list string.

The xvar Element

When you want to specify an individual generic container of information, you use the **xvar** element. You can use **xvar** to specify formulas, additional address information, reference pointers to external information sources, or anything else that is considered a container of generic information.

Mathematical Markup Language (MathML)

The MathML vocabulary was created primarily for supporting the need to display and exchange mathematical formulas and symbols. This language is useful if you need to include mathematical formulas in your Web site. It's also an excellent XML application for learning how elements and subelements work and how attributes further explain the elements. Be forewarned, however, that there's a lot to the MathML vocabulary, and we cannot outline all the features here. We highly recommend that you check out the latest version of MathML at **www.w3.org/TR/MathML2**.

It may sound strange to hear that MathML is an XML application, because XML is more about structuring data than displaying it. However, if you think about standard mathematical equations and how they're structured, you'll soon realize that you need to create the structures before you can construct a formula. Like CML data files, MathML data files require that you use a specialized viewer to see the parsed data, because the current browsers do not support the MathML results.

MathML can be used to create mathematical formulas as well as to represent such advanced mathematical equations as polynomials, calculus, and geometric and trigonometric equations on the Web. MathML has two sets of markup elements: one for content and another for presentation.

When you use MathML to create mathematical expressions, you must follow the guidelines specified in XML—for example, each element must be closed properly. To code your equation, follow the mathematical expression from left to right.

All MathML elements are contained in one of three categories:

- *Presentation*—Presentation elements describe mathematical notation structures. For example, **mrow** is used to indicate a horizontal row of characters. As a general rule, each presentation element corresponds to a single kind of notation schema, such as a row, subscript, or superscript. Currently, the

MathML presentation markup consists of over 25 elements that have more than 50 attributes combined. Each element corresponds to a two-dimensional notational device, such as a super- or subscript, a fraction, or a table. In addition, there are the **mi**, **mn**, and **mo** elements, which are presentation token elements. These are the only presentation elements in which characters and symbols can appear. The remaining few presentation elements are empty elements and are used primarily for alignment.

- *Content*—Content elements describe mathematical objects instead of just the notation that represents them. The **plus** element is an example of a content element; it represents the addition operator. Each content element corresponds to a carefully defined mathematical concept.

- *Interface*—Interface elements don't fall into the category of either content or presentation elements. The **math** element is an example of an interface element.

In the following sections, we describe some MathML elements (both presentation and content elements) that are used to define mathematical equations.

Presentation Elements

Presentation elements give you the ability to specify a notation's expression structure. The presentation elements come in two flavors: elements that declare the type of data and elements that denote the layout definition. The layout definition may include elements that specify rows, scripts, or fractions. Here are several presentation elements you might want to familiarize yourself with:

- **mfenced**—Represents a fence (such as parentheses, brackets, or braces). The content between the start and end tags is displayed within the fences.

- **mi**—Specifies variables, function names, and constants.

- **mn**—Represents numerical data.

- **mo**—Represents a mathematical operator.

- **mrow**—Groups a number of subexpressions in a horizontal fashion.

- **msup**—Represents the superscript notation to a base number.

Arithmetic and Algebraic Content Elements

Most of the arithmetic and algebraic element tags are relatively easy to understand and are either empty elements (meaning they have no content) or have no attributes. The empty elements are specified by following the name of the element with the forward slash, as follows.

- *Addition*—**<plus/>**

- *Subtraction*—**<minus/>**

- *Division*—**<over/>**

- *Multiplication—***<times/>**
- *To the power of—***<power/>**
- *Exponentiation—***<exp/>**
- *Remainder—***<rem/>**
- *Factorial—***<factorial/>**
- *Maximum—***<max/>**
- *Minimum—***<min/>**

Using Content Elements

The **apply** element is perhaps the single most important content element. It's used to group operators with arguments. If we used the **apply** element to present the formula

```
(x - y) / 2
```

the code would look like this:

```
<apply>
    <divide/>
        <apply>
            <minus/>
                    <ci>x</ci>
                    <ci>y</ci>
        </apply>
    <cn>2</cn>
</apply>
```

Open Software Description (OSD)

Microsoft and Marimba understood that a standard was needed for distributing software over the Internet. Their proposal, called the Open Software Description (OSD), uses unique XML elements to describe such things as the version of the product, the platform the product should work on (such as a Macintosh or Windows 98 operating system), and the upgrade mechanism. Then, CDF can be used to deliver software packages over the Internet.

OSD is an XML application because it uses XML to create the elements and attributes that describe how the software will be distributed over an intranet or the Internet. The OSD elements and attributes have the same rules and restrictions that XML elements and attributes have. As with any XML document, OSD should have a single root element from which all other subelements branch.

Why would you use OSD to help distribute software over a network? In a large organization, upgrading software one machine at a time can be very time consuming. The cost of employing software technicians to keep software up-to-date increases the cost of software ownership substantially. With so many computers, networks, and systems running the same type of software (for example Windows ME, Internet Explorer 5.5, and Microsoft Office 2000), offering a quick way to upgrade software over a network without the need to employ additional resources is paramount for most networked corporations and many individuals.

Remote software distribution provides the end user and the corporation with the following features:

- *The ability for hands-off installation*—The end user does not need to manually install software.

- *Software can be updated in a timely fashion from a single designated source*—End users no longer have to search for upgrades.

- *Upgrades can work across platforms*—The correct software gets to the correct platform based on the version and operating system used.

OSD can be used not only to upgrade standalone commercial software packages, but also to deploy Java packages, Java standalone applications, and platform-native code across a network.

Each OSD data file specifies a particular archive file (which can be a JAR or CAB file) in the URL attribute of the **CODEBASE** element. You can also embed the OSD vocabulary within the archived files. Examples of how to implement OSD can be found in this chapter's Immediate Solutions section.

Major and minor elements are available in OSD. The minor elements are children of one of the major elements and are used to further clarify the OSD package. In the following sections, we'll cover the OSD elements you need to be familiar with before you create an OSD file.

Major OSD Elements

You need to understand the following major elements before creating OSD files:

- **SOFTPKG**—The document element for any OSD document. It defines the general software package and the overall features of that package. All other elements are subelements of the **SOFTPKG** element.

- **IMPLEMENTATION**—Used to describe an implementation of the client-specific software package.

- **DEPENDENCY**—Used to indicate the dependency between software distributions or components.

The **ACTION=(Assert | Install)** attribute can be used with the **DEPENDENCY** element. If the **ACTION** value is **Assert**, the software package should be ignored entirely if the dependency is not already present on the client machine. If the value is **Install** and the dependency is not already present on the client machine, the browser should get the package and install it on the client machine.

Minor OSD Elements

You need to understand the following minor elements before creating OSD files:

- **IMPLTYPE**—Nests within the **IMPLEMENTATION** major element and describes the type of implementation.

- **TITLE**—The name of the software package (usually the consumer-oriented name).

- **ABSTRACT**—Used to provide a short description that summarizes the nature and purpose of the software distribution. This description should let the user know what the software package contains.

- **LICENSE**—Indicates where the user can retrieve the license agreement or copyright notice. It usually indicates a Web site, which can be used to verify that the user has read the license agreement.

- **DISKSIZE**—Used with the **VALUE** attribute to specify how much disk space is required by the software package. All sizes are specified in kilobytes.

- **CODEBASE**—Indicates where an archive of the software distribution exists. Basically, it sets up the location of the software package. Multiple URLs can be specified to load-balance when software packages are updated on an intranet or on the Internet. The following attributes can be used with the **CODEBASE** element:

  - **SIZE="*max-KB*"**—Specifies the maximum allowable size for the software in kilobytes.

  - **HREF="*url*"**—Points to the archive of the software package to be downloaded.

  - **FILENAME="*string*"**—Specifies a file contained within the archive that contains the OSD. If the OSD file is a standalone file, this attribute is ignored.

- **OS**—Indicates which operating system the software package requires. If you leave this element set to zero, the existing software platform will be used and specified to run on all operating systems, as is the case with Java applets.

- **OSVERSION**—Works in conjunction with the **OS** element. It specifies the operating system version required to use the software package. If no version is specified, it is assumed that the software package will run on all versions.

- **PROCESSOR**—Indicates the computer processor required to run the software package. If no **PROCESSOR** value is specified, the particular implementation of the software is assumed to run on all processors.

- **LANGUAGE**—Indicates the natural language used in the software user interface. If none is specified, it's assumed that the software package will use all languages.

- **VM**—Defines the virtual machine used by the software package.

- **MEMSIZE**—Specifies how much memory (runtime) is required by the software package. If the machine does not meet the specifications, the software package is not sent.

Synchronized Multimedia Integration Language (SMIL)

With SMIL, developers can create Web sites with multimedia-rich content. SMIL allows sites to have almost TV-like content with low bandwidth requirements for transmitting content over the Internet. When SMIL becomes more widely used, users won't need to configure their browsers to use specific helper or plug-in applications. Instead, SMIL will provide a cross-platform, standardized way to deliver multimedia without the need for proprietary software. It also means that additional programming languages won't be required to create multimedia documents. Like any XML application, all that is needed is a simple text editor.

SMIL also allows the developer to create and embed hyperlinking within the multimedia file. As a result, the developer can create time-based Web presentations, and media objects can be reused repeatedly.

TIP: *If you don't want to hard-code your SMIL files, you can download Real Networks' RealProducer G2 Authoring Kit. This application, located at **www.realnetworks.com/products/authkit/**, contains the SMIL Wizard. It's a great application for learning SMIL, because it offers a View Source option for viewing the SMIL code.*

Design Principles for SMIL

Similar to all XML applications, SMIL follows the standard design principles, but it also has a set of design principles all its own:

- All objects specified in any URLs must be available online.

- All objects specified in SMIL files must have a start time and end time based on temporal parameters.

- User options, such as stop, play, forward, and reverse, should be made available, and all components must react to these options in a synchronized fashion.

Hyperlinking is a key component to SMIL, and you should develop SMIL files with hyperlinks embedded in the files. However, SMIL doesn't just use simple hyperlinks. Instead, SMIL uses the advanced hyperlinking mechanisms used in XML.

Related solution:	*Found on page:*
Creating a Simple Link	333

SMIL Elements

The following list includes some of the SMIL elements you can use to create a SMIL document. They follow the same convention used in any XML-based application: Each element must be closed properly. The SMIL elements include:

- **head**—Specifies head information, such as meta content and layout
- **layout**—Specifies how the elements in the document's body are positioned on the rendering surface
- **body**—Specifies the section where the multimedia elements are displayed
- **smil**—Specifies that the document is a SMIL document
- **audio**—Specifies an audio object
- **video**—Specifies a video object
- **text**—Specifies a text object
- **img**—Specifies an image object
- **par**—Specifies that the objects will play in a parallel fashion
- **seq**—Specifies that the objects will play in a sequence (for example, first A, and then B)

TIP: Both the **par** and **seq** elements can have **begin** and **end** attributes to specify when an object will begin playing and when one will end.

- **switch**—Used to specify alternative media files for users based on bandwidth, language, screen resolution, and other variables
- **a**—Specifies a link to a multimedia file (used just as the HTML **a** element—it's an empty element)

TIP: Remember, there's a lot more to SMIL than the simple elements we've just listed. Although Real Networks has created some powerful design tools, if you want to know more about SMIL, be sure you check out **http://smw.internet.com/smil/smilhome.html**. The site includes additional information about how you can put this multimedia XML-based application to good use.

SMIL in Depth

To give you a better idea of how SMIL works, let's examine how to create a SMIL file. First, like HTML files, a SMIL file has two parts: a head and a body. The head specifies metacontent, such as copyright, author, and comment information. The head section is used to define various layout features of the document. If no layout information is specified in the head section, the application playing the SMIL file will control the layout of the media. A SMIL head section looks something like this:

```
<head>
  <layout>
    <region id="a" top="5" />
  </layout>
    <meta name="author" content="N. Pitts"/>
    <meta name="title" content="My Summer Vacation"/>
    <meta name="copyright" content="(c)2000 Natanya Pitts"/>
</head>
```

Information about the various multimedia elements and the synchronization of these objects is specified in the body of the SMIL document. Three presentation styles can be defined within the body of the SMIL document. Parallel presentation styles define how objects can be presented at the same time and how each object relates to another. The code for specifying parallel presentations looks like this:

```
<par>
  <audio src="audio.wav"/>
  <video src="video.avi"/>
</par>
```

Sequence is another presentation style. Sequence specifies the order of two individual multimedia objects. In a sequence presentation, the first object displays or plays at the specified time. The rest of the objects listed in the body of a sequence presentation start whenever the preceding object ends. The code to specify a sequence of multimedia elements looks like this:

```
<body>
  <seq>
    <audio src="audio/songone.wav"/>
    <audio src="audio/songtwo.snd"/>
  </seq>
</body>
```

It's amazing to see the tremendous support XML has garnered, and nowhere is it more evident than in the number of XML-based applications that have been created in a relatively short time. You can use XML to do just about anything you can think of, including deliver software updates remotely, transmit multimedia objects in a standard way, and design and display mathematical equations. In this chapter, we've examined what applications are available, the types of elements used in the most popular XML-based applications, and how some of these elements can be put to good use.

Immediate Solutions

Locating New XML Applications

The most important thing to do in your XML development career is to keep abreast of the new XML applications. Two of the best places to find new XML applications are James Tauber's XML Info site at **www.xmlinfo.com** and XML.com at **www.xml.com**. You can also find information about other XML activities at the W3C site at **www.w3c.org/XML**.

Creating a Mathematical Equation with MathML

In this example, you use content elements to create the equation for a circle, $x^2 + y^2 = 1$. You'll need to group each operation with the **apply** element, using the **ci** and **cn** token elements to hold the variables and the exponents. The **plus** element precedes the operations and applies the addition operation to the two products. The sum of the equation is entered between the **cn** tags after the last **apply** element is closed. The code for this equation looks like this:

```
<apply>
    <plus/>
    <apply>
       <power/>
       <ci>x</ci>
       <cn>2</cn>
    </apply>
    <apply>
       <power/>
       <ci>y</ci>
       <cn>2</cn>
    </apply>
</apply>
<cn>1</cn>
```

Creating an OSD Software Package

To use OSD to create a software package, you need to know several things about the software package and the intended audience or program you're distributing the software package to. The first thing you should do is create the main element that will define the application and where the application is located. To do that, follow these steps:

1. Create the main element by using the **SOFTPKG** element to define where the program is located (note that this is a completely fictional software program):

```
<SOFTPKG NAME="Go Fish Distribution 2" VERSION="2,0,0,0">
```

2. Specify the title of the package by supplying the **TITLE** element like this:

```
<TITLE>Go Fish</TITLE>
```

3. You can add additional abstract information that specifies what's contained in the package by adding this line of code:

```
<ABSTRACT>Go Fish by Dolphin Corporation</ABSTRACT>
```

4. Specify the location of the licensing agreement by adding the **LICENSE** element along with the URL of the location where the license is stored:

```
<LICENSE HREF="http://www.dolphin.com/gofish/license.html" />
```

5. Specify the implementation of the software, which includes the OS versions, the processor required, and the location of the CAB or JAR files of the actual application. You can also specify the language required for the application within the **IMPLEMENTATION** section. You can specify more than one implementation for different types of code and the dependencies required for the other types of code implementations to run. The code would look something like this:

```
<!-- Go Fish is implemented in native code for Windows 32-bit
applications,and Java code for other platforms -->
<IMPLEMENTATION>
  <OS VALUE="WinNT"><OSVERSION VALUE="4,0,0,0"/></OS>
  <OS VALUE="Win98"/>
```

```
    <PROCESSOR VALUE="x86" />
    <LANGUAGE VALUE="en" />
    <CODEBASE HREF="http://www.dolphin.com/gofish.cab" />
  </IMPLEMENTATION>
  <IMPLEMENTATION>
    <IMPLTYPE VALUE="Java" />
    <CODEBASE HREF="http://www.dolphin.com/gofish.jar" />
  <!-- The Java implementation needs the SchoolofFish object -->
    <DEPENDENCY>
      <CODEBASE HREF="http://www.dolphin.com/gofish.osd" />
    </DEPENDENCY>
  </IMPLEMENTATION>
```

6. To complete the software package, add the following end-tag element:

```
    </SOFTPKG>
```

The entire code should be similar to Listing 16.1.

Listing 16.1   A complete OSD file.

```
<?xml version="1.0"?>
<SOFTPKG NAME="Go Fish Distribution 2" VERSION="2,0,0,0">
<TITLE>Go Fish</TITLE>
<ABSTRACT>Go Fish by Dolphin Corporation</ABSTRACT>
<LICENSE HREF="http://www.dolphin.com/gofish/license.html" />
<!-- Go Fish is implemented in native code for Windows 32-bit applications,
and Java code for other platforms -->
<IMPLEMENTATION>
  <OS VALUE="WinNT"><OSVERSION VALUE="4,0,0,0"/></OS>
  <OS VALUE="Win98"/>
  <PROCESSOR VALUE="x86" />
  <LANGUAGE VALUE="en" />
  <CODEBASE HREF="http://www.dolphin.com/gofish.cab" />
</IMPLEMENTATION>
<IMPLEMENTATION>
  <IMPLTYPE VALUE="Java" />
  <CODEBASE HREF="http://www.dolphin.com/gofish.jar" />
<!-- The Java implementation needs the SchoolofFish object -->
  <DEPENDENCY>
    <CODEBASE HREF="http://www.dolphin.com/gofish.osd" />
  </DEPENDENCY>
</IMPLEMENTATION>
</SOFTPKG>
```

16. XML Applications

Creating a SMIL Data File

A SMIL file has an .smi extension and can be created with any text editor. Within the **smil** root element, you define how the file will be displayed, how the video will be synchronized with the audio, and how it will play other multimedia files within the file itself.

To create a SMIL file, follow these steps:

1. Declare the file as a SMIL file by adding this code to your blank text-only file:

```
<smil>
```

2. Specify the header information, which sets the size dimensions and the background color along with the text and image areas. It can also include the meta-information about the presentation. To create the header section, include the following code after the **smil** element:

```
<head>
  <layout>
   <root-layout height="252" width="340"
   background-color="white"/>
    <region id="region_images" left="0" top="32"
    height="180" width="300"/>
  </layout>
    <meta name="author" content="N. Pitts"/>
    <meta name="title" content="My Summer Vacation"/>
    <meta name="copyright" content="(c)2000 Natanya Pitts"/>
</head>
```

3. Specify the body of the SMIL document. In the body, you determine what elements will be loaded, and in what order, by using the sequence element, **seq**, and the parallel element, **par**. The following example demonstrates how one audio file can be loaded after the first has played. **Songone.wav** is loaded with the SMIL file; after it is completed, **Songtwo.snd** begins:

```
<body>
  <seq>
    <audio src="audio/Songone.wav"/>
    <audio src="audio/Songtwo.snd"/>
  </seq>
</body>
```

4. Close the document with the end SMIL element:

```
</smil>
```

The entire code should be similar to Listing 16.2.

Listing 16.2   A complete SMIL file.

```
<?xml version="1.0"?>
<smil>
<head>
  <layout>
   <root-layout height="252" width="340"
   background-color="white"/>
    <region id="region_images" left="0" top="32"
    height="180" width="300"/>
  </layout>
    <meta name="author" content="N. Pitts"/>
    <meta name="title" content="My Summer Vacation"/>
    <meta name="copyright" content="(c)2000 Natanya Pitts"/>
</head>
<body>
  <seq>
    <audio src="audio/Songone.wav"/>
    <audio src="audio/Songtwo.snd"/>
  </seq>
</body>
</smil>
```

Complex Sequencing

Through careful use of the **seq** and **par** elements, you can specify more complex sequencing of audio and visual elements. In the following example, the intro screen loads first, followed by the narrative track and the main image, which load simultaneously. Notice how these elements are nested in the proper order:

```
<body>
  <seq>
  <!--This shows the intro screen-->
    <img src="title.imf" region="region_images" fill="remove"/>
    <par>
    <!--This starts the narrative track-->
      <audio src="audio.rm"/>
    <!--This loads the main image -->
      <img src="images.imf" region="region_images" fill="remove"/>
    </par>
  </seq>
</body>
```

16. XML Applications

437

Specifying Bandwidth Options

You can use the **switch** element to load alternative content for users based on bandwidth, screen size, language, and other factors. For instance, you could use lightweight images for a user with a 28Kbps modem, or load the text "Guten Tag! Wie geht es Ihnen?" if the user's default language is German.

Listing 16.3 tests the user's bandwidth, and downloads a text file depending on how fast the user's connection is.

Listing 16.3   Switchable content.

```
<?xml version="1.0"?>
<smil>
  <head>
    <meta name="author" content="N. Pitts"/>
    <meta name="title" content="Switchable Content"/>
    <meta name="copyright" content="(c)2000 Natanya Pitts"/>
  </head>
  <body>
    <switch>
    <!-- if your bitrate is greater than 56000-->
      <text src="bigfile.txt"
          system-bitrate="56000" />
    <!-- if your bitrate is greater than 28000 -->
      <text src="smallfile.txt"
          system-bitrate="28000" />
    </switch>
  </body>
</smil>
```

Finding Tools to Build Documents for XML Applications

In this section of Immediate Solutions, we let you know what tools are available for the various XML applications and where you can find them.

Tools for Creating SMIL Documents

A wide variety of tools are currently available for creating SMIL documents. Many of these tools are free or have a free version available, and you can download them over the Internet:

• *SMIL Composer*—Sausage Software's SMIL Composer helps you create synchronized multimedia content for RealSystem G2. It features a WYSIWYG layout interface, so no knowledge of SMIL code is required. You can add media files and arrange their layout and the sequence in which they are played. The program then generates the SMIL code for you. SMIL Composer can be downloaded from **www.sausage.com/supertoolz/toolz/stsmil.html**.

- *Allaire HomeSite*—Allaire's HTML authoring tool, HomeSite, includes support for SMIL in release 4.0. HomeSite provides a WYSIWYG interface for the creation of SMIL graphics, and it generates the correct code for you. HomeSite prides itself on its generation of *clean code*, free from the extraneous tags that plague many HTML authoring tools. HomeSite can be purchased and downloaded from Allaire's Web site at **www.allaire.com/Products/HomeSite/**.

- *Free RealProducer G2 Authoring Kit*—RealNetwork's Free RealProducer G2 Authoring Kit features a SMIL Wizard for specifying the layout and sequencing of RealAudio and RealVideo files, as well as other Real Media file types. This tool can be downloaded from **www.realnetworks.com/products/authkit/**.

Tools for Editing and Viewing CML Documents

The only software currently available for viewing and editing CML documents is the JUMBO Java application. It can be run as a standalone application or as a Java applet served remotely. JUMBO can read many current non-CML files and convert them to CML. It's one of the first tools for editing molecular documents, and provides file importing, tree merging and deletion, and exporting of results. Find out more about JUMBO and download it from **http://ala.vsms.nottingham.ac.uk/vsms/java/jumbo/**.

Tools for Creating MathML Documents

MathML is perhaps the most complicated XML application currently in use. A MathML authoring tool is invaluable if you plan to use MathML frequently:

- *MathType*—Created by Design Science, Inc., MathType is an equation editor and authoring tool for creating mathematical expressions for word-processing and Web-publishing documents. It can output in MathML, but has support for only presentation elements at the time of this writing. MathType comes with four MathML translators to accommodate the differences in software that supports MathML. MathType features a keyboard-like interface with mathematical functions ranging from simple to extremely complex. You can also drag-and-drop equations onto the application window, and MathType will generate MathML code on the fly. To find out more about MathType, visit the official MathType site at **www.mathtype.com**.

- *WebEQ*—WebEQ, also from Design Science, Inc., is an application that provides two authoring tools: an Equation Editor and a Translator Wizard. You use the Equation Editor to graphically lay out equations, and the Wizard

16. XML Applications

to process WebTeX or MathML commands to lay out equations. You can use both tools to output images of equations, MathML, or interactive math applets. To find out more about WebEQ, visit the WebEQ site at **www.mathtype.com/webmath/webeq/features.stm**.

TIP: *To stay current on the latest MathML software, visit the W3C's Math Home Page at* **www.w3.org/Math/**.

Chapter 17

Implementing CDF

In Depth

In this chapter, we'll get pushy. In other words, we're going to delve into the world of push technology. Specifically, we examine Microsoft's implementation of push technology, which is an application XML-based called the Channel Definition Format (CDF). In this chapter, you'll learn what CDF is, how to use the correct syntax, how to create a CDF file, and how to create your own channels to push content to subscribers through applications such as screen savers, HTML-formatted email, and the Active Desktop channel.

Microsoft introduced the Active Channel technology and its structural base, CDF, when it introduced Internet Explorer 4.0. Although Active Channels are not incorporated into Internet Explorer 5.0, Active Channel Desktop items are a common use of CDF for users who have upgraded their browsers. Push technologies that use XML (such as CDF) give you, the developer, a way to organize and deliver specific, personalized Web-based information at predetermined times to users who request it. It's one of the easiest XML applications to learn and implement within a site, regardless of whether the site is on the Internet or is part of an intranet.

With CDF, developers can create content for distribution to a wide range of users and through a variety of delivery formats. For example, current stock prices could be sent to subscribers of a CDF push channel via an Active Desktop item, HTML-formatted email, Web pages, or a desktop screen saver. Automated software updates and company announcements can be pushed to the desktops of every user on a company's network. After the information's sent, it can be viewed offline, because all the graphics and textual content are delivered together in a single subscription package.

CDF provides a standard set of elements for defining channels, which automatically send data from a Web server to an Active Channel. CDF also lets you create a schedule for downloading updated content from the Web server to the browser. The content is labeled with a brief description and includes navigational buttons to allow the user to move through it easily. Let's examine how CDF relates to XML, the design concepts used in developing channels, and the CDF vocabulary.

A Closer Look at Channels

The concept of channels is relatively easy to understand. In its most basic form, a channel is a collection of information the developer has defined for delivery to those users who have subscribed to receive it. The easiest way to explain channels and their potential is to step out of the computer world for a moment and think about the television world—specifically, cable television. When you subscribe to cable television, you normally get access to an option called pay-per-view. Pay-per-view channels are channels you can subscribe to for specific content that is aired at a specific time. The cable company tells you what's available, usually through a preview channel. You subscribe to the content that appeals to you—the latest boxing match or a movie, for example—by dialing the phone, entering your cable account number, and selecting the program identification number shown on the preview channel; or by selecting the appropriate option through an automated menu on your TV. At a predetermined time, the cable company delivers the content you requested directly to your cable box.

With Active Channels, the theory is similar, except you normally don't have to pay. The content is usually free and can be accessed with the click of a button. Channels deliver a collection of information, graphics, sounds, and possibly movie files. The file that outlines what's available in the channel is called the CDF file. Included in the CDF file's channel index is a schedule that outlines when the information in the channel will be updated. Depending on how the channel is coded, the subscriber can specify whether that information is pushed to his or her email address, computer's desktop, and/or screen saver. After the content is received, the user can then view, manipulate, or print the information without connecting to the Internet, because all the content is saved on the user's computer.

Advantages of Channels for the User

For the user, channels offer easy access to information. The Channels button on the Internet Explorer 4.0 toolbar gives single point-and-click access to the channels that are available. Channels can also be viewed as windows in the Windows Active Desktop. Channels offer the same accessibility that Web pages offer by providing the same navigational controls. Links are still incorporated within the content, and depending on the level of the subscription, the information can be more than just a single Web page deep. The user is not required to learn new navigational techniques, special commands, or other controls to subscribe to, gather, or read the information. Because the information pushed to the user's desktop is presented in standard HTML format, the subscriber uses the information supplied in the channel in the same fashion he or she would use the information in a standard Web page.

For the user, subscribing to channels is as simple as clicking on an image on a Web page, such as the icon shown in Figure 17.1. The image links to your channel in much the same way as an HTML hyperlink. All the information the user subscribes to is automatically updated according to the default schedule specified in the CDF file, or as specified by the subscriber. The user does nothing in terms of seeking or finding the new information on your site. Better still, the updating is

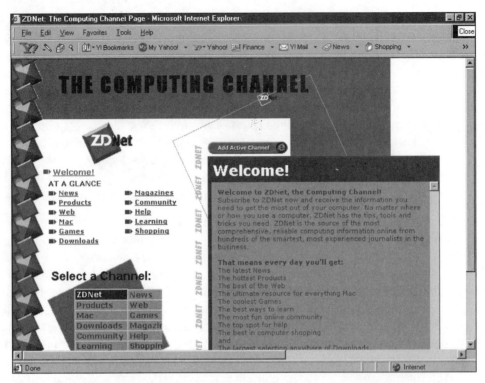

Figure 17.1   To subscribe to a site, all a user has to do is click on the channel logo.

done at a predetermined time, which means the user doesn't have to download content or wait for the channel to load. Simply viewing the channel brings up the latest information. And because the information is downloaded automatically, the user can view it offline.

Advantages of Channels for the Developer

All of this automation provides plenty of advantages to the Web developer. With CDF, the developer can extend the content on a Web site by delivering it to users who may not know about the content or who don't have the time to browse for it. As mentioned earlier, CDF is an excellent mechanism for delivering content through the Active Desktop, email, and/or screen savers. It offers developers the following benefits:

- *Full control over the delivery of information*—You can specify exactly what and how much information is pushed to the user. This control ensures that the user at least sees the information you want him or her to see, unlike just posting it on a Web page that may or may not be accessed by the users you want to target.

- *The ability to personalize content for the subscriber*—Subscribers can pick and choose what content will be delivered to their desktops.

- *The ability to provide access to authorized users only through password protection*—Because you can request a login name and password within the CDF file you create, you can request that only users who have login names and passwords subscribe to the content information. This option, however, does not provide full digital certification.

- *The ability to track and log page hits*—You can track users to learn what pages are being viewed and what pages are downloaded but never touched. Doing so helps you determine what information should be updated and what information users aren't interested in reading.

- *Options to deliver information based on subscriber's preference*—You can give the user a choice to view the information through email, a desktop screen saver, or an Active Desktop channel.

When you employ CDF files within your site, you set up information that is targeted to an interested audience, which means the information is more likely to be read. When users subscribe to your channel, they know the information is updated on a regular basis.

In terms of development, you can use the knowledge you already have to develop channel content:

- No new development tools or knowledge are needed to create the content. Because channels are simply HTML pages, you can use your Web development skills in layout, graphics, and programming to create channel content.

- The CDF file can be customized with Active Server Pages technology and other Common Gateway Interface (CGI) scripting—plus client-side scripting such as cookies—to extend and customize the content of the channel.

- You can automate the production of CDF files with such products as Microsoft FrontPage or Microsoft CDF Generator, which is a separate application that allows you to create CDF files without using FrontPage.

TIP: *An overview of the Microsoft CDF Generator is available at MSDN Online Web Workshop's Content & Component Delivery section at **http://msdn.microsoft.com/workshop/**. You can download the CDF Generator from **http://msdn.microsoft.com/downloads/tools/cdfgen/cdfgenerator.asp**.*

- CDF files let you organize your information in a hierarchy in the same structure as any other XML document, which means CDF files can be viewed through many of today's parsers. As a result, you can easily organize your information and present it to your subscribers in a logical order.

- When you package content in channels, you can target different sets of audiences for different types of information.

17. Implementing CDF

XML's Relationship with CDF

All content sent to the subscriber through a channel is created in HTML. XML doesn't format the content. So, how does CDF relate to XML? XML provides the framework through which the browser finds, describes, and delivers the channel content. CDF is an XML-based application, which means Microsoft has developed a list of specific CDF elements that follow the XML syntax and conventions but have been defined with their own attributes. These elements are used to create a channel. Microsoft's CDF processor is much more lenient than an XML processor, however, which allows for inconsistent element and attribute name cases, among other violations of the strict XML standards. Therefore, although CDF is built on an XML foundation, it doesn't adhere strictly to XML, like other XML applications do.

If you're a little fuzzy about the concept of elements, Chapters 6 and 8 outline exactly what elements and attributes are.

Related solutions:	Found on page:
Declaring and Specifying a Single Element with Parsed Character Data	163
Planning for Element Attributes	200

Specifically, CDF is based on a specification that contains information that points the user's browser to the information source, descriptive information about the content, and the schedule for downloading the information. The CDF application consists of a single root element, the element from which all other items within the channel branch. This single root element is called the **CHANNEL** element. The branches from this root element are called **ITEM** elements. You can also use additional **CHANNEL** elements within the root **CHANNEL** to specify subchannels. You can have multiple **ITEM** elements within a **CHANNEL**, but you can have only one **CHANNEL** element to describe the channel. The **ITEM** elements specify the individual pages or subpages that are the children of the channel.

In this chapter's Immediate Solutions section, you'll learn how to create both the CDF file that specifies the XML declaration and the CDF elements that create the channel information. Because the information is automatically sent to the user at a predetermined time, when the user clicks on the Channels button in Internet Explorer 4 (see Figure 17.2) or accesses the Active Desktop Channel window, the content is automatically available. There's no waiting for the text, pictures, sounds, or even movies to download.

Figure 17.2   The Channels button allows the user to view information that was delivered to the computer at a predetermined time.

The Development of Channels

There are five major steps for developing the CDF file, the accompanying images, and the information needed for a user to subscribe to your channel. Here are the steps in the order in which they should be performed:

1. Design the channel.
2. Create the channel logo icons and images.
3. Create the CDF file.
4. Upload or post the CDF file to the Hypertext Transfer Protocol (HTTP) server.
5. Offer the channel to potential subscribers.

Designing the Channel

Before you create the logos and the content or tell potential subscribers about your channel, you should design its structure. It doesn't matter if your channel is simply a recreation of your Web site, a subset of it, or new content—you still need to sketch the channel content hierarchy. The hierarchy is the actual structure of your channel and is created in the CDF file using the **CHANNEL** and **ITEM** elements, which represent the channel's content as well as its hierarchy.

When you design your channel, make sure the first level contains no more than eight subitems. Not only does this limit information overload for the subscriber, but it also reduces the download time needed to send the information. In addition, make sure your channels fall into one of the channel types, which makes it easier for the potential subscriber to understand exactly what type of content you're making available. After you outline the hierarchy and the type of channel your content falls into, you're ready to design the logos that represent it.

17. Implementing CDF

Creating the Channel Logo Icons and Images

Channels rely on three different types of icons that appear in various locations within your Web site and within the user's desktop and Internet Explorer 4 application. These logo icons make it easier for the subscriber to identify and locate the information within your channel, both online and offline. Each of the following icons needs to be designed within a certain size to match the design of Internet Explorer:

- *Channels Explorer Bar*—This bar must be 32 pixels high by 192 pixels wide and appears in the Internet Explorer 4 Channel pane. An example of this image is shown in Figure 17.3.

- *Desktop Channels Explorer Bar*—This bar must be 80 pixels high by 32 pixels wide and, as the name implies, appears on the user's Windows desktop. This image is shown in Figure 17.4.

Figure 17.3   The Channels Explorer Bar appears in the Channel pane located in the user's Internet Explorer application.

Figure 17.4   The desktop Channels Explorer Bar appears on the user's desktop.

- *Icons for each item in the channel subcategory*—Each icon must be 16 pixels high by 16 pixels wide. These icons appear in the Internet Explorer 4 Channel pane to display the additional subcategories when the channel is expanded. This type of icon is shown in Figure 17.5.

It's imperative that you create these images and icons so your channel will display properly on the user's computer and within Internet Explorer 4. Without them, the default icons Microsoft supplies will show instead, and your channel won't look much different than other channels. Each icon should have a transparent color background. The icons and images should also be fairly simplistic in design because they will occupy only a small amount of screen space. The code for including these elements is outlined in the CDF file in the following fashion:

```
<CHANNEL HREF="http://www.site.com/topchannel.html">
<!--This Logo is for the Channels Explorer Bar -->
<LOGO HREF="http://www.site.com/explorerlogo.gif" STYLE="IMAGE-WIDE"/>
<!--This Logo is for the desktop Channels Explorer Bar -->
<LOGO HREF="http://www.site.com/desktoplogo.gif" STYLE="IMAGE"/>
<!--This Logo is for the Channels Category Folder -->
<LOGO HREF="http://www.site.com/icon.gif" STYLE="ICON"/>
</CHANNEL>
```

Each top-level **CHANNEL** element should have three **LOGO** child elements. Each child element should contain a **STYLE** attribute that defines the type of icon. Again, if you don't specify these images and icons, Microsoft supplies default images for each category.

Also, note that you supply the **STYLE="ICON"** attribute just in case the subscriber puts your Active Channel in a category folder. The icon then displays properly in the subscriber's Channel pane by appearing in the list of available channels in the Channels Explorer Bar when the group to which it belongs is selected.

Figure 17.5   These icons appear in the Internet Explorer Channel pane when the channel is expanded.

Creating the CDF File

After you define the structure of your channel and design all the logos and icons, you're ready to create the actual CDF file. This file, which describes the channel itself, is an XML application even though the syntax is very similar to HTML. Remember, however, that XML is extremely particular about syntax. Each element must have a closing tag in order to make the CDF file a well-formed and valid document. You also need to make sure all attribute values are in quotes and that you close any open quotes. (You can use both single and double quotation marks. We suggest you pick one or the other and be consistent.)

Each CDF file must have at least one **CHANNEL** element that declares the channel and its elements. The **CHANNEL** element is used to define the top-level channel and any subitems that are nested below the main channel. The **CHANNEL** element actually defines the hierarchy of the channel and its elements. Within the **CHANNEL** element, **ITEM** elements are used to specify which Web pages are part of the channel's content. You can update this information when you want to redefine or update the channel content.

After you specify the hierarchy with the **CHANNEL** element and the content with the **ITEM** elements, you must include the proper **LOGO** elements for each icon and image. The order in which you specify them is not important. Remember, however, if you don't specify them, Internet Explorer uses the default icons.

Notice that the simple CDF file in Listing 17.1 is declared as an XML file. Also notice where the icons and images are outlined with the **LOGO** element and the items for the channel content are tagged with the **ITEM** element.

Listing 17.1   A simple CDF file.

```
<?xml version="1.0"?>
  <CHANNEL HREF="http://www.site.com/mainpage.html">
  <ABSTRACT>This is a sample channel.</ABSTRACT>
  <TITLE>Sample Channel</TITLE>
     <LOGO HREF="http://www.site.com/logo_icon.ico" STYLE="ICON" />
     <LOGO HREF="http://www.site.com/logo_img.gif" STYLE="IMAGE" />
     <LOGO HREF="http://www.site.com/logo_wide.gif" STYLE="IMAGE-WIDE" />
      <ITEM HREF="http://www.site.com/channel/item1/">
       <ABSTRACT>This is the first channel page.</ABSTRACT>
       <TITLE>First Channel Item</TITLE>
      </ITEM>
      <ITEM HREF="http://www.site.com/channel/item2/">
         <ABSTRACT>This is the second channel page.</ABSTRACT>
        <TITLE>Second Channel Item</TITLE>
      </ITEM>
  </CHANNEL>
```

TIP: *For more information about active channel logos and recommendations, check out the MSDN Online Web Workshop's Guidelines for Active Channel Logo Images at **http://msdn.microsoft.com/workshop/delivery/ channel/tutorials/images.asp**.*

Uploading or Posting the CDF File to the Web Server

For people to subscribe to your channel, you need to place the CDF file, the logo and graphics, and the content on a Web server and make sure the directory in which the files are stored is available to the public. These files can be transferred to your server via a File Transfer Protocol (FTP) utility. You can upload files in a batch format using a standard FTP client, such as the one included with Windows. Locate the directory where you'll place the files, and use the **MPUT** command to place multiple files on the Web server.

This chapter's Immediate Solutions section outlines the steps required to upload your CDF files. See "Adding the Channel to the Web Site."

Offering the Channel to Potential Subscribers

After you place the CDF file and the content on a publicly accessible Web server, you need to provide a mechanism for potential subscribers to not only find, but also to subscribe to the channel. Provide potential subscribers with a button image or a text link on one of your Web pages or via HTML email that links directly to the CDF file.

Channel Features

Channel content can be identical to standard Web page content. When you design channels, however, you can follow several guidelines to take advantage of the slightly different delivery mechanisms that are offered through the channel feature. Because you don't have control of the subscriber's bandwidth, you need to remember that the information you deliver should accommodate all the users who want to subscribe to the channel. This might mean sending information at non-peak hours, compacting information as much as possible, and warning users about large downloads.

CDF offers three features that developers can use to design channels that take advantage of the capabilities of CDF:

- Notification
- Site map options
- Offline content-caching features

Notification

The notification capability informs the user that the channel information has changed and that new information is available. Along with notifications of new information, a site map of the channel in which the new information is located can be sent. The site map can be viewed offline if the **PRECACHE** value is set to **YES**. This map lets the subscriber glimpse what that new data is without having to download all the channel content.

Subscribers can also request that an email message be sent to them when channel content has been updated. They can make the request through the Subscription Wizard when they first subscribe to the channel or later when they change the options of the channel subscription. If the subscriber is using Microsoft Outlook, the main page of the channel content will be sent as well as notification of the changed content.

Site Map Options

Most Windows users are familiar with the Windows Explorer interface that displays directory content in a treelike structure. Because CDF is an XML-based application, and because XML uses the same type of tree structure, the Channels Explorer Bar can display an outline of all the available page URLs that are specified in the CDF file. The tree structure/outline is fully navigational and displays the **ABSTRACT** information for each **ITEM** element found in the CDF file. The subscriber can navigate through the channel and pick and choose what content to download. All the user needs to do is subscribe to the channel; the CDF file specifies what is cached to the user's computer, and specifies what is displayed in the channel's site map.

Offline Content-Caching Features

With CDF, the developer can specify that channel content be downloaded for offline or off-site viewing. By caching or downloading not only Web pages, but also all graphics and scripts, the entire page renders properly even though the subscriber isn't connected to the Internet. The user can browse the entire content of a channel regardless of whether he or she is connected to the Internet or to the intranet that served the original channel content. However, the user must specify during the subscription process that caching is allowed by selecting the Download Content option in the channel's Subscription Wizard.

Active Channel Types

You can create a variety of channel types to facilitate delivery of information. Microsoft recommends that you fit your channel content into one of four categories:

- Immersion channels
- Notification channels
- News channels
- Hybrid channels

---

*TIP: For more information about channel content development, be sure to check out MSDN Online Web Workshop's Content & Component Delivery section at **http://msdn.microsoft.com/workshop/delivery/**.*

Immersion Channels

Immersion channels provide an immersion into the total content of the channel. You could use an immersion channel for an online game, a serialized soap opera, or a report on a particular topic.

Typically, all of an immersion channel's content is precached to the subscriber's site so the channel can be browsed offline. Therefore, you should consider the subscriber's bandwidth constraints when you design the content.

WARNING! Because you can specify other resources, such as ActiveX controls, Dynamic HTML (DHTML), scripts, and graphic files, all channel content should be designed for offline browsing and not have external references that need to be shown.

Because the channel is meant to immerse the subscriber into all of its content, its items and subchannels should not appear in the Channels Explorer Bar. However, all the elements should be precached so the subscriber is not required to reconnect to the Internet to continue exploring the channel. The CDF file is used mainly to specify what content needs to be downloaded and when the subscriber is notified that the content is updated. In the CDF file, the developer should specify a list of items that need to be updated and the schedule to update the list. Each item in the CDF file must include the **USAGE** child element, as follows:

```
<USAGE VALUE="NONE"></USAGE>
```

The **USAGE** element with a **VALUE** set to **NONE** tells the browser not to display the channel's subchannel or any other item in the Channels Explorer Bar. However, it allows the subchannel items to download and caches the content to the subscriber's computer. See "Creating an Immersion Channel" in this chapter's Immediate Solutions section for instructions on how to define an immersion channel.

Notification Channels

Notification channels also do what their name implies: They notify the user that content has been updated for a particular channel. A site map is sent to the subscriber when the notification is sent, so the subscriber can quickly access the desired content. However, the site map does not include the actual content. Instead, the **PRECACHE** attribute of each subchannel is set to **NO** because a notification channel is only meant to notify.

When you create a notification channel, each item and subchannel should be displayed in the Channels Explorer Bar. Either the **ABSTRACT** or subscription information should alert the subscriber that only the outline of the notification channel is sent to his or her computer, not the entire content of each subchannel. This type of channel is only intended to notify the subscriber of the updated content. For instructions on how to create this type of channel, see "Creating a Notification Channel" in this chapter's Immediate Solutions section.

News Channels

According to Microsoft, a news channel provides breaking news to its subscribers. It should provide a hierarchical structure with a list of other channel items available through the CDF file. This information can be cached to the subscriber's machine for offline viewing.

News channels can use all three channel capabilities: notification, a site map, and offline caching content. The site map provides an overview of all the late-breaking news available in the channel. The offline caching content allows the subscriber to view both the site map and the channel content offline. You use the notification capabilities to send the subscriber an email message or a CDF file with an overview of your new content.

TIP: *For some good examples of news channels, check out the News section of the Microsoft Active Desktop Gallery at* **www.microsoft.com/windows/ie/ie40/gallery/**.

Microsoft suggests the following guidelines for developing a news channel:

- Each news item page should be small and consist of only the most important text. Each page should have minimal graphics or reuse existing graphics.

- Each news item should be self-contained and dedicated to a single news story. Instead of using frames, you should use DHTML whenever possible. Also, the **TITLE** element of the story should specify the news item headline, and the **ABSTRACT** element should summarize the content of the story.

For more information, see "Creating a News Channel" in this chapter's Immediate Solutions section.

Hybrid Channels

Hybrid channels are a mix of news, immersion, and notification channels. For example, you can create a notification channel that provides news or you can create an immersion channel that also provides news.

When you develop a hybrid channel, remember to minimize the strain on bandwidth. You should also define those items that can be browsed offline and those that should only be accessed online.

Channel Delivery Mechanisms

You can use three different delivery mechanisms to push data to the user:

• Screen savers

• HTML email

• Desktop items

Screen Savers

Screen savers can deliver limited channel information to the user's screen. Internet Explorer allows HTML pages and files saved in the SCR format to be displayed on the subscriber's screen in the form of a screen saver. Any type of HTML element can be used to define the content shown on the user's screen. Animated Graphic Interchange Format (GIF) images, DHTML, and even JavaScript can be used in the channel content and viewed through the screen saver.

When the user subscribes to a channel that offers a screen saver as an **ITEM** of the **CHANNEL** element, the Channel Screen Saver dialog box appears. The user can then choose to have the information delivered through the screen saver or through another method.

The option to replace the existing screen saver with the channel's screen saver can be selected at any time, not just during the subscription process. The Channel Screen Saver can be selected as the default screen saver. First, you right-click on the Windows desktop, and select Properties from the pop-up menu. Next, you select the Screen Saver tab and select the Channel option in the list of screen savers. When the user selects the Channel Screen Saver as the default screen saver, Windows rotates through all the screen savers provided by the channel.

To designate an HTML page as a screen saver, the developer must identify it as an **ITEM** element in the CDF file. The **USAGE** value of **ITEM** is what determines that the **ITEM** element will be a screen saver. The **VALUE** attribute describes the content as a screen saver. There is no content for the **USAGE** element. Here's the code you would use:

```
<ITEMHREF="http://www.site.com/screensavers/default.htm">
  <USAGE VALUE="ScreenSaver">
  </USAGE>
</ITEM>
```

HTML Email

Subscribers have the option of receiving email notifications when the channel's content has been updated. The user can choose this option through the Subscription Wizard, and by default, the user is sent an HTML-formatted email. The HTML message includes a link to the top-level channel page. If the subscriber's email client is Outlook Express, the actual top-level page is sent and loads when the content is updated.

As with screen savers, HTML email is specified in the **ITEM** element in the top-level channel in the CDF file. The code for HTML email looks almost identical to the code for specifying a screen saver, with one exception: The value of the **USAGE** element's **VALUE** attribute is **"Email"**. Here's the code snippet:

```
<ITEM HREF="http://www.site.com/email/default.htm">
<USAGE VALUE="Email">
</USAGE>
</ITEM>
```

Desktop Items

In Windows 98, an option called the Active Desktop gave developers the ability to code information directly to the user's Windows desktop. The user can thus receive information in the form of *desktop items* without launching a browser or opening an email client. When a user has subscribed to an Active Channel and added it to his or her desktop, the channel appears as a window on the user's screen. See Figure 17.6 for an example of a computer with four Active Desktop items. The **USAGE** element for a desktop item features a number of child elements that are specific to desktop items.

Users subscribe to desktop items the same way they subscribe to any channel: through a Subscription Wizard. As with all channels, the top-level **ITEM** element's **HREF** value specifies the main page of the desktop item's content.

Elements for a desktop item help define the size of the item, the ability of the item to move, and whether the item can be resized. They also specify how the item will be interpreted and opened if the user double-clicks on it. The following elements are specific to desktop items:

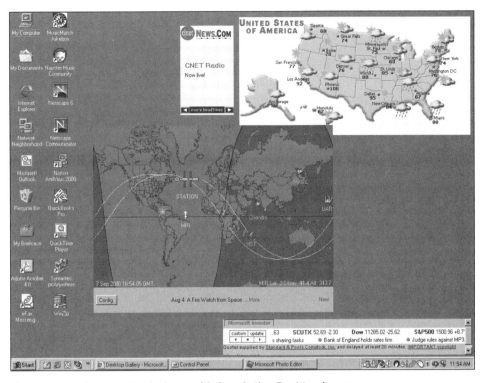

Figure 17.6   A computer desktop with four Active Desktop items.

- **OPENAS**—Specifies the file format in which the item opens. The two allowed values for this element are **HTML**, which is the default if no value is specified, and **Image**.

- **HEIGHT**—Specifies (in pixels) the height of the item as it appears on the Active Desktop.

- **WIDTH**—Specifies (in pixels) the width of the item as it appears on the Active Desktop.

- **CANRESIZE**—Specifies whether the user can resize the item after it's loaded onto the Active Desktop. Use a value of **YES** or **NO**.

- **CANRESIZEX**—Specifies whether the user can resize the item on the x-axis (horizontally).

- **CANRESIZEY**—Specifies whether the user can resize the item on the y-axis (vertically).

Other elements that can be used for—but are not specific to—desktop items include **SCHEDULE**, **TITLE**, and **ITEM**. You can use the **SCHEDULE** element to specify the schedule for updating content to the user's desktop. **TITLE** specifies the title that appears in the Web tab of the Desktop Properties dialog box and the Favorites|Subscription window.

The code for defining a desktop item looks something like this (notice that **USAGE VALUE** is set to **DesktopComponent**):

```
<ITEM HREF="http://www.site.com/channels/desktop/main.html"
PRECACHE="YES">
<TITLE>Daily Stock Quotes</TITLE>
<USAGE VALUE="DesktopComponent">
<OPENAS VALUE="HTML"/>
<HEIGHT VALUE="200"/>
<WIDTH VALUE="420"/>
<CANRESIZE VALUE="YES"/>
</USAGE>
</ITEM>
```

TIP: *The **PRECACHE** attribute you've seen in the various delivery mechanism code examples specifies whether items other than the HTML page are downloaded to the user's cache. For example, you might have several logo files, a photo, and an animated GIF that make up the top-level main page of the channel. If you set this attribute's value to **YES**, all the items associated with the Web page are cached locally and the page can be viewed offline.*

Design Guidelines for Channels

According to Microsoft, you should follow several design guidelines for developing channels. These guidelines include:

- Develop channels so they conform to the type of Active Channels outlined by Microsoft and described in "Active Channel Types" earlier in this chapter.

- Match the size of the content to the delivery capabilities of the subscribers. Consider how much data the average user can download in a few minutes. For example, if a subscriber uses a modem, the amount of data you supply should be far less than if the user is on an Ethernet network.

- Ensure that the channels are self-contained and don't require content from other sources that may not be online all the time.

- Personalize your channel, so users receive only the information they've requested.

Let's examine each channel design guideline in more detail.

Channels Should Conform to Active Channel Types

The channel you design should conform to one of the Active Channel types: news, immersion, notification, or hybrid. See "Active Channel Types" earlier in the chapter for more information on these categorizations.

Channel Content Should Match Bandwidth Constraints

You need to be aware of the bandwidth constraints your channel imposes, not only on your subscribers' connections, but also on your own connections. Ensure that your channel doesn't contain so many graphic files and so much content that you end up overloading your network and your subscribers must spend hours to download your channel content to their computers. Table 17.1 charts the average download time for 100K of data on several common connection speeds. Keep in mind that these speeds are greatly influenced by the Web server speed, the user's ISP, and the quality of the user's phone line (where applicable).

Channels Should Be Self-Contained

All content in a channel should be self-contained so it can be browsed offline. If it's not self-contained, subscribers may find that subitems are unavailable or their system is constantly reconnecting to fetch the content that isn't cached. According to Microsoft, you should minimize, hide, or consider not including links to noncached resources, particularly for content meant to be browsed offline. CGI scripting, DHTML, or JavaScript can be used to determine when the subscriber is offline. If the subscriber is offline, the script could perform functions to redisplay the data and check when the subscriber gets back online so the information could then be updated automatically.

You should reuse as many graphics as possible throughout the channel's site map. Use highly minimized graphics when you can. Consider investing in a graphics-optimizing program such as Equilibrium's Debabelizer or Macromedia Fireworks.

Channels Should Be Personalized

With the use of HTTP cookies, it's relatively easy to create a personalized browsing experience for each subscriber. By using cookies to generate a personalized CDF file, channel information can be sent faster, because content that is not applicable to the subscriber is not sent—only pertinent information is sent. See

Table 17.1 Download times for common connection speeds.

Connection Speed	Download Time for 100K
28.8Kbps	28 seconds
56Kbps	14 seconds
ISDN (64Kbps)	12 seconds
ISDN (128Kbps)	6 seconds
Cable Modem (1.5Mbps)	1 second (varies)

"Using Cookies To Create Personalized Channels" in this chapter's Immediate Solutions section for more information.

Developing for Netcaster

In theory, because CDF and HTML are so similar, browsers other than Microsoft Internet Explorer (such as Netscape Navigator) should be able to interpret the information found in the CDF file and parse it to the subscriber. However, as you may have guessed, issues exist that prevent full cross-browser compatibility. Netscape uses its own push technology—called Netcaster—to accommodate push information. When you design the CDF file and its accompanying content, be aware of the compatibility issues between the two browsers.

First, Netcaster cannot use the CDF file for full processing because it does not fully implement CDF as an XML application. However, Netcaster can use the CDF file to crawl the site, which means it retrieves and processes information for the user. The process differs only slightly from the process of retrieving information for a channel subscription:

1. An HTML page is retrieved.
2. The page is cached locally on the user's system.
3. The browser locates the links in the page.
4. For each link specified in the page, the browser retrieves and caches pages until all links have been followed or the process has been repeated enough times, as specified by certain criteria.
5. Non-HTML documents are retrieved for each link that specifies either an image file or a text file.

Netcaster treats the CDF file as if it were a standard HTML page to gather the information about where to crawl the site, but not for full CDF processing. For Netcaster to know where to start, you need to place an anchor element (**A**) within the **ITEM** and **CHANNEL** elements of the CDF file. You specify this anchor element as you would any other normal anchor element. For example, the following anchor element provides Netcaster with the information needed to start crawling the site:

```
<A HREF="http://www.site.com/netcaster/default.html">Welcome to Our Site</A>
```

The anchor element defines which links Netcaster should follow. The rest of the information found in the CDF file is normally ignored. The anchor element is nested inside the **ITEM** and **CHANNEL** elements of the CDF file. The anchor element identifies which pages are displayed when the items and channels are selected. The CDF file would look something like this:

```
<CHANNEL>
<A HREF="http://www.site.com/netcaster/mainpage.htm"></A>
<ITEM>
<A HREF="http://www.site.com/netcaster/page1.htm"></A>
<TITLE>This is Page 1 of the Site</TITLE>
</ITEM>
<ITEM>
<A HREF="http://www.site.com/netcaster/page2.htm"></A>
<TITLE>This is Page 2 of the Site</TITLE>
</ITEM>
</CHANNEL>
```

To use a CDF file to crawl a site, Netcaster must process the file as an HTML file. The CDF file must have either the .html or .htm extension, and the server storing the CDF file must return the MIME (content) type as **text/html** to the non-CDF-enabled browser. Also, the browser must be configured so that the MIME type for CDF files—specified in the browser as the **cdf** file type needing the **application/x-cdf** definition—is set to open as HTML.

TIP: *For CDF files to be processed correctly to CDF-enabled browsers, the MIME (content) **application/x-cdf** must be set on the server.*

When the browser uses the CDF file, it identifies the links in the **ITEM** element—such as **mainpage.htm**, **page1.htm**, and **page2.htm**—and crawls these pages. Much of the CDF file will be ignored. For example, Netcaster will not use the **BASE** attribute of the CDF file. Relative URLs are resolved by Netcaster against the base URL instead of the **BASE** attribute. You may decide to omit the **BASE** attribute or, if you want, to use the **BASE** attribute to make sure the name is the same as the base URL of the CDF file.

After these options are set on both the server and browser, the user can use Netcaster to subscribe to a channel defined by the CDF file. The subscription process is the same as the one used with Internet Explorer, with one exception: The user doesn't enter the URL for the CDF file. If the user specifies the URL of a CDF file, the initial page for the channel is not a normal HTML page. Instead, it's a CDF file rendered as an HTML page. The page will probably not appear correctly because the CDF file is not formatted to display HTML-formatted information.

Subscribing to CDF Files with Netcaster

The process of subscribing to a CDF-defined channel with Netcaster is the same as the process of subscribing to a channel, which is actually a Web page or Web site in Netcaster. However, if the user specifies the URL of the CDF file, the initial page of the channel is obviously not an HTML file. As a result, the page will not render properly in Netcaster. You can fix this problem by creating a transitory Web page that represents the channel content and contains a reference to the CDF file.

To make this transitory page and have it display properly in Netcaster, you can use Netscape's **LAYER** element. With a hidden **LAYER** element that references the new CDF file, users can use the transitory page rather than the URL of the CDF file when they subscribe. Use the following code to create the reference to the CDF file using the **LAYER** element:

```
<LAYER SRC="cdf_file.html" VISIBILTY="HIDDEN"></LAYER>
```

To subscribe to the channel automatically, the user clicks on the Subscription button on the transitory page. See "Creating a CDF File for Netcaster Users" in this chapter's Immediate Solutions section for the code and instructions on how to create the CDF file and the transitory page.

Examining the CDF Vocabulary

The best way to learn the CDF vocabulary is to look at an example of a CDF file. The CDF file serves to define the structure of the channel in much the same format that HTML defines a Web page. Remember, however, because CDF is an XML application, all elements must have ending tags and all attribute values must be in quotes. Each CDF file contains five main elements:

- *The document header*—Defines the file as an XML file and specifies the version of XML used.

- *The CHANNEL element*—Identifies the main page of the channel and all information about the subpages contained within the channel.

- *The TITLE element*—Provides navigational aides and identifies the title of the channel (which is displayed in the list of channels).

- *The ABSTRACT element*—Provides navigational aides and defines the tooltip text that displays when the user moves the mouse over the channel logo in the Channels Explorer Bar in Internet Explorer 4.0.

- *The LOGO element*—Defines the two different logos and the individual icon displayed in the Channels Explorer Bar, Active Desktop, and the Channel listing.

- *The ITEM element*—Defines the subpages used in the channel.

- *The SCHEDULE element*—Defines the schedule for updating channel content.

The Individual Elements and Their Attributes

In Chapter 1, you learned about markup languages and how they work. Now, you can put that information to good use. The following elements (and their attributes) were created by Microsoft developers using the XML syntax. These elements, which define the CDF XML application, are relatively simple, and their attributes are fairly limited.

The ABSTRACT Element

The **ABSTRACT** element provides a short description of the channel. This text is displayed when the user moves the cursor over the channel or item title.

The **ABSTRACT** element has one attribute, **XML-SPACE**, and is placed within the **CHANNEL** element section or within an **ITEM** subsection. **XML-SPACE** has a value that specifies how white space is treated: **DEFAULT** allows white space to be filtered out during file processing; **PRESERVE** dictates that all white space characters will be retained.

The **ABSTRACT** element must be placed after the **CHANNEL** element and before any nested **ITEM** or **CHANNEL** children. The following code is an example of how the **ABSTRACT** element is used:

```
<CHANNEL>
<ABSTRACT XML-SPACE="DEFAULT">
This channel provides information about my Web site.
</ABSTRACT>
<ITEM>
.
.
.
</ITEM>
</CHANNEL>
```

The CHANNEL Element

The **CHANNEL** element defines a channel or subchannel, and uses the following syntax:

```
<CHANNEL BASE="url" HREF="url" LASTMOD="date" LEVEL="number"
PRECACHE="YES" | "NO">
</CHANNEL>
```

The **CHANNEL** element contains information about the channel via the following attributes:

- **BASE**
- **HREF**

- **LASTMOD**
- **LEVEL**
- **PRECACHE**

The **CHANNEL** element defines the channel, all its subchannels, and other elements and attributes. The top-level channel is defined by whatever is placed within the first occurrence of the **CHANNEL** start and end tags. Every **CHANNEL** element contained within the top-level channel represents a subchannel, creating the hierarchy of the channel items.

The **BASE** attribute is used to provide a root directory for the relative URLs of the **ITEM** and **CHANNEL** subelements. If declared, the **BASE** attribute applies to all the child elements within the current channel. The **BASE** attribute of the current channel supercedes the **BASE** attribute of any parent channels. The URL must end with a trailing forward slash (/) or the last word will be removed.

The **HREF** attribute specifies a location and instructs the browser to navigate to that location when the user activates the channel. This attribute should be omitted if the **CHANNEL** element contains an anchor (**A**) as a child element.

The **LASTMOD** attribute specifies the date and time the page indexed by the **HREF** attribute was modified. This date is specified in Greenwich Mean Time (GMT), also known as Universal Time Coordinated (UTC). This time may or may not be your local time, depending upon whether you're in the same time zone as the system that is modifying the page. This attribute is used to help the client determine whether the content has changed since the last time it was downloaded. The item is downloaded only if the date associated with the cached item is older than the **LASTMOD** value in the CDF file. The date format used in the **LASTMOD** attribute is *yyyy-mm-ddThh:mm*; for example, **2000-01-01T12:01**.

The **LEVEL** attribute value specifies the number of links deep the client should crawl the site and precaches the content specified in the **HREF** attribute of the channel. If no value is set, the default is zero, which specifies that the browser should only cache the top-level content of the channel. If the URL uses frames, the client will also retrieve the content of the frameset.

The **PRECACHE** attribute specifies whether the content should be downloaded and cached on the subscriber's computer. The content is downloaded only if subscribers specify when they first subscribe to the channel that channel content should cached. If the value is set to **NO**, the content is not cached. If the value is set to **YES** or omitted, the content is cached to the subscriber's computer.

TIP: *For additional information about any CDF element, check out the Content & Component Delivery section of the MSDN Online Web Workshop located at **http://msdn.microsoft.com/workshop/**.*

Here's an example of **CHANNEL** element markup:

```
<CHANNEL HREF="http://www.site.com/channel/mainpage.htm"
BASE="http://www.site.com/channel/"
LASTMOD="2000-01-01T12:01" LEVEL="3" PRECACHE="YES">
<ITEM HREF="http://www.site.com/channel/page1.htm">
<TITLE>This is Page 1 of the Site</TITLE>
</ITEM>
<ITEM HREF="http://www.site.com/channel/page2.htm">
<TITLE>This is Page 2 of the Site</TITLE>
</ITEM>
</CHANNEL>
```

The ITEM Element

The **ITEM** element defines an item within a channel, and uses the following syntax:

```
<ITEM HREF="url" LASTMOD="date" LEVEL="number"
PRECACHE="YES" | "NO" ></ITEM>
```

ITEM can represent any type of information, but it's almost always a Web page. In the Channels Explorer bar, an **ITEM** will appear in a hierarchy pertaining to the child/subelement relationships of the **CHANNEL**. If you do not want the **ITEM** to show up in the Active Channels Explorer Bar, you can set the value of the child element **USAGE** to **NONE**.

The **HREF** attribute is required and represents the location of the item content file. When the subscriber clicks on the channel item, the browser navigates to the location specified in the **HREF**. There can be only one **HREF** attribute for each **ITEM** element.

The **LASTMOD** attribute specifies the date and time the Web page specified in the **HREF** attribute was last modified. The **LASTMOD** attribute is specified in the form *yyyy-mm-ddThh:mm*.

The **LEVEL** attribute specifies the number of links or levels deep the client should crawl and cache the Web site and graphics from within the location specified in the **HREF** attribute. If **NONE** is specified (which is the default), the client caches only the Web page of the item and the images it references. If the Web page contains frames, the client also retrieves all content inside the frames. The **PRECACHE** specification indicates whether the content should be cached on the subscriber's computer.

WARNING! You must specify the end-tag </ITEM> for the ITEM element to be processed properly.

The following code shows how the **ITEM** element could be used:

```
<ITEM
  HREF="http://www.site.com/channel/item1/mainpage.html"
  LASTMOD="2000-10-11T10:30">
  <TITLE>
    Welcome to this page.
  </TITLE>
  <ABSTRACT>Information on this page.
  </ABSTRACT>
</ITEM>
```

The SCHEDULE Element

The **SCHEDULE** element allows you to set the frequency and time for subscribers to receive channel updates. Channel updates involve downloading and saving or precaching the content specified in the **CHANNEL** and **ITEM** elements. Updating also includes sending page-hit logging information to the target server specified in the **LOGTARGET** element. The following attributes can be included in the **SCHEDULE** element:

- **STARTDATE**—Specifies the day on which the schedule starts. If you omit this attribute, updating starts on the current day.

- **STOPDATE**—Specifies the day on which the updating expires. If omitted, the schedule never expires.

- **TIMEZONE**—Specifies the difference between local time and UTC.

The following elements are children of the **SCHEDULE** element:

- **INTERVALTIME**—Declares how often the update occurs. This element is required.

- **EARLIESTTIME**—When used with the **INTERVALTIME** value, it specifies the earliest time the updating schedule applies.

- **LATESTTIME**—When used with the **INTERVALTIME** value, it specifies the latest time the updating schedule applies.

The **SCHEDULE** element must be placed within the top-level **CHANNEL** element. After the schedule is designated, all the channel items are updated at the same date and time according to the schedule outlined in the **SCHEDULE** element. You can set only one schedule per CDF file, and it's important to schedule the update for when your server load is lightest and the most bandwidth is free.

One of the children elements of the **SCHEDULE** element, **LATESTTIME**, is a very important element to include if you want to reduce server load. With **LATESTTIME**, you can set an interval, the latest time (**LATESTTIME**) minus the earliest time (**EARLIESTTIME**), during which subscribers' channel content is updated at random. This random updating prevents all subscribers from having their channel content updated at exactly the same local time.

TIP: *Dates are specified as year-month-day, as in **2000-09-22**.*

Speaking of time, the schedule is set to use the subscriber's local time zone. If you want to force updates of channel content to occur at a specific absolute time—when you know the server is not in use, for example—you can use the optional **TIMEZONE** attribute of the **SCHEDULE** element. **TIMEZONE** is expressed relative to UTC (or GMT). The following example specifies the Pacific Time Zone, which is eight hours earlier than UTC:

```
<SCHEDULE TIMEZONE="-0800"></SCHEDULE>
```

The following code snippet gives you an example of a schedule that updates content weekly between midnight and noon starting on January 1, 2000, and ending on December 31, 2001:

```
<SCHEDULE STARTDATE="2000-01-01" STOPDATE="2001-12-31">
<INTERVALTIME DAY="7" />
<EARLIESTTIME HOUR="0"/>
<LATESTTIME HOUR="12" />
</SCHEDULE>
```

TIP: *For those subscribers on local area networks (LANs), the **AutoSchedule** option applies; but dial-up users may find that their systems, if left on, dial in to the Internet unless they specify manual or custom-scheduled updates in the Channel Properties dialog box when they subscribe to your channel. Also remember that the end-tag **</SCHEDULE>** is required for the code to be valid.*

The INTERVALTIME Element

The **INTERVALTIME** element specifies the period of time that should pass before the schedule is repeated. The following syntax is used:

```
<INTERVALTIME DAY="value" HOUR="value" MIN="value"/>
```

The days, hours, and minutes are totaled to determine the length of the interval. **DAY** specifies the number of days that should pass, and the **HOUR** and **MIN** values are added to that time. Any **INTERVALTIME** value greater than half a day but less than a day is rounded up to one day. This element is a required child element of **SCHEDULE** and must always contain a value to be valid.

The following code specifies that a channel will be updated every day between 10 A.M. and 2 P.M. during the month of December 2000:

```
<SCHEDULE STARTDATE="2000-12-01" STOPDATE="2000-12-31">
<INTERVALTIME DAY="1" />
<EARLIESTTIME HOUR="10" />
<LATESTTIME HOUR="14" />
</SCHEDULE>
```

The EARLIESTTIME Element

The **EARLIESTTIME** element is a child of the **SCHEDULE** element, and specifies the earliest time the channel content can be updated. The following syntax is used:

```
<EARLIESTTIME DAY="value" HOUR="value" MIN="value"/>
```

This element adds days, hours, and minutes to the value from **INTERVALTIME** to determine when the earliest time for updating the channel content begins. If omitted, the earliest time is set to the beginning of the **INTERVALTIME** value.

The LATESTTIME Element

The **LATESTTIME** element specifies the latest time during **INTERVALTIME** that the schedule will be applied and updated:

```
<LATESTTIME DAY="value" HOUR="value" MIN="value"/>
```

This element adds the days, hours, and minutes to the value from **INTERVALTIME** to determine the latest valid time to update a channel. If you omit it, the latest time is set to the beginning of the **INTERVALTIME** value.

TIP: *If you omit both the **EARLIESTTIME** and **LATESTTIME** attributes, all of the content updates take place at the same time.*

The following code outlines how the **LATESTTIME** element would be used in a channel:

```
<SCHEDULE>
<INTERVALTIME DAY="1" />
<EARLIESTTIME HOUR="2" />
<LATESTTIME HOUR="6" />
</SCHEDULE>
```

The HTTP-EQUIV and LOGTARGET Elements

You can supply information to the server through the HTTP response headers via the **LOGTARGET** element. This element indicates that an HTTP header parameter should be added. The **NAME** attribute specifies the name of the HTTP header parameter that should be sent with the log file. For example, you may want to send the value **encoding-type** when you send back a compressed log file to the server. The **VALUE** attribute specifies the value of the corresponding parameter. The following example shows how to send a compressed log file back to the server:

```
<LOGTARGET HREF="http://www.mysite.com/logging/" METHOD="POST">
    <HTTP-EQUIV NAME="encoding-type" VALUE="gzip" />
</LOGTARGET>
```

The LOGIN Element

The **LOGIN** element specifies that the channel requires authentication for updates. A CDF file containing this element prompts the user for a name and password during the channel subscription process. Include this element by using the following code:

```
<LOGIN />
```

The LOGO Element

The **LOGO** element specifies an image that can be used to represent a channel or channel item. The following syntax is used:

```
<LOGO HREF="url" STYLE="ICON" | "IMAGE" | "IMAGE-WIDE" />
```

The **HREF** attribute specifies the URL link to the channel logo or icon image. Table 17.2 lists the values that can be associated with the **STYLE** attribute.

TIP: *GIF, JPEG, and other standard image formats supported by Internet Explorer can be used for logo images. However, animated GIF files are not supported with this element. Image formats and styles are subject to change.*

Here's an example of the code used to specify a logo image:

```
<LOGO HREF="http://www.site.com/images/logo.gif" STYLE="IMAGE"/>
```

Table 17.2   STYLE values you can specify.

Value	Size	What the Image Represents
ICON	16H x 16W	Appears in the Channels Explorer Bar hierarchy.
IMAGE	32H x 80W	Placed in the desktop Channels Bar to provide a quick launching mechanism for the main channel page.
IMAGE-WIDE	32H x 194W	Displayed in the Channels Explorer Bar to provide a link to the main channel page. When clicked, this image also expands or contracts the channel's hierarchy (if one exists) in the Channels Explorer Bar.

17. Implementing CDF

The LOGTARGET and LOG Element

The **LOGTARGET** and **LOG** elements provide you with a mechanism for tracking the number of hits to the individual channel pages you've created:

```
<LOGTARGET HREF="url" METHOD="POST" SCOPE="ALL" | "OFFLINE" | "ONLINE" >
```

Pages are tracked even while they're viewed offline. Viewing is logged with the World Wide Web Consortium (W3C) Standard Extended Log File Format, which is initially stored on the user's machine and later sent back and posted to the server during subsequent channel updates. Two elements, **LOGTARGET** and **LOG**, are required for page-view logging to be enabled.

The **LOGTARGET** element is always located in the top-level **CHANNEL** element and defines where the logged information is stored. Three attributes are used with this element: **HREF**, **METHOD**, and **SCOPE**. The **LOGTARGET** element's **HREF** attribute specifies the directory where the log file is posted. The **METHOD** attribute then specifies the transmission method used to post the file. At the time of this writing, **POST** is the only method supported, although that may change in the future. The **SCOPE** attribute specifies whether logging occurs when pages are viewed offline (**OFFLINE**), online (**ONLINE**), or both (**ALL**). In the following code example, the page is tracked, even though it's viewed offline:

```
<LOGTARGET HREF="http://www.site.com/logs/channelog.pl"
    METHOD="POST" SCOPE="OFFLINE">
    <PURGETIME=HOUR="12" />
</LOGTARGET>
```

TIP: *You can use a variety of methods to process log files, including Perl scripts or Microsoft Internet Information Server's ISAPI Dynamic Link Library (DLL).*

Each individual **ITEM** element to be logged needs to be marked with a **LOG** child element. At the time of this writing, only **DOCUMENT:VIEW** is a loggable user activity. Specify the **LOG** item as follows:

```
<ITEM HREF="http://www.site.com/channel/item1.html">
    <LOG VALUE="DOCUMENT:VIEW"/>
</ITEM>
```

The PURGETIME Element

The **PURGETIME** element is placed within a **LOGTARGET** element, and specifies the number of hours for which the logging information is considered valid. When the log file is being uploaded, any page hits older than the value specified by **PURGETIME** are not reported. In the following example, the maximum age of page hits is 12 hours:

```
<LOGTARGET HREF="http://www.site.com/logs/channelog.pl"
METHOD="POST" SCOPE="BOTH">
   <PURGETIME HOUR="12" />
</LOGTARGET>
```

The TITLE Element

The **TITLE** element defines the title of the channel content. This element has no attributes. It's used much like the **TITLE** element in an HTML document. For example, if you want to name your channel "A Day in the Life...", you include the following code within the **CHANNEL** element:

```
<CHANNEL>
<TITLE>A Day in the Life...</TITLE>
</CHANNEL>
```

The USAGE Element

The **USAGE** element appears as follows:

```
<USAGE VALUE="Channel" | "Email" |
"DesktopComponent" | "NONE" | "ScreenSaver"
| "SoftwareUpdate" > </USAGE>
```

Sometimes you may want to specify additional files—such as sound or video files—to be downloaded and placed in the user's cache for later viewing offline. To do so, you use **USAGE VALUE="NONE"**, which tells the browser that this item should be downloaded, but no usage is assigned to it at this point. The following code caches an AVI movie that can be played later:

```
<ITEM HREF="http://www.site.com/channel/movie.avi">
   <USAGE VALUE="NONE"></USAGE>
</ITEM>
```

The **USAGE** element can also be used as a parent element of **ITEM** if you want to precache multiple files. Set the subchannel's **USAGE** element to **NONE**, specify each item within the **USAGE** element, and set the **ITEM PRECACHE** attribute to **YES**. The following code caches multiple items:

```
<CHANNEL>
  <USAGE VALUE="NONE">
    <ITEM HREF="http://www.site.com/channel/sound.wav" PRECACHE="YES">
    <ITEM HREF="http://www.site.com/channel/movie.avi" PRECACHE="YES">
```

17. Implementing CDF

```
    <ITEM HREF="http://www.site.com/channel/moresound.wav" PRECACHE="YES">
  </USAGE>
</CHANNEL>
```

Table 17.3 contains a list of values for the **USAGE** element. Each value specifies the delivery-type mechanism you can use to deliver your content to the subscriber.

By now, you should realize exactly how pushy you can be, particularly with your Web-site content. CDF is one of the most exciting and easy-to-implement XML applications available. It extends the possibilities of your site by allowing users to receive information with little involvement. Channels are better than mailing lists because they offer the full content of a site instead of just the text, and they offer that content for offline browsing.

You can use the various predefined elements in the CDF in the same fashion you would use any other XML elements. All the conventions used in XML are applicable, because CDF is an XML-based application. If you have a good grasp of XML, you can quickly and easily implement channel technology within your site and start offering personalized content to visitors.

Table 17.3   USAGE values.

Value	What the Value Does
Email	Specifies that the item listed is emailed when the channel content has been updated.
NONE	When used within an **ITEM** element, the **ITEM** element will not appear in the Channels Explorer Bar.
DesktopComponent	Specifies that items will be displayed in a frame on the subscriber's Active Desktop. You can only use this value within the context of an Active Desktop item. You need to use a separate CDF file when you use this value.
ScreenSaver	Specifies that the item will be displayed as a screen saver on the subscriber's computer.
SoftwareUpdate	Specifies that the CDF file is being used for a software update channel. Software update channels let you send automatic software updates over the Web to the subscriber. You can only specify this value in a top-level channel.

Immediate Solutions

Creating a Channel

In this section, you learn how to create a CDF file that will house all the items to which the user can subscribe. You set the intervals at which the channel will update the subscriber's machine with new content, and specify what logos will be used to indicate your channel's content.

Creating the CDF File

The CDF file defines the structure of the channel. You need to create the CDF file after you've created the content and know exactly which options you're going to offer your subscribers. The syntax of a CDF file is much like the syntax in any XML or HTML document. Remember, however, that XML files require the proper syntax. Make sure elements have start and end tags, and that references to attributes are in the right case.

To create a CDF file, follow these steps:

1. Open your XML editor or a text editor, such as Notepad.

2. In the first line of the document, create the XML declaration that specifies that this is an XML document by typing the following code:

```
<?xml version="1.0"?>
```

3. Specify where the top-level main page of the channel is located, for example:

```
<CHANNEL HREF="http://www.site.com/channels/default.htm">
```

4. Use the **ABSTRACT** element as shown in this following code to define the text that displays for subscribers to see before they subscribe to the channel:

```
<ABSTRACT>This is a sample channel.</ABSTRACT>
```

5. Specify the channel's title:

```
<TITLE>The Channel Title</TITLE>
```

17. Implementing CDF

6. Specify the logo graphics for defining the channel's icons, for example:

```
<LOGO HREF="http://www.site.com/channels/channel.ico" STYLE="ICON" />
<LOGO HREF="http://www.site.com/channels/channel.gif" STYLE="IMAGE" />
<LOGO HREF="http://www.site.com/channels/channel-w.gif"
            STYLE="IMAGE-WIDE" />
```

7. Use the **ITEM** element to specify the channel's subpages (the **ITEM** element defines the subpage and various **ITEM** information):

```
<ITEM HREF="http://www.site.com/channels/subpage.html">
  <ABSTRACT>This is the subpage for the Channel</ABSTRACT>
  <TITLE>Subpage Title</TITLE>
</ITEM>
```

8. Complete the XML file by specifying the channel end tag:

```
</CHANNEL>
```

9. Use the .cdf extension to save the files as a CDF file.

TIP: *Remember to include references for pages if you plan to offer this channel to Netcaster users.*

Identifying the Main Page or CHANNEL Element

The main page of the channel is identified by the top-level **CHANNEL** element, and the information about the channel's subpages is contained between the start tag, **<CHANNEL>**, and the end tag, **</CHANNEL>**. In the opening **CHANNEL** element, identify the URL of the channel's main page with the **HREF** attribute, for example:

```
<CHANNEL HREF="http://www.site.com/channels/mainpage.html">
```

Describing the Channel and Its ABSTRACT and TITLE Elements

The **ABSTRACT** element appears as a tooltip when the subscriber moves the mouse over the channel logo in the Channels Explorer bar. It also helps relay information about what's contained in the channel. The **TITLE** element is a short description of what is displayed in the list of channels provided in the Favorites menu. The **ABSTRACT** and **TITLE** elements are used within both the **CHANNEL** element and the **ITEM** element. To define **ABSTRACT** and **TITLE** elements, type the following code within either the **CHANNEL** or **ITEM** element:

```
<TITLE>The Channel Title</TITLE>
<ABSTRACT>This is the abstract information.</ABSTRACT>
```

Describing the ITEM Element

The **ITEM** element helps define the channel's subpage. Within the **ITEM** element, specify the **HREF** attribute, which points to the URL of the subpage. The **ABSTRACT** and **TITLE** elements further define for the subscriber the information held within each **ITEM** by giving short descriptions of what will appear in the channel, via the Channels Explorer Bar and the tooltip. The code snippet used to define an **ITEM** subpage looks like this:

```
<ITEM HREF="http://www.site.com/channels/subpage.html">
  <ABSTRACT>The subpage for the Channel would be listed here.</ABSTRACT>
  <TITLE>The Channel Subpage</TITLE>
</ITEM>
```

Specifying the Logos for the Channels Explorer Bar

The **LOGO** element identifies the two logo images and one icon that will be used within the Channels Explorer Bar. The logo images should be saved in GIF format and the icon should be saved in ICO format. You should use images no more than 194 by 32 pixels and 80 by 32 pixels for the images and 16 by 16 pixels for the icon. The **LOGO** element does not have a content model specification, which means it does not have an end tag. You close it by placing a forward slash (/) at the end of the element declaration. Here's code you could use to specify both the images and icon graphics:

```
<LOGO HREF="http://www.site.com/channels/icon.ico" STYLE="ICON" />
<LOGO HREF="http://www.site.com/channels/image1.gif" STYLE="IMAGE" />
<LOGO HREF="http://www.site.com/channels/image-w.gif" STYLE="IMAGE-WIDE" />
```

Specifying Content to Be Precached

Information that should be cached (such as content used with immersion channels) or any content that should be available for offline viewing needs to be specified by using the **ITEM** element's **PRECACHE** attribute. For example, here's some code to define content that should be downloaded and cached on the subscriber's computer:

```
<ITEM HREF="http://www.site.com/channels/subpage.html"
PRECACHE="YES">
  <ABSTRACT>Abstract information for the page</ABSTRACT>
  <TITLE>Page Title Information</TITLE>
</ITEM>
```

17. Implementing CDF

You can precache individual files by using the **USAGE VALUE** element/attribute. For example, you can precache sound files with the following code:

```
<ITEM HREF="http://www.site.com/channels/sound.wav">
  <USAGE VALUE="NONE"></USAGE>
</ITEM>
```

You can also precache multiple items by setting a subchannel's **USAGE VALUE** to **NONE** and then specifying child **ITEM**s, as follows:

```
<CHANNEL>
  <USAGE VALUE="NONE">
    <ITEM HREF="http://www.site.com/channels/sound1.wav" PRECACHE="Yes">
    <ITEM HREF="http://www.site.com/channels/sound2.wav" PRECACHE="Yes">
    <ITEM HREF="http://www.site.com/channels/sound3.wav" PRECACHE="Yes">
  </USAGE>
</CHANNEL>
```

Specifying the Delivery Schedule

You can set the frequency for channel-content updates by using the **SCHEDULE** element to specify the schedule, for example:

```
<SCHEDULE STARTDATE="2000-01-01">
  <INTERVALTIME DAY="7" />
  <EARLIESTTIME HOUR="0" />
  <LATESTTIME HOUR="12" />
</SCHEDULE>
```

This code defines a schedule to update the channel content once a week between midnight and noon starting January 1, 2000. You should definitely include the **LATESTTIME** element. If you omit it, all users' channels will be updated at exactly the same local time, which can result in server overload.

You can set an interval by using **EARLIESTTIME** and **LATESTTIME**. Doing so will update the content randomly within this interval, thereby reducing server load. All channel items are updated according to the schedule you've outlined for the top-level **CHANNEL** element. Only one schedule can be specified in a CDF file. After an update has taken place, an email message can be sent to the subscriber if the CDF file has changed.

TIP: *LAN-connected users will automatically adhere to the schedule for content updates that is defined in the CDF file. Dial-up users will need to update their channels manually or create a custom schedule in the Channel Properties dialog box when they subscribe to a channel.*

Adding the Channel to the Web Site

After you've created the CDF file, have the graphics for your various channel logos, and know where you want to place the channel, all that's left is to place the file on a Web (HTTP) server. Users can then subscribe to the channel by clicking on a link to the CDF file. Again, the link can be a text link or an icon with the **HREF** attribute specifying its value. It should be apparent to the user that the icon or text is a link to subscribe to the channel.

If you're not using a FrontPage-enabled Web server, you can use an FTP program or Internet Explorer to connect to your Web server and upload the channel. Specify the login name, password, FTP location, and directory in the Address field of the browser or open the folder for the site and the browser will open a new window.

Follow these steps to use Internet Explorer to upload the CDF file and all the accompanying graphics to the Web site:

1. Store CDF file, graphics, and content in a folder or subfolder. You may want to store the CDF file and the graphics in the main folder, and the actual content in the subfolder.

2. Connect to the Internet and launch Internet Explorer.

3. Type "**ftp://login:password@ftpsite.com/directory/**" in the Address field, substituting the login name, password, and directory locations with your own information.

4. Upload your CDF file, your icon graphic, your channel graphics, and the content. You'll have to upload your files individually, because browsers do not offer batch uploading options at this point.

Creating Various Types of Channels

In this section, you'll learn how to create the various types of channels that Microsoft specifies. You will create immersion, notification, and news channels. You'll see how the channel types differ and what each channel does.

Creating an Immersion Channel

Each item in the CDF file of an immersion channel must include child elements with the **USAGE VALUE** element set to **NONE**. The following code is an example of a simple maze game. Different Web pages serve as the various hallways subscribers move through to find their way out. Listing 17.2 shows the markup for the CDF file.

Listing 17.2   The markup for a CDF file of an immersion channel.

```xml
<?xml version="1.0"?>
<CHANNEL HREF="http://www.site.com/games/maze/startpage.html"
BASE="http://www.site.com/games/maze/">

<TITLE>The Maze Game</TITLE>
  <ABSTRACT>Find your way out of our maze!</ABSTRACT>
    <LOGO HREF="maze_icon.gif" STYLE="ICON"/>
    <LOGO HREF="maze_image.gif" STYLE="IMAGE"/>


<SCHEDULE STARTDATE="2000-10-10" STOPDATE="2000-10-10">
   <INTERVALTIME DAY="1"/>
</SCHEDULE>

<ITEM HREF="hallway1.html" LASTMOD="2000-10-10T11:00">
   <USAGE VALUE="NONE"></USAGE>
</ITEM>

<ITEM HREF="hallway2.html" LASTMOD="2000-10-10T11:00">
   <USAGE VALUE="NONE"></USAGE>
</ITEM>

<ITEM HREF="hallway3.html" LASTMOD="2000-10-10T11:00">
   <USAGE VALUE="NONE"></USAGE>
</ITEM>

<ITEM HREF="hallway4.html" LASTMOD="2000-10-10T11:00">
   <USAGE VALUE="NONE"></USAGE>
</ITEM>

<ITEM HREF="roomNN.html" LASTMOD="2000-10-10T11:00">
   <USAGE VALUE="NONE"></USAGE>
</ITEM>

</CHANNEL>
```

You start this CDF file by declaring the channel, and then you declare the various items within the channel. The **TITLE** element specifies the game's title, and the **ABSTRACT** element displays descriptive information about the game. The **SCHEDULE** element specifies when new hallways will be updated. Each item defined specifies a hallway in the maze. Each time the CDF file is updated, you dynamically generate a new CDF file that creates new hallways. You could also modify existing hallways.

Creating a Notification Channel

The only purpose of a notification channel is to notify the subscriber of new content. Therefore, all items should display abstracts, but content should not be precached to the subscriber's computer. Suppose, for example, that you work in the human resources department and you want to notify employees about new employee benefits, changes in the payroll process, and upcoming company holidays. You can use a notification channel to tell employees about new information in the human resources section on the company Web site. The following code is an example of how a CDF file for a notification channel is constructed:

```
<CHANNEL HREF="http://www.site.com/notify/hr/main.html"
BASE="http://www.site.com/notify/hr/" PRECACHE="NO">

  <TITLE>Available HR Info</TITLE>
  <ABSTRACT>Information about your human resources department.</ABSTRACT>
  <LOGO HREF="logo16x16.gif" STYLE="ICON"/>
  <LOGO HREF="logo32x80.gif" STYLE="IMAGE"/>

  <SCHEDULE STARTDATE="2000-12-12" STOPDATE="2000-12-12">
     <INTERVALTIME DAY="1"/>
  </SCHEDULE>
</CHANNEL>
```

Creating a News Channel

News channels deliver information to subscribers in the form of stories. They are different from notification channels, because the content is actually cached to the subscriber's computer and subchannels are used to define the various stories. You can use the **ABSTRACT** element to identify the information that is contained in the channel. The **TITLE** element defines the news story headline. Also, each page contains the same graphics, which create the consistent look of a newspaper but alleviate the bandwidth requirement.

The CDF file creates the hierarchy and serves to organize the channel's items into subchannels, which are actually the individual stories. This example uses one channel, the Business Channel; within it are the stories for one section. The CDF file is shown in Listing 17.3.

Listing 17.3   The markup for a CDF file of a news channel.

```
<?xml version="1.0"?>
<CHANNEL HREF="http://www.site.com/channels/news/news.html"
BASE="http://www.site.com/channels/news/">

  <TITLE>Today's News</TITLE>
  <ABSTRACT>Today's News delivered to your electronic doorstep.</ABSTRACT>
```

17. Implementing CDF

```
    <LOGO HREF="logo16x16.gif" STYLE="ICON"/>
    <LOGO HREF="logo32x80.gif" STYLE="IMAGE"/>

    <SCHEDULE STARTDATE="2000-12-12" STOPDATE="2000-12-12">
       <INTERVALTIME DAY="1"/>
    </SCHEDULE>

<CHANNEL HREF="news1.html">
  <TITLE>Business News</TITLE>
  <ABSTRACT>Today's Business News</ABSTRACT>
  <LOGO HREF="street.gif" STYLE="ICON"/>

<ITEM HREF="news2.html" LASTMOD="2000-12-12T01:00">
  <TITLE>Today's News Headline</TITLE>
  <ABSTRACT>News Headline</ABSTRACT>
  <LOGO HREF="bizlogo.gif" STYLE="ICON"/>
</ITEM>

<ITEM HREF="news3.html" LASTMOD="2000-12-12T01:00">
  <TITLE>News Headline
  <ABSTRACT>Today's News Headline</ABSTRACT>
  <LOGO HREF="bizlogo.gif" STYLE="ICON"/>
</ITEM>
</CHANNEL>
</CHANNEL>
```

In this example, "Today's News" is shown in the Channels Explorer Bar. Because you do not include a **PRECACHE ITEM** attribute, all the content will be cached on the subscriber's computer. This caching allows the subscriber to view the news offline.

Creating Various Delivery Channels

In this section, you learn how to create the various types of delivery channels, including desktop channels, desktop screen savers, and HTML email.

Creating a Desktop Channel

Desktop channels require a separate CDF file. The file's **USAGE** element uses a number of child elements to specify various attributes for the desktop item channel. These attributes include **OPENAS**, **HEIGHT**, **WIDTH**, and **CANRESIZE**. See "Desktop Items" earlier in this chapter for explanations of the attributes used with desktop items.

The CDF files for desktop items can also have a **SCHEDULE** element to specify when automatic updates can occur. The markup in Listing 17.4 creates a desktop item.

Listing 17.4   Creating a desktop item using CDF.

```
<?xml version="1.0"?>
<CHANNEL>
  <SCHEDULE STARTDATE="2000-01-01">
    <INTERVALTIME DAY="7" />
    <EARLIESTTIME HOUR="0" />
    <LATESTTIME HOUR="5" />
  </SCHEDULE>

  <ITEM
   HREF="http://www.site.com/channels/desktopitem.htm"
    PRECACHE="YES">
    <TITLE>The Desktop Item</TITLE>
    <USAGE VALUE="DesktopComponent">
      <OPENAS VALUE="HTML" />
      <HEIGHT VALUE="200" />
      <WIDTH VALUE="320" />
      <CANRESIZE VALUE="NO" />
    </USAGE>
  </ITEM>

</CHANNEL>
```

In this example, the **HREF** attribute in the top-level **ITEM** element specifies which page to display on the subscriber's Active Desktop. When the subscriber opens the item, the page is displayed in HTML format.

Creating a Desktop Screen Saver

You can present your channel content as a screen saver on the subscriber's computer. In the CDF file, specify which page you want to turn into a screen saver and specify the **USAGE VALUE** as **ScreenSaver**, as shown in the following code:

```
<ITEM
HREF="http://www.site.com/channels/screensaver.html"
PRECACHE="yes">
<USAGE VALUE="ScreenSaver"></USAGE>
</ITEM>
```

The screen saver **ITEM** must be placed in the top-level **CHANNEL** element. When the user subscribes to the channel, a dialog box that provides a choice between the channel screen saver and the existing (nonchannel) screen saver will be presented.

17. Implementing CDF

Windows will rotate through all screen savers provided by the subscriber's channels. All screen saver behavior can be controlled through the Screen Saver Properties dialog box.

Creating HTML Email

To create an HTML email message that notifies subscribers of changes to your channel, set **USAGE VALUE** to **Email**. If subscribers elect to receive email notifications, they will be sent a link to the main top-level channel page as HTML. If a subscriber is using Microsoft Outlook, the main channel content page will load in the email message. Here's the code used to create an HTML email notification:

```
<ITEM HREF="http://www.site.com/channels/emailchannel.htm">
<USAGE VALUE="Email"></USAGE>
</ITEM>
```

Creating Advanced Channel Features

In this section, you learn how to create some advanced channels, including a multilevel channel and a channel that crawls a site for new content. You also learn how to track the usage of a particular channel. These advanced features go beyond the creation of a simple channel with a few channel items.

Creating a Multilevel Channel

To create multiple levels within your channel, place the **CHANNEL** elements within the main **CHANNEL** declaration and then place the **ITEM** elements within the subchannels, as shown in Listing 17.5.

Listing 17.5   Markup that creates a multilevel channel.

```
<CHANNEL HREF="http://www.site.com/channels/main.html"
BASE="http://www.site.com/channels/">
   <ITEM HREF="item_1/main.html">
      <ABSTRACT>This is the first item in the top-level channel.
      </ABSTRACT>
   </ITEM>
   <ITEM HREF="item_2/main.html">
      <ABSTRACT>This is the second item in the top-level channel.
      </ABSTRACT>
   </ITEM>
   <CHANNEL HREF="subchannel_1/main.html">
      <ITEM HREF="subchannel_1/item_1/main.html">
      <ABSTRACT>This is the first item in the first subchannel.
      </ABSTRACT>
   </ITEM>
```

```
        <ITEM HREF="subchannel_1/item_2/main.html">
        <ABSTRACT>This is the second item in the first subchannel.
        </ABSTRACT>
    </ITEM>
    </CHANNEL>
    <CHANNEL HREF="subchannel_2/main.html">
    <ITEM HREF="subchannel_2/item_1/main.html">
        <ABSTRACT>This is the first item in the second subchannel.
        </ABSTRACT>
    </ITEM>
    <ITEM HREF="subchannel_2/item_2/main.html">
        <ABSTRACT>This is the second item in the second subchannel.
        </ABSTRACT>
    </ITEM>
    <ITEM HREF="subchannel_2/item_3/main.html">
        <ABSTRACT>This is the third item in the second subchannel.
        </ABSTRACT>
    </ITEM>
    </CHANNEL>
</CHANNEL>
```

The preceding code creates second-level subchannels. The first subchannel contains two items, and the second contains three items. Unlike the top-level channel, subchannels containing items do not require an associated page. In other words, you do not have to specify an **HREF** attribute. This is what happens when you don't specify an **HREF** page:

- If a **BASE** parameter has not been declared for the top-level channel, the page that is displayed in the subscriber's current browser window is shown when the subscriber clicks on the subchannel's folder.

- If you have defined a **BASE** parameter, the base page is displayed in the browser window when the subscriber clicks on the subchannel's folder.

- If you specify the **HREF** attribute for the subchannel, the page to which the **HREF** attribute refers loads in the subscriber's browser window when the subscriber clicks on the subchannel folder.

Make sure every start tag has an accompanying end tag (unless it is an empty element). Also, remember that you can have only one top-level **CHANNEL** element per CDF file. Multiple channels must be nested within a single, root **CHANNEL** element. A document with the following structure would be invalid, and only the first **CHANNEL** element would be recognized:

```
<CHANNEL>
    <ITEM>
    </ITEM>
</CHANNEL>
```

17. Implementing CDF

```
<CHANNEL>
   <ITEM>
   </ITEM>
</CHANNEL>
```

The graphic used to signify subchannels is a simple default "book" graphic unless you use the **LOGO** element to specify another one. The following code specifies a specific icon instead of the default icon:

```
<LOGO HREF="http://www.site.com/channels/logo.gif" STYLE="ICON" />
```

Creating Crawling Options

Internet Explorer can connect to the Internet and check Web pages during channel updates. This process is called *site crawling*. The CDF file can specify the number of link levels deep the browser should crawl as it works its way through the channel. Within the CDF file, you can specify whether the pages that are crawled should be cached.

You can set the level of crawling by specifying the **LEVEL** attribute of the **CHANNEL** and **ITEM** elements. A value of **0** indicates that Internet Explorer should visit only the page defined in the **CHANNEL** or **ITEM HREF** attribute. A value of **1** tells Internet Explorer to crawl the **HREF** page and all the pages to which **HREF** links. The higher the number, the deeper Internet Explorer crawls.

You can mix and match the **PRECACHE** options to specify which pages should and shouldn't be cached as the site is crawled. The code for instructing a browser to crawl a site follows this format in the CDF file:

```
<ITEM HREF="http://www.site.com/channels/mainpage.htm"
PRECACHE="yes" LEVEL="0">
   <ABSTRACT>Channel Abstract Information</ABSTRACT>
   <TITLE>Channel Title Information</TITLE>
</ITEM>
```

The preceding code tells the subscriber's browser to precache the page **mainpage.htm**. No other pages or links will be crawled, because the **LEVEL** value is set to **0**.

Tracking Channel Usage

If you want to know who's getting the information you're sending, you can use the mechanisms in the CDF language to track hits to individual channel pages. Tracking allows you to find out who's viewing which pages, even if the pages are normally set to cache offline. Logging is done through the W3C Standard

Extended Log File Format. The log file is initially stored on the subscriber's computer and then later posted to the server when the channel updates are performed.

To track usage, you need to use two elements: **LOGTARGET** and **LOG**. The **LOGTARGET** element should be located in the top-level **CHANNEL** element because it specifies where the log file will be placed. The **HREF** attribute of the **LOGTARGET** element specifies the directory or location of the log file. The **METHOD** attribute specifies the method of transmission. Currently, the only method you can use is the **POST** method, but that may change soon. The **SCOPE** attribute specifies whether offline (**OFFLINE**), online (**ONLINE**), or all (**ALL**) page views should be logged in the log file. The following code specifies that all page views should be logged:

```
<LOGTARGET HREF="http://www.site.com/channels/log.pl"
           METHOD="POST" SCOPE="ALL">
  <PURGETIME=HOUR="12" />
</LOGTARGET>
```

Each individual item to be logged must be marked as such with a **LOG** child element. Currently, only **DOCUMENT:VIEW** is supported as loggable user activity. The following line of code causes an entry to be made in the log file every time the page is viewed:

```
<LOG VALUE="DOCUMENT:VIEW" />
```

You can use a number of methods to process log files, including Perl scripts or the ISAPI DLL (if you're running your channels off IIS server). Logs of individual **ITEM** elements are stored on your server, so you should specify what you wanted logged with some care.

Creating a CDF File for Netcaster Users

To make CDF files available for Netcaster users, you need to create both the CDF file and a transitory page that gives users the ability to subscribe to and view the content in Netcaster. To make this process clearer, let's look at the code for the CDF file, followed by the code for the transitory page that enables the user to subscribe to the channel. The CDF file code should have the .cdf extension. The file that includes the following code is named **cdf_file**:

```
<?xml version="1.0"?>
<CHANNEL HREF="http://www.site.com/netcaster/mainpage.htm">
  <ABSTRACT>This is the main page of the Channel</ABSTRACT>
  <LOGO HREF="http://www.site.com/netcaster/logos/logo.gif" STYLE="IMAGE"/>
  <SCHEDULE>
    <INTERVALTIME DAY="1"/>
  </SCHEDULE>
```

```
<!--These items allow the Netcaster user
    to view the Channel content offline. -->
    <ITEM><A HREF="http://www.site.com/netcaster/page1.htm"></A></ITEM>
    <ITEM><A HREF="http://www.site.com/netcaster/page2.htm"></A></ITEM>
    <ITEM><A HREF="http://www.site.com/netcaster/page3.htm"></A></ITEM>
</CHANNEL>
```

Notice that the **ITEM** elements specify the additional pages that will be downloaded to the client and made available for offline browsing. The next step is to create a copy of this file and name it **cdf_file.htm** so the CDF file can be viewed and used by Netcaster users.

Now, you need to create a section of code for the transitory Web page that allows the Netcaster user to subscribe to the channel. Notice that the **LAYER** element is used. You should name this second file something like **channel.htm** and it should reference the **cdf_file.cdf**. The code for this transitory page, shown in Listing 17.6, contains not only HTML, but also JavaScript to display the pages accurately.

Listing 17.6   Code for a transitory page.

```
<HTML>
<BODY>
<LAYER SRC="cdf_file.htm" VISIBILITY="HIDDEN"></LAYER>

<SCRIPT language="Javascript 1.2">
var nc - components["netcaster"];
nc.activate();
var chan = nc.GetChannelObject();
chan.url = "http://www.site.com/netcaster/channel.htm";
chan.name = "My Channel";
chan.desc = "This is a JavaScript
generated Channel using the JavaScript
API extensions";
chan.cardURL = "http://www.site.com/netcaster/logos/logo.gif";
function openDialog() { nc.AddChannelObject (chan);}
</SCRIPT>

</BODY>
</HTML>
```

Using Cookies to Create Personalized Channels

It's possible to customize channel content based upon user preferences saved in HTTP cookies. You can integrate CDF files with Internet Explorer browser cookies to present specific information to each of your subscribers. You do so using the subscriber's browser preferences to create a dynamically generated, customized CDF file.

To create a personalized channel, you should be familiar with cookies. If you don't know how to create cookies, check the MSDN Online Web site, located at **http://msdn.microsoft.com**, for more information. Search for the keyword "cookies."

Perform the following steps to create personalized channel content:

1. Create a form to request specific information from a visitor to your site who is a potential subscriber. The information will be used to customize the content for the user.

2. Save the information in the form to the Web server or within a cookie on the user's computer.

3. When the subscriber's Internet Explorer browser requests an updated CDF file from the server, the server downloads an existing CDF file specified by the preferences stored in the cookie file. The other option is to create a dynamically generated file to match the user's profile.

If you're using an IIS server to dynamically generate personalized CDF files, you must insert the following line of code at the top of your CDF file so the server will send the personalized CDF file. This code returns the correct MIME content type to the browser and will perform the expected actions for CDF files:

```
<% Response.ContentType = "application/x-cdf"%>
```

Optimizing the Delivery of Active Channels

Aside from cutting down on the amount of content pushed to a subscriber and making sure you only cache the required content, you should follow a few more steps to ensure that delivery of your channel is optimized. These steps support various HTTP headers. These headers check to make sure the server is not unnecessarily transferring data when it shouldn't be. Specifically, you should follow these suggestions for your HTTP headers:

• Use the **ITEM** element's **LASTMOD** attribute. Doing so prevents the user's computer from hitting the server again and again trying to retrieve content based on the last modified date for each item you reference in your channel's CDF file. As a result, the browser will download only the changes you've made. If your Web pages don't change often, using **LASTMOD** won't be a problem. Of course, if your content changes frequently, a dynamically generated CDF file is in order.

• Use the **If-Modified-Since** request header in the CDF file.

• Make sure you use the **EXPIRES** response header to indicate the lifetime of the response (in other words, the length of time the resource should remain active).

- Within the CDF file, make sure you use the **HEAD** and **GET** requests in the **Last-Modified** response header. By specifying these elements in the response header, the CDF client can monitor changes made to the channel without having to download any channel resources.

- Make sure you don't send the **Pragma:no-cache** response header unless you absolutely have to.

- Consider scheduling. The **SCHEDULE** element dictates the server load. It's important to manage schedules if you plan to facilitate your subscribers' demand for information. Make sure you list the update schedule near the beginning of your CDF file. The most effective update interval is once a day. Be sure to set the **INTERVALTIME** and **LATESTTIME** elements properly. And, schedule your updates for when your subscribers will most likely be connected if your content is important—stock quote updates need to be scheduled during the day, not at night or on the weekends.

- Let the client browser do the load balancing. Without the **INTERVALTIME** attribute, your channel is updated randomly. As a result, you have no control over when the content updates. If you specify a value for the **INTERVALTIME** attribute, you can control exactly what time the content should be updated. Scheduling the updates to download during wide time frames helps reduce server load. You could create a 23-hour interval to accomplish a wide time-frame parameter.

- Make sure you keep your updates reasonably sized to accommodate the average subscriber's connection rate.

Internet Explorer and Active Desktop can handle your updates, and you should let them. Because many subscribers may not have their machines on all the time, their computers will queue up the next updates. However, be aware of the following problems associated with allowing the client to update content automatically:

- If a user cancels the update, the browser will not attempt the update again until the next scheduled update.

- Updates interrupt the subscriber's computer, which could confuse or annoy subscribers who might decide to cancel the update or even the subscription.

- If the auto-dialer connection fails to update the CDF file, it will not try again during that update. It will wait until the next update is scheduled.

- If the computer gets a time-out error during a scheduled update, it will not try to reconnect to the server. This is why it's important to balance the load and keep the size of updates small.

- If the computer is able to connect to the server but there's a download failure, it will not attempt the update again during that scheduled update.

Optimizing a Channel for the Subscriber

Here are a few tips for optimizing your CDF file and channel content for the subscriber:

- Change the CDF file so the subscriber is notified of new content. Doing so will cause the notification item to be sent to the user, if you include such an item in your CDF file. Changing the CDF file can be as simple as adding a blank space somewhere and saving the file on the server.

- If appropriate, personalize your content for the subscriber. Doing so will give your subscribers more of what they are looking for. Give the subscriber options for specifying content and delivery mechanisms.

- Use Active Server Pages to give the subscriber a uniform and simple interface.

Using CDF Generator to Build Channels

Coding CDF files by hand can be time-consuming and error-prone. Fortunately, tools are available that will create CDF files for you. Microsoft FrontPage 98 features a CDF Wizard, and Microsoft also has a free CDF Generator application available for download from its Web site.

Because its sole purpose is to create CDF files, CDF Generator offers more advanced features than the FrontPage 98 CDF Wizard. It supports all CDF elements, has a simple and easy-to-understand user interface, and can edit your existing CDF files to eliminate code errors. Please note, however, that although CDF Generator creates valid CDF documents, the documents it produces will not be considered well formed and valid by an XML processor. Because it's free software, there's no reason not to use the CDF Generator when programming your channels.

TIP: Microsoft's CDF Generator is available for download from the MSDN Online Web site at **http://msdn.microsoft.com/downloads/tools/cdfgen/cdfgenerator.asp**.

CDF Generator makes creating a CDF file incredibly easy—as long as you have planned your channel content, schedule, and logging procedures beforehand. The following are the steps you need to take to create a new CDF file using CDF Generator:

1. In the CDF Generator application window, select File|New to open the Channel Creation Wizard.

17. Implementing CDF

2. The first page of the wizard, shown in Figure 17.7, allows you to set up your top-level channel. Decide if you would like the **HREF** of your **CHANNEL** element to be an attribute or an anchor (**A**) element, and select the appropriate radio button. Enter the URL of your main channel's content page. You can also enter a value for the channel's **BASE** and **SELF** attributes. Click Next when you're ready to continue.

3. In the next window, you can enter a **TITLE** value and an **ABSTRACT** value for your channel. You can also specify that you would like this channel logged by clicking the **LOG** checkbox. Click Next to continue.

4. The next window specifies the **LOGO** elements. It contains a checkbox and field for each **STYLE** of logo (**ICON**, **IMAGE**, and **IMAGE-WIDE**). Select the checkboxes of those logos that you're using, and enter the names of the image files. Click Next when you're ready.

5. The channel update schedule is specified in the next window, shown in Figure 17.8. Here, you can select the attributes of the **SCHEDULE** element that you would like to use and set values for them. Click Next to continue.

6. The following window is used to specify the destination of the log file. If you're using CDF's logging function, specify an **HREF** for the **LOGTARGET** element, the values of the **METHOD** and **SCOPE** attributes, and the **PURGETIME** subelement. If you're not using a log file, uncheck the Log Target checkbox. Click Next to continue.

7. The final window shows a preview of your CDF code. If the code is as intended, click Finish. If not, click Back to change information in previous screens.

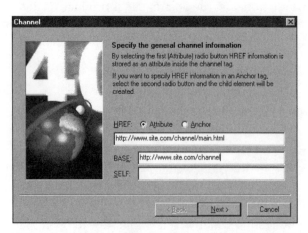

Figure 17.7   The first page of the Channel Creation Wizard.

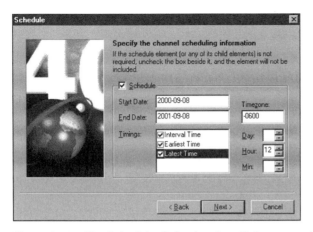

Figure 17.8   The Schedule dialog box in which you specify the channel update schedule.

8. When you're finished with the wizard, the code is shown in the right pane
    of the CDF Generator application window (see Figure 17.9). You can now
    add subchannels, items, logins, and all other CDF elements by using the
    Tag|New menu item and selecting one of the element options there. Each
    element has a wizard similar to the one for the top-level channel.

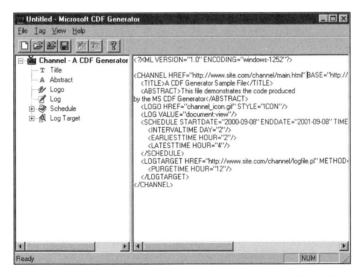

Figure 17.9   The CDF Generator application window displaying the CDF code.

Chapter 18

Building Web Pages with XHTML

In Depth

In this chapter, you'll learn what the Extensible Hypertext Markup Language (XHTML) is, how it compares to HTML, and how to make an XHTML document well-formed. In addition, you'll find out the specifics of browser support for XHTML and learn a little about its specification.

XHTML: XML-Compliant HTML

XHTML is the latest World Wide Web Consortium (W3C) Recommendation for the unification, or merger, of HTML 4 and XML: XML for syntax and HTML for the vocabulary of elements. This merger allows authors many options. One option is to stick with what you know and use the HTML 4 elements much like you've probably been doing for the last year or so. Another option is to extend the HTML 4 element set and introduce your own XML elements. And finally, you can combine XML vocabularies—for example, an XHTML document could include Scalable Vector Graphics (SVG), the Mathematical Markup Language (MathML), or any other predefined XML vocabulary.

XHTML sets the stage for a compliant Web that conforms to multiple user agents, such as browsers, screen readers, and other Web-access tools. In addition to offering the features of traditional browsers, XHTML is designed to encourage automated exchange and retrieval of documents, as well as to expand the scope of user agents.

The early goals of XHTML are best described as transitional. Whereas HTML mixes content- with presentation-based markup, XHTML focuses more on structure-driven markup. This transition encourages a wider base of accessibility, because XML stresses document structure and content and relies on Cascading Style Sheets (CSS)—or the Extensible Stylesheet Language (XSL)—for presentation.

This move toward XHTML has created both positive and negative reactions within the Web community. Developers who need documents to be machine readable, while maintaining human readability, seem to be enthusiastic. However, those developers are also concerned about widespread acceptance. Meanwhile, traditional Web designers fear that they will be faced with learning yet another variation of HTML, while still bemoaning the lack of presentation consistency between browsers.

For those who are learning Web markup for the first time, XHTML is just as easy to learn as HTML. In fact, many students seem to respect the well-formedness and consistency of elements that XHTML offers. As for dyed-in-the-wool HTML users, the transition can be made easier by using one of the several code-checking tools available, such as HTML Tidy. (See "Converting a Document Using HTML Tidy" in the Immediate Solutions section of this chapter for more information.)

XML is the *X* (Extensible) in XHTML, and it provides extensibility to HTML. Simply put, an extensible language allows the declaration of elements and attributes as outlined in a Document Type Definition (DTD), which creates a greater scope of usability for a document. Special DTDs are becoming available for e-business and many other document-rich sectors. XHTML is expressed through three XML DTDs: Strict, Transitional, and Frameset. You'll find out more about these DTDs in the "XHTML-Specific Rules" section later in this chapter.

Straight from the horse's mouth (this is a direct quote from W3C, at **www.w3.org/TR/xhtml1/#xhtml**), the benefits of XHTML are as follows:

- XHTML documents are XML conforming. As such, they are readily viewed, edited, and validated with standard XML tools.

- XHTML documents can be written to operate as well or better than they did before in existing HTML 4-conforming user agents as well as in new, XHTML 1.0-conforming user agents.

- XHTML documents can utilize applications (e.g. scripts and applets) that rely upon either the HTML Document Object Model (DOM) or the XML DOM.

- As the XHTML family evolves, documents conforming to XHTML 1.0 will be more likely to interoperate within and among various XHTML environments.

The benefits of XHTML will become more apparent as the transition to XML gathers momentum. Instead of being saddled with a lot of almost-useless HTML documents, with XHTML, you can be prepared for the transition and know that any changes and retro-coding will not be in vain.

As a starting point, most current HTML 4 pages can be automatically validated and brought up to XHTML standards with a utility such as Dave Raggett's HTML Tidy. This wonderful tool can assist in many of the mundane re-coding chores that XHTML compliance requires.

TIP: *To see how to convert an HTML document to XHTML using HTML Tidy, read the "Converting a Document Using HTML Tidy" section of the Immediate Solutions later in this chapter.*

For the most part, however, HTML and XHTML are much more similar than they are different. Unlike HTML, all elements, attributes, and values in XHTML must be in lowercase (unless specified otherwise in an associated DTD). The days of "anything goes" are behind us. Believe it or not, incorrect coding is a very easy habit to break, and most WYSIWYG editors will allow you to set lowercase as the default in the software's preferences menu.

Another major change is the need to close all element tags. Unfortunately, the built-in forgiveness (and bulk) of most browsers has allowed sloppiness to go unpunished for years. With XHTML, all tags must be closed or accommodated. For most tags, you will use the familiar code ***<tagname>...</tagname>***. However, empty elements, or elements that do not contain text to be marked up, are handled differently than you're used to. Empty elements are closed by putting a backslash (*/*) at the end before the closing greater-than sign. In addition, for backward compatibility, you should insert a space before the closing slash. For example, in XHTML, the familiar **
** element is now written as **
**. See the "XHTML Documents are Well-Formed" section later in this chapter for more information on the requirements of XHTML.

If you take the initiative to make the leap to XHTML from HTML, the benefit will be a head start toward understanding the markup of the future—namely, XML and beyond.

HTML and XHTML Compared

In this section, we'll compare HTML and XHTML from a practical standpoint, as opposed to a theoretical one. A great number of HTML documents exist in various states of disarray, and today's Web designers are faced with bringing them into compliance or replacing them. To effectively achieve this goal, you need to understand how HTML and XHTML differ, how they remain the same, and what you must change in HTML documents to make them compatible with XHTML.

Comparing HTML 4 with XHTML 1.0 is very much a matter of "mostly the same, only different." Whereas HTML has traditionally been an anything-goes-if-it-works type language, XHTML brings some new, stricter rules to the party:

- Element and attribute names must be lowercase. In other words, they're case sensitive.

- Tags must be nested correctly.

- All elements must be closed. In other words, nonempty elements require close (end) tags and empty elements must be terminated correctly.

- All attribute values must be quoted (single or double quotation marks will do; you just need to be consistent).

- The element hierarchy must follow that defined by the document's DTD.

- All documents must have a root element. For XHTML, that root element must be the **html** element.

- All documents must follow XHTML-specific rules (see the "XHTML-Specific Rules" section later in this chapter).

Case-Sensitive Tags

Looking at the most sweeping changes, we start with *case sensitivity*. In HTML, the case of attributes and attribute values does not really matter—except in the context of file names or within the content itself. Many of us even use uppercase markup to improve readability. In XHTML, however, case *does* matter (because XML is case sensitive). All XHTML elements and attributes must be lowercase, and attribute values are case sensitive. The conversion to lowercase has the potential to be a very laborious step in document conversion. Luckily, however, many of the HTML editors provide you with the option of lowercasing tags and attributes. Looking more closely, a traditional HTML element could be written as follows:

```
<A HREF="somefile.htm">
```

or

```
<A href="somefile.html">
```

However, in XHTML, the previous code must be written as follows:

```
<a href="somefile.html">
```

Note that in both examples, the file name (which is quoted) should be treated as though it's case sensitive.

The case sensitivity of XHTML elements also greatly expands the use of the elements. In HTML, **<B>** and **<b>** are the same element: They both render boldface text. Therefore, most browsers will interpret the text between the start and end tags as boldface text. However, an XHTML-compliant browser with a DTD reference will be able to take advantage of the expanded definitions as defined in the DTD. Doing so will allow a great degree of backward compatibility, and still allow for a much smoother transition to XHTML and beyond.

Proper Tag Nesting

The next important change from HTML to XHTML deals with element nesting. Again, in HTML, the order in which you opened and closed nested (or *concurrent*) elements was not terribly important. Okay, it really was illegal in HTML to nest your tags incorrectly; however, browsers implemented a feature that allowed overlapping of elements so they could make sense of incorrectly nested tags and wouldn't return an error. Therefore, many Web developers didn't nest their tags correctly. However, in XHTML, nesting is critical.

Nesting is one of the main tenets of a well-formed document. Because the goal of XHTML is to allow the *structure* of the document to be defined (as does XML), nesting and well-formedness are paramount. Overlapping (incorrectly nested) elements create confusion and invalidate a document in XHTML.

The following markup is illegal in XHTML because the bold (**b**) element is closed before the italic (**i**) element:

```
<b>This text is boldfaced, whereas <i>this text is
    italicized and boldfaced.</b></i>
```

The previous markup *will* display correctly in HTML. However, it's not well-formed in XHTML, which requires the following markup:

```
<b>This text is boldfaced, whereas <i>this text is
    italicized and boldfaced.</i></b>
```

Notice how the **i** element is closed before the **b** element. As mentioned, the first example is presented without question in almost any HTML browser, but it will not pass the well-formed test in XHTML. Again, the motivation for this change comes from XML, in which data containment and structure are the main goals of the markup. In the past, HTML authors were concerned with correct nesting only in the case of table row (**tr**) and table data (**td**) elements, because improper nesting of these elements would cause random or unpredictable table cell placement or would crash the page without displaying anything. The same idea holds in XHTML, but it applies to *all* elements, not just table elements.

As with making all elements lowercase, checking element nesting looks intimidating. However, software tools are available to help you fix your documents—they will either repair the documents for you or identify the lines that need fixing. (See the "Converting a Document Using HTML Tidy" section later in this chapter in the Immediate Solutions section.)

Element Closure and Termination

In XHTML, all element tags must be properly terminated, or closed—this means empty elements as well as closing tags. Ending element tags are a component of strict HTML, but they were considered optional by most HTML authors. If you've followed good practice in HTML coding, then this issue (with the exception of empty elements) will not be as challenging as some of the other requirements.

Many common HTML elements must be properly closed, simply as a result of their display properties. For example, if you don't close an anchor (**a**) or bold (**b**) element, you can see the error when the document is displayed. Therefore, for any element that uses *both* starting (opening) and ending (closing) element tags, practice remains the same in XHTML as it was in HTML.

However, with elements such as the paragraph (**p**) element, the closing tag was assumed, or optional. The following was valid in HTML:

```
<p>I'm a paragraph.
<p>I'm another paragraph.
```

But with XHTML, you must *always* close the paragraph element with **</p>**. So, the previous code becomes:

```
<p>I'm a paragraph.</p>
<p>I'm another paragraph.</p>
```

This one element will probably create more headaches than any other when you're changing your code to XHTML.

Empty elements are those that do not contain any other content, but stand-alone. For example:

```
<img src="image.gif">
```

The **img** element does not use a closing tag in HTML or XHTML. However, in XHTML, it does require an indication of closure, or termination; you signal closure by putting a backslash (*/*) before the greater-than bracket, like so:

```
<img src="image.gif" />
```

You'll notice in this code that a space appears before the slash. This space is necessary for backward compatibility with older browsers.

You need to add this markup to commonly used empty elements, such as **img**, **br**, and **hr**. The markup for these empty elements becomes:

```
<img />
<br />
<hr />
```

Quoted Attributes

In HTML, you could be a bit sloppy when it comes to quoting attribute values. Usually, the browser would figure out what you meant; and if it didn't, the element was ignored. For example, in HTML, you could use the following markup:

```
<a href=http://www.lanw.com>LANWrights, Inc.</a>
```

However, in XHTML, you must quote all attribute values to ensure a document is well-formed.

Quotes must be used for all values and file names. You can use either single or double quotation marks; we suggest that you just be consistent in your usage. We prefer to use double quotation marks because they're a little easier to see:

```
<a href="http://www.lanw.com">LANWrights, Inc.</a>
```

XHTML-Specific Rules

With HTML, you could get away with leaving out certain elements, such as the **head** and **title** elements; however, XHTML isn't as forgiving. The format for an XHTML document requires that you:

• Validate against one of the three available XHTML DTDs.

• Use a document type (DOCTYPE) declaration before the root element.

• Include an **html** root element that designates the XHTML namespace.

You can also enter an XML declaration. The XML declaration looks like this:

```
<?xml version="1.0" encoding="UTF-8"?>
```

It is considered good practice to include this reference on the first line, before the DTD. You can read more about XML declarations and DTDs in Chapter 5.

Related solution:	Found on page:
Creating and Specifying the DTD	142

The Three DTDs

As we mentioned, XHTML documents must be validated against a DTD, which provides the ground rules for the document to follow. In HTML, the DTD was automatically assumed by the browser. In XHTML, however, you must declare a DTD using a DOCTYPE declaration. You can choose from three DTDs: Strict, Transitional, and Frameset.

***WARNING!** Case is important in the DOCTYPE declaration, as is choosing the correct DTD. To be sure you choose the proper DTD, study either the DTD itself or the information on the W3C site at www.w3.org/TR/xhtml1/#dtds.*

The first of the three DTDs, *XHTML Strict*, is best used in the case of a document that must have very clean structural markup, with no presentation elements of any kind. This DTD requires a proper CSS style sheet to provide the information for presentation—fonts, colors, and so on. (You can read more about style sheets in Chapter 10.) The DOCTYPE declaration for the XHTML Strict DTD is:

```
<!DOCTYPE html PUBLIC "-//W3C//DTD XHTML 1.0 Strict//EN"
"http://www.w3.org/TR/xhtml1/DTD/xhtml1-strict.dtd">
```

The second DTD type (or *flavor*) is *XHTML Transitional*. This DTD allows the greatest public access and flexibility. It's also supported by older browsers that still use presentation markup that is independent of a required style sheet. You can include CSS in an XHTML document that has the Transitional DOCTYPE declaration, but it's optional. Most authors will opt for this flavor of XHTML, and it should be treated as the default DTD. The DOCTYPE declaration for the Transitional DTD is:

```
<!DOCTYPE html PUBLIC "-//W3C//DTD XHTML 1.0 Transitional//EN"
"http://www.w3.org/TR/xhtml1/DTD/xhtml1-transitional.dtd">
```

Last, we have *XHTML Frameset*, which allows the creation of documents with multiple frames in the browser window. When you use this DOCTYPE declaration, you use the **frameset** element in place of the **body** element. The DOCTYPE declaration for the Frameset DTD is:

```
<!DOCTYPE html PUBLIC "-//W3C//DTD XHTML 1.0 Frameset//EN"
"http://www.w3.org/TR/xhtml1/DTD/xhtml1-frameset.dtd">
```

The DOCTYPE Declaration

Because this use of the DTD is new to many HTML authors, some description of its use is in order. Let's use the XHTML Transitional DOCTYPE declaration for our example:

```
<!DOCTYPE html
PUBLIC "-//W3C//DTD XHTML 1.0 Transitional//EN"
"http://www.w3.org/TR/xhtml1/DTD/xhtml1-transitional.dtd">
```

This entire code snippet is placed on the very first line of the document, before any other markup—except the XML declaration (**<?xml version="1.0" encoding="UTF-8"?>**) if you decided to use it. It appears even before the **html** element itself. This code indicates to the browser (or validator) that the DTD should be referred to for parsing the document's structure.

This declaration states that all markup (elements, attributes, and values) should be used within the context of

```
"-//W3C//DTD XHTML 1.0 Transitional//EN"
```

This snippet indicates a DTD in English (**EN**) for XHTML 1.0 provided by W3C. Therefore, any markup found in this document is compared to the XHTML 1.0 Transitional DTD and used in the manner prescribed. If markup that isn't defined by the DTD is found, the browser or parser will display the raw source code. This reference is crucial for XHTML to work properly.

The XML Namespace

As is true for XML, XHTML is well-formed only if it contains a root element. Unless you're referencing a DTD other than one of the three XHTML DTDs, the **html** element will be your root element. Within the root element, you need to declare a namespace. An XHTML namespace uniquely identifies all elements as XHTML elements. Namespaces are fairly complicated, and you can find out more about them as they apply to XML in Chapter 15.

In an XHTML document that uses one of the three XHTML DTDs, you should use the following namespace:

```
<html xmlns="http://www.w3.org/1999/xhtml">
```

The style and script elements

We must also note the change to the **style** and **script** elements. It's now suggested that you declare these elements using

```
<script> <![CDATA[ ... script content goes in here ... ]]> </script>
```

and

```
<style> <![CDATA[ ... style content in here ... ]]> </style>
```

Note that the XHTML version of the **script** element does not include a **language** attribute. In addition, both elements must include the **CDATA** section, which is XML syntax stating that the contained instructions are of the type **CDATA**. **CDATA** markup specifies that the text enclosed contains characters that would otherwise be considered markup. This section can be viewed almost as a meta-escaped sequence. The characters **]]** delimit the **CDATA** and indicate the end of the character block.

If you use an external style sheet or script, these changes can be ignored. They're only meant for proper, self-referring, well-formed XHTML documents that contain script or style information.

Also, in the past, it was acceptable to use the comments (<!--...-->) to hide script or style contents; however, we don't suggest you use this method anymore. It may cause the XML processor to remove the script or style content.

It is a bit more complex than the traditional **html** element of HTML; but by declaring the XML namespace, (**xmlns=**), you meet compatibility requirements of XML and continue on your way to a well-formed XHTML document.

Putting It All Together

The following are examples of a typical HTML document and a minimal XHTML document. First, here's a typical HTML document:

```
<html>
  <head>
   <title>A typical HTML Document</title>
  </head>
    <body>
      <p>This is a typical HTML Document, but not technically correct.
    </body>
</html>
```

The HTML in this example is *not* well-formed, but it's typical of the code HTML authors write every day. In fact, if you asked someone if it seemed correct, chances are that he or she would say, "yes."

Next, here are the bare bones for a well-formed XHTML document:

```
<?xml version="1.0" encoding="UTF-8"?>
<!DOCTYPE html PUBLIC "-//W3C//DTD XHTML 1.0 Transitional//EN"
"http://www.w3.org/TR/xhtml1/DTD/xhtml1-transitional.dtd">
<html xmlns="http://www.w3.org/1999/xhtml" xml:lang="en" lang="en">
  <head>
   <title>A Proper XHTML Document</title>
  </head>
    <body>
      <p>This is a proper XHTML Document.</p>
    </body>
</html>
```

By this time, you should notice the differences between a properly marked up HTML document and an improperly marked up one.

XHTML Documents Are Well-Formed

The concept of a well-formed document has its roots in the Standard Generalized Markup Language (SGML) and XML. To be honest, the idea of a well-formed document has not been of much concern for most HTML developers. In the past, simply testing a Web page on a variety of browsers and on various platforms was deemed adequate. If a page displayed correctly, it was often assumed to be written correctly. With XHTML, and its goal of compliance with XML, the consideration of and need for well-formed documents becomes much more critical.

In XML 1.0, the W3C defines (this is a direct quote from the W3C) a well-formed document as follows (see **www.w3.org/TR/REC-xml#sec-well-formed**):

- It contains one or more elements.

- There is exactly one element, called the *root*, or *document element*, no part of which appears in the content of any other element. For all other elements, if the start-tag is in the content of another element, the end-tag is in the content of the same element. More simply stated, the elements, delimited by start- and end-tags, nest properly within each other.

In addition, if you need to use markup characters such as **<** and **&** as part of your content, you must escape them properly (in other words, they must appear as character references, built-in entities, or be enclosed in **CDATA** sections). Basically, if you read the previous section that compared XHTML to HTML, and you follow all those rules (recognizing case sensitivity, nesting all tags correctly, closing all elements, quoting attributes, and making sure all the necessary pieces and parts are in your XHTML document), your document will be well on its way to being well-formed.

Browser Support for XHTML

Browser support for XHTML 1.0 is best described as elusive. As of this writing, no native browsers support *just* XHTML. However, because one of the foundations of XHTML is the extension of HTML 4.0, browsers that support HTML 4 will in turn support XHTML, with some gaps.

When an HTML 4 browser (such as Amaya, Netscape Navigator 4 and higher, Microsoft Internet Explorer 4 and higher, or Opera) encounters an XHTML document, the results will most likely be acceptable. As we stated previously, the HTML component of XHTML exists to ensure backward compatibility with legacy browsers. In the case of each browser flavor, the more recent the browser, the better the results.

In the case of XHTML, a strong push is being made to accommodate non-browser type access agents. These include (but are not limited to) Web appliances, mobile phones, personal digital assistants (PDAs), and other non-traditional browsing tools. The XML-derived components of XHTML are more capable of matching up content and markup, devices, and style sheets than HTML 4—for example, the application of CSS for non-Web applications, and the ability of XML to be parsed by software.

Numerous elements are being deprecated in XHTML 1.0. When an element is deprecated, it will not be used in future versions of the XHTML specification. For the most part, the presentational elements have been deprecated in favor of the use of style sheets. By exploring these elements, you can get a sense of how the current crop of Web browsers may render your document.

Elements that will be unsupported in the future (most likely omitted from XHTML 1.1) include:

• **base**

• **basefont**

• **center**

• **font**

• **frame**

• **frameset**

• **iframe**

• **isindex**

• **menu**

• **noframes**

• **s**

• **strike**

• **u**

For each of these elements, alternatives or replacements will be suggested. As is the case with XHTML elements, older browsers that do not recognize the newer elements will simply ignore them.

Changes are also planned for many element attributes, primarily in position attributes and color attributes. Most of these attributes will be controlled in CSS; but that is another sticky issue for browser support, especially CSS 2. See Chapter 10 for more information on CSS.

The XHTML Specification in Review

Let's go over the specification for XHTML 1.0 as presented by the W3C in their January 26, 2000 Recommendation. This specification can be found in its entirety at **www.w3.org/TR/xhtml1/**. We'll examine the key points of the recommendation in relation to HTML 4 and XML 1.0, and then explore how each point impacts actual Web applications.

Overview

The XHTML 1.0 Specification is defined by W3C as "a reformulation of HTML 4 as an XML 1.0 application." To the Web developer, this means that XHTML 1.0 is an evolutionary step in HTML. Because it's not a dramatic departure from HTML 4 and considers backward compatibility of great importance, it remains in the spirit of earlier revisions of HTML.

The way that XHTML is designed allows it to evolve with the needs of the Internet, especially regarding the growth of non-browser agents, such as mobile phones, Internet appliances, and the like. It's estimated that these alternative platforms for Internet document viewing will compose as much as 75 percent of all platforms by the year 2002. Bear in mind, however, that this figure is for *all* Internet documents (the bulk of which are email), *not* specifically Web pages.

The XHTML specification states very clearly that XML is a driving force behind the reformulation. In one of the bullet points, it states specifically that, "XHTML documents are XML conforming." This means that XHTML documents can be viewed, edited, and validated using XML tools. You do so through the proper use of one of the three XHTML 1.0 DTDs (Strict, Transitional, or Frameset).

The specification goes on to assure us that, "XHTML documents can be written to operate *as well or better* than they did before in existing HTML 4-conforming user agents…." Through the use of proper nesting, case sensitivity, and the correct DTD, documents can be presented much more predictably and uniformly.

Another benefit of the XHTML guidelines is a document's ability to use either the HTML DOM or the XML DOM when calling scripts or applets. Simply put, this benefit provides for a vastly greater choice of DOM applications dictated by the scope and purpose of the authored document. (See Chapter 19 for more information on the XML DOM.)

Finally, the point is strongly made that XHTML is "…the next step in the evolution of the Internet." This fact allows the XHTML standards to incorporate new accessibility tools and methods, and to adapt more readily to the proliferation of non-traditional Internet devices. Unfortunately, HTML—though serving so gallantly for so long—has finally painted itself into a corner for any application beyond presentation.

The XML Factor

A small portion of the XHTML specification describes XML and its heritage as a subset of SGML. Although HTML was based on principles of SGML, XML adheres more closely to the format and specificity of SGML. The goals of XML include power and flexibility, both of which are assets of SGML. However, SGML can be intimidating in its complexity. XML maintains most of the positive features of SGML through its extensibility, power, versatility, and flexibility, while avoiding most of the complexity.

By blending the strength of XML with the familiarity of HTML, the W3C hopes to create a bridge standard that can be understood and applied by the majority of Web authors. The W3C states that one of the benefits of the migration to XHTML 1.0 is that many Web developers and user agent designers will be able to expand their ideas more readily through the extensibility factor brought in by XML. Because most of these developers are already pushing the envelope with markup, providing a framework for developing and sharing new techniques will enhance the entire community. One of these new frameworks is *XHTML Modules*.

The concept of XHTML modularization is based on creating feature sets that can be easily incorporated into existing and new designs by combining new XML elements and attributes into XHTML modules. You can find more information about XHTML Modularization at **www.w3.org/TR/2000/WD-xhtml-modularization-20000105/**.

As we stated earlier, XHTML also addresses the new limitations placed on HTML by non-traditional Internet user agents. HTML met the challenge of Web browsers, but began to fall short with the rapid proliferation of PDAs, mobile phones, and so on. XML and its associated components allow XHTML to meet the needs of these users and to continue to expand and meet the needs of future hardware advances.

In the heart of the basis of XHTML, however, remains the concept of familiarity along with extensibility; and this goal seems to be met in the XHTML 1.0 recommendation.

Definitions and Terminology

Although many of the terms and definitions used in the XHTML specification are consistent with other W3C publications, a bit of a review never hurts. Therefore, in this section of the specification, you find out how various words in the specification are used. You're already familiar with most of the terms in this list, so we won't bore you with the details again. However, if you need a refresher, visit **http://www.w3.org/TR/xhtml1/#terms**. For a complete list of definitions, see RFC2119 at **www.w3.org/TR/xhtml1/#ref-rfc2119**.

Strict Conformance

An XHTML document must meet four criteria for strict conformance:

- It must validate against one of the three DTDs: Strict, Transitional, or Frameset.

- The document must have a root element, such as **html**.

- The root element must designate the XHTML namespace, using the **xmlns** attribute.

- The DTD must be referenced in a DOCTYPE declaration prior to any other markup (except the optional XML declaration, which indicates the version of XML referred to in the **version** attribute).

Strict conformance is validated against one of the three DTDs, which is specified in the document.

User Agent Conformance

Criteria also exist for user agent conformance. You won't be interested in this topic unless you plan to create a browser (see **www.w3.org/TR/UAAG/** for more details). Nine major points and many minor ones appear in the specification, but some key concepts are:

- The user agent must parse and validate the XHTML document for well-formedness.

- If a user agent claims to support facilities, as defined in the specification, then it must remain consistent with the facilities definition.

- If a user agent doesn't recognize an element, it should still render the element's content.

- If an agent doesn't recognize an attribute, it must ignore it.

- If an agent doesn't recognize an attribute value, it should use the default value.

This short list is not complete, by any means, and the rest of the guidelines deal mainly with characters and their representation. The essence of what is presented in the previous list is that if a user agent does not now how to present an element, attribute, or value, it should not crash or return an error as a result, but instead should ignore the confusing portion or use a default. You can find the complete list at **www.w3.org/TR/2000/WD-xhtml-modularization-20000105/ conformance.html#s_conform_user_agent**.

The XHTML 1.0 specification defines and describes many of the differences from HTML 4. A few of these have been covered in other areas of this chapter (see "HTML and XHTML Compared").

Immediate Solutions

Converting a Document from HTML to XHTML

The steps required for document conversion from HTML 4 to XHTML 1 are fairly simple. Document conversion can be done either by hand or using various tools. We first cover how to convert an HTML document by hand, and then we use HTML Tidy to convert the same document.

Converting a Document by Hand

You will use the requirements outlined in the section "HTML and XHTML Compared" to convert this incorrect HTML document to a correct XHTML document, all by hand:

```
<html>
  <head>
   <TITLE>My XHTML Document</Title>
  </head>
    <body>
      <p>This is an XHTML document. Our Web site can be found at
      <a href=http://www.lanw.com>LANWrights, Inc.</a>
      <p>I want to put a line break here. <br>
      <p>I want this to be <em>emphasized.</p></em>
    </body>
</html>
```

Let's start by correcting the existing code. Then you will add the necessary information at the beginning of the document. Follow these steps:

1. Make sure all elements and attributes are lowercase. Change this line of markup

    ```
    <TITLE>My XHTML Document</Title>
    ```

    to read

    ```
    <title>My XHTML Document</title>
    ```

2. Make sure all documents are nested correctly. Change this markup

```
<p>I want this to be <em>emphasized.</p></em>
```

to read

```
<p>I want this to be <em>emphasized.</em></p>
```

3. Make sure all elements are terminated properly. You need to close all the **p** elements and put the appropriate markup (*/*) at the end of empty elements. In addition, you need to quote all attribute values. This markup

```
<p>This is an XHTML document. Our Web site can be found at
<a href=http://www.lanw.com>LANWrights, Inc.</a>
<p>I want to put a line break here. <br>
```

needs to look like this:

```
<p>This is an XHTML document. Our Web site can be found at
<a href="http://www.lanw.com">LANWrights, Inc.</a></p>
<p>I want to put a line break here.</p> <br />
```

4. Optionally, place the following line of code as the first line of the document:

```
<?xml version="1.0" encoding="UTF-8"?>
```

5. Assess which DTD (of the three) should be used. More often than not, the Transitional DTD is the preferred choice. Add the following markup under the XML declaration added in Step 4:

```
<!DOCTYPE html
PUBLIC "-//W3C//DTD XHTML 1.0 Transitional//EN"
"http://www.w3.org/TR/xhtml1/DTD/xhtml1-transitional.dtd">
```

6. Follow this line with the **html** element, including the XML namespace attribute:

```
<html xmlns="http://www.w3.org/1999/xhtml" xml:lang="en" lang="en">
```

7. Put it all together, and your final document looks like this:

```
<?xml version="1.0" encoding="UTF-8"?>
<!DOCTYPE html
PUBLIC "-//W3C//DTD XHTML 1.0 Transitional//EN"
"http://www.w3.org/TR/xhtml1/DTD/xhtml1-transitional.dtd">
<html xmlns="http://www.w3.org/1999/xhtml" xml:lang="en" lang="en">
  <head>
   <title>My XHTML Document</title>
  </head>
    <body>
        <p>This is an XHTML document. Our Web site can be found at
        <a href="http://www.lanw.com">LANWrights, Inc.</a></p>
        <p>I want to put a line break here.</p><br />
        <p>I want this to be <em>emphasized.</em></p>
    </body>
</html>
```

This process can be accomplished in any text editor that is suitable for HTML documents, such as Notepad or WordPad. However, the task can be daunting and tedious. Luckily, you can use some widely available tools—such as HTML Tidy—to speed the task along.

Converting a Document Using HTML Tidy

HTML Tidy does all the things you did manually in the previous section automatically. HTML Tidy is currently available for the following platforms and operating systems:

- AIX 4.3.2 (and later)
- Amiga
- Atari
- BeOS
- FreeBSD
- HP-UX
- Linux
- Mac OS
- MiNT (Atari) OS
- MSDOS
- OS/2
- RISC OS
- Solaris
- UnixWare
- Windows 95/98/NT/2000

18. Building Web Pages with XHTML

HTML Tidy is very easy to configure with a configuration file or from the command line. The HTML Tidy Web site at **www.w3.org/People/Raggett/tidy/** contains adequate documentation and information about an HTML Tidy users' group.

HTML Tidy has several front ends available for Microsoft Windows 9x. For our example, we'll use TidyGUI (available at **http://perso.wanadoo.fr/ablavier/ TidyGUI/**). It's a graphical front end to HTML Tidy that makes the process much more user-friendly for Windows users.

After you download TidyGUI, follow these steps to convert your document to XHTML:

1. Open the TidyGUI.exe file.
2. Click on the Configuration button, which displays the Tidy Configuration dialog box.
3. On the Markup tab, shown in Figure 18.1, choose the Loose DTD from the Doctype pull-down menu.

NOTE: *The Loose DTD is actually from HTML; however, when you choose it from TidyGUI or HTML-Kit (covered in the following section), the XHTML Transitional DTD markup is inserted into your document.*

4. Choose the XML tab and check the Output As XHTML and Add XML Declaration checkboxes, as shown in Figure 18.2. Click on Apply. (Note that because you checked the Add XML Declaration checkbox, the Output As XML checkbox is checked automatically when you click Apply.)
5. Close the Tidy Configuration dialog box. Click the Browse button to search for the HTML file you want to convert.

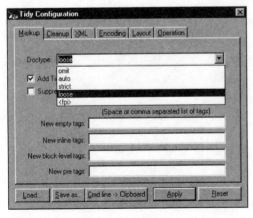

Figure 18.1   The Tidy Configuration dialog box Markup tab.

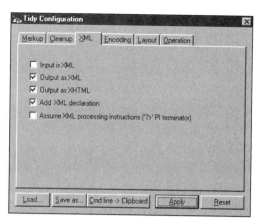

Figure 18.2   The Tidy Configuration dialog box XML tab with the appropriate checkboxes checked.

6. After you choose the file, click on the Tidy! button. The results are shown in Figure 18.3. You'll notice that the errors found are listed in the bottom pane by line number.

7. Click the Show Output button. The results are displayed in all their glory (see Figure 18.4).

8. Click the Save As button. Save the file with a new name, and you're done: You have a well-formed XHTML document.

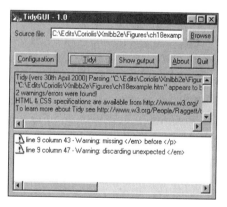

Figure 18.3   The results shown when you click on the Tidy! button.

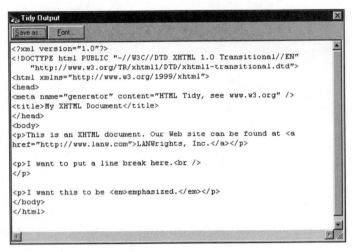

```
Tidy Output                                                              X
Save as    Font
<?xml version="1.0"?>
<!DOCTYPE html PUBLIC "-//W3C//DTD XHTML 1.0 Transitional//EN"
    "http://www.w3.org/TR/xhtml1/DTD/xhtml1-transitional.dtd">
<html xmlns="http://www.w3.org/1999/xhtml">
<head>
<meta name="generator" content="HTML Tidy, see www.w3.org" />
<title>My XHTML Document</title>
</head>
<body>
<p>This is an XHTML document. Our Web site can be found at <a
href="http://www.lanw.com">LANWrights, Inc.</a></p>

<p>I want to put a line break here.<br />
</p>

<p>I want this to be <em>emphasized.</em></p>
</body>
</html>
```

Figure 18.4   Well-formed XHTML document output created by TidyGUI.

Using HTML-Kit to Build and Implement XHTML

Because XHTML is relatively new, few tools are available yet that are designed specifically for XHTML. However, you can use HTML tools or XML tools to achieve the necessary results. (See Chapter 23 for a list of XML tools.)

In this section, you'll use HTML-Kit to create the beginning of a well-formed XHTML document. You can download HTML-Kit from **www.chami.com/html-kit/**. After you install HTML-Kit, follow these steps to create a new XTHML document:

1. Launch HTML-Kit and choose Create A New File, as shown in Figure 18.5. Click OK.

2. An untitled document is displayed. Notice that the DOCTYPE declaration and the required elements are already displayed (see Figure 18.6).

3. Notice that you're missing a couple of elements necessary to create a well-formed XHTML document. As with TidyGUI, you need to make sure the preferences are set to produce the desired input. Choose Edit|Preferences from the toolbar.

4. In the Preferences dialog box's Tidy tab (which appears by default), make the following changes:

   - Change the Output setting to XHTML.

   - Make sure the Add XML Processing Instruction and Assume XML Processing Instructions checkboxes are checked in the Switches list.

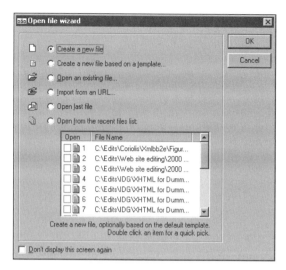

Figure 18.5   The Open File Wizard of HTML-Kit.

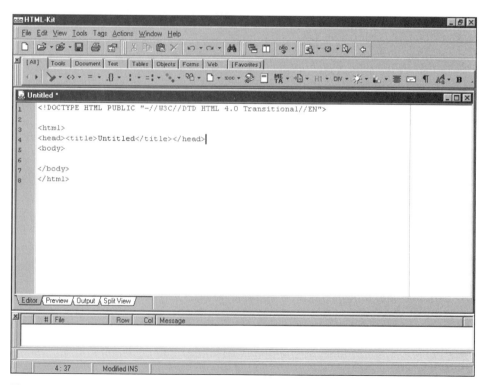

Figure 18.6   An untitled document in HTML-Kit.

- Choose the appropriate DTD for your document. For this example, choose the Loose DTD (which produces the markup from the Transitional DTD).

  Your Tidy tab should now look similar to Figure 18.7.

5. Make any other changes you desire and click OK to save your preferences.

6. Choose Actions|Tools|HTML Tidy|Convert To XTHML. The HTML-Kit screen changes to Split View, and the XHTML is generated in the right pane, as shown in Figure 18.8. Notice that the XML declaration and the XML namespace have both been added to the markup.

7. To save this change and use it to create your well-formed XHTML document, choose Edit|Copy Output To Editor. Alternatively, you can right-click in the right pane and choose Copy All To Editor from the pop-up menu.

8. Click the Editor tab at bottom left on the screen and begin creating your XHTML document.

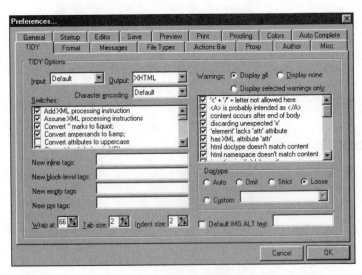

Figure 18.7   The Tidy tab of the HTML-Kit Preferences dialog box.

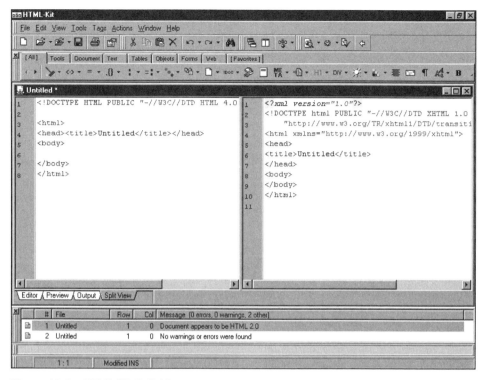

Figure 18.8   HTML-Kit Split View.

Chapter 19

Processing XML

In Depth

To see the results of the markup and content of the XML documents and Document Type Definitions (DTDs) you've created, you must process the information contained within them. When an XML document is processed, it actually goes through several steps before the content is finally displayed or handled in some other way by the application using it. These steps—which often include parsing and style-sheet formatting or transformation but may also include being inserted into a database or sent across the Internet to control the behavior of an application—make up the overall concept of XML document processing.

In this chapter, we'll examine your XML-processing options. We'll review parsers and how they work, and we'll look at the application programming interfaces (APIs) that are available for XML document objects so you can display or work with the contents of any given XML document. In addition, we'll show you how you can use Java and C++ to create bridges to XML documents and objects within those XML documents. In this chapter's Immediate Solutions section, we'll show you how to create the code used to help connect XML documents with browsers and other programs.

The Basics of Processing XML Documents

What is an XML processor? In the most basic terms, a *processor* is a software module that reads XML documents and provides access to their structure and content. Processing in the XML world can be done with parsers and processors, both of which survey the structure of the XML document and pass the results to an XML application, which in turn does something with the content. The purpose of processing is to interpret the structure, report errors, and then—assuming the errors aren't too grave—pass the interpretation to another XML application.

NOTE: *In XML 1.0, the terms parser and processor used interchangeably ususally when referring to Web browsers.*

A good example of a processing application is a Web browser. Remember that the browser's goal is to display the contents of the XML file, so the paces it puts an XML document through are to achieve that end. A browser goes through four basic steps to get the XML structure and content you've created to the point where the information can be displayed:

1. Parse the XML document and associated DTD to gather the structural information about the document the browser needs to display its content. The parser may be a validating parser that checks whether the document is valid and well formed, or it may be a non-validating parser that checks for only well formedness.

NOTE: *Remember that you can build XML documents that don't have DTDs and still use the documents. Because we recommend that you build DTDs for most documents, we include them in all our examples. If the XML processor uses a validating parser, you need to supply a DTD for your document.*

---

2. Process the parsing results and check for errors. Most browsers that support XML will not continue processing an XML document if it contains errors. To be sure that your document isn't halted during processing because of errors, be sure to validate it during development.

3. Process any Cascading Style Sheet (CSS) or Extensible Stylesheet Language (XSL) style sheets associated with the document.

4. Display the information according to the style-sheet formatting instructions.

These processing steps are particular to an XML browser, but they represent the kind of processing an XML document goes through to be useful to either a person or an application. An application designed to insert information from an XML document into a database will follow steps similar to these:

1. Parse the XML document and associated DTD. Because database structures can be fairly strict and you want to make sure all the required fields in the database are populated from an XML document, most XML-to-database applications use validating parsers to be sure the XML document's structure is correct.

2. Process the parsing results and check for errors. Any errors in the information to be added to the document should be caught during parsing rather than during the database insert process. This step ensures that the data is ready to be added to the database.

3. Insert information from the XML document into the database. The parsing steps exposed the structure of the XML document to the processing application that can now grab bits and pieces from the document—based on instructions given to the processing application—and insert them into the database.

As you can see, the steps an XML document goes through are slightly different depending on the way the XML-described content is used. Our browser display and database insert are just two examples of many. Often, one application handles all the processing steps; however, other times a collection of applications performs some but not all of the steps. For example, you can use a parser (validating or non-validating) to parse your document and prepare the results for a particular application. You can also use an XSL or XSL Transformations (XSLT) parser to specifically handle style documents. After the data is parsed, it may be sent to a processing application that displays it in a particular way, uses it to drive an automated process, or directs the activities of an application.

When you create an XML file, you're actually creating a standard text file that can be interpreted by a variety of products, including browsers, Java applications, databases, and even page-layout programs. The type of product you use to interpret the file depends on what you want to do with the content contained in the file. Do you want to send the information to a database, display the information in a browser, or pull the content into a page-layout program? What you can do with the results of your processed XML files depends on the steps you take when you process the XML files, related DTDs, and style sheets.

Your specific XML solution and the tools you use will define what combination of parsing and processing tools you finally assemble. It's entirely possible that these tools may all communicate directly with each other and, in a sense, behave as one tool. You can also purchase or build a single tool that performs all the processing steps for you. Regardless, it's important to have a good handle on the many different tools that can be used to process XML as well as the role each tool is designed to play.

XML Editors

The first step in processing an XML document is to have an XML document to process. To create an XML file, you can use an XML editor; or, because XML files and DTDs are simply text files, you can use a simple text editor, such as Notepad.

TIP: *Notice that we recommend Notepad and not WordPad. WordPad natively saves its files in the Microsoft Word binary format instead of the requisite text-only format. If you use WordPad, you must remember to change the file type to text (with .xml or .dtd extension) when you save the document.*

You don't have to use a simple text editor to build XML documents. More robust XML editors are available, and even more are slated for release over the next several months. Some products offer easy-to-use interfaces that walk you through the process of creating XML elements, attributes, and entities and their related values. Such editors automatically put the correct brackets in the correct locations and include all the quotation marks, semicolons, and other grammatical notations. You simply provide the names of the elements and other XML components, and the editor does the rest.

In addition to performing the laborious tasks involved in marking up documents properly, many editors offer tools that help you write the XML DTDs and will then validate your XML documents against the DTDs. An XML editor is a great tool to keep in your XML software toolbox. For a more complete list of XML editors, refer to Chapter 23.

Related solution:	*Found on page:*
Identifying Your Tool Needs	634

TIP: XML filters and plug-ins are now available for many word processors, including Microsoft Word. These additional pieces of code allow you to use the familiar interface of your word processor when you create XML files.

Although we highly recommend you use such editors, here's what we recommend you do first: Create a few simple XML files in a basic text editor to get used to writing XML code and to learn how to form XML documents correctly. It's important that you understand how to construct a simple XML document before you use third-party editors; for example, it's easy to create an element when, in fact, the document requires an attribute. Creating XML files manually will give you valuable experience and help you understand how XML elements, attributes, entities, and notations are formed. It will also help you troubleshoot the code you write in an XML editor, because you'll understand exactly what's required where and when.

After you have some experience hand-coding a few pages, we recommend you explore and work with some of the XML editors on the market. They can help you quickly create XML documents and limit the amount of typing you have to do. Just make sure you carefully read and check the code generated by the XML editor you use, which will help prevent errors. You can also add comments to your code if the XML editor does not include such an option.

Although many XML editors are available, any XML editor you choose should have the following capabilities:

• The ability to display your document in a tree structure, which will help you visualize your document and quickly reference the elements and attributes that become objects in programming and scripting languages.

• The ability to quickly organize and reorganize your DTD and document, usually with a drag-and-drop interface.

• Support for both UTF-8 and UTF-16. Whichever encoding scheme you decide to use, your XML editor should be able to support it. (Some only support 8-bit.)

NOTE: For a complete list of editors we highly recommend, all of which meet the preceding specifications, refer to Chapter 23.

XML Parsers

The processes of creating and then processing XML data are very much akin to the processes involved in writing a book. First, you write the text. Then, you send it to an editor, who checks to make sure it's grammatically correct and warns you if there are any problems in the construction of your sentences. If the book is a technical book that needs to adhere to a specific set of rules and be particularly accurate, you send it to a technical editor who checks it for technical accuracy. And finally, the entire book is sent to the designer who, with the help of style sheets, creates the display of the book. Each step and each person's job ensure that the final product is as the original author intended it to be.

With XML files, software applications and components perform these functions. After you create the XML file and/or the DTD, the next step is to check the file to ensure you've used the correct XML grammar. The XML counterpart to the editor is a software program called a *parser*. The Random House Dictionary defines the word *parse* as "the act of describing grammatically, or the telling of the part of speech." Therefore, when your XML document is parsed, the program figures out what the various parts of the XML speech mean and ensures that you've used the correct grammar. On the most basic level, parsers break the XML document into its element tree so either the processor or another application can do something with the content.

Before you can display or work with the content of your XML file, the document and its DTD must go through a parser. The parser reads the element tags and all other document components, and checks to make sure the grammatical structure of the document conforms to the standards in the XML specification. If there are problems with your grammar, the processor will report errors.

Parsers are small programs that check not only the grammar of the XML file, but also the well formedness and possibly the validity of the document. The two types of parsers that know what rules are required for the document to be either well formed or valid are:

- *Non-validating parsers*—Software programs that check XML documents for well formedness but not validity. This type of parser ignores information provided in an external DTD. If the document is missing a DTD, the parser will not report errors.

TIP: *Non-validating parsers don't read DTDs. However, according to the XML 1.0 specification, all parsers—whether they're validating or non-validating—need to be able to read and properly interpret DTDs. The next time you use your parser, run one of your DTDs through it to see what happens. If it doesn't read the DTD, you may want to find one that can. A parser that doesn't interpret DTDs may not interpret XML documents correctly.*

- *Validating parsers*—Software programs that check XML documents for validity, which means they check for the presence of the document's DTD and whether the document conforms to it. If a document doesn't have a DTD or if it has one but doesn't conform to its rules, the document is considered invalid.

TIP: *Whether you decide to use an internal or external DTD is entirely up to you, but this choice will affect what type of parser you can use. Both validating and non-validating parsers are currently available. Validating parsers check external DTDs, but non-validating parsers don't.*

Parsers usually take the form of some sort of code library, often written in C++, Java, or another language. Both Netscape Navigator and Microsoft Internet Explorer use Java and C++ parsers. These parsers consist of a code library that contains all the necessary programming to parse both valid and well-formed XML documents. If you don't have the code library, you can download it from the company that provides it and then reference it when you parse the document. Parsers can also be standalone applications: You specify the file you want parsed and then get back the results of the parsing process.

XML documents can be parsed a variety of ways and with a variety of products. Although you may assume parsing is done when the XML document processing starts, it can happen anywhere along the way. If the document is sent to a browser for display, it's parsed on the client side by the browser. If XML drives an application or it's used as part of a database interaction, the document may be parsed by a server. You don't even have to parse all pieces of the document at one time. For example, you can parse a document, process it, and then parse the links contained within it on a secondary level.

The product or method you use to parse or when you parse the document is almost entirely up to you. Some parsers are part of the final display application; others are separate pieces of software you load on your computer and use to evaluate your XML files. You'll find a variety of free XML parsers available on Internet sites, such as James Tauber's XMLSoftware (**www.xmlsoftware.com**). Microsoft also offers both a Java and a C++ parser in both Internet Explorer 4 and Internet Explorer 5. The Java parser, called MSXML, is actually a Java code library. You can learn more about the MSXML parser at **http://msdn.microsoft.com/xml/default.asp**. IBM's Alphaworks project also offers a very good Java-based validating parser. You can find it at **www.alphaworks.ibm.com/tech/xml4j**. Chapter 23 includes a more complete listing of XML parsers written in many different languages.

The parser compares the code in the XML document with the rules set forth in the XML specification to make sure the document is well formed. The parser must be able to read UTF 8-bit and 16-bit encodings and character entities. A validating parser reads the internal XML document before it interprets internal or external DTDs; this sequence ensures that local declarations are processed before external ones. If comments are stored in the document or in the external DTD, most parsers ignore them, but some report the context of the comment's text. When the parser encounters an attribute that's not defined in the DTD, an error is reported, depending on the type of parser used. An XML parser also normalizes any white space, character strings, or character references.

A parser sends the XML application names of notations and the notations' external identifiers. When it encounters an entity, the parser warns the XML application of multiple entity declarations. The parser also tells the application where entity references have occurred and provides the application with the names of the entities. The parser replaces the reference with the actual character or text and passes this information to the application. The parser must recognize the five built-in entities used within XML, even if they aren't declared in the document. Parameter entity references are always expanded when the parser encounters them.

When the parser interprets the information in the XML document and/or DTD, it passes specific information to the next application—or to the next piece in the same application if the parser is part of a bigger processing application. Although you still have to check your document for errors, parsers display errors so you don't have to hunt and peck through your document to find them.

Using Validating and Non-Validating Parsers

Which should you use to process your documents—a validating parser or a non-validating parser? It depends on the types of XML documents you're creating. If you use a non-validating parser, you run the risk of XML markup that doesn't conform to a DTD, which is a problem if you need to conform to one. If you use a validating processor, all code—regardless of whether it appears in the XML document or the DTD—must follow a specific set of defined rules. That's why using validating parsers is preferred. Because a validating parser reads and interprets both DTDs and XML documents, you can be sure the documents you create are correct in their structural content according to the XML 1.0 specification and to the DTD of your choice.

However, if speed is what you need, a non-validating parser will work faster than a validating parser, especially if you're using an external DTD stored on a remote site. A non-validating parser isn't required to check the DTD against the document, which can save processing time. All the information parsed is sent to the next processing application more quickly than if you were using a validating processor. Less computing resources are required with a non-validating parser, which most likely means that less bandwidth is required. Regardless of whether you use an external or internal DTD, you should consider using a non-validating parser if your computer resources are limited and you have network bandwidth constraints.

If you choose to use a non-validating parser, remember that a document must meet the following requirements to be considered well-formed:

- The XML document must begin with a valid XML declarative statement.
- Only one element acts as the root element, which is the parent to all other elements.
- Elements must be closed properly. All elements must have an end tag. For elements with no content defined, as in the **img** element—where the location of the image is actually an attribute and not specified as content—the element must either have both an open tag **<img>** and a close tag **</img>**; or, you can indicate the close of the element within the tag, like this: **<img/>**. (The latter is the preferred method for closing empty elements.)
- With the exception of the root element, all elements are contained within another element, which is referred to as the element's *parent*; all contained elements are referred to as the parent element's *children*.
- Character data that should not be processed as XML is enclosed within **CDATA** sections.
- Documents can include comments, white space, and processing instructions.

XML Processors

After the XML document has been parsed, an XML processor takes over. It reads the document and offers other applications access to the XML components stored within the XML document. A processor can be a search application used to retrieve information from a database. Or, as in the case of the Mathematical Markup Language (MathML, an XML application), a processor can take the results of the parsed XML document, process the information through a statistical application, and pass the results to another viewer that allows the client to see the results. A processor can also simply pass the results of the parsed file to a browser and let the browser display the data.

When a processor intercepts the parsed information, software developers can quickly access the structure of an XML document and work with the components in a variety of ways. All elements, attributes, entities, and notations are then considered objects, which can be further manipulated by other programs. After a document has been parsed, developers can take the parsed information and use additional editors, browsers, and databases to search or pull XML objects from the parsed document. The various parsed XML objects can then be referenced, manipulated, or displayed using additional programming languages or browsers.

With most XML processors and parsers, the role of the processor overlaps the role of the parser. The parser is responsible for checking the syntax of the DTD or XML document, and the processor is responsible for providing access to the content and structure of the document.

If a Web browser is capable of displaying or interpreting XML files, the browser must normally have an XML parser attached to it. The parser parses the data and then passes the results to the processor. The built-in processor identifies the style formats specified in the file and displays the XML data in the format specified in the style sheet.

TIP: *Current browsers, such as Netscape 6 and Microsoft Internet Explorer 5, can interpret and display XML files. In other words, they have built-in XML parsers. However, older browsers can't display or parse XML documents—they can only parse and display HTML documents. If you plan to use XML to drive your Web site, you must keep your audience in mind and identify whether users' browsers have the capabilities to view the data you're offering.*

Internet Explorer versions 4 and 5 are good examples of how this parser/processor relationship works. Both browsers offer Java-based XML parsers and also ActiveX components that are used to parse XML files. However, the ActiveX parser does not use external DTDs—only the built-in Java parser does. Older browsers (such as Internet Explorer 3 and Netscape Navigator 4) are limited because they don't include built-in XML parsers, but that doesn't mean they're incapable of displaying XML. They simply don't have the built-in programming code that enables XML files to be processed. As a developer, you could display XML files by processing them through a Java interpreter that turns the results of a parsed XML file into HTML or by displaying XML files in Java applets embedded in HTML files. As long as the browser offers a Java component, such as those included in Internet Explorer 4 and 5 and Netscape 6, external Java-based parsers can be used to parse XML data and then display the results in a Web browser window.

TIP: *If you have one of the original versions of Internet Explorer 4, you need to download the latest Java class libraries for XML parsing to work. You can find them on Microsoft's XML site,* **http://msdn.microsoft.com/xml**. *Also note that the XML Java parser included with Internet Explorer 4 can be used with Netscape Navigator. That's the glory of Java— it's never machine specific and, in most cases, it's portable across applications.*

XML and Browsers

Because browsers can display XML content using CSS or XSL style sheets, XML can be used on a wide scale. However, for a Web site built on XML to succeed, the browsers your visitors use must have XML capabilities. If they don't, the document will be displayed in text-only format or it will signal to the browser that the file should be downloaded and saved.

An alternative to directly serving XML to browsers and hoping that your users' browsers support XML is to translate your XML into HTML on the server side using XSLT and serve pure HTML to all users. This approach to building a Web site on XML means that you're planning ahead and converting your content to

XML; therefore, your site is more extensible and accessible, and you're still meeting the needs of an audience using a variety of browsers. When XML browsers become standard, you'll be able to use XSL or CSS to drive the display of the XML documents and skip the XML to HTML translation.

A Brief History of XML-Enabled Browsers

For the first two years of XML's existence, developers knew XML had great potential. However, it didn't catch on quickly because they couldn't demonstrate the results of their XML code and DTDs in any standard, widely used browser. Few, if any, Web browsers understood XML files, let alone offered built-in parsers and processors. Software developers quickly realized that for all the hype about XML to be universally embraced, the masses must have a tool to view XML content.

Although native XML support was available in Microsoft Internet Explorer 4 by early 1998, Netscape Navigator didn't offer real support for it until mid-1998. XML remained a relatively obscure markup language because there were far more Navigator users than Internet Explorer users in 1998. Navigator users had to download additional Java code and code libraries that allowed them to use their Java-enabled browser to parse and then process the XML data into a tree-structured display. Even with Java-enabled parsers and processors, many Java implementations within the popular browsers were unstable, and users were still stymied by systems that regularly crashed when they tried to display XML files and structures.

It wasn't until late 1998 that Netscape announced widespread support for XML in its Navigator 4.7 browser. Although Internet Explorer 4 already had XML support (albeit on a limited basis), it wasn't until early 1999 with the release of both Navigator 6 and Internet Explorer 5 that users had not only a choice, but also full XML support in the latest browsers.

Today's browsers fully implement all the features found in the XML 1.0 specification. They not only understand what XML and DTD files are, but they also parse, process, and display the content. The latest versions of both Navigator and Internet Explorer let you view XML documents using CSS. Internet Explorer 4 and 5 also offer the ability to interface with XML documents through the Document Object Model (DOM), which lets developers use or display any of the objects found in an XML document.

TIP: *Because new features are added almost monthly, make sure you visit both Netscape's and Microsoft's developer sites, located at **www.mozilla.org** and **http://msdn.microsoft.com/xml/**, respectively.*

XML and Application Programming Interfaces

Application programming interfaces (APIs) are tools that work with XML processors. Some APIs might be included in the processor to provide additional processing functionality and services. In addition to numerous XML processors and parsers, API kits for XML have been popping up recently. With an API kit, you can use modules to process well-formed XML documents in a variety of ways. For example, you can use certain API modules to sort the data within an XML document. Other API modules might allow you to create reports from an XML data source. And still others can help you convert HTML documents to XML by cleaning up the HTML code so the file can successfully function as an XML document. Here's a partial list of available APIs (you can find more at **www.xmlsoftware.com**):

- *Free-Dom*—An API written in Java to sit on top of any XML parser.

- *Saxon*—An API written in Java for processing XML documents. This API assists in transforming XML documents to HTML and HTML to XML documents.

- *Tidy*—An API written in the C programming language and used to clean up HTML documents so you can convert them to XML.

Processing XML in Other Ways

After parsing the document, the XML parser passes the tree structure and other document information to a processor. The processor can be a scripting language, such as JavaScript or VBScript, or it can be Java itself. Representatives of Sun Microsystems, the creators of Java, have said that XML finally gives Java something to do. With compatible structures, Java and XML complement each other, and Java helps extend the functionality you can incorporate with XML data sources. In the Immediate Solutions sections, we'll describe how you can use scripting languages to process XML data sources. We'll start with a simple example that uses ActiveX (a component found in Internet Explorer) and Java components to present XML data within a browser.

XML and the Document Object Model

To further explain how XML processing works, let's crank it up a notch and discuss something that may be confusing for some people—the Document Object Model (DOM). The DOM is a way to describe an XML document to another application or programming language in an effort to further manipulate the information. You can use the DOM to place XML data sources with browsers. More specifically, however, you can use the DOM to collect information about an XML document's structure and then use that information to create connections between the document's structure and other applications or data sources.

A relatively easy way to use DOM is to use a scripting language, such as JavaScript or VBScript, to load an XML document, manipulate it, and send the data or results to another application. Depending on the application and scripting language you use, you can even use the DOM to display the content of the XML file or to provide a mechanism to search the XML document.

One of the joys of Internet Explorer 5.0 and later is that when you load an XML document into the browser, the various parts of the document are exposed to the DOM. They're available for manipulation just like the pieces of an HTML document are available for manipulation via the DOM. In Internet Explorer 4.0 and earlier, you have to use an Active X component or Java applet to load the XML document into the browser and access it via the DOM.

XML's tree structure enables you to quickly retrieve the information or XML component you need. Everything in the tree is an object, from the first root node to the value of an entity. Being able to navigate this tree allows you to retrieve important information concerning the data source.

To help you further understand how the DOM works in relationship to XML, let's look at how a simple script used in Internet Explorer 4 can access XML. After you've accessed the objects you need, you can use JavaScript to display the final results in a Web page.

First, you should know that the DOM uses three objects to access an XML file:

• The XML document

• The XML node

• The XML node list

The XML Document as an Object

Think of the XML document as an object. That object, although it represents the entire XML source document, can be accessed through the use of a script, which can be placed in a Web page. The script can load the XML document, because to the scripting language, it's just an object. After it's loaded, the script can manipulate the XML document like it manipulates any object. Because XML requires you to follow a structured pattern to form your XML documents, the DOM can access any XML document, and the document represents an object you can manipulate. In theory, you could use and reuse scripts to access XML documents. In addition, because the structure of XML documents follows a pattern, with a few simple changes, your script would apply to just about any XML document.

The XML document, as defined in DOM, consists of the root element along with all of its descendants. For example, in the following code, **newspaper** is the root element, and the rest of the elements, such as **section**, are considered its descendants, or children. The entire XML document object is all the code contained in the following:

```
<newspaper>
    <section>
        <story>
        </story>
    </section>
</newspaper>
```

The XML Node

The XML node object represents a node within an XML document. The following are considered nodes in Internet Explorer 5:

- Element
- Parsed character data (PCDATA)
- Comment
- The document type (DOCTYPE) declaration
- Any processing instructions
- Character data (CDATA) sections
- Namespaces
- Entity references (EntityRef)
- White space
- Attributes
- The XML declaration

The XML Node List

The node list in the XML document model represents a collection of nodes. Several properties and methods are used in the XML node list:

- *Property*—**Length**
- *Methods*—**CurrentNode**, **Item**, **MoveTo**, **MoveToNode**, **NextNode**, and **previousNode**

Using XML DOM

When you use the DOM, you can assign various XML objects to variables. The variables can then be accessed and manipulated by any number of applications. After you create an XML document object, you can access information about the object and manipulate the object by using the DOM's properties and methods. A full reference to all the XML DOM properties and methods is available from the World Wide Web Consortium's site located at **www.w3.org/DOM**. Microsoft offers information about the DOM on its XML Web site, located at **http://msdn.microsoft.com/xml**.

Immediate Solutions

Parsing an XML File

Parsing simply means reading through the document and making sure the grammar conforms to the XML specification, so the information can be passed to the XML processor and, finally, to the intended application for display. Parsers can be written in a variety of languages, including Java and C++.

There are two types of XML parsers: validating and non-validating. Validating parsers match the XML document structure to the referenced DTD to ensure all the elements, attributes, and entities specified in the XML document match those described in the DTD. Non-validating parsers only check if a document's well formed. Some parsers even act as both validating and non-validating, depending on the parameters you provide them. In the following example, you'll use the XML Parser RXP both locally and on the Web to parse an XML document. Follow these steps for downloading, installing, and parsing your XML documents:

1. Point your Web browser to **www.cogsci.ed.ac.uk/~richard/rxp.html** to access the RXP Web page. Click on the MSDOS/Windows executable link to **ftp://ftp.cogsci.ed.ac.uk/pub/richard/rxp.exe** to download a Windows version of the parser that you can run from the DOS prompt. The entire parser is contained in the executable, so you only download one small file.

2. Choose where you want to save the executable **rxp.exe** and download the file to your hard disk. Our example command in Step 4 assumes the executable is saved to your hard disk on the C drive. If you save the executable elsewhere, you need to move to that directory in the DOS window before you run the executable.

3. A collection of switches associated with the parser controls how an XML document is parsed and what format the parsed output is in. The switch to validate a document is **-V**. To have the parsing results output in bits, use **-o b**. Be sure to save a copy of the switch list at **ftp://ftp.cogsci.ed.ac.uk/pub/richard/rxp.txt** so you can see how the various switches change the parsing and the output.

4. To validate and parse an XML document and report the results of the parser in bits, use the following command at the DOS prompt:

```
c:rxp.exe -V -o b xml_file_name.xml
```

5. If your XML file has errors, RXP will stop processing the document and deliver an error message in the DOS window. If the document is valid and well formed, RXP returns parsed data in the format you specify.

6. To parse an XML document without validating it, simply omit the **-V** switch when you run RXP.

7. If you're connected to the Internet and want to parse an XML file that is on the Internet, you can replace the file name with a URL, like this:

```
c:rxp.exe -V -o b url
```

A Web version of RXP is also available that doesn't require downloading an executable or working from the DOS prompt. To use it, your XML files and DTDs must be available via the Internet. To use the RXP Web interface, visit **www.cogsci.ed.ac.uk/~richard/xml-check.html** and type the XML document's URL.

NOTE: *If you just want to check if your XML is well formed and don't care about parsing it, use the RUWF (are you well formed?) tool provided by XML.com at* ***www.xml.com/xml/pub/tools/ruwf/check.html***.

Browsers in Action: Parsing, Processing, and Displaying XML Data

Remember the key component of XML: The content is separate from the presentation. XML separates the presentation markup from the structural markup, and this feature makes it easy for developers to embed specific instructions on how to display the same XML content a variety of ways. The browser or display software is responsible for downloading and displaying the data in a format that best suits its needs. This process allows the user to view the data in a variety of ways after it has been downloaded to the client computer. It also reduces the amount of server traffic, which makes it appear as if the browser is processing the information faster than it does for traditional HTML.

Because of this flexibility in content display, the developer must specify ways for the data to be presented. You must include a style sheet (the markup language that defines how the content will look) in the code. Without a style sheet, the XML application won't know what to do with the parsed and processed data. A style sheet is the link to the content and the client. Let's look at how the parser, processor, and XML application use the document's structure, tree, and style sheet to display the content in a browser or through another XML-based application or vocabulary.

In this section, we demonstrate how the XML processing instruction, document structure, and document elements are processed. We use the Channel Definition Format (CDF) to demonstrate this. Following the XML declaration, the actual document structure—the content of the channel—is created. With most XML documents, you can include an internal DTD or specify a reference to a DTD. In the case of CDF (an application based on XML), the CDF file does not contain any references to a DTD file. Instead, the structure of the document is defined within the declared element tags.

NOTE: *CDF is an XML vocabulary developed specifically by Microsoft to drive its Active Channels. Although any XML parser can read and parse well-formed CDF files, only processors such as Internet Explorer that know how to handle CDF data are able to do anything productive—such as display an active channel—using CDF.*

The root element, from which all other elements branch, is the **CHANNEL** element. Contained within the **CHANNEL** element are the elements that further describe the channel, including **ICON**, **ITEM**, and **ABSTRACT**. These elements create the tree structure from which Internet Explorer can parse and display the data. The code is shown in Listing 19.1.

Listing 19.1 A CDF document.

```
<?xml version="1.0" encoding="UTF-8"?>
    <CHANNEL HREF="http://www.site.com/channels/index.htm"
        BASE="http://www.site.com/">
     <TITLE>The Channel</TITLE>
     <ABSTRACT>The Site's Channel</ABSTRACT>
        <LOGO HREF="http://www.site.com/logos/wide_logo.gif"
         STYLE="IMAGE-WIDE"/>
        <LOGO HREF="http://www.site.com/logos/logo.gif"
         STYLE="IMAGE"/>
        <LOGO HREF="http://www.site.com/logos/icon.gif"
         STYLE="ICON"/>
     <SCHEDULE>
       <INTERVALTIME DAY="1"/>
       <EARLIESTTIME HOUR="0"/>
       <LATESTTIME HOUR="12"/>
     </SCHEDULE>
     <ITEM HREF="http://www.site.com/channels/
      dailyupdate.htm">
        <LOGO HREF="http://www.site.com/logos/icon.gif"
         STYLE="ICON"/>
        <ABSTRACT>The Channel's Daily Update</ABSTRACT>
     </ITEM>
```

```
<ITEM HREF="http://www.site.com/channels/info.htm">
    <LOGO HREF="http://www.site.com/logos/icon.gif"
     STYLE="ICON"/>
    <ABSTRACT>Information About the Channel
    </ABSTRACT>
  </ITEM>
</CHANNEL>
```

This is the XML document structure from which Internet Explorer creates a tree structure. Using this structure, Internet Explorer can display the various channel elements you've created with your code.

TIP: *Notice that the code in Listing 19.1 isn't a document in the traditional sense; it contains no real content, only references to content. The mechanism to describe where the XML content can be found is called metadata. Netscape uses this term frequently when referring to XML-enabled applications. This is also an example of a document that drives a process—the gathering of channel content for display—but isn't designed to be displayed.*

When you use Internet Explorer to access the CDF file, the browser parses the information and knows it's using XML instead of HTML. It then opens a dialog box that asks if you want to subscribe to the site's channel. The document was first parsed and then processed; Figure 19.1 shows an example of the processor's results.

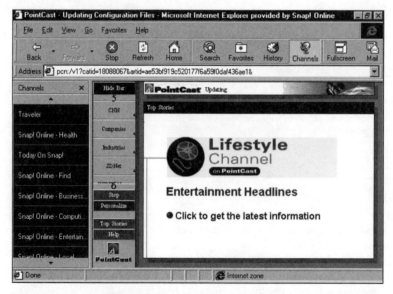

Figure 19.1   Our XML data file was parsed and processed, and the result is the channel in our Channels Explorer bar.

After the channel and all its elements are loaded in the browser, you can see how channels show the tree structure of the XML document from which they were based. You can then decide to view the individual channel elements or collapse the tree structure.

Processing XML Documents with ActiveX and Java Components

As you know, presentation and data are separate in XML. Although the code to display XML is built in to newer browsers, many people still use HTML-only browsers that cannot interpret XML code. Therefore, you need some mechanism to display the content you've structured in XML. You can point to and display the XML content with either ActiveX or Java—both are commonly used to get XML data to HTML-specific browsers. You can create your XML document, define a style sheet, and add programming code to marry the XML data to the browser, essentially processing the XML data into readable code that an HTML-specific browser can handle. Follow these steps:

NOTE: You can also use an XSLT style sheet and an XSLT processor on the server side to perform the same functions listed here. The more conversion you do on the server side, the less time it takes for data to display on the client side. However, if you serve up millions of pages a day, it may make more sense to let clients (Web browsers) handle the majority of the conversion. Server-side processing offers a key benefit over client-side processing: You only have to create Java or Active X code that works in one place, your server. Client-side code has to work on many different platforms, computer configurations, and browser configurations.

1. Define the XML document from which the information will be parsed and then processed into the browser. Although such a document doesn't need a DTD, if you want valid XML code, you should include one. Listing 19.2 includes the DTD within the XML document.

Listing 19.2   An XML document with a DTD included in it.

```
<?xml version="1.0" ?>
<!DOCTYPE bookstore[
<!ENTITY bk "Borders Books">
<!ELEMENT bookstore (book)*>
<!ELEMENT book (subject)*>
<!ELEMENT subject (title,publisher,author,price,pages)>
<!ELEMENT title (#PCDATA)>
<!ELEMENT publisher (#PCDATA)>
<!ELEMENT author (#PCDATA)>
```

```
<!ELEMENT price (#PCDATA)>
<!ELEMENT pages (#PCDATA)>
]>

<bookstore>
  <book>
   <subject>
    <title>XML Black Book, 2nd Edition</title>
    <publisher>Coriolis</publisher>
    <author>Natanya Pitts </author>
    <price>$49.99</price>
    <pages>844</pages>
   </subject>
  </book>

  <book>
   <subject>
    <title>Dynamic HTML Black Book</title>
    <publisher>Coriolis</publisher>
    <author>Natanya Pitts, C.C. Sandars, and Ramesh Chandak</author>
    <price>$49.99</price>
    <pages>700</pages>
   </subject>
  </book>
</bookstore>
```

2. After you've defined the XML data, you need to create the style sheet that will be referenced by the Java parser. The code for such a style sheet will look something like Listing 19.3.

Listing 19.3   The code for a style sheet that will be referenced by the Java parser.

```
<xsl:stylesheet version="1.0"
    xmlns:xsl="http://www.w3.org/1999/XSL/Transform">

<xsl:output method="html" version="4.01"
    encoding="ISO-8859-1"
    omit-xml-declaration="yes"/>

<xsl:template match="/">
 <html>
  <head><title>Books</title></head>
  <body background-color="#FFFFFF">
   <xsl:apply-templates/>
  </body>
 </html>
</xsl:template>
```

```
<xsl:template match="bookstore">
 <xsl:apply-templates/>
</xsl:template>

<xsl:template match="book">
 <div background-color="white" color="blue">
  <xsl:apply-templates/>
 </div>
</xsl:template>

<xsl:template match="subject">
 <xsl:text>Title: </xsl:text>
  <b><xsl:value-of select="title"/></b><br />
 <xsl:text>Author: </xsl:text>
  <i><xsl:value-of select="author"/></i><br />
 <xsl:text>Publisher: </xsl:text>
  <xsl:value-of select="publisher"/><br />
 <xsl:text>Price: </xsl:text>
  <xsl:value-of select="price"/><br />
 <xsl:text>Pages: </xsl:text>
  <xsl:value-of select="pages"/>
</xsl:template>
</xsl:stylesheet>
```

3. Define code that points the ActiveX component or Java applet to the XML file. If you plan to use the ActiveX parser (a component shipped with Internet Explorer 5) to point to the style sheet and XML file, essentially marrying them, the HTML code you create will look like this:

```
<object id="XSLControl"
classid="CLSID:2BD0D2F2-52EC-11D1-8C69-0E16BC000000"
codebase="http://www.microsoft.com/xml/xsl/msxsl.cab"
style="display:none">

<param name="documentURL" value="xmldocument.xml">

<param name="styleURL" value="stylesheet.xsl">

</object>
```

4. Define a target in which the information can be placed. This information is formatted using the style-sheet mechanism. The HTML code looks like this:

```
<div id="styleTarget"></div>
```

5. Create a script that will specify to the parser that the information stored within the XML document, xmldocument.xml, will be displayed within the **div** target created. Here's how the code looks:

```
<script for="window" event="onload">
var xslHTML = XSLControl.htmlText;
document.all.item("styleTarget").innerHTML = xslHTML;
</script>
```

Processing XML Data with JavaScript

But wait, there's more! Not only can you use the document from the previous project to view channels if you use Internet Explorer, you can also pass the XML document structure to another processing language to do more than just process the document structure. You can do something as simple as printing the contents of each **item** element, or you could do something more complex, such as store the list of channels and their **item** elements in a database.

This example uses JavaScript to pull the information from the XML document and display it in another window. You might use this feature to give the visitor more information about what's contained in each channel or to add banner advertising to a separate window. The example uses JavaScript and the Microsoft MSXML processor to take the data contained in the previous XML CDF file, open a new window, and display more information about the channel. The JavaScript code could look like Listing 19.4.

Listing 19.4   Javascript code that will display more information about the channel.

```
<script language="jscript">
<!--
var doc = new ActiveXObject("msxml");
var wndw = null;

function DisplayElements(cdffile)
{
// This is where the new window opens to display the info
wndw = window.open("","CDFFile",
"resizable,scrollbars=yes");
wndw.document.open();
doc.URL = cdffile;

// The next line displays the elements or ITEMS
// starting with the root element
displayElement(doc.root);
```

```
wndw.document.write("</body>");
wndw.document.close();

}

function displayElement(elem) {
if (elem == null) return;
wndw.document.writeln("<p>");
if (elem.type == 0)
    wndw.document.writeln("Document with element: " + elem.tag);
else
    wndw.document.writeln("Document contains element with no tag.");
wndw.document.writeln("<br>Element is of type: " +
GetType(elem.type) +"<br>");
wndw.document.writeln("Element text: "
+ elem.text + "<br>");
wndw.document.writeln("Element href: "
+ elem.getAttribute("href") + "<br>");
wndw.document.writeln("Element base: "
+ elem.getAttribute("base") + "<br>");
wndw.document.writeln("Element style: "
+ elem.getAttribute("style") + "<br>");
wndw.document.writeln("Element day: "
+ elem.getAttribute("day") + "<br>");
wndw.document.writeln("Element hour: "
+ elem.getAttribute("hour") + "<br>");
wndw.document.writeln("Element minute: "
+ elem.getAttribute("min") + "<br>");

// Next we move to any children elements
var elem_children = elem.children;
if (elem_children != null)
    for (var i = 0; i < elem_children.length; i++) {
       element_child = elem_children.item(i);
        displayElement(element_child);
    }

}

// This is where we specify the element type
function GetType(type) {
if (type == 0)
        return "ELEMENT";
if (type == 1)
        return "TEXT";
```

```
if (type == 2)
        return "COMMENT";
if (type == 3)
        return "DOCUMENT";
if (type == 4)
        return "DTD";
else
        return "OTHER";
}


//-->
</script>
```

Processing Databases with ASP

Until now, we've concentrated on processing XML data within a Web browser. But the beauty of XML is that it can also connect the data in XML documents with applications such as databases to make information more accessible. In this section, we give you an overview of how XML database processing works. We show you how a simple Access database can be interfaced with XML to create an interesting integrated database system.

NOTE: *We cover the relationships between XML and databases in more detail in Chapter 21. The following example represents one method of linking databases to XML files but does not tell you everything about how you can use XML with databases.*

When you work with desktop databases such as Access or even Excel, the biggest problem is that only users who have Access or Excel stored on their systems can access the data. With XML, you can easily create a few simple scripts, an Active Server Page (ASP), and an XML data source that pulls the information from the Access database and populates the XML database every time someone requests information from it. This can all be done with the help of VBScript and Open Database Connectivity (ODBC), found in Windows 95, 98, NT, and 2000.

After the scripts convert the data in the Access database into an XML source file, the information can easily be manipulated by other applications and shown in standard HTML Web pages. This process makes the data accessible to anyone who has a Web browser, even if they don't have Access loaded on their computer. Let's step through it and see how ASP can help process XML data. In the following example, the actual act of processing the information into and out of XML involves more than just a simple browser application.

You have a database that lists all the employees in a particular department along with their phone numbers and addresses. This data is stored in an Access database, so you can quickly find and sort information about whoever you're looking for at a particular time. The problem is, not everyone has Access installed on his or her computer. You need to make the data accessible across your company's intranet. Doing so requires your Access database, a few lines of code, the Microsoft Internet Information Server (IIS), ASP, and XML. Table 19.1 shows the structure of your database.

NOTE: *In Windows 2000 products, IIS is expanded as Internet Information Services.*

You need to connect your database to the Web using an intranet server, running Microsoft's IIS with its accompanying ASP technology, to make the information in the database accessible via a Web page. ASP will help you transform the Access data into an XML data source. The data source will reside on your intranet server in the form of an ASP file that can be accessed with Internet Explorer. ASP does more than just transform the Access file into an ASP file—it actually converts the data to XML. The data can then be evaluated using the DOM or other XML-based technologies. ASP also makes it possible for scripts to access the file. Scripts can query the database, as well as populate it, if necessary. And because the XML data source is generated dynamically from the Access database, Access users can still use Access to add new information.

To create the XML data source on the server, follow these steps:

1. Create an ASP file that is used to create the Access data and turn it into XML data. (You might have seen something similar done with ASP to generate HTML pages. The theory is the same, but the output will be XML instead of HTML.) The code for generating an ASP file looks like this:

```
<%@LANGUAGE = VBScript%>
   <?xml version="1.0"?>
   <employees>
```

Table 19.1   The Access database structure.

Name	Department	Phone
Jane Doe	Human Resources	555-2300
Harry Smith	Accounting	555-2301
Jeff North	Accounting	555-2310
Bobby Diggins	Information Systems	555-4458

As you can see, the ASP file starts with a declaration that indicates which scripting language is used. The next line indicates that XML version 1.0 is used, and the third line specifies the main root element of the XML document.

2. Name the Access database stored on the company's server. Because you're going to make a connection between Access, ASP, and VBScript, you need to invoke ODBC and make the Access database accessible to the VBScript. You do that by opening the Control Panel's ODBC applet and adding the Access database to the list of ODBC-accessible items.

3. Connect the Access database to the ASP script by using an Active Data Object declaration in another VBScript. This script creates an object from the Access database, which in turn accesses a table called **Employeelist**. At that point, the following script will populate the XML data source:

```
<%
    Set Conn = Server.CreateObject("ADODB.Connection")
    Conn.Open "EMPLOYEES"
    Set EMPLOYEE = Conn.Execute("select * from EMPLOYEELIST")
    Do While Not Tape.EOF
    %>
```

4. Create the basic structure of the elements. It's important that you pay special attention to the structure; if you don't, the information that is displayed could be incorrect or point to the wrong element. Working with data that is stored in tabular format makes it easier to create your XML structure. In this example, you have three subelements within the employee database: **employeename**, **department**, and **phone**. You can turn this information into an XML document structure with the following code to specify each employee's record:

```
<employee>
        <employeename></employeename>
        <department></department>
        <phone></phone>
</employee>
```

5. Create an XML data source that contains the various elements. The idea is to have the script populate each of the employee elements in the XML document. The script does this by pulling the information from the Access database and placing it in the XML document where the elements for the employees match the fields in the database. To do this, you simply need to create a framework for the employee element. Then, you populate the framework with declared variables representing the various fields in the employee database. The script looks like this:

```
<employeerecord>
      <employeename><%=Info("Name")%></employeename>
      <department><%=Info("Department")%></department>
      <phone><%=Info("Phone")%></phone>
</employeerecord>
```

6. Tell the Active Server Page to continue through each entry in the Access table. This code creates a loop that pulls out the information:

```
<% Info.MoveNext
   Loop
   %>
   </employees>
```

From the previous code, the accompanying script will create the code in Listing 19.5, which is a data source in a well-formed XML structure.

Listing 19.5   The data source in a well-formed XML structure.

```
<?xml version="1.0"?>
  <employees>
    <employeerecord>
      <employeename>Jane Doe</employeename>
      <department>Human Resources</department>
      <phone>555-2300</Phone>
    </employeerecord>

    <employeerecord>
      <employeename>Harry Smith</employeename>
      <department>Accounting</department>
      <phone>555-2301</phone>
    </employeerecord>

    <employeerecord>
      <employeename>Jeff North</employeename>
      <department>Accounting</department>
      <phone>555-2310</phone>
    </employeerecord>

    <employeerecord>
      <employeename>Bobby Diggins</employeename>
      <department>Information Systems</department>
      <phone>555-4458</phone>
    </employeerecord>

  <employees>
```

Using the XML DOM to Access XML Objects

To access XML objects, you first have to create an instance of the parser. You can do this by using an ActiveX object. You can use the object model to walk the document tree structure. After creating this object (actually an object that is the document), you can access the information by calling the properties and methods that are associated with the XML document object you've created. To do so, follow these steps:

TIP: *The method for accessing an XML data source in Microsoft Internet Explorer 5 is similar to that of accessing an XML data source in Internet Explorer 4.*

1. Create an XML document object by creating a new ActiveX object. The code you use to create the document object assigns the XML document object to the variable **xml**, which you specify in the following code:

```
var xml = new ActiveXObject("microsoft.xmldom");
```

2. Call the **load** method and pass it a valid URL by including the following code in your document:

```
xml.load("xmlDataSource.xml");
```

3. Use the document node property to identify the root element of the XML data source to which you're pointing in the URL in the preceding line of code:

```
var docRoot = xml.documentNode
```

After you locate the document root, you can move up and down the document's tree structure by using the node object to navigate and manipulate the document's tree.

Creating a Script to Access the Object Model

After you create the code to access an XML data source, you can create a JavaScript to reveal the contents of the XML document to a browser such as Internet Explorer 5. The script shown in Listing 19.6, an example from Microsoft's XML site, creates an ActiveX object that represents an XML data source. From there, the root of the document is passed to the function **output_doc**. The code in Listing 19.6 provides access to the object model.

Listing 19.6   Script that creates an ActiveX object that represents an XML data source.

```jscript
<SCRIPT LANGUAGE="JScript" FOR=window EVENT=onload>
var indent_array = new String(" ");
var str = "";

var xml = new ActiveXObject("microsoft.xmldom");
xml.load("pdcxml.xml");

var docroot = xml.documentNode;

output_doc(docroot,0);

function output_doc(node,indents)
{
    var i;

    if (node.nodeType == 0)  // 0 is an ELEMENT node
    {
        document.all("results").insertAdjacentText("BeforeEnd",
            indent_array.substring(0,(4 * indents)) +
            "<" + elem.tagName + ">" + "\n");

    if (node.childNodes != null)
    {
        for (i = 0 ; i < node.childNodes.length ; i++)
        output_doc(node.childNodes.item(i),(indents + 1));
        }

        document.all("results").insertAdjacentText("BeforeEnd",
            indent_array.substring(0,(4 * indents)) +
            "</" + elem.tagName + ">" + "\n");
    }
    else if (node.nodeType == 1) // 1 is a TEXT node
    {
        document.all("results").insertAdjacentText("BeforeEnd",
            indent_array.substring(0,(4 * indents)) +
            "\"" + elem.text + "\"\n");
    }
    else
        alert("unknown element type: " + node.nodeType);
}
```

Chapter 20

The Components of a
Total XML Solution

In Depth

Although a strong knowledge of XML Document Type Definitions (DTDs), documents, syntax rules, and so on is a practical requirement for any XML developer, a solid understanding of all the pieces of a complete XML solution is essential to XML development. Moving away from the cut-and-dry world of syntax and coding requirements and into the more abstract world of solution design, this chapter looks at all the pieces—data and software alike—that you need to build a complete XML solution. In addition, we include a discussion of the different roles XML documents play in information delivery, and we look at the parts that make up some real-world XML solutions. The chapter ends with a look at how to build a concrete plan for your XML solution and methods for evaluating canned XML solutions compared to build-to-suit XML solutions.

What It Takes to Deploy an XML Solution

Designing an entire XML solution involves combining many different components to build and process XML to achieve a particular result. The role XML plays in the total solution can be wide ranging and include:

- Describing the data that the solution relies on, such as financial records passed from system to system.

- Describing the commands and parameters that drive the solution, such as the particulars of software applications to be installed across a network.

Whether you use XML to store data, drive a system, or perform any other activity, you need a collection of components to work with the XML to produce a final result, including:

- DTD

- Parsing and processing tools

- Style sheets

- Display tools

When you think of the overall design of an XML solution, you can divide the components into two distinct categories:

- *Technical design components*—The pieces that make the system function and process data.

• *Interface design components*—The pieces that drive the display (if there is one) of data for the user.

The truth is that some XML solutions use XML strictly to command a system—the user doesn't see the data described with XML. More often than not, however, XML solutions display information to a user in some way. Our discussion in this chapter assumes that most solutions have a display component. If yours doesn't, you don't need to worry about the display components; you should focus on the technical components that drive your system.

Technical Design Components

By themselves, XML documents can't do much. For an XML document to be useful, it has to be parsed and processed. The components that parse, process, and do something with XML-described data make up the technical, or system, design components of an XML solution. These elements don't affect how the browser displays a document as directly as elements such as fonts and colors do, but they can often drive what data is passed to the style sheet for display, or what information is passed to another application for display. The technical design components include:

• DTDs and documents

• Parsing and processing tools

At first glance, these elements are a bit more amorphous than the interface elements, but the following discussions should make them more concrete.

DTDs and Documents

DTDs and documents make up the XML piece of any XML-driven solution. Although a DTD isn't required, it is helpful (see Chapter 5 for more on DTDs). DTDs are useful when you have more than one XML document—and chances are, you will. The majority of the other chapters in this book are devoted to the building of XML DTDs and documents, so we won't repeat ourselves here unnecessarily by discussing the intricacies of building either DTDs or documents. Instead, as you begin to assemble the components of an XML-based solution, you need to keep in mind some DTD- and document-related issues:

• The goal and purpose of the XML application (DTD) that guides the development of your XML documents—if one is used.

• The requirement that all XML documents be well formed and at the very least, valid.

• The potential and limitations of markup.

Related solution:	*Found on page:*
Creating and Specifying the DTD	142

The next three sections investigate these issues in more detail.

The Goal and Purpose of the XML Application

Because XML allows DTD designers to create markup to provide a solution to a specific problem, each XML application has its own particular purpose. A quick look at a handful of existing applications in Table 20.1 shows how the purposes can change drastically from one application to another.

Obviously, a document written for the MathML application would be very different from one written for the OSD application. When XML first came on the scene, the distinctions between the different XML applications were fairly clear. However, as XML has become a more prevalent technology, applications that are more similar in purpose have begun to arise.

If you're using an XML application developed by someone else for an industry or particular type of content, you need to know that application—and its purpose—inside and out. You should examine the documentation and resources that support each application to discover its exact purpose and make sure your documents use the markup elements that it defines correctly. "Evaluating an XML Application," in this chapter's Immediate Solutions section, provides some guidelines for how to evaluate an XML application for use within your XML solution.

Table 20.1   Various XML applications and their purposes.

Application	Acronym	Purpose
Channel Definition Format	CDF	To facilitate the delivery of Internet content via server-side push.
Open Software Description	OSD	To guide the installation of software over a network via server-side push.
Resource Description Framework	RDF	To describe Internet resources in a standard metadata format that is usable by a wide variety of clients and servers.
Meta Content Framework	MCF	To describe collections of documents residing on a network in a standard metadata format.
Web Interface Definition Language	WIDL	To describe Web application programming interfaces (APIs).
Mathematical Markup Language	MathML	To describe and process mathematical data.
Chemical Markup Language	CML	To describe and process chemical compound data content.

The Requirement That a Document Be Well-Formed and/or Valid

For an XML processor to work with any XML document, the document must be at least well formed. Well-formed documents have the following characteristics:

• All entities used in the document body are declared in the internal DTD.

• All formal rules for the physical document structure are followed.

Basically, a well-formed document is not checked against any DTD except the internal one that specifies the entities for the document. A valid XML document is a well-formed document that also adheres to all the rules set down in its associated DTD.

An XML document must be well formed and, if it's being validated, valid. If it's not, the document is in error. All other design issues are irrelevant. Just about every XML editor available let's you know if your XML document is in error. Many XML editors will also validate your XML document against a DTD.

Part of the decision you have to make about the XML in your solution is whether the XML needs to validate against a particular DTD and where in the solution you want to validate it. The benefit of validating a document is that you know it conforms to the structure you've defined in the DTD. The downside to validating a document within a system is that it takes a parser longer to parse and validate a document than it does to simply parse the document.

If your solution needs to process quite a bit of data, you may opt to validate documents in some way before they come into the system—as part of a development workflow, perhaps. If for some reason a document does make it into your system without being validated, and your solution relies on valid data, the system may produce an error message instead of the expected result. The decisions on when and if to validate your XML are based on the specific needs of the system, including its reliance on valid data and a need for quick and efficient performance.

Often, the best way to determine when (or if) to validate a document with respect to system performance is to try several validation schemes to judge how each affects the solution and its performance. Try using a validating parser to check documents as they are parsed. If that takes too long, try validating documents with an editor beforehand, but take into account that you need to be sure this step happens before documents come into the system. Send a test document that you know is invalid through the system to see what kinds of errors it produces. Would you rather trap for errors before or after the data is in the system? There's no right or wrong answer—just the best one for your solution.

The Potential and Limitations of the Markup

Hypertext Markup Language (HTML) authors who come to the world of XML comfortable with defying all the rules to achieve an end result may have some adjusting to do. XML markup can't be forced to do what it wasn't created to do; therefore, it's important to know both the potential and the limitations of any given XML application. By researching an application, you can put together a reasonably accurate picture of how the elements in the application are supposed to function. By all means, use them to their fullest potential, but don't try to force them beyond their capabilities.

Parsing and Processing Tools

At the very least, XML documents will be parsed by a parser and evaluated by a processing tool of some kind. The role of the parser is to make the document available to the processor. The role of the processor is to evaluate the document and then do something with the parsed content. For presentation-based markup, this "something" will usually be to display the content with a browser. The latest versions of the major Web browsers will read an XML document, apply a style sheet, and display the content. In this case, the browser is a parser and a processor all in one.

For every XML document you create, you need to know how an XML processor will deal with documents written for a specific application and what happens to the content of the document after it's processed. For example, the XML-based application CDF was expressly designed to describe channels for display in Web browsers. CDF files are processed by XML processors built into Web browsers that support CDF (specifically, Microsoft Internet Explorer 4 and later). Then, the information inside the files is shown to the user in the Web browser. Armed with this knowledge, CDF document developers should realize that their CDF documents are best viewed with Internet Explorer 4 and later and probably can't be viewed with Netscape Navigator. In addition, CDF files are at least well-formed XML files; therefore, any generic XML processor will parse them—but that doesn't necessarily mean the processor will know what to do with the CDF content when the parsing is done.

If you're developing documents for an XML application associated with a specific software package or packages (for example, CDF), make sure your audience has access to the tools needed to access and view your documents. If you don't, your efforts will be wasted.

The bottom line is that your XML solution needs a parser and a processing tool. As we mentioned, one tool may possibly do both tasks. A whole collection of XML parsers written in just about every programming language and for just about every operating system are available—usually for free or a minimal charge. If your solution requires that you distribute the parser as part of an application (similar to the parser built in to Web applications), you may have to work out a licensing agreement with the parser's developer.

The processing piece of your application is often a custom tool that you use to do something with your XML. If the XML application is one that you've developed and is designed to drive a particular development effort, you'll most likely need to build your own processor. If you're using XML to drive a Web site, intranet, or other content-publishing activity, you may be able to buy a XML-based system that also delivers HTML, Portable Document Format (PDF), Wireless Markup Language (WML), or any other content format. For information on such systems, visit **www.xmlsoftware.com/dms/**.

Your decision to build or buy a processing tool depends entirely on the goal of your XML solution. The "Defining the Components in Your XML Solution" section in this chapter's Immediate Solutions will help you identify the different pieces in your solution.

Interface Design Elements

XML is all about information. The same can be said for its parent, Standard Generalized Markup Language (SGML), and its distant cousin—or child, depending on how you look at it—HTML. The Internet and the Web provide the creators of information with a powerful mechanism for sharing information with others around the world. No matter which way you look at it, the Internet—including its services, protocols, hardware, and software—is all about information.

But you knew that already, and that's probably why you've turned to XML as a document creation tool. Existing Internet and Web mechanisms don't provide you with the exact solution you need, but an XML application—yours or someone else's—does. So, why kill all these trees to talk about design? In the end, the design of a document can make or break its ability to convey the information it contains. Granted, good design is more important in presentation-based documents than in content-based documents, but half, if not more, of the documents created for XML applications will be presentation-based. As a whole, a document's design includes:

- *Styles*—Fonts, colors, placement of page elements
- *Bells and whistles*—Images, multimedia components
- *Well formedness*—The correct use of markup
- *Congruity*—How well it fits with other documents in a document collection
- *Appropriateness*—How well it adheres to the spirit of the XML application for which it was created

Together, these design elements form the *user interface (UI)* for the document as a whole; the UI is guided entirely by the document's content. In a nutshell, the UI provides a way for the user to interact with the information in the document. Even colors and font selection can contribute to users' success or failure in getting what they need from a document.

Whereas technical design elements work almost invisibly in the background of a document, user interface design elements work up front in center stage. They include:

- Style sheets
- Display tools

Each element is at work in individual documents as well as in document collections. Together, they guide users through the information you present.

Style Sheets

Font faces, heading levels, and colors are all components of page and site styles. They should always be created to reflect the purpose and content of the site. As an example, check out the *Dynamic HTML Black Book* site shown in Figure 20.1.

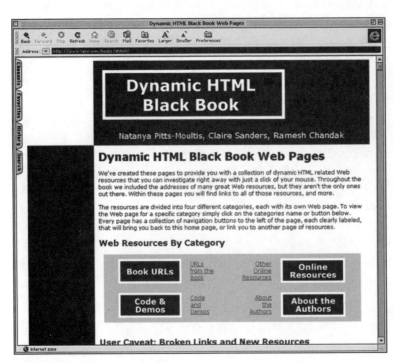

Figure 20.1   The *Dynamic HTML Black Book* site at **www.lanw.com/books/dhtml**.

Style sheets play one of two roles in XML: They either drive the display of a document using flow objects (Extensible Stylesheet Language, or XSL) or they convert your XML structures into HTML for display in a standard Web browser or other HTML-compliant tool (Extensible Stylesheet Language Transformations, or XSLT). Because XSL is still under development, it makes sense to use XSLT to convert your XML to HTML for display in a Web browser. To use XSLT as part of an XML solution to display HTML, you need the following:

- An XSLT style sheet or collection of style sheets to drive the conversion of your XML content to HTML or Extensible HTML (XHTML)

- An XSLT parser and processor to do the document conversion

Even though XSLT style sheets are valid and well-formed XML documents, they are an example of XML documents that require a processor that knows what to do with the markup. An XSL processor is simply a parser that applies the transformation rules described with XSLT to an XML document.

The latest Web browsers have XSLT processors built into them; so if you're planning to deploy your content for Web browsers, you could, in theory, send XML documents with XSLT style-sheet links to the browser and let it handle the transformations. The issues to consider with this approach are:

- *Only the latest versions of the browsers support XML.* Older browsers won't know what to do with your XML, so you're limiting who can access your content. You can detect which browser a user accesses your site with and send either an XML document or an HTML document based on the browser, but then you must maintain two versions of the same content. Until Web browsers that support XML are commonplace, this isn't the best approach to XML conversion.

- *The browser must download both the XML document and the XSLT style sheet to perform the conversion.* Although doing so makes life easier for your server, it puts more responsibility on the client and may cause the page to take longer to download and display.

For now, the best approach to using XSLT style sheets to convert XML to HTML is to perform the transformation on your server and send HTML to Web browsers. Many Web servers will let you cache converted HTML if it isn't going to change often, so the XML transformation doesn't have to happen each time a user requests an XML document.

Entire XML systems, such as those discussed in Chapter 23, are set up to make the XML processing as efficient as possible. A good example of such a complete system that processes style sheets and caches the results is the Cocoon XML-based publishing system, which is part of the open source Apache project. Find out more at **http://xml.apache.org/cocoon/index.html**.

XSLT parsers are available for most platforms and are written in common programming languages such as Java, C++, and Perl. Along with a parser, this is one of the pieces of an XML solution that you can most likely buy (or license for not much money) instead of build yourself. For a listing of XSLT processing tools, visit **www.xmlsoftware.com/xslt/**.

Display Tools

We didn't title this section "Browsers," because a Web browser isn't your only option for a display tool. Granted, the proliferation of the Web makes a Web browser one of the more common XML display tools, but it certainly isn't the only one. A display tool is simply an XML processor that takes XML, applies a Cascading Style Sheet (CSS), XSL, or XSLT style sheet to it, and displays the markup content for the user. A display tool also interprets hyperlinks to make it possible for users to navigate from one piece of content to the next.

The hope in the XML community is that eventually you'll be able browse from XML file to legacy HTML file back to XML file and not know the difference. Of course, the reality of this scenario depends entirely on the vendors that build the browsers. Keep that in mind when you're thinking about what kind of display tool to use in your XML solution (assuming your solution has anything to display, of course).

The attraction of standard Web browsers is that they are just that—standard Web browsers. Users are comfortable with them and know what to expect. A developer, however, may not be as comfortable with a Web browser when it comes to XML, and developers are resigned to the fact that they can never quite know what to expect from a browser, no matter how well documented that browser might be.

Choosing to use a standard Web browser as your display tool means you don't have to build your own display tool. It also means that you're stuck with the functionality the browser comes with. If you decide to build your own display tool, you can customize it to your heart's content—but, of course, you have to build it.

One solution to the display dilemma is to convert all your XML to HTML on the server side using XSLT, as described in the previous section. This may be the safest approach to displaying XML content—for the time being, anyway. However, with this approach, you lose much of the flexibility and extensibility of XML. In general, you're reverting to HTML for display, and you may have started using XML simply because HTML isn't the best vehicle for your content. Before you decide on an XML-to-HTML transformation, be sure it's the best way to display your content.

If HTML simply won't do because your content is more complex than HTML can support well or easily, but you want to take advantage of the familiar standard

Web browser interface your users know and love, you aren't out of luck. Another solution to the XML display dilemma, especially for very complex data, is to build a Java applet display tool that you can embed in a Web page. The applet is responsible for the display of the content, so you can customize it to your heart's desire. However, because the applet is embedded in a Web page, your viewers get to use their familiar Web browser and they won't have to install any special software.

As you can see, the resources you need to implement these two display scenarios are different. If you convert XML to HTML using XSLT, you'll need an XSLT guru on hand, especially if your content is complex. You'll also need an HTML guru who can provide the best combination of HTML elements to display your content. If you go with the applet-in-a-Web-page solution, you'll need a Java guru who can build the applet to display your content. You'll probably also need an interface design specialist who can help you build an applet that is intuitive and easy to use.

Regardless of which solution you choose, know that you aren't alone in your development efforts. Some developers are already delivering XML styled with CSS directly to Web browsers, especially on intranets where they have better control over which browsers people use. Other developers are building server-side XSLT conversion systems, whereas others are taking the applet approach to display.

---

*TIP: If you want to find out what others are doing with XML, visit XMLTree at **www.xmltree.com**. This site details the particulars for a large collection of XML solutions that you can use, in the site's words, "as examples and for inspiration."*

The Components in Two Real-World Solutions

To see how the various pieces of an XML solution work together, it's useful to see how others have built their XML solutions. In the following two sections, we look at two XML solutions and the different components they include.

Solution 1: Email on a Mobile Phone

WappyMail (**www.wappymail.com**) delivers standard Post Office Protocol (POP) mail to mobile phones and other remote digital devices. Because mobile phones aren't designed to be POP mail clients, WappyMail uses WML (which is specifically designed for delivering content to wireless devices) to allow users to access their existing POP mail via their mobile phone or other wireless device. The components in this XML solution are:

- *DTD/application: Wireless Markup Language (WML).* WML is an XML application being developed by companies in the wireless market to deliver Internet content to mobile phones and other wireless devices. WML is managed by the WAP Forum (**www.wapforum.org**).

- *XML documents: WML documents that drive access to a user's POP mailbox as well as the request for mail, display of mail, and other interactions with the mailbox.* Because WML is an established DTD, the XML document developers had to work with the structures provided in the DTD. Because WML is designed for activities such as accessing email from a mobile phone, this was easy to do. For an example of a WML document delivered by the system, visit **www.xmltree.com/resource/testForm.cfm?ResourceID=5896** and click the Get XML Content button.

- *Parser and processor: Specialty parser and processing system built into the digital device.* The WML documents are delivered to the wireless device over a wireless network. It's then up to the device to parse and interpret the WML documents.

- *Display tool: The wireless device.* Part of processing the WML information is preparing it for delivery on a specific wireless device. Because each device may have a different display configuration, each device displays the parsed and processed WML data as appropriate to its particular display.

WML is the driving force behind this solution. It not only describes the content of the mobile phone's display, but it also drives all email activities performed on the phone. Without the parser and WML processor built in to each mobile phone, the WML would be useless. The wireless device has to know what to do with the WML content it receives.

This solution is a good example of how an XML application developed by a group of organizations in a market can make information available to a wide variety of users. WappyMail isn't a mobile phone company; it's a service provider. Because the wireless device vendors have agreed on WML as an XML application for delivering content to wireless devices, WappyMail has a common set of structures to work with as it delivers POP mail access to mobile phones. The same can be said for news providers, stock tickers, and any other services that want to deliver content to wireless devices. WML provides the common ground.

Solution 2: Online Testing

Professional certification and Web-based training are two of the most rapidly growing industries. The ability to deliver test materials via the Web for either practice testing or as part of an online training initiative is key. HTML forms provide a nice way to present limited kinds of test questions. However, building a complete testing engine using HTML and Common Gateway Interface (CGI) is a huge undertaking, simply because the test results and the different ways to use them are more complex than HTML is equipped to deal with. LANWrights, Inc. (**www.lanw.com**)

built an XML-based testing engine to provide a flexible tool for a variety of purposes, including simulating certification testing and as part of an online training solution. The components in this XML-based solution include:

- *DTD/application: A test data DTD defined specifically to describe test questions.* The DTD accounts for different kinds of test questions (multiple choice with one answer, multiple choice with multiple answers, and more). It's also human readable and easy to use.

- *XML documents: Test questions described using the test data DTD.* Because all the questions are saved in the same XML format, they can easily be imported into a database-driven question bank.

- *Parser: Java validating parser from Sun.* Because this is a Java-based solution, a Java-based parser was required. The Sun parser is free and built using pure Java.

- *Processor: A Java applet or servlet specifically designed to process test data.* The applet and servlet depend on the parsed XML data to drive the testing aspects of the testing engine. Other functionality such as grading, marking skipped questions, and navigating the test are also built into the applet and servlet.

- *Display tool: A Web browser.* The testing engine must be delivered in a standard Web browser; this requirement hasn't changed over time. When users want to access the testing tool, they fire up their Web browsers and type in a URL. From the user's perspective, it's very easy to access the testing tool.

It's interesting to note that the testing engine originally used a proprietary text-based scripting language to store test questions for a Java applet to process and display. When it became clear that XML was a safe technology to use, all question content was converted to XML, and the Java applet was reworked to accept XML content. The original applet was also ported to server-side Java servlets to allow more flexibility in deployment.

This solution is a good example of how XML can become part of an existing solution. Because the testing engine now supports XML, it will be easier to import text questions from other sources. If those questions are stored in a different set of XML markup, an XSLT style sheet can convert the questions to the applet's preferred flavor of XML. If a standard test DTD or XML application is developed in the future, existing test questions can be converted to the standard DTD. The applet and servlet will have to be tweaked, but, in reality, both are much more extensible than they were when the test questions were stored in a proprietary format.

Immediate Solutions

Defining the Components in Your XML Solution

The first step in defining the components you need in your XML solution is to perform both a business requirements analysis and an information analysis. From these two analyses, you should gather the following information:

- What does the solution need to do?
- Who will be using the solution?
- What content will the solution use?
- How is the content created and managed?
- How will the solution use the content?

After you perform your business and information analysis, you can start to define your XML component requirements. Some questions to ask are:

- Do you need to create your own DTD, or can you use an existing industry-specific DTD?
- How much content will you need to deal with, and who will develop most of it? If you have non-technical staff building XML content, you need to find the right combination of tools and training to be sure they develop well-formed and, possibly, valid XML documents.
- Do you want to work with data stored in a database?
- Is content display part of the solution?
- Is a certain display tool required (such as a Web browser)?
- In what format must the content be delivered to the display tool (for example, HTML, PDF, XML)?
- Do you need to write style sheets to convert data from one XML vocabulary to another?
- What platform(s) are you developing the application for?

These questions will get you started thinking about your complete XML solution. Process flows for how information will move through your system are helpful, as are data-analysis documents and system-design plans. In reality, an XML solution is a software solution, and it requires the same processes and methods.

Evaluating an XML Application

The goal of an XML application drives document creation and design. If an application and its documents are largely content-based, there won't be much design work to do—except for ensuring that the document is well formed and/or valid and that it doesn't stretch the bounds of the application's markup. For presentation-based applications and documents, design extends past well formedness to the documents' look and feel. Of course, before you begin developing a document for an application, you should make sure its goals match your own. Follow these steps to match an application to your needs:

1. Define your goals. Answer the following questions to help you determine them:

   - What kind of information are you trying to describe with an XML application?

   - What other applications have you looked at as possible solutions and where have they fallen short?

   - Who is your audience?

   - What do you want your audience to get/learn from your information?

   - Is your information based on content or presentation?

2. Define the goal of the application. Turn to application documentation and other XML documents to see how the application has been used as a solution by others.

3. Compare the information you've found for the XML application with your findings about your own goals and see if they're compatible. Remember that you must play by the rules set down by the DTD for creating documents for the application. If you think you might have to bend the rules, the application may not be your best choice.

4. In the end, if you can't find an existing application that meets your needs, consider building your own.

Chapter 21

XML and Databases

In Depth

Data store is a term that can be used to describe any medium that is used to store data. It may be a structured text file, an Extensible Markup Language (XML) file, a relational database, or even some proprietary binary format. In this chapter, we'll compare and contrast how relational databases and XML can be used to store information, and we'll also look at how the two can be used together to provide a reliable and accessible data store.

Databases and XML have many similarities: They both provide ways to structure and store information. Relational databases store information in the form of records and fields, and it's a characteristic of relational databases that the order and relationship one field or record holds to another is not necessarily significant. XML documents can also be structured to store information in a manner similar to databases. In other words, an XML document can be structured to mimic a relational database. However, in XML documents, the order and the relationship of one part of a document to other parts of a document are always significant, and usually important.

For most packets of information, the same information set can be stored either as a relational database or as an XML document. In many cases, little difference exists between the benefits of using either as a storage medium; however, in other cases, it's clearly preferable to use one or the other. Which medium should be used as a data store depends not only on the nature of the data, but also on how the stored data will be used. By and large, if the stored data is going to be used to provide large numbers of subsets of information, and if retrieval speed is imperative, it's better to store data as a database. However, if the data is complex in form or if the data is positionally or sequentially related to other data (as, for example, in most medical and legal records), it's better to store it as XML.

The first section of this chapter quickly reviews the fundamental aspects of a relational database. We'll briefly look at some of the terminology surrounding databases and also briefly examine the way information can be retrieved from a database using the Structured Query Language (SQL). Then, we'll see how the same kinds of procedures can be carried out on an equivalent XML file.

Relational Databases

Table 21.1 is an excerpt from a real-world database. It's a table that logs every admission to a hospital and gives information about the admitting doctor (**doccode**), the doctor's specialty, the date of discharge (**discdate**), the diagnosis code (**drg**), and the length of the patient's stay (**los**). Note that for reasons of brevity and privacy, numerous fields have been deleted. The total number of fields in this table was originally 21, and the total number of records was more than 12,000.

Database Terminology

Here's a brief review of the terminology used in describing databases.

Databases

A *database* comprises any collection of related information. This information is gathered into one or more tables, all of which are usually interrelated in some manner.

Tables

A *table* is divided into a number of rows and columns, known in database terminology as records and fields.

Records and Fields

A *record* is a single entry in a table. For example, one row from Table 21.1 (which is a recordset) is a single record. Note that in a relational database, the order of the records has no semantic significance.

A *field* is a column of information of the same data type. For example, in database theory, it's not possible to have one entry in the same field as a date type and another as a text type. Again, note that in a relational database, the order of the fields has no semantic significance.

If you look at the **los** column, or field, in Table 21.1, the data type of each entry is an integer that represents the number of days the patient was in the hospital.

Table 21.1   An excerpt from a real-world database.

ID	specialty	drg	discdate	los	doccode
21	CD	483	1/4/99	33	4355
22	PUD	416	1/6/99	24	6640
23	CD	476	1/2/99	15	4355
24	IM	204	1/6/99	19	6557
25	U	308	1/14/99	23	6478

The first field in Table 21.1, the **ID** field, is a special field called a *primary index* field. This field must have a unique value for each record. Although a primary index field is not compulsory, most tables will have such a field, and it's essential if the table is going to be related to other tables in the database.

Data Types

Every field must contain information of the same data type. The different data types supported vary with each brand of database. Most, however, support text, numeric, binary, and date fields.

Text Data Types

Text fields are usually limited to a certain number of characters, and this number differs with each brand of database. In Access, for example, the maximum number is 255 characters. If it's required to store a body of text larger than this number, then the database usually stores a pointer to a text file. Again, the name given to this data type varies with each proprietary database. In Access, this field type is called a *memo*; in SQL server, it's called a *text field*.

In general, databases are not optimized to handle this kind of field, and if a database includes several fields of this type, performance will be markedly slowed. If the information to be stored requires several of these fields, it may be better to store the information as an XML file. It should also be noted that most databases use only one-byte characters and, therefore, do not handle Unicode well. If your data contains numerous non-ASCII characters, either get a database designed for the job or use XML, which is designed for two-byte characters.

Recordsets

A *recordset* is any subset of your database. Table 21.1 is a recordset of the original very large table, and you can in fact create recordsets of this subset. A single record can be a recordset, or you can create recordsets with different subsets of information. For example, here's a recordset of all the records where the ID field has a value of 22:

```
22    PUD    416    1/6/99    24    6640
```

Here's a recordset of the **drg**, **los**, and **doccode** fields of the specialty CD:

```
483    33    4355
476    15    4355
```

These recordsets are usually created using a process called *querying* the database. In fact, a standard language exists for this purpose: the Structured Query Language (SQL).

SQL

Numerous proprietary relational databases are on the market. Luckily, it's not necessary to learn a separate set of rules for each database. Most databases conform to an international standard called SQL (pronounced "sequel"). SQL is both an International Organization for Standardization (ISO) and an American National Standards Institute (ANSI) standard. For the record, most current databases conform to the ISO standard SQL92, although there is a later standard, SQL99.

Using SQL, standard statements can be made into a database that will select and construct recordsets. SQL can also be used for updating and inserting new data and fields into a database. What follows is not meant to be a tutorial on SQL: These examples are just to show some of the more common things that are done with SQL, as a basis to show how similar manipulations can be carried out on an XML file.

Queries and Selections

Probably the most common use of SQL is to select various fields and records from a table to create a recordset of selected data. To produce the last example (the recordset of the **drg**, **los**, and **doccode**), you would write the following SQL statement:

```
SELECT drg,los,doccode FROM mytable WHERE specialty = "CD"
```

The SQL keywords are capitalized, and **mytable** is the name of the table. The statement instructs the database engine to search through its records and make a recordset containing the values for the **drg**, **los**, and **doccode** fields, where the value of the **specialty** field is **CD**.

Note that if you use the wildcard (*) in place of the **drg**, **los**, and **doccode** fields, as follows

```
SELECT * FROM mytable WHERE specialty = "CD"
```

all the fields would have been selected.

Insertions and Updates

Tables can also be updated and/or new rows and columns inserted using the SQL language. Doing so is out of scope for an XML book; we mention it because, as you will see in the "XQL and XML Data Stores" section, the Document Object Model (DOM) can be used to produce similar functionality in an XML data store.

DISTINCT and Grouping

SQL allows the user to eliminate redundant data. For example, if you want to make a list of all the **doccode** numbers, you would provide a query such as:

```
SELECT doccode FROM mytable;
```

The following recordset would be returned.

```
4355
6640
4355
6557
6478
```

Note the duplication of **4355**. To get rid of the duplication, you need to use the **DISTINCT** keyword. So, the query

```
SELECT DISTINCT doccode FROM mytable;
```

would return the following recordset:

```
6640
4355
6557
6478
```

This recordset can even be ordered, by using this code:

```
SELECT DISTINCT doccode FROM mytable ORDER BY doccode
```

The query will return this recordset:

```
4355
6478
6557
6640
```

Aggregates

It's also possible to summarize data using aggregate functions. For example, the query

```
SELECT COUNT(doccode) FROM mytable;
```

would return the integer **5**.

However, the query

```
SELECT COUNT(DISTINCT doccode) FROM mytable;
```

would return the integer **4**.

Other aggregate functions are **SUM**, **MAX**, **MIN**, and **AVG**. Here, they are applied to the **los** (length of stay) field:

```
SELECT MAX(los) FROM mytable; returns 33

SELECT MIN(los) FROM mytable; returns 15

SELECT SUM(los) FROM mytable; returns 115

SELECT AVG(los) FROM mytable; returns 23
```

RADBMS

Each database has an engine that allows it to search, filter, and collate the records in its memory. The engine working in conjunction with the database is known as a Random Access Data Base Management System (RADBMS). Over the years, every company that produces a database puts a lot of work into optimizing the code that runs the databases. The net result is that most databases are extremely fast and efficient at performing searches. As of yet, engines that search XML documents cannot begin to approach the speed of performance of a database, although the MSXML3 Active X object is very fast (more of this later in the "XQL and XML Data Stores" section). This means that if speed of retrieval is of the essence for your application, XML still cannot rival a database as a data store. However for data stores of up to about 20,000 records where you're not expecting more than one hit per second, the difference in speed probably will not be noticeable.

The following section looks at an XML data store and shows how it can be sorted and collated in the same way that a database sorts and collates its information into recordsets using SQL.

XML Data Stores

Here's the same information that appeared in Table 21.1 structured as an XML file. The element types have been selected to describe the fields of the "XML table":

```
<recordset>
<record id="a21">
   <id>21</id><spec>CD</spec><drg>483</drg>
      <dd>1/4/99</dd> <los>33</los><dc>4355</dc>
</record>
<record id="a22">
   <id>22</id><spec>PUD</spec><drg>416</drg>
      <dd>1/6/99</dd><los>24</los><dc>6640</dc>
</record>
```

```
<record id="a23">
   <id>23</id><spec>CD</spec><drg>476</drg>
      <dd>1/2/99</dd><los>15</los><dc>4355</dc>
</record>
<record id="a24">
   <id>24</id><spec>IM</spec><drg>204</drg>
      <dd>1/6/99</dd><los>19</los><dc>6557</dc>
</record>
<record id="a25">
   <id>25</id><spec>U</spec><drg>308</drg>
      <dd>1/14/99</dd><los>23</los><dc>6478</dc>
</record>
</recordset>
```

Superficially, the information in the previous code is exactly the same as the information in Table 21.1. However, note that the XML file uses a tree structure, and order is important. In a database, the order of the records and the fields is unimportant; the query language, SQL, is designed to be independent of any ordering. In XML, however, the order is important. Each of the records is indexed; and, more important, the fields have a parent/sibling relationship. The element type **dc** is the **lastChild** of the element type **record**, and element type **id** is the **firstChild**.

Data Types in XML

Unlike in a database, each cell in an XML data store can hold only one type of data—namely, character data. If you're retrieving data that represents a date from an XML data store for use in a program, you must cast it from a string data type to a date data type before you can use it. Doing so uses computer resources, and if speed is critical or if your application is making copious use of date manipulations, it may be better to store this snippet of data in a database.

The XML Schema specification—a technique for describing XML markup using XML notation, rather than a Standard Generalized Markup Language (SGML)-based Document Type Definition (DTD)—is not yet a recommended World Wide Web Consortium (W3C) standard. Until it becomes one, there's no way to control or verify what type of data is entered into an XML element's cell. As far as a DTD is concerned (the only officially-supported method for defining XML document structure at present), every entry is character data. Even when XML Schema becomes a recommendation and applications implement it, you should remember that even though you'll be able to control the form of the data that's entered into an element cell, it will still be a character representation of that form and not the form itself.

Take, for example, the long integer value 120,000. In a database, it's stored in memory as a single three-byte data element. However, in XML it must be stored as the character representation **120,000**, which takes up 12 or 14 bytes of memory. Further, if you tried to enter **apples** into this field in a relational database, the database would generate an error message automatically. In XML, unless you write a *hand-rolled* function, a DTD-based application will happily accept either **120,000** or **apples**, because both are valid strings.

XQL and XML Data Stores

The W3C is in the process of defining a language that is to XML what SQL is to a database: the XML Query Language (XQL). However, at the time of writing (August 2000), this process is very much in the early design stage. The latest working draft can be found at **www.w3.org/TR/query-datamodel/**. Don't be too alarmed by the apparent complexity of this document, because experience indicates that a working draft progresses from complex to more understandable. We hope the final draft will match much of the simplicity that characterizes the SQL standard documents.

One of the problems encountered by XQL is that an element is a much more complicated container than a data store cell. Data store cells are all the same size in memory, and they contain only one type of information. Each cell also has only two relationships: to a record or to a field.

In XML, an element cell has several relationships: to its ancestors, to its siblings, and to its descendants. Also, each element cell can be modified by encumbering it with attributes, which an XML query language must be able to analyze.

Although all these factors add to the richness of XML as a storage medium, they also add to the problems and complexity for any query language designed to access objects stored in XML form.

Queries and Selections

Until the XQL language matures and offers working implementations, it's necessary to query and make selections from XML documents using the DOM, XSLT, and hand-rolled functions. It's relatively easy to retrieve a single record from our example XML data store, provided we've tagged each record with a unique ID, as we have here. For example, to retrieve the following record

```
<record id="a22">
   <id>22</id><spec>PUD</spec><drg>416</drg>
      <dd>1/6/99</dd><los>24</los><dc>6640</dc>
</record>
```

you simply use the DOM level II **getElementByID("a22")** method.

To mimic the following SQL statement, the equivalent XML markup is more complex:

```
SELECT drg,los,doccode FROM mytable WHERE specialty = "CD"
```

For example, using the DOM and ECMAScript, you would first have to retrieve all the records as a list, search them individually, and then build up an XML recordset. Listing 21.1 shows the ECMAScript code to perform this task.

Listing 21.1 Building a recordset from an XML data store.

```
var xrec=recordset

    document.write ( "&lt;xql:recordset><br />");
 var reclist=xrec.getElementsByTagName("record")
  var recset=""
  for(var i=0;i<reclist.length;i++)
    {
    if(reclist.item(i).firstChild.nextSibling.firstChild.data=="CD")
      {
       recset=recset + "&lt;drg>" +
reclist.item(i).firstChild.nextSibling.nextSibling.firstChild.data +
"&lt;/drg>"
       recset=recset + "&lt;los>" +
reclist.item(i).firstChild.nextSibling.nextSibling.nextSibling.
nextSibling.firstChild.data + "&lt;/los>"
       recset=recset + "&lt;doccode>" +
reclist.item(i).lastChild.firstChild.data + "&lt;/doccode></br>"

      }
    }
    document.write (recset + "&lt;/xql:recordset>");
```

As you can see, if you want to do complex queries on an XML data store today, you must do a lot of the query processing work yourself. However, the good news is that XML software is improving tremendously. For example, the Microsoft MSXML3 Dynamic Link Library (DLL) object is about 100 times faster than the original DLL. XSLT can also be used for complex queries.

Updates and Inserts
Updating and inserting records can easily be done using the factory methods of the DOM. This topic is covered in Chapter 19.

Related solution:	Found on page:
Using the XML DOM to Access XML Objects	546

Grouping and DISTINCT

If you want to mimic the SQL **DISTINCT** keyword, you again have to write your own code. Listing 21.2 shows how you do it using ECMAScript.

Listing 21.2   Deleting redundant dc values from a list of dc elements.

```
var reclist=xrec.getElementsByTagName("dc")
  alert(reclist.length)
  var docarray = new Array();
  var doccode
  var docname
  var docpresent
  var counter=0

  for(var i=0;i<reclist.length;i++)
    {
    docpresent=false
    docname=reclist.item(i).firstChild.data

    //document.write(docname+"<br />");
     for(var j=0;j<docarray.length;j++)
      {
      if (doccode==docarray[j])
        {docpresent=true;break;}
      }
      if(docpresent==false)
        {
        docarray[counter]=docname
        counter++
        }
    }
  for(i=0;i<docarray.length;i++)
    {document.write (docarray[i] +"<br />");}
```

If you want to sort the values, you have to write your own **bubble** or **Shell** sort.

Aggregates

Again, if you want to mimic the SQL aggregate functions, you must write your own. The following is a script that mimics the **MAX** function:

```
var reclist=xrec.getElementsByTagName("los")
  //alert(reclist.length)
  var losmax=0
  var templos=0
```

```
for(var i=0;i<reclist.length;i++)
  {
  templos=reclist.item(i).firstChild.data;
  if(templos > losmax)
    {
    losmax=templos;
    }
  }
document.write (losmax +"<br />");
```

Using XML as a Data Store

The preceding sections have shown how you can accomplish most of the things that you want to do with XML. They have perhaps also left you wondering why you should bother with XML—at least until the XQL standards have matured and accompanying software is available to manipulate XML files as easily as you can manipulate databases with SQL. After all, who wants to write and debug code when the same thing can be accomplished by writing a few SQL queries to a database?

Furthermore, over the years, the makers of relational databases have optimized their code for efficiency and speed. As a result, queries to databases will probably run much more quickly than any code that you can write to search an XML document (or at least more quickly than any code we can write).

This is all true; however, certain types of data are difficult to store in databases. Maintaining a list of addresses or hospital admissions is one thing, but how about complex documents such as medical records or legal records? Consider Table 21.2.

Some visits to a doctor's office are simple and others are complex. If you use a database to record all such visits, they will all be stored using the same flat format. Therefore, this information would be more efficient if stored in an XML file. (Another example would be a complex office note that has several subsections

Table 21.2   A sample medical record.

Date	Clinic Number	Attending Practitioner	Office Note	Prescriptions and Disposition
Jan 4 2001	123	Dr. Crippen	Patient is anemic following childbirth.	Iron 300mg TID for 1 month.
Jan 4 2001	456	Dr. Strangelove	This patient has numerous problems (...2000 words follow).	(A whole number of complex transactions and tests are detailed.)

you would like to be able to collate and search; you'd be unable to do this if you stored the information in a database.)

Furthermore, it's unlikely that you would have to make numerous searches or complex correlations (two areas in which it's better to use a database as your data store) with this medical-record data. Because you probably won't have to perform those functions, that's all the more reason to store these records as XML rather than in a database.

Here's what Table 21.2 might look like if it was stored as XML (note that we include some additional information in this markup):

```
<clinNotes>
<officeNote>
 <date>Jan 4 2001<date>
 <clinicNumber>123</clinicNumber>
 <attPract>Dr. Crippen</attPract>
 <simpleOfficeNote>Patient is anemic following childbirth.</
simpleOfficeNote>
 <disposition>
  <prescriptions>Iron 300mg TID for 1 month</prescriptions>
  <return>One month</return>
  <note>Get hemoglobin prior to visit</note>
</disposition>
</office-note>
<officeNote>
 <date>Jan 4 2001<date>
 <clinicNumber>456</clinicNumber>
 <attPract>Dr. Strangelove</attPract>
 <complexOfficeNote>
  <history>[Complex note with own child elements]</history>
  <pe>[Complex note with own child elements]</pe>
  <other></other>
</complexOfficeNote>
  <disposition>
  <prescriptions>[Numerous]</prescriptions>
  <tests>[Numerous]</tests>
  <consultations>[Numerous]</consultations>
  <return>[detailed instructions]</return>

</disposition>
</office-note>
<clinNotes>
```

Note that the hierarchical nature of XML allows you to add layer upon layer of granularity to the more complex aspects of an office note, giving a richness of structure that is just not possible with a database. These substructures will be easily retrievable using XQL or the DOM. For example, you could do a search and find out which patients had a consultation with Dr. Y in the year 2000. Building a database with the same functionality would be extremely difficult!

When to Use XML as a Data Store

This section and the next provide you with a brief account of some of the reasons you should consider when deciding whether to use XML or a database as a data store. Consider using XML as the primary storage for information when the following criteria are met:

- *The information is in a complex form.* Some forms of records do not scale well to databases. This is clearly the case with the medical record in the previous example. Furthermore, a doctor's patient record may contain a few office visits or a hundred or more. It's difficult for a database to be structured to cope with this variation; however, XML can handle this situation with ease.

- *The individual fields are large and complex.* Again, records such as medical records in which an office note can be anything from a few words to several pages do not store well in databases. In a database, each field must be the same size unless (for example, in Access, text fields can only be up to 255 characters) it provides a pointer to an outside file. Although databases handle the problem of variable size by providing pointers, most databases do not handle this situation well.

- *Speed of searching is not an issue.* As mentioned, database engines are optimized for speed. Although the DOM enables you to carry out any search you want on an XML document, it's still a slow process compared to a database search. At peak periods, it's said that the ESPN server carries out 12,000 searches per second! There's no way (at present) that an XML search can cope with numbers like these.

- *Data typing is not important.* Everything in XML is stored as a string. Although schemas will allow data descriptions, the information is still stored as a string. Databases, on the other hand, can store data types in their native formats, making it easy to pass data to programs that need to manipulate the data (for example, an Astronomy program with the coordinates of stars). Using a traditional database to store information of this type is more efficient.

- *The data will be archived for a long time.* If you plan on keeping the data for a number of years, it makes sense to store it as XML. Because XML is readable by any agent that can read ASCII (including humans), it means that whereas you can almost guarantee that the software in 40 years time will not be able to read today's databases, software will exist that will be able to read an XML file. The Y2K problem of recent memory should serve as a reminder of the importance of persisting data over time.

- *The data needs to be accessed by different systems.* Every platform that understands ASCII (or Unicode) can read XML. Therefore, programs and applications running on Unix, Linux, Macs, PCs, or any other system can easily access data stored as XML.

- *The database is small but the need for scalability is important.* XML is ideal for small data stores, such as the type that will meet the needs of a start-up company. Because it's so easy to pass the information to a DBMS if necessary, XML data stores are extremely scaleable.

- *Information needs to be archived.* Even information that is better stored in a database is often more effectively archived as XML. Not only does XML take up less space in many instances (compressed XML files take up only a little more space than compressed ASCII files), but there's also a guarantee that the data can be read by any system on any platform at any time in the future.

When Not to Use XML as a Data Store

If the data that needs to be stored matches any of the following criteria, it's probably better *not* to use XML as a data store:

- *Complex searches are necessary.* As mentioned previously, databases are optimized for query speed. If you expect numerous hits per second to your data store, use a database.

- *Complex queries are required.* Again, over the years, databases have been optimized to work with SQL. It's tedious to write the code to mimic this functionality in an XML document. Chances are that you won't be prepared to invest the time and energy it takes to write tight, fast code that comes anywhere close to the code professional database coders have accomplished over the years.

- *Speed of searching is an issue.* Again, databases have been optimized for speed. Although the speed of some of the recent XML engines is impressive, they still, for the most part, do not match the speed of a database engine. However, because of recent advances, there may be other compelling reasons to use XML. You may be pleasantly surprised!

- *The data store will be under high peak loads.* Again, databases have been designed to take a high rate of hits. For now, it's unlikely that your server will be able to match this functionality.

- *Data needs to be typed (categorized).* XML treats everything as a string. You can't check entries for the correct data type when you use XML (short of writing your own verification scripts). In addition, when the data is retrieved, it's necessary to cast it to the correct data type. All this uses computer resources and slows down your applications.

- *Different data needs to be indexed.* When you select a recordset from a database, it's relatively easy to index it by one of the fields; for example, you can sort your database contacts by state, by ZIP code, or alphabetically by name. To do this in XML, you'd have to write your own sorting code. Although sorting is a fairly common task (most programming books have entire sections on the subject), chances are that the database will do it more efficiently and quickly than you can (or at least more quickly than any code we can write).

Immediate Solutions

Knowing When to Use XML with a Database

In previous sections, we've considered an either/or option. In fact, XML and data-bases fit together very nicely, and most applications that process data can use both forms to their advantage. Here are some of the uses that can be made of XML in such a hybrid system:

- To back up and archive a data store
- To store frequently requested queries
- To store resource-intensive queries
- As a package to ship data between various databases and data stores
- As a package to display data
- As a data store itself

Let's consider each of these in turn.

Using XML to Back Up and Archive a Data Store

Using XML to back up and archive a data store is probably the chief use of XML with databases at this time. You can write scripts that convert database tables to XML, and you can keep those XML files for future reference. It's also relatively easy to convert XML back to a recordset if you need to. Two Active Server Pages (ASP) scripts that accomplish this task are given at the end of this section.

Using XML to Store Frequently Requested Queries

In an Internet application, certain requests from a database make up about 90 percent of the activity. By converting these requests to XML or XHTML, down-load speed can be increased and server resources can be conserved.

Using XML to Store Resource-Intensive Queries

Some SQL operations are resource-intensive. For example, if you're running ag-gregate statements on numerous recordsets, the time to handle the transactions can become prohibitive in Internet terms. For example, in our example database (Table 21.1), if you wanted to calculate the standard deviation for **los** (length of stay) for each **drg** (diagnosis code) in 5,000 records, it would take about three minutes on an average server. It's much better to do this calculation once and store the results as an XML file. The XML file will take about two seconds to download.

Using XML as a Package to Ship Data between Various Databases and Data Stores

How do you send data from, for example, an Access database to a Database 2 (DB2—an IBM relational database) database? The answer is "with great difficulty," unless you employ XML. The trick is to convert the data to XML as an intermediary.

Using XML as a Package to Display Data

Data in data stores can be easily converted to either XML or XHTML for ease of display over the Internet. An example script for doing this using ASP is shown at the end of this chapter.

Using XML as a Data Store Itself

Data can be held entirely as XML. In fact, most data-driven Internet applications use a mixture of databases and XML to store their data. As the XML engines improve, expect to find more and more of the data stored as native XML.

Using Scripts to Manipulate XML and Data Stores

The scripts in the following section are executed using ASP and a Windows NT Server. However, they can easily be exported to other systems. For accessing the databases, we've assumed that your server administrator has already set up a *Data Source Name* (DSN) for them. For details on how to do this, grab a copy of *Beginning ASP Databases*, from Wrox Press, by John Kaufman.

Using Scripts to Archive a Database

As mentioned in the previous section, probably the most common use of XML in conjunction with a database is to archive the database content as XML. The following script shows how this is achieved. The process is quite fast; for example, to back up 5,000 records with the script shown in Listing 21.3 takes about three seconds. Performance will vary, of course, depending on the power of the server.

Listing 21.3   Backing up a database table as XML.

```
<%

Server.ScriptTimeOut =2000


response.write now & "<br />"
response.write  "Backing up pldata table<br />"
'make a scripting object

dim oFSO,oTS,fname

  set oFSO=server.createObject("Scripting.FileSystemObject")

  fname="c:\book_xmlbb\backup1.xml"

'open or create the xml file
  if oFSO.FileExists(fname) then
    set oTS=oFSO.OpenTextFile(fname,8) '8=for appending
  else
    set oTS=oFSO.CreateTextFile(fname)
  end if

%>

<%

dim oConn,oRS,oRS2,strSQL,counter,xrec

 'make a connection object
  set oConn=server.createObject("ADODB.connection")
  oConn.open "DSN=pldata"


 'recordset of all prinprocs
  set oRS=Server.CreateObject("ADODB.recordset")

  strSQL="SELECT  * from pldata "
  oRS.open strSQL,oConn

dim strXMLrec
counter=0
 strXMLrec = "<pldatabackup date=" & Now & ">" & chr(13) & chr(10)
  oTS.writeLine strXMLrec
```

```
do while NOT oRS.EOF
  strXMLrec=strXMLrec & "<record id=a" & oRS("ID") & ">"
  strXMLrec=strXMLrec & "<specialty>" & oRS("speciality")& "</specialty>"
  strXMLrec=strXMLrec & "<drg>" & oRS("drg")& "</drg>"
  strXMLrec=strXMLrec & "<dd>" & oRS("discdate")& "</dd>"
  strXMLrec=strXMLrec & "<los>" & oRS("los")& "</los>"
  strXMLrec=strXMLrec & "<dc>" & oRS("doccode")& "</dc>"
  strXMLrec=strXMLrec & "</record>" & chr(13) & chr(10)
  oTS.writeLine strXMLrec
  strXMLrec=""
  oRS.moveNext
   'counter=counter+1
   'if counter=999 then exit do
  loop

  strXMLrec= "</pldatabackup>"
  oTS.writeLine strXMLrec
response.write  Now & "</br>"
response.write "pltable backed up"

'housekeeping
oTS.close
set oTS=Nothing

oRS.close
set oRS=Nothing


oConn.close
set oConn=Nothing

%>
```

Now, let's analyze some of this script. Just in case you're backing up a very large database, you set the time-out property to a large number to give ASP time to do it, as follows:

```
<%

Server.ScriptTimeOut =2000
```

You can benchmark the procedure with a simple method. In this snippet, **now** is a Visual Basic (VB) method that gives the current date and time:

```
response.write now & "<br />"
response.write  "Backing up pldata table<br />"
```

You'll be writing a text stream, so you must make a scripting object to receive the stream:

```
'make a scripting object
```

Then, you declare the variables:

```
dim oFSO,oTS,fname

  set oFSO=server.createObject("Scripting.FileSystemObject")
```

This is the file name to which you'll be writing the backup stream:

```
  fname="c:\book_xmlbb\backup1.xml"
```

Check to see if the file already exists, and if not, open it. In the process, you create a text stream object to receive the text stream, as follows:

```
'open or create the xml file
  if oFSO.FileExists(fname) then
    set oTS=oFSO.OpenTextFile(fname,8) '8=for appending
  else
    set oTS=oFSO.CreateTextFile(fname)
  end if

%>
```

This next section opens the database that you want to back up:

```
<%
```

This code declares the variables and makes a connection and recordset object:

```
dim oConn,oRS,oRS2,strSQL,counter,xrec

 'make a connection object
  set oConn=server.createObject("ADODB.connection")
```

You're using a DSN to connect to your database. You could use a connection string, but using a DSN is preferable:

```
oConn.open "DSN=pldata"
```

```
'recordset of all prinprocs
set oRS=Server.CreateObject("ADODB.recordset")
```

The recordset is filled with all the contents of the **pldata** table:

```
strSQL="SELECT  * from pldata "
oRS.open strSQL,oConn
```

```
dim strXMLrec
counter=0
```

Now, write the opening tag for your latest backup and date it. **chr(13)** is a new line in VB, and **chr(10)** is a linefeed:

```
strXMLrec = "<pldatabackup date=" & Now & ">" & chr(13) & chr(10)
```

Write the line to your opened file

```
oTS.writeLine strXMLrec
```

Now, loop through all the records in your recordset and make a line of XML for each record:

```
do while NOT oRS.EOF
  strXMLrec=strXMLrec & "<record id=a" & oRS("ID") & ">"
  strXMLrec=strXMLrec & "<specialty>" & oRS("specialty")& "</specialty>"
  strXMLrec=strXMLrec & "<drg>" & oRS("drg")& "</drg>"
  strXMLrec=strXMLrec & "<dd>" & oRS("discdate")& "</dd>"
  strXMLrec=strXMLrec & "<los>" & oRS("los")& "</los>"
  strXMLrec=strXMLrec & "<dc>" & oRS("doccode")& "</dc>"
  strXMLrec=strXMLrec & "</record>" & chr(13) & chr(10)
  oTS.writeLine strXMLrec
```

Remember to empty your string before filling it with the next record. Failure to do this can produce a file in the gigabyte dimensions, which can seriously bog down your platform:

```
strXMLrec=""
oRS.moveNext
```

The following two lines have been commented out, but are kept to show you that it's easy to write a set number of records:

```
 'counter=counter+1
 'if counter=999 then exit do
loop

strXMLrec= "</pldatabackup>"
oTS.writeLine strXMLrec
response.write  Now & "</br>"
response.write "pltable backed up"
```

Close all the objects you've created, and set them to **Nothing**. Failure to do this with a text stream can lead to difficulties opening the file in another application, because the platform will think another application is still writing to it:

```
'housekeeping
oTS.close
set oTS=Nothing

oRS.close
set oRS=Nothing


oConn.close
set oConn=Nothing

%>
```

TIP: *If needed, this script can be set to run automatically at a set time of the day, making archiving of databases a very simple process.*

Converting XML to a Database Recordset

The following code shows how you would convert an XML file that's set up as a series of records to a database. All the records in this XML file are of the following format:

```
<record>
<spec>CD</spec><drg>483</drg><discdate>1/4/99</discdate><los>33</los>
<pd>40493</pd><pp>311</pp><doccode>4355</doccode>
</record>
```

The code in Listing 21.4 loops through the XML file and reads each XML record into a database record of the construct shown in Table 21.3.

Table 21.3   The construct of each XML record in the form of a database record.

specialty	drg	discdate	los	prindiag	prinproc	doccode
CD	483	1/4/99	33	40493	311	4355

Listing 21.4   Reading an XML file structured as a recordset into a database.

```
fname="c:\xmlbb\pldata.xml"

set xfile=server.CreateObject("Microsoft.XMLDOM")
xfile.load(fname)

set reclist= xfile.getElementsByTagName("record")


dim specialty, drg,discdate,los,prindiag,prinproc,doccode

dim oConn
  set oConn=Server.createobject("ADODB.connection")
'here we use a DSN
'Data Source Names must be set up us by the Server administrator

  oConn.open "DSN=pldata"


for i=0 to reclist.length-1
'i=1
specialty = reclist.item(i).firstChild.firstChild.data

drg= cint(reclist.item(i).firstChild.nextSibling.firstChild.data)

discdate=cdate(reclist.item(i).firstChild.nextSibling.nextSibling.
firstChild.data)

los=cint(reclist.item(i).firstChild.nextSibling.nextSibling.nextSibling.
firstChild.data )

prindiag=
clng(reclist.item(i).firstChild.nextSibling.nextSibling.nextSibling.
nextSibling.firstChild.data)

prinproc=
clng(reclist.item(i).firstChild.nextSibling.nextSibling.nextSibling.
nextSibling.nextSibling.firstChild.data)
```

```
doccode=
cint(reclist.item(i).firstChild.nextSibling.nextSibling.nextSibling.
nextSibling.nextSibling.nextSibling.firstChild.data)

strSQL="INSERT INTO pldata
(specialty,drg,discdate,los,prindiag,prinproc,doccode)
VALUES ("
strSQL=strSQL & "'" & specialty & "',"
strSQL=strSQL & drg &","
strSQL=strSQL & "#" & discdate & "#,"
strSQL=strSQL & los &","
strSQL=strSQL & prindiag &","
strSQL=strSQL & prinproc &","
strSQL=strSQL & doccode
strSQL=strSQL & ");"

response.write strSQL
oConn.Execute(strSQL)
next

response.write "XML string converted to access data base<br />"
response.write now


'housekeeping
  oConn.close
  set oConn=Nothing

%>
```

Here is a breakdown of the code. This variable contains the source of the XML file. Of course, this will be different on your server:

```
fname="c:\xmlbb\pldata.xml"
```

In VBScript (and VB), the **Set** keyword is used to instantiate an object. **Microsoft.XMLDOM** is an ActiveX object, and it must be registered on your server. If you have Internet Explorer 5 registered, then **Microsoft.XMLDOM** will automatically be registered. The latest version of this DLL is MSXML3.DLL:

```
set xfile=server.CreateObject("Microsoft.XMLDOM")
```

After the object has been instantiated, it must be loaded with appropriate data. The **load** keyword points to an XML file:

589

```
xfile.load(fname)
```

Next, make a **reclist** object of the file:

```
set reclist= xfile.getElementsByTagName("record")
```

Declare the variables you're going to use:

```
dim specialty, drg,discdate,los,prindiag,prinproc,doccode

dim oConn
```

Create an **ADODB** object:

```
set oConn=Server.createobject("ADODB.connection")
```

There are two ways to connect to a database in ASP. You can either use a connection string, which differs with each brand of database, or you can have your administrator set up a DSN. The later is preferable and faster:

```
'here we use a DSN
'Data Source Names must be set up by the Server administrator

oConn.open "DSN=p1data"
```

Loop through your nodeList of record elements. For each one, read in the value to a variable that has been previously declared:

```
for i=0 to reclist.length-1
'i=1
specialty = reclist.item(i).firstChild.firstChild.data

drg= cint(reclist.item(i).firstChild.nextSibling.firstChild.data)

discdate=cdate(reclist.item(i).firstChild.nextSibling.nextSibling.
firstChild.data)

los=cint(reclist.item(i).firstChild.nextSibling.nextSibling.nextSibling.
firstChild.data )

prindiag= clng(reclist.item(i).firstChild.nextSibling.nextSibling.
nextSibling.nextSibling.firstChild.data)

prinproc= clng(reclist.item(i).firstChild.nextSibling.nextSibling.
nextSibling.nextSibling.nextSibling.firstChild.data)
```

```
doccode= cint(reclist.item(i).firstChild.nextSibling.nextSibling.
nextSibling.nextSibling.nextSibling.nextSibling.firstChild.data)
```

Now, build up a SQL string. Note that this technique builds up the string in stages:

```
strSQL="INSERT INTO pldata
(specialty,drg,discdate,los,prindiag,prinproc,doccode)
 VALUES ("
strSQL=strSQL & "'" & specialty & "',"
strSQL=strSQL & drg &","
strSQL=strSQL & "#" & discdate & "#,"
strSQL=strSQL & los &","
strSQL=strSQL & prindiag &","
strSQL=strSQL & prinproc &","
strSQL=strSQL & doccode
strSQL=strSQL & ");"
```

As a debugging mechanism, it's often a good idea to write out the string:

```
'response.write strSQL
```

You now execute the string that reads the record into your database:

```
oConn.Execute(strSQL)
```

Repeat the procedure for each record in your XML file:

```
next
```

```
response.write "XML string converted to access data base<br />"
```

Finally, close the object and set its value to **Nothing** to conserve resources:

```
'housekeeping
  oConn.close
  set oConn=Nothing
```

```
%>
```

Converting a Recordset to X(HT)ML

Quite often, you want to present a recordset as an XHTML table or as a drop-down box in an HTML form so that further selections can be made. The following script will convert a recordset to an HTML stream. The example shows how to create an ordered drop-down box of all the **drg** codes in the example database (Table 21.1):

```
<html>
<title>Creating a dropdown list from pldata</title>
<%

   dim oConn,oRS

 'make a connection object
    set oConn=server.createObject("ADODB.connection")
    oConn.open "DSN=pldata"

       set oRS=Server.CreateObject("ADODB.recordset")

    strSQL="SELECT  DISTINCT drg FROM pldata order by drg;"

    oRS.open strSQL,oConn


%>

<div>Select a DRG for analysis from the list below.</div>
<form method="post" name="getdrg" action="drganal.asp">
<select   name="drg">
<%
  do while NOT oRS.EOF
  response.write "<option value='" & oRS("drg") & "'>"
  & oRS("drg")  & "</option>"
  oRS.moveNext
  loop
%>
</select>
<input type="submit" value="Analyse DRG" />
</form>
</html>
```

Now, let's analyze the previous markup. This is introductory XHTML markup:

```
<html>
<title>Creating a dropdown list from pldata</title>
<%
```

Declare the variables and instantiate them as objects:

```
    dim oConn,oRS

 'make a connection object
    set oConn=server.createObject("ADODB.connection")
```

Again, we assume you're using a DSN to connect to the database:

```
    oConn.open "DSN=pldata"

        set oRS=Server.CreateObject("ADODB.recordset")
```

This SQL statement selects all the values from the **drg** field, eliminates redundant and repeat information, and then orders the values:

```
    strSQL="SELECT  DISTINCT drg FROM pldata order by drg;"

    oRS.open strSQL,oConn
```

```
%>
```

This is pure XHTML code:

```
<div>Select a DRG for analysis from the list below.</div>
<form method="post" name="getdrg" action="drganal.asp">
<select  name="drg">
```

You now loop through the record and write the XHTML **option** elements with the values from the recordset:

```
<%
  do while NOT oRS.EOF
  response.write "<option value='" & oRS("drg") & "'>" & oRS("drg")  &
  "</option>"
  oRS.moveNext
  loop
%>
```

Finally, you end with some more XHTML code:

```
</select>
<input type="submit" value="Analyse DRG" />
</form>
</html>
```

Chapter 22

Programming with XML

In Depth

This chapter reviews the programming philosophy behind the different techniques for working with XML data in computer programs, and supplies examples of each approach that can start you on a solution to your programming problems.

A programmer can take three major paths when working with XML. Each involves a completely different approach. The paths are:

- *The Document Object Model (DOM)*—In this approach, the entire XML document is brought into memory as a hierarchical "tree" of nodes, all descended from a root. The programmer can then apply various methods to locate and manipulate the nodes.

- *The Simple Application Programming Interface (API) for XML (SAX)*—In the SAX approach, the XML document is read by a parser, which identifies each element as it's encountered and calls methods supplied by the programmer as the document is read.

- *The Extensible Stylesheet Language Transformations (XSLT) approach*— Rather than the procedural programming of DOM and SAX, XSLT uses a "declarative" style of programming that many people don't even recognize as programming. Nevertheless, a programmer can incorporate XSLT processing into a program in a variety of ways. XSLT processing can be used in cooperation with both DOM- and SAX-based programs.

The DOM Approach

Figure 22.1 is a conceptual diagram of the way programmers approach an XML document using the DOM. Essentially, you set up a parser with an XML source, stand back, and let it run. If there's an error, you get an error report; if there isn't, you get a DOM object that you can then manipulate.

Generally speaking, for any search or other manipulation of the DOM, you must start at the root element and work your way through the hierarchy. Because all parts of the document are present in memory, you can correlate and combine information at will.

The SAX Approach

Figure 22.2 is a conceptual diagram of the way programmers approach an XML document using SAX. You set up a parser with an input source and connect it to a set of *handler* methods. When you start the parser, it communicates *events* to the

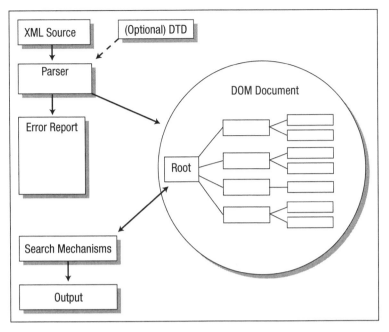

Figure 22.1   Information flow in DOM processing.

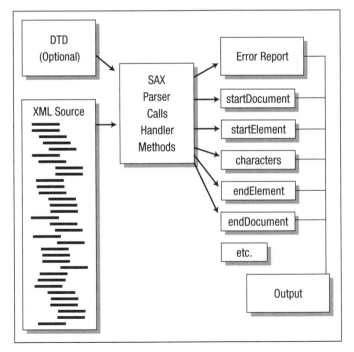

Figure 22.2   Information flow in SAX processing.

handler methods. Every time the parser detects an important part of the XML document, it calls the appropriate handler. An error can occur at any point in the process of scanning the input source, so you'll get useful information from all elements in the document before the error is hit.

When the parser reaches the end of the document, the only information your program has is what you saved in the handler methods or wrote to some form of output. Naturally, this result means you can tackle XML documents of any size— even those much larger than the available memory.

The XSLT Approach

XSLT processing applies the transformation rules created in an XSLT document to the data content of an XML document. Because the XSLT document must also be a valid XML document, both inputs to the transformation process are tree structures. The transformed data is output to create a new document.

You can think of this process as occurring in two separate phases: transformation of structure and formatting of the output, as suggested by Figure 22.3. Because most programmers will be using existing XSLT processor toolkits, the interesting events happen in the creation and control of the inputs and the output.

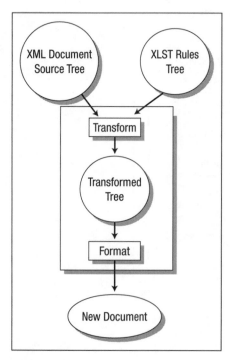

Figure 22.3   Data flow in a XSLT.

The DOM Application Programming Interface

The definitive API for working with the DOM is provided by a World Wide Web Consortium (W3C) recommendation. The Web page at **www.w3.org/DOM/** describes this recommendation as follows: "The Document Object Model is a platform- and language-neutral interface that will allow programs and scripts to dynamically access and update the content, structure, and style of documents."

The DOM considers the basic unit of a document to be a **Node**. The **Node** interface (set of allowed operations) is implemented by all the different subcategories of **Node**, listed in Table 22.1. This form of representation is obviously very much suited to modern, object-oriented computer languages such as Java. Every **Node** type in the DOM has a corresponding Java interface.

In addition to the various subtypes of **Node**, the DOM defines interfaces for collections of **Nodes**, such as:

- **NodeList**—An ordered collection of **Nodes**, with a provision for addressing individual nodes by an index number. The order of the collection is the order in which the **Nodes** occur in the document.

- **NamedNodeMap**—A collection of **Nodes** that can be addressed by name. The collection does not preserve the original order of the document.

Table 22.1   The subtypes of Node in the DOM.

Node Type	Explanation
Document	Represents the single root element of a document, containing all the others.
Element	Type of node that represents the majority of objects (apart from text) that programmers manipulate in XML documents.
Attr	Short for *attribute*; a name/value pair attached to an **Element**.
Text	Represents a collection of character data in an **Attr** or **Element**.
CDATASection	A block of text that may contain markup; if it does, that markup is not parsed.
EntityReference	Represents a reference to an entity that has not been expanded.
Entity	Represents an XML entity.
ProcessingInstruction	An instruction that controls the behavior of a parser.
Comment	Encapsulates the text of comments included in a document.
DocumentType	A representation of the Document Type Definition (DTD) for a document.
DocumentFragment	A subset of a **Document**, based at a **Node** and containing all of the **Node**'s children.
Notation	Represents a notation in a DTD.

The DOM also specifies a **DOMException** interface that can be used to communicate exceptional problems. Languages that do not directly support exceptions can use the error code constants defined in the specification.

The Java equivalent interfaces are provided in the **org.w3c.dom** package; this package consists entirely of interface definitions plus the single exception class. The naming of these interfaces exactly follows the DOM recommendation, as do most implementations of the DOM in other languages.

NOTE: *The string **org.w3c.dom** is a package name that is a Java naming convention; it's not a URL.*

The Principles of DOM Processing

The basic idea is that an XML document is turned into a DOM consisting of objects that implement these interfaces. Every part of the document becomes an object, and the connections between the objects reflect the hierarchy of the document.

The programming tool that reads the XML document and creates the DOM is called a *parser*. A variety of parsers are available from which you can select. Here are some of the considerations you should take into account before choosing a parser.

Validation

Parsers come in both *validating* and *non-validating* forms. Validating parsers can be configured to skip the validation step. Because validation of an XML document requires much more processing time, using a non-validating parser may speed up your program greatly, but you must be sure that your XML documents are all well-formed and valid.

Compliance

Given the rapid rate of evolution of XML and the many variants and alternatives floating around in the programming community, it should not be surprising that parser writers have had a hard time keeping up with the standards-writing working groups. When looking for a parser toolkit in any language, you should pay attention to the degree of compliance to standards.

Memory Requirements

Not long ago, it was assumed that every programmer would have plenty of memory to work with, and the size of parser toolkits was not a big concern. Then, everybody realized that small devices such as Palm Pilots and Internet-connected mobile phones would need parsers, as well. Naturally, you have to give up validating capability and some degree of compliance with the full XML standard to achieve a small parser; but generally, small devices deal with valid, relatively simple XML. Java seems to be the language of choice for small device parsers at this time.

Navigating the XML Document Object Model

Several methods in the DOM model **Node** interface define the relationships between **Nodes** and provide for movement along the connections between the **Nodes**. The diagram in Figure 22.4 illustrates this. Consider Elements A, B, and C, which are all at the same level in the XML tree. Element B has three child **Nodes** and can reach the first and last by the method calls **getFirstChild** and **getLastChild**, respectively. As an alternative, Element B can get a **NodeList** and then address the child **Nodes** by their position in the list, as follows:

```
NodeList list = B.getChildNodes();
Node firstN = list.item( 0 );
```

Element B can also get a reference to Element A by **getPreviousSibling** and to Element C by **getNextSibling**. Any of the **Nodes** can get a reference to the document root by the **getOwnerDocument** method. The children of Element B can get a reference to it by the **getParentNode** method.

The SAX API

The SAX standard grew out of a realization that the DOM approach was too complex and cumbersome for many applications. Furthermore, at the time, every Java parser available for XML followed its own interface standard. Programmers determined to bring order to this chaos produced the first drafts SAX—in an astonishingly short time.

The SAX standard is now widely accepted and forms the basis for parsers used to create DOM models as well as parsers that simply provide a SAX interface. This interface (actually a set of interface definitions, as shown in Table 22.2) is provided in Java in the **org.xml.sax** package.

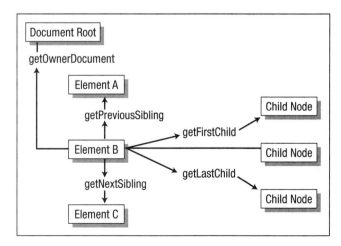

Figure 22.4   Methods used to define relationships and allow movement among nodes.

Table 22.2   The SAX interfaces.

SAX Interface	Purpose
Parser	Provides the basic methods for creating a parser and connecting it to input sources and event handlers.
DocumentHandler	Defines event-handling methods for the main events encountered during document parsing.
Locator	Defines the methods by which a SAX event can report the location in a document file where a parsing event occurred.
AttributeList	Defines the way a program can access the attribute list associated with an element.
DTDHandler	Defines methods that the parser will call to report entities and notations found in the DTD of an XML document.
ErrorHandler	Defines the methods by which the parser will report errors.
EntityResolver	Defines the methods by which an application can provide customized resolution of external entities.

The basic idea is that your program will create a SAX parser to read a specific input and will register an object or objects implementing the various interfaces with the parser. When the parser runs, it notifies the registered objects when parsing events occur.

SAX Parser Inputs

A generalization of possible inputs to a parser is provided by the **InputSource** class. An **InputSource** can be created from a stream of Unicode characters or a stream of bytes. Because Java's Input/Output (IO) classes are mostly oriented to reading and writing streams of bytes or characters, there are many ways to create an **InputSource** object.

The other form of parser input is specified in terms of a Uniform Resource Identifier (URI) naming a system resource. This resource can be a file name or a Uniform Resource Locator (URL) for the retrieval of a document over a network.

The SAX DocumentHandler Interface

Typically, most of the work in a program using a SAX approach takes place in the methods defined in the **DocumentHandler** interface. Table 22.3 summarizes these methods.

SAX Error Reporting

The **SAXException** class is the basic class for error reporting. Because a lot can go wrong inside a parser, the **SAXException** class is used as a generalized

Table 22.3   SAX parsing events in the DocumentHandler interface.

Parsing Event Handler	Event Interpretation
startDocument	Parsing has begun. This event is called once at the start of parsing.
endDocument	The end of the document has been reached. This is the last event handler called.
startElement	The start tag of an element has been parsed. An **AttributeList** containing all attributes in the element is provided.
endElement	The end tag of an element has been parsed. For empty elements, this event is called right after **startElement**.
characters	The parser has located a block of character data that is passed to this method. This event handler may or may not represent all the text content of a tag.
ignorableWhitespace	The parser has located a sequence of whitespace characters considered ignorable in the XML standard.
processingInstruction	The parser has located a processing instruction that is passed to the method as a **String**.
setDocumentLocator	This event passes an object implementing the **Locator** interface that points to the spot in the document where an event has been detected. This action occurs before the event handler for the event is called.

wrapper for such things as network and file IO errors. More specific details are provided by a **SAXParseException** in the event that a document structure error is discovered by a parser.

The **ErrorHandler** interface calls for three methods that receive a **SAXParseException**: **warning**, **error**, and **fatalError**. Obviously, the first two may be recovered from, but a **fatalError** is the last event a parser sends before dying. Methods in the **SAXParseException** class allow you to locate the exact point in a document, in terms of line number and character position, that caused the error.

The Java HandlerBase Class

The **org.xml.sax** package provides a utility class called **HandlerBase**. This class implements the **DocumentHandler**, **DTDHandler**, **ErrorHandler**, and **EntityResolver** interfaces with do-nothing methods. A programmer only has to implement those methods related to events of interest.

The XSLT API

As discussed extensively in Chapter 11, programmers who work with XSL style sheets quickly realize the power of a set of rules for transforming documents. The XSLT standard was rapidly developed using Java to create the prototypes.

Related solution:	Found on page:
Defining Basic XSLT Style Sheet Constructs	293

Generally, the programmer's role in working with XSLT is to control the inputs to a transformation engine and make use of the outputs. An obvious application is an application server that needs to provide information to users on a wide variety of platforms. Platforms that the server may have to deal with include desktop PCs, limited-display palm devices, or even more limited Internet-enabled mobile phones. Here's what happens when you incorporate XSLT into a program:

1. The initial user request is examined by the server, and a dialog format selected according to the platform is sent.

2. The user creates a specific information request.

3. The server queries a database and receives an XML-formatted reply.

4. The server selects an output transformation according to the user's platform. Possibilities include the Hypertext Markup Language (HTML), Extensible Hypertext Markup Language (XHTML), Wireless Markup Language (WML), XML, and even the Voice Markup Language (VML—which is currently under development).

5. The server feeds the data and the selected transformation to an XSLT engine.

6. The server directs output to the user in the format required for the particular device.

Programming Languages and XML

Because XML (and especially the DOM model of XML) lends itself to expression in object-oriented languages, it should not be surprising that most work with programming and XML has been done in Java and C++, the most widely used object-oriented languages.

Because Java is the most portable programming language and XML is the medium for portable data, the Java-XML combination is a logical and obvious one. Although the pioneers of XML processing have used a variety of languages (including Perl, C, C++, and JavaScript), Java currently offers the best-developed programming toolkits, with Perl a close second.

Perl, which is a text manipulation-oriented language, is a natural candidate for XML manipulation. Although originally a strictly procedural language for small utilities, recent Perl extensions have added many object-oriented capabilities. Perl parsers are available that meet both the W3C DOM interface recommendations and the SAX standard.

Immediate Solutions

Deciding How to Access an XML Document

As we already discussed, there are three completely different approaches to accessing an XML document in a program: the DOM, SAX, and XSLT processing. Table 22.4 is intended to suggest the criteria you should consider before deciding which approach to take.

Table 22.4   Decision matrix for selecting an XML processing approach.

Criterion/Capability	DOM	SAX	XSLT
Document size	Small to medium	Any	Any
Access multiple elements at the same time	Easy	Tricky	Possible
Rearrange elements	Yes	No	Yes
Create a new document	Yes	No	Yes
Modify an existing document	Yes	Tricky but possible	Yes

Creating and Manipulating a DOM in Java

In this example, we use the current XML parser toolkit from Sun: the JAXP API parser toolkit, which replaces several different earlier XML toolkits. In this latest incarnation, Sun is trying for an extremely flexible toolkit, using two JAR files—jaxp.jar and parser.jar—that you should place in the directory for standard extensions. Your import statements should include these packages:

```
import java.io.* ;
import java.util.* ;
import javax.xml.parsers.* ;
import org.xml.sax.* ;
import org.w3c.dom.* ;
```

If you've worked with earlier Sun toolkits or class libraries from other vendors, be sure to remove them from your **classpath**. Failure to do so can result in some errors that are *very* hard to track down.

Because the parser does all the work, all you have to do is use **DocumentBuilder-Factory** to create a **DocumentBuilder** and hand it a file reference. This can be as simple as:

```
File xmlFile = new File( src ) ;   // where src is a String file name
DocumentBuilderFactory dbf = DocumentBuilderFactory.newInstance();
DocumentBuilder db = dbf.newDocumentBuilder();
Document doc = db.parse( xmlFile );
```

The **Document** reference is a reference to an object that implements the **Document** interface defined in the **org.w3c.dom** package. The specific class is one provided by the **DocumentBuilder**; but you don't need to know the internal details of that class, because the **Document** interface provides all the methods you need.

The parsing code also must provide for catching Java exceptions to report the various errors that might occur, such as:

- **ParserConfigurationException**—Thrown if the **DocumentBuilderFactory** can't create the required parser.
- **SAXParseException**—Thrown if the parser encounters a problem with the formatting of the XML. This might happen because of missing or incorrectly formatted elements. The **Exception** object carries information about the location in the file that caused the error.
- **SAXException**—The most general error thrown by a parser.
- **IOException**—Thrown if file errors occur.

Recognizing a DOM Library Class in Java

To illustrate the use of the DOM, we present a complete Java utility class for maintaining DOM objects in a memory-resident library. This class can be useful in Web server applications by keeping frequently used documents in memory instead of parsing them anew for every user request.

The start of the class appears in Listing 22.1, which shows the static method used to obtain a reference to the single **DOMlibrary** object and the instance variables.

Listing 22.1   Start of the DOMlibrary class.

```
import java.io.* ;
import java.util.* ;
import javax.xml.parsers.* ;
import org.xml.sax.* ;
import org.w3c.dom.* ;
```

22. Programming with XML

```
public class DOMlibrary
{
  private static DOMlibrary theLib ;

  public synchronized static DOMlibrary getLibrary(){
    if( theLib == null ) theLib = new DOMlibrary();
    return theLib ;
  }

  // instance variables below this
  private Hashtable domHash ;

  private String lastErr = "none" ;
  // private constructor to ensure singleton
  private DOMlibrary(){
    domHash = new Hashtable();
  }
```

A complete Java method to create a DOM is shown in Listing 22.2. This method is called with a **String** giving the location of an XML file and a **boolean** flag with the value **true** if validation is desired. The method returns a **Document** reference if it succeeds or a **String** containing an error message if it fails. Note that if the error message is due to a **SAXParseException**, the **String** will contain details of the location of the error.

Listing 22.2   The **loadXML** method.

```
// returns either a Document or a String if there was an error
  private Object loadXML( String src, boolean validate ) {
    File xmlFile = new File( src ) ;
    String err = null ;
    try {
      DocumentBuilderFactory dbf = DocumentBuilderFactory.newInstance();
      dbf.setValidating( validate );
      DocumentBuilder db = dbf.newDocumentBuilder();
      Document doc = db.parse( xmlFile );
      return doc ;
    }catch(ParserConfigurationException pce){
        err = pce.toString();
    }catch(SAXParseException spe ){
        StringBuffer sb = new StringBuffer( spe.toString() );
        sb.append("\n Line number: " + spe.getLineNumber());
        sb.append("\n Column number: " + spe.getColumnNumber() );
        sb.append("\n Public ID: " + spe.getPublicId() );
        sb.append("\n System ID: " + spe.getSystemId() + "\n");
        err = sb.toString();
```

```
        }catch( SAXException se ){
           err = se.toString();
           if( se.getException() != null ){
              err + = " caused by: " + se.getException().toString() ;
           }
        }catch( IOException ie ){
           err = ie.toString();
        }
        return err ;
     } // end loadXML
```

Other classes access documents in the library by calling the **getDOM** method shown in Listing 22.3. This method is called with a **String** giving the location of the XML file. If that file has already been parsed, the **Document** object reference is returned. If the file is not resident, it is parsed using the **loadXML** method.

Listing 22.3   The public method used to obtain a **Document**.

```
// either returns the document or null if a problem
public synchronized Document getDOM( String src, boolean validate ){
   Object doc = domHash.get( src );
   File f = null ;
   if( doc == null ){
      System.out.println("DOMlibrary.getDOM new " + src );
      doc = loadXML( src, validate );
      domHash.put( src, doc );
      if( doc instanceof String ){
          lastErr = (String) doc ;
      }
   }
   // if not a document, must be a string due to error
   if( doc instanceof Document ) {
      return (Document) doc ;
   }
   return null ;
}
```

The conclusion of the **DOMlibrary** listing with some utility methods is shown in Listing 22.4.

Listing 22.4   The **DOMlibrary** class continued.

```
// use this to force removal of a dom. it
// returns last copy of dom or null if dom not in hash
public synchronized Document removeDOM( String src ){
   Document dom = (Document)domHash.get( src );
   if( dom != null ){
      domHash.remove( src );
```

```
    // System.out.println("Removed " + src );
  }
  return dom ;
}


// call this to force a reload after src is modified
public synchronized Document reloadDOM( String src, boolean validate ){
  if( domHash.get( src ) != null ){
    domHash.remove( src );
  }
  return getDOM( src, validate );
}


public String getLastErr(){ return lastErr ; }


}
```

Locating Elements by Type

After the **Document** is created, all of your programming operations will use it as a starting point. The XML file is closed and the parser is discarded. Now, let's look at what you can do with the document.

In the W3C nomenclature for DOMs, every part of the document is represented by an object that is a type of **Node**. The subtypes of **Node** define the various kinds of behavior they require. The type of **Node** you will usually be working with in a DOM is **Element**. The DOM provides a special kind of collection interface called **NodeList** that is used to hold a list of **Node** references.

Suppose you have an XML-formatted list of books with a root element **Publications**, where each **Book** tag pair encloses a number of other elements as shown in Listing 22.5. You would obtain a **NodeList** of **Book Elements** as follows:

```
Element dE = doc.getDocumentElement();
NodeList booklist = dE.getElementsByTagName( "Book" );
```

You get the number of **Elements** like this:

```
int bookCt = booklist.getLength() ;
```

and you get an individual **Element** like this:

```
Element bookE = (Element) booklist.item( n ) ;
```

Where **n** is an index between 0 and **bookCt** minus 1. Note that **Nodelist** preserves the order of **Elements** as found in the original document. Furthermore, a **Nodelist** is not a static structure but dynamically reflects changes to the DOM made by the program. Also, note that you must include a specific cast to **Element** when accessing the **n**'th item in the list, because this method is defined as returning a **Node** reference.

Navigating the DOM Model

For some practical examples of Java code to navigate with the DOM model, we'll use an XML document designed to store information about books and other publications. Listing 22.5 shows some elements of this document.

Listing 22.5   Elements from an XML document describing publications.

```
<?xml version="1.0" encoding="ISO-8859-1"?>
<!DOCTYPE Publications SYSTEM "publications.dtd" >
<Publications date="May 5, 2000">
<Book isbn="1576102912" >
   <Title>Java 2 Exam Cram</Title>
   <Author>Bill Brogden</Author>
   <Edition edition="1" />
   <DatePublished year="1999" />
   <Publisher>The Coriolis Group</Publisher>
   <Press>Certification Insider Press</Press>
   <Series>Exam Cram</Series>
   <Size pp="388"/>
   <Cover img="images/j2ec.gif" />
   <Topic>Java</Topic>
   <Topic>Certification</Topic>
   <Topic>Exam 310-025</Topic>
   <Topic>Certified Programmer for the Java 2 Platform</Topic>
   <Topic>Study Guide</Topic>
   <Errata code="ecj2" />
   <BriefDescription>This compact study guide concentrates on the topics
      covered in Sun's Java 2 programmer certification exam.
Numerous questions
similar to those on the real exam are presented and discussed.
   </BriefDescription>
</Book>
<Book isbn="076450360X">
   <Title>HTML 4 For Dummies</Title>
   <Edition edition="5"/>
```

```
<Publisher>IDG Books Worldwide</Publisher>
<Series>Dummies</Series>
<DatePublished month="7" year="1999" />
<Size pp="400"/>
<Author>Natanya Pitts</Author>
<Author>Ed Tittel</Author>
<Topic>HTML</Topic>
<Topic>WWW</Topic>
<BriefDescription> The fifth edition of this introductory book about the
  Hypertext Markup Language, the markup used to build documents for use
  on the Web. This book covers elements of page design, comprehensive
  markup definitions and examples, and includes a CD with examples
  taken from the text, along with a set of Web pages, templates,
  and online resources built specifically for the book's readers.
  </BriefDescription>
</Book>
</Publications>
```

Given an **Element** representing a **Book**, you can get a list of the children of this element. For example, the following code fragment gets a **Nodelist** of **Author Elements** belonging to a particular book. If no **Elements** of that type are found, the **Nodelist** will have a length of zero:

```
Nodelist authors = bookE.getElementsByTagName( "Author");
```

The text associated with the **Author Element** is treated as a child **Node**; therefore, to print the authors in the example, you use the following code:

```
for( int i = 0 ; i < authors.getLength() ; i++ ){
  Element aE = (Element) authors.item( i );
  String txt = aE.getFirstChild().getNodeValue();
  System.out.println("Author " + txt );
}
```

Locating Child Nodes

The text content of an **Element** may be held in the DOM in more than one child **Node**. In the following XML example from a questionnaire form, a **CDATA** section is used so that HTML markup can be incorporated:

```
<Qtext>
<![CDATA[Please fill in <b>all</b> Fields
]]>
</Qtext>
```

The resulting DOM model has three child **Nodes**. The line end after **<Qtext>** is one **Node**, the **CDATA** section is a **Node**, and the line end after **]]>** is a **Node**. To collect all the text inside the **Element**, you must use the following method:

```
String getChildrenText( Element e ){
    StringBuffer sb = new StringBuffer();
    NodeList nl = e.getChildNodes();
    for( int i = 0 ; i < nl.getLength() ; i++ ){
        sb.append( nl.item(i).getNodeValue() );
    }
    return sb.toString();
}
```

Navigating between Siblings

An **Element** object also knows its close relations in the DOM. You can locate the preceding and following **Elements** at the same level of the hierarchy with these methods:

```
Element prev = aE.getPreviousSibling();
Element next = aE.getNextSibling();
```

These methods return null if no sibling exists at that point.

Accessing Attributes by Name

Attributes attached to an **Element** can be accessed by name to get the value, as in:

```
String isbnStr = bookE.getAttribute("isbn" );
```

The **String** returned will be empty if no attribute by that name is found. That works in XML where the attribute values are simple text. If your XML may have entity references in attributes, you will have to work with the **Node** representation of an attribute, as in the following, where **Attr** is an extension of the **Node** interface:

```
Attr isbn = bookE.getAttribute( "isbn");
```

You can get all the attributes attached to an **Element** as a **NamedNodeMap**, as in:

```
NamedNodeMap map = bookE.getAttributes();
```

The contents of a given attribute can then be accessed by name:

```
Node nd = map.getNamedItem( "isbn" );
```

Note that what you retrieve is a **Node** of the **Attr** type, or **null** if the attribute does not exist. To get the actual **String** value, you do this:

```
String value = nd.getNodeValue();
```

Modifying a DOM

When you have a **Document** in memory, you can modify it by a variety of methods. For example, if you want to add a **"printing"** attribute to the **Edition** tag of a particular **Book Element**, you can do so like this:

```
NodeList editNL = bookE.getElementsByTagName( "Edition");
Element edition = (Element) editNL.item( 0 );
edition.setAttribute("printing", "3");
```

The **Document** interface specifies methods for creating **Node** objects of all of the various types. For example, if you want to add a new **Book** to the example **Document**:

```
Element addBook = doc.createElement( "Book");
doc.appendChild( addBook ) ;
```

Title, **Author**, and other **Elements** can be created and added as children of the **addBook** object. There's also a method to insert a child **Node** before a given **Node**.

For extracting portions of a **Document** or rearranging the parts of a document, the DOM provides the **DocumentFragment** interface.

Understanding SAX Processing in Java

Programming with SAX requires a major change in viewpoint from DOM programming. The SAX parser takes one pass through the source document, and you have to accomplish everything in the course of that one pass. One advantage of SAX processing is that the parser takes very little memory, and the amount of memory is independent of the size of the XML document.

As an example, we're going to use a document downloaded from the **moreover.com** headline news syndication service. This free service allows you to download current headlines drawn from more than 1,500 Web sites. Depending on the number of topics you subscribe to, this document could be quite large. The tags used for each article are illustrated in Listing 22.6. This is a subset of the full headline file used as the input for the **SaxTest** program described later.

Listing 22.6   Part of a headline download from moreover.com.

```
<?xml version="1.0" encoding="iso-8859-1"?>
<!DOCTYPE moreovernews SYSTEM "moreovernews.dtd">
<moreovernews>
<article id="_8510757">
<url>http://c.moreover.com/click/here.pl?x8510756</url>
<headline_text>Cyclone Commerce Poised to Fulfill Promise
of E-Signature Legislation</headline_text>
<source>Java Industry Connection</source>
<media_type>text</media_type>
<cluster>Java news</cluster>
<tagline> </tagline>
<document_url>http://industry.java.sun.com/javanews/more/hotnews/
</document_url>
<harvest_time>Jul 25 2000  8:34AM</harvest_time>
<access_registration> </access_registration>
<access_status> </access_status>
</article>
<article id="_8514989">
<url>http://c.moreover.com/click/here.pl?x8510853</url>
<headline_text>Schlumberger Showcases Integrated Smart Card-Based
Solutions for Campus Market at Nacubo 2000</headline_text>
<source>Java Industry Connection</source>
<media_type>text</media_type>
<cluster>Java news</cluster>
<tagline> </tagline>
<document_url>http://industry.java.sun.com/javanews/more/hotnews/
</document_url>
<harvest_time>Jul 25 2000  8:34AM</harvest_time>
<access_registration> </access_registration>
<access_status> </access_status>
</article>
```

Understanding Parser InputSources

Sun's implementation of SAX parsers in the **javax.xml.parsers** package is very flexible. You obtain a parser via a **SAXParserFactory** like this:

```
SAXParserFactory fac = SAXParserFactory.newInstance();
SAXParser parser = fac.newSAXParser();
```

The parser is started by calling one of the **parse** methods provided. These differ only in respect to the way the XML source is specified. You can use an **InputStream**, a **File** object, a URI, or an **org.xml.sax.InputSource** object. The **parse** method also requires a reference to an object extending the **HandlerBase** class. The **Thread** calling the **parse** method calls these so-called *call-back* methods and only returns when the parsing is complete.

An **InputSource** can be created from any object extending the abstract classes **java.io.InputStream** or **java.io.Reader**. The following code snippets illustrate creation of an **InputSource** from a file, an array of bytes, and a **String**.

```
InputSource is = new InputSource( new FileReader("myFile"));
InputSource is = new InputSource( new ByteArrayInputStream( myArray ) );
InputSource is = new InputSource( new StringReader( myBigString ) );
```

The wide variety of sources that can be fed to a SAX parser gives you tremendous flexibility as a programmer. It is clear that object-oriented programming fits well with the requirements of XML processing.

Building on **HandlerBase**

HandlerBase is a utility class that provides a "do-nothing" method for each of the call-back methods that the parser will call as it detects various parsing events. Your custom class must extend **HandlerBase** and provide overriding methods for the events you're interested in. In a typical application, these are the methods you have to create:

```
public void startDocument(){}
public void endDocument(){}
public void startElement( String name, AttributeList attrib ){}
public void endElement( String name ){}
public void characters( char[] buf, int start, int length ){}
```

The **characters** method delivers the text contents of elements, such as the **headline_text** element in our example. However, there's no guarantee that a call to **characters** will contain all the text belonging to an element. The parser does not try to assemble large blocks of text; that is up to you, as the programmer. Let's look at the sequence of calls to your methods as the parser runs through the following lines:

```
<article id="_8510757">
<url>http://c.moreover.com/click/here.pl?x8510756</url>
<headline_text>Cyclone Commerce Poised to Fulfill Promise
of E-Signature Legislation</headline_text>
```

These are the method calls in order:

- **startElement** called with **name="article"**, **attrib** containing a single attribute for **id**

- **startElement** called with **name="url"**

- **characters** called one or more times with the contents of the **url** tag

- **endElement** called with **name="url"**

- **startElement** called with **name="headline_text"**

- **characters** called one or more times with the **headline_text** contents

- **endElement** called with **name="headline_text"**

The real trick to programming with SAX is realizing that you get only one chance to capture any data. If you're watching for a headline that contains the word *Amazon*, then when you detect that word, the **url** that belongs to that headline has already been parsed. If you didn't save it, too bad—it's gone for good.

The **SaxTest** class shown in Listing 22.7 illustrates how to work with a SAX parser. In this simple example, you're going to scan an XML file in the moreover.com news headlines format as shown in Listing 22.6. Only the **url** element and the **headline_text** element text will be saved and output to **System.out**. If a keyword is provided on the command line, only headlines that contain that word will be output.

Listing 22.7   An example use of SAX.

```
import java.io.* ;
import java.util.* ;
import org.xml.sax.* ;
import javax.xml.parsers.* ;

public class SaxTest extends org.xml.sax.HandlerBase
{
  public static void main(String[] args){
    if( args.length < 1 ){
      System.out.println("Expects xml file name on command line");
      System.exit(1);
    }
    try {
      SaxTest st = new SaxTest( args );
      st.parse();
    }catch(Exception ex){
      ex.printStackTrace( System.out );
    }
  }
```

```
// instance variables
File sourceFile ;
String keyword ;
StringBuffer urlSB, headlineSB ;
boolean inUrl, inHeadline ;

SaxTest(String[] args ) {
  sourceFile = new File( args[0] ) ;
  if( args.length > 1 ){
    keyword = args[1].toUpperCase();
  }
}

void parse() throws Exception {
  SAXParserFactory fac = SAXParserFactory.newInstance();
  fac.setValidating( true );
  SAXParser parser = fac.newSAXParser();
  parser.parse( sourceFile, this );
}

public void startDocument(){
  System.out.println("Start parsing " + sourceFile.getAbsolutePath() );
}
public void endDocument(){
  System.out.println("End parsing " );
}

public void startElement( String name, AttributeList attrib ){
  if( inUrl = name.equals("url")){
    urlSB = new StringBuffer( 50 );
  }
  else if( inHeadline = name.equals("headline_text")){
    headlineSB = new StringBuffer(200);
  }
}

public void endElement( String name ){
  if( name.equals("headline_text") ){
    String tmp = headlineSB.toString();
    if( keyword != null ){
      if( tmp.toUpperCase().indexOf( keyword ) < 0 ){
          return ;
      }
    }
    String url = urlSB.toString();
    System.out.println( "<a href=\"" + url + "\" >" + tmp + "</a>");
  }
```

```
  }
  // we are only interested in characters in two fields
  public void characters( char[] buf, int start, int length ){
    if( inUrl ) {
      urlSB.append(buf, start, length)  ;
    }
    else if( inHeadline ){
      headlineSB.append( buf, start, length );
    }
  }
}
```

Note that to capture all the text in the two elements of interest, you append characters supplied in calls to the **characters** method to **StringBuffer** objects. Flag variables of type **boolean** are set and cleared by the **startElement** methods. This general approach is typical of SAX processing in any language. Listing 22.8 shows the program output from a recent headline news XML file using the keyword *virus*. The original long lines have been broken for this listing.

Listing 22.8 Output of the SaxTest program searching for *virus* in headlines.

```
<a href="http://c.moreover.com/click/here.pl?x8391420">
Pretty Park: Hoax or virus?</a>
<a href="http://c.moreover.com/click/here.pl?x8281612" >
Sophos calls for calm over Smash virus hype</a>
<a href="http://c.moreover.com/click/here.pl?x8275969" >
'Smash' Virus Could Attack Today</a>
```

Locating Parse Errors

Serious parsing errors will cause a **SAXParseException** to be thrown. Listing 22.9 shows how to extract the maximum information from an exception into a **String**.

Listing 22.9 Extracting information from a SAXParseException.

```
}catch(SAXParseException spe){
      StringBuffer sb = new StringBuffer( spe.toString() );
      sb.append("\n Line number: " + spe.getLineNumber());
      sb.append("\n Column number: " + spe.getColumnNumber() );
      sb.append("\n Public ID: " + spe.getPublicId() );
      sb.append("\n System ID: " + spe.getSystemId() + "\n");
      return sb.toString();
```

Modifying an XML Document with SAX

Any attempt to use SAX to modify an XML document faces serious obstacles. Every parsing event would have to be caught and used to write text to an output file. Doing so could get quite complicated if entities are present in the document.

Modifications that affect only a single element, such as substituting one phrase for another in element text or adding an attribute to selected elements, would be fairly straightforward. Rearranging the order of elements could get quite complicated.

Using XSLT in a Java Program

As of this writing, Sun has not created a release version of a toolkit to do XSLT processing in Java. However, the Apache organization has been very active in this area; therefore, the example we discuss uses the Xalan toolkit, which can be found on the Web at **http://xml.apache.org/xalan/**. This toolkit requires the XML parser toolkit named Xerces, which was also developed by the Apache organization and is included in the downloadable package.

To work with XSLT in a Java program, you need to have both the xalan.jar and xerces.jar files on your **classpath**. An extremely simple example from the samples provided in the Xalan download is shown in Listing 22.10. This example applies the **foo.xsl** transformation to the **foo.xml** document and writes the results to **System.out**.

Listing 22.10   The SimpleTransform class.

```
import org.xml.sax.SAXException;
import org.apache.xalan.xslt.XSLTProcessorFactory;
import org.apache.xalan.xslt.XSLTInputSource;
import org.apache.xalan.xslt.XSLTResultTarget;
import org.apache.xalan.xslt.XSLTProcessor;

public class SimpleTransform
{
  public static void main(String[] args)
    throws java.io.IOException,
           java.net.MalformedURLException,
           org.xml.sax.SAXException
  {
    XSLTProcessor processor = XSLTProcessorFactory.getProcessor();
    // Have the XSLTProcessor processor object transform "foo.xml" to
    // System.out, using the XSLT instructions found in "foo.xsl".
    processor.process(new XSLTInputSource("foo.xml"),
                      new XSLTInputSource("foo.xsl"),
                      new XSLTResultTarget(System.out));
  }
}
```

In practice, your program should provide for catching the exceptions and displaying error messages.

The Xalan toolkit is extremely flexible in terms of the inputs and outputs the **XSLTProcessor** class will work with. You can create **XSLTInputSource** objects from input streams of bytes or characters, or from a DOM object. Similar flexibility is available on the output side—an **XSLTResultTarget** can be created to output streams of bytes or characters, a file, or a DOM-style **Node** object. What we have here is a mind-boggling degree of flexibility. With this toolkit, you can combine DOM documents with XSL transformation scripts created on the fly to accomplish very specific formatting tasks.

Finding Help on the Web

When you're ready to begin writing programs to process XML, you'll find plenty of help on the Web.

Locating Standards

- Information on DOM—**www.w3.org/** and **http://www.w3.org/TR/REC-DOM-Level-1/**

- Information on SAX—**www.megginson.com/SAX/index.html**

Locating Resources

- A huge collection of programming resources—**www.xml.com/pub/Programming**

- XML parsers in Java, C++, and Perl, plus the XSLT processor project—**http://xml.apache.org/**

- An open source Java- and XML-based application server—**www.enhydra.org/**

- A Java publishing framework that uses only XML and XSL to create content—**http://xml.apache.org/cocoon/index.html**

Fascinating But Still in Beta Test

Sun has released an early version of an XSLT compiler. The XSLT Compiler works by parsing an input XSL file and then creating a Java class file that performs the required transformation. The resulting class is very compact and suitable for downloading into small devices. You can find the compiler at **www.sun.com/xml/developers/xsltc/**.

Chapter 23

The XML Toolbox

In Depth

Although XML applications and documents can be created by using a simple text editor, complex Document Type Definitions (DTDs) and extensive document collections are better managed using tools specifically created for XML. Because XML is a child of the Standard Generalized Markup Language (SGML), tool vendors are already in place and quality XML tools have been cropping up left and right. This chapter examines the types of XML development tools available and provides descriptions and links to important Web resources for each tool. The Immediate Solutions section focuses on choosing the right XML tool to meet your needs.

There's nothing like a good tool to make a tough job easier. The same holds true for the design and development of XML DTDs and documents. Because XML is so robust and can be used to create complex and extensive documents, it's easy to see why the right set of tools can be an XML developer's best friend. Grounded in the strong history of quality SGML development tools, the first generation of XML development tools is proving to be excellent.

XML tools generally fall into these categories:

- XML DTD and document editors
- XML parsers and processors
- XML browsers
- Conversion tools
- Database systems

NOTE: *Note that there are also Extensible Stylesheet Language (XSL) and XSL Transformation (XSLT) processors but we don't go into detail about them in this book.*

In this chapter, we'll look at the role each type of tool plays in the development of XML applications and documents; we'll also provide you with information about some of the tools currently available on the market in each category. Several companies have put together suites of XML development tools that include all or most of the tools you'll need to build a complete XML solution; we list those companies and a catalog of their toolsets at the end of the In Depth section. The Immediate Solutions section at the end of this chapter provides a set of diagnostic tools you can use to determine which tools are right for you.

XML DTD and Document Editors

To use XML, you need to be able to build XML DTDs and documents. A variety of XML DTD- and document-development tools are available. Some tools only help you build DTDs or documents, but others are DTD editors and document editors. Many of these tools are based on SGML development tools. Some of them are very expensive, and others are freeware or shareware.

NOTE: *For each tool listed in this section, we include pricing information that falls into one of four categories: freeware/ shareware, low-end commercial, moderate commercial, or high-end commercial. Freeware/shareware tools are distributed for free or on the honor system. Low-end commercial products cost less than $500, moderate commercial products cost more than $500 but less than $1,000, and high-end commercial products cost more than $1,000. Keep in mind that many high-end tools—especially entire publishing systems—can cost hundreds of thousands of dollars. If you really want to know the cost of a particular tool, visit the vendor Web site for current pricing information.*

CLIP! XML Editor

- *Vendor*—Techno2000
- *Version*—1.5
- *Platform(s)*—Windows 95/98/2000/NT and Solaris
- *URL*—**www.t2000-usa.com/**
- *What the vendor says*—"Primary purpose of CLIP! is to let you create valid XML documents. Its advanced features and user-friendly authoring environment let you focus on the content of your document rather than the technicalities of XML. Its helper tools can be utilized to create and edit documents in both Structure and Text Mode. CLIP! is more than an editor. It is a viewer as well as a search tool. Graphical representation in Structure Mode lets you visualize document structure in one glance and powerful search features grant you every piece of information in documents you are composing."
- *Cost*—Low-end commercial

Epic Editor

- *Vendor*—ArborText
- *Version*—4.0 (An evaluation version is avilable on the CD-ROM.)
- *Platform(s)*—Windows 95/98/2000/NT and Sun Solaris 7, 8
- *URL*—**www.arbortext.com/Products/Selection_Guide/Epic_Editor/ epic_editor.html**

- *What the vendor says*—"Epic Editor allows authors to write text, create tables, place graphics and configure links. Authors can use Epic Editor to author Web content, books, manuals, catalogs, encyclopedias, and other business and technical documents. Because Epic Editor supports the creation of multi-level compound documents, which both enables and encourages reuse, many authors can collaborate simultaneously on the same document."

- *Cost*—Lite version: moderate commercial; Full version: high-end commercial

Schema Central

- *Vendor*—XMLSolutions
- *Version*—1.0
- *Platform(s)*—Windows 95/98/2000/NT
- *URL*—**www.xmls.com/products/schemacentral/?id=sc**
- *What the vendor says*—"Schema Central allows organizations to actively manage a centralized repository of schemas; and provides tools to import, categorize, validate, generate, edit, browse, version, export, and manage the development of XML schemas and DTDs."
- *Cost*—High-end commercial

WebWriter

- *Vendor*—Stilo
- *Version*—None
- *Platform(s)*—Windows 95/98/2000/NT
- *URL*—**www.stilo.com/webwriter.htm**
- *What the vendor says*—"Stilo WebWriter is an industrial strength XML Editing tool, providing all of the functionality expected of leading XML Editors, but made so simple to use that it is not necessary to have any prior knowledge of XML in order to be productive."
- *Cost*—Low-end commercial

XMetaL

- *Vendor*—SoftQuad
- *Version*—2.0
- *Platform(s)*—Windows 95/98/2000/NT
- *URL*—**www.softquad.com/**

- *What the vendor says*—"SoftQuad XMetaL, the premier enabler for XML-based content applications, has the power and flexibility you need to create and work with XML content in a real world production environment. Combining state-of-the-art XML editing features and the ideal front-end to your applications, XMetaL makes it easy for your entire user base to create content."

- *Cost*—Moderate commercial

XML Notepad

- *Vendor*—Microsoft
- *Version*—Beta 1.5
- *Platform(s)*—Windows 95/98/2000/NT
- *URL*—**http://msdn.microsoft.com/xml/notepad/intro.asp**
- *What the vendor says*—"XML Notepad offers an intuitive and simple user interface that graphically represents the tree structure of XML data. Working with the standard building blocks of XML supported in Microsoft Internet Explorer 4.0, authors are able to create reproducible data structures that can be easily filled, allowing greater emphasis to be placed on application development instead of manual data structuring."
- *Cost*—Freeware/shareware

XML Pro

- *Vendor*—Vervet Logic
- *Version*—2.0 (An evaluation version is avilable on the CD-ROM.)
- *Platform(s)*—Windows 95/98/NT/2000, Linux, and Solaris
- *URL*—**www.vervet.com/xmlpro.html**
- *What the vendor says*—"By combining the features expected in a professional XML solution with the pricing expected from consumer products, XML Pro is a perfect tool for XML developers, content providers, and authors. XML Pro provides the quick, functional editing solution missing from many high-end packages, and fits well into any XML toolkit."
- *Cost*—Low-end commercial

XML Spy

- *Vendor*—Icon Information Systems
- *Version*—3.0 (An evaluation version is avilable on the CD-ROM.)
- *Platform(s)*—Windows 95/98/2000/NT

23. The XML Toolbox

- *URL*—**www.xmlspy.com/**

- *What the vendor says*—"XML Spy is centered around a professional validating XML editor that provides four advanced views on your documents: an Enhanced Grid View for structured editing, a Database/Table view that shows repeated elements in a tabular fashion, a Text View with syntax-coloring for low-level work, and an integrated Browser View that supports both CSS and XSL style-sheets."

- *Cost*—Low-end commercial

NOTE: *CSS stands for Cascading Style Sheets, and XSL means Extensible Stylesheet Language.*

XML Parsers and Processors

An XML parser is the most basic XML tool. Its main job is to read XML documents and make their content available to a processing tool such as a browser, a mobile phone, or even a piece of manufacturing software. All parsers check to see if an XML document is well-formed, and generate an error message or collection of error messages if errors exist in the document. Other parsers also check whether a document is valid in addition to checking if it's well-formed. Validating parsers are most often used with applications that depend on valid XML data to function properly.

Ælfred

- *Vendor*—OpenText

- *Language*—Java

- *Type*—Non-validating

- *Version*—1.1 (An evaluation version is avilable on the CD-ROM.)

- *URL*—**www.opentext.com/services/content_management_services/ xml_sgml_solutions.html#aelfred_and_sax**

- *What the vendor says*—"We've designed Ælfred for Java programmers who want to add XML support to their applets and applications without doubling their size: Ælfred consists of only two core class files, with a total size of about 26K, and requires very little memory to run."

Expat

- *Vendor*—James Clark

- *Language*—C

- *Type*—Non-validating

- *Version*—1.1 (An evaluation version is avilable on the CD-ROM.)
- *URL*—**www.jclark.com/xml/expat.html**
- *What the vendor says*—"Expat is an XML 1 parser written in C. It aims to be fully conforming. It is currently not a validating XML processor."

Lark

- *Vendor*—Textuality
- *Language*—Java
- *Type*—Non-validating
- *Version*—1 final beta (An evaluation version is avilable on the CD-ROM.)
- *URL*—**www.textuality.com/Lark**
- *What the vendor says*—"Lark is a non-validating XML processor implemented in the Java language; it attempts to achieve good tradeoffs among compactness, completeness, and performance."

Larval

- *Vendor*—Textuality
- *Language*—Java
- *Type*—Validating
- *Version*—0.8 (An evaluation version is avilable on the CD-ROM.)
- *URL*—**www.textuality.com/Lark**
- *What the vendor says*—"Larval is a validating XML processor built on the same code base as Lark."

Microsoft XML Parser

- *Vendor*—Microsoft
- *Language*—Java
- *Type*—Validating
- *Version*—Beta release
- *URL*—**http://msdn.microsoft.com/code/sample.asp?url=/msdn-files/027/ 000/541/msdncompositedoc.xml**
- *What the vendor says*—"This latest release of MSXML represents a step beyond the May 2000 release, providing improved XSLT/XPath standard compliance, Microsoft Visual Basic support for SAX2 (Simple API for XML), a number of bug fixes, and the closest conformance yet with the Organization for the Advancement of Structural Information Standards (OASIS) Test Suite."

Xerces

- *Vendor*—Apache
- *Language*—Java
- *Type*—Validating
- *Version*—1.2.0
- *URL*—**http://xml.apache.org/xerces-j/index.html**
- *What the vendor says*—"The Xerces Java Parser 1.2.0 supports XML 1.0 recommendation and contains advanced parser functionality, such as XML Schema, DOM Level 2 version 1.0, and SAX Version 2, in addition to supporting the industry-standard DOM Level 1 and SAX version 1 APIs.

XP

- *Vendor*—James Clark
- *Language*—Java (JDK 1.1)
- *Type*—Non-validating
- *Version*—none (An evaluation version is avilable on the CD-ROM.)
- *URL*—**www.jclark.com/xml/xp/index.html**
- *What the vendor says*—"XP is an XML 1 parser written in Java. It is fully conforming: It detects all non well-formed documents. It is currently not a validating XML processor. However, it can parse all external entities: external DTD subsets, external parameter entities and external general entities."

XML Browsers

XML browsers are designed to display XML content in a graphical interface that is navigable by users. Generally, browsers are developed with a specific XML application in mind, such as the Jumbo viewer created expressly for viewing Chemical Markup Language (CML) documents. The latest versions of the major Web browsers also support XML using either CSS or XSL to drive display.

Internet Explorer

- *Vendor*—Microsoft
- *Platform*—Windows 95/98/2000/NT and Macintosh
- *Version*—5.5
- *URL*—**www.microsoft.com/windows/ie/default.htm**

JUMBO

- *Vendor*—Peter Murray-Rust
- *Language*—Java
- *Version*—1
- *URL*—**http://ala.vsms.nottingham.ac.uk/vsms/java/jumbo/**

Mozilla

- *Vendor*—The Mozilla Organization
- *Platform*—Windows 95/98/2000/NT, Macintosh, and Linux
- *Version*—Milestone 17 (An evaluation version is avilable on the CD-ROM.)
- *URL*—**www.mozilla.org/**

Navigator

- *Vendor*—Netscape
- *Platform*—Windows 95/98/2000/NT, Macintosh, and Linux/Unix
- *Version*—4.7
- *URL*—**http://developer.netscape.com/tech/xml/**

Opera

- *Vendor*—Opera Software
- *Platform*—Windows 95/98/2000/NT, beta version for Macintosh, and alpha version for Linux
- *Version*—4.02
- *URL*—**www.opera.com/index.html**

Conversion Tools

Because XML is a relatively new content format, and legacy content may be stored in any number of other formats—from Microsoft Word to Lotus Notes—a collection of content conversion tools has begun to appear in the XML world. A content conversion tool helps you convert content from a particular content format (or set of content formats) into XML. You may still have to clean up some of the converted content by hand, but using a good conversion tool beats a hands-on-only approach to conversion.

TIP: *For a conversion tool to work well, you should be sure that your original source document is as consistent as possible. If you're converting a document in Microsoft Word, for example, be sure that you apply styles consistently to the different pieces of the document. This bit of tidying up in the source document will make the conversion and post-conversion clean-up process much smoother.*

TIDY

- *Content converted*—HTML to XHTML or XML

- *Vendor*—Dave Raggett

- *Platform*—Windows 95/98/2000/NT with GUI available for Macintosh, BeOS, Linux, Solaris, and OS/2

- *Version*—4th August 2000

- *URL*—**www.w3.org/People/Raggett/tidy/**

- *What the vendor has to say*—"When editing HTML it's easy to make mistakes. Wouldn't it be nice if there was a simple way to fix these mistakes automatically and tidy up sloppy editing into nicely laid out markup? Well now there is! Dave Raggett's HTML TIDY is a free utility for doing just that. It also works great on the atrociously hard to read markup generated by specialized HTML editors and conversion tools, and can help you identify where you need to pay further attention on making your pages more accessible to people with disabilities."

upCast

- *Content converted*—RTF

- *Vendor*—Infinity-loop

- *Platform*—Windows 95/98/2000/NT, Unix, and Macintosh

- *Version*—1.2.6

- *URL*—**www.infinity-loop.de/en/prodUpcast.html**

- *What the vendor has to say*—"upCast takes into account not only RTF information explicitly present in the document, but also looks for certain layout characteristics to recreate the logical structure of your document that got lost when using your layout-driven word processing application. This means that you'll get the best possible XML from your source document, which enables you to process and edit it with your XML tools of choice without spending the usual hours on editing and tweaking the generated XML."

Database Systems

Data stored in databases naturally integrates with structured data described with XML. Because many information solutions utilize databases to store and organize information, it makes sense to formulate ways to connect data in databases with XML documents.

ODBC2XML

- *Vendor*—Intelligent Systems Research
- *Platform*—Windows 95/98/2000/NT
- *Version*—2.1
- *URL*—**http://members.xoom.com/gvaughan/odbc2xml.htm**
- *What the vendor has to say*—"ODBC2XML simplifies the generation of complex XML documents. It allows non-programmers to generate sophisticated XML files without the need for scripting languages, report writers, or other more complex processing tools."

XMLDB

- *Vendor*—Cerium Component Software
- *Platform*—Java
- *Version*—1.0
- *URL*—**http://209.196.47.141/jackBeans/XMLDB.html**
- *What the vendor has to say*—"XMLDB reads the XML from XMLOutline and writes corresponding database table definitions. Used this way, XML may be a UML for the many, or an Everyman's Universal Modeling Language."

XML-DBMS

- *Vendor*—Ron Bourret
- *Platform*—Java and Perl
- *Version*—1.01
- *URL*—**www.informatik.tu-darmstadt.de/DVS1/staff/bourret/xmldbms/**
- *What the vendor has to say*—"XML-DBMS is a set of Java packages for transferring data between XML documents and relational databases. It views the XML document as a tree of objects in which element types are generally viewed as classes and attributes and PCDATA as properties of those classes.

It then uses an object-relational mapping to map these objects to the database. An XML-based mapping language is used to define the view and map it to the database."

Complete XML Tool Sets

Three different companies have put together complete XML tool sets. Whereas you can use any of the tools independently, you can also use them together to build a complete XML solution. The benefit of using them all together is that they are designed to communicate with each other and to support the different elements in an XML solution. The following three sections provide an overview of the vendors and list the tool that each provides.

IBM AlphaWorks Visual XML Tools

AlphaWorks is a Java-based, IBM XML project that provides a complete XML toolset. The majority of the tools in the set are freeware, but some of the more robust tools are also available via a commercial license. In addition to a solid toolset, the IBM AlphaWorks site also includes a collection of XML developer resources and is on the cutting edge of XML development. The Visual XML Tools include:

- Visual XML Builder (new)
- Visual DTD
- Visual XML Creation
- Visual XML Transformation
- Visual XML Query

To learn more about the Visual XML Tools, visit **http://www.alphaworks.ibm.com/tech/visualxmltools**.

Oracle Toolset

Oracle has developed a collection of tools specifically designed to help Oracle users integrate an Oracle database into an XML solution, or vice versa. Although not as extensive as the AlphaWorks system, the Oracle tools go a long way toward building an XML solution that involves Oracle. If you're running an Oracle database and are building an XML solution, you should look to these tools first before attempting to integrate similar XML tools from other vendors. The official Oracle XML Developers Kit contains these tools:

- XML Schema Processor—Available for Java, C, and C++
- XSL Processor
- Validating XML parsers—Available for Java, C, C++, and PL/SQL

- XSQL servlet
- XML Class Generator
- XML Transviewer Java Beans

Read more about them at **http://technet.oracle.com/tech/xml/index.htm**.

Sun Toolset

Sun Microsystems recognizes that many developers use Java to build XML solutions. So, the company has built a couple of tools to make it easier for Java developers to work with XML. If you're a Java developer, look to these tools before you try to integrate tools developed by another vendor:

- Java Project X validating parser
- JAXP (Java API for XML Parsing)

To access information about these tools, visit **http://developer.java.sun.com/ developer/**, register with the site (it's free), and search for XML.

Finding New Tools

Although this chapter couldn't contain an exhaustive list of all the XML tools available today, we've attempted to provide a good sampling of what's out there to help you with your application and document development. To keep up with the development of new tools, we suggest you keep weekly tabs on the following three sites:

- James K. Tauber's XML site software list at **www.xmlsoftware.com**
- Robin Cover's XML site at **www.oasis-open.org/cover**
- The World Wide Web Consortium's (W3C's) XML site at **www.w3.org/XML**

23. The XML Toolbox

Immediate Solutions

Identifying Your Tool Needs

Answer the following questions to help identify your needs and wade through the swamp of available XML tools to find the best match.

Step 1: What's Your Budget?

XML tools come with a variety of prices, from free to extremely expensive. Usually, the free tools are under development or are part of an initiative by the W3C. The high-priced development tools are often part of a larger SGML document-management suite. They can be powerful and provide you with slick interfaces and custom APIs. The middle-of-the-road tools are a bit better than the free ones, but they don't have the advanced management capabilities of the high-end tools.

If you're working in an enterprise or intranet environment and are planning a wholesale move to XML as your document type of choice, you'll want to invest in a high-end tool. If you're a serious but small Internet developer on a budget, go for a middle-of-the-road tool; you'll enjoy its frills, but you won't pay for advanced capabilities you'll never need. Finally, if you're just learning XML or aren't sure that it's the right solution for you, take advantage of one of the many free XML tools available today.

Step 2: What's Your Platform?

This is almost a no-brainer, but we had to mention it. Make sure the tool you're interested in is available for your primary platform. Users running Windows and Unix have a few more choices than the Mac crowd. Also, if a tool claims to work well on all platforms, do a bit of research to find out if the claim is true. If a tool is constantly crashing your system, it's not doing you much good, regardless of its XML development qualities.

Step 3: Do You Need a Parser or a Development Kit?

Are you looking for just an XML parser to add to existing applications (Java, C, and so forth), or do you want an entire development kit devoted to document and application development? Many of the existing XML parsers specifically designed to be compact and fast. Most of them are Java based, so they will fit neatly with existing Web applications. However, if you need a full document-development kit, you'll want more than just a parser. In general, these development kits include XML-specific editors and tools to make document generation easier. They'll probably have a small parser, as well, to help you check your documents; but a parser is not a requirement in a good development tool.

Step 4: Do You Need Manuals and a Lot of Tech Support?

Free software packages generally don't come with extensive manuals or tech support (although some do). Often, a readme file is the only material you get in addition to the code package. You can email the developer, but it could be weeks before you get a reply, if ever. However, middle-of-the-road and high-end tools usually come with solid manuals and tech support. Generally, the more expensive the product, the more extensive the manuals and support. If you're not used to working with beta or test-bed freeware, you might want to consider a mid-range tool. Although it will cost you a bit, the headaches you'll avoid while trying to use it will be well worth the cost.

23. The XML Toolbox

Appendix A

Online Resources

XML and its associated specifications—Extensible Stylesheet Language (XSL), XML Linking Language (XLink), the XML Pointer Language (XPointer), and others—will grow and change rapidly in the coming months. Although we're confident that this book provides you with the most current and up-to-date information about XML, as veteran developers, we're aware that nothing in this industry stays the same for long. The best way to stay abreast of the most current developments in XML, or any Web technology, is to visit those Web sites with the most reliable and current information and to visit them regularly.

To help you get started, we've sorted through the growing collection of online XML resources to provide you with a list of the best XML sites. If you take the time once a week or so to visit these sites and read about the latest updates and changes to XML, you'll always be aware of the developments in the XML world. In addition to a list of general XML sites that you can always count on for reliable information, this appendix includes links to information on the majority of XML vocabularies under development at press time. The appendix ends with a list of links to information on many of the XML parsers and development applications currently available.

General Resources

The following sections describe general XML resources.

W3C's XML Page

www.w3.org/XML

The World Wide Web Consortium's (W3C's) XML page is the ultimate resource for any XML developer. This site includes links to current and past XML specifications as well as useful resources, information on works in progress, and the most up-to-date news about XML. Although it's the most current and accurate, the information at the W3C site is also the most technical. However, after you've got the XML lingo down, the information on this site will be invaluable.

CSS2 Specification

www.w3.org/TR/REC-CSS2/

The Cascading Style Sheets, level 2 (CSS2) specification is the current, official CSS specification. It provides a style mechanism that you can use to drive the display of both XML and HTML documents. Because Web browsers support CSS better than XSL (the style mechanism designed specifically for XML), you may find that using CSS to style your XML pages is a good first step towards delivering XML content on the Web.

XSL Working Draft

www.w3.org/TR/xsl/

Style sheets for XML are being developed as the XSL specification. This Webified version of the specification is the best place to begin learning about XML style sheets and will always contain the most current information about XSL. Because XSL is the bridge that will allow many XML documents to be served on the Web, you'll want to visit this site frequently to catch up on the latest XSL news.

XLink Candidate Recommendation

www.w3.org/TR/xlink/

XML's linking element is separate from XML proper and has its own specification—XLink. The XLink candidate recommendation on the Web includes the most current information about the status of XLink. When XLink is finally released as an official specification, all the particulars will be posted to this site first. Because XLink will be the mechanism you use to connect your XML documents, this site is a resource you will want to visit time and again.

XPath Recommendation

www.w3.org/TR/xpath

XPath works with XPointer, XLink, and XSL to identify unique elements in an XML document and do things with those elements, such as include them in hyperlinks, transform them into other elements, or specify how they should be displayed. XPath is an official recommendation, so it's a good place to start as you learn how to point at different pieces of an XML document.

XPointer Candidate Recommendation

www.w3.org/TR/WD-xptr

XPointers work with XLinks to create internal references in an XML document. As with XLink, XPointer has been removed from the general XML candidate recommendation so it can be more fully developed. The XPointer candidate recommendation is the most accurate account of the mechanisms and syntax specifics that make XML references tick. XPointers are powerful tools, and as you begin to integrate them into your own XML documents, you'll find that this Web site is the best way to learn all you need to know.

Namespaces in XML

www.w3.org/TR/REC-xml-names/

Namespaces link XML vocabularies and allow you to take advantage of elements from one Document Type Definition (DTD) in another DTD. Namespaces help XML processors figure out how to handle different kinds of elements, and save you, as a developer, from having to rebuild what someone else has already done well. You'll want to familiarize yourself with the XML namespaces recommendation so you can use namespaces correctly and frequently.

XML FAQ

www.ucc.ie/xml

Got questions about XML? The XML FAQ, maintained by Peter Flynn on behalf of the W3C's XML Working Group, answers many of the most commonly asked XML questions. The FAQ is regularly maintained, and it contains basic questions and answers about XML as well as the most current and hot XML topics. Once you're XML savvy, you'll want to keep an eye on this site for quick, concise, and accurate descriptions of what's new in XML.

Robin Cover's XML/SGML Pages

www.oasis-open.org/cover/

Robin Cover has compiled *the* list of XML resources. This site includes links to virtually every XML-related resource on the Web. Linked resources are grouped under the following categories:

- News
- Introductions
- XML, XSL, XLink
- Related Standards
- Applications
- Publications
- Software
- Support
- Events
- Special Topics
- Contacts

The site is a smorgasbord of information and a good starting point when you're researching a particular topic. XML developers should visit Cover's site at least once a week.

XML.com

www.xml.com

Produced by the folks at Seybold Publications, a subsidiary of O'Reilly & Associates, XML.com is one of the best independent sources of XML information available on the Web. The site includes a wonderfully annotated version of the XML 1.0 specification, articles about XML, and the Are You Well Formed? (RUWF) XML validator. As XML develops as a Web technology, look to this site for interesting and useful information.

XML Info

www.xmlinfo.com

Created by James Tauber, XML Info is yet another site chock full of useful and up-to-date information. The site includes links to general XML information, books about XML, sample XML documents, and more. The site is frequently updated and keeps up with the almost daily happenings in the world of XML. Bookmark this must-visit site, and check it regularly for important XML developments.

Application Profiles and Document Types

www.schema.net

Also from James Tauber, schema.net focuses specifically on XML vocabularies that are both standard and under development. If you're searching for the right vocabulary for your documents, or if you're searching for examples of the work others have already done with XML, this site is a virtual gold mine of information.

XML Software

www.xmlsoftware.com

Yet another exceptional site from James Tauber (this makes three in a row), XMLSoftware.com is the best place on the Web to find out about the software available to XML developers. The site includes a parser comparison chart and a frequently updated list of XML software. When you're looking for the right tool for the job, turn to XMLSoftware.com.

XML Exchange

www.xmlx.com

XML Exchange is a Web site specifically for those developers who are designing their own DTDs. Visitors can check out examples of good DTDs, exchange information, and swap solutions. If you're working hard to get your own XML vocabulary up and running, this site is an invaluable resource.

XML Resources at Textuality

www.textuality.com/xml

Tim Bray has created a set of XML links that are useful to every XML developer. Although it's not as extensive as some of the other sites listed in this appendix, Bray's collection of resources and information is highly selective and useful. You won't have to sort through any fluff to get right to what you need, and because Bray is the primary editor of the XML 1.0 specification, the information on these pages is truly from the proverbial horse's mouth.

WebReview's XML Reference Guide

http://webreview.com/xml

WebReview, a solid Web information resource in general, has some excellent XML resources. Included are source code, articles about implementing XML, and links to other resources. All in all, this is a good resource for any XML developer.

Microsoft XML Pages

http://msdn.microsoft.com/xml/default.asp

Microsoft is on the XML bandwagon and has created a set of extremely useful Web pages housed at the Microsoft site. You'll find an XML FAQ and information about Channel Definition Format (CDF) and Open Software Description (OSD)— two Microsoft-sponsored XML vocabularies—as well as links to demos and other related information. This site focuses its implementation information on Internet Explorer, but even so, the information is factual and usable without a lot of marketing hype.

Support for XML in Internet Explorer

http://msdn.microsoft.com/workshop/xml/general/xmlxsldemo.asp

Unlike the general XML resources on the Microsoft site, this set of Web pages specifically discusses the use of XML in Internet Explorer 5 (IE5). Issued as a developer's release at the time of publication, IE5 includes a much broader implementation of XML than is found in IE4. Because Web browsers are users' windows to the Web, it's important to keep up with their level of support for XML.

XML in Mozilla

www.mozilla.org/rdf/doc/xml.html

When the Mozilla source code for what would have been Navigator 5 was released, many were surprised to find support for XML. You never know which browser your users may be using to view the Web, so you'll want to learn as much as you can about how XML is implemented in Navigator 5.

XML Software

The following sections contain links to XML parsers and document-development software.

Parsers

- *Expat*—**www.jclark.com/xml**
- *Java API for XML Parsing (JAXP)*—**http://java.sun.com/xml/ download.html**
- *Lark*—**www.textuality.com/Lark**
- *Larval*—**www.textuality.com/Lark**
- *MSXML*—**http://msdn.microsoft.com/code/sample.asp?url=/msdn-files/ 027/000/536/msdncompositedoc.xml**
- *TclXML*—**www.zveno.com/zm.cgi/in-tclxml/**
- *Oracle's XML Parser for Java*—**http://technet.oracle.com/tech/xml/ parser_java2/**
- *Oracle's XML Parser for C*—**http://technet.oracle.com/tech/xml/parser_c/**
- *Oracle's XML Parser for C++*—**http://technet.oracle.com/tech/xml/ parser_cpp/**
- *Oracle's XML Parser for PL/SQL*—**http://technet.oracle.com/tech/xml/ parser_plsql/**
- *Xerces Java Parser*—**http://xml.apache.org/xerces-j/index.html**
- *Xerces C++ Parser*—**http://xml.apache.org/xerces-c/index.html**
- *Xerces Perl Parser*—**http://xml.apache.org/xerces-p/index.html**
- *XML Parser for Java*—**http://alphaworks.ibm.com/tech/xml4j**
- *xmlproc*—**www.stud.ifi.uio.no/~larsga/download/python/xml/ xmlproc.html**
- *XP*—**www.jclark.com/xml/xp/index.html**
- *Xparse*—**www.jeremie.com/Dev/XML**

Document Development Software

- *Cocoon publishing framework*—**http://xml.apache.org/cocoon/**
- *Epic*—**www.arbortext.com/Products/products.html**
- *Jumbo Java XML browser*—**http://ala.vsms.nottingham.ac.uk/vsms/java/ jumbo/index.html**

- *Microsoft XML Notepad*—**http://msdn.microsoft.com/xml/notepad/ intro.asp?**
- *Near & Far Designer*—**www.opentext.com/near_and_far/**
- *Visual XML Tools*— **www.alphaworks.ibm.com/tech/visualxmltools**
- *Xeena XML editor*—**www.alphaworks.ibm.com/tech/xeena**
- *XMetaL*—**www.softquad.com/products/xmetal**
- *XML PRO (beta 2)*—**www.vervet.com**
- XML *Spy*—**www.xmlspy.com/**
- *XPublish*—**http://interaction.in-progress.com/xpublish/index**
- *Zydeco XML browser and development environment*—**www.dn.net/zydeco**

**Appendix A
Online Resources**

Appendix B

The XML 1.0 Specification

The XML specification is the ultimate resource for any Web developer using XML, because it is the official XML rule book. Although you can find the most current version of the specification at the World Wide Web Consortium's (W3C's) Web site, we decided to include a copy of it here for quick reference.

NOTE: *The second edition of the XML specification was released on October 6, 2000. This version incorporates the errata found at www.w3.org/XML/xml-19980210-errata. You can find the updated specification at www.w3.org/TR/REC-xml. And as always, check www.w3.org/XML/ for the latest info if you come across a W3C URL that doesn't take you where it's supposed to.*

Tim Bray, the primary editor of the specification, has compiled a Web-based annotated version of it that is available at **www.xml.com/xml/pub/axml/axmlintro.html**. This annotated version of the specification serves as a guide to its many parts and includes extended explanations of terminology as well as historical information. You may want to visit the annotated version and mark the annotations in this appendix that are most relevant to your needs or that you think you'll want to remember. Regardless of which version of the specification you're using for reference—annotated or not—remember that the specification is the first and best source for answers to questions about XML rules and syntax.

NOTE: *The W3C owns the copyright for the XML 1.0 specification. It was written by Tim Bray, Jean Paoli, and C. M. Sperberg-McQueen and can be found online at **www.w3.org/TR/REC-xml**.*

Extensible Markup Language (XML) 1.0 REC-xml-19980210

W3C Recommendation 10-February-1998

This version:

- **http://www.w3.org/TR/1998/REC-xml-19980210**

- **http://www.w3.org/TR/1998/REC-xml-19980210.xml**

- **http://www.w3.org/TR/1998/REC-xml-19980210.html**

- **http://www.w3.org/TR/1998/REC-xml-19980210.pdf**

- **http://www.w3.org/TR/1998/REC-xml-19980210.ps**

Latest version:

- **http://www.w3.org/TR/REC-xml**

Previous version:

- **http://www.w3.org/TR/PR-xml-971208**

Editors:

- Tim Bray (Textuality and Netscape) **<tbray@textuality.com>**

- Jean Paoli (Microsoft) **<jeanpa@microsoft.com>**

- C. M. Sperberg-McQueen (University of Illinois at Chicago) **<cmsmcq@uic.edu>**

Abstract

The Extensible Markup Language (XML) is a subset of SGML that is completely described in this document. Its goal is to enable generic SGML to be served, received, and processed on the Web in the way that is now possible with HTML. XML has been designed for ease of implementation and for interoperability with both SGML and HTML.

Status of This Document

This document has been reviewed by W3C Members and other interested parties and has been endorsed by the Director as a W3C Recommendation. It is a stable document and may be used as reference material or cited as a normative reference from another document. W3C's role in making the Recommendation is to draw attention to the specification and to promote its widespread deployment. This enhances the functionality and interoperability of the Web.

This document specifies a syntax created by subsetting an existing, widely used international text processing standard (Standard Generalized Markup Language, ISO 8879:1986(E) as amended and corrected) for use on the World Wide Web. It is a product of the W3C XML Activity, details of which can be found at **http://www.w3.org/XML**. A list of current W3C Recommendations and other technical documents can be found at **http://www.w3.org/TR**.

This specification uses the term URI, which is defined by [Berners-Lee et al.], a work in progress expected to update [IETF RFC1738] and [IETF RFC1808].

The list of known errors in this specification is available at **http://www.w3.org/XML/xml-19980210-errata**.

Please report errors in this document to **xml-editor@w3.org**.

Extensible Markup Language (XML) 1.0

Table of Contents

1. Introduction

Extensible Markup Language, abbreviated XML, describes a class of data objects called XML documents and partially describes the behavior of computer programs which process them. XML is an application profile or restricted form of SGML, the Standard Generalized Markup Language [ISO 8879]. By construction, XML documents are conforming SGML documents.

XML documents are made up of storage units called entities, which contain either parsed or unparsed data. Parsed data is made up of characters, some of which form character data, and some of which form markup. Markup encodes a description of the document's storage layout and logical structure. XML provides a mechanism to impose constraints on the storage layout and logical structure.

A software module called an *XML processor* is used to read XML documents and provide access to their content and structure. It is assumed that an XML processor is doing its work on behalf of another module, called the *application*. This specification describes the required behavior of an XML processor in terms of how it must read XML data and the information it must provide to the application.

1.1 Origin and Goals

XML was developed by an XML Working Group (originally known as the SGML Editorial Review Board) formed under the auspices of the World Wide Web Consortium (W3C) in 1996. It was chaired by Jon Bosak of Sun Microsystems with the active participation of an XML Special Interest Group (previously known as the SGML Working Group) also organized by the W3C. The membership of the XML Working Group is given in an appendix. Dan Connolly served as the WG's contact with the W3C.

The design goals for XML are:

1. XML shall be straightforwardly usable over the Internet.
2. XML shall support a wide variety of applications.
3. XML shall be compatible with SGML.
4. It shall be easy to write programs which process XML documents.
5. The number of optional features in XML is to be kept to the absolute minimum, ideally zero.
6. XML documents should be human-legible and reasonably clear.
7. The XML design should be prepared quickly.
8. The design of XML shall be formal and concise.
9. XML documents shall be easy to create.
10. Terseness in XML markup is of minimal importance.

This specification, together with associated standards (Unicode and ISO/IEC 10646 for characters, Internet RFC 1766 for language identification tags, ISO 639 for language name codes, and ISO 3166 for country name codes), provides all the information necessary to understand XML Version 1.0 and construct computer programs to process it.

This version of the XML specification may be distributed freely, as long as all text and legal notices remain intact.

1.2 Terminology

The terminology used to describe XML documents is defined in the body of this specification. The terms defined in the following list are used in building those definitions and in describing the actions of an XML processor:

- *may*—Conforming documents and XML processors are permitted to but need not behave as described.

- *must*—Conforming documents and XML processors are required to behave as described; otherwise, they are in error.

- *error*—A violation of the rules of this specification; results are undefined. Conforming software may detect and report an error and may recover from it.

- *fatal error*—An error which a conforming XML processor must detect and report to the application. After encountering a fatal error, the processor may continue processing the data to search for further errors and may report such errors to the application. In order to support correction of errors, the processor may make unprocessed data from the document (with intermingled character data and markup) available to the application. Once a fatal error is detected, however, the processor must not continue normal processing (i.e., it must not continue to pass character data and information about the document's logical structure to the application in the normal way).

- *at user option*—Conforming software may or must (depending on the modal verb in the sentence) behave as described; if it does, it must provide users a means to enable or disable the behavior described.

- *validity constraint*—A rule which applies to all valid XML documents. Violations of validity constraints are errors; they must, at user option, be reported by validating XML processors.

- *well-formedness constraint*—A rule which applies to all well-formed XML documents. Violations of well-formedness constraints are fatal errors.

- *match*—(Of strings or names:) Two strings or names being compared must be identical. Characters with multiple possible representations in ISO/IEC 10646 (e.g., characters with both precomposed and base+diacritic forms) match only if they have the same representation in both strings. At user option, processors may normalize such characters to some canonical form. No case folding is performed. (Of strings and rules in the grammar:) A string matches a grammatical production if it belongs to the language generated by that production. (Of content and content models:) An element matches its declaration when it conforms in the fashion described in the constraint "Element Valid".

- *for compatibility*—A feature of XML included solely to ensure that XML remains compatible with SGML.

- *for interoperability*—A non-binding recommendation included to increase the chances that XML documents can be processed by the existing installed base of SGML processors which predate the WebSGML Adaptations Annex to ISO 8879.

2. Documents

A data object is an *XML document* if it is well-formed, as defined in this specification. A well-formed XML document may in addition be valid if it meets certain further constraints.

Each XML document has both a logical and a physical structure. Physically, the document is composed of units called entities. An entity may refer to other entities to cause their inclusion in the document. A document begins in a "root" or document entity. Logically, the document is composed of declarations, elements, comments, character references, and processing instructions, all of which are indicated in the document by explicit markup. The logical and physical structures must nest properly, as described in "4.3.2 Well-Formed Parsed Entities".

2.1 Well-Formed XML Documents

A textual object is a well-formed XML document if:

1. Taken as a whole, it matches the production labeled **document**.

2. It meets all the well-formedness constraints given in this specification.

3. Each of the parsed entities which is referenced directly or indirectly within the document is well-formed.

Document

```
[1]   document::= prolog element Misc*
```

Matching the **document** production implies that:

1. It contains one or more elements.

2. There is exactly one element, called the *root*, or document element, no part of which appears in the content of any other element. For all other elements, if the start-tag is in the content of another element, the end-tag is in the content of the same element. More simply stated, the elements, delimited by start- and end-tags, nest properly within each other.

As a consequence of this, for each non-root element **C** in the document, there is one other element **P** in the document such that **C** is in the content of **P**, but is not in the content of any other element that is in the content of **P**. **P** is referred to as the *parent* of **C**, and **C** as a *child* of **P**.

2.2 Characters

A parsed entity contains *text*, a sequence of characters, which may represent markup or character data. A *character* is an atomic unit of text as specified by ISO/IEC 10646 [ISO/IEC 10646]. Legal characters are tab, carriage return, line feed, and the legal graphic characters of Unicode and ISO/IEC 10646. The use of "compatibility characters", as defined in section 6.8 of [Unicode], is discouraged.

Character Range

```
[2] Char::= #x9 | #xA | #xD | [#x20-#xD7FF] | [#xE000-#xFFFD] |
    [#x10000-#x10FFFF]    /* any Unicode character, excluding the
    surrogate blocks, FFFE, and FFFF. */
```

The mechanism for encoding character code points into bit patterns may vary from entity to entity. All XML processors must accept the UTF-8 and UTF-16 encodings of 10646; the mechanisms for signaling which of the two is in use, or for bringing other encodings into play, are discussed later, in "4.3.3 Character Encoding In Entities".

2.3 Common Syntactic Constructs

This section defines some symbols used widely in the grammar.

S (white space) consists of one or more space (#x20) characters, carriage returns, line feeds, or tabs.

White Space

```
[3]  S::= (#x20 | #x9 | #xD | #xA)+
```

Characters are classified for convenience as letters, digits, or other characters. Letters consist of an alphabetic or syllabic base character possibly followed by one or more combining characters, or of an ideographic character. Full definitions of the specific characters in each class are given in "B. Character Classes".

A *Name* is a token beginning with a letter or one of a few punctuation characters, and continuing with letters, digits, hyphens, underscores, colons, or full stops, together known as name characters. Names beginning with the string "xml", or any string which would match **(('X'|'x') ('M'|'m') ('L'|'l'))**, are reserved for standardization in this or future versions of this specification.

NOTE: *The colon character within XML names is reserved for experimentation with name spaces. Its meaning is expected to be standardized at some future point, at which point those documents using the colon for experimental purposes may need to be updated. (There is no guarantee that any name-space mechanism adopted for XML will in fact use the colon as a name-space delimiter.) In practice, this means that authors should not use the colon in XML names except as part of name-space experiments, but that XML processors should accept the colon as a name character.*

An **Nmtoken** (name token) is any mixture of name characters.

Names And Tokens

```
[4] NameChar::= Letter |Digit |'.' |'-' |'_' |':' |CombiningChar |Extender
[5] Name::= (Letter |'_' |':') (NameChar)*
[6] Names::= Name (S Name)*
[7] Nmtoken::= (NameChar)+
[8] Nmtokens::= Nmtoken (S Nmtoken)*
```

Literal data is any quoted string not containing the quotation mark used as a delimiter for that string. Literals are used for specifying the content of internal entities (**EntityValue**), the values of attributes (**AttValue**), and external identifiers (**SystemLiteral**). Note that a **SystemLiteral** can be parsed without scanning for markup.

Literals

```
[9]  EntityValue::= '"' ([^%&"] |PEReference |Reference)* '"'
|  "'" ([^%&'] |PEReference |Reference)* "'"
[10] AttValue::= '"' ([^<&"] |Reference)* '"'
|  "'" ([^<&'] |Reference)* "'"
[11] SystemLiteral::= ('"' [^"]* '"') |("'" [^']* "'")
[12] PubidLiteral::= '"' PubidChar* '"' |"'" (PubidChar - "'")* "'"
[13] PubidChar::= #x20 |#xD |#xA |[a-zA-Z0-9] |[-'()+,./:=?;!*#@$_%]
```

2.4 Character Data and Markup

Text consists of intermingled character data and markup. *Markup* takes the form of start-tags, end-tags, empty-element tags, entity references, character references, comments, CDATA section delimiters, document type declarations, and processing instructions.

All text that is not markup constitutes the *character data* of the document.

The ampersand character (**&**) and the left angle bracket (**<**) may appear in their literal form only when used as markup delimiters, or within a comment, a processing instruction, or a CDATA section. They are also legal within the literal entity value of an internal entity declaration; see "4.3.2 Well-Formed Parsed Entities". If they are needed elsewhere, they must be escaped using either numeric character references or the strings "**&**" and "**<**" respectively. The right angle bracket (**>**) may be represented using the string "**>**", and must, for compatibility, be escaped using "**>**" or a character reference when it appears in the string "**]]>**" in content, when that string is not marking the end of a CDATA section.

In the content of elements, character data is any string of characters which does not contain the start-delimiter of any markup. In a CDATA section, character data is any string of characters not including the CDATA-section-close delimiter, "**]]>**".

To allow attribute values to contain both single and double quotes, the apostrophe or single-quote character (') may be represented as "**'**", and the double-quote character (") as "**"**".

Character Data

```
[14] CharData::= [^<&]* - ([^<&]* ']]>' [^<&]*)
```

2.5 Comments

Comments may appear anywhere in a document outside other markup; in addition, they may appear within the document type declaration at places allowed by the grammar. They are not part of the document's character data; an XML processor may, but need not, make it possible for an application to retrieve the text of comments. For compatibility, the string "—" (double-hyphen) must not occur within comments.

Comments

```
[15] Comment::= '<!--' ((Char - '-') |('-' (Char - '-')))* '-->'
```

An example of a comment:

```
<!--declarations for <head> & <body> -->
```

2.6 Processing Instructions

Processing instructions (PIs) allow documents to contain instructions for applications.

Processing Instructions

```
[16] PI::= '<?' PITarget (S (Char* - (Char* '?>' Char*)))? '?>'
[17] PITarget::= Name - (('X' | 'x') ('M' | 'm') ('L' | 'l'))
```

PIs are not part of the document's character data, but must be passed through to the application. The PI begins with a target (**PITarget**) used to identify the application to which the instruction is directed. The target names "**XML**", "**xml**", and so on are reserved for standardization in this or future versions of this specification. The XML Notation mechanism may be used for formal declaration of PI targets.

2.7 CDATA Sections

CDATA sections may occur anywhere character data may occur; they are used to escape blocks of text containing characters which would otherwise be recognized as markup. CDATA sections begin with the string "**<![CDATA[**" and end with the string "**]]>**":

CDATA Sections

```
[18] CDSect::= CDStart CData CDEnd
[19] CDStart::= '<![CDATA['
[20] CData::= (Char* - (Char* ']]>' Char*))
[21] CDEnd::= ']]>'
```

Within a CDATA section, only the **CDEnd** string is recognized as markup, so that left angle brackets and ampersands may occur in their literal form; they need not (and cannot) be escaped using "**<**" and "**&**". CDATA sections cannot nest.

An example of a CDATA section, in which "**<greeting>**" and "**</greeting>**" are recognized as character data, not markup:

```
<![CDATA[<greeting>Hello, world!</greeting>]]>
```

2.8 Prolog and Document Type Declaration

XML documents may, and should, begin with an *XML declaration* which specifies the version of XML being used. For example, the following is a complete XML document, well-formed but not valid:

```
<?xml version="1.0"?>
<greeting>Hello, world!</greeting>
and so is this:
<greeting>Hello, world!</greeting>
```

The version number "**1.0**" should be used to indicate conformance to this version of this specification; it is an error for a document to use the value "**1.0**" if it does not conform to this version of this specification. It is the intent of the XML working group to give later versions of this specification numbers other than "**1.0**", but this intent does not indicate a commitment to produce any future versions of XML, nor if any are produced, to use any particular numbering scheme. Since future versions are not ruled out, this construct is provided as a means to allow the possibility of automatic version recognition, should it become necessary. Processors may signal an error if they receive documents labeled with versions they do not support.

The function of the markup in an XML document is to describe its storage and logical structure and to associate attribute-value pairs with its logical structures. XML provides a mechanism, the document type declaration, to define constraints on the logical structure and to support the use of predefined storage units. An XML document is *valid* if it has an associated document type declaration and if the document complies with the constraints expressed in it.

The document type declaration must appear before the first element in the document.

Prolog

```
[22]   prolog ::=  XMLDecl? Misc* (doctypedecl Misc*)?
[23]   XMLDecl ::=  '<?xml' VersionInfo EncodingDecl? SDDecl? S? '?>'
[24]   VersionInfo ::=  S 'version' Eq (' VersionNum ' | " VersionNum ")
[25]   Eq ::=  S? '=' S?
[26]   VersionNum ::=  ([a-zA-Z0-9_.:] | '-')+
[27]   Misc ::=  Comment | PI |  S
```

The XML *document type declaration* contains or points to markup declarations that provide a grammar for a class of documents. This grammar is known as a document type definition, or *DTD*. The document type declaration can point to an external subset (a special kind of external entity) containing markup declarations, or can contain the markup declarations directly in an internal subset, or can do both. The DTD for a document consists of both subsets taken together.

A *markup declaration* is an element type declaration, an attribute-list declaration, an entity declaration, or a notation declaration. These declarations may be contained in whole or in part within parameter entities, as described in the well-formedness and validity constraints below. For fuller information, see "4. Physical Structures".

Document Type Definition

```
[28]  doctypedecl ::=  '<!DOCTYPE' S Name (S ExternalID)? S? ('['
(markupdecl | PEReference | S)* ']' S?)? '>' [ VC: Root Element Type ]
[29]  markupdecl ::=  elementdecl | AttlistDecl | EntityDecl |
NotationDecl | PI | Comment  [ VC: Proper Declaration/PE Nesting]
     [ WFC: PEs in Internal Subset ]
```

The markup declarations may be made up in whole or in part of the replacement text of parameter entities. The productions later in this specification for individual nonterminals (**elementdecl**, **AttlistDecl**, and so on) describe the declarations after all the parameter entities have been included.

Validity Constraint: Root Element Type
The **Name** in the document type declaration must match the element type of the root element.

Validity Constraint: Proper Declaration/PE Nesting
Parameter-entity replacement text must be properly nested with markup declarations. That is to say, if either the first character or the last character of a markup declaration (**markupdecl** above) is contained in the replacement text for a parameter-entity reference, both must be contained in the same replacement text.

Well-Formedness Constraint: PEs In Internal Subset
In the internal DTD subset, parameter-entity references can occur only where markup declarations can occur, not within markup declarations. (This does not apply to references that occur in external parameter entities or to the external subset.)

Like the internal subset, the external subset and any external parameter entities referred to in the DTD must consist of a series of complete markup declarations of the types allowed by the non-terminal symbol **markupdecl**, interspersed with white space or parameter-entity references. However, portions of the contents of the external subset or of external parameter entities may conditionally be ignored by using the conditional section construct; this is not allowed in the internal subset.

External Subset

```
[30]  extSubset ::=  TextDecl? extSubsetDecl
[31]  extSubsetDecl ::=  ( markupdecl | conditionalSect | PEReference | S )*
```

The external subset and external parameter entities also differ from the internal subset in that in them, parameter-entity references are permitted within markup declarations, not only between markup declarations.

An example of an XML document with a document type declaration:

```
<?xml version="1.0"?>
<!DOCTYPE greeting SYSTEM "hello.dtd">
<greeting>Hello, world!</greeting>
```

The system identifier "**hello.dtd**" gives the URI of a DTD for the document.

The declarations can also be given locally, as in this example:

```
<?xml version="1.0" encoding="UTF-8" ?>
<!DOCTYPE greeting [
  <!ELEMENT greeting (#PCDATA)>
]>
<greeting>Hello, world!</greeting>
```

If both the external and internal subsets are used, the internal subset is considered to occur before the external subset. This has the effect that entity and attribute-list declarations in the internal subset take precedence over those in the external subset.

2.9 Standalone Document Declaration

Markup declarations can affect the content of the document, as passed from an XML processor to an application; examples are attribute defaults and entity declarations. The standalone document declaration, which may appear as a component of the XML declaration, signals whether or not there are such declarations which appear external to the document entity.

Standalone Document Declaration

```
[32]  SDDecl ::=  S 'standalone' Eq (("'" ('yes' | 'no') "'") | ('"'
('yes' | 'no') '"')) [ VC: Standalone Document Declaration ]
```

In a standalone document declaration, the value "**yes**" indicates that there are no markup declarations external to the document entity (either in the DTD external subset, or in an external parameter entity referenced from the internal subset) which affect the information passed from the XML processor to the application. The value "**no**" indicates that there are or may be such external markup declarations. Note that the standalone document declaration only denotes the presence of external *declarations*; the presence, in a document, of references to external *entities*, when those entities are internally declared, does not change its standalone status.

If there are no external markup declarations, the standalone document declaration has no meaning. If there are external markup declarations but there is no standalone document declaration, the value "**no**" is assumed.

Any XML document for which **standalone="no"** holds can be converted algorithmically to a standalone document, which may be desirable for some network delivery applications.

Validity Constraint: Standalone Document Declaration
The standalone document declaration must have the value "**no**" if any external markup declarations contain declarations of:

- Attributes with default values, if elements to which these attributes apply appear in the document without specifications of values for these attributes, or

- Entities (other than **amp**, **lt**, **gt**, **apos**, **quot**), if references to those entities appear in the document, or

- Attributes with values subject to normalization, where the attribute appears in the document with a value which will change as a result of normalization, or

- Element types with element content, if white space occurs directly within any instance of those types.

An example XML declaration with a standalone document declaration:

```
<?xml version="1.0" standalone='yes'?>
```

2.10 White Space Handling

In editing XML documents, it is often convenient to use "white space" (spaces, tabs, and blank lines, denoted by the nonterminal **S** in this specification) to set apart the markup for greater readability. Such white space is typically not intended for inclusion in the delivered version of the document. On the other hand, "significant" white space that should be preserved in the delivered version is common, for example in poetry and source code.

An XML processor must always pass all characters in a document that are not markup through to the application. A validating XML processor must also inform the application which of these characters constitute white space appearing in element content.

A special attribute named **xml:space** may be attached to an element to signal an intention that in that element, white space should be preserved by applications. In valid documents, this attribute, like any other, must be declared if it is used. When declared, it must be given as an enumerated type whose only possible values are "**default**" and "**preserve**". For example:

```
<!ATTLIST poem   xml:space (default|preserve) 'preserve'>
```

The value "**default**" signals that applications' default white-space processing modes are acceptable for this element; the value "**preserve**" indicates the intent that applications preserve all the white space. This declared intent is considered to apply to all elements within the content of the element where it is specified, unless overridden with another instance of the **xml:space** attribute.

The root element of any document is considered to have signaled no intentions as regards application space handling, unless it provides a value for this attribute or the attribute is declared with a default value.

2.11 End-of-Line Handling

XML parsed entities are often stored in computer files which, for editing convenience, are organized into lines. These lines are typically separated by some combination of the characters carriage-return (#xD) and line-feed (#xA).

To simplify the tasks of applications, wherever an external parsed entity or the literal entity value of an internal parsed entity contains either the literal two-character sequence "#xD#xA" or a standalone literal #xD, an XML processor must pass to the application the single character #xA. (This behavior can conveniently be produced by normalizing all line breaks to #xA on input, before parsing.)

2.12 Language Identification

In document processing, it is often useful to identify the natural or formal language in which the content is written. A special attribute named **xml:lang** may be inserted in documents to specify the language used in the contents and attribute values of any element in an XML document. In valid documents, this attribute, like any other, must be declared if it is used. The values of the attribute are language identifiers as defined by [IETF RFC 1766], "Tags for the Identification of Languages":

Language Identification

```
[33]  LanguageID ::=  Langcode ('-' Subcode)*
[34]  Langcode ::=  ISO639Code | IanaCode | UserCode
[35]  ISO639Code ::=  ([a-z] | [A-Z]) ([a-z] | [A-Z])
[36]  IanaCode ::=  ('i' | 'I') '-' ([a-z] | [A-Z])+
[37]  UserCode ::=  ('x' | 'X') '-' ([a-z] | [A-Z])+
[38]  Subcode ::=  ([a-z] | [A-Z])+
```

The **Langcode** may be any of the following:

- A two-letter language code as defined by [ISO 639], "Codes for the representation of names of languages."

- A language identifier registered with the Internet Assigned Numbers Authority [IANA]; these begin with the prefix "**i-**" (or "**I-**").

- A language identifier assigned by the user, or agreed on between parties in private use; these must begin with the prefix "**x-**" or "**X-**" in order to ensure that they do not conflict with names later standardized or registered with IANA.

There may be any number of **Subcode** segments; if the first subcode segment exists and the Subcode consists of two letters, then it must be a country code from [ISO 3166], "Codes for the representation of names of countries." If the first subcode consists of more than two letters, it must be a subcode for the language in question registered with IANA, unless the **Langcode** begins with the prefix "**x-**" or "**X-**".

It is customary to give the language code in lower case, and the country code (if any) in upper case. Note that these values, unlike other names in XML documents, are case insensitive.

For example:

```
<p xml:lang="en">The quick brown fox jumps over the lazy dog.</p>
<p xml:lang="en-GB">What colour is it?</p>
<p xml:lang="en-US">What color is it?</p>
<sp who="Faust" desc='leise' xml:lang="de">
  <l>Habe nun, ach! Philosophie,</l>
  <l>Juristerei, und Medizin</l>
  <l>und leider auch Theologie</l>
  <l>durchaus studiert mit heißem Bem‚h'n.</l>
  </sp>
```

The intent declared with **xml:lang** is considered to apply to all attributes and content of the element where it is specified, unless overridden with an instance of **xml:lang** on another element within that content.

A simple declaration for **xml:lang** might take the form

```
xml:lang  NMTOKEN  #IMPLIED
```

but specific default values may also be given, if appropriate. In a collection of French poems for English students, with glosses and notes in English, the **xml:lang** attribute might be declared this way:

```
<!ATTLIST poem    xml:lang NMTOKEN 'fr'>
   <!ATTLIST gloss  xml:lang NMTOKEN 'en'>
   <!ATTLIST note   xml:lang NMTOKEN 'en'>
```

3. Logical Structures

Each XML document contains one or more *elements*, the boundaries of which are either delimited by start-tags and end-tags, or, for empty elements, by an empty-element tag. Each element has a type, identified by name, sometimes called its "generic identifier" (GI), and may have a set of attribute specifications. Each attribute specification has a name and a value.

Element

```
[39] element::= EmptyElemTag
                                | STag content ETag[ WFC: Element Type Match ]
                                              [ VC: Element Valid ]
```

This specification does not constrain the semantics, use, or (beyond syntax) names of the element types and attributes, except that names beginning with a match to (('X'|'x')('M'|'m')('L'|'l')) are reserved for standardization in this or future versions of this specification.

Well-Formedness Constraint: Element Type Match
The **Name** in an element's end-tag must match the element type in the start-tag.

Validity Constraint: Element Valid
An element is valid if there is a declaration matching **elementdecl** where the **Name** matches the element type, and one of the following holds:

1. The declaration matches **EMPTY** and the element has no content.
2. The declaration matches **children** and the sequence of child elements belongs to the language generated by the regular expression in the content

model, with optional white space (characters matching the nonterminal **S**) between each pair of child elements.

3. The declaration matches **Mixed** and the content consists of character data and child elements whose types match names in the content model.

4. The declaration matches **ANY**, and the types of any child elements have been declared.

3.1 Start-Tags, End-Tags, and Empty-Element Tags

The beginning of every non-empty XML element is marked by a *start-tag*.

Start-tag

```
[40] STag::= '<' Name (S Attribute)* S? '>'[ WFC: Unique Att Spec ]
[41] Attribute::= Name Eq AttValue[ VC: Attribute Value Type ]
                              [ WFC: No External Entity References ]
                                [ WFC: No < in Attribute Values ]
```

The **Name** in the start- and end-tags gives the element's *type*. The **Name-AttValue** pairs are referred to as the *attribute specifications* of the element, with the **Name** in each pair referred to as the *attribute name* and the content of the **AttValue** (the text between the ' or " delimiters) as the *attribute value*.

Well-Formedness Constraint: Unique Att Spec
No attribute name may appear more than once in the same start-tag or empty-element tag.

Validity Constraint: Attribute Value Type
The attribute must have been declared; the value must be of the type declared for it. (For attribute types, see "3.3 Attribute-List Declarations".)

Well-Formedness Constraint: No External Entity References
Attribute values cannot contain direct or indirect entity references to external entities.

Well-Formedness Constraint: No < in Attribute Values
The replacement text of any entity referred to directly or indirectly in an attribute value (other than "<") must not contain a <.

An example of a start-tag:

```
<termdef id="dt-dog" term="dog">
```

The end of every element that begins with a start-tag must be marked by an *end-tag* containing a name that echoes the element's type as given in the start-tag:

End-tag

[42] ETag::= '</' Name S? '>'

An example of an end-tag:

</termdef>

The text between the start-tag and end-tag is called the element's *content*:

Content Of Elements

[43] content::= (element | CharData | Reference | CDSect | PI | Comment)*

If an element is *empty*, it must be represented either by a start-tag immediately followed by an end-tag or by an empty-element tag. An *empty-element tag* takes a special form:

Tags For Empty Elements

[44] EmptyElemTag::= '<' Name (S Attribute)* S? '/>'[WFC: Unique Att Spec]

Empty-element tags may be used for any element which has no content, whether or not it is declared using the keyword **EMPTY**. For interoperability, the empty-element tag must be used, and can only be used, for elements which are declared **EMPTY**.

Examples of empty elements:

<IMG align="left" src="http://www.w3.org/Icons/WWW/w3c_home" />

</br>

3.2 Element Type Declarations

The element structure of an XML document may, for validation purposes, be constrained using element type and attribute-list declarations. An element type declaration constrains the element's content.

Element type declarations often constrain which element types can appear as children of the element. At user option, an XML processor may issue a warning when a declaration mentions an element type for which no declaration is provided, but this is not an error.

An *element type declaration* takes the form:

Element Type Declaration

```
[45] elementdecl::= '<!ELEMENT' S Name S contentspec S? '>'
                         [ VC: Unique Element Type Declaration ]
[46] contentspec::= 'EMPTY' | 'ANY' | Mixed | children
```

where the **Name** gives the element type being declared.

Validity Constraint: Unique Element Type Declaration

No element type may be declared more than once.

Examples of element type declarations:

```
<!ELEMENT br EMPTY>
<!ELEMENT p (#PCDATA|emph)* >
<!ELEMENT %name.para; %content.para; >
<!ELEMENT container ANY>
```

3.2.1 Element Content

An element type has *element content* when elements of that type must contain only child elements (no character data), optionally separated by white space (characters matching the nonterminal **S**). In this case, the constraint includes a content model, a simple grammar governing the allowed types of the child elements and the order in which they are allowed to appear. The grammar is built on content particles (**cps**), which consist of names, choice lists of content particles, or sequence lists of content particles:

Element-Content Models

```
[47] children::= (choice | seq) ('?' | '*' | '+')?
[48] cp::= (Name | choice | seq) ('?' | '*' | '+')?
[49] choice::= '(' S? cp ( S? '|' S? cp )* S? ')'
                 [ VC: Proper Group/PE Nesting ]
[50] seq::= '(' S? cp ( S? ',' S? cp )* S? ')'[ VC: Proper Group/PE Nesting]
```

where each **Name** is the type of an element which may appear as a child. Any content particle in a choice list may appear in the element content at the location where the choice list appears in the grammar; content particles occurring in a sequence list must each appear in the element content in the order given in the list. The optional character following a name or list governs whether the element or the content particles in the list may occur one or more (**+**), zero or more (*****), or zero or one times (**?**). The absence of such an operator means that the element or content particle must appear exactly once. This syntax and meaning are identical to those used in the productions in this specification.

The content of an element matches a content model if and only if it is possible to trace out a path through the content model, obeying the sequence, choice, and repetition operators and matching each element in the content against an element type in the content model. For compatibility, it is an error if an element in the document can match more than one occurrence of an element type in the content model. For more information, see "E. Deterministic Content Models".

Validity Constraint: Proper Group/PE Nesting
Parameter-entity replacement text must be properly nested with parenthesized groups. That is to say, if either of the opening or closing parentheses in a **choice**, **seq**, or **Mixed** construct is contained in the replacement text for a parameter entity, both must be contained in the same replacement text. For interoperability, if a parameter-entity reference appears in a **choice**, **seq**, or **Mixed** construct, its replacement text should not be empty, and neither the first nor last non-blank character of the replacement text should be a connector (l or ,).

Examples of element-content models:

```
<!ELEMENT spec (front, body, back?)>
<!ELEMENT div1 (head, (p | list | note)*, div2*)>
<!ELEMENT dictionary-body (%div.mix; | %dict.mix;)*>
```

3.2.2 Mixed Content
An element type has *mixed content* when elements of that type may contain character data, optionally interspersed with child elements. In this case, the types of the child elements may be constrained, but not their order or their number of occurrences:

Mixed-Content Declaration

```
[51] Mixed::= '(' S? '#PCDATA' (S? '|' S? Name)* S? ')*'
            | '(' S? '#PCDATA' S? ')'
                [ VC: Proper Group/PE Nesting ]

                [ VC: No Duplicate Types ]
```

where the **Names** give the types of elements that may appear as children.

Validity Constraint: No Duplicate Types
The same name must not appear more than once in a single mixed-content declaration.

Examples of mixed content declarations:

```
<!ELEMENT p (#PCDATA|a|ul|b|i|em)*>
<!ELEMENT p (#PCDATA | %font; | %phrase; | %special; | %form;)* >
<!ELEMENT b (#PCDATA)>
```

3.3 Attribute-List Declarations

Attributes are used to associate name-value pairs with elements. Attribute specifications may appear only within start-tags and empty-element tags; thus, the productions used to recognize them appear in "3.1 Start-Tags, End-Tags, And Empty-Element Tags". Attribute-list declarations may be used:

- To define the set of attributes pertaining to a given element type.
- To establish type constraints for these attributes.
- To provide default values for attributes.

Attribute-list declarations specify the name, data type, and default value (if any) of each attribute associated with a given element type:

Attribute-list Declaration

```
[52] AttlistDecl::= '<!ATTLIST' S Name AttDef* S? '>'
[53] AttDef::= S Name S AttType S DefaultDecl
```

The **Name** in the **AttlistDecl** rule is the type of an element. At user option, an XML processor may issue a warning if attributes are declared for an element type not itself declared, but this is not an error. The **Name** in the **AttDef** rule is the name of the attribute.

When more than one **AttlistDecl** is provided for a given element type, the contents of all those provided are merged. When more than one definition is provided for the same attribute of a given element type, the first declaration is binding and later declarations are ignored. For interoperability, writers of DTDs may choose to provide at most one attribute-list declaration for a given element type, at most one attribute definition for a given attribute name, and at least one attribute definition in each attribute-list declaration. For interoperability, an XML processor may at user option issue a warning when more than one attribute-list declaration is provided for a given element type, or more than one attribute definition is provided for a given attribute, but this is not an error.

3.3.1 Attribute Types

XML attribute types are of three kinds: a string type, a set of tokenized types, and enumerated types. The string type may take any literal string as a value; the tokenized types have varying lexical and semantic constraints, as noted:

Attribute Types

```
[54] AttType::= StringType | TokenizedType | EnumeratedType
[55] StringType::= 'CDATA'
[56] TokenizedType::= 'ID'[ VC: ID ]
                                            [ VC: One ID per Element Type ]
                                            [ VC: ID Attribute Default ]
                    | 'IDREF'[ VC: IDREF ]
                    | 'IDREFS'[ VC: IDREF ]
                    | 'ENTITY'[ VC: Entity Name ]
                    | 'ENTITIES'[ VC: Entity Name ]
                    | 'NMTOKEN'[ VC: Name Token ]
                    | 'NMTOKENS'[ VC: Name Token ]
```

Validity Constraint: ID

Values of type **ID** must match the **Name** production. A name must not appear more than once in an XML document as a value of this type; i.e., ID values must uniquely identify the elements which bear them.

Validity Constraint: One ID per Element Type

No element type may have more than one ID attribute specified.

Validity Constraint: ID Attribute Default

An ID attribute must have a declared default of **#IMPLIED** or **#REQUIRED**.

Validity Constraint: IDREF

Values of type **IDREF** must match the **Name** production, and values of type **IDREFS** must match **Names**; each **Name** must match the value of an ID attribute on some element in the XML document; i.e. **IDREF** values must match the value of some ID attribute.

Validity Constraint: Entity Name

Values of type **ENTITY** must match the Name production, values of type **ENTITIES** must match **Names**; each **Name** must match the name of an unparsed entity declared in the DTD.

Validity Constraint: Name Token

Values of type **NMTOKEN** must match the **Nmtoken** production; values of type **NMTOKENS** must match Nmtokens.

Enumerated attributes can take one of a list of values provided in the declaration. There are two kinds of enumerated types:

Enumerated Attribute Types

```
[57] EnumeratedType::= NotationType | Enumeration
[58] NotationType::= 'NOTATION' S '(' S? Name (S? '|' S? Name)* S? ')'
                     [ VC: Notation Attributes ]
[59] Enumeration::= '(' S? Nmtoken (S? '|' S? Nmtoken)* S? ')'
                    [ VC: Enumeration ]
```

A **NOTATION** attribute identifies a notation, declared in the DTD with associated system and/or public identifiers, to be used in interpreting the element to which the attribute is attached.

Validity Constraint: Notation Attributes

Values of this type must match one of the notation names included in the declaration; all notation names in the declaration must be declared.

Validity Constraint: Enumeration

Values of this type must match one of the **Nmtoken** tokens in the declaration.

For interoperability, the same **Nmtoken** should not occur more than once in the enumerated attribute types of a single element type.

3.3.2 Attribute Defaults

An attribute declaration provides information on whether the attribute's presence is required, and if not, how an XML processor should react if a declared attribute is absent in a document.

Attribute Defaults

```
[60] DefaultDecl::= '#REQUIRED' | '#IMPLIED'
                                 | (('#FIXED' S)? AttValue)
[ VC: Required Attribute ]

[ VC: Attribute Default Legal ]

[ WFC: No < in Attribute Values ]

[ VC: Fixed Attribute Default ]
```

In an attribute declaration, **#REQUIRED** means that the attribute must always be provided, **#IMPLIED** that no default value is provided. If the declaration is neither **#REQUIRED** nor **#IMPLIED**, then the **AttValue** value contains the declared *default* value; the **#FIXED** keyword states that the attribute must always have the default value. If a default value is declared, when an XML processor encounters an omitted attribute, it is to behave as though the attribute were present with the declared default value.

Validity Constraint: Required Attribute

If the default declaration is the keyword **#REQUIRED**, then the attribute must be specified for all elements of the type in the attribute-list declaration.

Validity Constraint: Attribute Default Legal

The declared default value must meet the lexical constraints of the declared attribute type.

Validity Constraint: Fixed Attribute Default

If an attribute has a default value declared with the **#FIXED** keyword, instances of that attribute must match the default value.

Examples of attribute-list declarations:

```
<!ATTLIST termdef
          id     ID       #REQUIRED
          name   CDATA    #IMPLIED>
<!ATTLIST list
          type   (bullets|ordered|glossary)  "ordered">
<!ATTLIST form
          method  CDATA    #FIXED "POST">
```

3.3.3 Attribute-Value Normalization

Before the value of an attribute is passed to the application or checked for validity, the XML processor must normalize it as follows:

- A character reference is processed by appending the referenced character to the attribute value.

- An entity reference is processed by recursively processing the replacement text of the entity.

- A whitespace character (#x20, #xD, #xA, #x9) is processed by appending #x20 to the normalized value, except that only a single #x20 is appended for a "#xD#xA" sequence that is part of an external parsed entity or the literal entity value of an internal parsed entity.

- Other characters are processed by appending them to the normalized value.

If the declared value is not CDATA, then the XML processor must further process the normalized attribute value by discarding any leading and trailing space (#x20) characters, and by replacing sequences of space (#x20) characters by a single space (#x20) character.

All attributes for which no declaration has been read should be treated by a non-validating parser as if declared **CDATA**.

3.4 Conditional Sections

Conditional sections are portions of the document type declaration external subset which are included in, or excluded from, the logical structure of the DTD based on the keyword which governs them.

Conditional Section

```
[61] conditionalSect::= includeSect | ignoreSect
[62] includeSect::= '<![' S? 'INCLUDE' S? '[' extSubsetDecl ']]>'
[63] ignoreSect::= '<![' S? 'IGNORE' S? '[' ignoreSectContents* ']]>'
[64] ignoreSectContents::= Ignore ('<![' ignoreSectContents ']]>' Ignore)*
[65] Ignore::= Char* - (Char* ('<![' | ']]>') Char*)
```

Like the internal and external DTD subsets, a conditional section may contain one or more complete declarations, comments, processing instructions, or nested conditional sections, intermingled with white space.

If the keyword of the conditional section is **INCLUDE**, then the contents of the conditional section are part of the DTD. If the keyword of the conditional section is **IGNORE**, then the contents of the conditional section are not logically part of the DTD. Note that for reliable parsing, the contents of even ignored conditional sections must be read in order to detect nested conditional sections and ensure that the end of the outermost (ignored) conditional section is properly detected. If a conditional section with a keyword of **INCLUDE** occurs within a larger conditional section with a keyword of **IGNORE**, both the outer and the inner conditional sections are ignored.

If the keyword of the conditional section is a parameter-entity reference, the parameter entity must be replaced by its content before the processor decides whether to include or ignore the conditional section.

An example:

```
<!ENTITY % draft 'INCLUDE' >
<!ENTITY % final 'IGNORE' >

<![%draft;[
<!ELEMENT book (comments*, title, body, supplements?)>
]]>
<![%final;[
<!ELEMENT book (title, body, supplements?)>
]]>
```

4. Physical Structures

An XML document may consist of one or many storage units. These are called *entities*; they all have *content* and are all (except for the document entity, see below, and the external DTD subset) identified by *name*. Each XML document has one entity called the document entity, which serves as the starting point for the XML processor and may contain the whole document.

Entities may be either parsed or unparsed. A *parsed entity's* contents are referred to as its replacement text; this text is considered an integral part of the document.

An *unparsed entity* is a resource whose contents may or may not be text, and if text, may not be XML. Each unparsed entity has an associated notation, identified by name. Beyond a requirement that an XML processor make the identifiers for the entity and notation available to the application, XML places no constraints on the contents of unparsed entities.

Parsed entities are invoked by name using entity references; unparsed entities by name, given in the value of **ENTITY** or **ENTITIES** attributes.

General entities are entities for use within the document content. In this specification, general entities are sometimes referred to with the unqualified term entity when this leads to no ambiguity. Parameter entities are parsed entities for use within the DTD. These two types of entities use different forms of reference and are recognized in different contexts. Furthermore, they occupy different namespaces; a parameter entity and a general entity with the same name are two distinct entities.

4.1 Character and Entity References

A *character reference* refers to a specific character in the ISO/IEC 10646 character set, for example one not directly accessible from available input devices.

Character Reference

```
[66] CharRef::= '&#' [0-9]+ ';'
                  | '&#x' [0-9a-fA-F]+ ';'[ WFC: Legal Character ]
```

Well-Formedness Constraint: Legal Character

Characters referred to using character references must match the production for Char.

If the character reference begins with "**&#x**", the digits and letters up to the terminating ; provide a hexadecimal representation of the character's code point in ISO/IEC 10646. If it begins just with "**&#**", the digits up to the terminating ; provide a decimal representation of the character's code point.

An *entity reference* refers to the content of a named entity. References to parsed general entities use ampersand (**&**) and semicolon (;) as delimiters. *Parameter-entity references* use percent-sign (%) and semicolon (;) as delimiters.

Entity Reference

```
[67] Reference::= EntityRef | CharRef
[68] EntityRef::= '&' Name ';'[ WFC: Entity Declared ]
                                             [ VC: Entity Declared ]
                                             [ WFC: Parsed Entity ]
                                             [ WFC: No Recursion ]
[69] PEReference::= '%' Name ';'[ VC: Entity Declared ]
                                        [ WFC: No Recursion ]
                                             [ WFC: In DTD ]
```

Well-Formedness Constraint: Entity Declared

In a document without any DTD, a document with only an internal DTD subset which contains no parameter entity references, or a document with "**standalone='yes'**", the **Name** given in the entity reference must match that in an entity declaration, except that well-formed documents need not declare any of the following entities: **amp**, **lt**, **gt**, **apos**, **quot**. The declaration of a parameter entity must precede any reference to it. Similarly, the declaration of a general entity must precede any reference to it which appears in a default value in an attribute-list declaration. Note that if entities are declared in the external subset or in external parameter entities, a non-validating processor is not obligated to read and process their declarations; for such documents, the rule that an entity must be declared is a well-formedness constraint only if **standalone='yes'**.

Validity Constraint: Entity Declared

In a document with an external subset or external parameter entities with "**standalone='no'**", the **Name** given in the entity reference must match that in an entity declaration. For interoperability, valid documents should declare the entities **amp**, **lt**, **gt**, **apos**, **quot**, in the form specified in "4.6 Predefined Entities". The declaration of a parameter entity must precede any reference to it. Similarly, the declaration of a general entity must precede any reference to it which appears in a default value in an attribute-list declaration.

Well-Formedness Constraint: Parsed Entity

An entity reference must not contain the name of an unparsed entity. Unparsed entities may be referred to only in attribute values declared to be of type **ENTITY** or **ENTITIES**.

Well-Formedness Constraint: No Recursion

A parsed entity must not contain a recursive reference to itself, either directly or indirectly.

Well-Formedness Constraint: In DTD
Parameter-entity references may only appear in the DTD.

Examples of character and entity references:

```
Type <key>less-than</key> (&#x3C;) to save options.
This document was prepared on &docdate; and
is classified &security-level;.
```

Example of a parameter-entity reference:

```
<!-- declare the parameter entity "ISOLat2"... -->
<!ENTITY % ISOLat2
         SYSTEM "http://www.xml.com/iso/isolat2-xml.entities" >
<!-- ... now reference it. -->
%ISOLat2;
```

4.2 Entity Declarations

Entities are declared thus:

Entity Declaration

```
[70] EntityDecl::= GEDecl | PEDecl
[71] GEDecl::= '<!ENTITY' S Name S EntityDef S? '>'
[72] PEDecl::= '<!ENTITY' S '%' S Name S PEDef S? '>'
[73] EntityDef::= EntityValue | (ExternalID NDataDecl?)
[74] PEDef::= EntityValue | ExternalID
```

The **Name** identifies the entity in an entity reference or, in the case of an unparsed entity, in the value of an **ENTITY** or **ENTITIES** attribute. If the same entity is declared more than once, the first declaration encountered is binding; at user option, an XML processor may issue a warning if entities are declared multiple times.

4.2.1 Internal Entities

If the entity definition is an **EntityValue**, the defined entity is called an *internal entity*. There is no separate physical storage object, and the content of the entity is given in the declaration. Note that some processing of entity and character references in the literal entity value may be required to produce the correct replacement text: see "4.5 Construction Of Internal Entity Replacement Text".

An internal entity is a parsed entity.

Example of an internal entity declaration:

```
<!ENTITY Pub-Status "This is a pre-release of the specification.">
```

4.2.2 External Entities

If the entity is not internal, it is an *external entity*, declared as follows:

External Entity Declaration

```
[75] ExternalID::= 'SYSTEM' S SystemLiteral
                 | 'PUBLIC' S PubidLiteral S SystemLiteral
[76] NDataDecl::= S 'NDATA' S Name[ VC: Notation Declared ]
```

If the **NDataDecl** is present, this is a general unparsed entity; otherwise, it is a parsed entity.

Validity Constraint: Notation Declared

The **Name** must match the declared name of a notation.

The **SystemLiteral** is called the entity's *system identifier*. It is a URI, which may be used to retrieve the entity. Note that the hash mark (**#**) and fragment identifier frequently used with URIs are not, formally, part of the URI itself; an XML processor may signal an error if a fragment identifier is given as part of a system identifier. Unless otherwise provided by information outside the scope of this specification (e.g., a special XML element type defined by a particular DTD, or a processing instruction defined by a particular application specification), relative URIs are relative to the location of the resource within which the entity declaration occurs. A URI might thus be relative to the document entity, to the entity containing the external DTD subset, or to some other external parameter entity.

An XML processor should handle a non-ASCII character in a URI by representing the character in UTF-8 as one or more bytes, and then escaping these bytes with the URI escaping mechanism (i.e., by converting each byte to %HH, where HH is the hexadecimal notation of the byte value).

In addition to a system identifier, an external identifier may include a *public identifier*. An XML processor attempting to retrieve the entity's content may use the public identifier to try to generate an alternative URI. If the processor is unable to do so, it must use the URI specified in the system literal. Before a match is attempted, all strings of white space in the public identifier must be normalized to single space characters (#x20), and leading and trailing white space must be removed.

Examples of external entity declarations:

```
<!ENTITY open-hatch
        SYSTEM "http://www.textuality.com/boilerplate/OpenHatch.xml">
<!ENTITY open-hatch
```

```
            PUBLIC "-//Textuality//TEXT Standard open-hatch boilerplate//EN"
            "http://www.textuality.com/boilerplate/OpenHatch.xml">
<!ENTITY hatch-pic
            SYSTEM "../grafix/OpenHatch.gif"
            NDATA gif >
```

4.3 Parsed Entities

4.3.1 The Text Declaration
External parsed entities may each begin with a *text declaration*.

Text Declaration

```
[77] TextDecl::= '<?xml' VersionInfo? EncodingDecl S? '?>'
```

The text declaration must be provided literally, not by reference to a parsed entity. No text declaration may appear at any position other than the beginning of an external parsed entity.

4.3.2 Well-Formed Parsed Entities
The document entity is well-formed if it matches the production labeled **document**. An external general parsed entity is well-formed if it matches the production labeled **extParsedEnt**. An external parameter entity is well-formed if it matches the production labeled **extPE**.

Well-Formed External Parsed Entity

```
[78] extParsedEnt::= TextDecl? content
[79] extPE::= TextDecl? extSubsetDecl
```

An internal general parsed entity is well-formed if its replacement text matches the production labeled **content**. All internal parameter entities are well-formed by definition.

A consequence of well-formedness in entities is that the logical and physical structures in an XML document are properly nested; no start-tag, end-tag, empty-element tag, element, comment, processing instruction, character reference, or entity reference can begin in one entity and end in another.

4.3.3 Character Encoding in Entities
Each external parsed entity in an XML document may use a different encoding for its characters. All XML processors must be able to read entities in either UTF-8 or UTF-16.

Entities encoded in UTF-16 must begin with the Byte Order Mark described by ISO/IEC 10646 Annex E and Unicode Appendix B (the ZERO WIDTH NO-BREAK

SPACE character, #xFEFF). This is an encoding signature, not part of either the markup or the character data of the XML document. XML processors must be able to use this character to differentiate between UTF-8 and UTF-16 encoded documents.

Although an XML processor is required to read only entities in the UTF-8 and UTF-16 encodings, it is recognized that other encodings are used around the world, and it may be desired for XML processors to read entities that use them. Parsed entities which are stored in an encoding other than UTF-8 or UTF-16 must begin with a text declaration containing an encoding declaration:

Encoding Declaration

```
[80] EncodingDecl::= S 'encoding' Eq ('"' EncName '"' |  "'" EncName "'" )
[81] EncName::= [A-Za-z] ([A-Za-z0-9._] | '-')
     */* Encoding name contains only Latin characters */
```

In the document entity, the encoding declaration is part of the XML declaration. The **EncName** is the name of the encoding used.

In an encoding declaration, the values "**UTF-8**", "**UTF-16**", "**ISO-10646-UCS-2**", and "**ISO-10646-UCS-4**" should be used for the various encodings and transformations of Unicode / ISO/IEC 10646, the values "**ISO-8859-1**", "**ISO-8859-2**", ... "**ISO-8859-9**" should be used for the parts of ISO 8859, and the values "**ISO-2022-JP**", "**Shift_JIS**", and "**EUC-JP**" should be used for the various encoded forms of JIS X-0208-1997. XML processors may recognize other encodings; it is recommended that character encodings registered (as charsets) with the Internet Assigned Numbers Authority [IANA], other than those just listed, should be referred to using their registered names. Note that these registered names are defined to be case-insensitive, so processors wishing to match against them should do so in a case-insensitive way.

In the absence of information provided by an external transport protocol (e.g., HTTP or MIME), it is an error for an entity including an encoding declaration to be presented to the XML processor in an encoding other than that named in the declaration, for an encoding declaration to occur other than at the beginning of an external entity, or for an entity which begins with neither a Byte Order Mark nor an encoding declaration to use an encoding other than UTF-8. Note that since ASCII is a subset of UTF-8, ordinary ASCII entities do not strictly need an encoding declaration.

It is a fatal error when an XML processor encounters an entity with an encoding that it is unable to process.

Examples of encoding declarations:

```
<?xml encoding='UTF-8'?>
<?xml encoding='EUC-JP'?>
```

4.4 XML Processor Treatment of Entities and References

The table below summarizes the contexts in which character references, entity references, and invocations of unparsed entities might appear and the required behavior of an XML processor in each case. The labels in the leftmost column describe the recognition context:

- *Reference in Content*—As a reference anywhere after the start-tag and before the end-tag of an element; corresponds to the nonterminal **content**.

- *Reference in Attribute Value*—As a reference within either the value of an attribute in a start-tag, or a default value in an attribute declaration; corresponds to the nonterminal **AttValue**.

- *Occurs as Attribute Value*—As a **Name**, not a reference, appearing either as the value of an attribute which has been declared as type **ENTITY**, or as one of the space-separated tokens in the value of an attribute which has been declared as type **ENTITIES**.

- *Reference in Entity Value*—As a reference within a parameter or internal entity's literal entity value in the entity's declaration; corresponds to the nonterminal **EntityValue**.

- *Reference in DTD*—As a reference within either the internal or external subsets of the DTD, but outside of an **EntityValue** or **AttValue**.

| | | Entity Type | | | |
| | | Internal | External | | |
	Parameter	**General**	**Parsed General**	**Unparsed**	**Character**
Reference in Content	Not recognized	Included	Included if validating	Forbidden	Included
Reference in Attribute Value	Not recognized	Included in literal	Forbidden	Forbidden	Included
Occurs as Attribute Value	Not recognized	Forbidden	Forbidden	Notify	Not recognized
Reference in Entity Value	Included in literal	Bypassed	Bypassed	Forbidden	Included
Reference in DTD	Included as PE	Forbidden	Forbidden	Forbidden	Forbidden

4.4.1 Not Recognized

Outside the DTD, the % character has no special significance; thus, what would be parameter entity references in the DTD are not recognized as markup in **content**. Similarly, the names of unparsed entities are not recognized except when they appear in the value of an appropriately declared attribute.

4.4.2 Included

An entity is *included* when its replacement text is retrieved and processed, in place of the reference itself, as though it were part of the document at the location the reference was recognized. The replacement text may contain both character data and (except for parameter entities) markup, which must be recognized in the usual way, except that the replacement text of entities used to escape markup delimiters (the entities **amp**, **lt**, **gt**, **apos**, **quot**) is always treated as data. (The string "**AT&T;**" expands to "**AT&T;**" and the remaining ampersand is not recognized as an entity-reference delimiter.) A character reference is *included* when the indicated character is processed in place of the reference itself.

4.4.3 Included if Validating

When an XML processor recognizes a reference to a parsed entity, in order to validate the document, the processor must include its replacement text. If the entity is external, and the processor is not attempting to validate the XML document, the processor may, but need not, include the entity's replacement text. If a non-validating parser does not include the replacement text, it must inform the application that it recognized, but did not read, the entity.

This rule is based on the recognition that the automatic inclusion provided by the SGML and XML entity mechanism, primarily designed to support modularity in authoring, is not necessarily appropriate for other applications, in particular document browsing. Browsers, for example, when encountering an external parsed entity reference, might choose to provide a visual indication of the entity's presence and retrieve it for display only on demand.

4.4.4 Forbidden

The following are forbidden and constitute fatal errors:

- The appearance of a reference to an unparsed entity.

- The appearance of any character or general-entity reference in the DTD except within an **EntityValue** or **AttValue**.

- A reference to an external entity in an attribute value.

4.4.5 Included in Literal

When an entity reference appears in an attribute value, or a parameter entity reference appears in a literal entity value, its replacement text is processed in place of the reference itself as though it were part of the document at the location the reference was recognized, except that a single or double quote character in the replacement text is always treated as a normal data character and will not terminate the literal. For example, this is well-formed:

```
<!ENTITY % YN '"Yes"' >
<!ENTITY WhatHeSaid "He said &YN;" >
```

while this is not:

```
<!ENTITY EndAttr "27'" >
<element attribute='a-&EndAttr;>
```

4.4.6 Notify
When the name of an unparsed entity appears as a token in the value of an attribute of declared type **ENTITY** or **ENTITIES**, a validating processor must inform the application of the system and public (if any) identifiers for both the entity and its associated notation.

4.4.7 Bypassed
When a general entity reference appears in the **EntityValue** in an entity declaration, it is bypassed and left as is.

4.4.8 Included as PE
Just as with external parsed entities, parameter entities need only be included if validating. When a parameter-entity reference is recognized in the DTD and included, its replacement text is enlarged by the attachment of one leading and one following space (#x20) character; the intent is to constrain the replacement text of parameter entities to contain an integral number of grammatical tokens in the DTD.

4.5 Construction of Internal Entity Replacement Text
In discussing the treatment of internal entities, it is useful to distinguish two forms of the entity's value. The *literal entity value* is the quoted string actually present in the entity declaration, corresponding to the non-terminal **EntityValue**. The *replacement text* is the content of the entity, after replacement of character references and parameter-entity references.

The literal entity value as given in an internal entity declaration (**EntityValue**) may contain character, parameter-entity, and general-entity references. Such references must be contained entirely within the literal entity value. The actual replacement text that is included as described above must contain the replacement text of any parameter entities referred to, and must contain the character referred to, in place of any character references in the literal entity value; however, general-entity references must be left as-is, unexpanded. For example, given the following declarations:

```
<!ENTITY % pub    "&#xc9;ditions Gallimard" >
<!ENTITY   rights "All rights reserved" >
<!ENTITY   book   "La Peste: Albert Camus,
&#xA9; 1947 %pub;. &rights;" >
```

then the replacement text for the entity "**book**" is:

```
La Peste: Albert Camus,
© 1947 …ditions Gallimard. &rights;
```

The general-entity reference "**&rights;**" would be expanded should the reference "**&book;**" appear in the document's content or an attribute value.

These simple rules may have complex interactions; for a detailed discussion of a difficult example, see "D. Expansion Of Entity And Character References".

4.6 Predefined Entities

Entity and character references can both be used to *escape* the left angle bracket, ampersand, and other delimiters. A set of general entities (**amp**, **lt**, **gt**, **apos**, **quot**) is specified for this purpose. Numeric character references may also be used; they are expanded immediately when recognized and must be treated as character data, so the numeric character references "**<**" and "**&**" may be used to escape **<** and **&** when they occur in character data.

All XML processors must recognize these entities whether they are declared or not. For interoperability, valid XML documents should declare these entities, like any others, before using them. If the entities in question are declared, they must be declared as internal entities whose replacement text is the single character being escaped or a character reference to that character, as shown below.

```
<!ENTITY lt    "&#38;#60;">
<!ENTITY gt    "&#62;">
<!ENTITY amp   "&#38;#38;">
<!ENTITY apos  "&#39;">
<!ENTITY quot  "&#34;">
```

Note that the **<** and **&** characters in the declarations of "**lt**" and "**amp**" are doubly escaped to meet the requirement that entity replacement be well-formed.

4.7 Notation Declarations

Notations identify by name the format of unparsed entities, the format of elements which bear a notation attribute, or the application to which a processing instruction is addressed.

Notation declarations provide a name for the notation, for use in entity and attribute-list declarations and in attribute specifications, and an external identifier for the notation which may allow an XML processor or its client application to locate a helper application capable of processing data in the given notation.

Notation Declarations

```
[82] NotationDecl::= '<!NOTATION' S Name S (ExternalID |  PublicID) S? '>'
[83] PublicID::= 'PUBLIC' S PubidLiteral
```

XML processors must provide applications with the name and external identifier(s) of any notation declared and referred to in an attribute value, attribute definition, or entity declaration. They may additionally resolve the external identifier into the system identifier, file name, or other information needed to allow the application to call a processor for data in the notation described. (It is not an error, however, for XML documents to declare and refer to notations for which notation-specific applications are not available on the system where the XML processor or application is running.)

4.8 Document Entity

The *document entity* serves as the root of the entity tree and a starting-point for an XML processor. This specification does not specify how the document entity is to be located by an XML processor; unlike other entities, the document entity has no name and might well appear on a processor input stream without any identification at all.

5. Conformance

5.1 Validating and Non-Validating Processors

Conforming XML processors fall into two classes: validating and non-validating.

Validating and non-validating processors alike must report violations of this specification's well-formedness constraints in the content of the document entity and any other parsed entities that they read.

Validating processors must report violations of the constraints expressed by the declarations in the DTD, and failures to fulfill the validity constraints given in this specification. To accomplish this, validating XML processors must read and process the entire DTD and all external parsed entities referenced in the document.

Non-validating processors are required to check only the document entity, including the entire internal DTD subset, for well-formedness. While they are not required to check the document for validity, they are required to *process* all the declarations they read in the internal DTD subset and in any parameter entity that they read, up to the first reference to a parameter entity that they do not read; that is to say, they must use the information in those declarations to normalize attribute values, include the replacement text of internal entities, and supply default attribute values. They must not process entity declarations or attribute-list declarations encountered after a reference to a parameter entity that is not read, since the entity may have contained overriding declarations.

5.2 Using XML Processors

The behavior of a validating XML processor is highly predictable; it must read every piece of a document and report all well-formedness and validity violations. Less is required of a non-validating processor; it need not read any part of the document other than the document entity. This has two effects that may be important to users of XML processors:

- Certain well-formedness errors, specifically those that require reading external entities, may not be detected by a non-validating processor. Examples include the constraints entitled Entity Declared, Parsed Entity, and No Recursion, as well as some of the cases described as forbidden in "4.4 XML Processor Treatment Of Entities And References".

- The information passed from the processor to the application may vary, depending on whether the processor reads parameter and external entities. For example, a non-validating processor may not normalize attribute values, include the replacement text of internal entities, or supply default attribute values, where doing so depends on having read declarations in external or parameter entities.

For maximum reliability in interoperating between different XML processors, applications which use non-validating processors should not rely on any behaviors not required of such processors. Applications which require facilities such as the use of default attributes or internal entities which are declared in external entities should use validating XML processors.

6. Notation

The formal grammar of XML is given in this specification using a simple Extended Backus-Naur Form (EBNF) notation. Each rule in the grammar defines one symbol, in the form

```
symbol ::= expression
```

Symbols are written with an initial capital letter if they are defined by a regular expression, or with an initial lower case letter otherwise. Literal strings are quoted.

Within the expression on the right-hand side of a rule, the following expressions are used to match strings of one or more characters:

- **#xN**—Where **N** is a hexadecimal integer, the expression matches the character in ISO/IEC 10646 whose canonical (UCS-4) code value, when interpreted as an unsigned binary number, has the value indicated. The number of leading zeros in the **#xN** form is insignificant; the number of leading zeros in the corresponding code value is governed by the character encoding in use and is not significant for XML.

- **[a-zA-Z], [#xN-#xN]**—Matches any character with a value in the range(s) indicated (inclusive).

- **[^a-z], [^#xN-#xN]**—Matches any character with a value outside the range indicated.

- **[^abc], [^#xN#xN#xN]**—Matches any character with a value not among the characters given.

- **"string"**—Matches a literal string matching that given inside the double quotes.

- **'string'**—Matches a literal string matching that given inside the single quotes.

These symbols may be combined to match more complex patterns as follows, where **A** and **B** represent simple expressions:

- (**expression**)—**expression** is treated as a unit and may be combined as described in this list.

- **A?**—Matches **A** or nothing; optional **A**.

- **A B**—Matches **A** followed by **B**.

- **A | B**—Matches **A** or **B** but not both.

- **A – B**—Matches any string that matches **A** but does not match **B**.

- **A+**—Matches one or more occurrences of **A**.

- **A***—Matches zero or more occurrences of **A**.

Other notations used in the productions are:

- **/* ... */**—Comment.

- **[wfc: ...]**—Well-formedness constraint; this identifies by name a constraint on well-formed documents associated with a production.

- **[vc: ...]**—Validity constraint; this identifies by name a constraint on valid documents associated with a production.

Appendices

A. References

A.1 Normative References

IANA
(Internet Assigned Numbers Authority) Official Names for Character Sets, ed. Keld Simonsen et al. See **ftp://ftp.isi.edu/in-notes/iana/assignments/character-sets**.

IETF RFC 1766
IETF (Internet Engineering Task Force). RFC 1766: Tags for the Identification of Languages, ed. H. Alvestrand. 1995.

ISO 639
(International Organization for Standardization). ISO 639:1988 (E). Code for the representation of names of languages. [Geneva]: International Organization for Standardization, 1988.

ISO 3166
(International Organization for Standardization). ISO 3166-1:1997 (E). Codes for the representation of names of countries and their subdivisions—Part 1: Country codes [Geneva]: International Organization for Standardization, 1997.

ISO/IEC 10646
ISO (International Organization for Standardization). ISO/IEC 10646-1993 (E). Information technology—Universal Multiple-Octet Coded Character Set (UCS)—Part 1: Architecture and Basic Multilingual Plane. [Geneva]: International Organization for Standardization, 1993 (plus amendments AM 1 through AM 7).

Unicode
The Unicode Consortium. The Unicode Standard, Version 2.0. Reading, Mass.: Addison-Wesley Developers Press, 1996.

A.2 Other References

Aho/Ullman
Aho, Alfred V., Ravi Sethi, and Jeffrey D. Ullman. Compilers: Principles, Techniques, and Tools. Reading: Addison-Wesley, 1986, rpt. corr. 1988.

Berners-Lee et al.
Berners-Lee, T., R. Fielding, and L. Masinter. Uniform Resource Identifiers (URI): Generic Syntax and Semantics. 1997. (Work in progress; see updates to RFC1738.)

Brüggemann-Klein

Brüggemann-Klein, Anne. Regular Expressions into Finite Automata. Extended abstract in I. Simon, Hrsg., LATIN 1992, S. 97-98. Springer-Verlag, Berlin 1992. Full Version in Theoretical Computer Science 120: 197-213, 1993.

Brüggemann-Klein and Wood

Brüggemann-Klein, Anne, and Derick Wood. Deterministic Regular Languages. Universität Freiburg, Institut für Informatik, Bericht 38, Oktober 1991.

Clark

James Clark. Comparison of SGML and XML. See **http://www.w3.org/TR/NOTE-sgml-xml-971215**.

IETF RFC1738

IETF (Internet Engineering Task Force). RFC 1738: Uniform Resource Locators (URL), ed. T. Berners-Lee, L. Masinter, M. McCahill. 1994.

IETF RFC1808

IETF (Internet Engineering Task Force). RFC 1808: Relative Uniform Resource Locators, ed. R. Fielding. 1995.

IETF RFC2141

IETF (Internet Engineering Task Force). RFC 2141: URN Syntax, ed. R. Moats. 1997.

ISO 8879

ISO (International Organization for Standardization). ISO 8879:1986(E). Information processing—Text and Office Systems—Standard Generalized Markup Language (SGML). First edition—1986-10-15. [Geneva]: International Organization for Standardization, 1986.

ISO/IEC 10744

ISO (International Organization for Standardization). ISO/IEC 10744-1992 (E). Information technology—Hypermedia/Time-based Structuring Language (HyTime). [Geneva]: International Organization for Standardization, 1992. Extended Facilities Annexe. [Geneva]: International Organization for Standardization, 1996.

B. Character Classes

Following the characteristics defined in the Unicode standard, characters are classed as base characters (among others, these contain the alphabetic characters of the Latin alphabet, without diacritics), ideographic characters, and combining characters (among others, this class contains most diacritics); these classes combine to form the class of letters. Digits and extenders are also distinguished.

Characters

```
[84] Lettet::= BaseChar | Ideographic
[85] BaseChar::=  [#x0041-#x005A] | [#x0061-#x007A] | [#x00C0-#x00D6] |
    [#x00D8-#x00F6] | [#x00F8-#x00FF] | [#x0100-#x0131] | [#x0134-#x013E] |
    [#x0141-#x0148] | [#x014A-#x017E] | [#x0180-#x01C3] | [#x01CD-#x01F0] |
    [#x01F4-#x01F5] | [#x01FA-#x0217] | [#x0250-#x02A8] | [#x02BB-#x02C1] |
    #x0386 | [#x0388-#x038A] | #x038C | [#x038E-#x03A1] | [#x03A3-#x03CE] |
    [#x03D0-#x03D6] | #x03DA | #x03DC | #x03DE | #x03E0 | [#x03E2-#x03F3] |
    [#x0401-#x040C] | [#x040E-#x044F] | [#x0451-#x045C] | [#x045E-#x0481] |
    [#x0490-#x04C4] | [#x04C7-#x04C8] | [#x04CB-#x04CC] | [#x04D0-#x04EB] |
    [#x04EE-#x04F5] | [#x04F8-#x04F9] | [#x0531-#x0556] | #x0559 |
    [#x0561-#x0586] | [#x05D0-#x05EA] | [#x05F0-#x05F2] | [#x0621-#x063A] |
    [#x0641-#x064A] | [#x0671-#x06B7] | [#x06BA-#x06BE] | [#x06C0-#x06CE] |
    [#x06D0-#x06D3] | #x06D5 |
    [#x06E5-#x06E6] | [#x0905-#x0939] | #x093D |
    [#x0958-#x0961] | [#x0985-#x098C] | [#x098F-#x0990] | [#x0993-#x09A8] |
    [#x09AA-#x09B0] | #x09B2 |
    [#x09B6-#x09B9] | [#x09DC-#x09DD] | [#x09DF-#x09E1] | [#x09F0-#x09F1] |
    [#x0A05-#x0A0A] | [#x0A0F-#x0A10] | [#x0A13-#x0A28] | [#x0A2A-#x0A30] |
    [#x0A32-#x0A33] | [#x0A35-#x0A36] | [#x0A38-#x0A39] | [#x0A59-#x0A5C] |
    #x0A5E |
    [#x0A72-#x0A74] | [#x0A85-#x0A8B] | #x0A8D |
    [#x0A8F-#x0A91] | [#x0A93-#x0AA8] | [#x0AAA-#x0AB0] | [#x0AB2-#x0AB3] |
    [#x0AB5-#x0AB9] | #x0ABD | #x0AE0 | [#x0B05-#x0B0C] | [#x0B0F-#x0B10] |
    [#x0B13-#x0B28] | [#x0B2A-#x0B30] | [#x0B32-#x0B33] | [#x0B36-#x0B39] |
    #x0B3D |
    [#x0B5C-#x0B5D] | [#x0B5F-#x0B61] | [#x0B85-#x0B8A] | [#x0B8E-#x0B90] |
    [#x0B92-#x0B95] | [#x0B99-#x0B9A] | #x0B9C |
    [#x0B9E-#x0B9F] | [#x0BA3-#x0BA4] | [#x0BA8-#x0BAA] | [#x0BAE-#x0BB5] |
    [#x0BB7-#x0BB9] | [#x0C05-#x0C0C] | [#x0C0E-#x0C10] | [#x0C12-#x0C28] |
    [#x0C2A-#x0C33] | [#x0C35-#x0C39] | [#x0C60-#x0C61] | [#x0C85-#x0C8C] |
    [#x0C8E-#x0C90] | [#x0C92-#x0CA8] | [#x0CAA-#x0CB3] | [#x0CB5-#x0CB9] |
    #x0CDE |
    [#x0CE0-#x0CE1] | [#x0D05-#x0D0C] | [#x0D0E-#x0D10] | [#x0D12-#x0D28] |
    [#x0D2A-#x0D39] | [#x0D60-#x0D61] | [#x0E01-#x0E2E] | #x0E30 |
    [#x0E32-#x0E33] | [#x0E40-#x0E45] | [#x0E81-#x0E82] | #x0E84 |
    [#x0E87-#x0E88] | #x0E8A | #x0E8D | [#x0E94-#x0E97] | [#x0E99-#x0E9F] |
    [#x0EA1-#x0EA3] | #x0EA5 | #x0EA7 | [#x0EAA-#x0EAB] | [#x0EAD-#x0EAE] |
    #x0EB0 | [#x0EB2-#x0EB3] | #x0EBD | [#x0EC0-#x0EC4] | [#x0F40-#x0F47] |
    [#x0F49-#x0F69] | [#x10A0-#x10C5] | [#x10D0-#x10F6] | #x1100 |
    [#x1102-#x1103] | [#x1105-#x1107] | #x1109 |
    [#x110B-#x110C] | [#x110E-#x1112] | #x113C | #x113E | #x1140 | #x114C |
    #x114E | #x1150 | [#x1154-#x1155] | #x1159 | [#x115F-#x1161] | #x1163 |
    #x1165 | #x1167 | #x1169 |
```

```
               [#x116D-#x116E] | [#x1172-#x1173] | #x1175 | #x119E | #x11A8 | #x11AB |
               [#x11AE-#x11AF] | [#x11B7-#x11B8] | #x11BA | [#x11BC-#x11C2] | #x11EB |
               #x11F0 | #x11F9 | [#x1E00-#x1E9B] | [#x1EA0-#x1EF9] | [#x1F00-#x1F15] |
               [#x1F18-#x1F1D] | [#x1F20-#x1F45] | [#x1F48-#x1F4D] | [#x1F50-#x1F57] |
               #x1F59 | #x1F5B | #x1F5D |
               [#x1F5F-#x1F7D] | [#x1F80-#x1FB4] | [#x1FB6-#x1FBC] | #x1FBE |
               [#x1FC2-#x1FC4] | [#x1FC6-#x1FCC] | [#x1FD0-#x1FD3] | [#x1FD6-#x1FDB] |
               [#x1FE0-#x1FEC] | [#x1FF2-#x1FF4] | [#x1FF6-#x1FFC] | #x2126 |
               [#x212A-#x212B] | #x212E |
               [#x2180-#x2182] | [#x3041-#x3094] | [#x30A1-#x30FA] | [#x3105-#x312C] |
               [#xAC00-#xD7A3]
   [86]  Ideographic::= [#x4E00-#x9FA5] | #x3007 | [#x3021-#x3029]
   [87]  CombiningChar::=  [#x0300-#x0345] | [#x0360-#x0361] |
               [#x0483-#x0486] | [#x0591-#x05A1] | [#x05A3-#x05B9] | [#x05BB-#x05BD] |
               #x05BF | [#x05C1-#x05C2] | #x05C4 | [#x064B-#x0652] | #x0670 |
               [#x06D6-#x06DC] | [#x06DD-#x06DF] | [#x06E0-#x06E4] | [#x06E7-#x06E8] |
               [#x06EA-#x06ED] | [#x0901-#x0903] | #x093C | [#x093E-#x094C] | #x094D |
               [#x0951-#x0954] | [#x0962-#x0963] | [#x0981-#x0983] | #x09BC | #x09BE |
               #x09BF |
               [#x09C0-#x09C4] | [#x09C7-#x09C8] | [#x09CB-#x09CD] | #x09D7 |
               [#x09E2-#x09E3] | #x0A02 | #x0A3C | #x0A3E | #x0A3F | [#x0A40-#x0A42] |
               [#x0A47-#x0A48] | [#x0A4B-#x0A4D] | [#x0A70-#x0A71] | [#x0A81-#x0A83] |
               #x0ABC |
               [#x0ABE-#x0AC5] | [#x0AC7-#x0AC9] | [#x0ACB-#x0ACD] | [#x0B01-#x0B03] |
               #x0B3C |
               [#x0B3E-#x0B43] | [#x0B47-#x0B48] | [#x0B4B-#x0B4D] | [#x0B56-#x0B57] |
               [#x0B82-#x0B83] | [#x0BBE-#x0BC2] | [#x0BC6-#x0BC8] | [#x0BCA-#x0BCD] |
               #x0BD7 |
               [#x0C01-#x0C03] | [#x0C3E-#x0C44] | [#x0C46-#x0C48] | [#x0C4A-#x0C4D] |
               [#x0C55-#x0C56] | [#x0C82-#x0C83] | [#x0CBE-#x0CC4] | [#x0CC6-#x0CC8] |
               [#x0CCA-#x0CCD] | [#x0CD5-#x0CD6] | [#x0D02-#x0D03] | [#x0D3E-#x0D43] |
               [#x0D46-#x0D48] | [#x0D4A-#x0D4D] | #x0D57 | #x0E31 | [#x0E34-#x0E3A] |
               [#x0E47-#x0E4E] | #x0EB1 |
               [#x0EB4-#x0EB9] | [#x0EBB-#x0EBC] | [#x0EC8-#x0ECD] | [#x0F18-#x0F19] |
               #x0F35 | #x0F37 | #x0F39 | #x0F3E | #x0F3F |
               [#x0F71-#x0F84] | [#x0F86-#x0F8B] | [#x0F90-#x0F95] | #x0F97 |
               [#x0F99-#x0FAD] | [#x0FB1-#x0FB7] | #x0FB9 | [#x20D0-#x20DC] | #x20E1 |
               [#x302A-#x302F] | #x3099 | #x309A
   [88]  Digit::= [#x0030-#x0039] | [#x0660-#x0669] | [#x06F0-#x06F9] |
               [#x0966-#x096F] | [#x09E6-#x09EF] | [#x0A66-#x0A6F] | [#x0AE6-#x0AEF] |
               [#x0B66-#x0B6F] | [#x0BE7-#x0BEF] | [#x0C66-#x0C6F] | [#x0CE6-#x0CEF] |
               [#x0D66-#x0D6F] | [#x0E50-#x0E59] | [#x0ED0-#x0ED9] | [#x0F20-#x0F29]
   [89]  Extender::= #x00B7 | #x02D0 | #x02D1 | #x0387 | #x0640 | #x0E46 |
               #x0EC6 | #x3005 | [#x3031-#x3035] | [#x309D-#x309E] | [#x30FC-#x30FE]
```

The character classes defined here can be derived from the Unicode character database as follows:

- Name-start characters must have one of the categories Ll, Lu, Lo, Lt, Nl.

- Name characters other than Name-start characters must have one of the categories Mc, Me, Mn, Lm, or Nd.

- Characters in the compatibility area (i.e., with character code greater than #xF900 and less than #xFFFE) are not allowed in XML names.

- Characters which have a font or compatibility decomposition (i.e., those with a "compatibility formatting tag" in field 5 of the database—marked by field 5 beginning with a "<") are not allowed.

- The following characters are treated as name-start characters rather than name characters, because the property file classifies them as alphabetic: [#x02BB-#x02C1], #x0559, #x06E5, #x06E6.

- Characters #x20DD-#x20E0 are excluded (in accordance with Unicode, section 5.14).

- Character #x00B7 is classified as an extender, because the property list so identifies it.

- Character #x0387 is added as a name character, because #x00B7 is its canonical equivalent.

- Characters ':' and '_' are allowed as name-start characters.

- Characters '-' and '.' are allowed as name characters.

C. XML and SGML (Non-Normative)

XML is designed to be a subset of SGML, in that every valid XML document should also be a conformant SGML document. For a detailed comparison of the additional restrictions that XML places on documents beyond those of SGML, see [Clark].

D. Expansion of Entity and Character References (Non-Normative)

This appendix contains some examples illustrating the sequence of entity- and character-reference recognition and expansion, as specified in "4.4 XML Processor Treatment Of Entities And References".

If the DTD contains the declaration

```
<!ENTITY example "<p>An ampersand (&#38;#38;) may be escaped
numerically (&#38;#38;#38;) or with a general entity
(&amp;amp;).</p>" >
```

then the XML processor will recognize the character references when it parses the entity declaration, and resolve them before storing the following string as the value of the entity "**example**":

```
<p>An ampersand (&#38;) may be escaped
numerically (&#38;#38;) or with a general entity
(&amp;amp;).</p>
```

A reference in the document to "**&example;**" will cause the text to be reparsed, at which time the start- and end-tags of the "**p**" element will be recognized and the three references will be recognized and expanded, resulting in a "**p**" element with the following content (all data, no delimiters or markup):

```
An ampersand (&) may be escaped
numerically (&#38;) or with a general entity
(&amp;).
```

A more complex example will illustrate the rules and their effects fully. In the following example, the line numbers are solely for reference.

```
1 <?xml version='1.0'?>
2 <!DOCTYPE test [
3 <!ELEMENT test (#PCDATA) >
4 <!ENTITY % xx '&#37;zz;'>
5 <!ENTITY % zz '&#60;!ENTITY tricky "error-prone" >' >
6 %xx;
7 ]>
8 <test>This sample shows a &tricky; method.</test>
```

This produces the following:

- In line 4, the reference to character 37 is expanded immediately, and the parameter entity "**xx**" is stored in the symbol table with the value "**%zz;**". Since the replacement text is not rescanned, the reference to parameter entity "**zz**" is not recognized. (And it would be an error if it were, since "**zz**" is not yet declared.)

- In line 5, the character reference "**<**" is expanded immediately and the parameter entity "**zz**" is stored with the replacement text "**<!ENTITY tricky "error-prone" >**", which is a well-formed entity declaration.

- In line 6, the reference to "**xx**" is recognized, and the replacement text of "**xx**" (namely "**%zz;**") is parsed. The reference to "**zz**" is recognized in its turn, and its replacement text ("**<!ENTITY tricky "error-prone" >**") is parsed. The general entity "**tricky**" has now been declared, with the replacement text "**error-prone**".

- In line 8, the reference to the general entity "**tricky**" is recognized, and it is expanded, so the full content of the "**test**" element is the self-describing (and ungrammatical) string. This sample shows an error-prone method.

E. Deterministic Content Models (Non-Normative)

For compatibility, it is required that content models in element type declarations be deterministic.

SGML requires deterministic content models (it calls them "unambiguous"); XML processors built using SGML systems may flag non-deterministic content models as errors.

For example, the content model **((b, c) | (b, d))** is non-deterministic, because given an initial **b** the parser cannot know which **b** in the model is being matched without looking ahead to see which element follows the **b**. In this case, the two references to **b** can be collapsed into a single reference, making the model read **(b, (c | d))**. An initial **b** now clearly matches only a single name in the content model. The parser doesn't need to look ahead to see what follows; either **c** or **d** would be accepted.

More formally: a finite state automaton may be constructed from the content model using the standard algorithms, e.g., algorithm 3.5 in section 3.9 of Aho, Sethi, and Ullman [Aho/Ullman]. In many such algorithms, a follow set is constructed for each position in the regular expression (i.e., each leaf node in the syntax tree for the regular expression); if any position has a follow set in which more than one following position is labeled with the same element type name, then the content model is in error and may be reported as an error.

Algorithms exist which allow many but not all non-deterministic content models to be reduced automatically to equivalent deterministic models; see Brüggemann-Klein 1991 [Brüggemann-Klein].

F. Autodetection of Character Encodings (Non-Normative)

The XML encoding declaration functions as an internal label on each entity, indicating which character encoding is in use. Before an XML processor can read the internal label, however, it apparently has to know what character encoding is in use—which is what the internal label is trying to indicate. In the general case, this is a hopeless situation. It is not entirely hopeless in XML, however, because XML limits the general case in two ways: each implementation is assumed to support only a finite set of character encodings, and the XML encoding declaration is restricted in position and content in order to make it feasible to autodetect the character encoding in use in each entity in normal cases. Also, in many cases other sources of information are available in addition to the XML data stream itself. Two cases may be distinguished, depending on whether the XML entity is presented to the processor without, or with, any accompanying (external) information. We consider the first case first.

Because each XML entity not in UTF-8 or UTF-16 format must begin with an XML encoding declaration, in which the first characters must be '<?xml', any conforming processor can detect, after two to four octets of input, which of the following cases apply. In reading this list, it may help to know that in UCS-4, '<' is "#x0000003C" and '?' is "#x0000003F", and the Byte Order Mark required of UTF-16 data streams is "#xFEFF".

- **00 00 00 3C**: UCS-4, big-endian machine (1234 order)
- **3C 00 00 00**: UCS-4, little-endian machine (4321 order)
- **00 00 3C 00**: UCS-4, unusual octet order (2143)
- **00 3C 00 00**: UCS-4, unusual octet order (3412)
- **FE FF**: UTF-16, big-endian
- **FF FE**: UTF-16, little-endian
- **00 3C 00 3F**: UTF-16, big-endian, no Byte Order Mark (and thus, strictly speaking, in error)
- **3C 00 3F 00**: UTF-16, little-endian, no Byte Order Mark (and thus, strictly speaking, in error)
- **3C 3F 78 6D**: UTF-8, ISO 646, ASCII, some part of ISO 8859, Shift-JIS, EUC, or any other 7-bit, 8-bit, or mixed-width encoding which ensures that the characters of ASCII have their normal positions, width, and values; the actual encoding declaration must be read to detect which of these applies, but since all of these encodings use the same bit patterns for the ASCII characters, the encoding declaration itself may be read reliably
- **4C 6F A7 94**: EBCDIC (in some flavor; the full encoding declaration must be read to tell which code page is in use)
- **other**: UTF-8 without an encoding declaration, or else the data stream is corrupt, fragmentary, or enclosed in a wrapper of some kind

This level of autodetection is enough to read the XML encoding declaration and parse the character-encoding identifier, which is still necessary to distinguish the individual members of each family of encodings (e.g., to tell UTF-8 from 8859, and the parts of 8859 from each other, or to distinguish the specific EBCDIC code page in use, and so on).

Because the contents of the encoding declaration are restricted to ASCII characters, a processor can reliably read the entire encoding declaration as soon as it has detected which family of encodings is in use. Since in practice, all widely used character encodings fall into one of the categories above, the XML encoding declaration allows reasonably reliable in-band labeling of character encodings, even when external sources of information at the operating-system or transport-protocol level are unreliable.

Once the processor has detected the character encoding in use, it can act appropriately, whether by invoking a separate input routine for each case, or by calling the proper conversion function on each character of input.

Like any self-labeling system, the XML encoding declaration will not work if any software changes the entity's character set or encoding without updating the encoding declaration. Implementors of character-encoding routines should be careful to ensure the accuracy of the internal and external information used to label the entity.

The second possible case occurs when the XML entity is accompanied by encoding information, as in some file systems and some network protocols. When multiple sources of information are available, their relative priority and the preferred method of handling conflict should be specified as part of the higher-level protocol used to deliver XML. Rules for the relative priority of the internal label and the MIME-type label in an external header, for example, should be part of the RFC document defining the text/xml and application/xml MIME types. In the interests of interoperability, however, the following rules are recommended:

- If an XML entity is in a file, the Byte-Order Mark and encoding-declaration PI are used (if present) to determine the character encoding. All other heuristics and sources of information are solely for error recovery.

- If an XML entity is delivered with a MIME type of text/xml, then the **charset** parameter on the MIME type determines the character encoding method; all other heuristics and sources of information are solely for error recovery.

- If an XML entity is delivered with a MIME type of application/xml, then the Byte-Order Mark and encoding-declaration PI are used (if present) to determine the character encoding. All other heuristics and sources of information are solely for error recovery.

These rules apply only in the absence of protocol-level documentation; in particular, when the MIME types text/xml and application/xml are defined, the recommendations of the relevant RFC will supersede these rules.

G. W3C XML Working Group (Non-Normative)

This specification was prepared and approved for publication by the W3C XML Working Group (WG). WG approval of this specification does not necessarily imply that all WG members voted for its approval. The current and former members of the XML WG are:

Jon Bosak, Sun (Chair); James Clark (Technical Lead); Tim Bray, Textuality and Netscape (XML Co-editor); Jean Paoli, Microsoft (XML Co-editor); C. M. Sperberg-McQueen, U. of Ill. (XML Co-editor); Dan Connolly, W3C (W3C Liaison); Paula Angerstein, Texcel; Steve DeRose, INSO; Dave Hollander, HP; Eliot Kimber, ISOGEN; Eve Maler, ArborText; Tom Magliery, NCSA; Murray Maloney, Muzmo and Grif; Makoto Murata, Fuji Xerox Information Systems; Joel Nava, Adobe; Conleth O'Connell, Vignette; Peter Sharpe, SoftQuad; John Tigue, DataChannel.

Glossary

absolute location path—In XPath, a location path that starts at the document root.

action—The portion of a construction rule that describes how the document element (pattern) should be formatted.

Active Channel—A Microsoft technology that uses the Channel Definition Language (CDF, an XML vocabulary) to create channels of regularly updated information that users can subscribe to within Internet Explorer.

ActiveX controls—A stripped-down version of Object Linking and Embedding (OLE) controls, whose size and speed are optimized for use over the Internet.

API (application programming interface)—A set of instructions that allows one program to invoke the functions of a second program.

ASCII (American Standard Code for Information Interchange)—A method of encoding characters that translates letters, numbers, and symbols into digital form.

ASP (Active Server Page)—A Web programming technique that enriches commerce and business communications by improving script management. ASPs can execute with a transaction so the transaction is aborted if the script fails.

attribute—An item that is added to an element to provide additional information about the element.

attribute list declaration—A listing in the DTD of all the attributes that can be used with a given element. This listing includes the attributes, their values and defaults (if the values are fixed), and whether the attribute is required or optional.

attribute name—The name used to identify the attribute in the DTD and reference it in a document.

attribute specification—An individual listing for a single attribute within the attribute list declaration.

attribute type—The value that identifies the attribute as a string, tokenized, or enumerated attribute.

attribute value—A list in the specification of all the possible values an attribute can take. In a document, this is the specific value assigned to the attribute by the document developer.

axis—In XPath, the first section of each location path step. The axis specifies the relationship between the context node and the nodes that are selected by the step.

bidirectional link—A hyperlink that can be traversed in more than one direction. Bidirectional links are an XLink convention.

box properties—A group of CSS properties and values that governs the margins, padding, height, width, and border aspects of any element.

BSML (Bioinformatic Sequence Markup Language)—A developing XML vocabulary intended to provide a standard method for encoding and displaying DNA, RNA, and protein sequence information between programs and over the Internet.

CDF (Channel Definition Format)—A vocabulary based on XML that lets a developer use a variety of delivery mechanisms to publish collections of information called *channels* from any Web server to any Internet-compatible appliance. CDF was developed by Microsoft.

CGI (Common Gateway Interface)—Scripts that execute programs on a Web server.

channel—A server-push mechanism defined using CDF that allows developers to send collections of Web data to users. Channel content is delivered to users who have subscribed to receive it.

character data—The text (other than markup) included within document elements. Not all elements must necessarily allow character data as content.

character reference—All the text used in the document to create declarations, markup, and text inside XML elements.

child element—An element that is contained (nested) within another element. A child element may also be a parent of other, lower-level elements.

Glossary

CKML (Conceptual Knowledge Markup Language)—An XML vocabulary used to represent knowledge and data analysis, which serves to create models for rational thinking, judgement, and decision making.

classification properties—A group of CSS properties and values that govern the way white space and lists are displayed.

CML (Chemical Markup Language)—A content- and presentation-based XML vocabulary that is used to describe and process chemical compound data.

comments—Notes in an XML document that are ignored by an XML processor.

Competence Gap Analysis Tool—An elaborate system created by RivCom, a consulting firm in England (**www.rivcom.com**), for Shell Services International. This system was designed to be an interactive tool to help people define the skill levels needed for certain jobs within the organization and how those skills rated in the overall job requirements.

content—Anything found between the start and end tags of an element. Content can include element content, character data, or mixed content.

content model—The definition in a DTD of what content is allowed within any given element.

content-based markup—Markup that is robust enough to describe information so it can be processed by one or more applications or delivered in ways other than traditional visual presentation (such as aurally or in Braille).

CSS (Cascading Style Sheets)—A set of style rules that governs how HTML, XHTML, and XML elements are displayed by a browser or other mechanism.

data model—A representation of an XML document created by and kept in an XPath processor.

data store—Any medium that is used to store data.

declaration—Markup that gives the XML processor special instructions on how to process a document.

document element—The main element of an XML document. The document element holds all the text and markup in the document. Also called the *root element*.

document type declaration—Used to associate the XML document with its corresponding DTD. Also called the *DOCTYPE declaration*.

DOM (Document Object Model)—A way to describe an XML document to another application or programming language as a series of objects in a hierarchical tree. The DOM makes it easier to access and manipulate the elements in the document.

DSO (Data Source Object)—*See* XML DSO.

DTD (Document Type Definition)—An SGML or XML specification for a document that organizes structural elements and markup definitions so they can be used to create documents.

dynamic HTML—HTML that is combined with style sheets and scripts to create Web pages that change in response to user interactions. Also called *DHTML*.

EAD (Encoded Archival Description)—An XML vocabulary used to develop a nonproprietary encoding standard for library documents, including indexes, archives, and any other type of holdings that may be found in libraries and museums.

element—A component of a document. An element consists of markup and the text contained within the markup. The combination of elements, as defined by the document's related DTD, makes up the main part of an XML document.

element content—Other elements (tag pairs) that can be included within an element. The elements that can be nested within a tag (and the order in which they must appear) are defined for each element in the DTD.

empty element—An element that has no element content of any kind. An empty element is typically represented by the markup *<element/>*.

entity—Essentially, a unit of storage whose contents are associated with a name. Whenever the name is invoked in an XML document, the unit's contents are inserted in place of the name, just as a less-than sign (<) is displayed in place of the entity <. Entities allow developers to include binary and non-ASCII text resources in XML documents.

extended link—In XLink, a link that is stored in an external file and that allows you to express relationships between more than two resources.

extended link groups—In XLink, special types of extended links that are used to store a list of links to other documents.

Extended Pointers—*See* XPointer.

Extensible Linking Language—*See* XLink.

external DTD—The portion of a document's DTD stored in an external file.

external entity—An entity that describes information stored in a file that is external to the document that references the entity.

font properties—A group of CSS properties and values that provide font specifics for document elements.

forward axis—In XPath, an axis that selects the context node or nodes after the context node in the document.

GedML (Genealogical Data in XML)—An XML vocabulary created to provide a standard method for presenting, exchanging, and manipulating genealogical data across a network and with other users.

general entity—A parsed entity that's created for use in the content of a document.

HTTP (Hypertext Transfer Protocol)—The protocol for communication between a Web server and a Web browser (uses HTML).

hybrid channel—A channel that combines news, immersion, and notification channels.

HyTime—A standard used within the SGML specification that defines the inline and out-of-line link structures and some semantic features, including traversal control and presentation of objects.

ICE (Information & Content Exchange)—An XML vocabulary intended to provide automatic, controlled exchange and management of online assets between business partners. ICE gives businesses a standard way to set up online relationships with other businesses and to transfer and share information.

IIS (Internet Information Server)—Web server software by Microsoft that is included and implemented with Windows NT Server. The Windows 2000 version of this software is called Internet Information Services.

immersion channel—A channel that provides an immersion into the total content of the channel.

IMS Metadata Specification—A specification that uses XML to offer effective delivery of high-quality training materials over the Internet. It also supports the management of materials and types of data relating to Web sites.

inline link—In XLink, a link that serves as one of its own resources. More specifically, in an inline link, the content of the linking element acts as a resource. An example of such a link is the HTML anchor (a) element.

Glossary

interface element—An XML element that doesn't fall into the category of either a content or presentation element. The **math** element, found in the MathML vocabulary, is an example of an interface element.

internal DTD subset—The portion of a document's DTD that is included within the document.

internal entity—An entity whose contents are included directly within the entity's declaration in the DTD. Internal entities are self-contained and do not reference any content outside the DTD.

intranet—An internal, private network that uses the same standards and protocols as the Internet.

ISO 10646—The International Organization for Standardization's official name for the Universal Character Set (UCS), which is equivalent to Unicode.

Java—An object-oriented programming language developed by Sun Microsystems that is used for Web application development.

Java class files—The file or set of files behind a Java applet or application that contains the instructions that drive the applet.

JavaScript—A scripting language, supported by Netscape 2 and higher and Internet Explorer 4 and higher, that is used to script Web pages. Also known as ECMAScript.

language processor—*See* parser.

linking element—In XLink, an element that specifies the existence of a link and describes its characteristics.

local resource—In XLink, the content of an inline linking element. It specifies the content-role and content-title of the link.

location term—The key ingredient and basic addressing information unit in an XPointer that describes the exact spot within a resource that is linked to.

locator—In XLink, a piece of data (provided as part of a link) that identifies a resource and can be used to locate it.

MathML (Mathematical Markup Language)—A content- and presentation-based XML vocabulary that is used to describe and process mathematical data.

metadata—Data that provides information about other resources.

metalanguage—A set of rules used to define other languages.

mixed content—A combination of element and character data that can be included as content for any given element.

MSXSL (Microsoft Extensible Style Sheet Language)—A language processor that allows you to turn XML data into HTML data by means of style sheets. MSXSL was developed by Microsoft.

multidirectional link—In XLink, a link that can be traversed from more than one of its resources. It's more than just a link that provides a mechanism to go back to a previously visited resource or link. Instead, a multidirectional link gives the user the ability to move up, down, left, right, or backward—in other words, in just about any direction.

namespace—A collection of element types and attribute names.

nesting—A description of how elements are contained within one another.

news channel—According to Microsoft, a channel that provides breaking news to its subscribers.

nodes—The various branches found on an XML data tree.

node test—In XPath, the second part of the location path step, separated from the axis by a double colon (::).

node-set function—In XPath, a function used in location path predicates to further refine the members of a node-set.

notation—An XML declaration that associates a type of uparsed entity, such as a GIF or JPEG file, with a processing application, such as LView or Paint Shop Pro.

notification channel—A channel that notifies users when content has been updated for a particular channel.

Object Model—See *XML OM (Object Model)*.

ObjectStore—An object database management system that provides native storage for structured data, such as XML, C++ objects, or Java objects.

ODBC (Open Database Connectivity)—A Microsoft standard API that allows database files of various formats to communicate effectively.

OFX (Open Financial Exchange)—An XML vocabulary that is a spin-off of the SGML applications that work behind the scenes in Microsoft's Money and Intuit's Quicken packages.

OML (Ontology Markup Language)—An XML vocabulary that allows Web-page authors to annotate their Web pages so the pages can be read by machines and processed with intelligent agent software.

OpenTag—An XML vocabulary designed to create a standardized way to code diverse file types through the use of a common markup method.

OSD (Open Software Description)—An XML vocabulary used to describe software components, software versions, and the underlying structure of software packages and their components for delivery over a network. OSD can work in conjunction with CDF to update software over the Internet or an intranet.

OTP (Open Trading Protocol)—An XML vocabulary proposed by MasterCard International, along with AT&T, Hewlett-Packard, and Wells Fargo, and used for the exchange of financial information. It can help financial companies transfer information about their clients through disparate financial systems without the need to replace their existing systems.

out-of-line link—In XLink, a link whose content does not serve as one of the original link's resources. Out-of-line links don't even have to occur in the same document. They are used within multidirectional links and when read-only resources have outgoing links.

parameter entity—An entity used strictly within a DTD to create an alias for a group of elements (usually attributes or element content) that is used frequently within the DTD.

parent element—An element that has one or more elements as content. A parent element of a child element or elements may also be the child of another, higher-level element.

parsed entity—Character data assigned as content to an entity name. When a parsed entity is referenced, the content of the entity is inserted in the document in place of the entity reference.

parser—A software program that breaks an XML document into its element tree and checks its syntax.

participating resource—In XLink, a resource that belongs to a link.

pattern—The part of a template rule that specifies the set of conditions in which an element in the source tree matches the template rule.

PCDATA (parsed character data)—Element content made up of only plain text.

Perl—The most commonly used programming language for CGIs.

PostScript—An Adobe page-description language used to create print images for output on suitably equipped print engines.

predicate—Markup used in a location path step to filter the resulting node-set into a new node-set. That is, a predicate further refines the set of nodes selected by the location path.

presentation-based markup—Markup whose primary function is to describe text that will be rendered visually by a browser. HTML is a presentation-based markup language.

processing instructions (PIs)—Instructions from the XML document that are passed through the parser to the display software to tell the software how to process all or part of the document. A PI can be included anywhere in an XML document.

production rule—Information in the XML specification that is necessary for creating well-formed or valid XML code.

QName (Qualified Name)—The name of an element type, preceded by a prefix and followed by a colon. An attribute that is so prefixed it is also called a qualified name. In XPath, a QName is an element name that contains the prefix that represents the namespace URI.

RADBMS (Random Access Data Base Management System)—The engine that works in conjunction with the database that allows it to search, filter, and collate the records in its memory.

RDF (Resource Description Framework)—A content-based XML vocabulary used to describe Internet resources in a standard metadata format that is usable by a wide variety of clients and servers. This vocabulary provides a mechanism for organizing, describing, and navigating Web sites.

recordset—Any database subset that contains at least one record.

relational database—A database that stores information in the form of records and fields. In relational databases, the order and relationship that one field or record holds to another are not necessarily significant.

relative location path—In XPath, a location path that starts at the current node.

remote resource—In XLink, any participating resource of a link to which a locator points. It specifies the **role**, **title**, **show**, **actuate**, and **behavior** attributes of the link.

resource—In XLink, a service or group of information (an object) that is specified in a link. A resource could be a file, an image, documents, programs, database query results, or a sound file. More generally, a resource can be anything that can be accessed via a URI.

Glossary

result tree—The tree of elements and element content in a document after XSLT transformation.

reverse axis—In XPath, an axis that selects the context node or nodes that come before the context node.

root element—See *document element.*

root node—The document element of the XML document tree. All the nodes in a tree are the descendants of the root node.

SAX (Simple API for XML)—An event-based interface created specifically for XML parsers that are written in object-oriented applications, such as Java.

scripting language—One of several interpreted languages used to control the behavior of Web pages in response to user activities.

selector—In a CSS, one of the two parts of a style rule. The selector defines the markup element to which the style rule is applied.

SGML (Standard Generalized Markup Language)—A generic text-based markup language used to describe the content and structure of documents.

simple link—An XML link that uses the **href** attribute to point to only one re-source. All HTML links are simple links.

SMIL (Synchronized Multimedia Integration Language)—An XML vocabu-lary that assists developers in integrating multimedia into their sites. SMIL pro-vides a standardized way to describe multimedia and the various components needed to use, display, and manipulate it on the Internet.

source tree—The tree of elements and element content in an XSLT original document.

SQL (Structured Query Language)—An IBM-developed language for inter-acting with relational databases.

string attributes—XML attributes that allow the user to define any value for the attribute.

style rules—The rules in an XML document that drive the display of a Web page.

style sheet—A document that uses markup to provide information about the structure and content of another document or set of documents. A style sheet also provides information about the document's style and presentation to the soft-ware package used to parse and process the document.

SVG (Scalable Vector Graphics)—A language that can be used to describe two-dimensional graphics in XML.

TecML (Technical Markup Language)—An application-independent XML vocabulary used to describe technical information.

TEIP3 (Text Encoding Initiative Guidelines)—The guidelines on which the entire XLink language is based. These guidelines provide structures for creating links, aggregate objects, and link collections.

template—The part of a template rule that specifies what is instantiated in the result tree when the template rule is applied (i.e., when the template rule's pattern matches an element in the source tree).

template rule—The cornerstone of an XSLT style sheet. Template rules consist of a pattern and a template.

text properties—A set of CSS properties and values that provides text specifics for document elements.

TIM (Telecommunications Interchange Markup)—An XML vocabulary used to provide a standard mechanism for offering industry standards associated with the provision, procurement, and use of telecommunications equipment, products, and services.

TML (Tutorial Markup Language)—An XML vocabulary designed specifically for creating and working with educational applications.

TMX (Translation Memory Exchange)—An XML vocabulary designed to allow easier exchange of translation memory data between tools and/or translation vendors with little or no loss of critical data during the process.

tokenized attribute—A name for seven different types of predefined attributes that play a specific role in XML documents and that must have a particular kind of value.

traversal—In XLink, the action of using a link to access a resource. Traversals are usually initiated by a user action or by some sort of program control.

tree structure—A hierarchical organizational scheme that is roughly pyramidical in shape.

Unicode—The ISO 10646 character set that uses 16-bit patterns to represent characters.

unparsed entity—Anything that's not an XML-encoded resource. For example, audio and video files are binary entities.

Glossary

URI (Uniform Resource Identifier)—A name or an address that identifies a network resource. URLs are subsets of URIs.

URL (Universal Resource Locator)—An Internet specific point that is part of a resource's URI set that defines how to access the resource over the Internet.

URN (Universal Resource Name)—A persistent name that is part of a resource's URI set that doesn't change over time. A resource's URL and URN may be the same.

UXL (UML eXchange Format)—An XML vocabulary created for software developers as a mechanism for transferring Unified Modeling Language (UML) models. The application format is powerful enough to allow developers to express, publish, and exchange UML models universally.

valid XML document—A document that is well formed and adheres to its DTD.

validating parser—A software program that checks an XML document for validity, meaning that it checks for the presence of the document's DTD and whether the document conforms to it.

VBScript (Visual Basic Scripting Edition)—A Microsoft proprietary scripting language for markup language documents whose syntax resembles Visual Basic. VBScript is used only in Microsoft Web products.

WAP (Wireless Application Protocol)—An XML vocabulary that offers standards for wireless network transmissions and scaling across various transport options and device types.

WebDAV (Distributed Authoring and Versioning on the World Wide Web)— An XML vocabulary intended to define HTTP methods and semantics for creating, removing, querying, and editing Web pages remotely.

well-formed documents—Documents that conform to the XML specification.

WIDL (Web Interface Definition Language)—A content-based XML vocabulary used to describe Web APIs.

XHTML (Extensible Hypertext Markup Language)—The current World Wide Web Consortium (W3C) recommendation for the merger of HTML 4 (for the vocabulary of elements) and XML (for syntax). The *X* in XHTML stands for XML because it's XML-compliant HTML.

XLink—XML's linking language that allows users to create powerful links in XML documents.

XML application—A specific implementation of XML that is a DTD or set of DTDs designed to serve a specific purpose. Also known as an *XML vocabulary.*

XML declaration—A declaration that tells the processor to use a specific version of the XML specification to process the document as an XML document. It also specifies the type of character encoding that will be used for the document and whether the XML document is a standalone document.

XML DSO (XML Data Source Object)—A Microsoft proprietary technology that uses the data-binding facility found in dynamic HTML to bind structured XML data to HTML.

XML processor—A software module that is used to read XML documents and provide access to their structure and content.

XML Schema—A technique for describing XML markup using XML notation, rather than an SGML-based DTD. This is not yet a recommended World Wide Web Consortium (W3C) standard.

XML specification—A technical description that outlines exactly how elements must be declared and how XML must be constructed for XML processors (which interpret XML code) to process the XML information properly and send it to the Web browser for display.

XPath (XML Path Language)—A language used by both XSL and XLink to address parts of XML documents.

XPointer (XML Pointer Language)—The mechanism that provides developers with a way to designate various resources by using terms that specify locations in documents or resources. XPointer is a companion to XLink.

XQL (XML Query Language)—A language currently under development by the World Wide Web Consortium (W3C) that is to XML what SQL is to databases.

XSL (Extensible Stylesheet Language)—A style sheet mechanism that is customized for XML.

XSLT (XSL Transformations)—A component of XSL that provides a language for changing one XML document into another.

Index

C

Recordset, 568
Relational databases, 567–571
Relative location path, 350
Remote resource, 311, 315
#REQUIRED, 198
Reserved characters, 120
Resource, 310–311, 314
Resource Description Framework (RDF),
   30–31, 415
resource element, 327–328
Result tree, 279–280
Reverse axis, 354–355
Reverse document order, 360
Rich Text Format (RTF), 3–4
Rivcom's competence gap analysis tool, 102–103
role attribute, 324
Root node, 361
RTF, 3–4
RUWF, 534

S

SAX, 596–598, 601–603, 613–619
   conceptual diagram (information flow), 597
   DocumentHandler interface, 603
   error reporting, 602–603, 618
   HandlerBase, 603, 615–618
   interfaces, 602
   Java, and, 613–619
   modifying XML documents, 618–619
   overview, 605
   parser inputs, 602, 614–615
Saxon, 304, 530
Scalable Vector Graphics (SVG), 416
SCHEDULE element, 466–468
Schema Central, 624
Scheme, 380
Scientific applications, 418
Screen savers, 455, 481
Script element, 502
Scriplets, 30
Server-side processing, 537
SGML, 6–8, 162
show attribute, 321–322, 335–336
Siblings, 155
Siemens TimeCard System, 97–102
Simple Application Programming Interface
   (API) for XML. *See* SAX.
Simple link, 312–313, 315, 319–320, 333–334

Singleton, 380
Site crawling, 484
Site design, 67–70, 73–74
Skonnard, Aaron, 370
SMIL, 416, 429–432
   bandwidth options, 438
   complex sequencing, 437
   creating data file, 436–438
   design principles, 429
   elements, 430
   more information, 416
   tools, 438–439
SMIL Composer, 438
Solution design. *See* Total XML solution.
Source tree, 280
Special characters, 217, 226–244
Specification, 31–37, 43–44
SQL, 569–571
Standalone document attribute, 113
Standard character set/encoding, 93
Standardization, 88–91
Start tags, 57
Starting resource, 311
String attributes, 188, 194
String functions, 358–359
String ranges, 386–388
Style element, 502
Style sheets, 253–255, 556–558. *See also* CSS,
   XSLT.
Stylus, 304
Sub-elements, 155
Sub-resource, 380
Sun Toolset, 633
SVG, 416
Symbols character set, 244
Synchronized Multimedia Integration
   Language. *See* SMIL.
Syntax, 56–62
SYSTEM, 115, 122, 123
System DTD, 115

T

Table, 567
Tags
   nesting, 59
   starting/ending, 57
   terminology, 153
Tauber, James K., 433, 525, 633

Related Coriolis Technology Press Titles

Active Server Pages Solutions

By Al Williams, Kim Barber, and Paul Newkirk
ISBN: 1-57610-608-X
Price: $49.99 U.S. • $74.99 CAN
Media: CD-ROM • Available Now

Explores all the components that work with Active Server Pages, such as HTML (including Dynamic HTML), scripting, Java applets, Internet Information Server, Internet Explorer and server-side scripting for VBScript, Jscript, and ActiveX controls. Offers practical examples using commonly used tools.

HTML Black Book

By Steven Holzner
ISBN: 1-57610-617-9
Price: $59.99 U.S. • $89.99 CAN
Media: CD-ROM • Available Now

Explores HTML programming thoroughly, from the essentials up through issues of security, providing step-by-step solutions to everyday challenges. This comprehensive guide discusses HTML in-depth, as well as covering XML, dynamic XML, JavaScript, Java, Perl, and CGI programming, to create a full Web site programming package.

Java Black Book

By Steven Holzner
ISBN: 1-57610-531-8
Price: $49.99 U.S. • $74.99 CAN
Media: CD-ROM • Available Now

A comprehensive reference filled with examples, tips, and solved problems. Discusses the Java language, Abstract Windowing Toolkit, Swing, Java 2D, advanced java beans, the Java Database Connectivity Package, servlets, internalization and security, streams and sockets, and more.

C++ Black Book

By Steven Holzner
ISBN: 1-57610-777-9
Price: $59.99 U.S. • $89.99 CAN
Media: CD-ROM • Available: December 2000

NEW

From the basics to the most advanced topics, this book provides complete coverage of everything needed to master C++, including all C++ compilers. The book explores working with data and C++ operators, storing data in strings and arrays, creating functions, and standard library functions for data processing and I/O, plus much more.

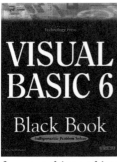

Visual Basic 6 Black Book

By Steven Holzner
ISBN: 1-57610-283-1
Price: $49.99 U.S. • $69.99 CAN
Media: CD-ROM • Available Now

Completely explains the crucial Visual Basic tool set in detail. Jam-packed with insight, programming tips and techniques, and real-world solutions. Covers everything from graphics and image processing, to ActiveX controls, database development and data-bound controls, multimedia, OLE automation, Registry handling, error handling and debugging, Windows API, and more.

Visual Basic 6 Core Language Little Black Book

By Steven Holzner
ISBN: 1-57610-390-0
Price: $24.99 U.S. • $36.99 CAN
Available Now

Provides a detailed reference on all Basic control structures, data types, and other code mechanisms. Includes step-by-step instructions on how to build common code structures in VB, from simple if statements to objects and ActiveX components. Not merely a syntax summary, but a detailed reference on creating code structures with VB6 code and data elements.

THE CORIOLIS GROUP, LLC   Telephone: 800.410.0192 • www.coriolis.com
Coriolis books are also available at bookstores and computer stores nationwide.

What's on the CD-ROM

The contents of the companion CD-ROM will help you start creating XML documents right away. The CD-ROM features the following:

- *Shareware and demonstration software packages*—Try out several of the most popular XML parsers, browsers, and development systems to find the ones that fit your specific needs.

- *HTML files that link to all the URLs mentioned in the book*—The book's Web site provides you with quick access to all of the URLs listed in the book and includes contact information for the *XML Black Book, 2ⁿᵈ edition* author.

- *Code files*—Code listings from the book allow you to easily edit and change existing XML files in your favorite text or XML editor.

Requirements

- A PC with a 486 or better processor
- 16MB of RAM minimum, 32M recommended
- Windows 95, 98, 2000, or NT
- A Web browser capable of displaying Java; Internet Explorer 4 or later is recommended